A GAMELAN MANUAL

Richard Pickvance

A GAMELAN MANUAL

a player's guide to the central Javanese gamelan

Jaman Mas Books

Published by Jaman Mas Books, London, United Kingdom

Associated website: *www.gamelan.org.uk*,
linked to *www.jamanmasbooks.co.uk*

ISBN 0-9550295-0-3

First published in the UK 2005

Designed and typeset by the author, using Corel Ventura, Corel Draw, Corel PhotoPaint and Adobe Photoshop software

Set in Monotype Ehrhardt, Monotype Gill Sans Book and other members of the Gill Sans family, Adobe Tekton, Monotype Javanese NLC, and custom-designed fonts

Printed and bound in Europe by the Alden Group, Oxford

The paper used in this book is acid-free and conforms to ISO 9706 Permanence of Paper

Preface

This book on the gamelan of central Java has been written for several groups of readers.

The main target is the gamelan player brought up in the Western musical environment, and particularly those who have not had the opportunity to study in Java. Among other things, this is the book that I should like to have found when I first started playing the gamelan.

The second category of readers would be those who have been instantly impressed, as Debussy was, by the beauty and evident complexity of gamelan music, but now wish to get beneath the surface and understand in detail how the gamelan and its music work.

Another group might be teachers and composers interested in using elements of gamelan music as resources in their own work, especially since music from other cultures was included in the national curriculum for UK schools.

I take it as axiomatic that central Javanese gamelan music—*karawitan*—represents one of the great musical cultures of the world, and that its virtues are the reason why it has taken firm root in the alien cultures of Europe, North America and Australasia. No further justification need be given for studying it: if more is sought, it may be found in the fact that, for students coming from the Western classical tradition, *karawitan* differs in almost every respect from the music they are used to, and therefore presents a stimulating challenge—especially to those who are already experienced players. On the other hand, the gamelan possesses the unusual merit that novice players can participate alongside skilled ones, achieving results satisfying to all.

Gamelan music is ensemble music, and the Western student's principal learning situation is usually in class with a teacher. The learning process ideally should be based mainly on listening. In Java, this may be the only method used. Written material is of limited value in class, and the teacher may actively discourage its use. In any case, it is not practical to teach the playing of instruments entirely via the printed page, so that most of this book is more suitable for leisurely background reading. Also some students do not benefit from reading instructional material: clearly this book is not for them.

As is inevitable in a book specifically for readers outside Java, this one takes a more analytical approach than a typical Javanese teacher would: most players in the West start late by Javanese standards, and are in a hurry.

Initially I hoped to be able to declare the book free of theory, but it became clear that students of the gamelan inevitably encounter various theories, from both Western and Javanese sources, and that it would be advisable to examine them critically here. While I would have preferred to discuss Javanese music entirely in Javanese terms, it seemed likely that part of the target audience would benefit from comparisons between *karawitan* and the music that is more familiar to them.

I have kept in mind that the writer's task in a technical manual—such as this book—is to make the subject (in the words attributed to Einstein) 'as simple as possible, but no simpler'. It would be too much to expect to dispel the reader's every confusion. At best an author can only aspire to leave readers confused about the right things.

Students of *karawitan* like to be given rules, but soon find that rules are not altogether helpful, because an exception can always be found. (Even less productive, perhaps, is any attempt to explain **why** a particular feature of *karawitan* is the way it is.) To deal with the diversity of Javanese musical practice, the writer must often qualify statements by means of words such as 'may', 'sometimes', 'tend to', 'usually', etc. If there are rules governing *karawitan*, they are what computer scientists would call 'fuzzy' rules: there are few certainties.

No work by a single author—even a Javanese one—could hope to encompass the full range of Javanese performance practice. If such a work were possible at all, it would certainly be of encyclopedic length. The present work goes far beyond the beginner level, and seems to include a wider range of practice than is to be found in other sources. Nevertheless it is a personal view; any other writer would record a different collection of practices. It is also an outsider's view as to what is important, noteworthy or difficult. No criticism of other writers is intended. I have tried to describe what actually happens in Java, rather than what some experts give as the standard (or even the only) practice.

This is therefore a book about some ways in which the Javanese play their music, not a comprehensive prescription for how it should be played. Teachers of gamelan classes must concentrate on the most generally applicable techniques and those that they can teach to a whole class. This is particularly true in the early stages. Readers should therefore not be surprised if their teachers discourage them from following some of the practices described here.

Karawitan is a living tradition. The book describes how the Javanese currently treat their musical heritage, but does not pretend to be up to date with musicians' latest innovations. It also refers to the historical background, and to some current forces for change.

In keeping with its practical emphasis, the book does not try to deal with every aspect of *karawitan*. The bibliography lists books, theses, journals and other sources that cover topics deliberately omitted from the present work or given only limited coverage. This said, the book (unlike most in the field) is a player's book, and may contribute to the understanding of performance both for its own sake and as an element of ethnomusicological research.

Readers' comments, corrections and suggestions are welcome, especially where the text resorts to question marks.

Acknowledgements

The principal acknowledgement is to all my teachers, both in the United Kingdom and in Java. They are too numerous to list, and it would be unfair to single out any of them. I am also grateful to all the gamelan groups in Java who welcomed me in without asking embarrassing questions about my abilities.

Generally I have depended heavily on the library of the School of Oriental and African Studies, London, and those of STSI in Solo and ISI at Sewon, Yogyakarta. The library of the Royal Botanical Gardens, Kew, provided specialised help. The book occasionally touches on my researches into foreign visitors' accounts of early contacts with the Javanese gamelan. In this field, I have been greatly assisted by Jennifer Wraight, the Admiralty librarian, and by Dr Andrew Cook of the Oriental and India Office Collection at the British Library.

It is a pleasure to acknowledge inspiration from Edward Tufte's works *The Visual Display of Quantitative Information*, *Visual Explanations* and *Envisioning Information* during the preparation of diagrams for this book.

Apologies and acknowledgements are due to Paul Crum for the cartoon on p. 53.

Andrew Timar, Joan Suyenaga and Professor Roger Vetter provided valuable information on aspects of instruments and instrument-making.

Special thanks are due to Professor Judith Becker for permission to use the material that forms the basis of the Glossary; to Professor Roger Vetter for permission to quote from his PhD thesis; to Nikhil Dally, Murwanto, Prasadiyanto, Cathy Eastburn and Jonathan Roberts for acting as photographic models to demonstrate playing techniques; and to *dhalang* Tim Byard-Jones for his contributions to the margins throughout the book. I am particularly delighted to have been able to make use of Marcus Risdell's very recent research into what were probably the first gamelan performances heard in the UK, and some of the first in Europe.

Besides the acknowledgements, a semi-apology is in order. Unlike the Indonesian and Javanese languages, English is not blessed or cursed with a set of gender-free pronouns. The usage of pronouns in this book tends to conform to a reality in Java in which most performers are male.

Richard Pickvance
London, 2005

webmaster@gamelan.org.uk

Using the book

This is intended as a resource book. Readers should feel free to traverse the content in any way that suits them. That can mean skipping over parts rather than reading the book straight through from cover to cover. To assist such an approach, the material has been extensively cross-referenced and indexed. The introduction is still a good place to start.

Books on the gamelan usually begin with the instruments. Here we start with the music, and the instruments are left until later—partly because most of the likely readers will be more or less familiar with the instruments already.

While the basic approach of the book is practical, there is also background material that should help players to understand not only what they are playing but why they are playing it. The introductory part 'sets the scene', by introducing numerous aspects of the environment in which the music exists.

The second part deals in general terms with the musical material played by the gamelan, and describes the various fundamental principles on which it is based. It also explains the principal notation system used, and the differences between the standard forms of compositions.

The third part focuses on the instruments and their performance practice, and on what each contributes to the ensemble. Each instrument is dealt with individually and as a member of a group with a wider function. One of the features of gamelan music is interaction between several instruments within the ensemble; something that can conveniently be described under a separate subheading. This part also describes the different ways in which the instruments are combined into ensembles.

The fourth part is a library of notation for specific pieces, with notes on details of performance practice. Notation for drumming, since most of it is generic and not confined to a single piece, is covered in a separate subsection.

After the four main parts come a glossary and various appendices. The glossary is intended to cover the terms used in this book and also in other related material that readers might pursue. One appendix lists references and further reading, with comments on the value of some of the items. There is also a discography. The other appendices mostly deal with subjects of more specialised interest, and are not included in the printed book. They are available, together with other supplementary material, via the associated website *www.gamelan.org.uk*.

When the book refers to Western music, it is obliged to use the relevant terminology. Readers who have no knowledge of the theory of Western music should not feel at a disadvantage: indeed, they benefit by having less to unlearn when they approach gamelan music. However, they may need to consult a dictionary of music. They should be aware that, in addition to their everyday meanings, words can also be technical terms in music; a **bar** (in British English), a **measure** (in American English), **key**, **tonic**, to **resolve**, and many more. The word 'note' here refers, as usual in British English, mainly to pitch rather than duration.

The associated website includes exercises related to the book. These are of two types, neither having any formal academic purpose. One type tests the reader's understanding at a more theoretical level. The other is more practical, and usually allows the reader to try out the sort of thinking that is regularly required of players. (Where appropriate, answers are also given.)

Each major part of the book begins with a detailed contents list.

Web resources

Additional resources that might help the reader are available on the World Wide Web. (As usual, these are of varying quality.) The URLs listed in Appendix 7 were correct at the time of writing, but are liable to change, as are the structures of websites: the information mentioned here may therefore still be accessible, but no longer in the place specified. Readers may need to resort to search engines in order to locate material that has moved.

Part 1 — Introduction

Part 2 — Music

Illustrations

Front cover

A central Javanese gamelan group, presumably in Yogyakarta (from the white ground colour of the *batik*, the blue *lurik* jacket worn by the *bonang* player, and the *bonang cacad*), by a local artist, from the *Radèn Panji Semara Bangun* manuscript in the John Rylands Library (Javanese MS 16, unnumbered folio). The manuscript is dated by an obscure chronogram, possibly indicating a date towards the end of the 18th century or towards the end of the 19th century. Reproduced by courtesy of the Director and University Librarian, The John Rylands Library, The University of Manchester.

Back cover

The author in natural habitat

Figures and plates

Maps

Tables

Locations of instruments illustrated

Frontispiece, Figs 3.9(b), 3.12, 3.15, 3.16, 3.26, 3.34, 3.41, 3.53, 3.54, 3.57, 3.58, 3.59, 3.60, 3.64, 3.68, 3.78, 3.81, 3.82, 3.97, back cover: *Kyai Lebdhåjiwå*, South Bank Centre, London
Fig. 1.7: *Kyai Kanyut Mèsem*, *Purå Mangkunegaran*, Solo
Fig. 2.1: Horniman Museum, London
Fig. 3.9(a): *Kangjeng Kyai Medharsih/Kangjeng Kyai Mikatsih*, *Kraton Yogya*
Figs 3.10, 3.43, 3.44, 3.50, 3.62, 3.65, 3.69, 3.71, A10, A11, A12: *Kyai Madu Sari* (author's own instruments), London
Figs 3.11, 3.18, 3.20, 3.35, 3.40, 3.48, 3.49, 3.56: Pendhopo Ageng, STSI Solo
Figs 3.13, 3.63 (mostly): house of the late Ki Suhardi, Gedong Kuning, Yogya
Figs 3.17, 3.42, 3.72, 3.75, 3.90: *Kyai Sekar Tunjung*, home of K. P. H. Notoprojo (Pak Cokro), Mergangsan, Yogya
Figs 3.32, 3.66, 3.73: generic
Figs 3.24, 3.74, 3.79, 3.80, A13: workshop of Suhirdjan, Gedong Kiwo, Yogya
Fig. 3.27: *Gamelan kodhok ngorèk*, Pendhopo Ageng, STSI Solo
Fig. 3.28: *Kangjeng Kyai Surak*, *Kraton Yogya*
Fig. 3.29: *Kyai-Nyai Riris Manis*, Sonobudoyo Museum, Yogya
Fig. 3.30: *Kyai Megamendhung* from *Kraton Kasepuhan*, Cirebon, in Sonobudoyo Museum, Yogya
Fig. 3.31: *Kangjeng Kyai Pengawé Sari/Kangjeng Kyai Telågå Muncar*, *Purå Pakualaman*, Yogya
Fig. 3.67: Dr David Hughes, SOAS, London
Fig. 3.83: *Kraton Yogya*
Fig. 3.91: Condong Catur, Yogya
Fig. 3.92: Dr Tim Byard-Jones, Reading, UK
Fig. 3.96: *Kangjeng Kyai Kaduk Manis/Kangjeng Kyai Manis Renggå*, *Kraton Solo*
Fig. 3.98: Pak Sutarjan's group, Solo
Fig. 3.99: *Kangjeng Kyai Guntur Laut*, *Kraton Yogya*
Fig. 3.101: *Kangjeng Kyai Någåwilågå*, *Kraton Yogya*

Bathik patterns

Tips and tricks

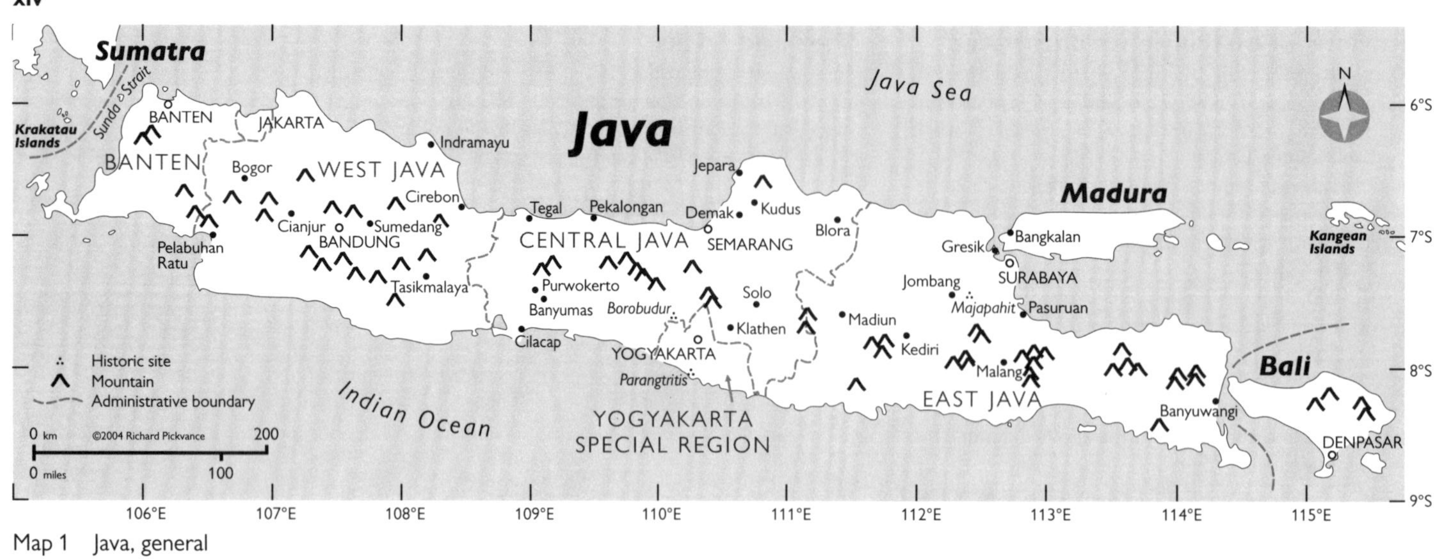

Map 1 Java, general

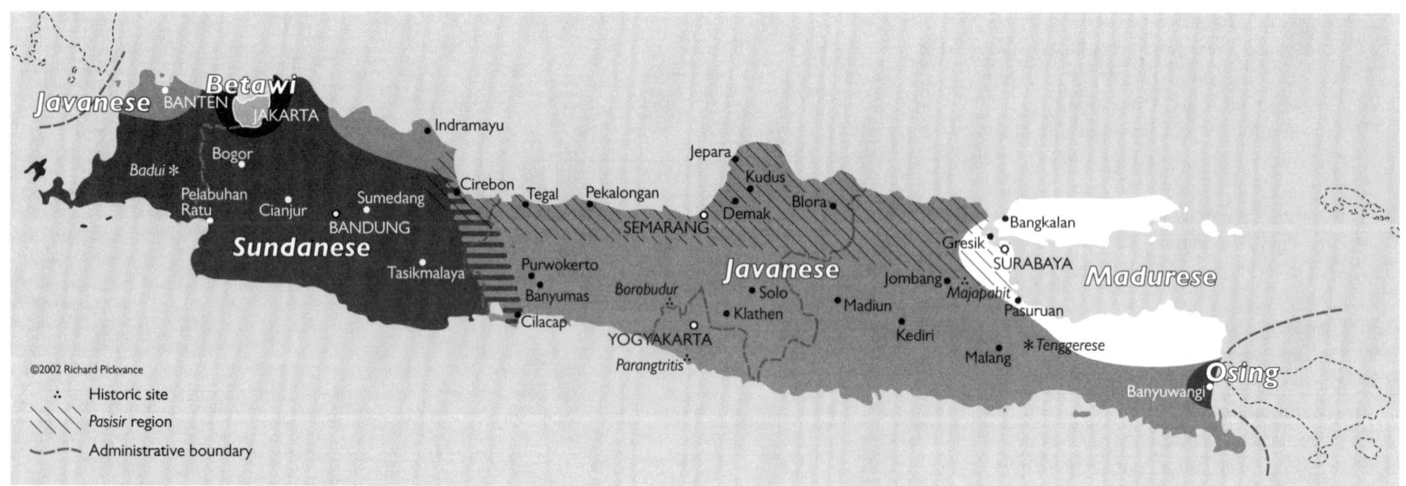

Map 2 Cultural and linguistic divisions of Java

Introduction

Encountering the gamelan

Scope

This book is about *karawitan*, the classical music of central Java. The term *karawitan*, widely used only since the mid-twentieth century, is related to the root *rawit* = refined, perfect. It allows the Javanese to distinguish their own musical culture from Western music, called *musik* or—to make it even clearer—*musik barat*.[1] For a piece of music to qualify as *karawitan*, it must use one or both of the characteristic tuning systems *sléndro* and *pélog*, neither of which corresponds to any Western scale. In some places this principle is challenged: see **Gamelan abroad**.

It is advisable to point out that the word 'Javanese' has cultural significance that outsiders may miss. The home territory of the Javanese ethnic group is the province of Central Java and the autonomous *Daerah Istimewa Yogyakarta* (DIY) or Yogyakarta Special Region.[2] Politically dominant at the national level, they are also widely diffused across the Indonesian archipelago, partly as a result of the policy of resettlement (*transmigrasi*) to the less-populated islands. Elsewhere in Java (see Map 2), groups with their own languages and cultures, such as the Sundanese in West Java and Banten provinces, are not Javanese any more than the Scots are English.[3]

Since the founding of the Indonesian republic, education throughout the country has been based on the use of the Indonesian language. In most areas of the country, however, Indonesian is only a second language, and a regional first language is used for everyday purposes, forming an important element of cultural identity. Music sessions in central Java normally use Javanese throughout, unless the presence of a Westerner (*londo*) makes it necessary to resort to Indonesian.

The book concentrates on the main traditions of central Java, based around the twin cities of Surakarta (Solo) and Yogyakarta (Yogya), which are sometimes referred to as the Principalities. There is only passing reference to the related musical cultures of Bali, Sunda, East Java and Madura.[4] The common origins of all these traditions can be seen not only in the obvious fact that they all use forms of gamelan (and other clearly related ensembles) and the same or similar scales, but also from the construction of their music and their instruments.

Within its chosen field, the book tries to reflect a wide range of performance practice, although still only a small fraction of the exuberant variety actually in use.

One overall aim of the book is to equip readers with enough techniques to be able to make an acceptable interpretation of any new piece that they encounter. 'Acceptable' implies that it will not necessarily be what an experienced Javanese musician, more familiar with the piece, would play: in other words, it should be compatible with what other players are likely to be contributing, but need not be ideal (assuming that such a description had any meaning in the context of *karawitan*).

Ultimately it is impossible to draw limits for performance practice and say that x is right but y is wrong (see **Orientation**, opposite). The boundaries would have to vary from place to place, from group to group within a place, from occasion to occasion, (most importantly?) from piece to piece, and even from player to player: less is expected of some players than of others.

Terminology

Any student of the gamelan and its music must tackle a large quantity of technical terms in Javanese. This is inevitable, since Javanese music works on different principles from Western music. There are simply no English equivalents for most of the terms needed, and attempts to translate Javanese terms literally into English can produce ludicrous results.

For some concepts, even quite important ones, the Javanese seem to manage without a dedicated term. Those terms that do exist are not used consistently by different sources (see **Orientation** again). The text here generally follows the academies in their usage of terms, but points out where other usages exist. A few English terms for Javanese concepts have become established and will be used here, with due caution.

Technical terms in Javanese and Indonesian are printed in italics here, with two exceptions. The word 'gong' when used in its most general sense is treated as being (after some 400 years) fully naturalised into English. The word 'gamelan' is treated slightly differently: it is used with both singular and plural meanings,

1 *Musik* also means Javanese music played on instruments other than the gamelan.

2 The province of Central Java (*Jawa Tengah*) and the DIY are here referred to collectively as 'central Java'.

3 For a convenient overview of the ethnic, linguistic and cultural differences within the island, see Hatley (1984).

4 For an introduction to these, see Garland (1998) or the appropriate sections under INDONESIA in Grove (1980, 2001).

Orientation

The situation confronting the Western student of gamelan music can be crystallised in a few observations and anecdotes.

- Speaking to a Western audience after an Indonesian dance performance, the leader of the troupe encouraged his listeners to try to understand the culture, but 'don't try to **become** Indonesian'.
- The following conversation took place between an experienced British gamelan player and a Javanese teacher.

  PLAYER: Can you give me a *gambang* part for [a certain piece]?

  TEACHER: Why?

  PLAYER: Because I want to do it right.

  TEACHER: You are a *gambang* player. What you do **is** right.

  Conclusion To be regarded as fully competent, a player need not be perfect, but must have reached the stage of being trusted to play something acceptable. It is possible for a *londo* to aspire to this level.
- An exchange:

  STUDENT: Should I play *pinjalan ngedhongi* here?

  TEACHER: No, play it like this.

  The teacher then plays what the student recognises as *pinjalan ngedhongi*.

  Conclusion Technical terms are of limited value. Many of the terms appear in treatises that musicians do not read—indeed, the terms may have been invented quite recently by the writers (Western as well as Javanese)—and teachers do not necessarily use them. Since the process of learning in Java has traditionally been based on imitation, technical terms have not been strictly necessary.
- For the same reasons, the meaning of a technical term can vary between one source and another.
- Words from Old Javanese are often used in texts, and as the titles of pieces and the names of gamelan. In terms of distance from the present day, Old Javanese is roughly equivalent to Chaucer for an English-speaker. Musicians are seldom expert in Old Javanese, and therefore cannot be relied on for translations. It is likely that many mistranslations have been passed on to Western players.
- The secondary- and tertiary-level music schools and academies in Java are, like the universities, a relatively new development. Many expert players and teachers never attended any such institution. They may preserve performance practices that are just as valid, 'traditional' or widespread as those now taught in the institutions.
- Western students may find the relationship between Javanese teachers and their students old-fashioned. Teachers still receive respect by right rather than having to earn it. This does not inhibit students in their development of individuality and independence.
- Because the Javanese musical culture was transmitted orally for a long period, the question of mobility becomes important. Musicians may have experienced only a small part of the range of current usage: nevertheless they may make confident statements about what is normal, and thereby mislead their students. This is no criticism, merely a statement about a society where people have traditionally moved around rather less than Westerners are used to.
- Every student of the gamelan who has played for a Javanese teacher has received a comment along the lines of 'It isn't wrong, but ….' In other words, the teacher would never consider playing it that way.

  Conclusion Players are confronted with a variety of possible performance practices, and are expected to make artistic judgements.
- A group of players may all have the same notation in front of them, but nevertheless all deviate from it in the same way when playing.

  Conclusion Notation is only a rough guide to performance practice: group experience overrides it. Also some Javanese musicians are not actually very good at notating pieces that they know.
- The Javanese are said to prefer indirectness: this certainly applies to aspects of social relationships, and may explain a love of allusion and wordplay that also contributes to their music.
- When seeking reliable information on music, gamelan students in Indonesia experience the same difficulty as tourists in general. Asking three informants can elicit at least three different replies. The cultural obligation to make some kind of reply is stronger than the obligation to give the **right** answer.

as any Indonesian or Javanese noun can be. (For the benefit of newcomers, it may be useful to point out that 'gamelan' always refers to the instruments, not the players.) Spelling has deliberately been left unstandardised.

To help the reader with the technical terms, a comprehensive glossary is provided (p. G-1). It begins with an introduction that covers various problems in reading and understanding Javanese words.

Sources

There is a bewildering range of information, sometimes mutually contradictory, in current Indonesian writings about *karawitan*. Often the writers have described what was familiar to them without indicating the existence of equally valid alternative practices. Whether they were even aware of the other practices is impossible to say.

On the other hand, the risk of standardisation has grown with the development of *karawitan* as a subject at educational institutions in Java and beyond, with the broadcasting and recording of music, with the increased use of notation and with the advent of printed editions of both musical compositions and instructional material. The Javanese have noted the effect of a group of musicians sharing the same sources, thereby running the risk of sounding like 'clones'.[5] Ideally any book, including this one, will not contribute to any such tendency. Experienced players of the gamelan should find here things that are new to them but nevertheless 'correct'.

Apart from direct experience and the evidence of several decades of sound recordings, the sources used here include numerous books. Those written by Indonesians often suffer from the limitations mentioned below and under **Orientation** (as well as from the depressingly high incidence of misprints in Indonesian printing). Most of them are at the primer level anyway, and therefore the coverage in this book goes well beyond them.

Even recordings are not necessarily authoritative: some well-known recordings undoubtedly contain mistakes by players. Any performance practice described here as exceptional might be regarded by other musicians as an error.

Dissertations or theses written by ISI and STSI students have been a useful source. These describe living practices at the time of the research, and were independently assessed.

No definitive collection of notation exists for the corpus of classical compositions, although many small collections have been issued. The three typescript volumes by the distinguished Solonese musician Mloyowidodo, published by ASKI in 1975,[6] are the nearest thing to definitive in recent years. However, the nearly 900 items therein exclude pieces that have no *balungan*, pieces in the 'editable' and other irregular forms, some well-established recent compositions, and pieces in other genres that are regularly played on the gamelan (see **Relationship with other music**, p. 15). The Yogyanese tradition is even less well served by published notation. Players tend to accumulate their own large collections of notation, with multiple variants of well-known pieces.

A special warning must be issued about Javanese folk-etymologies (*jarwådhåså* or *jarwådhosok*). Normally etymologies would be expected to supply clues to the original or true meanings of words, but it has been said that etymologies in Java are a branch of literature rather than of linguistic science.[7] Students of the gamelan can expect to hear numerous competing explanations of the origins of words, all given by the informants with total conviction. Thick fog now surrounds some of the most important terms (e.g. *pélog*, *pathet*, *sekati/sekatèn*).

Some topics that might seem important to players or to researchers in this field are apparently not regularly discussed or written about by the Javanese—perhaps another result of the oral traditions of *karawitan*. These 'non-subjects' are mentioned below where relevant.

Despite the limitations of Javanese sources, they must form a writer's point of departure. More weight is given here to what Javanese players do than to what they say they do.

History and tradition

At various points it seems worth looking backwards into the history of *karawitan*, but the available material is of limited value.

The history of notation stretches back only into the nineteenth century (see p. 44). From before that time we have a few writings about music, but they must be treated with a degree of scepticism.

The word 'traditional' is too readily applied to *karawitan*, and requires comment. It is the oldest elements recalled by teachers and performers, and those evidenced by the oldest recordings and literary references, that attract the description 'traditional'. Notation has very

5 K. R. T. Wasitodiningrat, reported by Brinner (1995), p. 150. The sources may be, for example, the same small group of teachers at an academy.

6 Although actually compiled in the 1950s.

7 And are therefore perhaps best treated like poems or 'urban legends'.

little value as evidence. 'Traditional' features therefore are not necessarily very old. Whenever the word 'traditional' is used below, the proviso '(as far as we can now ascertain)' should be understood.

If such-and-such a composition is mentioned as dating from a certain period, is it the piece that we know by the same name today? Is the present-day *gendhing Lipur érang-érang* identical to the *Ngérang-ngérang* of 400 years ago or the thirteenth-century *Lipur érang-érang*?[8] Without notation we cannot be sure. The existence of unrelated pieces that share a name today must make us suspicious. For example, it is hard to see any relationship between *gendhing bonang Babar layar* in *pélog limå* and the *gendhing rebab* of the same name in *pélog barang*. The Solonese *ladrang Semar mantu* (soft-style, *pélog nem*) bears little resemblance, as performed, to its Yogyanese namesake (loud-style, *sléndro manyurå* or *nem*).

It is also possible for compositions to fall out of use. If a ruler decides that a certain gamelan should no longer be played or a certain art form or ceremony no longer be performed, any associated pieces may be lost. Long compositions, or more complex treatments of a certain piece, may be neglected if people who order performances decide there is no time for them. We do not know how much has been lost.

Similarly, the history of instruments, ensembles and performance practice lacks a solid base. Even if early notation had survived, we would still not necessarily know how the music was originally performed. Pieces may have very ancient origins, but do they now sound the same as they did when first played? In some respects we can be sure that the answer is no: for example, certain instruments (*siter*, *ciblon*, *gendèr panerus*) have not been in the gamelan for long, and *pesindhèn* too are a relatively recent addition. The sound of the music must have been affected by the increased number of *kenong* and *kempul* notes now available. If the ceremonial gamelan are evidence, there used to be fewer but larger instruments, and pitch has risen over the years. As will be shown later, some elements of present-day performance practice were introduced only recently.

We have independent evidence from the beginning of the sixteenth century, in the form of accounts by foreign visitors, of ensembles that seem to fit the description of gamelan. They also show that most major artistic forms tied to *karawitan*, i.e. dance and drama including various forms of *wayang*, were already established at that time. Earlier dates have been ascribed by the Javanese to some surviving sets of instruments that are similar in their make-up to modern gamelan (allowing for the absence of the recently developed instruments).

The *Wédhå Pradånggå* gives dates as far back as the third century AD for the first gamelan, although the account lacks the corroboration that Western historians would expect.[9] These gamelan (whatever their true dates) were different and simpler in their instrumentation than today's ensembles. Certainly they would not have been able to perform in most styles familiar today. The general shape of the historical development is from a few simple ensembles, owned by the rulers and probably with a ceremonial function, to a large number of ensembles spread throughout the population and capable of playing a much wider range of music.

(Also see **Origins of *karawitan*** in Part 2, p. 24.)

Authenticity and authorship

Where the text is concerned (if it is allowable to refer to musical notation by this term), there is a basic difference in attitude between the Javanese and Western traditions.

In Western classical music, the composer's original score tends to be treated as sacrosanct. Musicians may go to elaborate lengths to find the most 'correct' version of a score. The assumption is that the score tells all the players what to do at all times. The players actually interpret a work within a strict set of performance conventions, although they take them for granted in the case of modern works. For older works, musicians research the historically appropriate performance practice—or at least this had become normal by the end of the twentieth century.

For Javanese musicians the notation (if they use it at all) is at most a starting point. In fact its main purpose was originally to ensure that the stock of compositions was not forgotten, or perhaps to discourage the performance of 'incorrect' versions, rather than as a precise guide to how a piece should be played.[10] The inventors of the notation schemes would probably never have expected players to use notation in performance.

As is explained later, none of the instruments plays exactly what is usually notated, i.e. the standard form of notation is not the part for any specific instrument.[11] Every musician interprets the piece in accordance with the performance practice of his/her particular instrument.

8 Both dates come from the *Wédhå Pradånggå*, a history of *karawitan*: see Becker & Feinstein (1987).

9 Documentary evidence for the arts only begins towards the end of the first millennium AD (Holt, 1967; Kunst, 1968).

10 For a recent review of the evidence pointing to a Western role in the adoption of notation, see Perlman (2004).

11 Vocal parts have usually been notated separately.

Complete parts for individual instruments are rarely written out except by students.

The 'traditional' repertoire for the gamelan must have been formed over a period of several centuries. Even if detailed information existed about changes in performance practice since *karawitan* began, one wonders whether today's musicians would take account of it and revive superseded performance practices.

In Western classical music, the nearest equivalent to the Javanese performer's role is a keyboard player's realisation of the basso continuo line in a baroque piece. There the player must expand the bare bass line into suitable chords, or perhaps something more ambitious.[12]

Javanese musicians, like their Western counterparts, are therefore working within conventions. However, they come from a background that gives a different status to the composer and the act of composition, as compared to the Western classical tradition. (See also **Authority and the royal courts**, p. 14, and **Improvisation**, p. 25.)

This situation can be compared to literary practice. Indonesian writers leave the reader to sort out the meaning of the text, in contrast to the English-speaking world, where it is the writer's duty to make everything clear. These are respectively 'reader-responsible' and 'writer-responsible' cultures.

It follows from the above that, for each instrument that interests them, players must study general performance practice for that instrument as much as individual pieces.

Why play the gamelan?

Most readers will already have their own answers for this question. Playing the gamelan demands cooperation—*gotong royong*, to use the Indonesian political term—and is thus seen by the Javanese as having a moral value.

Westerners with other political beliefs will still commend the listening skills and responsiveness developed by gamelan-playing—seen as valuable when transferred to any other musical culture, and even to activities outside music (see under **Gamelan abroad**, p. 19 foll.). The sound of the gamelan has appealed immediately to most (though by no means all) foreigners.

Much of the merit of *karawitan* for Westerners lies in the ways in which it challenges familiar musical principles: it differs in its scales, its instruments and playing techniques, the roles of the instruments, its musical forms (including the concept of development), the character of melodic lines, the relationships between the various players and their parts, the player's responsibilities, the extent to which the course of a performance is predetermined, and the attitude towards errors, variation and personal contributions.

The gamelan can be, and frequently is, played by people of widely differing abilities. The many 'seats' in the ensemble are useful for teaching large classes. In both these respects, the central Javanese gamelan offers more than some other Indonesian musical traditions.

Further study

Those who wish to pursue their gamelan studies beyond the level of this book will now find an extensive literature in English. The available material is mostly in the form of theses, or papers on limited topics published in academic journals. Also see under **Gamelan abroad**.

Ultimately there is no substitute for studying in Java itself. Westerners up to the age of 35 can apply for the *dharmasiswa* arts studentships offered by the Indonesian government for study at institutions such as STSI or ISI.

Health warnings

At a time when the matter of health and safety at work enjoys a higher profile than formerly, a few warnings should perhaps be given.

Gamelan instruments, like the Western orchestra, can certainly develop volume levels that are dangerous to the hearing. On the other hand, a *demung* player who has not experienced a temporary threshold shift by the end of a *gendhing bonang*, or perhaps in a dance accompaniment for a fight scene involving a *gagah* character, has arguably not been playing loud enough.

The *placak* of various instruments—perhaps especially the long thin pins of the *gambang*—present a risk of injury to anyone falling against the instrument.

Various forms of repetitive strain injury (RSI)—or **upper limb disorder**, to give it the name now preferred—are a hazard when playing almost any instrument other than a punctuating instrument.

Finally, many gamelan players suffer long-term addiction, and withdrawal symptoms appear after only a week or two without playing.

12 In this context it is possible for a player to be considered too creative with the composer's text. For example, some people used to say that Thurston Dart's keyboard continuo contributions went too far.

Gamelan at home

Where?

The gamelan and where to find it

One of the most interesting items in *Music in Java*[13] is a gamelan census showing 12,477 gamelan in Java and Madura together, ignoring minor types of ensemble, for a population of 40.9 million (1930 figures). The Principalities[14] accounted for 10 per cent of the population but over 21 per cent of the gamelan. With this many gamelan in central Java, a village or community (*kampung*) would have its own gamelan or at least would not be far from one. It is unlikely that the quantity of gamelan has kept pace with the trebling of the population since 1930.

The *kampung* may now be a small district within a city, still having a community identity. Under Indonesia's hierarchical local government structure (Fig. 1.1), there are plenty of centres where a gamelan may be based. Besides the many gamelan in the royal courts, others can be found in educational institutions—not only those devoted to music—and in workplaces and hotels. Sets of instruments exist in the homes of musicians, music-lovers and members of the royal families: the latter can of course be music-lovers and performers too.

Instruments are sometimes transported to allow performances away from their usual homes, but normally the players go to where the instruments are.

Religion and music

As a generalisation, musical styles in Java are associated with the cultural/linguistic groups rather than with religion. Java, like Indonesia as a whole, is reckoned to be about 85–90 per cent Muslim. Here and there the Christian missionaries have had an impact. Within the Chinese ethnic group, Buddhism is still common, and not all Hindu believers fled to Bali when Islam arrived. There are also isolated groups practising pre-Islamic religion (the Badui and Tenggerese, see Map 2).

Significant regional differences exist in the practice of Islam. The Sundanese are considered more strictly observant, whereas central Java is known for its syncretistic form of religion, in which mysticism (*kebatinan*) and Hindu and Buddhist elements still play a part.

Beneath or alongside Islam, earlier animist beliefs persist everywhere. The *dhukun*, the Indonesian version of the shaman and healer, has made the transition from traditional village figure to urban professional with consulting rooms and office hours. Christianity is probably stronger in Solo and Yogyakarta than in most other areas of Java, and Christian villages are found in the area too. It is quite practical to organise an all-Christian gamelan group in Yogyakarta, without calling in *londo*.

According to the standard account, the Islamic 'saints' or holy men (*wali*) who introduced Islam to Java exploited the traditional arts, including the gamelan and *wayang*, to spread their message. This goes against the general perception that Islam has no place for music. An alternative view[15] is that the early stages of Islam in Java were associated with the Sufis, who were heavily involved in the dissemination of Islam. In Sufism, music is not only not forbidden but forms an essential part of religious practice.

Whatever may have happened in the past, instrumental music is not found in present-day mosques. (The only tenuous connection is that many mosques have a *bedhug* for summoning the faithful to Friday midday prayers.) However, Islamic religious music does exist, in the form of the chants heard from the mosques' loudspeakers and the *rebånå* groups that meet in people's homes.

Islam affects *karawitan* in that many gamelan events or performances cease during the fasting month (*Påså*: see **Appendix 6**) or during Friday, the Muslim day of prayer. In the royal palaces (*kraton*), perhaps because their traditions go back to before the arrival of Islam, these prohibitions are observed less strictly.

Because *karawitan* is detached from the prevailing religion, the titles of pieces and the texts that they use rarely contain references to Islam. On the other hand, the divinities, heroes and heroines of the Hindu myths (in distinctive Javanese versions) regularly figure in these places. Individual pieces of music are treated as having ritual or religious significance, a situation that appears incompatible with Islam. For example, *ldr Wilujeng* (= fortunate, blessing) is frequently used to bring good fortune to any ceremony or event, while the Solonese

13 Kunst (1973), Appendix 57.

14 The regional boundaries used by Kunst differ from the present-day boundaries.

15 Which does not necessarily invalidate the whole of the standard account: see Sumarsam (1995).

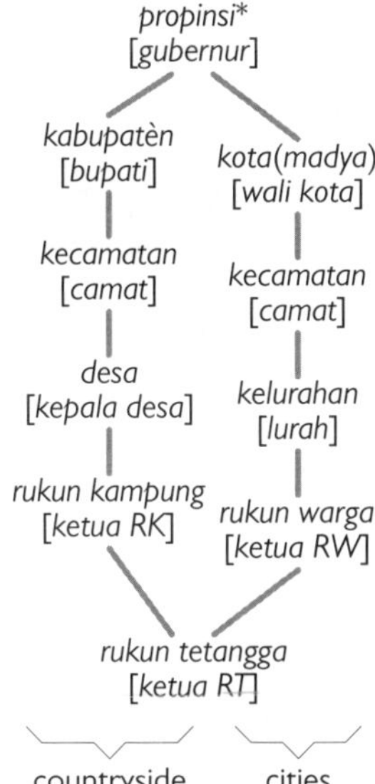

1.1 Local government structure from province level downwards: title of head shown in brackets

version of *ldr Semar mantu* (= Semar holds a wedding) serves a similar purpose specifically for weddings. Another piece with special sacred meaning is *Ayak-ayakan Gadhung mlathi*, linked to Ratu Kidul, the queen of the southern ocean and mythical consort of the rulers of Solo and Yogya.

The full gamelan receives an occasional welcome into Christian churches in Java, e.g. in a Catholic Mass with gamelan accompaniment. It is even possible for a *pélog* gamelan to accompany a congregation singing hymns in Western diatonic scales.

Gamelan etiquette

1.2 *Pesindhèn* from a *siteran* group on the streets of Solo at night

Players observe certain rules of behaviour around the gamelan instruments. They always remove their footwear before playing, and avoid stepping over the instruments, or even touching instruments with their feet. All this can be seen as part of a foot taboo, because the feet are considered the least sacred part of the body, being in contact with the ground, and the head is the most sacred —which is why Western tourists must resist the temptation to pat the head of a Javanese child. However, Indonesians normally take off their shoes or sandals anyway when entering any building other than an office or place of business. Another habit that may relate to the same taboo is to replace the beaters on the instruments, not on the ground, after playing.

In the royal palaces, gamelan are classed as possessions of the ruler (*kagungan dalem*), deserving additional respect. Players may apologise to the instruments if they are obliged to move them, and will perform a *sembah*—a gesture of greeting and respect—to the instruments when entering or leaving the *pendhåpå*. Ceremonial gamelan are sacred heirlooms (*pusåkå*) and are accorded even higher status.

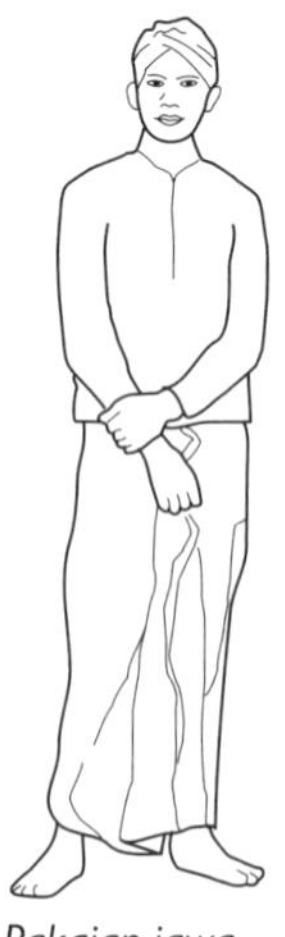

1.3 *Pakaian jawa*

Traditional animist beliefs are no doubt behind all this behaviour. Another indication of the same tradition is that musicians sometimes think of the notes as being resident in the instrument, just waiting to be released when the instrument is struck. Offerings of flowers and food may be made to the *gong ageng*, as embodying the spirit of the gamelan, on appropriate anniversaries or before important performances. The performance of certain pieces calls for additional offerings.

In most playing sessions—even in live broadcasts, whatever the house rules may say—eating, drinking and smoking are normal. Western players tend to be rather more concerned than the Javanese to keep their instruments and beaters clean. In Java the trough resonators of instruments are often full of cigarette ends, dried-up leaves, dead insects and other detritus.

Pesindhèn normally sit on their heels or on a very low stool, whereas men normally sit cross-legged. These postures are not unusual anyway for the Javanese, but they incidentally keep the performers at a lower level than the ruler, and prevent the soles of the feet from being seen.

For the more formal occasions, players dress appropriately. Women wear *kain kebaya* (Fig. 1.2)—the combination of a *bathik* or print blouse with a *bathik* piece as a skirt—plus a tight corset and often a diagonal sash, and extend their hair with a chignon (*sanggul*).

Men wear 'court dress' (*pakaian jawa*, Fig. 1.3), which includes a *bathik* headdress (*blangkon*) and a *kain panjang* —a *bathik* piece of extra length that allows for a set of seven narrow pleats at the front. Short jackets (*beskap*, *jas*, *pranakan*) are found in both Solo and Yogya: long jackets (*surjan*) are perhaps more common in Yogya than in Solo. Yogya *kraton* ensembles often wear *lurik*, a coarse cotton homespun with a vertical stripe, and both prints and embroidered silk are found too. *Bathik* jackets are unusual. Some ensembles wear a uniform of their own. Not seen in Fig. 1.3 are a sash (*stagèn*) and belt into which a *kris* should be tucked (see Fig. 3.101).

When?

Occasions for performances

It has been said that gamelan performances not accompanying dance or drama (including *wayang kulit*) are the exception not the rule in Java. So far as public performances by professional players are concerned, this may be the case. At the domestic level and for amateur players (accounting for the majority of sessions), the opposite is true: amateur groups play mainly for their own pleasure or for events on a modest scale without dance or drama. Sessions that are independent of drama or dance are usually called *klenèngan* in Solo or *uyon-uyon* in Yogya.

Apart from regular rehearsals (*latihan*) and sessions for the players' own pleasure, occasions for performances are numerous:

- the 'playing-in' or try-out (*percobaan*) of a new gamelan before shipment,

- the 35-day birthday (*tingalan*, *wetonan*: see **Appendix 6**) of someone important, e.g. a member of the royal family (see Table 1.1) or a distinguished musician,
- a coming-of-age,
- the morning before a wedding—or, in deference to present-day working patterns, the previous night,[16]
- a wedding reception,
- a *mitoni* or *tingkeban*, a ceremony for the seventh month of a pregnancy—especially the first,
- the birth of a child,
- the fifth day after the birth (*sepasaran*), to mark the withering of the umbilical cord, or the 35th day,
- a circumcision (*supitan*, *tetakan*),
- any fortunate event,
- the making of a vow (*kaul*), or its fulfilment,
- a funeral,
- the one-thousandth day (*nyèwu*) after a death,[17]
- rituals related to the harvest and the rice goddess Dewi Sri, including the annual ritual of cleansing the village (*bersih désâ*, *bersih dhusun*),
- an exorcism (*ruwatan*) ceremony to protect a child thought to be in danger,
- to welcome important visitors,
- public holidays,
- as an element of a political campaign, a government campaign or an advertising promotion,
- an anniversary of an institution, e.g. of the founding of a university or a business, or the establishment of a local government structure, or Indonesia's Independence Day (17 August),
- other public ceremonies of institutions, e.g. the opening of a new supermarket or other building, a university's degree day, a church dedication,
- other public events, e.g. the opening of a sports event, a conference or an arts festival,
- regular broadcasts (*siaran*) from the palaces or from the RRI studios, such as the weekly *Uyon-uyon Månåsukå* (RRI Yogyakarta) and *Klenèngan Hamengsukå* (RRI Surakarta),
- background music in the foyer of a first-class hotel (although *siteran* ensembles are often used in preference to a full gamelan).

Within the list are several items where the gamelan performance is an adjunct to a ceremonial meal (*selamatan/wilujengan*). In most sessions, the musicians can expect to be fed or at least watered—not unreasonable when a session can last for four hours or more.

16 The previous night is also the time for the traditional *malam widadarèni*, when the bride and groom meet. These days it is unlikely to be the first time they have met.

17 The last of the various ceremonies associated with a death.

Table 1.1
Central Javanese courts and their *wetonan/tingalan*, with dates applicable to the rulers in 2003

	Surakarta		Yogyakarta	
	Senior court	Junior court	Senior court	Junior court
Full name[a]	*Kraton Surakarta Hadiningrat*	*Purå Mangkunegaran*	*Kraton Ngayogyakarta Hadiningrat*	*Purå Pakualaman*
Short name	*Kasunanan*	—	*Kasultanan*	—
Title of ruler	*Susuhunan/Sunan*	*Pangeran, Adipati*	*Sultan*	*Pangeran, Adipati*
Name of ruler	*Pakubuwånå*	*Mangkunegårå*	*Hamengkubuwånå*	*Pakualam*
Title of *tingalan*			*Uyon-uyon (H)adiluhung*	*Uyon-uyon Muryåraras*
Date of *tingalan*[b]	?*malam Selasa-Legi*[c]	*malam Sabtu-Pon*	*malam Selasa-Wagé*	*malam Sabtu-Paing*
Time of *tingalan*	?2200[c]	2200	2130–0030	2130–0000
Opening piece	*Ldr Srikaton pl 7*	*Ktw Puspåwarnå sl m*	*Ldr Prabu Mataram sl 9*, *ldr Råjåmanggålå pl 6*	*Ktw Puspåwarnå sl m*
Closing piece	*Ay²an Umbul dongå sl m*	*Ay²an Kaloran sl m*	*Ldr Srikondur sl m*, *ldr Tedhak saking pl 7*	*Bub Hudan mas pl 7*

a. Some sources apply the term *kraton* to all four courts, but the term *purå* is normally used for the junior courts when the full name of the court is given, as here.
b. Days begin at sunset. *Malam* means the evening before, so *malam Selasa* is Monday evening. See **Appendix 6**. c. This information applied to Pakubuwånå XII, who died in June 2004. As a result of a contested succession, the new ruler (and therefore the new *wetonan* date) was still unknown at the time of writing.

The above list embraces both public and domestic occasions. A wealthy household or organisation may commission a *wayang* rather than just a concert. The performance of a *wayang* is believed to have a moral influence, and is therefore most likely to be mounted in connection with one of the major milestones of life.[18]

Clearly not all families will be able to afford a *wayang* performance, even if the invited guests are contributing towards the costs, or a *klenèngan* from a professional ensemble. Two alternatives are a local amateur group or a commercial recording. Cassettes and CDs of music suitable for wedding receptions (*gendhing-gendhing resepsi*) can be bought. The hosts may also hire professional singers to sit in with an amateur group in order to raise the standard of this highly valued element of *karawitan*.

In another exception to the list, some leading *dhalang* use their *tingalan* as a platform for shows by other *dhalang*, including young performers.

The relationship between the audience and the music is not as Westerners might expect.[19] By attending a performance associated with a ceremony, the Javanese demonstrate their respect for tradition, but the music is essentially background. Whether they are also showing appreciation for 'high art' is debatable, because high art is a Western concept.

The audience does not always feel an obligation to arrive at the beginning and stay until the end. At *wayang* performances, it is common practice to leave early, typically after the clown scene in the second 'act'. Also the audience may move around to get different views or to be able to talk to their friends. At weddings or other family ceremonies they are more likely to stay in their seats. One may ask who are the real audience: the official guests who leave early, or the uninvited villagers (including young children) who stay until the end?

1.4 The death of Jathayu, from the 'Ramayana ballet'

'Concert conditions' are therefore not to be expected in any Javanese musical event, and in any case few of these events resemble concerts as Westerners know them. Performances often take place in *pendhåpå* with open sides (Figs 1.6 and 1.7), guaranteeing extraneous noises.

Performances with dance or drama

By custom, performances of *wayang* are usually sponsored by an organisation (these days including radio stations) or by a rich individual or family. The audience may be invited, or the performance may be open to all, but anyone who attends does not expect to pay. This may reflect a different view of the relationship between host and guest: for a Westerner, it is an honour to be invited to a party or an event, whereas in Java the guests honour the host by their presence.

There are exceptions to the custom of free performances. *Wayang* is now often presented on a normal commercial basis. Some dance academies and performing groups such as the Sriwedari *wayang wong* troupe in Solo run scheduled performances, to say nothing of the events aimed mainly at tourists, e.g. the 'Ramayana ballet' at the Prambanan temple complex (Fig. 1.4) and elsewhere.

All-night *wayang* and *kethoprak* performances are broadcast regularly by radio stations, complete except for interruptions from news and advertisements.

In the list above, there are items where dance may feature. The presence of dance items in a wedding reception recalls the tradition of *tayuban* dancing at weddings.[20] *Tingalan* performances at the royal palaces (see Table 1.1) include court dances of the *srimpi* or *bedhåyå* types —a little surprising, because these events are broadcast live, and the audience present in person may number only a dozen, perhaps mainly foreign tourists.

These *srimpi* or *bedhåyå* performances, performed to an empty throne, retain an element of ritual: the event

18 During the political crisis of 1998, performances of a rare *lakon* were organised all over Java to stiffen the nation's moral fibre.

19 See Pemberton (1987) for an amusing investigation of the subject.

20 See Sumarsam (1995), pp. 30–6. *Tayuban* dancing could also occur at other ceremonies.

takes place regardless of whether an audience is present, and continues, once started, to its conclusion. One of these dances, the Solonese *Bedhåyå Ketawang*, is so sacred that restrictions apply even to its rehearsals. Its Yogya counterpart had fallen completely out of use until it was recently reconstructed.[21] These dances too are classed as *pusåkå*, and it is only in the twentieth century[22] that they were first performed outside the palaces.

There are several other dance forms without sacred or ritual associations, but they require similar training, make the same physical demands on the dancer (in spite of the apparently slow pace of the dance), and equally represent dance-as-performance. In contrast, *tayuban* (in spite of its ritual origins) looks like a form of social dance: only the female participants (known as *tlèdhèk*, *ronggèng*, etc.: Fig. 1.5) are trained professionals.[23]

The musical needs of *wayang* and dance are outlined in Part 2.

What?

Programme content

There is a classic format for a *klenèngan* or *uyon-uyon*. Pieces in all *pathet* are played, starting with the lowest (*sl 6* or *pl 5*) and working upwards, in the same sequence as is used for the 'acts' of a *wayang* performance (p. 97). The pieces alternate between the two *laras* if both are available. If the concert is long enough, pieces in the pair of 'related' *pathet* in *sléndro* and *pélog* alternate before the players move on to the next pair of *pathet*. If the programme includes a *gendhing bonang*, it comes first, regardless of its *pathet*. *Gendhing bonang* traditionally feature in wedding ceremonies too, and programmes consisting entirely of *gendhing bonang* also occur.

The *gendhing*, typically with an added 'third section', take about half an hour each. They could be performed with fewer repetitions to save time, but this is not what normally happens. Some individual *gendhing* or standard combinations of pieces can last considerably longer. Add opening and closing pieces to a set of *gendhing* in all six *pathet*, perhaps with a dance item inserted, allow some refreshment breaks for players and listeners, and a duration of four hours is not unusual. Enthusiasts view this as a normal evening's music-making.

The following is an actual programme, with a *gendhing bonang* to start, showing the normal sequence of *laras* and *pathet* except that there is no closing piece in *pélog barang*. There is also no dance item:

- □ *gd bonang Tukung kt 4 kp mg 8 pl 7*,
- □ *gd Måråsånjå kt 4 aw mg 8 sl 6*,
- □ *gd Logondhang kt 2 kp mg ldr Éling-éling kal ktw Gondhang kasih pl 5*,
- □ *gd Menyan kobar kt 4 kp mg 8 kal ktw Mijil dhempel sl 9*,
- □ *gd Onang-onang kt 4 kp mg 4 kal ldr Surung dhayung pl 6*,
- □ *gd Lobong kt 2 kp mg Kinanthi kt 4 kas andhegan Puspanjånå kal ldr Kembang pépé sl m*.

The programme above lasted about four hours and was performed by and for serious gamelan enthusiasts, with some leading local professionals participating. All the pieces are 'heavyweight', and some of them are not among the best-known in the repertoire.

All-night *klenèngan* also occur, again divided into three sections according to *pathet*, like *wayang* performances. In this case there will certainly be time for several compositions in the same *laras* and *pathet*, but again the two *laras* are used alternately. All pieces in *sléndro nem* and *pélog limå* are considered serious. In the later sections of the session, serious pieces are played first, then more cheerful ones.

Other groups regularly choose much lighter fare, consisting mainly of shorter pieces, and including some items in more popular style—*lagu dolanan* and *langgam*, or even *dangdut*—and pay little or no attention to the 'correct' sequence of *laras* and *pathet*. Linked sequences of pieces, e.g. a *ladrang* performed in several *iråmå*, with an inserted *langgam* and one or more *ketawang* to follow, can equal the length of a full-sized *gendhing*.

Groups often have standard opening and/or closing pieces (e.g. as shown in Table 1.1). There may be standard short opening and closing pieces for each *laras*. A *bubaran* is by definition a closing piece, although *ayak-ayakan* are also commonly used for the same purpose. *Hudan mas* is particularly well known, to the extent that it can be used to tell wedding guests when to leave.

The royal courts' opening pieces have a special status. By convention, the entrance of the ruler causes the musicians to stop whatever they are playing and start the appropriate piece—a major departure from standard performance practice. It has been extended to the arrival of the Indonesian president at official functions.

21 This is the *Bedhåyå Semang*, in which no living dancer had ever participated. The dance has been performed again but not yet restored to regular rehearsal.

22 Earlier in Yogya than in Solo.

23 On the origins of various dance forms, and their interrelationships and mutual influences, see Choy (1984) and Brakel-Papenhuyzen (1995). For a Western dancer's view of the technique involved, see Hoskin (2001).

1.5 A *ronggèng* (after an aquatint by William Daniell in Raffles (1817))

Solo vs. Yogya

The present four royal courts resulted from a series of splits in the Mataram kingdom during the colonial era.[24] They could only exercise limited political power, but could apply their resources to artistic activities. They also asserted their individuality via their performance styles. So far as gamelan playing is concerned, Solo and Yogya are rivals and are known for distinct styles: Solo for its soft-style playing, and Yogya for its loud style. It is possible that the *kraton Yogya* preserves more of the musical tradition from before the splits, but the evidence is inconclusive. Whether logical or not, the term *Mataram* is synonymous with Yogyakarta when it appears in the title of a piece or as a description of the playing style.

Perhaps because of marriages between the courts, there has been significant mutual influence, especially from Solo on the Pakualaman court, and, to a lesser extent, from Yogyakarta on the Mangkunegaran court. Current practice at the Pakualaman, as for several decades past, is noticeably mixed. The instrumentation of the principal gamelan there includes *kenong japan*, *bonang panembung*, and a *kempyang* with notes 6 and 7, all of which are expected only in a Yogyanese gamelan. On the other hand, there is a Solo-style *engkuk-kemong*, and the instruments of the *saron* family use Solo-style frames —but the whole *balungan* section in *sléndro* lacks the low 6 of Solonese instruments. The present playing style could be described as basically Solonese with some obvious Yogyanese elements.

The two cities exhibit major differences of performance practice (*garap*) for certain instruments, summarised in the list on page 108. There are also individual compositions that are considered to belong to one tradition, and whole categories that are only found in one. Many pieces are typically played in different versions or known by different names in the two cities.

To be able to make statements about differences of style between Solo and Yogya, one must qualify them. When central Javanese gamelan music is heard outside its home, Solonese style is the **default** style[25]—the one that will be used unless someone has chosen otherwise. Similarly, there are elements of *garap* that can be considered as the default option in one style or the other.

Equally one can refer to a feature as **characteristically** Yogyanese or Solonese: in other words, something that will be recognised by musicians as belonging to one tradition. Other features can be described as **typical** of one tradition, although they may be found in either city.

It is important to distinguish 'characteristic' from 'typical'. Not every group performs in a style 100 per cent characteristic of its home: an element of *garap* may be typical performance practice for a particular playing group, although not characteristic of the wider tradition that the group belongs to.

Musicians from one tradition borrow as they please from the other, if not always very accurately. For example, Solonese musicians refer to 'Yogya-style' *kendhangan* for *ladrang*, which they often choose to use in a loud-style piece, but there are actually at least six types of Yogya-style drumming for *ladrang*.

Rather than ask how the Yogyanese play, for example, it is necessary to ask how they play when consciously following a Yogyakarta style. Because so many Yogyanese groups play in a Solo-influenced style, Yogyanese musicians on average probably know more about Solonese style than Solonese musicians know about Yogya style. It is also possible that the Solonese style is more standardised than the Yogyanese, but statements of this kind are dangerous because they are not supported by the current state of research.

There is therefore no glass wall located somewhere between Solo and Yogya, defining where one style stops and the other begins. Also stylistic features should not be

24 This is the Muslim Mataram kingdom (1575 onwards), not the earlier Hindu Mataram kingdom of the eighth and ninth centuries AD. Map 3 shows the locations of the courts: in both cities the junior court is to the north of the *kraton*. The *kraton Yogya* was established close to the site of the old capital of the Muslim Mataram kingdom at Kota Gedhé.

25 See Sutton (1991).

1.6 The Pendhopo Ageng, principal performance space at STSI Solo, housing various types of gamelan including ceremonial gamelan

regarded as confined to one city: a 'Yogyanese' feature may be found frequently in areas east of Solo.

Elsewhere in the region

Outside the Principalities, further regional variations exist within central Java as regards both performance practice and the ensembles themselves. The *calung* ensemble from the Banyumas area is only one folk ensemble based on bamboo instruments.

By saying that the royal courts stand at the cultural centre of the region, one implies that local styles also exist. *Kébar* is one widely used playing style that is always said to be of village origin. The same may be true of *imbal* on the *bonang*. Playing practices can also be described as 'village' (*désȧ*) to mock their crudeness. Influences in the other direction can also be identified: elements of *kraton* style may be consciously imitated outside the *kraton*.

Some distinguished players in the central Javanese tradition were born well away from the Principalities; some even in East Java. Good players do not necessarily return home after training at the academies. The number of students who have returned to their origins must still be small in relation to the number of gamelan groups. Broadcasts and visits by well-known *dhalang* are among other routes by which 'central' performance practices may be diffused through the region. The extent of these influences and the degree of stylistic variation within the region are essentially unknown;[26] these are under-researched aspects of *karawitan*.

An observer visiting a group for the first time may find that practically all the performance practice is already familiar. It will be impossible to tell whether any unfamiliar element is widespread or unique—and, in the latter case, whether it is unique to the player, the piece (if it is not a familiar one), the group or the locality. It is likely that playing styles vary gradually from place to place, so that there are clines rather than dividing lines.

Other regional styles

Map 2 shows no cultural boundary between central Java and East Java, and thus suggests a continuum across a large area of the island. This picture is reasonably accurate for gamelan music: there are strong similarities as well as differences in many of the ensembles found across the two regions, and in the pieces played on them.

Although Map 2 shows Madurese culture present on the mainland of Java, the true situation is more complicated than can easily be depicted on a map. In parts of East Java there are outposts of Madurese culture rather than large areas. So far as music is concerned, Madurese and East Javanese styles overlap. Around Banyuwangi various styles can be found, including some distinctive local ones showing Balinese influence.

The boundary between West Java and central Java represents a greater cultural divide. (See also **Religion and music**, p. 7.) The theoretical basis of Sundanese music is different, and the notation system works 'upside down' relative to that of central Java (see p. 39n). The gamelan and related ensembles, of which there are several different kinds, tend to contain fewer instruments than those further east. The practical result is that East Javanese pieces can be adapted and played on central Javanese instruments more easily than Sundanese pieces.

Cirebon on the north coast is an interesting case. The city contains several ancient royal courts—older, indeed, than those of the Principalities—and shows evidence of influences from various regions, rather than belonging wholly to the Sundanese cultural region as might be expected. (In any case, cultural boundaries have shifted over the centuries.) Cirebon lies towards one end of the *pasisir* area of the north coast (see Map 2), where the coastal cities maintained overseas trading contacts, and where Islam was first introduced to the island.[27]

Cultural connections

Karawitan does not exist in isolation from the rest of Javanese culture. The connections between *karawitan* and literature are mentioned later at various points. The character of a piece may be determined by the text sung by the *gérong* and/or the *pesindhèn*. In a few cases (e.g. *ldr Kijing miring/Gonjing miring*) alternative texts are sung with the same instrumental parts, and set quite different moods. The popular end of the gamelan repertoire includes many pieces with very earthy texts, full of double meanings, although the Javanese love of wordplay is much in evidence throughout the repertoire.

An important axis in the Javanese world view is the contrast between *(h)alus* (= refined) and *kasar* (= coarse or unrefined). These terms can be applied both to individuals and to activities.[28]

The contrast between *alus* and *kasar* sometimes corresponds to other contrasts. For the Yogyanese, *alus* may

26 The subject is mentioned by Becker (1980). Students at ISI and STSI have written *skripsi* (dissertations) that report on local musical practice in a number of parts of Java. Sutton (1991) examines the situation at specific points in the wider Javanese cultural area.

27 The gamelan delivered to the Paris Conservatoire in 1887 came from Cirebon. It is thought that Debussy may have had an opportunity to play the instruments, but there were no musicians to give a performance on the gamelan.

28 *Londo*, of course, are irredeemably *kasar*.

even be a way of indicating a Solonese treatment of a piece. *Wayang* puppets have distinctive features that allow audiences to identify *alus* and other character types.

In a battle between an *alus* character and a *kasar* character—a frequent scenario in *wayang* and dance—the former is victorious because he has better control of his emotions. The Javanese prize the calm exterior that hides everything that may be going on internally.

On other links with Javanese philosophy and *Weltanschauung*, see **Character of music**, p. 37.[29]

Authority and the royal courts

The various rulers exercise ultimate artistic control in the palaces, deciding where, when and whether musical performances should take place.[30] They are not immune to changing economic circumstances. The amount of artistic activity in the courts is certainly lower than a few decades ago. Indonesia's economic crisis of 1997–8 had effects inside as well as outside the palaces.

The rulers have therefore fostered the cultural activities of the royal courts to differing degrees. In the *Wédhå Pradånggå* we often read that such-and-such a ruler 'composed' a certain piece. Statements of this kind should be taken as suggesting only that the piece was written during the reign of the said ruler. This is not to deny that some of the rulers have been notable practitioners as well as promoters of the arts.

At times, the courts have made conscious decisions to admit influences from outside Java.[31] Instruments from European military bands were adopted by the courts of Solo and Yogya, played either in separate ensembles or together with gamelan instruments. Trumpets and the European tenor drum are still to be heard in gamelan pieces at the *kraton Yogya*: see ***Gati/mares***, p. 72.

Scholarship

As indicated above, Javanese historical writings on gamelan instruments and their music are not very helpful to the practical musician: they lack detail and tend towards a belles-lettres rather than a technical character.[32] For an orally transmitted musical tradition, this is no great surprise. Some writings may have been lost because

1.7 Players at a regular informal dance rehearsal at the Mangkunegaran palace

29 Also Becker (1993).

30 The task may be delegated to another member of the royal family.

31 See Sumarsam (1995), pp. 69–70.

32 Verse rather than prose was the usual mode of literary expression.

they were on perishable materials. Although the datable manuscript sources go back twelve centuries,[33] the references in early documents are in any case difficult to relate to present-day instruments.

When Javanese musicians started writing about *karawitan* in a recognisably 'modern' manner, regrettably they were too influenced by Western scholars: they introduced irrelevant categories from Western music, and got involved in theoretical issues that simply do not apply to *karawitan*.

More recently, Javanese musicians have come to universities in the West and combined Western research methods with their deep knowledge of *karawitan*. The resulting studies are among the most valuable contributions to scholarship.

Relationship with other music

The audience for gamelan music is not exclusively loyal to *karawitan*. Most people listen to more popular styles of music too. The radio stations that broadcast *karawitan*—whether in the form of 'concerts', *wayang* or *kethoprak*—play several other kinds of music, including (increasingly) Western pop music. All these styles compete, and go in and out of fashion.

Some Javanese popular music styles exert an influence on *karawitan*. For example, a *langgam* may be played as a *selingan* in a classical piece or suite. Gamelan players sometimes relax by playing *dangdut*, which suits the gamelan. Another popular form, the Portuguese-influenced *kroncong* (using an ensemble mainly of bowed or plucked string instruments), does not. In fact, *langgam* as found in the context of *karawitan* represents a re-creation of *kroncong* in gamelan terms (although the gamelan has influenced *kroncong* too). *Dangdut*, *kroncong* and *langgam* are non-regional, but there are also regional popular styles such as Sundanese *jaipongan*.[34]

Twentieth-century composers of music for the gamelan incorporated elements of regional and/or popular styles into their works, or combined styles that would traditionally never have been found in the same composition. Pieces of this type are simply accepted without comment rather than being specially marked out. Some have become 'standards' (in the terminology of Western popular music) and receive performances in a variety of styles, not limited to those of central Java. For example, Ki Nartosabdho's *dangdut*-influenced piece *Gambang suling* (also known by its original name *Suårå suling*) has been performed in Balinese and country-and-western styles too.[35]

Experimentation and innovation

Javanese musicians are concerned to innovate. If anything, it is Western gamelan enthusiasts who tend to want to maintain the status quo. There is even an intriguing prospect of 'marginal survival', where usages that have been copied or borrowed elsewhere—by the West, in this case—continue after they have been superseded in their place of origin. This effect has already been noted in the expatriate Javanese community in Suriname, South America. In contrast, musical life within the royal courts offers less scope for innovation, and this is one reason why musicians have sought employment elsewhere.

Experimentation takes various forms. There are new ensembles that include unconventional instruments, and Western instruments have sometimes been used with the gamelan. Because Western and Javanese scales differ so much, mixing the two systems may involve building new instruments of traditional Javanese form but with chromatic or diatonic tuning.

Composers have bent or broken traditional rules—to switch between *sléndro* and *pélog* within a melodic line, for example. They have used triple rhythms instead of the hierarchy of binary divisions on which *karawitan* is normally based. Compositions have departed from the rather limited range of standard forms (*bentuk*), and used instruments outside their conventional fixed roles.

Musicians distinguish the degree of innovation: on one hand, works within the established structures of *karawitan*; on the other, works using gamelan instruments (perhaps together with others) but not within the standard forms of *karawitan*. Two terms, *komposisi baru* and *kréasi (baru)*, are applied, but not consistently.

Campur sari means a mixture of styles—different Indonesian styles, including those mentioned under the previous heading, or mixed Indonesian and Western styles. *Campur sari* is increasingly popular. Radio stations broadcast a full-orchestral version, with elements of *karawitan* played in a diatonic *pélog* scale. Traditional gamelan groups play it in addition to pure *karawitan*, and *campur sari* versions of *wayang* can be heard.[36]

Pieces are also created by writing new sections or

33 See the list in Kunst (1968).

34 The latter was developed relatively recently from the *kethuk tilu* form. This was the Sundanese version of the music of the itinerant *ronggèng/ tlèdhèk*, and shared their associations with sexual immorality.

35 Also in *sléndro*, even though its melodic lines might seem to make sense only in *pélog*.

36 On innovation in *wayang kulit*, see Byard-Jones (2001).

treatments for items in the existing repertoire. The word *rinenggå* (= embellished) used in the title of a piece can indicate this process. It is noticeable that new compositions, whatever the degree of innovation, are mainly in the smaller forms.

A group style

Every individual gamelan group has its favourite pieces and develops its own ways of doing things, from a range of influences (Fig. 1.8). Dominant personalities, contacts with other groups, and practices accidentally heard from radio and TV can all play their part.

Who?

There are of course both amateur and professional gamelan players. In amateur groups, players come from the widest range of backgrounds. For example, the members of one gamelan group in a Yogya *kampung* included a *becak*[37] driver, a chauffeur, a motor mechanic, a carpenter, a stonemason, teachers, retired teachers, other university employees, and housewife *pesindhèn*. Only one or two of them could be considered expert players, able to cope with all the instruments and the most difficult pieces. This group used a bronze gamelan in *sléndro* owned by one family. Besides its regular Saturday night *uyon-uyon* sessions, it played for events within the *kampung*.

37 Tricycle rickshaw, pedicab.

38 Even Western *pesindhèn* performing in Java have been paid at these rates.

39 Supanggah (1985).

40 For the record, there have also been female *dhalang* and male *pesindhèn*.

academies (STSI, ISI)
our regular pelatih
TV advertising jingles
neighbouring villages
kroncong
kraton performances
visiting experts
our group
other regional styles
kethoprak
experimental groups
langgam
dangdut
published collections
broadcast performances
commercial recordings

1.8 Network of influences on a gamelan group

Professional players tend to work in more than one place in order to earn an adequate living. If they take part in *kraton* performances, these days it is not for the money, because the pay is low. Leading players are associated with the radio stations and/or the music academies. They can also boost their income by giving private lessons to foreign students of the gamelan. Such is the disparity in the cost of living that these lessons are good value for money for Westerners, and very lucrative for the Javanese.

The situation is somewhat different for *dhalang* and *pesindhèn*: these are the performers who currently enjoy star status, although work has been harder to find during the harsher economic climate of the post-Soeharto era. For a single session, a *pesindhèn* can be paid more than several instrumental players together, and more than most Indonesians earn in a month.[38] The pay rates for expert instrumental players can sometimes allow them to survive on just a few performances a month.

The situation just described represents a reversal of the traditional status of players in the *kraton*.[39] Formerly the players stood at the top of the hierarchy of palace servants (*abdi dalem*), above the *dhalang*, *pesindhèn*, dancers and practitioners of the other arts.

There are *dhalang* who employ permanent groups of musicians. Sometimes a *dhalang* takes only a couple of key players—the *gendèr barung* and *kendhang* players—to a performance, and relies on local people (professionals and/or amateurs) to provide the rest of the ensemble.

There was a strong tendency for the music profession to run in families. It has often been assumed that players used to be exclusively male. Evidence from drawings in eighteenth- and nineteenth-century manuscripts suggests this may not always have been the case: they show women playing in mixed groups, and even in all-female groups, although it is not certain that they relate to central Java. Even after *pesindhèn* began to perform with the gamelan, women players remained rare. Female *gendèr* players married to *dhalang* were a regular exception: the function of the *gendèr* is so important to a *dhalang* that it is convenient if the player is a family member.[40] In any case the instrument is considered specially appropriate for a woman because of the elegance of the player's hand movements.

These days mixed groups are less unusual, and women players are now increasingly common in the formerly all-male *kraton* groups. All-women (*ibu-ibu*) groups also exist now. Both sexes are represented among the students, whether from Indonesia or from the West, who attend the graduate-level academies (STSI and ISI).

Players' skills

How well must a gamelan player play? This interesting topic—musical competence—has been addressed by several researchers.[41] For readers of this book, perhaps the more relevant question is how well they must play before being accepted into a group of Javanese players.

One of the unusual features of the gamelan is that it can accommodate players of widely differing capabilities. Some members of a group, as in the *kampung* group mentioned above, stick rigidly to one of the simpler instruments and would be out of their depth on the more difficult ones. Other players, though amateurs in the sense that they are not paid for playing, are fully competent on most instruments—possibly on all of them.

Strangers may be welcomed as equal participants—Javanese singers or players, both amateur and professional, as well as visiting *londo*. Javanese musicians are liable to ask Western players which instrument they play, because they are used to players specialising in one instrument. A *londo* may, embarrassingly, be treated as something between a curiosity and a status symbol for a Javanese group. *Londo* will not necessarily be the least competent members of the group, but can in any case expect their errors to be indulged up to a point.

Age and education

Ability also does not necessarily depend on age. The academies now enable stars of the future to be recognised while still young. Before they were founded, the process of musical education was informal and highly diverse.

In the past, many distinguished musicians, by their own accounts, began their careers by being invited to play at a young age when there was an empty 'seat' in an ensemble, or simply when a player wanted to take a break, for whatever reason, during a performance. After growing up surrounded by *karawitan*, and able to attend all local performances without the deterrent of admission charges, they had already picked up enough knowledge to play one of the easier instruments.[42]

Players might acquire their skills entirely in this way. At its most formal, the learning process might rely on the personal relationship between a would-be player and one or more experienced masters. It was left to the student to decide what his objectives were and when he had achieved them. Such a situation was likely to lead to great variety in personal playing styles.

The academies follow more systematic methods of teaching. So also do the primary and secondary schools[43] in central Java: some education in *karawitan* has been a feature of the curriculum since roughly the 1950s, although by no means all schools have actually provided it. Naturally most pupils are not destined to go on to the academies or to become professional musicians, with or without further training. Some of them do not complete the full school programme anyway, since education in Indonesia is neither compulsory nor free in practice. With the growth of *campur sari* and with bookshops full of guitar tutors, there is even some anxiety about the possible lack of a younger generation of players who will take over the classical tradition of *karawitan*.

Javanese respect for age means that the *gong ageng*, as the most important instrument in the gamelan, is often played by someone at the opposite end of the age range. The combination of age, tropical heat and the often long intervals between gong strokes has been known to result in other players throwing objects at the gong player to wake him up.

Easy and difficult instruments

Some instruments have higher status than others. This is not purely a matter of technical difficulty. The *gong ageng*, for example, is easy to play: on the other hand, playing it in the wrong place constitutes a major disaster. In classes at the academies, students play the various instruments in a set sequence that reflects their status and relative difficulty.

There is an important distinction between 'front-row' and 'back-row' instruments. The former category (*ricikan depan* [*in*], *instrumen mukå*) consists of the more difficult decorating instruments: *gendèr*, *rebab* and *gambang*. For professional players, the distinction translates into higher pay rates on the front row.

Handling errors

Even Javanese professional musicians make mistakes. Playing the right note in the wrong place is arguably a worse error than the wrong note in the right place.

41 Especially Brinner (1995).

42 For more on musical education and training in Java, see Supanggah (1985); for a Westerner's viewpoint, see Steptoe (2001). Sumarsam (2004) and Susilo (2004) write about training in Java and their several decades of teaching gamelan in the West.

43 Elementary schools (*sekolah dasar*) cover ages 6 to 12, junior high schools (*sekolah menengah pertama*) 12 to 15, and senior high schools (*sekolah menengah atas*) 15 to 18.

Getting the notes right is obviously desirable. Just as important is the ability to recover after errors or to learn from one's mistakes and develop a correct performance. As the course of a performance is not fully predictable, and the musical cues that players must respond to are audible rather than visible, there is a premium on the players' listening skills. This is true if the players have notation to work from, but becomes even more important when playing from memory. All players therefore need to learn how to recover from errors.

The following account of rehearsals for a broadcast *tingalan* performance in the Yogya *kraton* describes a typical situation, from a time when notation was never used within the *kraton*:[44]

> I transcribed *in situ* all the rehearsals of *Taliwangsa*[45] and its broadcasted performance. Of these ten playings only the final rehearsal and the actual broadcast were correct in the sense that each repetition of the gong-phrase had the correct number of beats and a consistent rendering of the *saron* part (*balungan*). During the early rehearsals there would often not be a single gong-phrase repetition with the correct number of beats (much less the correct *balungan*), the phrases ranging in length from four to sixty-four beats short of 256 beats, to eight to forty-eight beats too long. As the rehearsals approached the broadcast, the mistakes became more minor and the gong-phrase lengths consistent and correct.
>
> During the early rehearsals of *Taliwangsa*, even though a state of musical chaos existed during the thirty to forty minutes it was played, the music never once stopped. The structural and melodic designs of the piece were totally obscured; but somehow the last thirty-two or so melodic beats would eventually emerge, the *gong ageng* would be struck, and they would return to the beginning of the repeated cycle for another attempt. Upon completing a playing of the piece, the musicians never once discussed the problems that were encountered, nor did they isolate any section that was unclear and work on it.
>
> The successful performance of *Taliwangsa* for the Hadiluhung broadcast seems to have been based on a confidence that problems will be resolved through musical repetition rather than through verbal discussion. The cyclic organisation of gamelan music allows the musicians several opportunities within a single performance to clarify a difficult or vaguely remembered passage. Because experienced musicians do have good memories, several repetitions of a troublesome passage or an entire piece are often all that is necessary to straighten out the problem.

The rehearsal procedure described above contrasts with the way that, say, an orchestral rehearsal in the West would be run. There the conductor would stop the music for much smaller errors than those described above. A Javanese teacher or *pelatih* will generally stop only after a complete musical breakdown or—perhaps a more frequent event?—when the players and/or singers have demonstrated a gross failure of interpretation. Although notation is now used routinely, and players are thus less likely to commit major errors in the *balungan* line, rehearsals still tend to follow the pattern described above, and pieces are rarely repeated in the same rehearsal.

Players can recover from situations that are potentially even more serious. For example, some pieces exist in several alternative versions, and it would seem obvious that the musicians ought to decide in advance which one is to be used. Nonetheless, performances may start without any such decision having been made, yet the players (even without the benefit of notation) will work their way towards agreement on one version.

The situation described in the quotation above represents only one approach to rehearsal. Another is exemplified by a troupe of full-time professional players who regularly play for a *dhalang*, and scarcely need rehearsals: here the repertoire is relatively fixed, and includes items that are played several times in a single *wayang* performance. It is no real exaggeration to say that the players could play the music in their sleep, because in the small hours, by all accounts, they do respond correctly to the musical cues and start playing while half-asleep. To avoid problems, the work of accompanying an all-night performance may be divided between two teams of players.

In other public performances—even broadcasts—the musicians again play without rehearsal, relying on their professional skills and experience alone.

44 Vetter (1986), describing events in 1982–3.

45 In the Yogya *kraton* tradition, this is played as a *gendhing bonang*.

Gamelan abroad

Where?

Gamelan would be expected in the Netherlands, as the former colonial power in Indonesia. A particularly wide range of Indonesian musical cultures is indeed represented there.

However, gamelan (Sundanese, Balinese and Javanese) are now to be found in a number of other countries in the West. There are several hundred gamelan groups in North America (United States and Canada). On the opposite side of the Pacific, gamelan exist in Australia, the People's Republic of China, Japan, Malaysia, New Zealand, the Philippines, Singapore and Taiwan.

Although Stamford Raffles brought two nearly complete sets of instruments back from Java in 1816,[46] the current gamelan activities in the United Kingdom date only from the late 1970s, well after gamelan-playing started in the Netherlands and the USA.

Elsewhere in Europe, gamelan communities are active in Belgium, France, Germany, the Irish Republic, Italy and Norway, among other countries. The UK probably now has more gamelan and more playing groups than any other country in Europe, mainly as a result of two developments: first, a series of gifts of instruments arranged by the Indonesian government, and then (somewhat later) changes in the education system: see below.

Some groups in the West are taught by resident Indonesian teachers, and others by Westerners who have studied in Indonesia.[47]

Museums

Gamelan often found their way to museums, together with *wayang* puppets, literary manuscripts, *bathik* and other important artefacts of Javanese culture. The handling of museum objects by members of the public tends to conflict with the principles of good curatorship, but some of these institutions do permit public access. For example, the Übersee-Museum in Bremen, Germany, devoted to 'the whole world under one roof', runs an educational programme around its gamelan. A gamelan was given to the Bate Collection of instruments at Oxford University specifically to be played.

Universities

Possession of a gamelan is now regarded as a prerequisite for university ethnomusicology departments. In addition to their use of the gamelan as part of their courses, some of these departments run classes open to outsiders.

Numerous gamelan-related theses and dissertations have been written by students in these departments. Most aspects of Javanese culture have now been the subject of at least one thesis. Selected examples of these, some republished as books, are listed in **Appendix 7**. (Also see **Scholarship** above, p. 14.)

Other educational institutions

The connections between the gamelan and education in the West date from early in the twentieth century. When Carl Orff (1895–1982) and his collaborators developed new music education methods for German elementary schools,[48] two of their key elements are said to have been inspired by the gamelan: the focus on percussion instruments and the choice of pentatonic scales. (Much else in the scheme owed nothing to gamelan or *karawitan*.) The *Schulwerk* principles remained very influential in other countries for the rest of the century.

In the UK a National Curriculum for schools,[49] developed in the late 1980s, requires contact with music of other cultures.[50] A workshop based around a gamelan is one method of meeting this requirement. A group having no previous experience of the gamelan can perform a simple piece by the end of a two-hour workshop; something that is not realistically achievable with other well-known 'exotic' musical cultures such as flamenco, Indian classical music or West Indian steel bands. The gamelan has also been used to implement the curriculum's more general requirements on listening, appreciation, performance and composition.

The UK National Curriculum has therefore resulted in some schools acquiring their own gamelan, and others booking workshops at arts centres or other institutions that make their gamelan available for this purpose.[51]

Besides schools, some UK local authorities have acquired gamelan for their Social Services departments. For them the attraction is that children and adults with

46 He only brought one musician to play on them. It is not clear when the first full performance on a gamelan took place in the West. Marcus Risdell has recently brought to light extensive documentation of a three-month season given by a Javanese gamelan group in London in 1882 (personal communication, 2005). This visit preceded one to the Netherlands by another group in the following year, as well as the better-known event at the Paris *Exposition* of 1889 attended by Debussy and other French musicians.

47 Gamelan groups in the USA and elsewhere in the West do not depend on the presence of a local expatriate Indonesian community.

48 Leading to the *Schulwerk* publications (1930–).

49 Detailed at *www.nc.uk.net*

50 For some responses to this need, from both before and after the National Curriculum, see Vulliamy and Lee (1982), Floyd (1996) and Steptoe (2001).

51 To dispel any impression that all these sessions are 'educational', it must be recorded that workshops are also booked as birthday treats.

learning difficulties can feel the same sense of musical achievement on the gamelan as anyone else. The gamelan also offers a rewarding musical experience to those with impaired eyesight or hearing.

Another initiative tried in the USA, UK and France is gamelan in prisons. Apart from its musical virtues and its value simply as a break from prison routine, prisoners have enthused about the calming effect of the gamelan. The real value of the exercise, however, lies in the development of listening, communication, self-expression, concentration, problem-solving and teamwork. Many prisoners lack these skills, which are important in making them employable after they leave prison.

When?

Concerts

There are very few professional gamelan groups or players in the West, although most groups give public performances. Various types of gamelan also feature in 'world music' festivals, and have sometimes appeared at the annual BBC Promenade concerts, which are essentially a festival of Western classical music. Playing skills in the West have developed to the point where Javanese dancers and *dhalang* who visit Europe or North America no longer need to bring teams of musicians with them.

Film

One of the more notable public appearances of a gamelan in the West occurred in Sergio Leone's film *Once upon a Time in America* (1984). In this a Javanese gamelan was seen accompanying a shadow-puppet play that was apparently being performed next to a Chinese opium den. There is in fact an independent tradition of shadow-puppet performance in China, but Kunst records the Chinese in Java as connoisseurs of *karawitan* and owners of gamelan.

Theatre

Gamelan compositions by westerners include music-theatre pieces, but the gamelan has also been used in incidental music for existing plays.

There is almost a tradition in the UK for using the gamelan in plays by Shakespeare and his contemporaries.[52] Alec Roth used only the Javanese gamelan in his full suite of music for *The Tempest* in 1989. Later Adrian Lee wrote music for *A Midsummer Night's Dream*, combining a Javanese gamelan with Western instruments.

In 2002, Adrian Lee again used the Javanese gamelan in his music for John Fletcher's play *The Island Princess* (1621), which is set in the actual 'spice islands' of Ternate and Tidore in what is now Indonesia. The music was played mainly by actors who were not required on stage at the time, rather than by specialist musicians.

What?

Most gamelan instruments in the West were obtained from Indonesia and use the traditional *pélog* and *sléndro* tunings. Some were ordered with a diatonic tuning[53]—normally a diatonic *sléndro*, i.e. without any semitone intervals—so that they could be played with Western instruments.

Western composers have engaged with the gamelan in various ways:

- Some evoke the sound-world of the gamelan (with varying degrees of inaccuracy) in compositions for Western instruments, but without regard for its musical structures. After Debussy and Ravel,[54] several others responded in a similar way to the Javanese gamelan,[55] although the Balinese gamelan has probably had at least as much influence.[56]
- Some use selected principles of *karawitan* and/or other gamelan music in compositions for Western instruments. For example, the repeating cyclic structures of gamelan music are among the techniques of the 'minimalists', such as Steve Reich.
- Some write works to be played on the gamelan or similar instruments of their own construction, sometimes in combination with Western orchestral instruments. The works range from those that try to conform to the principles of *karawitan* to others that apply Western concepts of harmony and structure, ignoring the implications of the Javanese tunings, and simply use the gamelan for its sonorities. In this category the best-known name is Lou Harrison (1917–2003), who wrote extensively for several kinds of Indonesian gamelan as well as for an 'American gamelan' consisting of home-made instruments tuned to scales based on 'just intonation'.

52 All these plays were written at a time when voyages to the East Indies, and the consequent trade conflicts between the European nations, were in the news. See *Twelfth Night*, III.ii, MARIA: 'He does smile his face into more lines than is in the new map with the augmentation of the Indies.' *A Midsummer Night's Dream* is dated to about 1595, before the first voyage of the British East India Company (1601–3), but after Drake's and Cavendish's circumnavigations (respectively 1577–80 and 1586–8), and James Lancaster's expedition (1591–4), all of which reached Java. *Twelfth Night* is dated to about 1601, and *The Tempest* to about 1611.

53 i.e. with only whole-tone and semitone intervals.

54 Not forgetting Percy Grainger's remarkable orchestrations of Debussy's *Pagodes* (1928) and Ravel's *La Vallée des Cloches* (1944).

55 e.g. Henry Eichheim, Charles Griffes, Dirk Schäfer, Leopold Godowsky, Olivier Messiaen.

56 Bartók, Poulenc, McPhee, Cage, Britten, Ligeti, Peter Sculthorpe, etc.

Music

Karawitan — the art of music

When discussing the basic principles of *karawitan*, it is difficult to avoid giving examples, which means using standard notation. On the other hand, certain aspects of the notation system make no sense without some understanding of the principles of *karawitan*. Therefore there is no ideal order for dealing with these topics.

General principles

Comparisons: Java vs. the West

Some readers may wish to start with comparisons between musical cultures, which will help to explain *karawitan* by describing what it is **not**.

A crude generalisation has been made about the guiding principles of the musical cultures of the world:

- Western tradition (Europe and elsewhere): **harmony**
- Africa: **rhythm**
- Asia: **melody**

This can only be a starting point. For example, it says nothing about the differences between north Indian classical music and Indonesian gamelan, which are among the Asian musical traditions best known outside Asia.

Starting with Western classical music on the assumption that all readers should be familiar with it, we can identify its key features as melody, harmony, rhythm and (in general terms, since no single technical term covers it) the relative motion of the voices or instrumental lines that are heard simultaneously.

Harmony

Western musical theory talks about **intervals**, i.e. relationships between two notes, but the concept of a **chord** is more important. Any combination of two or more simultaneous notes constitutes a chord. Western harmony is based on the use of chords of three or more notes. These principles apply regardless of whether the notes are sung or played, and represent a 'vertical' view of music. For 'horizontal' views, see the next heading.

Harmony is a form of restriction on the notes that may be heard simultaneously, or at least a system of preferences for some combinations over others. This is a subjective matter, and what is currently felt to be 'harmonious' in a culture does not necessarily apply to other cultures or to the same culture at other times.

The principle of harmony in Western music goes much further: for example, certain combinations of notes are felt to give a sense of incompletion, and thus traditionally only a few harmonies can end a piece of music. Emotional or 'expressive' effects are attributed to combinations of notes, and certain specific sequences of different harmonies are treated as giving a sense of progression. To summarise, harmony in Western music has both expressive and structural implications.

Harmony is partly dependent on the concept of **key**, which is discussed in several places below. In *karawitan*, keys do not exist, harmony in the sense of chord sequences is an unknown concept, and there is only limited acknowledgement of the significance of certain intervals. Any consideration of intervals is related to the principle of *sèlèh* (see **Principles of structure**, p. 28). For the Javanese understanding of 'harmony', see ***Laras***, p. 45.

Relationships between parts

Various types of relationship are possible between a basic melody and other instrumental or vocal lines. Some of these models are found more often than others in Western music.

Frequently there is a melody plus an accompaniment. The latter consists of notes that harmonise with the melody, but are not equal in importance to the melody. At any given moment, the number of simultaneous notes varies. These notes within the accompaniment do not necessarily form additional melodic lines.

In **homophonic** music, a fixed number of accompanying parts move at the same rate as the melody, and thus are not truly independent.

In **polyphony**, there are several melodic lines present at once, each moving independently while conforming to the rules of harmony as well as to the rules of **counterpoint** (which are themselves related to the rules of harmony). Of the various lines, one called the **cantus firmus**[1] forms the basis of the music and has the highest status: the other lines must fit against it. In **fugue** and

1 Referring to a pre-existing melody that has an independent life, e.g. a secular song serving as *cantus firmus* in a Christian liturgical work. Compare the sense in which Kunst (1973) uses the term (see p. 36).

canon, the various lines are required to imitate each other to a high degree.

Of the other models, **diaphony** is two-part singing or playing without regard to the usual rules of harmony. It is known from folk music[2] rather than art music. Homophony and polyphony are the two principles most commonly used in Western classical music. Polyphony was the basis of Western art music for several centuries, but became progressively less important from about 1600 on. Relationships of all these kinds are irrelevant to *karawitan*.

Heterophony is the simultaneous performance of different versions of the same melody. In Western music, the occurrence of 'plain' and ornamented versions of a melody in different parts of a musical texture is not unknown, but heterophony does not amount to an important organising principle of the music. In the music of the gamelan, on the other hand, heterophony is the nearest thing to a fundamental model controlling the relationships among all the instrumental and vocal lines.[3]

Some writers object to the application of the term 'heterophony' to *karawitan*, on the grounds that it implies inferiority to Western-style polyphony. They point out that heterophony is not inferior but simply different.

One characteristic treatment (*garap*) in *karawitan* involves splitting a sequence of notes between two instruments, making an interlocking pattern. Such patterns can also be shared between two players on the same instrument, or even between the two hands of one player. This is a treatment with very ancient origins, being found on all the old ceremonial gamelan of the Principalities (see **Origins of *karawitan***, p. 24). Under the name 'hocketing' it has been used in Western music too, although it does not play a major role there.

Rhythm

The term 'rhythm' describes time relationships of all kinds. Music in most cultures (at least for part of the time) uses regular beats that can be counted and grouped. In Western classical music, there can be a hierarchy of groupings. Within groups of two, three, four or more beats, the individual beats may be subdivided—usually into 2, 4, 8, etc., but sometimes into multiples of 3.

In *karawitan* the various forms of triple time (i.e. where sequences of notes have a stress on every third beat and/or beats are subdivided into three) are almost unknown. Some Javanese composers in the twentieth century decided this was one aspect of Western music that they ought to copy, but triple time has never become established as a regular feature. However, triplet rhythms, i.e. three notes in the time usually occupied by two or (more often) four, occur in the parts played by individual instruments.[4]

The rhythms of *karawitan* are therefore basically binary. Beats are repeatedly divided by two—with great regularity, on most instruments.[5] The details of these binary relationships are described later. On the other hand, the basic tempo of a piece, i.e. the speed at which the melodic material moves, can have a particularly wide range.

The Javanese word for rhythm in the widest sense is *irâmâ*, but this word also has an extremely important technical meaning that requires discussion under a separate heading: see below, p. 58 foll.

Melody and structure

Melody and treatment

Focusing now on *karawitan*, one must explain exactly what the terms 'melody' or 'basic melody' correspond to in the complex texture generated by the gamelan. It is in fact a difficult subject.

The 'melody' recorded in collections of notation for the gamelan is called the *balungan*, meaning 'skeleton' or 'framework'—it is also the word for the structural framework of a building—or sometimes *balunganing gendhing*.[6] The term correctly suggests that what is notated is only part of the picture.

Most melody instruments do not play the *balungan* line as written. Some play it substantially as written except that they must translate it so that it fits into the single octave available on the instrument. Others play much more or much less than is notated. Those that play more are the **decorating** or **elaborating** instruments, and those that play less are the **punctuating** instruments.

All the instruments realise the melodic material in their own individual styles, and this realisation is known as *garap* (literally, 'working-out' or 'processing'): the word could be defined as the difference between this melodic material and what the instruments actually play.

Furthermore, there is the question of what is the 'real' melody of a composition. The *balungan* usually has a very stylised form, often consisting of standard four-note patterns. The melodic lines of the *rebab* and some vocal parts

2 For example, that of Bulgaria, although it is perhaps necessary to add that the recordings well known under the name *Le Mystère des Voix Bulgares* stand at some distance from the folk tradition, and owe much to the arranger's art.

3 Another non-Western usage of heterophony is in the singing of the cantor and the congregation in a Jewish synagogue—an effect imitated in Jody Diamond's *Sabbath Bride* for gamelan and voices.

4 The word 'triplet' is used in its correct sense here. Patterns of three notes of normal duration, creating a cross-rhythm in a melodic part or drumming pattern, are **not** triplets.

5 As a result, Western writers sometimes say that *karawitan* is entirely written in $\frac{4}{4}$ time.

6 Some writers use the term *balungan* to refer to the simplified, single-octave version of this melody played by the *saron*.

Origins of *karawitan*

It is sometimes said that all music derives from dance or song. (The remark may be accompanied by a stated or implied criticism of Western classical music for losing touch with its roots.) While no exact history can be established, dance and song certainly figure in the origins of *karawitan*. However, several other sources can be identified.

The *pencon* instruments of the Javanese gamelan are related to bronze 'frog drums' (Fig. 2.1) made since the fourth century BC in adjacent parts of mainland Asia.[7] Frog drums were associated with dance and rain-making ceremonies, and thus prefigure the various types of ceremonial gamelan that are found in the Principalities (see pp. 239 foll.). Some of these ensembles are of ancient origin,[8] and their repertoire of music is purely instrumental.

7 For a conjectural reconstruction of the historical evolution of the gamelan, see Hood (1980).

8 As evidenced, for example, by a *gamelan sekatèn* at Cirebon, dated to 1495 and thus earlier than any in Solo or Yogya.

Several of the Hindu and Buddhist religious monuments in central Java dating from the tenth century or earlier, notably Borobudur, are decorated with stone carvings that show musical instruments. Strictly speaking, these carvings only imply that the sculptors (whoever they were) were familiar with the instruments. Most of the instruments shown are not found in gamelan as we know them, although some occur elsewhere in Java. Hanging gongs that may date from the same period—or earlier—have been excavated in the region, but gongs are not to be seen among the carvings.

2.1 Bronze 'frog drum' or kettle gong from Myanmar, date unknown (Horniman Museum, London)

The Borobudur carvings include at least one *wilah* instrument, although not of a type currently used in the gamelan. It is possible that *wilah* instruments were late additions to the gamelan: some of the surviving ceremonial gamelan consist only of *pencon* instruments and drums. From various evidence, including its Arabic name, the *rebab* is believed to be an import from the Islamic world. However, the *Wédhå Pradånggå* suggests another history when it includes a '*gendhing*'—said to be a *rebab*—among the instruments of a fourth-century ensemble.

In Java's complicated early history, cultural boundaries differed from today's. The central Javanese tradition therefore cannot be considered in isolation. Even the history of Bali may be relevant, because many Javanese took their culture there when Islam arrived in Java.

2.2 *Lesung*-pounding

Accounts by the earliest foreign visitors to Java (up to the fifteenth century) do not usually include descriptions of ensembles that can be recognised as gamelan. If they mention music or musical instruments at all, they describe gongs and other instruments being used for signalling purposes—in battle, for example. (Since these accounts do not report any actual battles, they can also be dismissed as second-hand.)

The characteristic hocketing patterns of *karawitan* (and other forms of Indonesian music) may have a serendipitous origin—from the rhythms set up by groups of people pounding rice with wooden pestles (*alu*) in the long rice-mortar (*lesung*), made from a hollowed-out tree-trunk, to separate the husks from the grain (Fig. 2.2). These rhythms are called by names (*kothèkan*, *béndrong(an)*, *géjog(an)* or *gendhong(an)*) that have been given to compositions for the gamelan.

Rice-pounding still takes place as part of certain annual *kraton* ceremonies, and is pursued by groups as a musical hobby. In an interesting parallel with the fixed roles of gamelan instruments, each of the pestle-wielders has a named role, and plays a specific rhythm on a specific part of the *lesung*. It has been suggested that work is made less onerous by the cooperation involved in producing the interlocking rhythms. The element of pleasure is obvious when, for example, Indonesian postal clerks cancel stamps in interlocking rhythms. Similar interlocking patterns occur in the music of adjacent areas of mainland Asia and nearby Pacific islands.

(Ce)ciblon, a children's game of slapping the surface of water to produce a variety of musical sounds, has given its name to one of the drums regularly used with the gamelan, and to the patterns that it plays, and thus forms another of the sources of *karawitan*.

The nature of the relationship between the gamelan and its music is uncertain: are the instruments the way they are because of the music played on them, or was the music determined by the instruments? This can be regarded as either a philosophical or a historical question, but in either case the evidence to answer it does not exist.

A present-day gamelan consists of a combination of soft-style and loud-style ensembles, which have different origins. The latter clearly derive from those used outdoors for ceremonial and signalling purposes. The origins of the soft-style ensemble are less obvious, but it is assumed to have been used indoors and to be associated with voices. Javanese legend associates vocal music, using existing song in traditional metres (see **Appendix 1**), with the earliest gamelan. If this account is incorrect, song may have spread to 'concert' music from traditional dramatic forms where it was an essential element. Originally only male singers participated.

are much freer in style, and must sometimes be taken into account when deciding how to realise the *balungan*.

Some writers[9] refer to an 'inner melody', not heard in any instrumental or vocal part but imagined by the players, and representing the true composition. Sometimes the term *lagu* is used for this 'inner melody', but *lagu* is simply the general Javanese word for the concept of melody or for a specific melody.

The concept of an inner melody may perhaps be supported by the evidence of *siteran* groups. These do not contain *balungan* instruments, so that only vocal parts and decoration are obvious. The pieces that such groups perform are undoubtedly the same (in their essentials) as established gamelan pieces, but their vocal parts are different. In some performances on normal gamelan, the *balungan* disappears completely: see **Pinjalan**, p. 233.

If the *balungan* as notated is not the real composition, why should discussion of performance practice be based on the *balungan* notation? One answer is that the alternatives are not practical. The inner melody remains unnotated: it is a virtual melody, to use current terminology from the computer field. Since Javanese musicians themselves discuss *balungan*, issue collections of *balungan* notation—not collections of inner melodies—and write about performance practice in terms of the realisation of the *balungan*, it seems reasonable to do the same.

A related question concerns the dividing line between *balungan* and *garap*. There are signs that some elements of *garap* have become so well established that they are now recorded in *balungan* notation. Nevertheless, they are not truly part of the *balungan*, let alone of the inner melody, and therefore must be ignored when working out what certain instruments should play. Various examples of situations where a *balungan* line must be 'undone' will be presented later; e.g. *ldr Surung dhayung pl 6* in Part 4.

Improvisation

Each decorating instrument has a range of possible treatment for the same *balungan*. Some writers therefore refer to 'improvisation', but this word gives the wrong impression about the role of the decorating instruments, suggesting that they play something new each time. However, a certain amount of variation in the realisation of a given piece of *balungan*, i.e. when playing the passage more than once or when the same melodic figure recurs at another point in the piece, is considered good style.

In fact players generally select suitable *garap* from the existing body of performance practice. If they do create new *garap* as they play, it is still unlikely to depart greatly from existing *garap*.

The Javanese concept of *garap* can be contrasted with improvisation as practised in other music cultures that may be familiar to Westerners. In performances of north Indian classical music, the main melody instrument (e.g. *sitar* or *sarod*) and the drums (*tabla*) frequently take turns improvising, the other player maintaining a fixed pattern for the improviser to play against. Similar practices can be found in jazz and to some extent in flamenco.

In *karawitan*, the *balungan* line and the musical 'punctuation' can be considered to constitute the fixed part of the composition, assigned permanently to certain instruments. The (somewhat variable) decoration is normally supplied by other players. However, in *karawitan* the decorating instruments never revert to a fixed pattern in order to allow improvisation by the players supplying the *balungan* or punctuation: roles remain unchanged.

In jazz, the chord sequence and the melody are the defining elements of a composition. It often seems that improvisation in jazz aspires to depart as far as possible from the melodic line without completely losing contact with the chord sequence. Usually only one jazz player at a time improvises freely: the process is described as taking a solo. The concept of a soloist is alien to *karawitan*, and in a wider sense it would be somewhat un-Javanese to draw attention to oneself in this way.

The performance of *karawitan*, where many players are applying *garap* simultaneously, has been described as group improvisation. From the discussion above, it should be clear that such a description is at least misleading, if not wholly inaccurate.[10]

Characteristics of melody

In *karawitan* the melodic line characteristically moves stepwise. In Western music, stepwise movements are considered 'weak', and large jumps are thought of as 'strong'. By this measure, the melodic contours of *karawitan* tend to be weak. Melodies could also be said to lack internal contrast—as against contrasts of *garap*.

The range of the basic melodies exceeds two octaves, and is thus greater than is expected of male or female voices in the West, at least if untrained. It is usual for a piece to start in the low or medium register, then go high

9 See particularly Sumarsam, 'Inner Melody in Javanese Gamelan', 1975, in Becker and Feinstein (1984). Perlman (2004) covers the topic in much greater depth than is possible here.

10 For more on the player's responsibilities, see Sutton (1998) and Suyenaga (1984). Discussion of improvisation is generally in terms of who decides on variations, and when. On the gamelan, even the *balungan* can have variants, but it is the teacher rather than the player who decides on their use.

at some point before finishing relatively low—but not necessarily on the note where it started. Sometimes the piece includes a section identified as *(nge)lik*, which starts high and ends low: further details are given later.

Although the instruments that play the basic melody are limited to a single octave, the decorating instruments all have a wider range—and exploit it. Therefore the gamelan as a whole does indicate the true contour of the inner melody, if not always very clearly or accurately.

One of the most fundamental characteristics of *karawitan* is that its basic melody can be played at a wide range of speeds, but the *garap* changes accordingly. (See **Iråmå**, p. 58.) A decorating instrument may play many notes against each note in the basic melody.

The *balungan* itself can exist in several versions with different densities (Fig. 2.3, top three lines). The regular form of *balungan* is called *balungan mlaku*. The form with the lowest density is described as *balungan nibani*, and has notes only on the even-numbered beats—the stronger beats of the structure (see **Principles of structure**, p. 28). There are specific relationships between these two forms of *balungan*: see **Rules of *balungan nibani***, p. 31.

Similar rules relate *balungan mlaku* to another form of *balungan* with twice as many notes. The latter has no single established name, but is sometimes called *balungan ngracik* or *balungan mulur*.[11] Here it will be described as **double-density** *balungan*. (*Balungan nibani* and *balungan mlaku* could also be described as half-density and normal-density *balungan*, respectively.) *Balungan* with quadruple or even higher density also occurs, but usually only in short stretches.

In pieces where there are two versions of the *balungan*, played in different contexts, there is sometimes good evidence that the double-density version is the original, representing the true inner melody.[12] The other version, with *balungan mlaku*, is clearly more regular, simplified or abstracted. *Mulur* means 'expanded', but in this situation it is rather that the *mlaku* version is contracted. *Ldr Pangkur* is one of many pieces of this kind.

Another term, used particularly for short stretches of double density, is *balungan ngadhal*. *Ngadhal* means 'move like a lizard', and refers to the undulating sideways body movements of the lizards (*kadhal*) that frequent every Javanese house and garden. It is a very appropriate description for the relationship between each pattern in Fig. 2.3 and the next simpler version: in each case, the more complex version keeps the same overall contour, but inserts additional notes above and below the contour.

Fig. 2.4 repeats the content of Fig. 2.3 in graphical form for increased clarity. The dotted line in each case represents the final or target note of the pattern (or *sèlèh* in Javanese—see under the next heading). Both diagrams include not only three forms of *balungan* but examples of the parts played by some decorating instruments, using the same expansion principle. (The examples are not all on the same timescale.) The diagrams could have been extended by a further step, representing (for example) the part played by the *gambang* in *ir IV*, but this would not have fitted on the page.

This process of expansion can be compared to zooming in or zooming out with a camera lens. The simplest form of *balungan* represents a distant, zoomed-out view

11 In another interpretation it is called *balungan mlampah* or *balungan ngracik* in contrast to the basic *balungan lugu*.

12 Sumarsam (1995), pp. 205ff.

13 Slightly simplified from the original two-handed version.

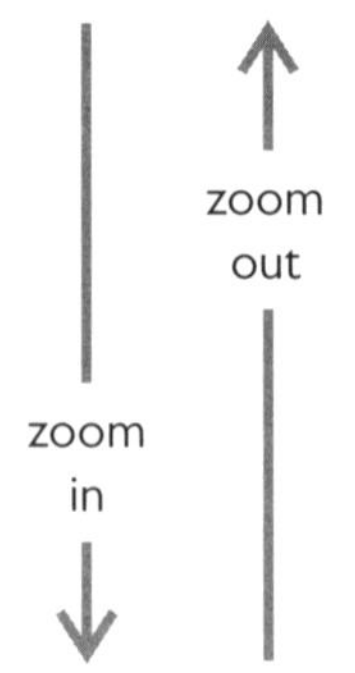

. 3 . 2	*balungan nibani*
3 5 3 2	*balungan mlaku*
3 5 6 5 3 2 1 2	double-density *balungan*
1 2 3 5 5 3 2 3 3 2 1 . 3 2 1 2	*bonang barung, ir II* (Yogya-style *nglagu*)
6̣ 1 6̣ 1 2 3 5 6 3 5 6 1̇ 2̇ 1̇ 2̇ 3̇ 3̇ 3̇ 1̇ 2̇ 6 6 3 3 1 2 6̣ 1 2 6̣ 1 2	*gambang, ir II*
6̣ 1 6̣ 1 2 3 2 3 2 1 6̣ 1 6̣ 1 2 3 5 6 3 5 6 1̇ 2̇ 3̇ 3̇ 5̇ 2̇ 1̇ 6 2̇ 1̇ 6 2̇ 1̇ 2̇ 3̇ 2̇ 3̇ 5̇ 2̇ 6 1̇ 6 5 3 2 1 6̣ 6̣ 1 6̣ 1 2 3 5 6 6 1̇ 5 3 2 3 1 2	*gambang, ir III* [13]

2.3 Expansion and contraction of a *balungan* contour

of the basic contour of the *balungan*. To get more detail, one zooms in. In the most expanded versions of the *balungan*, segments of the melodic line still have the same shape as the more contracted versions: in other words, the melodic lines possess a fractal geometry.[14]

Melodic lines do not always move at an even rate. The basic assumption, reflected in the notation system, is that a note continues until a new note is played or sung. This means that rests are not a regular feature, and the melodic instruments normally play continuously without gaps. If a new note is not played on one of the stronger beats, the result is known as *balungan pin mundur*, and there is some special *garap* associated with this type of melodic shape. Most of the decorating instruments also play continuously if they are playing at all.

It is also possible for the *balungan* to stop moving, i.e. stay on one note, for extended periods—sometimes for the best part of half a minute. The word *gantung(an)* is applied to such areas (see the display box **Gantungan**, p. 30). All the decorating instruments give special treatments to stretches of *gantungan*.

The patterns played by the decorating instruments when realising the *balungan* are known as *céngkok* or *wilet*. Some sources use the terms interchangeably; others distinguish between them, e.g. giving the term *céngkok* to the general shape of the pattern and *wilet* to the specific set of notes played. Certain melodic shapes, sometimes having a number of alternative fixed forms, are recognised and known by name: see Table 2.1. The table tries to divide these into two groups (not necessarily a distinction that would be accepted by Javanese musicians). The first group, known to all performers, consists of contours (strictly) in the inner melody, and it may be misleading to give an equivalent *balungan* line. Often the name is derived from the words that are (or were) sung with the melodic formula: for example, *kacaryan* takes its name from a phrase sung in the very well-known *ketawang Puspâwarnâ*. The second group consists of (more or less) standardised *garap* formulae used by some soft-style decorating instruments for other contours. In this group, the names now belong to the *garap* rather than the contour. These *céngkok* again often take their names from vocal lines, e.g. in *senggakan* or popular songs.

In the table, the formulae are mainly quoted in versions used in *sléndro manyurâ*. Some can be transposed for other *sèlèh* notes in the same *pathet*, or for other *pathet*. Sometimes the connection between the *céngkok* and the original vocal line is hard to see. For example, Fig. 2.5 shows two examples of such vocal lines, with two *gendèr* realisations of the *céngkok kuthuk kuning* for different *irâmâ*. The relationship between the vocal and *gendèr* versions of the *céngkok* is not equally clear.

The word 'contour' has been used frequently above, and will be used again. Within their respective limits, the various instruments and vocal lines all try to represent the contour of the melody.[15]

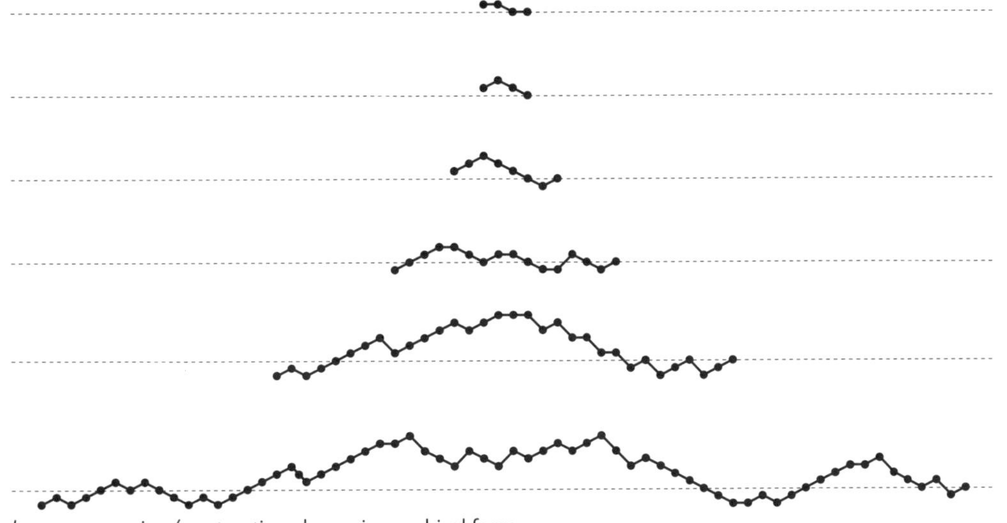

2.4 *Balungan* expansion/contraction shown in graphical form

14 See, for example, Gleick (1988). Web searches on the term 'fractal music' will return examples of the principle of fractal structure applied to many aspects of music.

15 In Javanese there seems to be no word for 'contour', in spite of the importance of the concept, but *kalimat lagu* [*in*] sometimes gets close to it.

Principles of structure

In most instrumental pieces, the *balungan* notation is divided into units of regular length. The smallest structural unit is simply a pair of notes. In such a pair, the second note is called the *dhong*, and carries the greater weight. The first note of the pair is called the *dhing*.

The *dhing–dhong* relationship is only one manifestation of a fundamental principle of *karawitan*: that of **end-weightedness**. The whole of any composition consists of a journey towards its final note, marked by the last stroke on the *gong ageng*, although the principle operates on shorter timescales too.

Table 2.1
Named *céngkok*, named contours

Céngkok	Corresponding form(s) of *balungan*: *ir II*	*ir III*	Notes
Contours in the inner melody			
Ayu kuning[a] (pretty yellow)	61̇3̇2̇ 6321, ..32 5321		
Gantung (hanging)	any *gantungan*		
Kacaryan[a] (spellbound, astonished)	3̇2̇65 1̇653, 6523, .5.3, .6.5 .2.3	.5.3	
Puthut gelut (quarrelling disciples)[b]	33.. 6532, 3565 3212, ..12 3532, ..23 6532, .3.6 .3.2, etc.	.3.2	
Puthut semèdi (disciples at prayer)[b,c]	6532, 3532, 1232, 1̇632	.2	
Other named *céngkok*			
Åjå ngono (not like that)			
Dhebyang-dhebyung (a bit of this, a bit of that)	16̣13 16̣12	.3.2	typically follows *puthut gelut*
Dua lolo[d]	2321, 6321, .2.1, 3231	.1, .1̇	
Duduk(an) (?)	5653 2126̣, .2.6, .2.3 .1.6̣, etc. 5653 216̣5̣, 2352 216̣5̣, etc. 5635 2121, .5.3 .2.1, etc.	.6	*sl m* *sl m* *sl m*, *sl 9*
Elå-elå (care about?)	5653, .5.3 .1.6̣		to 3, *sl 9* to 6, *sl 9*
Gendhuk kuning (yellow girl)			
Jarik kawung[a] (sugar-palm *bathik* pattern)	.3.2, 3512, 6532, 6132		
Kuthuk kuning[a] (yellow chick)	61̇ 5653 .1.6̣		to 1̇ to 3 to 6̣
Nduduk (?)	(signals high 6)		
Nyå tali nyå emping[a] (?)	see *Dhebyang-dhebyung*		
Ora butuh[a] (no need)	6523 3265	.5.3	to 3 to 5
Rambatan (creeping, climbing)	5653		*sl 9*
Rujak-rujakan[a] (fruit salad)	2321 3216̣	.1.6̣	
Yå suråkå[a]	see *Dudukan*		
Tumurun[a] (descending)	1̇653 3216̣, .2.6̣, .126̣, .1.6̣, 2126̣	.6	to 3 to 6̣

a. Named after vocal phrases using these or similar words. b. The disciples are those of a holy man: alternatively *Puthut* may be one of the names of Yudhistirå. c. = second half of *puthut gelut*. d. The most appealing suggestion for the meaning of *Dua lolo* is that *dua*, undoubtedly the Indonesian for 'two', is followed by a young child's attempt to pronounce *loro*, its Javanese equivalent.

Kacaryan (two vocal versions)

. . 61̇ 2̇ .3̇ 6 565 . . 6 6 1̇2̇ 6.53
. . 61̇ 2̇ .3̇ 1̇2̇6 5 . . 6 6 1̇2̇ 61̇653
ka-car- yan ang- gung ci- na- tur

Corresponding *wilet* for *gendèr*:
lampah 2

6 .	1̇ 6	3 5	3 2	5 6	5 1̇	5 6	5 3
. 3	5 2	. 6̣	. 5̣	. 2̣	. 1̣	. 2̣	. 3̣

Kuthuk kuning

. . . . 2 2 2 2 . 6̣ . 5̣ . 6̣ . 1
kuthuk kuning a- dang ka- tul

Corresponding *wilet* for *gendèr*:
lampah 2

6 1̇	6 2̇	6 1̇	6 5
2 2	2 2	6̣ 5̣	6̣ 1

lampah 4

6 1̇ 6 .	6 1̇ 6 2̇	6 1̇ 6 2̇	6 1̇ 6 5
. . 6̣ 1	2 2 2 2	. 6̣ . 5̣	. 6̣ . 1

2.5 Examples of céngkok based on vocal phrases

At the most important structural points, i.e. those that end the larger units of structure, all the melodic instruments in principle land on the same note, normally the appropriate note of the *balungan*. According to another somewhat fuzzy rule, the more important the structural point, the more likely it is that the instruments will come together in this way. At these points, the Javanese are thinking vertically. This is arguably the nearest that *karawitan* gets to the Western concept of harmony.

The Javanese refer to the lines separating and converging (*misah* and *nunggal*, respectively). The principle of coming together at particular points is called *sèlèh*, and the note at such a point is the *sèlèh* note. The word *sèlèh* means 'settle' or 'come to rest'. There is no room for doubt as to whether end-weightedness and *sèlèh* are basic principles. The patterns played by all the decorating instruments (and vocal parts with an equivalent function) work towards a specific *sèlèh* note, and usually coincide with the *sèlèh* note in both time and pitch.

Gamelan players coming from the Western musical tradition are used to hearing melodies where the strongest note comes first—which is the way that the bar lines of Western staff notation mark out the music. When they apply the same approach to *karawitan*, it simply does not work. Some players therefore have great difficulty with the concept of end-weightedness: unable to hear the music as the Javanese do, they suffer a long period of puzzlement until road-to-Damascus enlightenment arrives. End-weightedness also has important implications for the notation of *karawitan*: see **Notation**, p. 38.

Within the overall composition, various units of structure, from the shortest to the longest, are terminated by a stroke on one of the punctuating instruments.

These characteristic stress patterns in *karawitan* do not relate to syllable stresses or any other feature of the Javanese language.

Small-scale structure

The principle of a *dhing–dhong* pair of notes has been mentioned. In practice the four-note *gåtrå* is the smallest unit of *balungan* notation normally considered. Its second and fourth notes are both *dhong*, so they become respectively the minor and major *dhong* if it is necessary to label them. The four notes of the *gåtrå* can then be distinguished as, in order, the *dhing cilik*, *dhong cilik*, *dhing gedhé* and *dhong gedhé*. To confirm the importance of the *gåtrå* as a structural unit, each pattern (= *céngkok* or *wilet*) played by any soft-style decorating instrument usually corresponds to one *gåtrå*.

Out of the three forms of *balungan* (*nibani*, *mlaku* and double-density), no more than two forms are usually found in any individual piece; either *nibani* and *mlaku* or *mlaku* and double-density. In those pieces (e.g. soft-style *ladrang*) that have a *balungan mlaku* in *ir I* and *ir II* alongside a double-density version in *ir III*, the question arises: what is a *gåtrå* in the latter? Do four notes of the double-density *balungan* constitute a *gåtrå*, because a *gåtrå* is supposed to consist of four notes? On the other hand, these four notes correspond to only half of the *gåtrå* in *ir II*. Either of the two possible answers may be valid, and both views may be relevant when deciding how to realise the notes.

Players normally interpret pieces *gåtrå* by *gåtrå* (assuming that interpretation is required), although for some instruments it is also necessary to take account of the preceding or following *gåtrå*. (Also see the **Cross-rhythms** display box, p. 31.) Sometimes the player responds to two successive *gåtrå* rather than one, and plays patterns that do not coincide with the *sèlèh* note of the

Gantungan

When the 'inner melody' hovers around a single note, as evidenced by the *balungan* and/or by vocal lines, the terms *nggantung*, *gantung* and *gantungan* are used. The basic meaning of *gantung* is 'hang'. Such a contour may be described as *gantungan*. The *balungan* around a *gantungan* may be called *balungan nggantung*, or a single *gåtrå* called *gåtrå gantung*.

The presence of *gantungan* affects what various instruments play: in particular, characteristic patterns (*céngkok gantungan*) are played by the decorating instruments in response to it.

Gåtrå gantung occur more often as odd-numbered *gåtrå* of the *balungan*. (This has special implications for the notes played on the *kenong*, q.v.) A *gantungan* may last for more than one *gåtrå*, e.g. for the first 2½ *gåtrå* in the second line of this example from the *mérong* of *gd Sambul gendhing kt 4 kp pl 6*:

5323̂
. . . . 33 . . 33 . 2 3521

In *balungan* notation there are standard ways of indicating *gåtrå gantung*. On the basis that a *pin* represents a continuation of the previous note, the *gåtrå* 22 . . clearly shows a *gantungan* on the note 2. An apparently empty *gåtrå* . . . . represents a continuation of the *sèlèh* note of the previous *gåtrå*. Thus the second *gåtrå* of *xyz*5 . . . . is interpreted as *gantung* 5. The *balungan* instruments normally interpret such a *gåtrå* by playing the *gantung* note on the third beat, and *balungan* notation is often written in that form, i.e. *xyz*5 . . 5 . in this case. A doubling of the note at the beginning of the *gåtrå gantung* would signify that the previous *sèlèh* note was not being continued: e.g. *xyz*5 1̇1̇ . .

Gåtrå gantung in *balungan* notation can be identified in other ways, but with less certainty. A player may suspect or presume—presumption is perhaps more frequent among the Yogyanese—that a *gåtrå* of the form *xyzx* represents a *gantungan* on *x*. There is a slightly higher probability that a *gåtrå* of the form *xxyx* represents a *gantungan*. Therefore 5235 and 5565 can both indicate a *gantungan* on 5.

However, exceptions can always be found. For example, here are two versions of the same piece (*ldr Ondhé-ondhé pl 7*). In version (a), the fifth *gåtrå* is of another form that commonly indicates a *gantungan*. (Repetition of a note in the middle of a *gåtrå* is rare otherwise.) There is indeed a *gantungan* at this point in one version of the vocal line. In version (b) the *balungan* gives no evidence of the *gantungan*, but the source still specifies a *gantungan* on the note 7 for the same *gåtrå*.

(a) 7653 5235̂ 7653 5235̂
. 77 . 6672̇̂ . 72̇3̇ 2̇76⑤

(b) 7653 5235̂ 7653 5235̂
672̇7 2̇3̇4̇2̇̂ 7672̇ 767⑤

In these examples, the *gåtrå* 2̇3̇4̇2̇ and the various *gåtrå* 5235 do not signify *gantungan*, despite their *xyzx* form.

The examples illustrate the principle that the inner melody determines where the *gantungan* occur. The *balungan* notation may or may not give unambiguous evidence.

The term *gantungan* seems to be reserved for stretches of one *gåtrå* or more. However, a *balungan* can also be static for a half-*gåtrå*, and may then require the same interpretative response as for a longer *gantungan*. A *gåtrå* of the form 232 . (one type of *balungan pin mundur*) attracts the rule about continuing the previous note through a *pin*. The rule applies similarly to a pair of *pin*, as in *xyz*6 . . 51̇, where the second *gåtrå* is treated as 6651̇. A *gåtrå* in which a note is repeated in one half, as in 3356, is a *balungan kembar*.

first *gåtrå*. This can be seen as another form of 'zoom-out', i.e. taking a broader view of the melodic line.

There are several further possible reasons for a player not to treat a certain note as a *sèlèh* point, as will be discussed later, in Part 3. Vocal lines too may not coincide at all the obvious *sèlèh* points. All this can be seen as further evidence that the *balungan* is only an approximation to the 'inner melody', which ideally should always inform the basis of the *garap*—subject to the difficulty of deciding exactly what the inner melody is.

Padhang and *ulihan*

Javanese musicians describe the structure of musical phrases in terms of *padhang* and *ulihan*. Of the two words, *ulihan* is the easier to explain: it simply means 'return'. Martopangrawit[16] understood *padhang* to mean 'clear', 'bright' (as in *padhang bulan* = moonlight), but it seems more than possible that *padhang* relates to the word *(a)dhang*, meaning 'wait'.[17]

Each *padhang* is followed by an *ulihan*—sometimes of the same length, sometimes shorter or longer. These two

16 In Vol. 1 of Becker and Feinstein (1984).

17 *Padhang* then means 'the thing that waits'.

sub-phrases can be viewed as a question followed by an answer, a proposal and a response, departure and return, tension and relaxation, thesis and antithesis, etc. There can also be several *padhang* in succession, then one *ulihan* that responds to all of them. The sequence of three *padhang* and one *ulihan* is a common arrangement that fits the structures of various *bentuk*. One or more *padhang–ulihan* pairs can themselves be considered as a *padhang* or an *ulihan* at a higher level in a hierarchy.

At the lowest level in the hierarchy the *padhang* or *ulihan* is normally quite short, amounting to only one or two *gåtrå*. The lengths of *padhang* and *ulihan* are often exact numbers of *gåtrå*, but this is not an absolute requirement. It is the phrase structure that matters, rather than its relationship to *gåtrå* boundaries.

For each of the standard forms of composition in *karawitan* there is at least one characteristic overall *padhang–ulihan* structure, with a hierarchy of two, three or even more levels. Details are given under **Bentuk**. p. 63. Pieces in the 'editable' forms (see p. 85 foll.) and other irregular forms can be analysed in the same way as the regular forms, although their *padhang* and *ulihan* are harder to identify.

Fig. 2.7 applies this type of analysis to a piece from the Western classical tradition, and the example was deliberately chosen for its unequal phrase lengths. Here the first three staves of the notation fall naturally into *padhang* and *ulihan* corresponding to the lines of verse that Berlioz set. The first three staves together form a longer *padhang* that is answered by the *ulihan* in the final stave. This particular structure can be found in the *ladrang* form, e.g. *ldr Mugirahayu sl m* as shown in Fig. 2.6.

Cross-rhythms

While the music is usually analysed in terms of four-note *gåtrå*, cross-rhythms are sometimes set up by patterns of three notes that ignore *gåtrå* boundaries, e.g.

5325 3253 2523 5653

where the pattern 532 is repeated. This particular passage is found in several *gendhing bonang*.[18] Another three-note pattern found in more than one piece is . 6̣2, usually also preceded by 2, e.g.[19]

4̣5̣6̣2
. 6̣2 . 6̣2 . 6̣ 2123 2165

Cross-rhythms in drumming are discussed later.

Rules of *balungan nibani*

Balungan nibani conforms to a certain pattern, and its principles also apply when it is necessary to convert *balungan mlaku* to *balungan nibani*. In a conversion the *sèlèh* note always remains unchanged (see **Principles of structure**, p. 28).

According to the basic rule, the note at the mid-point of the *gåtrå* is the note above the *sèlèh* note, e.g. . 5 . 3. However, the mid-point note must not repeat the final note of the previous *gåtrå*. To avoid the repetition, the next higher note or, less often, the note below the expected one will be used. Thus . 3 . 2 cannot follow . 5 . 3, so it is replaced by . 5 . 2 or . 1 . 2. Some cases where the mid-point note is not the note above the *sèlèh* note may reflect the presence of the note in the 'inner melody' or a vocal line.

A *gåtrå gantung* is treated the same way as any other. Thus 6 6 . . or . 6̣6̣ . in *balungan mlaku* may become . 1̇ . 6 or . 1 . 6̣ respectively.

Standard cadential phrases exist in more than one *nibani* version: . 2 . 6̣ as well as . 1 . 6̣ in *sl m*, etc., and . 1 . 5̣ as well as . 6̣ . 5̣ in *sl 9*, etc.

Special considerations apply when *balungan nibani* is played on the *bonang panembung*, q.v.

The rules are reversed if a *balungan nibani* needs to be expanded to *mlaku* form: additional notes, adjacent to the existing notes, are inserted in such as way as to maintain the shape and *sèlèh* note of the *gåtrå*: e.g. . 5 . 3 may become 5653. The same principles apply if a *balungan mlaku* is expanded to double density, as in the *garap* called *kinthilan* (Yogya style), q.v.

The actual content of the *padhang* and *ulihan* is another matter. The case may be as simple as a *padhang* with a rising contour followed by an *ulihan* with a falling contour. A given phrase can even be a *padhang* at one point in the piece and an *ulihan* at another (e.g. in the *mérong* of *gd Lobong sl m*). Sometimes the same *padhang–ulihan* pair occurs more than once in the overall structure. For

18 *Gd bonang Babar layar pl 5, gd bonang Sidåmukti sl 6*, etc.

19 *Gd bonang Slébrak pl 5*. Cf. *gd Okrak-okrak sl m, ldr Banthèng warèng sl 6*, etc. Also . 5̣1 in *sl 9*, etc.

P						U	
P		P		P		U	
P	U	P	U	P	U	P	U
36̣1 .	36̣12	36̣1 .	36̣12	3523	61̇65	1̇653	6̣13(2)

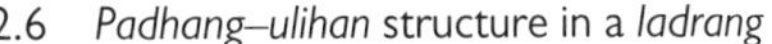

2.6 *Padhang–ulihan* structure in a *ladrang*

Berlioz: *Villanelle* from *Nuits d'Été*, Op. 7
P = padhang; U = ulihan
Allegretto ♩= 96
P
U
Quand vien- dra la sai- son nou- vel- le, Quand au- ront dis- pa- ru les froids,
Tous les deux nous i- rons, ma bel- le, Pour cueil- lir le mu- guet aux bois;
Sous nos pieds é- gre- nant les per- les Que l'on voit au ma- tin trem- bler,
Nous i- rons é- cou- ter les mer- les. Nous i- rons é- cou- ter les mer- les sif- fler.
(continues)

2.7 Example of *padhang–ulihan* analysis applied to Western classical music

example, an AABA structure, common in Western music, occurs in *karawitan* too, although the AAAB structure is more frequent. Many other structures are found, with or without repetition of particular *padhang–ulihan* phrases.[20]

The correct use of *padhang* and *ulihan* is, just like an understanding of *pathet* (one of the most difficult theoretical aspects of *karawitan*: see ***Pathet***, p. 52), essential to the character of a composition. Westerners have sometimes written gamelan pieces that appear to use standard *bentuk*, but their *padhang–ulihan* structures either are unclear or do not conform to the pattern expected for the *bentuk*. Such pieces cannot sound idiomatic to Javanese ears. The topics of *padhang–ulihan* structure and *pathet* can be considered in isolation, but they are certainly not independent: for example, within a given *pathet*, the important notes of that *pathet* are more likely to occur as the final note of an *ulihan* than as the final note of a *padhang*.

Large-scale structure

The major structural division in compositions is the *gongan*, i.e. a stretch of music terminated by a gong stroke. In this context, 'gong' means either the *gong ageng* or the *gong suwukan*, as appropriate. The length of a *gongan* is not standardised—in terms of either number of beats or duration in minutes and seconds—but is characteristic of the form of the piece (see ***Bentuk***, p. 63), with a few exceptions (especially in the 'editable' forms).

In most forms, *gongan* can also be subdivided into *kenongan*, i.e. stretches marked off by *kenong* strokes. The editable forms, however, use so many *kenong* strokes that a *kenongan* would not be a meaningful structural unit. Some other forms have no *kenong* strokes anyway.

A composition can consist of a single *gongan*, but usually there is more than one; the relationships between the *gongan* are discussed later in connection with each of the standard forms. An entire *gongan* can be analysed as a *padhang* or an *ulihan*.

As described later under ***Pathet***, the *balungan* note that falls on the gong stroke has special significance. It is commonly called the 'gong note'—not to be confused with the pitch of the note produced by the gong. A piece can be characterised as 'gong *x*' when note *x* in the *balungan* coincides with the gong. This shorthand description of a piece is regularly used by the Javanese. However, it is something of a simplification, because in pieces with several *gongan* the gong note is not necessarily the same in every *gongan*. Some gong notes or *sèlèh* points are more important than others; those at the end of the *bukå* and the end of the last *gongan* are the most important.

20 See Vetter (1977).

In performance, the one or more *gongan* that make up a piece—or section of a piece—are repeated (cycled) until the appropriate person gives the signal to stop or else to move to another section or another piece, as explained under the next headings. A single *gongan* can only be cycled if the notes at the *gong bukå* and the final gong are the same: otherwise the cycle must consist of more than one *gongan*. In Western terms, Javanese pieces are in strophic (i.e. cyclic) forms rather than being through-composed. There are some exceptions.

Sometimes there is a reason for a particular number of cycles. *Ktw Puspåwarnå* theoretically needs to be cycled nine times, because the words of its *gérongan* consist of nine stanzas concerning different flowers (the *Puspåwarnå* of the title) that correspond to the nine moods or sensations (*råså*)—six pleasant, three unpleasant—of Indian philosophy. In practice, the piece is only cycled about three times.

The melodic and harmonic conventions of Western art music suggest—to a listener who is familiar with them—such ideas as tension, relaxation, development, climax and resolution. The listener (whether consciously or not) expects to experience a beginning, a middle and an end in the composition.

In contrast, a strophic structure that is simply repeated without change (as just described for *ktw Puspåwarnå*) may give the listener no sense of inherent development or progression. Some Western composers describe this approach to musical construction—music without progression or climax—as 'process music',[21] and imitate it in their own compositions.

However, it would be wrong to imply that *karawitan* is a music without variation. On the contrary, a piece can often be played with several major variations and contrasts of *garap*, to the extent that listeners unfamiliar with the practices of *karawitan* may not even recognise it as the same piece.

Possible variations include

- the use of various types of vocal parts,
- major changes of volume level,
- the inclusion or omission of optional sections,
- the use of different *iråmå* (see **Iråmå**, p. 58),
- a switch of *garap* from 'plain' to decorated, or between alternative forms of decoration,
- the application of certain standard forms of multi-instrument *garap* that are described later, such as *kébar* or *pinjalan*.

Although there is no a priori reason why all available *garap* variations should not be applied to a given piece, in practice each piece is conventionally given only a certain range of *garap*, and any individual performance will not necessarily use the whole of this range.

The variations of *garap* listed above may still convey no sense of progression, but such a feeling is possible in suites that start with pieces in a longer form and end with pieces in shorter forms. One standard suite of this type is the introduction (*talu*) that precedes a full *wayang kulit* performance. Here a *gendhing* is typically followed by a *ladrang*, a *ketawang* and then pieces in the editable forms *ayak-ayakan*, *srepegan* and *sampak*.

In Western music it is common to perform the last cycle louder or softer than the others, or faster or slower, or with different instrumentation or harmonies, or with an additional or changed vocal line; the soloist may add an extra-high note or hold the final note longer.[22] In *karawitan*, sometimes the only hint of progression likewise comes with the ending of the piece. This effect is stronger with a *suwuk gropak* (see **... and finishing**, p. 35).

The term 'modulation' relates to the key system of Western music. Since key is absent from *karawitan*, modulation is theoretically not possible. In practice there can be a strong suggestion of modulation, i.e. a move to a distinctly higher or lower register,[23] in certain contexts. *Langgam*, which tend towards an AABA structure, often have a feeling of modulation in the B section. The display box overleaf includes another possible example, in which the second *gongan* of the *mérong* essentially repeats the first, but three notes higher (a *kempyung* higher, in the terminology of *karawitan*). Readers are left to try out this piece and analyse their reactions to it.

A standard optional section, and a place where something resembling modulation regularly occurs, is the *lik* or *ngelik* section. This is normally a vocal section. In some pieces it is the only section with vocal lines; in other pieces there is solo female singing (*sindhènan*) throughout, but male choral singing (*gérongan*) only in the *ngelik* section. It is usual for the singing to start in a relatively high register,[24] because this improves the chances of the vocal line penetrating the texture of the gamelan. Afterwards the vocal line may go low, and the *lik* section often closes with the same *balungan* line as the non-*lik* section.

21 Different writers use the term 'process music' to mean different things.

22 This last practice is not unknown among Javanese singers.

23 The registers are sometimes referred to as different scales, but this view raises awkward theoretical questions.

24 *Lik* is an abbreviation of *cilik*, meaning 'small'. *Ngelik* is its verbal form, meaning 'become small', i.e. 'go high'.

Transitions

The course of a performance is not predictable, because of the range of possible *garap* options, and because players do not know how many times the piece or its constituent parts will be cycled, nor how the tempo will change, nor whether another piece will follow on, possibly making a suite. The players therefore rely on receiving signals that indicate all the required transitions (see p. 222).

Most of the signals come from the drums. The signal to enter the *lik* section comes from the melodic leader instrument (see **Loud and soft styles**). Some other transitions cannot be indicated by any standard signal, and must therefore be understood in advance by all the performers. For example, an instantaneous transition from one piece to another may be signalled by the drummer playing a *kendhangan* pattern that indicates the form of the second piece. The drums cannot, however, specify **which** piece in that form is to be played. The melodic leader instrument could provide a *bukå* (see **Starting …**, p. 35), but would be doing so before the first piece had finished; this is not normal practice. Some sequences of pieces are standard. Thus, if the *kendhang* signals a *ladrang* at the end of *gendhing Lobong kinanthi*, the players will assume that *ldr Kembang pépé* is intended. In other situations the players can only guess.

In some circumstances the drum player takes cues from the *dhalang*, or from dancers or a dance-master or -mistress. On this and the complexity of the transitions that can be controlled by signals from the *kendhang*, see ***Irâmå***, p. 58, and **Principles of *kendhangan***, p. 222.

An example of modulation?

Gd bonang Dhenggung laras kt 2 kp mg 4 pl 5

bukå	5̣5̣3.	12.5̣	5̣5̣3.	12.5̣
	.6.6	.5.3	..25	.32(1̂)
mérong	...1	.5̣6̣1	..12	.321
	...1	.5̣6̣1	..12	.321̂
	...1	.5̣6̣1	..12	.321̂
	.3.2	3216̣	..6̣1	232(1̂)
	55..	5535	..56	.765
	...5	.235	..56	.765̂
	...5	.235	..56	.765̂
	.7.6	7653	..25	.32(1̂)
inggah	3231	3235	3635	3231
	.2.3	.5.3	.6.5	.2.1̂
	.5.3	.6.5	65653	.2.1
	.66.	2165	3235	323(1̂)

Methods of composition

As indicated earlier, the Javanese and Westerners take different views of composers and the act of composition. Even in the twentieth century, when many wholly new pieces were written, **centonisation**—the re-use of existing material to create new pieces—remained a common and accepted practice in Java. This may sound like a rather modern procedure, akin to sampling, or falling within the parameters of postmodernism, but it has in fact been used for centuries in Java, and was also found in Western music during the medieval period.[25]

The re-used elements can be quite substantial. The same *kenongan* may be found with little or no change in several *gendhing*. Even whole *gongan* recur; for example, standard *lik* sections for the *mérong* of *gendhing* in the same *laras–pathet* combination.

As a result of this principle, there are groups of compositions showing family resemblances; e.g. groups of *gendhing bonang* written at about the same time.

It is believed that new *garap* has sometimes resulted from players' mistakes when playing existing material. The same process is believed to have led to the unintentional creation of new pieces, e.g. when the *bonang barung* player made a mistake and the *balungan* players, in accordance with their duty, played the *balungan* implied by his patterns rather than the melodic line that they were expecting. Doubtless some of the *balungan* variants that groups regularly play for certain established pieces also arose in this way.

Roles of instruments

A key feature of the central Javanese gamelan is that each instrument has one or more fixed roles. As mentioned earlier, *karawitan* does not normally work on the principle of a soloist and an accompaniment.[26] In contrast, any instrument in a Western symphony orchestra may function as a soloist, although of course some orchestral instruments take on this role more often than others.

The roles of the instruments and the status of their players relate to the Javanese musical aesthetic. When a

25 On centonisation in Western music, see Grove (1980, 2001); on its use in *karawitan*, see Sutton (1993).

26 The standard balance heard on Indonesian recordings often suggests otherwise.

Starting ...

All instrumental pieces start with an introduction (*bukå*) of some kind. Its melodic line typically derives from the end of a *gongan* in the body of the piece. However, there are exceptions, and often the rhythm of the melodic unit from that *gongan* is distorted in the *bukå*. The *bukå* does not necessarily start with a whole *gåtrå*, but a *padhang–ulihan* pair is usually obvious within it.

Since the drums function as the nearest equivalent of an orchestral conductor, any piece may have a *bukå kendhang*, and some pieces always start in this way. More often the introduction is given by one of the decorating instruments (see **Loud and soft styles**, p. 36), and serves the further purpose (which a *bukå kendhang* cannot) of indicating which piece is to be played. The *kendhang* joins in with a pattern that leads to the gong stroke (the *gong bukå*). Some of the soft instruments, if used at all, may enter before the first gong stroke.

The *kendhang* has an additional function of setting the starting tempo. It is not the responsibility of the decorating instrument to do this, and its player may start some way from the correct tempo—in fact it is not bad style for the instrumental *bukå* to start a little fast and be brought down to the right speed.

In both loud-style and soft-style pieces, a solo vocal introduction is possible. Some pieces regularly start with a short *bukå celuk*, possibly leading into the middle of a *gongan*—this is common practice in *langgam* form. A longer vocal introduction (*båwå*) in one of the classical verse metres (see **Appendix 1**) is often performed before a soft-style *gendhing*. These vocal introductions —particularly *båwå*—are somewhat free in rhythm, although some *båwå* end with a *jineman* section in which a regular rhythm is established. As with instrumental introductions, the entry of the *kendhang* soon establishes the correct tempo.

piece is played, it is not heard as group *x*'s or player *y*'s interpretation of the piece.[27] Good musicians or ensembles are those who best express the character of the piece. Nevertheless, individual contributions are noted and appreciated—or sometimes criticised.

Writers in English often use the term **stratification**, meaning that the gamelan ensemble breaks down into layers with different functions and that each instrument belongs to one of these layers. It would be wrong to overemphasise the distinctions between the layers. Ultimately **every** tuned instrument in the gamelan is playing the inner melody or *lagu*, but is realising it via its own characteristic *garap*.

Ideally players should aspire to hear the music as a whole, rather than in layers. However, this 'whole' varies according to which instruments are present, and therefore is not the same in every performance. One must wonder whether the musicians feel that the music is reduced in any way if certain instruments are absent: are they mentally supplying the missing parts?

... and finishing

Most types of piece end with a stroke on the *gong ageng* or the *gong suwukan*. Some exceptions are mentioned later. In the usual closing sequence, the *kendhang* signals a speed-up in order to indicate that the piece is to end, then gradually slows down. When the end of the piece arrives, the gong player delays the final stroke, and the other instruments only play their final note after the gong stroke. The delay between the gong and final notes is only a fraction of a second (Western players often make it too long) and the gong stroke could even be considered as (in Western terms) an anacrusis before the other notes. These other notes are spread out in time: this is normal *garap*. For pieces in the editable forms, the conventions are a little different, and the delay before the final gong stroke is minimal or nil, so that all the instruments essentially finish together.

The last syllable of a vocal line is usually sung after the final gong stroke. Both the *pesindhèn* and the *gérongan* (if any) may sing the preceding syllable on the penultimate note of the vocal line, as might be expected. More often, perhaps, they may each start on that note but then change to the final note (the gong note) before the gong. The *pesindhèn* and the *gérongan* may even choose different options. In this area a group may have a typical performance style.

In some circumstances a piece can have a fast ending (*suwuk gropak*), possibly including a major acceleration that obliges the decorating instruments (including the *peking*) to change their *garap* or stop playing. All instruments including the gong then play their last note together. The approach of the final gong is signalled by obvious cross-rhythms in the *kendhangan* (see Part 4). This *garap* is associated with less refined characters in *wayang*, and may be used in *klenèngan* too. It is the standard form of *suwuk* for *gangsaran*.

27 Some recent musical innovations appear to break with this aesthetic.

Javanese writers too, at least since Martopangrawit,[28] have used a version of the stratification concept. In this, there is a broad division into 'melody' and 'rhythm' sections (respectively *bagian lagu* and *bagian irama* in Indonesian). Each section can be further divided.

Within the *bagian lagu*, there is a supervisor or controller of *lagu* (*pamurbå lagu*). Martopangrawit gave this role to the *rebab*, but we can deduce that it will fall to the *gendèr barung* or *bonang barung* if the *rebab* is absent for some reason. All other members of the *bagian lagu* are classed as 'upholders of *lagu*' (*pamangku lagu*), so this is the description of all *balungan* instruments, both types of *gendèr* (usually), *suling*, *gambang*, *celempung/siter*, and usually all the *bonang* family.

Within the *bagian irama*, the *kendhang* is the supervisor or controller of *iråmå* (*pamurbå iråmå*). The other instruments—gongs, *kempul*, *kenong*, *kethuk*, *kempyang*, *engkuk-kemong*, *kemanak* and *kecèr*—are classed as upholders of *iråmå* (*pamangku iråmå*).

The title *pamurbå* accurately describes the way in which one melody instrument determines which composition will be played and when the piece will progress into a *ngelik* section. It also describes the role of the *kendhang* (to be understood in the plural, because several kinds of drum may be involved) in determining progress between major sections of a piece, from one piece to another, and from one *tingkat iråmå* to another. Players know that on occasion almost any instrument, in the hands of an expert teacher, can supply all the necessary signals and become the *pamurbå* of everything.

Another earlier Javanese analysis[29] uses an analogy with *bathik* fabrics,[30] dividing the instrumental parts into *kalowongan* (outlines) on the one hand, and *plataran* (background) or *isèn-isèn* (filling-in) on the other. The first category consists of the punctuating instruments, and the second covers all the rest.

Kunst, writing before Martopangrawit, gave another version of stratification:

- *balungan* instruments (in his terminology, 'cantus firmus' or 'nuclear theme' instruments);
- punctuating instruments;
- instruments playing a more or less independent counter-melody;
- paraphrasing instruments;
- agogic or rhythm instruments.

He did not assign instruments permanently to these categories. He pointed out that not all 'paraphrasing' instruments stayed equally close to the *balungan*, and that roles could vary between pieces. The 'counter-melody' category should include vocal parts as well as *suling*.

In fact most comments made about instruments apply equally to vocal lines. Female, male and mixed vocal parts are independent of each other and of the instruments; female solo singing is particularly free in rhythm. More information on the character of decoration is given under **Decorating instruments—introduction**, p. 136, and **Vocal parts**, p. 226. 'Elaborating' is sometimes preferred to 'decorating', as it describes the function of the instruments more accurately, implying that this function is fundamental rather than an optional extra: on the other hand, all instruments arguably 'work out' the material.

Another characteristic of *karawitan* is found in other music too. This is the principle that the higher-pitched instruments play denser patterns, i.e. more notes per second or per *gåtrå*. The principle is not absent from Western music,[31] but *karawitan* follows it more thoroughly. Since much of the decoration is heard as lying above the *balungan*, and much of the punctuation sounds lower than the *balungan*, Westerners have the best chance of identifying the basic melodic material if they listen to the middle of the texture—another difference from Western music.

Loud and soft styles

A full gamelan (*gamelan gedhé*) incorporates both loud-style and soft-style ensembles. It can therefore play music written in either the soft style, which usually involves some form of singing—solo, chorus, or both—or the purely instrumental loud style. Programmes played by such ensembles may include pieces in both styles.

The style of the piece also determines which instrument plays the *bukå*. The *bonang barung* supplies it for loud-style pieces. For soft-style pieces there is a hierarchy of possible *bukå* players. If a *rebab* is available, it will take the role. Failing a *rebab*, the *gendèr barung* replaces it, and the *bonang barung* will only take over if both *rebab* and *gendèr barung* are missing. A few pieces have *bukå* on other instruments; e.g. *ktw Subåkaståwå*, a *gd gendèr*.

Whichever instrument plays the *bukå* normally has the additional responsibility for signalling the transition to the *lik* section, if there is one. The *bonang*, *rebab* and

28 *Catatan-catatan Pengetahuan Karawitan* (1972, 1975): English translation in Becker and Feinstein (1984).

29 R. A. A. Tjakrahadikusuma, described in Sumarsam (1995), p. 146.

30 Bearing complex designs created by up to about six successive stages of applying wax resist and then dyeing.

31 It is fundamental to the playing of Russian bells—an effect imitated in pieces such as the coronation scene in Musorgsky's *Boris Godunov*, 'The Great Gate of Kiev' from the same composer's *Pictures at an Exhibition*, and Rimsky-Korsakov's *Russian Easter Festival Overture.*

Descriptions of compositions

The full description of a piece consists of its *bentuk*, its name, and its *laras* and *pathet*, e.g. *ladrang Pangkur laras sléndro pathet manyurå*. Abbreviations (p. G-4) are common. Methods of distinguishing the different categories of the largest forms (*gendhing*) are explained later (p. 81 foll.). When several pieces are combined to make a sequence, terms are available to describe the interrelationships between the pieces:

dados	moving to another piece (typically of the same *bentuk*; or *båwå* to *gendhing*)
dipun	[passive prefix before a verb]
jangkep	complete
jugag	short, incomplete (cf. *wantah*)
kalajengakèn	followed by; and then
kapungkas mawi	ending with
kasambet	continuing with
kasuwuk	ending with
katampèn, ketompèn	using, including
katindakaké x	in *x* style
komplit	implies the inclusion of all expected optional elements, e.g. *gd Lobong Kinanthi komplit* should include *inggah* in *ir II* and *ir III*, *andhegan Puspanjånå* and *ldr Kembang pépé*
komplit mawi	complete with [an optional element]
lampah x	in *x* style
lanjutan	continuation (of)
malih	then
minggah	(Solo) moving to the second section of a *gendhing*; (Yogya) moving to a shorter piece after the second section of a *gendhing*
(n)dhawah, sadhawahipun	(Yogya) moving to the second section of a *gendhing*; (Solo) continuing with
rangkaian [in]	combination, sequence, suite
selingan, diseling, kaseling	inserting [a piece in a shorter form into a longer form]
suwuk	ending; also a complete stop before the next section
terus	continuing with
wangsul	returning to [a piece heard earlier in the sequence]
wantah, wetah	complete, full (cf. *jugag*)

pesindhèn are sufficiently audible to fill this role in a full gamelan. The *gendèr* is less able to make itself heard.

When a piece changes speed within the system of rhythmic relationships in *karawitan* (see **Iråmå**, p. 58), it may effectively be changing between loud and soft styles. Whereas the loud style is associated with the fastest *iråmå*, soft-style pieces usually start fast but then spend most of the time in slower *iråmå*. (In the Yogya tradition, loud-style pieces can be played in more *iråmå* than in the Solo tradition.) The *slenthem*—the sole soft-style *balungan* instrument—plays from the *gong bukå* onwards, but the soft-style decorating instruments may enter only if the tempo is comfortable for the *iråmå* level.

Character of music

The Javanese consider their music expressive, in that they believe it can induce a mood (*råså*) in the listener, or can have a specific character.[32] However, several elements of the music contribute to the expressive effect.

A piece may take its character from a particular text (*cakepan*), although many of the texts used are standard and are found in numerous pieces. Standard texts may be used in some parts of a piece, but unique texts (sometimes related to the title of the piece) in other parts. The verse metre (see **Appendix 1**) in which a text is written is considered to have a character in its own right, regardless of the particular words.

Each of the two tuning systems (*laras*) is taken to have a character—or rather several characters, because of the different modes (*pathet*) available within each *laras*.[33]

The gamelan itself can have a character. This depends largely on its specific intervallic structure (see **Embat**, p. 50). As a result, the gamelan may be judged more suitable for some *pathet* than for others. Other relevant factors are the manufacturing quality of the individual instruments, and the balance between their tonal characteristics in the overall ensemble.

With so many factors present, they can even potentially conflict with each other.

It would be wrong to suggest that everything about *karawitan* works in a formulaic manner. The results still depend on the players, and are at least as spontaneous and unpredictable as in any other music. Seasoned players know the experience of a piece 'catching fire' on one occasion but not on others.

32 These could be considered as respectively the active and passive aspects of *råså*, which is a difficult subject. The term is borrowed from Indian philosophy, but the Javanese use it differently: see Geertz (1973). For an extended survey of *råså* in *karawitan*, see Benamou (1998).

33 See Lindsay (1979), p. 25, and Sastrapustaka in Becker and Feinstein (1988), p. 316.

Notation

The standard notation system for *karawitan* is known as *kepatihan*.[34] It came into use at the end of the nineteenth century, and was based on the Galin–Paris–Chevé system, imported into Indonesia by Christian missionaries as a way of notating hymns to be sung by congregations.[35]

Although not without its problems, the system is efficient, and often allows a piece to be notated faster than it is played.

Principles of *kepatihan* notation

Except where noted, these principles follow the Galin–Paris–Chevé system.

Notation of pitch

Kepatihan represents notes by numbers, and is therefore sometimes called **cipher notation**. The five *sléndro* pitches are numbered 1, 2, 3, 5 and 6, with 1 as the lowest. The seven *pélog* pitches are numbered from lowest to highest as 1 to 7. The reason for omitting the number 4 from the *sléndro* numbering scheme was doubtless to clarify the relationship between *sléndro* and *pélog* (see **Sléndro–pélog comparisons**, p. 47).

Table 2.2 shows how the pitch numbers correspond to the names that musicians had earlier used for the notes. Some of the names represented numbers anyway; all were symbolic, mostly referring to parts of the body.[36]

34 From the name of the residence of the *patih* (= chief minister or grand vizier) at Solo, where it is said to have been introduced.

35 The name comes from the surnames of various French people who developed it in the 19th century, although the system originated in Jean-Jacques Rousseau's proposals dating from 1742. It came into widespread use in the second half of the 19th century. Churches in Java still use the system for its intended purpose.

36 See Becker (1993) and Sastrapustaka in Becker and Feinstein (1984).

Table 2.2
Names and numbers of notes[a]

Note	Short name	Javanese numerals		Old name		Indonesian numeral
		Ngoko	*Kråmå*	*Sléndro*	*Pélog*	
1	*ji*	*siji*	*satunggal*	*barang*	*bem, panunggal*	*satu*
2	*ro*	*loro*	*kalih*	*gulu, jånggå [ki]*	*gulu, jånggå [ki]*	*dua*
3	*lu*	*telu*	*tigå*	*dhådhå, tengah*	*dhådhå, tengah*	*tiga*
4	*pat*	*(pa)pat*	*sekawan*	–	*pélog*	*empat*
5	*ma*	*limå*	*gangsal*	*limå, gangsal*	*limå, gangsal*	*lima*
6	*nem*	*nem*	–	*nem*	*nem*	*enam*
7	*pi, tu*	*pitu*	–	–	*barang*	*tujuh*

a. For additional numerals, see Appendix 2

The table also shows short names that are used as mnemonics: these are derived from the *ngoko* numerals (see the introduction to the **Glossary**).

In the Galin–Paris–Chevé system, 1 always stands for the tonic of the scale: thus the significance of the numbers is not constant, because 1 has a different pitch in each key. In contrast, *karawitan* has no concept of a tonic (although some Western scholars have done their best to apply it). Apart from the difference between *sléndro* and *pélog*, and variations between one gamelan and another, the numbers in *kepatihan* always represent the same pitches.

A rest (= silence) is not consistently notated in *karawitan*, but is left largely to the player's understanding of the appropriate style for the particular instrument. The number 0 was used for a rest in the Galin–Paris–Chevé system. The zero is part of *kepatihan*, but is rarely if ever found in instrumental parts. However, it is often used in vocal notation to signify a rest. The 0 then corresponds to a pause for breath—a *pedhotan* in terms of Javanese traditional verse metres (see **Appendix 1**). Singers breathe at other points too, such as the ends of phrases (*gåtrå*, in the sense that applies to verse texts), but these points are not usually indicated in the notation.

Register dots

The basic numbers 1 to 6 or 1 to 7 represent a single octave, the middle octave of the range that *balungan* notionally occupy. Notes in the octave above are indicated by numbers with a dot above: $\dot{1}$ $\dot{2}$ etc. Notes in the octave below have a dot below the number: $\underset{\cdot}{1}$ $\underset{\cdot}{3}$ $\underset{\cdot}{6}$ etc. The full range of notes used in any *balungan* or vocal part falls within

$\underset{\cdot}{2}$ $\underset{\cdot}{3}$ $\underset{\cdot}{5}$ $\underset{\cdot}{6}$ 1 2 3 5 6 $\dot{1}$ $\dot{2}$ $\dot{3}$ $\dot{5}$

in *sléndro* or

$\underset{\cdot}{1}$ $\underset{\cdot}{2}$ $\underset{\cdot}{3}$ $\underset{\cdot}{4}$ $\underset{\cdot}{5}$ $\underset{\cdot}{6}$ $\underset{\cdot}{7}$ 1 2 3 4 5 6 7 $\dot{1}$ $\dot{2}$ $\dot{3}$ $\dot{4}$ $\dot{5}$

in *pélog*.

The next octave below $\underset{\cdot}{1}$ to $\underset{\cdot}{7}$ is denoted by two dots below the ciphers, and the next octave above $\dot{1}$ to $\dot{7}$ is shown by two dots over the ciphers. The two dots may be written side by side or one above the other. Three dots above the note indicate the next octave above, and so on.[37] Some writers use 7 without a dot instead of 7̣, but write other notes in the lower octave 'correctly', and follow the same pattern in other octaves; a phrase such as 2 7 5̣ 6̣ should then be read as 2 7̣ 5̣ 6̣.[38]

Few gamelan instruments have a compass as wide as the full *balungan* ranges shown above. Some are confined to a single octave. Only the *gambang* regularly has a range extending to three octaves or more. When register dots are used in the notation for an individual instrument, they indicate the octaves within the compass of that instrument; in other words, they do not indicate the absolute level of the octave within the full range of the gamelan (see Figs 3.1 and 3.2). Some writers have tried to use register dots to show absolute pitch, but this is neither practical, given the range of nearly seven octaves covered by the various instruments—i.e. needing more register dots—nor necessary.

In Yogya, *kepatihan* has characteristically been written without register dots. For *balungan* notation, confusion between 1 and 1̇ (= *barang alit*) in *sléndro* was resolved by writing 1̇ as 7. Some musicians continue this practice; others write 1̇ but use no other register dots in *balungan* notation. In notation for individual decorating instruments or vocal lines, the use of the register dots is unavoidable.

Miring notes

Miring notes (see ***Miring* relationships**, p. 49) are represented by strokes drawn through the *kepatihan* numbers. In the Galin–Paris–Chevé system, a flattened 7 is shown as 7̸, or a sharpened 5 as 5̸. (The notation runs from left to right, so that the forward slash points upwards.) *Miring* notes are flattened versions of regular notes, but the Javanese may use either a forward slash (solidus, oblique) or a backslash to indicate them.

Notation of duration

Every note symbol in *kepatihan* represents, by default, a standard duration. In the Galin–Paris–Chevé system the absolute duration of the note is implied by the tempo marking. In contrast, no tempo indication accompanies *kepatihan*, because convention sets a range of speeds, and within this range the players always follow the tempo given by the *kendhang*.

Obviously gamelan melodies do not proceed as a series of notes of the same duration. Two additional symbols allow more complex rhythms in the melodic lines to be notated.

Pin

A *pin*, sometimes called *tik*, is literally a dot. It represents a continuation of the previous note, and is therefore the usual way of indicating a note with more than the standard duration. It is **not** a rest—i.e. a period of silence —although Western players commonly say 'rest' when reading out a *pin* from a line of notation, and Javanese players follow their example.

A melodic pattern of the form 3 3 5 6 would represent four separate notes, of which at least the first three had equal durations. A pattern of the form 3 . 5 6 lasts just as long as 3 3 5 6, but differs in that only three notes are played: the first lasts twice as long as the second. To lengthen a note further, two or more *pin* can be written. For example, 3 3 . . 3 3 5 6 represents six notes, of which the second has three times the standard duration.

Overscore

Notes of less than the standard duration are indicated by an overscore. Here warnings must be given: for various reasons, this element of the Galin–Paris–Chevé system does not fit the structure of *karawitan* very well, and the Javanese do not use it in a consistent manner.

In the Galin–Paris–Chevé system, the basic principles are that all the notes under one overscore are of equal duration and collectively should last as long as one standard note. (A *pin* is treated in the same way as a note.) In *karawitan*, with its binary tendencies, the most usual situation has two notes under the overscore, e.g. 2 3 5 $\overline{6\dot{1}}$.

If two such pairs of half-duration notes are to be notated, a separate overscore is theoretically needed for each pair: 1 2 $\overline{65}$ $\overline{35}$. With only a single overscore over the last four notes (1 2 $\overline{6535}$), the meaning would theoretically be different, because the four notes 6 5 3 5 together should then last as long as the 1 or the 2. In practice, Javanese writers may use a single overscore when two would be 'right'.

An overscore over three notes should mean that each note has one-third the standard duration. In *karawitan*, triplet rhythms of this kind occur on rare occasions. The notation may then include a digit 3 written above the overscore (as for the equivalent structure in Western staff

37 The same notation scheme is used for Sundanese music, but the meanings are reversed: 1 is higher than 2, and dots over the ciphers indicate the octave below.

38 Similarly the 7 adjacent to 1̇ may be written 7̇, etc.

notation), although this is not required by the Galin–Paris–Chevé system.

More frequently, three notes occupy the space of two or four standard lengths, i.e. each note has two-thirds or one and one-third times the standard duration. Unfortunately, *kepatihan* (like the Galin–Paris–Chevé system) has no way of representing this. Such patterns are found in the parts played by various decorating instruments, i.e. they are *garap* rather than part of the *balungan*, so that the deficiency in the notation system is not too important. Any such cases will be mentioned specifically below.

To represent notes of one-quarter the standard duration, a double overscore is used. For example, in

$\overline{\dot{1}\dot{2}}\quad \overline{65}\quad \overline{6\dot{1}}\quad \overline{\dot{2}\,\overline{.\,\dot{3}}}$

the final *pin* and note $\dot{3}$ are each of one-quarter length, and all the others are half-length. The longer overscore is normally written above, as in the example.

Four notes of one-quarter duration add up to one standard-length note. Theoretically, a single overscore over all four notes suffices to show this: $\overline{3523}$. Probably in the interest of clarity, the Javanese normally use a double overscore:

$\overline{\overline{3523}}$

Considering all the ways that the Javanese actually use the overscore, we can deduce that they are trying to indicate half-length notes with a single overscore, quarter-length notes with a double overscore, and so on. More than two overscores are possible. Provided that this usage is fairly consistent, it is clear and helpful, although not in strict accordance with the Galin–Paris–Chevé system. But players cannot be sure which rules are being followed, so they need to check any uses of the overscore whose meanings are not immediately obvious.

According to the principles of the Galin–Paris–Chevé system, the overscore starts on a stronger note and ends on a weaker one—a situation that suits Western classical music but conflicts with the end-weighted character of melodic material in *karawitan*. This becomes a problem in longer stretches of *balungan* with double (or higher) density, as discussed under **Notation of structure**. p. 41. However, the difficulty is fundamental. A few Javanese musicians find the usage of the overscore in Galin–Paris–Chevé so inappropriate for *karawitan* that they reverse its meaning, and end the overscore on a stronger note; some do this only for triplets. In this book, the overscore starts on a stressed note, and any resulting problems or obscurities are noted in the text.

Quite apart from any deliberate decision to use the overscore in what seems a more suitable way, it is not surprising that many Javanese musicians have difficulty with the overscore and do not use it 'correctly'. In some cases, the overscore serves as little more than an indication that there are some half-duration notes somewhere in the vicinity. When encountering new notation, especially from an unfamiliar source, it is therefore advisable to check how the overscore is being used. It may even be necessary to add up the durations of all the notes and check that the totals make sense. Furthermore, the notation could be 'correct' yet not represent what is actually played.

Notation for punctuation

The *bentuk* of each piece defines the positions where the punctuating instruments are struck. In the traditional repertoire there are relatively few *bentuk*, and most pieces are entirely regular in form. It is therefore hardly necessary to mark the positions of the punctuating instruments unless the form is irregular.

In practice the *kenong* and gong strokes are usually shown by adding distinctive symbols to the *kepatihan* numbers. (These symbols are of course not part of the Galin–Paris–Chevé system.) This information helps to confirm the player's reading of the rest of the notation.

Use of the solidus in notation

The solidus (oblique) has a variety of uses in notation; not usually in *balungan* notation but in individual parts. Uses of the backslash are also listed here. Some of these uses are unambiguous, but others are not.

Solidus or backslash superimposed on note

6̸	note damped while it is struck or struck 'dead' (*saron, demung, peking, bonang, siter*, etc.), or damped immediately after being struck (*gendèr*)
6̸	flattened *miring* note (vocal parts, *rebab, suling*)
6⃥	flattened *miring* note (vocal parts, *rebab, suling*)
6̸	*gembyang* (on *bonang*)
6̸	*kempyung* or *gembyung* (on *bonang*)

Solidus or backslash in isolation

/	separator between *gåtrå*
/	'up-bow', right-to-left bow stroke (*rebab*)
\	'down-bow', left-to-right bow stroke (*rebab*)

Because different categories of *gendhing* are characterised by their *kethuk* patterns, notation for *gendhing* sometimes has the *kethuk* positions marked, at least in the first *kenongan*. Otherwise *kethuk* and *kempyang* strokes are not often shown. For the remaining punctuating instruments (*engkuk-kemong* and *kemanak*) there seem to be no established symbols anyway.

There is no single standard scheme of symbols for the punctuating instruments: in fact pages could be filled with variants. The scheme used here and shown in Table 2.3 is based on one in common use at STSI (but understood elsewhere), exploiting distinctive symbols above or around the ciphers. Only a few alternatives are shown.

Since there is always a *kenong* stroke coincident with the gong stroke, it is not strictly necessary to mark the *kenong* stroke there. It is always worth checking whether the notation distinguishes the *gong suwukan* from the *gong ageng*: not all notation does so, since most of their usage is characteristic of the *bentuk*, and experienced players are therefore well aware of the places where the *gong suwukan* is used instead of the *gong ageng*.

When it is important to indicate the particular *kenong* or *kempul* note to be used, usually because it is not the one that might have been expected, the number is written as a superscript to the right of the symbol. The same may be done for the *gong suwukan*, but in the form of a subscript. The display box (right) shows an example of standard notation, using the above scheme as it is most often used, i.e. before the addition of superscript/subscript numbers.

Mark-up other than the above for punctuating instruments is usually quite easy to understand, because of the regular form of most pieces.

When non-standard punctuating patterns must be notated, the position of the punctuating stroke may be indicated by position (i.e. spacing) alone, e.g. for *kethuk* strokes half-way between *balungan* notes:

Notation example

Inc Baitå kandhas pl 6

bukå	3 . 123 . 2 . 1 . 3 . 2 . 1 . (6)
A	[. 2 . 6̂ . 2̆ . 6 . 3̆ . 2̂ . 1̆ . (6̂) × II
B	. 3 . 5̂ . 3̆ . 2̂ . 5̆ . 3̂ . 5̆ . (6)
	. 3 . 5̂ . 3̆ . 2̂ . 5̆ . 3̂ . 5̆ . (6)]

Table 2.3
Symbols for punctuating instruments

Instrument	Standard symbol	Some alternatives
gong ageng	⬯ ◯	G ( )
gong suwukan	( ) ⬯ ◯	G ‿ □ (
kenong	ˆ ⌒	N)
kempul	˘ ˅	P
kethuk	+	t × ^
kempyang	–	○ '

+ + + +
. . . .

but errors may arise when the notation is reproduced. Especially for the more complex patterns, it is safer to use the full resources of *kepatihan* to represent the time relationships, e.g. for another non-standard *kethuk* pattern:

. . . . . or . t . t . t .

Notation of structure

In the Galin–Paris–Chevé system, notes are grouped by vertical bar lines. The same practice is followed in Java when the system is used to notate Christian hymns and sometimes words for *langgam*. In these contexts the bar line precedes the strongest beat, as in normal Western staff notation, of which there is an example in Fig. 2.7.

As described earlier, the strongest beat in *karawitan* is at the end of a phrase, so that it is more logical for the separator to come after the end of the phrase. The separator most often used in lines of *balungan* is simply a space between the *gåtrå*. Occasionally a vertical bar, a broken vertical line or a solidus is found instead, especially in notation for vocal parts in *langgam* or *lagu dolanan*.

Whether the notation is printed or handwritten, lines longer than four *gåtrå* can be difficult to follow. Depending on the *bentuk*, a line of four *gåtrå* amounts to anything from ⅛ *kenongan* to four *kenongan*. It is helpful to the player if successive lines are laid out so that the ends of *gåtrå* are vertically aligned, and likewise the ends of *kenongan*. Typically notes are spaced out so that occasional *balungan ngadhal* does not increase the length of the line. If there are places where the *balungan* density is more than double, neat spacing becomes difficult.

Vertical spacing can also be important. It may be used to separate the *gongan* of any piece, or the *kenongan* of a

long *gendhing*, or the different sections of a piece (*mérong* and *inggah*, or *ompak* and *ngelik*) in order to clarify the structure.

There are alternative methods of notating double-density *balungan*. For a *gongan* which is not double-density throughout, the overscore is often used, as in the *ir II* section of *ldr Angguk kudus pl 7*

ir I

5 3 5 3   2 7 6 7̂   3 2 3 2̆   7 6 7 6̂
2 7 2 7̆   2 6 7 2̂   6 7 2 3̆   6 5 3 (2)

ir II

. 5 35 353   . 2 76 767̂   . 3 23 232̆   . 7 67 676̂
. 2 72 72 7̆   2 6 7 2̂   6 7 2 3̆   6 5 3 (2)

but notation based on spacing alone may be clearer

ir II

. 535353   . 276767̂   . 323232̆   . 767676̂
. 272727̆   2 6 7 2̂   6 7 2 3̆   6 5 3 (2)

because the relationship with the unexpanded *ir I* version is then more obvious.

A writer who believed in using the overscore in a truly Javanese manner might prefer

. 53 53 53   . 27 67 67̂   . 32 32 32̆   . 76 76 76̂
. 27 27 27̆   2 6 7 2̂   6 7 2 3̆   6 5 3 (2)

but it must be emphasised that this is a minority taste.

For a piece that has a full double-density *balungan*, e.g. many *ladrang* when they enter *ir III*, it is normal to write in groups of four notes again, raising the question of whether each such group is a *gåtrå* or a half-*gåtrå*. For example, *ldr Asmarandånå* is shown here in *sl m*:

ir I/II	2126 2123̂ 5321̆ 3231̂
	6321̆ 3216̂ 5321̆ 321(6)
ir III/IV	2321 3216 2321 6123̂
	6132 6321̆ 3632 1561̂
	6132 6321̆ 3632 3126̂
	5353 2321̆ 3632 312(6)

Sections of *balungan nibani* that are to be performed in *ir III* are sometimes notated with additional dots; e.g. the *gåtrå* . 3 . 2 as

. . . 3   . . . 2

Repeated sections are enclosed within large square brackets. Where a repeated section occurs within another repeated section, Javanese writers do not always include correctly matching pairs of brackets. For example, the sequence [[A] B] is very frequent—i.e. section A can be played once or more before proceeding to section B, within the overall repeated structure—but it is often written [A] B].

The positions of *andhegan* are sometimes indicated by a superscript asterisk, with either an overscore or an underline showing where the instruments do not play, e.g. (from *ktw Brondong mentul sl m*)

ompak 323. 3261̂* 6123̆ 212(6)

where the underline stops before the point where the instruments re-enter: it may continue for one more note.

Otherwise there are no dedicated symbols for indicating transitions between sections.

Notation for individual instruments

As *balungan* notation is not the notation for any single instrument, some interpretation of the notation is necessary for most instruments, as explained in Part 3.

However, *balungan* notation almost gives sufficient information for certain players in the ensemble. If the notation does not distinguish between *gong ageng* and *gong suwukan*, the player will know which is appropriate for pieces in traditional forms. The gong player will also not usually find the *gong suwukan* notes specified in the notation. In any case the *kendhangan* may request additional (decorative) *gong suwukan* strokes in certain contexts (see Part 3). If the positions of the *kempul* and *kenong* notes are shown in basic *balungan* notation, usually the actual notes played on these instruments are not.

For some punctuating instruments, the default patterns change during treatments such as *kébar*, or are replaced by *salahan*. In either of these two situations, the experienced player will know what to add to the standard notation. If the players of any of these instruments wish to record the notes that they are to play, they will write them into the *balungan* notation.

Notation for decorating instruments follows the requirements of the individual instrument, and especially the density of the decoration. To minimise the number of *pin* needed in the notation, the ciphers usually represent the standard duration of each note for the combination of the instrument and the *iråmå*. Thus there could be up to 32 standard-duration notes in a *gambang* part for each note in the *balungan*.

Alternative forms of notation are possible, and not unusual when writing out (for example) *sekaran* for the *bonang*. A full *sekaran* can be treated as having eight beats

1̅6̣̅ 3̣ 6̣ 1 2 6̣̅1̅ 6̣̅1̅ 2

or 16 beats, so that overscores are not required

. 1 6̣ 3̣ . 6̣ . 1 . 2 . 6̣ 1 6̣ 1 2

or, with an off-beat lead-in,

2 1 6̣ 3̣ . 6̣ . 1 . 2 . 6̣ 1 6̣ 1 2

but a problem arises if an off-off-beat lead-in (.̅2̅1 etc.) starts this *sekaran*, because an overscore is then needed again:

.̅2̅ 1 6̣ 3̣ . 6̣ . 1 . 2 . 6̣ 1 6̣ 1 2

To avoid an overscore, it would be necessary to treat the *sekaran* as 32 beats:

. . 2 1 . 6̣ . 3̣ . . . 6̣ . . . 1 . . . 2 . . . 6̣ . 1 . 6̣ . 1 . 2

which is theoretically right too, but not actually found in practice—it uses a lot of space because of the many *pin*.

If the *sèlèh* note of the pattern or *gåtrå* is followed by a note on the off-beat, the off-beat note (strictly speaking) belongs to the following pattern or *gåtrå*. 'Off-beat', as the above example shows, also relates to the number of beats being used in the notation. Depending on the style of *kepatihan* are being used, the off-beat note may either be attached to the *sèlèh* note with an overscore or be written 'correctly' in the next *gåtrå*. This is a further example of the problems that result from using the overscore in the Galin–Paris–Chevé manner. Decisions must therefore sometimes be made on how to notate dangling off-beat notes in individual parts as well as in *balungan*. This problem often occurs when notating *kendhangan*.

For some instruments played with two beaters or plucked with both hands, the parts for the two hands are written on two lines, the right-hand part above the left-hand, usually with careful vertical alignment. In Yogyanese notation for the *bonang*, the separating line can have another meaning: see ***Bonang* notation**, p. 139.

For the *rebab*, several additional markings are generally included in the notation: solidus and backslash for bowing, Roman numerals for left-hand position, and lower-case letters for the left-hand fingerings.

Other forms of notation

Use of roman numerals

Since the arabic numerals represent notes, Javanese musicians are careful about using numerals in other contexts. Roman numerals are normal in various places:

- for *kenong*/*kenongan* numbers—for example, 'N II' after a line of notation indicates that it ends with the second *kenong* of the *gongan*—although the *kenong* **note** is still shown, if necessary, by an arabic numeral,
- left-hand positions on the *rebab*: 'I' above the note in *rebab* notation means that the left hand is in the highest position (furthest from the *srentèn*/bridge), corresponding to the first position on the violin, etc.,
- numbers of repetitions: '× II' to the right of notation indicates that a section is played twice (see the example on p. 41),
- *iråmå* levels (*tingkat iråmå*): see pp. 58–9, Table 2.13,
- indicating categories of *kendhangan*—'*kendhang I*' or '*kendhang II*' (abbreviated to '*kd I*' or '*kd II*') representing respectively *kendhang satunggal*/*kendhang siji* or *kendhang kalih*/*kendhang loro*—although arabic 1 and 2 are also found,
- to distinguish between two players in interlocking *garap*, e.g. *demung I* and *demung II* in *demung imbal*,
- octave numbers: occasionally numbers are used to distinguish the octaves in which instruments play, ranging from I for the lowest to VII for the highest: see also Figs 3.1 and 3.2,
- (in older sources, before *kepatihan* was so well established) pitches of notes: the roman number value is not necessarily the same as the value in *kepatihan*,
- as identification numbers for established *sekaran* in *ciblon* drumming.

Drum notation

Notation for *kendhangan* uses its own set of symbols, because different drumstrokes rather than different pitches must be represented: see p. 217.

Vocal notation

Vocal parts use basically the same notation symbols as instrumental parts, but 0 may be used to indicate a true rest. The punctuating instrument symbols are not usually included. The text is normally shown underneath,

and notes sung to the same syllable are joined by an underline. Because more than one note is usually sung per *balungan* note, vocal notation often treats the standard duration of a note as shorter, e.g. by a factor of two or four, so that fewer overscores are needed.

Variations of presentation

Details of notation vary according to the method of reproduction as well as the individual writer's style. If handwritten, notation can contain any symbol that the writer cares to use, although the symbols shown above are still very widely used.

Typewriters[39] offer only a limited set of characters, and fine adjustment of vertical position is difficult, so typewritten notation tends to use symbols that are on or in the line: G, N, P,), (, ( ). Underlining sometimes replaces register dots, because it is easier to use. Professional typesetting should be able to provide the widest range of symbols, but in practice the simplest in-line symbols are still much used. Unfortunately, Javanese typesetters often ignore the spacing and careful horizontal alignment that are necessary to make *kepatihan* easy to follow, and these errors are not corrected by proofreaders. Some books contain notation that is simply unintelligible.

Word processing and desktop publishing software should enable personal computer users to emulate the best professional typesetting for this sort of material. Special *kepatihan* fonts have been created.[40] These sometimes combine ciphers and register dots, with or without symbols for the punctuating instruments, as single characters: this avoids many problems, but creates a large special character set that must be learnt. Alternatively, another type of custom-made font (as used in this book) keeps the ciphers, the register dots and all the punctuating instrument symbols separate: then the characters are much easier to use, but at the price of requiring more detailed knowledge of how the WP or DTP software works.

Kepatihan symbols can also be treated as pure graphic objects and manipulated by any drawing software, preferably of the vector graphic type: this method is very straightforward but slow to use.

Alternatives to *kepatihan*

Kepatihan gradually replaced at least two home-grown forms of notation that also dated from late in the nineteenth century; *ranté* (chain) and *åndhå* (ladder). The latter (also sometimes called **chequer notation**) can occasionally be seen in quite recently published books: it allows punctuating instruments and *kendhangan* to be notated at the same time as the *balungan* line. *Titilaras* in Javanese or *notasi* in Indonesian are generic words for all types of notation.

Titilaras ranté resembles Western staff notation in using horizontal lines and reading from left to right. Apart from notating *balungan*, it was also used to record vocal lines complete with ornamentation. *Titilaras åndhå* in contrast uses parallel vertical lines—six for *sléndro*, seven for *pélog*—and reads from top to bottom and then from left to right.

At present the fragments of *rebab* melody recorded in Western staff notation by Stamford Raffles[41] seem to be the earliest gamelan notation of any kind. More recent writers have also used this type of notation, sometimes adapted for the five-note scales of *karawitan*, but it has no advantages over *kepatihan*, and arguably it is inherently unsuitable for *karawitan* because it conflicts with the principle of end-weightedness.[42]

Hand signals

In mid-performance, or whenever verbal commands are undesirable, hand signals (Fig. 2.8) can communicate note numbers to other players. (The right hand is shown, but either hand may be used: 6 and 7 can also be signalled by the combination of two hands.) The technique is used, for example, to tell the *kenong* and/or *kempul* players (if necessary) which notes to play during *palaran*, where these notes are relatively difficult to work out.

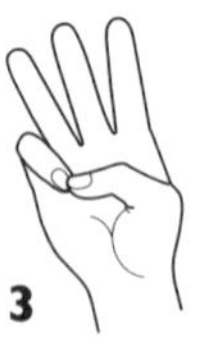

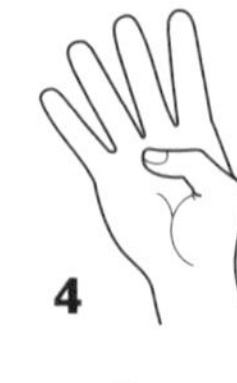

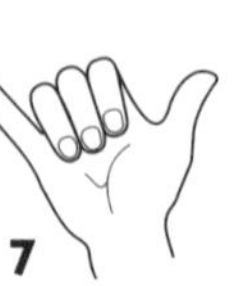

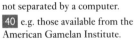

2.8 Hand signals for note numbers

39 For younger readers: a typewriter was a printing device in which the keyboard and the printing mechanism were mechanically connected, and not separated by a computer.

40 e.g. those available from the American Gamelan Institute.

41 Raffles (1817). Present-day musicians have had no difficulty in recognising the pieces when played from the notation.

42 Cf. Mantle Hood's account of an argument over three days and nights between himself and Colin McPhee about the use of staff notation for Balinese music (Hood, 1988).

Laras — 'tuning'

Some explanation is necessary, as *laras* has two principal meanings and some minor ones, while 'tuning' has three.

The main meaning of *laras*, to which this section is devoted, is the set of pitches that the instruments play and the singers sing—or, more precisely, one or other of the two sets of pitches that characterise *karawitan*. The word can also indicate any one of the pitches: essentially this is a singular version of the same usage. As explained below, it is slightly unsafe to translate this main usage of *laras* as 'scale', but the usual rendering as 'tuning' brings in more problems. The word 'tuning' in English commonly refers to the process of adjusting the pitch of the notes of an instrument, for which the Indonesian word would be *pelarasan*.

'Tuning' can also describe the relative sizes of the intervals between the pitches. The intervallic structure of a gamelan, called *embat* in Javanese, is discussed later in the present section.

The word *laras* can also be an adjective, translatable as 'harmonious', in the sense of sounding pleasant together. It can also represent the noun 'harmony' with the same sense, i.e. not the usual technical sense of the word in Western classical music, as mentioned on p. 22.

It is necessary to preface this section by saying that many aspects of gamelan tunings continue to be debated among scholars: the origins of the tunings, the relationship between *sléndro* and *pélog*, the extent to which practice conforms to theory, the degree of spread tuning used, the differences in pitch between the instruments of one gamelan, the amount and type of adjustment that occur when a gamelan is re-tuned, the variations between central Java and other areas that nominally use the same tunings, and so on.

Pitches are given in hertz (Hz), and intervals in cents: for explanations, see Appendix 4.

Sléndro vs. *pélog*

The two tunings of the central Javanese gamelan are sufficiently different to be implemented on separate instruments. A single gamelan is a complete set of instruments in one tuning. A double gamelan is a complete set in both tunings, although some instruments may be shared between the two tunings where possible. Single and double gamelan should be distinguishable by the terms *gamelan sepangkon* and *gamelan seprangkat*, but these terms are not applied consistently.

Neither of the tunings is absolute: note 3 (say) does not have the same pitch on every gamelan, nor are the sizes of the intervals the same on every gamelan. In theory, the *embat* of every gamelan is different: this is one of the most important aspects of *karawitan*. In practice, variations of *embat* are more widespread and noticeable in *laras sléndro*. Gamelan noted for their sound are taken as models (*babon*) when creating new sets of instruments. There used to be a ban on copying the much-admired court gamelan, but this restriction is no longer rigid.

Illustrations below are based on two specific gamelan, which are described by means of Fig. 2.9. It is important to emphasise that these cannot be considered as typical, average or representative in any way: they are simply two well-known gamelan, chosen because they illustrate a number of important features of gamelan tunings. The RRI Solo gamelan is of course widely heard because of its broadcasts, and is a frequent *babon*. *Kyai Kanyut Mèsem*[43] enjoys the highest reputation for its tonal quality, although it is a little unusual by today's standards, as a *tumbuk limå* gamelan (see **Tumbuk**, p. 49).

Any remarks about the pitch of a gamelan must be qualified by a warning that different instruments are not necessarily exactly in tune with each other. However, central Javanese instruments, unlike Balinese instruments, are not deliberately tuned to create beat notes.[44] When a gamelan is characterised, it is usually either the *demung* or the *gendèr barung* that is measured. For comparison, Fig. 2.9 shows the usual reference pitch for Western music, A = 440 Hz, but no assumptions should be made about the absolute pitch of other gamelan.[45]

Fig. 2.9 compares the two *laras* with each other and with the Western equal-tempered scale. In the latter, the span of one octave is defined as exactly 1200 cents. Comparing the pitches of the notes 1 and $\dot{1}$ on the gamelan with their nearest equivalents in the Western scale, it can be seen that the octave between them is not 1200 cents.

43 This name combines the names of its constituent parts: *Kyai Kanyut* (*sléndro*) and *Kyai Mèsem* (*pélog*).

44 Although old gamelan suggest that the Yogyanese may have preferred the instruments to be slightly out of tune with each other (*umyung*), as this was felt to favour loud-style playing (Sutton, 1991).

45 In particular, old gamelan and ceremonial gamelan have lower pitch.

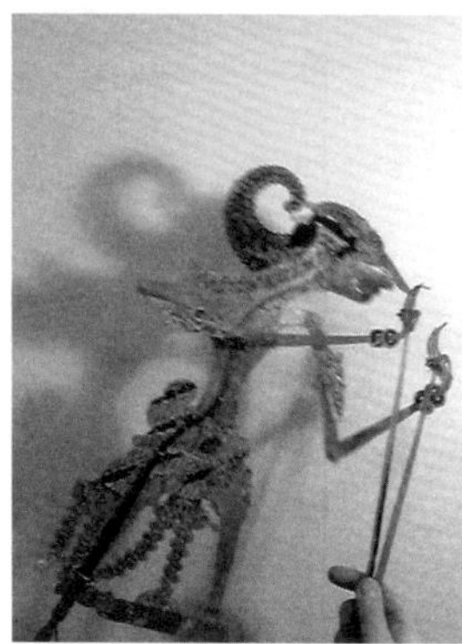

This applies to both *laras* on both gamelan. In fact the interval is variously 1213 and 1225 cents (RRI Solo, respectively *sléndro* and *pélog*), or 1218 and 1223 cents (*Kyai Kanyut Mèsem*, *sléndro* and *pélog*).

The explanation for the unexpected octave intervals is 'spread tuning' or 'octave-stretching'. Notes further and further up the range of the gamelan need to be tuned sharper and sharper relative to their theoretical pitches; otherwise they sound flat. Conversely, notes below the middle of the range must be tuned flatter.[46] Piano tuners in the West follow exactly the same principles, although there is some evidence that the 'spread' tends to be larger on the gamelan. If published measurements are right,[47] some gamelan have no spread tuning or even a negative spread, and there are reports that the degree of octave-stretching is deliberately varied between the instruments.

Sléndro scales

The *sléndro* tuning has five pitches per octave, making up a five-note scale.[48] The scale is used to form three *pathet*, which can be viewed as the equivalent of modes in Western terms, although they also have other associations, e.g. with the 'acts' of *wayang*. The *pathet* system is dealt with at length later: see ***Pathet***, p. 52.

In some *sléndro* compositions, additional pitches are used in the vocal parts and by the *rebab*. For further details, see **Miring relationships**, p. 49.

Pélog scales

The *pélog* tuning has seven pitches per octave. This is **not** the same as saying that *pélog* is a seven-note scale.

The most pragmatic view of *pélog* is that it actually possesses two five-note scales. The *bem* scale consists of the notes 1 2 3 5 6, and the *barang* scale of 2 3 5 6 7. Some decorating instruments are tuned to only one of these scales (see Figs 3.1 and 3.2). The two scales are used to make various modes or *pathet*. (Writers who say that *pélog* is a seven-note scale have to refer to the *bem* and *barang* 'sub-scales'.)[49]

At this point it is sufficient to say that *pathet limå* and *pathet nem* use the *bem* scale, whereas *pathet barang* uses the *barang* scale. The differences between *pathet limå* and *pathet nem* are disputed. It has been said (rightly or wrongly) that the note 4 is more often used in *pathet limå* than in *pathet nem*. At least one source goes so far as to say that the *pathet limå* scale is 1 2 4 5 6 rather than 1 2 3 5 6, but this is an extreme view. Many Yogyanese sources resolve the confusion over *pathet limå* and *pathet nem* by using the term *pathet bem* for both. This subject is revisited under ***Pathet*** below.

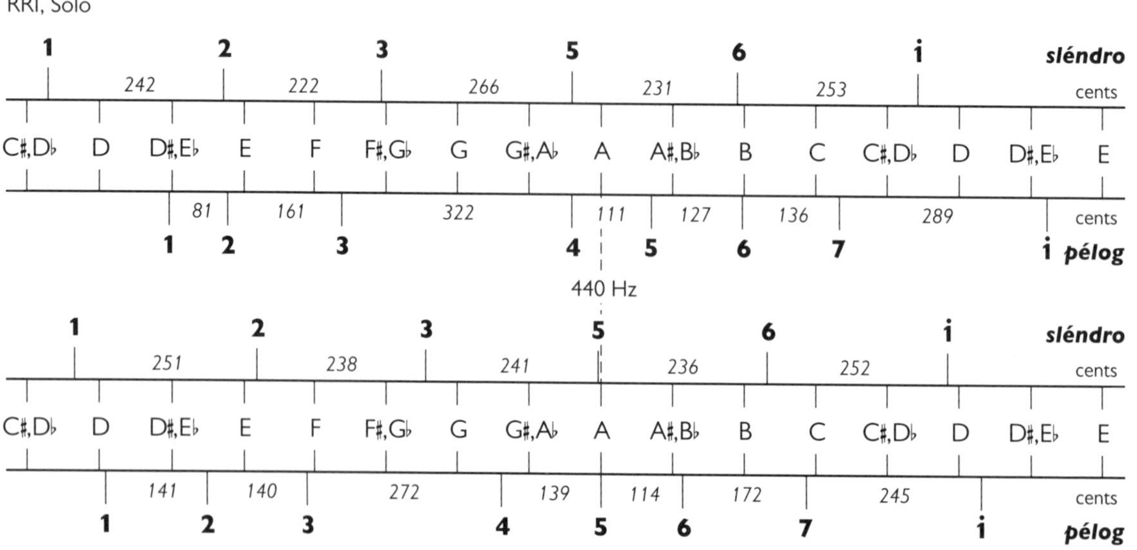

2.9 Interval structure in two double gamelan, compared against tempered scale

46 Kunst's (1973) measurements of gamelan tunings show no spreads (whereas later measurements on the same gamelan by other people find spreads). The reason why is unclear, since he mentions the use of spread tuning 'in olden times'. It is possible that he would have found spread tuning difficult to reconcile with the 'circle of fifths' theory, to which he devoted a large part of his book. For various reasons the theory does not fit the gamelan.

47 The measurements used here are taken from Wasisto Surjodiningrat et al. (1969/1972), who used more accurate measuring techniques than were available to Kunst. Several yet more accurate techniques now exist.

48 Elsewhere in Indonesia, *sléndro*-type tunings occur in the form of three-note or four-note scales.

49 Elsewhere in Indonesia too, five-note *pélog* scales are used.

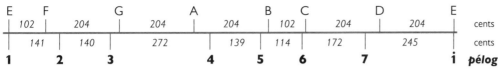

E	F	G	A	B	C	D	E	
102	204	204	204	102	204	204		cents
141	140	272	139	114	172	245		cents
1	**2**	**3**	**4**	**5**	**6**	**7**	**1̇**	***pélog***

Kyai Kanyut Mèsem

2.10 Comparison between *pélog* and 'white note' scale

The two *pélog* pitches that are not 'native' to the scale, i.e. 4 and 7 in the *bem* scale or 4 and 1 in the *barang* scale, are brought in as alternatives, sometimes called *sorogan* —or accidentals, in terms of Western music. In *pélog barang*, 4 is equivalent to a flattened 5, and 1 to a sharpened 7. In *pélog limå* and *nem*, 4 is equivalent to a sharpened 3, and 7 to a flattened 1. These relationships are of extreme importance in determining which notes players choose to play in all forms of 'decoration'.

The note 4 is thus never an equal member of the scale. Depending on the *pathet*, the same applies either to 1 or to 7. It is highly exceptional for the *sorogan* note and the basic note to be used in close proximity in the same part.[50] To do so would be the equivalent of 'false relation' in Western classical music.[51] The conflicting notes should be separated at least by a non-*sorogan* note. For example, the *gåtrå* 35 . 4 (in *gd Kombangmårå pl 5*) is possible because the note 5 serves to separate 3 from 4. Since instruments such as the *gendèr* and *gambang* do not have the note 4, clashes are unavoidable between 4 on some instruments and either 3 or 5 on others.

If an apparent exception to these principles occurs in classical *karawitan*, there is usually an explanation for it. In the first half of the fourth *kenongan* of the *mérong* of *gd bonang Tukung pl 7*, notes 5 and 4 occur adjacent to each other even though this is 'wrong' in *pathet barang*:

5 4 . 2   4 5 421   4 1 . 2   4 5 6 5

. . 5 .   5 5 . .   6̣ 7̣ 2 7̣   6̣ 5̣ 3̣ ⑤

The explanation here is that the *balungan* has temporarily modulated (to use a term from Western classical music) into *pathet limå*.[52] The return to *pathet barang* is signalled by the long *gantungan* on note 5, common to the *bem* and *barang* scales. On the other hand, no such explanation applies to the adjacent 1 and 7 in this passage from the *mérong* of *gd ktw Dårådasih kt 4 kp mg 8 pl 5*:

2̣ 4̣ . 2̣   4̣ 5̣ 4̣2̣1̣   7 7 . .   5 6 7 ⑥

although the 1̣–7 transition (from the lower limit of the *pathet* almost to the opposite extreme) is unusual.

Some modern compositions do treat the seven notes of *pélog* as if they are equal.

Singers and *rebab* players must, up to a point, adjust their notes to conform to the pitches of the fixed-tuned instruments. The note 4 is usually sung noticeably low, making the intervals 3–4 and 4–5 quite similar in size. The note 2 in *pélog* is also treated in a slightly anomalous manner. Musicians seem to hear the note 2 as higher, and therefore the interval 2–3 as smaller, in *pathet barang*. This suggests a resemblance between the intervallic structures of the two scales:

bem	1	2	3	5	6	1̇
barang	5̣	6̣	7̣	2	3	5

Note 2 is not necessarily tuned identically on the *bem* and *barang* instruments. Minor differences can be found with other notes too, but the case of note 2 is the most obvious. Singers too may adjust to the scale. Theorists say that any tuning is a compromise: see **Embat**, p. 50.

Fig. 2.10 shows how the notes of one *pélog* gamelan can be compared against a 'white note' scale from a Western instrument. Absolute pitch should be ignored: only the sizes of the intervals are relevant. The Western scale is assumed to use spread tuning, giving intervals around 102 and 204 cents instead of 100 and 200.

Sléndro–pélog comparisons

The *sléndro* scale contains five roughly equal intervals in the octave, i.e. about 240 cents each, and can therefore be called **equipentatonic** or **anhemitonic** (i.e. with no semitone intervals). It is unlikely that any gamelan has exactly equal intervals, but some approach it quite closely, e.g. with all intervals between 232 and 246 cents.[53] Differences between the interval structures of *sléndro* gamelan are discussed again under **Embat**.

The *pélog* tuning contains seven very unequal intervals in the octave, which cannot simply be characterised as 'large' and 'small'. The largest is almost invariably 3–4, although the interval 7–1̇ is often not much smaller. The

50 Hastanto (1985) gives an account of how unpleasant this can sound to Javanese ears.

51 This effect was deliberately cultivated by some Renaissance composers. The 40-part motet *Spem in alium* (1573?) by Thomas Tallis is one well-known piece where it can be heard.

52 Or else into an alternative scale within *pathet barang*: see **Pathet**.

53 The similarity of the intervals in a *sléndro* scale can be measured by the **standard deviation** (S.D.) of the intervals: the more similar the intervals, the lower the S.D. The gamelan just referred to had an S.D. of 5 cents. In other gamelan measured by Wasisto et al. (1969/1972) the values ranged up to nearly 18 cents, and the average was about 12 cents. For comparison, the diatonic pentatonic scale familiar from *Auld Lang Syne* would correspond to a *sléndro* scale with an S.D. of 49 cents.

interval 6–7 is intermediate in size, and normally the intervals 1–2 and 5–6 are the smallest. Therefore there are intervals in *pélog* that are consistently larger than others. The same could not be said of *sléndro*. In subjective terms, this means that *pélog* gamelan tend to sound more like each other than *sléndro* gamelan do.

For one collection of measurements,[54] excluding ceremonial gamelan because they are not typical of anything, the *pélog* intervals fall into groups as follows:

3–4	250 to 325 cents
7–1̇	215 to 310 cents
6–7	135 to 235 cents
2–3 and 4–5	95 to 165 cents
1–2 and 5–6	80 to 145 cents

Therefore the smallest intervals can be less than a semitone (100 cents) in Western terms, and the largest can exceed a minor third (300 cents).[55]

Javanese tradition and modern scholarship disagree as to whether *pélog* pre-dates *sléndro*.[56] From the sizes of the intervals in the two *laras*, it is difficult to see how one tuning could have been derived from the other, although this has sometimes been argued. There has also been a suggestion that *pélog* derives from a scale with nine roughly equal intervals, in which case any relationship with *sléndro* would be even more unlikely.

Writers who compare *sléndro* and *pélog* to the Western major and minor scales respectively have rather missed the point. Also the term *minir/minur* has another meaning anyway in *karawitan*. Neither can *sléndro* and *pélog* be compared to keys in Western music. A key has a **tonic**, the first note of its scale. Although some notes are more important than others in *karawitan* (see ***Pathet***, p. 52), there is no 'first note' in either *laras*.[57]

An obvious but unanswerable question is whether the Javanese prefer one *laras* to the other. Kunst's gamelan census (see p. 7) showed large regional variations in the relative numbers of gamelan in the two *laras*.

Intervals

The intervals of *sléndro* are such that one cannot easily compare the scale with the Western diatonic scales. Arguably the most important interval in *karawitan* is the *kempyung*, defined as two notes separated by two other notes in the scale. At around 720 cents on average, the *kempyung* in *sléndro* is not far from the perfect fifth in a Western scale, which in its equal-tempered version is 700 cents. The *gembyung* (= two notes separated by one other note), at around 480 cents, is flat relative to a Western equal-tempered perfect fourth (= 500 cents). No other intervals in *sléndro* sound familiar to a Western ear that is sensitive to tuning.

When intervals in a *pélog* gamelan are analysed, one or other of the scales must be chosen. For example, in the *bem* scale, 1–5 is a *kempyung*, because 4 is not native to the scale, and so is 7̣–5 (because 7̣ is a *sorogan* for 1). In the *barang* scale, 1–5 and 7̣–5 are still *kempyung*, but so are 1–4 (because 4 is a *sorogan* for 5) and 7̣–4. Table 2.4 shows how some of the intervals are calculated.

From examination of the data for any specific *pélog* gamelan, such as those in Fig. 2.9, it is clear that the sizes of *kempyung* vary greatly, so that the interval cannot simply be equated to a fifth in Western terms. The *kempyung* interval 3–1̇ in *pélog* regularly exceeds a major sixth (= 900 cents), whereas 4–7 (using the *sorogan* alternatives to the notes 3 and 1̇) can be less than a major third (= 400 cents). The most important *kempyung* in *pélog* are 1–5 and 2–6. Both gamelan in Fig. 2.9 are typical in having a smaller 1–5 interval in *pélog* than in *sléndro*. As for the 2–6 intervals, see ***Tumbuk***, p. 49. Similarly, a *gembyung* is only very approximately a Western fourth.

Most of the other possible intervals have names, as shown in the table below.

Notes apart	Examples	Name
1	1–2, 5–6	*kempyang, siliran*
2	1–3, 3–6	*gembyung, salah gumun*
3	1–5, 2–6	*kempyung, adu manis*
4	1–6, 2–1̇	?
5 (octave)	1–1̇	*gembyang*

To Javanese ears, as to Western ears, different intervals are not all equally pleasant. The absence of a name for intervals such as 1–6, corresponding most closely to the sixth in Western terms, is significant. This interval and its 'inversion', the third (e.g. 6̣–1), are not favoured in *karawitan*. The situation can be compared to continental Europe in the fourteenth century, where the third and sixth were not regarded as consonant.[58]

The question arises of how the Javanese (or other listeners) feel about the constantly changing intervals created between the *balungan* and the decoration, or

54 Wasisto et al. (1969/1972).

55 See Jones (1963) for an analysis of *pélog* scales that sees note 4 as a fixed point against which the other notes shift, and divides gamelan into three classes according to the amount of this shift.

56 Archaeological evidence makes *pélog* earlier, but Javanese musicians draw the opposite conclusion from the fact that much *garap* in *pélog* is based on *garap* in *sléndro*.

57 Although Javanese writers have translated 'tonic' as *dhasar* and used the term in connection with *pathet*. Among Debussy's perceptive comments on gamelan music is this from a letter to Pierre Louÿs (1895): '… remember the music of Java, which contained every shade of meaning, … in which the tonic and dominant were no more than empty phantoms for use by unenlightened children.' This translation is based on sources that have '… des petits enfants pas sages' at the end of the quotation. F. Lesure in *Debussy: Correspondance* (Coll. Savoir, 1993) omits 'pas'.

58 Both intervals were in common use in England, and were introduced to the Continent by John Dunstable in the fifteenth century. It would be an exaggeration to say that

between different decorating parts (which will be described in Part 3). In *pélog*, the playing style of the *peking*, for example, positively guarantees the frequent occurrence of intervals around 100 to 200 cents between the *peking* part and the *balungan*; these are the sizes considered least harmonious in Western music.

It has been suggested that the non-harmonic overtones of most gamelan instruments (see Appendix 4) make a wide range of intervals acceptable. Any pair of notes in the *sléndro* scale, it is generally agreed, sound satisfactory together. The same is not true of *pélog*. However, intervals due to decorative *garap* exist only briefly, and the *sèlèh* points are the most important places where the Javanese think in terms of 'harmony' or lack of it.

Tumbuk

In a double gamelan it is entirely possible that none of the notes in the *pélog* section will coincide with one in the *sléndro* section. However, it is usual for at least one note, with the same number, to have the same pitch in both sections. Such a note is called a *tumbuk* note: the word *tumbuk* means 'collision' or 'coincidence'.

On older gamelan, at least in Yogyakarta, any coincidence tended to be on note 5, leading to the gamelan being described as '*tumbuk limå*'. *Kyai Kanyut Mèsem* in Fig. 2.9 is an example. A *tumbuk limå* gamelan may have another *tumbuk* on note 1. The other common situation is exemplified by the RRI Solo gamelan (Fig. 2.9), with *tumbuk* note 6. In *tumbuk nem* gamelan, an additional *tumbuk* on note 2, or at least a very close approximation, is possible. It is also common for the *pélog* note 4 to coincide with the *sléndro* 5 (not strictly a *tumbuk*, since the note numbers differ). In some gamelan, *pélog* 7 is close to *sléndro* 1. To be counted as a *tumbuk*, the notes must be very close, but not necessarily identical to the last cent: perhaps a difference of less than 5 cents is sufficient.

In the latter part of the twentieth century, a conference was held in Java to discuss the standardisation of gamelan tuning. Its outcome was (fortunately) not the standardisation of intervallic relationships, but recent gamelan tend to agree in two other ways: firstly, on *tumbuk nem* as the norm, and secondly, on the absolute pitch of note 6.

Fig. 2.9 shows that, even with *tumbuk* notes, one *laras* cannot be derived from the other: the sizes of the intervals are too different.

Miring relationships

Miring scales are used within *sléndro*, but include non-standard intervals.[59]

As shown in Fig. 2.12,[60] there are several *miring* scales, not one. Each coincides with the *sléndro* scale at (a minimum of) two points—the open circles in the diagram—which can be seen as another form of *tumbuk*. The different *miring* scales can be characterised by their two principal *tumbuk* notes, separated by a *kempyung*. Between the two notes there are four *miring* intervals instead of the three of the standard *sléndro* scale. Additional *miring* notes above the upper *tumbuk* note and below the lower *tumbuk* note are also used. (All *miring* pitch locations in Fig. 2.12 should be regarded as approximate.)

Some writers say that *miring* scales amount to using *pélog* intervals in *sléndro*, but this description is too simple. More precisely, the space between the two *tumbuk* points is divided in a way that creates intervals typical of *pélog* scales. Taking the 5̣ – 2 scale as an example, the first *miring* interval (5̣–6̸̣) has the size of the 1–2 interval in *pélog*, the next interval is the size of 2–3, and so on. The 4 in the *miring* scale is a vocal 4, i.e. giving similar intervals for 3–4 and 4–5. Thus the notes shown in the diagram as 5̣ 6̸̣ 1̸ 1 2 3̸ 5̸ correspond to 1 2 3 4 5 6 7. The same pattern of intervals occurs in each of the *miring* scales. This means that the pitch of 5̸, for example, is not constant, but varies between the different *miring* scales.

It is possible for a piece to use more than one of the *miring* scales, potentially giving the feeling of modulation. Scales are chosen in relation to the *pathet* and the tessitura (relative pitch range) of the melodic line. Often the *sèlèh* note of the phrase is the same as one of the *tumbuk* notes of the *miring* scale, but this is not an absolute rule. For an example, see *langgam Ngimpi* in Part 4.

Table 2.4
Examples of intervals in various scales

	Sléndro	*Pélog*	
		bem scale	*barang* scale
Kempyung	6̣–3, 1–5, 2–6, 3–1̇, 5–2̇, 6–3̇, etc.	6̣–3, 6̣–4, 7̣–5, 1–5, 2–6, 3–7, 3–1̇, 4–7, 4–1̇, 5–2̇, 6–3̇, 6–4̇, etc.	6̣–3, 7̣–4, 7̣–5, 1–4, 1–5, 2–6, 3–7, 3–1̇, 4–2̇, 5–2̇, 6–3̇, etc.
Gembyung	6̣–2, 1–3, 2–5, 3–6, 5–1̇, 6–2̇, etc.	6̣–2, 7̣–3, 1–3, 1–4, 7̣–4, 2–5, 3–6, 4–6, 5–7, 5–1̇, 6–2̇, etc.	6̣–2, 7̣–3, 1–3, 2–4, 2–5, 3–6, 4–7, 4–1̇, 5–7, 5–1̇, 6–2̇, etc.

the Javanese have a preference for the Pythagorean intervals, since the intervals in *pélog* and *sléndro* deviate from the Pythagorean values.

59 The names *barang miring* or *sléndro miring* are also found. Some sources use the name *barang miring* for a scale in which only a flattened 1 is added.

60 Developed from unpublished analysis by Nikhil Dally. The theory of *miring* scales is not much discussed by Javanese musicians, and the application of the term *tumbuk* here owes nothing to Javanese sources.

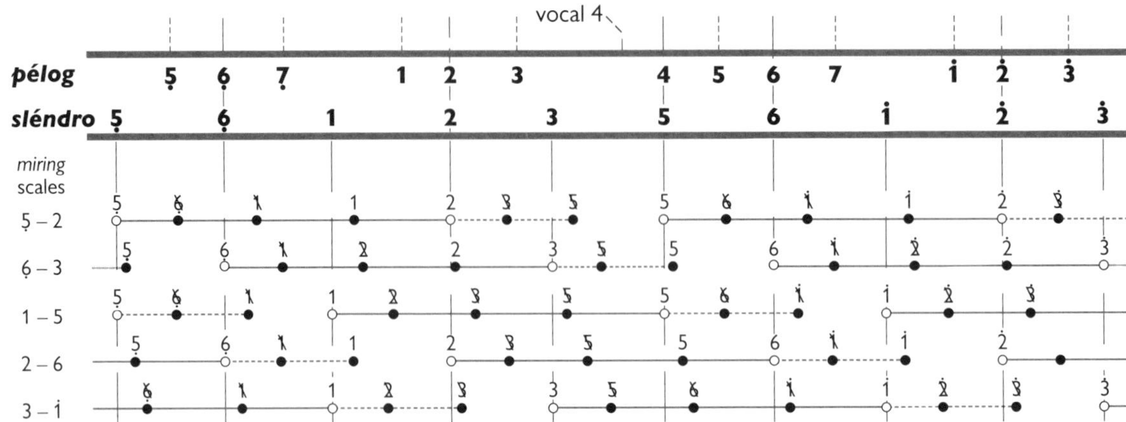

2.12 *Miring* relationships

Miring notes of course cannot be produced by any of the instruments with fixed tuning, so they are confined to vocal parts and the *rebab*, and sometimes the *suling*. In notation, notes that do not coincide with the standard scale are generally shown by the next higher note number with a backslash or forward slash (solidus) superimposed. (The word *miring* literally means 'oblique' or 'deviating', but has connotations such as 'crazy'.)

Miring scales can be used within any *pathet* in *sléndro*, but appear to be used most often in *pathet sångå*. They are particularly associated with moments of emotional stress in dance and drama, and are a feature of certain of the standard 'mood-songs' (*sulukan*), such as *Sendhon Tlutur*. *Miring* vocal lines are an established feature of specific compositions, e.g. *langgam Ngimpi*, *gd Mådyåratri*, *lnc Penghijauan*, *ldr Dirådåmetå* and some *sekar*. They are optional in other pieces. *Pesindhèn* have a repertoire of *cèngkok miring* for use in *sindhènan srambahan*, and use them instead of standard *céngkok* when the *rebab* itself switches to *céngkok miring*.

Miring notes can also be seen in vocal notation for pieces in *pélog*; for example, a 4̸ may indicate that the note is to be sung at the 'vocal 4' pitch, in contrast to the instrumental pitch.

Embat

The term *embat* refers to the relative sizes of the intervals of a gamelan—if theorists are right, only a gamelan in *sléndro*. The term does not refer to the absolute pitch of the gamelan.

Theorists say that all gamelan tunings derive from vocal pitches, as if there is a single vocal *embat* from which actual gamelan deviate. (The 'vocal 4' has already been mentioned.) A gamelan that did not deviate from this hypothetical tuning could then be said to have no *embat*.

RRI, Solo
1 2 3 5 6 i̇ *sléndro*
242 222 266 231 253 cents
200 200 300 200 300 cents
C D E F G A B C D
cents 300 200 200 200 300
cents 251 238 241 236 252
Kyai Kanyut Mèsem 1 2 3 5 6 i̇

2.11 Comparison of *sléndro* gamelan against 'white note' scales

Table 2.5
A history of tuning?

Kyai Kanyut (sléndro)

		1		2		3		5		6		1̇	Octave
A	Hz	291		331		383		439		500		582	
	cents		*223*		*253*		*236*		*225*		*263*		*1200*
B	Hz	288		333		382		439		503		582	
	cents		*251*		*238*		*241*		*236*		*253*		*1219*

Kyai Mèsem (pélog)

		1		2		3		4		5		6		7		1̇	Octave
A	Hz	295		317		345		399		439		465		512		590	
	cents		*125*		*146*		*252*		*165*		*100*		*167*		*245*		*1200*
B	Hz	295		320		347		406		440		470		519		598	
	cents		*141*		*140*		*272*		*139*		*114*		*172*		*245*		*1223*

Perhaps the most crucial intervals are those on either side of the note 3. The name *embat nyendari* describes a tuning where the interval 2–3 is relatively small, and 1–2 relatively large, as in the RRI Solo gamelan (see Fig. 2.11). The opposite situation, with a relatively large interval 2–3, is called *embat laras ati*. Another term, *embat colongan*, indicates that an interval has been reduced or enlarged according to the wishes of the tuner.[61]

Western ears may 'bend' the notes of the gamelan and hear them as fitting a more familiar scale. Fig. 2.11 shows how the *sléndro* scale may be made to conform to two different 'white-note' Western scales, i.e. scales that can be formed from the white notes of the piano. The intervals are then heard as either 200 or 300 cents (or about 204 or 306 cents with spread tuning). As with Fig. 2.10, the absolute pitch of the gamelan should be ignored.

Javanese musicians have been described as very sensitive to tuning. The naming of different *embat* would seem to support this comment. On the other hand, the comment may seem misplaced—or at least to imply a different kind of sensitivity—when the singers are singing a vocal 4 against an instrumental 4 on the *balungan* instruments, the *rebab* is playing a sharp vocal 4 to keep the *pesindhèn* up to pitch, and most of the decorating instruments are playing either 3 or 5 because they have no 4 at all: the air can throb with the dissonance.

Several of the observations above illustrate a more general principle: that the *embat* of any gamelan is a compromise between the needs of the various *pathet*, and affects the ease with which Javanese musicians can sing with the gamelan.[62]

Embat is an important element in the character of a gamelan. However, gamelan are tuned from time to time, so it would be interesting to know the basis on which the tuner makes the adjustments. Tuners do sometimes seem to introduce significant changes, and purely according to their own taste. Some possible evidence from *Kyai Kanyut Mèsem* is shown in Table 2.5, in the form of the pitches (in hertz) and their intervals (in cents). The figures labelled A are from Kunst, and those labelled B from Wasisto et al. Perhaps half a century separates the measurements. Allowing for possible errors in both sets of figures, especially the earlier ones, and for the absence of spread tuning in Kunst's, it seems possible that *Kyai Kanyut* has experienced an adjustment of its *embat*, whereas part of *Kyai Mèsem* has been tuned up slightly.

61 The terms *luruh*, *råtå* and *sigrak* are also used: see **Glossary**.

62 See Hatch (1980). Various aspects of tunings are examined by Vetter (1989).

Pathet — 'mode'

Pathet is the most contentious area of the theory of *karawitan*. The etymology of the word has failed to clarify its meaning.[63] What is beyond dispute is that *pathet* relates to the following:

- □ the tessitura or range of notes occupied by the melodic lines—i.e. *balungan*, parts for individual instruments, and vocal lines, etc.,
- □ a preference for certain notes, and the avoidance of certain others, at structurally important points, i.e. as gong notes or at the end of *kenongan*,
- □ the different 'acts' of *wayang* performances, and, more generally, certain times of day (Fig. 2.13),
- □ the mood and character of the composition—though not excluding other factors, as mentioned on p. 37.

The first two items in the list correspond more or less to the Western concept of **mode**, and therefore 'mode' has often been used as the most convenient translation of *pathet* in English.[64]

The Javanese see three *pathet* within each *laras*, arranged to correspond as in Table 2.6, which also shows the order of the *pathet* used for *wayang* accompaniments in both *sléndro* and *pélog* (see p. 97). The picture is complicated by the vestigial *pathet galong* in the third act of Yogyakarta *wayang kulit*,[65] but this will be ignored (following other writers) in the analysis below.

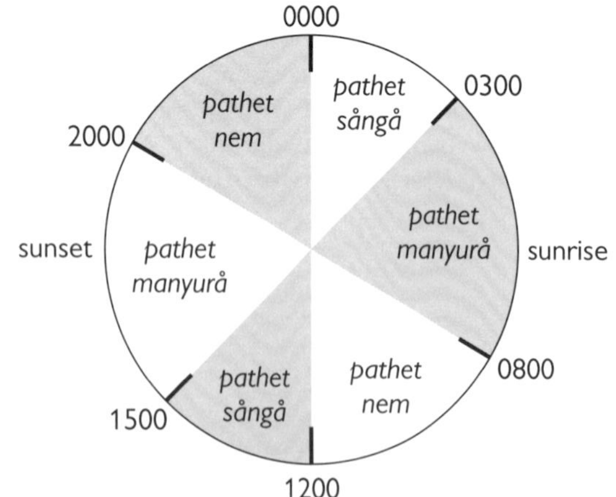

2.13 Usage of *pathet* according to time of day

Table 2.6
Notional relationships between *pathet*

Laras sléndro		*Laras pélog*	
Pathet nem	—	*Pathet limå*	lowest
Pathet sångå	—	*Pathet nem*	↓
Pathet manyurå	—	*Pathet barang*	highest

Every piece is assigned to a *pathet* as well as to a *laras*, and supposedly conforms to the characteristics of that *pathet*. Knowing the *pathet* of a piece, the player is then expected to choose appropriate *pathet*-specific *garap* when realising the piece. This duty has the most extensive implications for the players of the decorating instruments, especially those of the soft style, but affects even the players of punctuating instruments.

Each of the three *pathet* in *sléndro* has a characteristic cadential phrase that often occurs at the end of a piece

Pathet nem:	6̣5̣3̣2̣ or 6532
Pathet sångå:	216̣5̣
Pathet manyurå:	3216̣

and a set of fixed or 'dead' *balungan* contours (*céngkok mati*), unique to the *pathet* (Table 2.7).[66] Each is also characterised (Table 2.8) by its tessitura, a set of notes most likely to be found at stucturally important points, and an 'avoided' or 'enemy' note that is least likely to be found at such points. The enemy note is also the one note of the scale that does not occur in the cadential phrase.

The tessitura given is a little theoretical, but applies to the soft-style decorating instruments. Upper limits of 5̇ and 3̇ apply to vocal lines in *pathet manyurå* and *pathet sångå*, respectively. The *bonang* may use notes below the indicated range, especially in *imbal* and *sekaran*.

Table 2.7
'*Céngkok mati*' in *sléndro*

Sléndro nem		*Sléndro sångå*		*Sléndro manyurå*	
5653	216̣5̣	3532	.16̣5̣	5653	2126̣
.16̣5̣	1216̣	3532	.126̣	33..	6532
661̇6	5323	561̇6	5321	3561̇	6532
		1̇656	5321	3561̇	6523

[63] At first sight, the word *pathet* appears related to *mathet*, meaning 'pull tight', 'restrain' or 'curtail'; also 'damp', as of notes when playing the gamelan. It would make more sense if *pathet* were related to *pathut*, meaning 'fitting', 'proper'. It may be significant that the equivalent term in Balinese music is *patut*, and that a related term in Sundanese music is *surupan*, also meaning 'fitting', 'proper'—or it may be a complete coincidence.

[64] *Pathet* is treated under the MODE heading in Grove (1980, 2001).

[65] Anyone wishing to investigate *pathet* in greater depth should consider the situation in other parts of Java, where there can be more than three *pathet* per *laras*—see under *pathet* in the **Glossary**, Hastanto (1985) and Sutton (1991)—and the Balinese system of scales and *patut*. Elsewhere in central Java (although apparently not in Solo) this highest *pathet* is recognised and sometimes called *manyuri*.

[66] The list of *céngkok mati* is Martopangrawit's, with revisions (Hastanto, 1985).

Like Table 2.6, Table 2.8 oversimplifies the true situation in a number of ways. As will be shown below, the equivalent table for the *pathet* in *pélog* (Table 2.9) is even more unhelpful.

The *pathet* clock (Fig. 2.13) agrees with the earliest time (8 p.m.) that an all-night *wayang kulit* performance is likely to start. The start may be closer to 9 p.m., and the *wayang* proper usually follows a *talu* in another *pathet*.

As *pathet* are associated with different times of day, some pieces should theoretically not be performed at certain times. The principle applies most strongly with the lowest *pathet* in each *laras*, which are considered more serious than the others. The restrictions are more theoretical than practical, otherwise a range of pieces in all *pathet* could not be performed in *klenèngan*.

The problems

The description above simply does not explain how individual pieces are assigned to *pathet* and how musicians realise them in practice:

- In the *sléndro nem* act of *wayang kulit*, pieces in *sléndro manyurå* are often used. The shortage of *ketawang* and *lancaran* in *sléndro nem* is not a sufficient explanation.
- Many pieces usually considered as *sléndro manyurå* are sometimes assigned to *sléndro nem*—even *ldr Wilujeng*, which contains three of the four *céngkok mati* of *pathet manyurå*. In Mloyowidodo's collection of notation, more than one piece appears with identical notation in both the *sléndro manyurå* and the *sléndro nem* sections.
- Some pieces usually considered as *sléndro sångå* are sometimes assigned to *sléndro nem*. (However, there is no such confusion between *manyurå* and *sångå*.)
- Compositions do not always exhibit the 'correct' important notes; for example, nobody disputes that *gd (Per)kututmanggung* is in *sléndro manyurå*, yet it has note 1 at most of its important points—three out of four *kenong* including the gong note.
- The characteristics of the *pathet* in *sléndro* do not match the (supposedly) corresponding *pathet* in *pélog*. For example, the notes 1 and 5̣, important in *sléndro sångå*, have the equivalent status more regularly in *pélog limå* than in *pélog nem*. It is difficult to identify any 'enemy notes' in the *pathet* of *pélog*.
- (Related to the previous item) when pieces are converted from *sléndro* to *pélog*, they do not necessarily move to the 'corresponding' *pathet*, as in Table 2.6. Whereas pieces in *sléndro manyurå* are often converted to *pélog barang* by changing 1 to 7 and adjusting the shape of certain *gåtrå*, pieces in *sléndro sångå* can often be moved to *pélog limå* without changing the notes.
- The precise differences between *pélog limå* and *pélog nem* are debated, and the Yogyanese often group them together as *pélog bem*. Pieces are not assigned consistently to one or the other; for example, *ldr Tirtåkencånå* is usually labelled as *pathet nem*, but no less an expert than Martopangrawit assigned it to *pathet limå*.
- Some *pathet*, particularly *sléndro nem*, are described as having mixed characteristics. Musicians even subdivide *pélog nem* into 'gong 5' and 'gong 6' pieces, which they treat differently.
- If all *pathet* were created equal, as suggested by Table 2.6, players might need to learn six sets of *pathet*-specific *garap*, but this does not happen.
- Players of soft-style decorating instruments reportedly have difficulty in finding suitable *céngkok*, i.e. appropriate to the *pathet*, for realising certain pieces.
- Other *pathet* exist in both *laras*, and require explanation; besides *pathet galong* in *sléndro*, in *pélog* a *pathet manyurå* or *nyamat* certainly exists, as well as signs of a *pathet sångå*.

All this evidence tends to contradict the remark 'Pathet ... is not a problem for performers: only for theorists'.[67] Certainly *pathet* remains a problem for *londo*.

Table 2.8
Characteristics of *pathet* in sléndro

Pathet	Tessitura	Important notes	Enemy note
Manyurå	3̣ to 3̇	6̣, 2, 3	5
Sångå	5̣ to 2̇	5̣, 1, 2	3
Nem	2̣ to 3̇	2̣, 5̣, 6̣	1

Table 2.9
Characteristics of *pathet* in pélog

Pathet	Tessitura	Important notes	Enemy note[a]
Barang	3̣ to 3̇	5̣, 6̣, 2	?
Nem	2̣ to 3̇	5̣, 6̣, 2	?
Limå	1̣ to 2̇	5̣, 1	3?

a. Notes 1 and 7 are avoided in *pathet barang* and *pathet limå / nem* respectively because they do not belong to the scale, but they are not 'enemy notes' in the same sense as those in *sléndro*.

67 Hastanto (1985).

I keep thinking we're in *pathet sångå*

Addressing the problems

The earliest scholarly attempts to analyse the theory of *pathet* concentrated on the aspects that were easiest to identify and count.

First, the occurrence of notes at structurally important points—(in descending order of importance) the ends of *gongan*, *kenongan* and *gåtrå*—was studied. As indicated earlier, the evidence from the 'important notes' alone is not conclusive.

Second, similar attention was given to the frequency and position of use of certain *gåtrå*. This approach still fails to explain a number of apparent anomalies.

The analysis here is based largely on one source[68] which, though not beyond criticism, has proved best able to explain why players play what they play, and leaves the fewest questions unanswered. The approach is based on entire *padhang–ulihan* phrases in the notation, typically of two *gåtrå* but sometimes longer. It also takes into account the possibility of a *padhang* or *ulihan* not starting or finishing at a *gåtrå* boundary. (The rules for determining the location of phrase boundaries are too complex to be listed here.) It was further claimed to be based on the 'inner melody', not the *balungan*.

68 Hastanto (1985). The discussion here is necessarily simplified.

69 Not one of Hastanto's examples.

Table 2.10
Characteristic phrases in each *pathet* in *sléndro*

Sèlèh note	*Manyurå*			*Sångå*			*Nem*		
	↗	↘	→	↗	↘	→	↗	↘	→
3̇	MA3̇								
2̇				SA2̇					
1̇	MA1̇								
6	MA6	MD6		[SA6][a]			NA6	ND6	
5				SA5	SD5		NA5	ND5	
3	MA3	MD3	MR3					[ND3][a]	NR3
2		MD2		SA2	SD2[a]	SR2	NA2	ND2	NR2
1		MD1	MR1		SD1				
6̣		MD6̣			SD6̣		NA6̣		NR6̣
5̣					SD5̣			ND5̣	
3̣		MD3̣							
2̣								ND2̣	

After Hastanto (1985). a. ND3 and SA6, which Hastanto uses in analyses, are not supported by his sources and are included in brackets here. SD2 has been added because it is supported by his sources, although he omitted it from analyses as not unambiguous in *pathet*; this argument, however, would also exclude MD2 and ND2.

Analysis in *sléndro*

To identify the most characteristic shapes and final notes of phrases for each *pathet* in *sléndro*, Hastanto analysed certain material that is absolutely *pathet*-specific:

- *pathetan wantah*—the longer version of the *pathet*-defining piece that is played by the soft-style instruments before and/or after other pieces (usually suites or long *gendhing*), or at the start of a *wayang* 'act',
- *senggrèngan*—an introductory phrase on the *rebab* before the *bukå*, with a similar *pathet*-defining function but shorter, and
- *thinthingan*—an introductory phrase on the *gendèr barung*, also with a similar function but even shorter.

On the basis of these sources, he then created a table of characteristic phrases (Table 2.10), denoted by

- a letter indicating the *pathet*,
- a second letter indicating the direction of the phrase —ascending, descending or 'reciting', the latter including any phrase that starts and finishes on the same note, not restricted to pure *gantungan*,
- the final note of the phrase.

An important part of Hastanto's analysis was the acceptance of the possibility of mixtures of *pathet* in a piece; the piece would then be assigned to the *pathet* that was felt to predominate. In addition, many phrases are possible but not listed in the table. These can be interpreted as ambiguous or *pathet*-neutral, although sometimes they can usefully be analysed into sub-phrases—as can any other phrases that appear ambiguous.

This approach to the *bukå* and *ompak* of *ldr Wilujeng sl m*[69] gives:

132 6̣123　1132 .126̣
MA3　MD6̣/SD6̣

2123 2126̣　33.. 6532
MD6̣/SD6̣　MD2/SD2?/ND2

5653 2126̣　2123 2126̣
MD6̣/SD6̣　MD6̣/SD6̣

Only one phrase is unambiguous in *pathet*. It must be pointed out that the second and third *kenongan*, apparently ambiguous, are actually among the *céngkok mati* for *sléndro manyurå*. However, if some of the phrases are analysed further, the *manyurå* orientation becomes clearer:

2123	2126̣	33..	6532
MA3	MD6̣/SD6̣	MR3/NR3	MD2/SD2?/ND2
5653	2126̣	2123	2126̣
MD3/ND3?	MD6̣/SD6̣	MA3	MD6̣/SD6̣

Analysis in *pélog*

Any attempt to analyse the *pathet* of *pélog* along the same lines as the *sléndro* analysis immediately runs into several difficulties. The existence of two scales is one of them.

Table 2.9 shows that the important notes[70] are not helpful in characterising the *pathet*. Low 5 can be important in any of the three main *pathet* in *pélog*. There is little difference between *pathet barang* and *pathet nem*: low 6 is more than twice as frequent as 5̣ or 2 in *pathet barang*, but the three notes are equally common in *pathet nem*. Almost every note in the five-note scale can be found as a final gong note in each *pathet*: from 2̣ to 7 in *pathet barang*, 2̣ to 6 in *pathet nem*, 1̣ to 5 except 2̣ in *pathet limå*.

The analysis of *pélog barang* is made simultaneously simpler and more complicated by the realisation that it is not a *pathet* but a scale containing three *pathet*, corresponding to those of *sléndro*. A table of characteristic phrases (Table 2.11) can be drawn up, taking into account the *sorogan* notes of the *pathet*. Any composition can then be analysed as if it were in *sléndro*, giving clear guidance on how it should be realised.

Within the *pélog bem* scale, *pélog limå* is the easiest of the *pathet* to identify, sharing the same important notes as *sléndro sångå*. In the absence of *thinthingan* in most *pathet* in *pélog*, Hastanto's analysis replaced them with the *kemudå* when looking for the distinctive features of *pathet limå* and *pathet nem*. Rather than a table only of characteristic phrases, he created a table that included some of these but also other features (Table 2.12). The usage of note 7 in these two *pathet* is not mentioned in the table, because it is not a reliable indicator of *pathet*.

Using these principles, an analysis of *ldr Tirtåkencånå*, a piece that is usually classed as *pélog nem*,

2126̣ 216̣5̣	2126̣ 216̣5̣
Lb, Ld	Lb, Ld
15̣6̣1 3216̣	5̣4̣2̣4̣ 5̣6̣4̣5̣
Nb	Lc, Ld

suggests that the piece is clearly in *pathet limå*, which is further reinforced by the absence of 2̇ (except in the vocal line). Analysis of other *pélog nem* pieces with gong 5 yields the same result, but Hastanto does not provide an explanation for this.[71]

Pieces with 6̣ or 2 at important points are unlikely to belong in *pathet limå*: *pathet nem* is the obvious association, for example, *ktw Swålågitå / Wålågitå*

bukå	6̣ .123 .2.1	.3.2 .1.(6̣)
	Lc	Nb, Nd
ompak	.2.3 .2.1	.3.2 .1.(6̣)
	Lc	Nb, Nd
lik	33.. 3356	2̇3̇2̇1̇ 653(2)
	A	Nc, Ne
	5321 6654	6521 321(6̣)
	A	Nb, Nd

where 'A' marks phrases of ambiguous *pathet*.

However, a few pieces of this character, including

Table 2.11
Characteristic phrases in each *pathet* within *pélog barang* scale

Sèlèh note	*Manyurå*			*Sångå*			*Nem*		
	↗	↘	→	↗	↘	→	↗	↘	→
3̇	MA3̇								
2̇				SA2̇					
1̇/7	MA1̇, MA7								
6	MA6	MD6					NA6	ND6	
5/4				SA5, SA4	SD5, SD4		NA5, NA4	ND5, ND4	
3	MA3	MD3	MR3						NR3
2		MD2		SA2	SD2	SR2	NA2	ND2	NR2
1/7̣		MD1, MD7̣	MR1, MR7̣		SD1, SD7̣				
6̣		MD6̣			SD6̣		NA6̣		NR6̣
5̣/4̣					SD5̣, SD4̣			ND5̣, ND4̣	
3̣		MD3̣							
2̣								ND2̣	

After Hastanto (1985)

70 The statistics used here come from the final gong notes of the pieces in Mloyowidodo's collection.

71 His failure to analyse any pieces in *pélog nem* with gong 5 is the main weakness of his thesis.

well-known ones such as *gd Randhu kéntir mg ldr Ayun-ayun*, are classified as *pathet manyurå* or *nyamat*.[72] This *pathet* is supposed to be the result of transferring pieces straight from *sléndro manyurå* to *pélog* without changing the note numbers. Hastanto identifies a list of characteristics for the *pathet* (Table 2.12), showing the resemblances to *sléndro manyurå*. Its important notes include 6̣ but not 5̣, which already makes it distinctive within *pélog*. Mloyowidodo's collection does not support Hastanto's statement that the note 4 is never used in *pélog manyurå*.

Pathet in use

While a player's choices of *céngkok* (or *wilet*) to realise a particular piece are likely to derive mainly from the advice of teachers, the analysis above gives at least a rational basis on which the *céngkok* might originally have been chosen. Many of the remarks here about the use of *céngkok* on instruments apply equally to *sindhènan*.

Garap in *sléndro*

The corpus of *céngkok* for the decorating instruments usually divides into two sets, for *sléndro manyurå* and *sléndro sångå*. In *sléndro nem*, instruments tend to have specific *céngkok* only for the lower register, and in the main they use a mixture of *céngkok* belonging to the other two *pathet*; e.g. a *céngkok* from *pathet sångå* for a phrase falling to 5̣, since this is a characteristic *pathet sångå* phrase. On those instruments possessing a set of (usually named) *céngkok* for the various possible *sèlèh* notes, e.g. the *gendèr*, a *gåtrå* with a given *sèlèh* note is therefore played with different *céngkok* for different *pathet*.

Table 2.10 is compatible with the general principle that *céngkok* for *pathet sångå* are simply transposed down by one note from those for *pathet manyurå*: the characteristic phrases shown for the two *pathet* correspond as expected, e.g. SD5̣ paralleling MD6̣. This principle alone suffices to give each of the two *pathet* a distinct character. However, it is not the whole story. Certain 'harmonies' are characteristic of the *pathet*, i.e. the *pathet* determines which notes are preferable when played against a *sèlèh* note. Thus a *sèlèh* 1 can be accompanied by the 5 above it at the end of a *céngkok* on the *gendèr* in *pathet sångå*, but not in *pathet manyurå*, where 1̇ would be preferred. (The *gendèr* part therefore generally conveys more information about *pathet* than the *balungan* does.) Similarly, the *bonang* plays the combination of 3̣ with 1 in various contexts in *pathet manyurå*, but would not do so in *pathet sångå*, whereas it would play 6̣ with 2 or 2̣ there.

Table 2.10 also supports the general belief that *sléndro nem* is a mixed *pathet*. Most of the phrases listed for *sléndro nem* are to be found in the *manyurå* or *sångå* columns too. The main exceptions are NA6̣ and NR6̣. (ND2̣ should not have any equivalents in *manyurå* and *sångå*, because 2̣ is theoretically outside the range of those *pathet*.)

Table 2.12
Characteristics of each *pathet* within *pélog bem* scale

Pathet limå	
La[a]	1̣ as lowest or final note
Lb	Contours ending on 5̣, especially if preceded by 4̣
Lc	Contours ending on 1, preceded by some or all of 6, 5, 4, 2, or 6, 5, 3, 2
Ld	1 and 5̣ as important notes
Le	2̇ not an essential note
Lf	Contours with 6̣, 5̣, 4̣, 2̣, 1̣
Pathet nem	
Na[a]	3̣ as lowest or final note[b]
Nb	6̣ as final note
Nc	Contours ending on 2 preceded by some or more of 6, 5, 3, 2
Nd	2 and 6̣ as important notes
Ne	2̇ essential; final note of ascending phrase
Nf	Contours with 6̣, 5̣, 3̣
***Pathet manyurå* (usually labelled as *pélog nem*)**	
Ma	3̣ as lowest or final note (= Na)
Mb	6̣ as final note (= Nb)
Mc	1 as final note of descending phrase
Md	2 as final note of descending phrase (= Nc)
Me	6 as final note of ascending or descending phrase
Mf	1̇ as final note of ascending phrase
Mg	2̇ as final note of descending phrase (≠ Ne)
Mh	3̇ as final note of ascending phrase

After Hastanto (1985) a. Described as unique to the *pathet*.
b. Not supported by Mloyowidodo's collection, where there are three *gendhing* in *pélog limå* with final gong 3̣.

72 The list of pieces usually assigned to *pélog manyurå* is short: *ldr Ayun-ayun*, *gd Glathik incèng-incèng*, *gd Kembangdårå*, *gd Kembang nångkå*, *gd Randhu kéntir*, *gd Rendeng*, *gd Rujaksentul*, *ldr (?) Srundèng gosong*, *gd Tanjunggunung*. A version of *ktw Sinom Parijåthå* is sometimes added.

Garap in *pélog*

In *pélog*, the *céngkok* are as for *sléndro*, adapted only as necessary (7 replacing 1 in *pélog barang*), and the player's task is reduced to deciding which *pathet* to borrow from.

The three *pathet* within *pélog barang* suggest *sléndro manyurå*, *sléndro sångå* or a mixture, according to the important notes and other characteristics of the piece. *Pélog limå* implies *céngkok sångå*. (It is worth repeating that gong notes other than 1 and 5̣ are possible in *pélog limå*.)

The situation is least clear with *pélog nem*, and here players take account of the gong note. Gong 5 pieces with clear *pathet limå* characteristics are likely to be treated in the same way as pieces labelled as *pathet limå*. Gong 6 tends to imply *céngkok manyurå*. However, many gong 5 pieces in *pélog nem* are likely to be considered mixed, requiring *céngkok sångå* as well as *céngkok manyurå*. The same applies to some pieces with gong 6. *Pélog manyurå*, if it can be identified clearly, implies *céngkok manyurå*.

On the *pélog* instruments that have only the basic five-note scale (i.e. *gendèr*, *gambang*, etc.), players must realise a phrase containing a 4, even at a *sèlèh* point, with a *céngkok* that uses either 3 or 5. The governing principle is always that 4 is a sharpened 3 in the *bem* scale, but a flattened 5 in the *barang* scale.

Note 7 (= a flattened 1) can be found in any of the *pathet* of *pélog bem*, and will usually be treated as an isolated *sorogan* note, i.e. the player will continue using the instrument with the *bem* scale. The occurrence of the note 7 at a *sèlèh* point within *pélog bem* represents a change of *pathet*, and the players of the *gendèr*, *gambang*, etc., must respond by switching instruments, e.g. in the first two *kenongan* of the *inggah* of *gd Sambul gendhing*

. 3 . 2 . 1 . 6̣ . 3 . 2 . 6̣ . 7̣
. 2 . 7̣ . 2 . 7̣ . 5̣ . 6̣ . 3 . 2̂
. 3 . 2 . 3 . 2 . 3 . 2 . 6̣ . 7̣
. 2 . 7̣ . 2 . 7̣ . 5̣ . 6̣ . 3 . 2̂

where the underlining marks the part realised in *pathet barang* in an actual performance. Alternatively, the player can avoid a decision by playing a regular *céngkok* but to a different and theoretically 'wrong' *sèlèh* note.

The converse principle operates in *pathet barang*, although 1 (= a sharpened 7) in general occurs much less often there than 7 does in *pélog bem*. Isolated examples of the note 1 are again treated as *sorogan* notes. Note 1 at a *sèlèh* point may indicate a change of *pathet*—or a change to an alternative scale within the *pathet*, provided that one accepts the existence of such a scale: this is a theoretical point that need not concern the player. The decision for the *gendèr* or *gambang* player is whether the character of the melodic line has changed enough to demand a switch to the *pélog bem* instrument. Some such cases occur in *gendhing bonang* (*Siring*, *Tukung*, *Parigentang*, *Bondhèt kt 8 mg 16*), where these instruments are not involved, but there are others.

For players who have all seven notes of the scale available, the occurrence of 1 in *pélog barang* or 7 in *pélog bem* presents no problems; similarly 4 in either scale. They will usually play *céngkok* that include the *sorogan* note.

A 'foreign' phrase, i.e. one with the 'wrong' *pathet* orientation, or a phrase of uncertain *pathet* within a piece can be neutralised if it is followed by one or more phrases that are unambiguously in the right *pathet*. If players find that the *pathet* of a piece is unclear because it contains too many foreign or ambiguous phrases, they have problems in choosing suitable *céngkok*.[73] Hastanto gives this as the reason why *gd Okrak-okrak sl m* is played as a *gendhing bonang*: in *gendhing bonang*, the instruments that would suffer problems in choosing *céngkok* do not play. Similarly, some *sléndro* pieces such as *gd Bondhèt sl 9* are usually played in *pélog*, exploiting the greater tolerance of *pélog*, according to Hastanto, towards mixtures of *pathet*.

Review

To be able to realise pieces in all *pathet*, players do not have to learn at least six sets of *pathet*-specific *céngkok*. Instead (fortunately) they need only remember two important sets, for *sléndro manyurå* and *sléndro sångå*, and probably some additional *céngkok* for *sléndro nem*.

The main problem for players is deciding when to use each type of *céngkok*. It is of course possible for teachers to disagree as to which should be used where. A player who ventures to analyse a piece along the lines described here may still not obtain a clear answer about the *pathet* of the piece.

73 Not all musicians claim to experience these difficulties.

Iråmå — rhythm

Iråmå is the Javanese word for 'rhythm' in the widest sense. It is also sometimes used to mean 'tempo', i.e. the speed at which the basic melody of a piece moves; however, the Javanese word *låyå* has this specific meaning.[74]

The most important sense of the word *iråmå* is a more specialised one, referring to the system that allows the timescale of the melodic material to be expanded and contracted in a controlled manner. The basic melody in a given piece may move at widely differing speeds; a range exceeding 10:1 is possible, although not in most pieces.

The *iråmå* system also relates the basic tempo to the patterns played by the decorating instruments. The decorating instruments[75] play more than one note per beat of the *balungan*. Without some form of adjustment as the basic tempo changed, they would be obliged to play absurdly slowly or absurdly fast at various points. The *iråmå* system provides the required adjustment.

The *iråmå* system can be seen as a form of gearbox. A gearbox in a car allows it to travel at a wide range of road speeds while the engine stays within the more limited range of speeds where it is comfortable. Similarly, the *iråmå* system allows the *balungan* to move at a wide range of speeds while the decorating instruments always play a manageable number of notes per second.

The 'gears' or levels of the *iråmå* system—*tingkat iråmå* in Javanese—are mostly related by rough 2:1 ratios. In other words, when moving from one *iråmå* level to the next slower one, the basic tempo falls by about half: on the other hand, the decorating instruments start playing twice as many notes per *balungan* beat, so that they are playing much the same number of notes per second as before. For the *bonang barung* and *bonang panerus*, not only does the number of notes per *balungan* beat change in the different *iråmå*, but the style of decoration can be completely different.

A change of *iråmå* is something that all the players must be aware of. The transitions between *iråmå* are signalled by the *kendhang*, and players need to learn to recognise all the likely signals.

Western classical music has no equivalent to the *iråmå* system. Distortion of the timescale of melodic material at certain points is a regular procedure in fugues, but is not a general principle and is not as far-reaching in its effects as *iråmå*. The last movement of Beethoven's *Waldstein* Sonata, where the speed of the material exactly doubles,[76] is an isolated example.

Tingkat iråmå

The precise number of *tingkat iråmå* is disputable. For practical purposes, six can be recognised. As the basic tempo gets faster, more of the decorating instruments drop out. Because the *iråmå* principle is all about the relationship between *balungan* and decorating instruments,[77] arguably it becomes irrelevant at the fastest speeds.

The names of the various *tingkat iråmå* are another area of *karawitan* where there is no standardisation.[78] The names used here for the four slowest *iråmå* are those currently taught by the academies, but other sources use these names differently.

The Solonese sometimes refer to the six *tingkat iråmå* by fractions that represent the number of *peking* strokes per *balungan* beat. Thus *iråmå* ¼ represents *iråmå II*, which has four *peking* strokes to the *balungan* beat. In the Yogya style the *peking* patterns do not have these regular relationships with the *tingkat iråmå*, so that the fractions would not make sense.

For brevity and to minimise possible confusion, here the slowest four *tingkat iråmå* are normally referred to by roman numerals, giving the table below; this notation is understood in both Solo and Yogya. For the next *iråmå* faster than *ir I*, the designation *iråmå* ½ is sometimes seen, but here it is avoided on grounds of possible confusion. The abbreviation of *iråmå* to *ir* is standard.

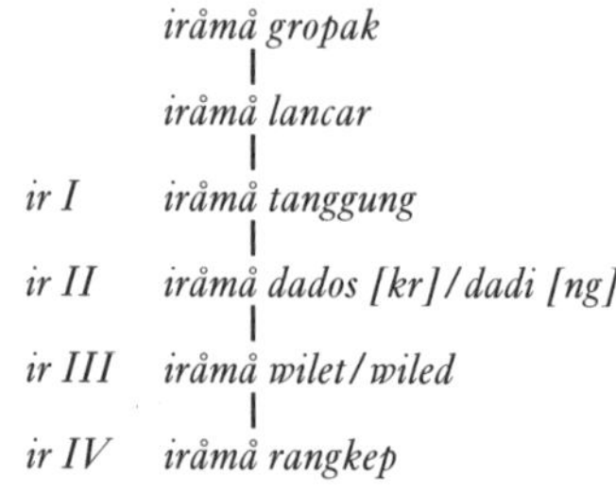

For the two fastest *iråmå*, the names *gropak*, *seseg* and *lancar* are all found, and without further information it is

74 The Old Javanese word *låyå* is, as Martopangrawit commented (in Becker and Feinstein, 1984), not in everyday use.

75 Excluding the *rebab* and *suling*, which do not have this kind of precise temporal relationship with the *balungan*.

76 Apparently in imitation of a feature of a Rhineland dance form.

77 Or between decorating instruments and punctuating instruments in those cases where there is no *balungan*.

78 Even in Becker and Feinstein (1984, 1987), the various Javanese sources disagree.

not clear whether one or two *irâmâ* are being referred to. For the purposes of this book, *irâmâ lancar* is the *irâmâ* in which a *lancaran* normally starts, and is also encountered, usually only briefly, in other pieces; for example, the *bukâ* of a *gendhing* is essentially in *irâmâ lancar. Irâmâ gropak* will be used to indicate an *irâmâ* faster than *irâmâ lancar*, such as often occurs during a *suwuk gropak*. This usage can be justified because in a *suwuk gropak* not only the *bonang* but even sometimes the *balungan* instruments are forced to play fewer notes than normal. The term *irâmâ seseg* will not be used here, although the adjective *seseg* will be used with other meanings.

Javanese sources commonly present the *tingkat irâmâ* as in the table above, implying that there is a simple hierarchy. The reality is different. In particular, the speed ratio between *ir III* and *ir IV* is normally not 2:1. *Ir IV* is always fast—typically about two-thirds the speed of the preceding *ir III*—and always light in character. *Ir IV* has been described as *nakal*, for which the dictionary definition is 'mischievous', although 'frivolous' might convey its flavour better. There are no established *gérongan* for use in *ir IV*.

Irâmâ rangkep is therefore as much a treatment (*garap*) option as a *tingkat irâmâ*.[79] In principle any *irâmâ* can be given a *rangkep* treatment, i.e. reducing the speed to two-thirds rather than one-half, and using characteristic *garap* such as *keplok*. To reflect these practices, a more accurate table of the *tingkat irâmâ* would be as below. This shows *irâmâ rangkep* as an option attached to both *ir III* and *ir II*. *Rangkep* treatment of *ir II*, a regular practice in the *langgam* form, is also found in the closely related *ketawang* form, as well as some *ladrang* and elsewhere.

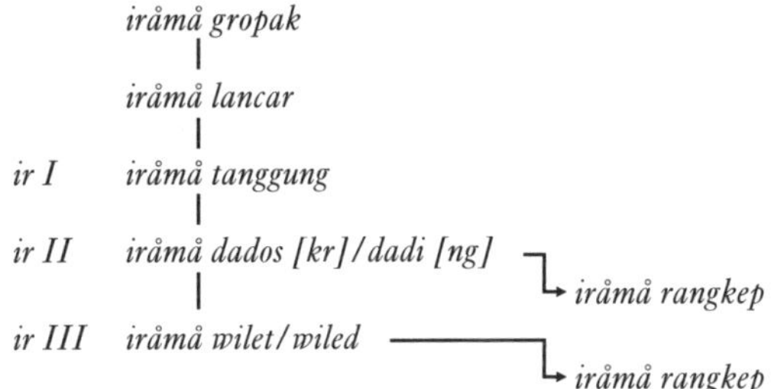

The term *ir IV* will be used here only to mean the *rangkep* version of *ir III*, which ought to be called *irâmâ wilet rangkep*. For the *rangkep* version of *ir II*, no unique term is established: confusingly, the Javanese simply refer to *irâmâ rangkep*. Here the term will be *ir II rangkep*.

Irâmâ and bentuk

There is no default *irâmâ*. Instead there is usually a range of possible *irâmâ* for each of the standard compositional forms (*bentuk*), represented in Table 2.13.

The Javanese say that a piece 'lives' in a certain *irâmâ*. A particularly wide range of *irâmâ* is to be found in the *ladrang* form, but many of them 'live' in *ir III*, meaning that the *ir III* version of the *balungan* is the basic one, and a simplified version is used in the faster *irâmâ*. Other *ladrang* 'live' in *ir II*, and there are also loud-style *ladrang* that are rarely heard outside *ir I*. The term 'home' in the table indicates an *irâmâ* in which the piece may spend all or most of the performance, though the piece may not 'live' there: thus *ldr Pangkur* lives in *ir III*, but a performance may remain entirely within *ir I*, or *ir I* and *II*.

The *irâmâ* described in the table as 'initial' are those in which the pieces start from scratch; a piece may start in a different *irâmâ*, especially a 'home' *irâmâ*, when it follows straight on from another piece.

79 It may be of relatively recent origin, as there are pieces that do not use it, even though they do not differ in style obviously from others that do use it.

Table 2.13
Usage of *irâmâ* according to *bentuk*

Bentuk	*Irâmâ*				*Suwuk gropak?*
	Initial	'Home'	Also possible	Closing	
Gangsaran	*gropak*[a]	*gropak*[a]	—	*gropak*[a]	Usual
Lancaran	*lancar, I*[b]	*lancar*	*I, II, III?*	*lancar, I, II*	Possible
Bubaran	*I*	*I*	*II*	*I*	
Ketawang	*I, II*[c]	*II*	*II rangkep*	*II*	
Langgam	*II*	*II*	*II rangkep*	*II, II rangkep*	
Ladrang, soft style	*I*	*I, II, III*	*IV, II rangkep*	*I, II, III*	Possible
Ladrang, loud style	*I*	*I, II*	*III*[c]	*I, II, III*[c]	Possible
Gati/marès	*I*	*I, II*	—	*I*	
Gendhing, vocal					
— *mérong*	*lancar*	*II*	*I,*[d] *III*[e]	*I, II, III*	—
— *inggah*[f]	*I, II, III*	*II, III*	*I, IV*	*I, II, III*	Possible
Gendhing bonang, Solo					
— *mérong*	*lancar*	*II*	*I*	*I*	
— *inggah*[f]	*I*	*II*	*I*	*I*	
Gendhing soran, Yogya					
— *lâmbâ–dados*	*lancar*	*II*	*I*	*I*	
— *ndhawah*[f]	*I*	*II*	*I*	*I*	

a. Can also be viewed as fast *irâmâ lancar*. b. Possible for *lancaran* with *balungan mlaku*. c. In Yogyakarta style. d. In some *srimpi/bedhâyâ* accompaniments. e. Possible during *janturan* in *wayang* accompaniment. f. For *inggah ladrang*, see *ladrang*; for *inggah ketawang*, see *ketawang*.

Table 2.14
Notional duration (min:s) of a *gongan* vs. *bentuk* and *iråmå*. [shaded] Combinations not normally encountered

Bentuk		Beats per *gongan*	*Iråmå*						
			gropak	*lancar*	*I*	*II*	*II rangkep*	*III*	*IV*
Gangsaran		16	0:04						
Lancaran and *bubaran*		16		0:08	0:15	0:30		1:00	
Ketawang and *langgam*		16			0:15	0:30	0:45		
Ladrang		32			0:30	1:00	1:30	2:00	3:00
Gati/mares		32			0:30	1:00			
Gendhing ketawang									
Mérong	*Kt 2 kp*	32			0:30	1:00		2:00	
	Kt 4 kp	64			1:00	2:00		4:00	
	Kt 8 kp	128			2:00	4:00		8:00	
Inggah	*Kt 4*	32			0:30	1:00		2:00	3:00
	Kt 8	64			1:00	2:00		4:00	6:00
	Kt 16	128			2:00	4:00		8:00	12:00
Gendhing									
Mérong	*Kt 2 kp*	64			1:00	2:00		4:00	
	Kt 4 kp/kt 2 ar	128			2:00	4:00		8:00	
	Kt 8 kp/kt 4 ar	256			4:00	8:00		16:00	
	Kt 8 ar	512			8:00	16:00			
Inggah	*Kt 4*	64			1:00	2:00		4:00	6:00
	Kt 8	128			2:00	4:00		8:00	12:00
	Kt 16	256			4:00	8:00		16:00	24:00

Iråmå and tempo

When the speed of the *balungan* varies over a sufficiently wide range, changes of *iråmå* must occur. However, speed can still vary considerably within one *iråmå*. A useful reference point is a figure of about one beat of *balungan mlaku* per second in *ir I* for a relaxed performance in *klenèngan/uyon-uyon* style. Table 2.14 illustrates the implications of this for the durations of entire *gongan* in the various forms (*bentuk*). Fig. 2.22 under **Gendhing** (pp. 76–7) shows how the tempo can vary in practice within one *iråmå*.

Essentially the tempo varies according to need. For *klenèngan* (concert) performances independent of dance or drama, tempo tends to stay within narrow limits, although it is still possible to speak of a fast performance or a more relaxed performance. In Solo style, the tempo for dance accompaniments tends to be faster than usual, whereas in Yogya style the tempo tends to be slower for dance. In the more dramatic parts of dances, tempo varies widely. *Wayang* tends to be fast throughout.

Iråmå and *garap*

As tempo (i.e. the speed of the *balungan* beats) is not a conclusive indicator, the current *iråmå* must be identified from the *garap* for certain of the decorating instruments.

A diagram such as Fig. 2.14 shows how the *garap* for one instrument can change with *iråmå*. The *balungan* is represented on a constant timescale, so that its expansion through the different *iråmå* can be seen clearly. The closer spacing of the *peking* notes for *ir IV* is a reminder that the speed ratio between *ir III* and *ir IV* would be about 2:3 in practice.

For the *peking* played in the Solo style as shown (although this is not the only possible *garap*), the relationship between *garap* and *iråmå* is very regular: the *peking* plays 1, 2, 4, 8, 16 or 32 notes per pair of *balungan* beats.

In *irâmâ gropak* the *peking* might still be able to play all the *balungan* notes. Alternatively it may simplify them as shown, i.e. one *peking* note per two *balungan* notes; the main *balungan* instruments are more likely to do so, especially the *slenthem* and *demung* because they are less able to move fast. The *bonang barung*, which would usually be playing at the same density as the *peking*, might manage to follow the *balungan* or might play two notes as shown. The *bonang panerus* would probably do the same as the *bonang barung*.

Irâmâ transitions

The *kendhangan* provides specific patterns to signal the transitions between one *irâmâ* and another. Some of the signals apply only to one *bentuk*, while others are general.

The various *irâmâ* and the transitions between them in a performance can be considered as a **finite-state machine** and represented by a **state diagram** such as Fig. 2.15. The finite-state model is usually used as a tool for describing control systems (mechanical, electronic, electrical or any combination thereof). A system of this kind is at all times in one or another of a finite set of states, and only moves between states on receipt of defined external signals.[80] If none of these signals occurs, the system state remains unchanged. In the case of the *ladrang* shown, the states are basically the different *irâmâ*, but *ir I* must be divided into *kébar* and non-*kébar* states. Remaining in the same state means cycling the same one or more *gongan* without change of *irâmâ* or *garap*.

Table 2.15 lists the transition signals that cause the changes of state/*irâmâ* seen in Fig. 2.15. During the speed-ups and slow-downs in *ir I*, the players of decorating instruments may briefly stop playing if they find the tempo uncomfortable. (Speed-ups and slow-downs are of course encountered in other *bentuk* too, and are illustrated in Fig. 2.22.)

Fig. 2.15 applies to *ladrang* such as *Asmarandânâ*, *Ayun-ayun* and *Pangkur*, which are played in the widest range of *irâmâ* and have a double-density *balungan* for *ir III* and *IV*. It does not cover all *ladrang*, because many are played only in *ir I* and *ir II* (e.g. *Wilujeng* and *Tirtâkencânâ*), and some only in *ir I* and/or without *kébar*. With *kosèk* drumming, *ir III* (but not *ir IV*) is possible as well as *ir I* and *II*, but the transition signals then differ from those listed. The diagram also does not cover the possibility of *ciblon* drumming in *ir II*.

Andhegan—often used as a method of switching in either direction between *ir III* and *ir IV*—can occur in some *ladrang*, but have been omitted from the diagram. Also omitted are transitions in either direction between *ompak* and *lik*, and situations where the *balungan* changes according to the *irâmâ*. In other words, the diagram represents only changes caused by *kendhangan*, and only some of them. More comprehensive diagrams could be created, taking into account these additional transitions, including those signalled by a melody instrument rather than the *kendhang*.

Not all transitions are of the same kind for the players of the *balungan* and the decorating instruments. In some, the *balungan* density changes gradually through the transition, whereas in others (signals (f1), (g), (i), (k), (n), (o)) the density halves or doubles at a particular point—usually a gong.

State diagrams could of course be created for other

80 In some systems, the time at which these external signals occur is irrelevant, and the system can be described as **asynchronous**. *Karawitan* is a **synchronous** system, because the timing of the signals is significant.

ir gropak:	*balungan*	5653
	peking	5 3
ir lancar:	*balungan*	5 6 5 3
	peking	5 6 5 3
ir I:	*balungan*	5 6 5 3
	peking	5 5 6 6 5 5 3 3
ir II:	*balungan*	5 6 5 3
	peking	5 5 6 6 5 5 6 6 5 5 3 3 5 5 3 3
ir III:	*balungan*	5 6 5 3
	peking	5 5 3 3 5 5 3 3 5 5 6 6 5 5 6 6 5 5 3 3 5 5 3 3 2 2 3 3 2 2 3 3
ir IV:	*balungan*	5 6 5 3
	peking	5533553355335533556655665566556655335533553355332233223322332233

2.14 Examples of *garap* changes for *peking* depending on *irâmâ*

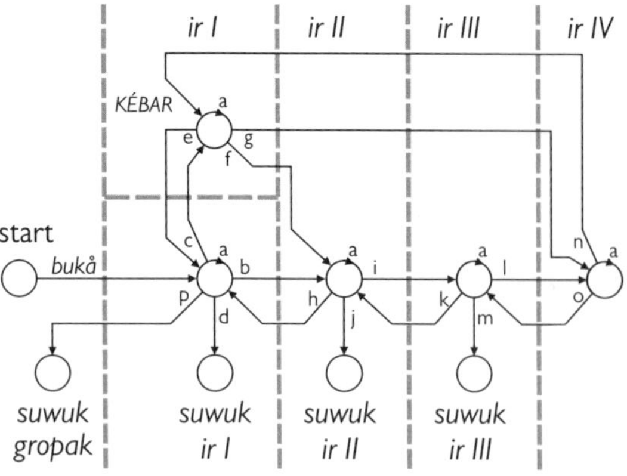

2.15 State diagram for the performance of a *ladrang*

Table 2.15
Kendhang signals for transitions shown in Fig. 2.15

	Transition	Description of *kendhangan* signal
a	none	no special signal
b	*ir I* to *ir II*	slow-down then doubling of density of *kendhangan*, with further slow-down, usually all during second *kenongan*
c	*ir I* to *ir I kébar*	*angkatan ciblon* in last *kenongan*, with slight relaxation of speed
d	*ir I* to *suwuk*	slow-down and *suwuk* pattern
e	*ir I kébar* to *ir I*	slight speed-up and switch to *kd II*, in last *kenongan*
f	*ir I kébar* directly to *ir II*	1: speed-up before gong, sustained after gong, then switch from *ciblon* to *kd II* and halving of speed mainly or entirely within second *gåtrå*. 2: switch from *ciblon* to *kd II* leading up to gong.
g	*ir I kébar* directly to *ir III*	slow-down then doubling of density in *kendhangan* immediately before gong
h	*ir II* to *ir I*	speed-up and halving of density of *kendhangan*
i	*ir II* to *ir III* (*ciblon*)	*angkatan ciblon* before gong, with slow-down and doubling of density within *ciblon* patterns
j	*ir II* to *suwuk*	slow-down and *suwuk* pattern
k	*ir III* (*ciblon*) to *ir II*	(not possible during *gérongan*) *seseg* then switch to *ir II*, then switch to *kd I*
l	*ir III* to *ir IV*	slow-down then doubling of density in *kendhangan* immediately before gong or *kenong*
m	*ir III* to *suwuk*	speed-up before penultimate gong, then return to normal speed; slight speed-up before third *kenong*, then switch from *ciblon* to *kd II* and slow-down with *suwuk* pattern
n	*ir III* to *ir I kébar*	slight speed-up before gong, then *angkatan kébar* and relaxation of speed just before gong
o	*ir IV* to *ir III*	slow-down immediately before gong or *kenong*, or where convenient
p	*suwuk gropak*	gradual doubling of speed (more or less), with cross-rhythms leading to final gong

bentuk, and would usually be simpler than Fig. 2.15. Fig. 2.16 illustrates transitions between related *bentuk* that are often played together. The transition from the *ayak-ayakan* to the *srepegan* can be as shown, but it is equally possible that the *ayak-ayakan* will go to the *suwuk*, followed by a new start for the *srepegan*. Fig. 2.16 includes examples of the use of one *kendhang* signal to serve multiple functions: the signal (e) that causes a *sirep* within the *srepegan* has a different effect within the *sampak*, causing a return to the *srepegan*. The signals (g, k) at the end of the *gongan* in the regular section of both *srepegan* and *sampak* to cause the transition to the *seseg* can again be similar. Fig. 2.16 omits various transitions that frequently occur, such as those in both directions between *srepegan* and *palaran*, and connections from other pieces—as when a *srepegan* or *ayak-ayakan* follows straight on from a *ladrang* or *ketawang*, for example.

Competent players have in their heads all the information corresponding to Figs 2.15 and 2.16 and their associated lists of signals—and the equivalent information for all the other *bentuk*. They know all the possible transition signals, and respond appropriately. Therefore a good *kendhang* player is one who presents the signals clearly and thus helps the players through the transitions, delivering tempi that the players can manage.

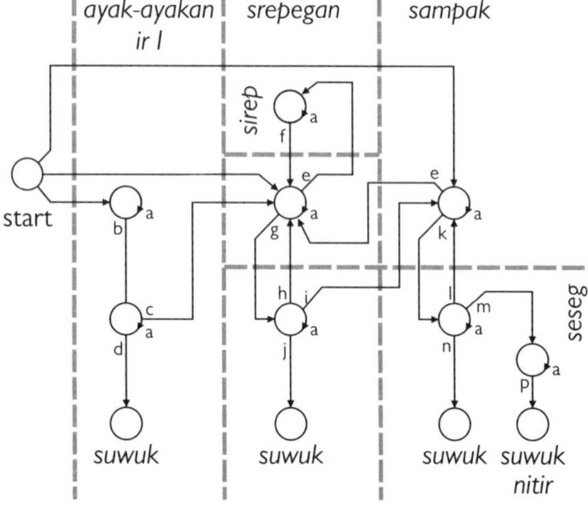

2.16 State diagram for *ayak-ayakan*, *srepegan*, *sampak*

Bentuk — form

Overview

Pieces in the traditional repertoire of *karawitan* conform to one or other of the fixed forms (*bentuk*).[81] Each *bentuk* is characterised by a particular pattern or cycle of strokes on the punctuating instruments. Writers in English[82] sometimes use the terms **colotomic structure** or **colotomy** for these. Fig. 2.18 shows (not on the same time-scale) the patterns for one *gongan* in some of the short forms, using single-syllable mnemonics for the names of the instruments

pyang = *kempyang*
thuk = *kethuk*
nong = *kenong*
pul = *kempul*

and using the weight of the text to show the relative importance of the punctuating instruments. The same information is sometimes shown in clock form (Fig. 2.17).

Many teachers believe that gamelan students should learn these patterns by heart as soon as possible.

The empty beats in the cycles, such as the fourth beat of the *ladrang* cycle, are not strictly rests, but 'rest' is the English term normally used when saying the mnemonic cycle out loud. The Javanese term is *welå*, meaning 'gap'. It is generally assumed that these gaps are intended to prevent the *kempul* from competing with the gong as the sound of the latter dies away. The gong has the highest status of all the gamelan instruments, and is never damped, so that its sound continues for several seconds into the new *gongan*.

The different forms can be grouped in various ways. It is necessary to point out the two main usages of the term *gendhing*: the more general one, which simply means

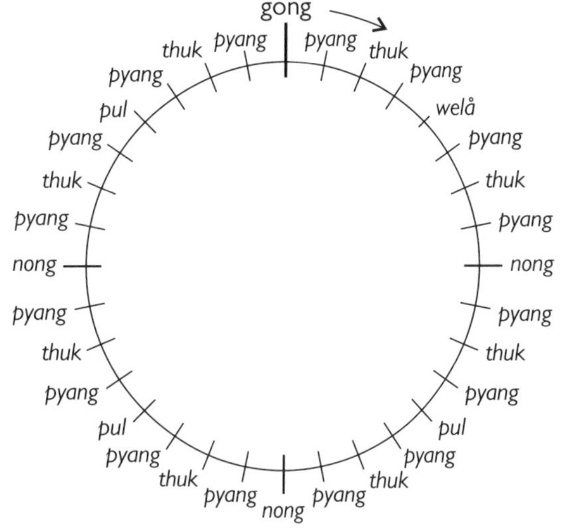

2.17 Colotomic structure of *ladrang* in clock form

81 *Bentuk* appears to be an Indonesian word, but is used regularly in the absence of a Javanese equivalent.

82 Following the English version of Kunst's *Music in Java*, where the words 'colotomy' and 'colotomic' were first introduced into English. Kunst is assumed to have invented the term in Dutch.

Ladrang															
pyang	*thuk*	*pyang*	—	*pyang*	*thuk*	*pyang*	**nong**	*pyang*	*thuk*	*pyang*	**pul**	*pyang*	*thuk*	*pyang*	**nong**
pyang	*thuk*	*pyang*	**pul**	*pyang*	*thuk*	*pyang*	**nong**	*pyang*	*thuk*	*pyang*	**pul**	*pyang*	*thuk*	*pyang*	**gong**
Ketawang															
pyang	*thuk*	*pyang*	—	*pyang*	*thuk*	*pyang*	**nong**	*pyang*	*thuk*	*pyang*	**pul**	*pyang*	*thuk*	*pyang*	**gong**
Lancaran															
thuk	—	*thuk*	**nong**	*thuk*	**pul**	*thuk*	**nong**	*thuk*	**pul**	*thuk*	**nong**	*thuk*	**pul**	*thuk*	**gong**
Gangsaran															
—	—	—	**nong**	*thuk*	*thuk*, **pul**	—	**nong**	*thuk*	*thuk*, **pul**	—	**nong**	*thuk*	*thuk*, **pul**	—	**gong**

2.18 Mnemonic patterns for punctuation of shorter *bentuk*

'composition' or 'piece', and the narrower sense referring to a family of longer *bentuk* that have certain features in common. Both usages are frequent, leading to some confusion, but the narrower meaning is normally used in this book.

One useful classification is into regular and irregular forms. Some irregular forms—*ayak-ayakan*, *srepegan* and *sampak*, or their Yogyanese equivalents (see p. 85 foll.)—are here called the **editable** forms, after their most important feature.

The other irregular forms are not editable, but all are basically vocal: the various 'mood-songs' (*sulukan*) associated with drama and dance, the *palaran/rambangan* form (which is related to *srepegan*, in the Solonese sense), and vocal introductions (*båwå*). The remaining irregular forms are usually classed as *jineman*. It would be unfair to describe *jineman* as a 'dustbin' category, containing everything that does not fit elsewhere, but the term *jineman* does have a number of meanings.

The regular forms can be divided by size. The shorter regular forms—*lancaran/bubaran*, *ketawang* and *ladrang* —are sometimes classified as *gendhing alit* or 'small compositions'.[83] Like *gendhing lampah*, this is an example of the term *gendhing* in its wider sense. As can be seen from Fig. 2.18, almost every beat in these structures is marked by a stroke on one or other of the punctuating instruments. The longer regular forms are the *gendhing* in the narrower sense. On the term *gendhing ageng*, see p. 84.

Another characteristic that distinguishes some *bentuk* from others is the number of *kenongan* in the *gongan*. As can be seen in Fig. 2.18, some forms have four *kenongan*. The *ketawang* has only two. In the editable and irregular forms, the *kenongan* is not a relevant concept.

The *gangsaran* form is usually left out of the classifications, but is in fact a short and entirely regular form that originated with one of the ceremonial gamelan. (The other ceremonial gamelan similarly have a repertoire in unusual forms.) *Langgam* too is often ignored, but can in any case be regarded as a variant of *ketawang* form.

Most *bentuk* consist of *gongan* whose lengths are multiples of four *gåtrå*—resulting in 16, 32, 64, 128, 256 or 512 *balungan* beats between gong strokes. Table 2.14 shows an **approximate, nominal** duration for a *gongan* in each of the regular forms, based mostly on speed ratios of 2:1 between adjacent *irâmå*.

These durations are given strictly for the purpose of estimating the duration of a piece, because in practice the tempo for a certain *irâmå* can vary on either side of the figures listed. *Irâmå IV* is always significantly faster than half the speed of *ir III*. *Irâmå I* can have a particularly wide speed range, as can *ir II* in dance performances.

Exceptions to these binary length relationships between *bentuk* are rare—basically examples of standard *bentuk* with too many or too few *kenongan*, or occasionally with a standard number of *kenongan* but a non-standard number of beats in one *kenongan*. Some other irregularities are mentioned later.

Although every piece in the classical repertoire can be assigned to one of the established *bentuk*, there are occasions when a piece may be performed in different *bentuk*: some examples are mentioned below.

Lancaran and bubaran

Lancaran are (or can be) simple, regular, loud-style pieces and are typically the first *bentuk* that non-Javanese students encounter. They are light in character and have short *gongan*.

Before describing *lancaran* further, it is necessary to minimise possible confusion between the terms *lancaran* and *bubaran*. There are at least three ways in which writers use these two terms. It is not simply a Solo–Yogya difference, although the two traditions often disagree on the use of the terms.

First, some writers do not treat the term *bubaran* as indicating a particular *bentuk* at all. For them a *bubaran* is simply a departure piece (*bubar* or *bibar* = disperse), so that *ladrang Tedhaksaking*, for example, becomes a *bubaran* if it is used to end a programme.

Second, many sources (especially in Yogya) treat *lancaran* and *bubaran* as two different *bentuk*; a *lancaran* having eight *balungan* notes per *gongan* and a *bubaran* having sixteen, e.g. (on the same timescale)

3 2̂   3̆ 2̂   3̆ 2̂   5̆ (3̂)

and

6356̂   76̆56̂   54̆24̂   21̆6(5̂)

This view ignores the important distinction between *balungan mlaku* and *balungan nibani*, and begs the question of why the *gongan* has the same duration in the two *bentuk*, and the same colotomic structure. Other sources —which will be followed here—prefer to speak of a

83 This term comes from just one of several classifications of compositions.

lancaran with *balungan nibani* and a *lancaran* with *balungan mlaku*, or simply *lancaran nibani* and *lancaran mlaku* respectively.

Third, sources may treat the terms *lancaran* and *bubaran* as referring to the same *bentuk*, but reserve the description *bubaran* for particular pieces that are usually played only in *ir I*. On this basis the popular piece *Hudan mas* is a *bubaran* (although it is also a *bubaran* according to the other two views). In contrast, the base *irâmâ* for a *lancaran* (with either type of *balungan*) is *irâmâ lancar*; however, pieces described by other people as *lancaran* are played in slower *irâmâ* too.

Lancaran is probably a relatively recent form. The term is not used at all by Kunst, who describes as *bubaran* various pieces (e.g. *Béndrong*) that are now usually classed as *lancaran*. There is also some evidence of the description *ladrang(an)* formerly being applied to pieces now called *lancaran*. It is impossible to tell whether there has been a change of *bentuk* for these pieces or simply a change of terminology/classification.

Structure

Ignoring the alternative interpretation just mentioned, a *lancaran* has a 16-beat, four-*gåtrå*, four-*kenongan* structure (Fig. 2.18). The punctuating instruments used are *gong ageng*, *gong suwukan*, *kenong*, *kempul* and *kethuk*. In the Yogya style a *kenong japan*, if available, may be used for all *kenong* strokes.

In some Yogyanese performances of *Hudan mas pl 7*, the *kempyang* is played mid-way between the *balungan* beats, i.e. 16 times per *gongan*, throughout the piece. Applied to a *lancaran* with *balungan nibani*, this pattern of usage would give two *kempyang* strokes per *balungan* note, which might be considered excessive. However, *lancaran* of this type may also have a *mlaku* version of the *balungan*, used in slower *irâmâ*.

A lancaran typically consists of a cycle containing between two and five *gongan*, but in some cases a *gongan* is repeated within the cycle. Cycles with any of the following structures occur

gongan A, *gongan* B
gongan A, *gongan* A, *gongan* B, *gongan* B
gongan A, *gongan* B, *gongan* C
gongan A, *gongan* B, *gongan* C, *gongan* D
gongan A, *gongan* B, *gongan* C, *gongan* C, *gongan* D

among others. Some recent compositions have longer cycles. Some *lancaran* include what looks like a *ngelik* section, but it is not usual to describe the other section as an *ompak*. In such pieces the non-*lik* section may be cycled by itself, as happens in other *bentuk*.

Because the gong strokes come so close together, the *gong ageng* is only played to mark the end of the overall cycle, and the *gong suwukan* is used at the ends of the other *gongan*. If only a single *gongan* is cycled, the *gong ageng* may be used, for example, in every fourth *gongan*.

Lancaran Béndrong(an) sl m/pl 6

bukå .5.2 .5.2 .5.③
A .5.3 .5.2 .5.2 .5.(3)
B .5.3 .5.2 .5.2 .5.(6)
C .1̇.6 .1̇.5 .1̇.5 .1̇.(6)
D .1̇.6 .1̇.5 .1̇.5 .1̇.(6)
E .2̇.3̇ .2̇.1̇ .6.5 .3.②

Gongan C to E constitute a *lik* section. *Gongan* B is simply a variant of A that provides a signal indicating the transition to the *lik*. *Gongan* A may be cycled by itself.

Lancaran Kebogiro glendheng pl 5

bukå 2.1 .2.1 .6̣.⑤̣
A ..4̣5̣ 4̣5̣4̣5̣ 4̣5̣4̣5̣ .6̣.(1)
B .6̣2. 6̣1.6̣ 2.6̣1 .6̣.⑤̣

A version in *pélog barang* is made by transposing the whole piece up by one note.

Lancaran Tropongbang pl 5/6

bukå 3132 5̣6̣12 16̣4̣⑤̣
balungan mlaku
3132 3132 5̣6̣12 16̣4̣(5̣)
3132 3132 5̣6̣12 16̣4̣(5̣)
1216̣ 1216̣ 5̣6̣12 16̣4̣(5̣)
1216̣ 1216̣ 5̣6̣12 16̣4̣⑤̣
balungan nibani
.3.2 .3.2 .1.6̣ .4̣.(5̣)
.3.2 .3.2 .1.6̣ .4̣.(5̣)
.1.6̣ .1.6̣ .4̣.2̣ .4̣.(5̣)
.1.6̣ .1.6̣ .4̣.2̣ .4̣.⑤̣

With note 4 replaced by 3, the piece can also be played in *sléndro*. A three-*gongan lik* section can be added.

```
         P               U
  P      P       P       U
. 3 . 5  . 6 . 5  . 6 . 5  . i̇ . (6)
```

2.19 *Padhang–ulihan* structure in *lancaran*

Some *lancaran* have only a *balungan nibani*, some only a *balungan mlaku*, and some have both. These variants are represented respectively by *Béndrong*, *Kebogiro glendheng* and *Tropongbang* in the examples shown. Sometimes there is a special version of the *balungan* played only by the *slenthem*. A few pieces have a double-density *balungan* for use in the slower *irâmâ*, e.g. *Manyar sèwu* and *Embat-embat penjalin*.

The typical *padhang–ulihan* structure of a single *gongan* of a *lancaran* is shown in Fig. 2.19.

Irâmâ and *garap*

As a loud-style piece, a *lancaran* usually has a *bukâ bonang*. Other options exist: for example, in *wayang* the piece may start after a vocal introduction from the *dhalang*, and the players will time their entry from the *bukâ kendhang*.

The home *irâmâ* for a *lancaran* with *balungan nibani* is *irâmâ lancar*. *Lancaran/bubaran* that have a *balungan mlaku* can also be started in *ir I*. Pieces that have both forms of *balungan* may start in *irâmâ lancar* with the *balungan nibani*, then switch to the *balungan mlaku* when entering *ir I*. If there is a *balungan mlaku* or a double-density *balungan*, *ir II* and *ir III* are also possible.

The default *garap* for the *bonang* in *irâmâ lancar* is *gembyangan cegat*. In both the Solonese and Yogyanese styles, the final *gâtrâ* of the *bukâ bonang* anticipates this *garap*: the *bonang barung* plays *gembyangan cegat* to the gong note, regardless of how the *bukâ* is notated. In *ir I* and below, a *balungan mlaku* is normal, and the *bonang* play standard *mipil*, or *gembyangan lâmbâ*, etc., where appropriate. In some dance suites, as when *lnc Béndrong* is used as part of the suite for *Topèng Klânâ*, the *balungan nibani* continues in *ir I* and the *bonang* play half-speed *gembyangan cegat*.

When playing *gembyangan cegat*, the *bonang* have difficulty in signalling changes of register. In *Béndrong*, for example, there are two places where such a signal would be useful; at the end of *gongan* B, to signal the transition to the *lik*, and for the first half of *gongan* E, to indicate the high register of the *balungan*. It is therefore desirable for the *bonang* to play *gembyang* 6 from the third *gâtrâ* of *gongan* B, and common for them to play *gembyang* 1 throughout the first half of *gongan* E.

Apart from the cases just described, there are still different approaches to the choice of *gembyang* notes on the *bonang*. Basically there is a choice between playing a separate *gembyangan cegat* pattern for each *gâtrâ* or the same pattern for a pair of *gâtrâ*. In the latter case, the *bonang* play to the *sèlèh* note of the second *gâtrâ* and the fourth *gâtrâ*; e.g. in *gongan* A of *Béndrong*, two *gâtrâ* of note 2 and then two *gâtrâ* of note 3. There is no standard practice in this area: different *gongan* of a *lancaran* may be treated differently, and teachers may disagree.

In *irâmâ lancar* the *peking* simply plays on every *balungan* beat. As a *pin* is interpreted as a continuation of the previous note, the *peking* regularly plays notes twice for a *balungan nibani*. At the start of *gongan* A of *Kebogiro glendheng* there are two *pin*, so the *peking* plays 5 three times in succession.

If a *lancaran* has both types of *balungan*, the *balungan mlaku* may be played as a counter-melody by the *saron* and perhaps the *demung*, while the *slenthem* continues playing the *balungan nibani*. The *peking* may base its part on either version of the *balungan*.

Core compositions

There is a short list of compositions that are sometimes described as core or essential pieces that every player must know. It is also suggested, with some exaggeration, that they contain all the *céngkok* that players of decorating instruments need to master. The list is:

- *Ktw Puspâwarnâ sl m*
- *Ktw Subâkastâwâ sl 9*
- *Ldr Wilujeng sl m*
- *Ldr Pangkur sl 9*
- *Gd Gambirsawit kt 2 kp mg 4 sl 9*

Ldr Pangkur can also be played in *pathet manyurâ*, and all the pieces exist in at least one *pélog* version too. Additional items could be suggested; e.g. the Yogyanese might add the version of *Gd Majemuk* with five *kenongan*, because of its irregular form, and others might add *bubaran Hudan mas pl 7*.

Whatever the precise status of these pieces, there is no doubt that they are all important and frequently played, and that they teach valuable *garap* principles that are applicable in other pieces.

Bonang imbal is used in response to some types of *ciblon* drumming. *Saron imbal* is established *garap* for some pieces, but the players may play *mbalung* for a full cycle of the piece before changing to *imbal*. In *wayang* or dance accompaniments, they may play *imbal* from the start.

The *garap* may also vary according to the tempo within one *irâmâ*. For example, the *saron* and *bonang* players may switch out of *imbal* and into *mbalung* and *gembyangan cegat* respectively when the tempo is fast.

Garap may change to accommodate the vocal parts, if any. At least the instruments are likely to play more softly during any *gérongan*, and the speed may be more relaxed.

Bubaran such as *Hudan mas* are played in a brisk *ir I* and possibly *ir II*, with *bonang* using *mipil* throughout except for certain *gembyang* signals: see *bub Runtung* on p. 169 and *Hudan mas* in Part 4.

Garap for the punctuating instruments is covered in Part 3.

Kendhangan

Separate forms of *kendhangan kalih* exist for *lancaran* and *bubaran*. When a *lancaran* is played for *wayang* or dance, it may be drummed on the *ciblon* throughout.

Use

With a variable number of short *gongan*, *lancaran* fit texts of various lengths, so they are often used for songs. In contrast to other *bentuk*, *lancaran* use words specific to the piece, rather than generic texts, and the title of the piece relates to the words. There are also purely instrumental *lancaran*. Some dance suites include *lancaran*.

Pieces in other *bentuk* are sometimes performed as *lancaran*. *Lnc Kebogiro glendheng*, also known simply as *lnc Glendheng*, is actually an extract from a *gendhing bonang*: the two *gongan* of *lancaran* correspond to half a *kenongan* of the *inggah* of *gendhing Glendheng kt 4 ar mg 8 pl 5*. The usual tempo for the *lancaran* version corresponds to the *seseg* section of the *gendhing*. The whole *inggah* of *gd Gambirsawit* is sometimes played as a four-*gongan lancaran*, but in this case the *balungan* runs at a much faster speed as a *lancaran* (in *irâmâ lancar*) than in the *gendhing* (usually *ir III*).

The *lancaran* category is fairly large. Since it includes many *lagu dolanan*, which are liable to prove ephemeral, the true number is uncertain.

Ketawang

The *ketawang* belongs mainly to the soft style and is best seen as a vocal form. Like the *lancaran*, it has short *gongan*, although the timescale is rather different. To distinguish it from the *gendhing ketawang* form, which can be much larger but does not use *kempul*, this one may be called *ketawang alit*.

Structure

Ketawang have a 16-beat, four-*gâtrâ*, two-*kenongan* structure (Fig. 2.18). The punctuating instruments used are *gong ageng*, *kenong*, *kempul*, *kethuk* and *kempyang*. As always, the Yogya style characteristically does not use the *kempyang* in *sléndro*.

Ketawang normally conform to an *ompak–lik* structure, with the *ompak* consisting of a single *gongan*. The length of the *lik* varies to suit the text used: most are in the range of two to five *gongan*, but a few exceed ten *gongan*. Because of the vocal character of *ketawang*, the *ompak* is not usually cycled on its own. A further indication of the unimportance of the *ompak* can be seen from the fact that one *ompak* often serves several *ketawang* in the same *laras* and *pathet*. For example, the *ompak* shown for *ktw Puspâwarnâ* is also found in *ktw Kinanthi pawukir*, *ktw Sri Utâmâ*, *ktw Pangrembé* and *ktw Sekartéjâ*. All of these also share the same *bukâ*.

Ketawang Puspåwarnå sl m

bukå	6̣.̅1̅23	.2.1	3312	.12(6̣)
ompak	.2.3	.2.1	.3.2	.1.(6̣)
lik	..6.	2̇3̇2̇1̇	3̇2̇65	1̇65(3)
	..32	5321	.3.2	.1.(6̣)
	.2.3	.2.1	.3.2	.1.(6̣)

For *pélog barang*, the note 1 is replaced by 7 throughout. One Yogya version has *balungan mlaku*, resulting from the addition of *pancer* 5: see Part 4.

Ketawang Subåkaståwå sl 9/pl 6

bukå	2.1	.2.1	2211	.6̣.(5̣)
ompak	.1.6̣	.1.5̣	.1.6̣	.1.(5̣)
lik	.2̇.1̇	.6.5	.2.1	.6̣.(5̣)
	.2̇.1̇	.6.5	.2.1	.6̣.(5̣)
	.2.1	.2.6̣	.2.1	.6̣.(5̣)

Lagu dolanan

The term *lagu dolanan* refers to the character of a piece rather than its *bentuk*. Many *lagu dolanan* are written in *lancaran* form (e.g. *É É É O O O, Witing klåpå, Suwé ora jamu*), but others use *ketawang, langgam, srepegan* or even *kemudå* form. They are always vocal pieces.

Dolan means 'play', and the *lagu dolanan* category is essentially light-hearted. Some pieces, though in similar style, have texts that are hardly *dolanan*; e.g. *K. B.* (= *Keluarga berencana*, 'Family planning') and *Penghijauan* ('Reafforestation', literally 'greening')—both of these titles being (significantly?) in Indonesian, not Javanese.

Some of these pieces are aimed at children, providing moral exhortation or encouraging citizenship and local pride. They may be about a town or *kebupaten* (*Sléman Sembada, Karanganyar Tentrem*), tourist attractions (the Gembira Loka zoo in Yogya, the Grojogan Sèwu waterfall at Tawangmangu, or others further afield), or aspects of everyday life (*Lumbung Désâ*, 'The Village Rice Barn'; *Witing klåpå*, 'The Coconut Tree'; *Ménthog-ménthog*, 'Manila Ducks').

The *ompak* may be played more than once before the transition to the *lik*. A very common practice is to play the *ompak* twice after the *bukå*, then only once on every subsequent iteration—again confirming the relative importance of the *lik*. The *suwuk* for a *ketawang* typically comes at the end of the *lik*.

The typical *padhang–ulihan* structure for one *gongan* of a *ketawang* is shown in Fig. 2.20.

Irâmå and *garap*

The home *irâmå* for *ketawang* is *ir II*. In the Solonese style, *ketawang* start in *ir I* but complete the transition to *ir II* around the *kempul* in the first *gongan*. In the Yogyanese style, the transition into *ir II* occurs during the *bukå*, so that the piece proper starts in *ir II*: for this reason, the usual *welå* is considered unnecessary, and *ketawang* performed in Yogya style characteristically have a *kempul* stroke at the mid-point of the first *kenongan* as well as the second.

In the Solo tradition, many *ketawang* have *balungan nibani*, at least in the *ompak*, and the *saron* and *demung* may add *pancer* notes: as usual, this happens more in *sléndro* than in *pélog*.

In the Yogya tradition, most *ketawang* have *balungan mlaku*—often because *pancer* notes have already been added—and some (*Gajah Éndrå, Gunungsari, Sesanti*) exceptionally have a double-density *balungan* (*balungan ngracik*).

Otherwise the parts played by the *balungan* instruments are straightforward, without the option of *saron imbal*. The standard *garap* for the *bonang* consists of the *mipil* patterns appropriate for *ir I* or *ir II*.

The *ompak* of *ktw Subåkaståwå* is derived from the music of the ceremonial *gamelan munggang*. It may optionally be performed with special *garap* known as *ompak klénangan*. The parts for the *bonang* are as described under **Klénangan** (p. 181), with *salahan* at the end of each *kenongan*. The *kempul* and *kethuk* play additional strokes: for details, see Part 3.

In the Solonese style, if the *bonang barung* provides the *bukå*, it can use special patterns to gong 5̣ or 6̣ in the last *gåtrå*, e.g. (showing the whole *bukå*):

theoretical:	3 . 2	. 3 . 2	3322	. 1 2 6̣
actual:	3 . 2	. 3 . 2	3322	. 1 5̣ 6̣ 1 6̣
similarly, *pl 7*:	3 . 2	. 3 . 2	3322	. 7̣ 5̣ 6̣ 7̣ 6̣
similarly, to 5̣:	2 . 1	. 2 . 1	2211	. 6̣ 3̣ 5̣ 6̣ 5̣

As soft-style pieces, *ketawang* usually involve the soft instruments from the start.

The vocal parts can take various forms. Female solo *sindhènan* is used in most *ketawang*, with male *gérongan* in the *lik* section, and *andhegan* are possible. For *Puspåwarnå* the *gérongan* is specific to the piece, whereas *Subåkaståwå* uses a generic text. Some *ketawang*, such as *ktw Barikan pl 5*, have a mixed chorus (*sindhènan bedhayan*).

Details of the regular *garap* for the punctuating instruments are covered in Part 3.

Kendhangan

The *ciblon* is sometimes used. *Ciblon* drumming calls for *bonang imbal* in the usual way, and the piece may then go from *ir II* to *ir II rangkep*. Otherwise *kendhangan loro* is normal, although a *kendhangan satunggal* also exists (see Part 4).

P		U	
P	U	P	U
. 2 . 3	. 2 . 1	. 3 . 2	. 1 . (6)

2.20 *Padhang–ulihan structure in ketawang*

Use

Ketawang are played by themselves, as 'third sections' for *gendhing*, and occasionally as *inggah*; also in various suites or sequences such as *talu* before a *wayang*. Another standard sequence consists of three *ketawang*: *ktw Sinom Parijåthå kal ktw Sinom Wenikenyå kal ktw Sinom Logondhang sl 9*. When a *ketawang* follows another piece, it may be entered at the *lik* section instead of the *ompak*.

Langgam

The *langgam* form, as played on the central Javanese gamelan, is essentially the same as *ketawang*, to the extent that some pieces may be assigned to either category. The differences are in the *garap*. Any *langgam* is liable to be played in a variety of *laras–pathet* combinations, sometimes with transposition. *Langgam* is again a vocal form, deriving ultimately from *kroncong*, a type of song heavily influenced by Portuguese popular song.[84]

Structure

Most *langgam* have the same 16-beat, four-*gåtrå*, two-*kenongan* structure as *ketawang* (Fig. 2.18), with the same pattern of punctuating instruments. There is a two-part structure with an *ompak*, but the other part is called *lagu* or *sekar* rather than *lik*. The most frequent overall pattern is an *ompak* consisting of a single *gongan*, and a *lagu* section consisting of four, typically in an AABA structure. Other patterns are found, but with a strong tendency towards multiples of four *gongan* in the *lagu*.

Langgam with 32 beats in each *gongan* also occur, but it is not clear whether these all follow *ladrang* structures.

Langgam Ngimpi sl 9 (miring)

ompak 1̇2̇61̇ 2̇1̇65 3561 216̣①
lagu 1̇2̇61̇ 2̇1̇65 3561 353②
1̇2̇61̇ 2̇1̇65 3561 216̣①
561̇6 1̇653 2̇1̇65 156①
1̇2̇61̇ 2̇1̇65 3561 216̣①

vokal
. . . . 1̇ 2̇1̇ .6 1̇ . .2̇ 1̇6 5 .3 32 35 5
. . . . 3 5 56 1 .3 21 15 5 .3 23 .1 2
. . . . 1̇ 2̇1̇ .6 1̇ . .2̇ 1̇6 5 .3 32 35 5
. . . . 3 5 56 1 .3 21 15 5 .3 21 .6̣ 1
. . . . .6 6 1̇1̇ 6 .1̇ 1̇6 .6 6 .1̇ 6 .5 3
. . . . .1̇ 1̇ 1̇6 5 .1 1 15 5 .3 21 .6̣ 1
. . . . 1̇ 2̇1̇ .6 1̇ . .2̇ 1̇6 5 .3 32 35 5
. . . . 3 5 56 1 .3 21 15 5 .3 21 .6̣ 1

Irâmå and garap

A *langgam* typically starts with a solo vocal introduction—a *bukå celuk* or a full *båwå*—leading into the start of the *lagu* section in *ir II*. The singer throughout is most often a *pesindhèn*, but sometimes a male soloist takes turns with her. A transition at some point from a slow *ir II* into a fast *ir II rangkep* is normal, therefore with little real change of tempo, and the same vocal line is used in both *irâmå*. The piece may finish in either *irâmå*.

In *kroncong* the instrumentation is not fixed, but it consists largely of a selection of bowed or plucked strings—violin, cello, string bass, mandolin, banjo, guitar and ukulele—together with flute, triangle and tambourine. When the *kroncong* form is adapted into *langgam* for the gamelan, the *garap* is generally as for *ketawang*. On the *peking*, two players play the same *imbal* patterns as for *saron imbal*, to the middle and the end of each *gåtrå*. For the two *bonang*, a special *garap* (see **'Salah gumun'**, p. 182) is often used, but *bonang imbal* and even *klénangan* (p. 181) can also be heard. The *slenthem* is typically the only *balungan* instrument.

In terms of syllables per second, vocal lines in *langgam* run faster than *gérongan* and *bedhayan* choruses, and more closely resemble vocal parts in *lagu dolanan*. The vocal style is rhythmically loose, although in a different way from standard *sindhènan*. The vocal line still runs through all or most of the *gongan*, with a *sèlèh* to all or most *gåtrå*, whereas *sindhènan srambahan* has a single *sèlèh* at the end of the *céngkok*. *Andhegan* are possible.

Garap for the punctuating instruments is covered in Part 3.

Kendhangan

The *kendhangan* for *langgam* is usually *kendhangan patut* on the *ciblon*.

Use

Langgam may be performed on their own, but they are often used as *selingan* in suites. One way of inserting a *langgam* is to start its vocal introduction in place of a standard *andhegan*. After the *langgam*, the next piece in the

84 According to legend, the Javanese imitated the songs of Portuguese sailors. The history can be explored via the notes with the *Kroncong, Dangdut and Langgam Jawa* CD from the Smithsonian/Folkways *Music of Indonesia* series: see Appendix 8.

sequence may be a repeat of the piece that preceded it, or a related *lik* section. One sequence of this type would be the *ir III* version of *ldr Ayun-ayun sl m*, then *langgam Ngidham sari*, followed by *lik Ilir-ilir* (the latter being closely associated with *Ayun-ayun*) also in *ir III*.

Ladrang

The *ladrang* category is an extensive one, comparable in quantity with *gendhing* (in the narrower sense). It embraces pieces of very different characters—instrumental (loud-style) and vocal (soft-style), long and short—some of which have a particularly wide range of possible *garap*, including the widest range of *irâmâ* options.

Structure

A *ladrang* has a 32-beat, eight-*gâtrâ*, four-*kenongan* structure (Fig. 2.18). The punctuating instruments used are as for *ketawang*: *gong ageng*, *kenong*, *kempul*, *kethuk* and *kempyang*. Again the *kempyang* is not used in *sléndro* in the Yogya style.

As with *ketawang*, there are some *bukâ* that serve several *ladrang* in the same *pathet*.

Most *ladrang* have an *ompak–lik* structure in which the *ompak* can be cycled by itself. The most frequent pattern has an *ompak* with a single *gongan* and a *lik* with one or more *gongan*. Further details of possible structures are given under the next heading. The *padhang–ulihan* structure illustrated in Fig. 2.6 is typical.

Irâmâ and *garap*

The widest range of *irâmâ* and *garap* is found in *ladrang* that have a double-density version of the *balungan* for use in *ir III* and *ir IV*. This is sometimes described as the standard pattern for a *ladrang*, but is in fact only one of several. In this subcategory, the possible *irâmâ* include *ir I* with or without *kébar*, *ir II* and, using the double-density *balungan*, *ir III* and *ir IV*. *Kébar* (p. 231)—or possibly *kinthilan* (p. 232) in the Yogya style—takes its usual form. The *ciblon* may also be used for *ir II*, again signalling *bonang imbal*. In *ir III* and *ir IV*, *ciblon* drumming and *imbal* on the *bonang* are normal, and *andhegan* are possible. There are typically *gérongan* for each of *ir I*, *ir II* and *ir III*.

Ldr Pangkur, in the display box opposite, is a good example of a *ladrang* with all these options. Although its

---

Ladrang Pangkur sl 9

bukâ	.2.1	.2.1	2211	.6̣.⑤̣	
ompak, ir I/II	[2126̣	216̣5̣	6521	3216̣	
	2321	5321	3216̣	216̣⑤̣	]
ompak, ir III/IV					
	[[.2.1	.2.6̣	.2.1	.6̣.5̣	
	66..	5561̇	2̇1̇52	.1.6̣	
	..32	5321	2132	5321	
	562̇1̇	5216̣	.2.1	.6̣.⑤̣	]
			↘	.56①̇	
ngelik	..1̇.	3̇2̇1̇2̇	..2̇3̇	5635	
	1̇1̇..	3̇2̇1̇6	2̇1̇53	6532	
	..23	5653	2356	5321	
	562̇1̇	5216̣	.2.1	.6̣.⑤̣	]

Vocal *ladrang* with optional *kébar* in *ir I*.

Ladrang Wilujeng pl 7

bukâ	7̣32	6̣7̣23	7̣7̣32	.7̣5̣⑥̣	
ompak	[[27̣23	27̣5̣6̣	33..	6532	
	5653	27̣5̣6̣	27̣23	27̣5̣⑥̣	]
ngelik	..6.	7576	3567	6532	
	66..	7576	7732	.7̣5̣⑥̣	] *suwuk*

Typical vocal *ladrang* with *gérongan* in *ngelik*.

Ladrang Sukarsih pl 6

(*bukâ* not used when *ladrang* follows an *inggah*)

ompak	[.2.1	.2.1	.3.5	.3.2	
	.6̣.5̣	.3.2	.5.4	.1.⑥	
ngelik	.5.6	.5.6	.2̇.1̇	.2̇.6	
	.3.2	.3.5	.1̇.6	.3.②	
	.3.2	.3.5	.1̇.6	.3.2	
	.6̣.5̣	.3.2	.5.4	.2.①	] *suwuk*

Ladrang Sigrâmangsah sl m

bukâ	.1.2	.1.6	3263	653②̂	
lâmbâ	.6.3	.6.2̂	.6.3̆	.6.2^{5}	
	.3.5̆	.6.3̂	6521̆	321⑥̂	
dados	[3561̇	3216̂	3561̇̆	3216^{3}	
	3523̆	1216̂	3263̆	653②̂	*suwuk*
	1̇61̇3	1̇61̇2̂	1̇61̇3̆	1̇61̇2^{5}	
	5235̆	1̇653̂	6521̆	321⑥̂	]

Loud-style *ladrang* in Yogya style with *lâmbâ* section.

'home' *pathet* is probably *sléndro sångå*, it is also played in *sléndro manyurå*, *pélog barang* and (less often) *pélog limå*. Others of this type include *ldr Éling-éling kasmaran sl 9*, *ldr Ayun-ayun sl m / pl 6* and *ldr Gonjing Miring sl m*. The pattern shown, with a *lik* used only in *ir III*, is typical.

Ldr Wilujeng sl m, also *pl 7* and *pl 5*, has a single *gongan* each of *ompak* and *lik*, and does not go beyond *ir II*. The usual *skema* is a transition to *ir II* around the first *kempul*, then a repeat of the *ompak* before the transition to the *lik*. The *lik* has *gérongan*: it is played once—as in most but not all cases—and the *ompak* usually twice. There is also a version of the *ladrang* with *bedhayan* chorus.

Ldr Sukarsih pl 6 represents a type with *bedhayan* chorus starting in the *lik* and then continuing into the *ompak*, and played only in *ir II* (not starting in *ir I*, because it follows an *inggah* in *ir II*). It is also among the *ladrang* usually played with *pinjalan*: this option seems to be rare in *laras sléndro*. *Ldr Gléyong pl 6* is a similar independent *ladrang* that has *gérongan* instead of the *bedhayan* chorus, starting in the *lik* but finishing in the *ompak*.

Ldr Sigråmangsah sl m in its Yogya version is a classic loud-style *ladrang*, played in *ir I* and *ir II*. The volume level remains high in *ir II*, and the only quiet part is a *sirep* lasting from the first *kenong* to the third in the final *gongan*. (A Solo version of the same piece, which uses both *sindhènan* and *gérongan*, has in *ir III* a single-*gongan* double-density *lik* in which the *balungan* is essentially the same as shown for the two *gongan* of the *dados* section of the Yogya version.) In the Yogya loud style, *ir III* is also possible, e.g. for *ldr Sumyar sl m*, and again the volume level remains high.

In the Solo tradition there are also *ladrang*, e.g. *ldr Singå-singå pl 7*, that are normally played in the loud style in *ir I*, sometimes filling the same role as Yogyanese *gati* (see below). However, they may also have vocal parts for use in soft-style performances.

The transition to the *lik* is usually signalled by the appropriate melodic leader instrument (and in the case of *ldr Pangkur*, involves a variant *balungan*). Sometimes, as with *ldr Sri katon sl m*, the *skema* for the piece is standardised, and no *lik* signal is used. (*Ldr Sri katon* also has vocal parts for *ir III*.)

For various *ladrang*, including *ldr Pakumpulan sl 9* and *ldr Dirådåmetå sl 6*, the *ompak* is cycled by itself in *ir I* to close the piece.

Ladrang can have *saron imbal* in *ir I* and *ir II* when performed in *wayang* style. In the same context and in others they can also have *suwuk gropak*.

Pancer notes are typically added to *ladrang* that have *balungan nibani* in *sléndro* (e.g. $\dot{1}$ in *ldr Sri katon sl m*), possibly from the start, but at least from the entry to *ir II* or the following gong, and will then continue until the end even if the piece goes to *ir I*. In *pélog*, *pancer* notes are less often used, but they are written into the *balungan* of some pieces, e.g. some versions of *ldr Sumyar pl 7*.

In the Yogya style, a *ladrang* may have a *låmbå* section with *balungan nibani*, lasting for most of a *gongan*. The transition to the *dados* section is accompanied by a change of speed, from a brisk *ir I* to a more relaxed tempo in the same *iråmå*. The special *garap* for a *låmbå* section and the start of the *dados* section are as described later for the Yogyanese *gendhing soran* category (p. 81), except that the transition to *ir II*, if any, usually happens after a few *gongan* in *ir I*.

In a *bukå bonang* in the Solo style, if used, the same special patterns to $\underset{\cdot}{5}$ or $\underset{\cdot}{6}$ are available as for *ketawang*.

Soft-style decorating instruments enter, as would be expected, at the transition to *ir II* in soft-style pieces, or at the *gong bukå*. They are silent in loud-style pieces.

Garap for the punctuating instruments is covered in Part 3.

Kendhangan

There is a wide range of *kendhangan* for *ladrang* in the Solo style:

- default *kendhangan kalih* for *ir I* and *II* (also for *ir III*, but rarely used), with a separate pattern for the *lik* section, although the Solonese often prefer *kendhangan Mataram* for loud-style *ladrang* in *ir I*;
- special *kendhangan kalih* for *ldr Embat-embat penjalin sl 9*, for *ir I* and *ir II*;
- special *kendhangan kalih* for *ldr Kagok Madurå sl 9*, for *ir I* and *ir II*;
- special *kendhangan kalih* for *ldr Lawung ageng sl m*, for *ir I* and *ir II*;
- special *kendhangan kalih* for *ldr Sobrang pl 7*, for *ir I* and *ir II*;
- a general *kendhangan satunggal* for *ir I* and *ir II*, with *kosèk alus* for *ir III*.

In addition the *ciblon* can be used in any *iråmå*. Besides *kébar*, it is possible for a *ladrang* in *ir II* to switch between

ciblon and *kendhangan kalih*. For example, in *ldr Tirtåkencånå pl 5/6*, the *ompak* is cycled in either *ir I* or *ir II* as long as *kendhangan kalih* continues, but a switch to the *ciblon* at the end of the *gongan* results in a transition to the *lik*, which is then played once or twice: a switch to *kendhangan kalih* at the end of the *gongan* signals the return to the *ompak*.

Apart from *ciblon* drumming, the Yogya style also offers various forms of *kendhangan* for *ladrang*, in all cases without a separate version for the *lik* section:

- default *kendhangan kalih*, going down to *ir III*: this is what the Solonese refer to as *kendhangan Mataram* for *ladrang*, although they change it in detail, and in any case are mainly interested in the *ir I* version,
- a *kendhangan satunggal* for *ir I*, *ir II* and *ir III*,
- *kendhangan råjå*, another *kendhangan kalih* for specific *ladrang* such as *ldr Lung gadhung pl 1* in *ir I* and *ir II*,
- special *kendhangan kalih* for *ladrang*, apart from *ldr Bimå kurdå*, played in *ir I* and *ir II* in connection with *gangsaran*,
- special *kendhangan kalih* for *ldr Bimå kurdå* when played in *ir I* and *ir II* in connection with *gangsaran*,
- *kendhangan sabrangan* in *ir I* only, which strictly belongs under the *gati* heading below.

Use

Ladrang are played by themselves, as *inggah* to many *gendhing*, e.g. *ldr Ayun-ayun* as the *inggah* to the popular *gd Randhu kéntir sl m/pl 6*, as 'third sections' to *gendhing*, and in suites, including *talu*. They are often used to accompany the entry and exit of the dancers in *srimpi* and *bedhåyå*, but see also under **Gati** below.

When a *ladrang* follows another piece, it may be entered at the *lik* section instead of the *ompak*.

Gati/mares

The *gati* or *mares* is a specifically Yogya form, exclusively in *pélog*. It is a *ladrang* in structure, and is only played in the loud style, but with distinct *garap*. Its most remarkable feature is the presence of European instruments. In the past, more of these instruments may have been used, but the trumpet and the tenor drum are still an essential part of the *bentuk*. There are fewer than 20 pieces in this category.

Irâmå and *garap*

Gati are usually played in *ir I*, although *ir II* is also possible. The trumpet plays the *balungan*, expressing its true range, i.e. exceeding the single octave of the *balungan* instruments.

Garap for the punctuating instruments is as for *ladrang*.

Kendhangan

Gati use *kendhangan sabrangan*, in which the *dhah* strokes are played on the *bedhug* instead of *kendhang ageng*. The tenor drum, with a separate player, contributes single strokes and rolls, including a long roll ending at the gong.

Use

Gati are used by themselves, but also provide the standard entry and exit pieces for *srimpi* and *bedhåyå* accompaniments in *pélog* in the Yogya style.

Gangsaran

The *gangsaran* is essentially an ostinato on one note—most often 2, although others are possible—a borrowing from the limited repertoire of the ceremonial *gamelan cåråbalèn* (p. 240). It is a loud-style form, and the soft-style instruments are not played.

Structure, *irâmå* and *garap*

Gangsaran has a four-*kenong*, 16-beat structure like that of *lancaran*, but the concept of a *gåtrå* is hardly relevant. The *kethuk* pattern, corresponding to the *penonthong* part in the original ensemble, differs fundamentally from those of other *bentuk* (Fig. 2.18). The other punctuating instruments—gong, *kenong* and *kempul*—play the same roles as in *gamelan cåråbalèn*, but not necessarily the same notes. As in *lancaran*, the *gong suwukan* is used most of the time, and the *gong ageng* is only used for (say) every fourth *gongan*.

The 'melodic' parts played by the *balungan* instruments do not correspond to anything in the *gamelan cåråbalèn*, which dates from before the time when *wilah* instruments are believed to have been added to gamelan.

In the *gamelan cåråbalèn* the *gambyong* and the interlocking *kenut* and *klénang* take the 'melodic' roles. For the *garap* that replaces their roles, see **Gangsaran**, p. 156, and **Klénangan**, p. 181, in the *bonang* section of Part 3.

The tempo varies within limits. Essentially *irâmå*

gropak—or arguably a fast *irâmâ lancar*—is the only *irâmâ* used. *Sirep* and *udhar* may be signalled by the *kendhangan*.

Kendhangan

Gangsaran use special *kendhangan kalih* based roughly on that played on the *peneteg ageng* and *peneteg alit* in the *gamelan cârâbalèn*, or can use elements of *ciblonan*. In the Yogya style, special variant *kendhangan* is used for *ladrang* when played in suites with *gangsaran*.

Use

Gangsaran are used in *wayang* and as part of dance suites, with special transitions on either side of the ostinato section (sometimes called the *ganjur*) to suit the context.

Another established practice is to play a sequence of *gangsaran – ladrang – gangsaran*. *Ldr Kagok liwung sl 6*, *ldr Lawung gedhé sl m*, *ldr Roning tawang pl 6* and *ldr Bimâ kurdâ pl 7* are all used in this way. The gong note of the *ladrang* is not necessarily related to the *gangsaran* note.

The sequence may be extended to two *ladrang* in different *laras*, with the *laras* changing on the *gangsaran* note in the middle, i.e. *gangsaran – ladrang – gangsaran A – gangsaran B – ladrang – gangsaran*. The *tumbuk* of the individual gamelan determines whether the order A–B is *sléndro–pélog* or *pélog–sléndro*: typically the order is chosen so that the second *gangsaran* note is higher than the first. These are suites for *klenèngan*/*uyon-uyon* use.

If the *gangsaran* does not lead to another piece, a *suwuk gropak* is normal.

Creating a *lâmbâ* section

The general principle of a *lâmbâ* section in a *ladrang* or *gendhing* is that it is a *balungan nibani* version of the *dados* section. In practice, the usual rules for changing *balungan mlaku* to *balungan nibani* are ignored to some extent, especially in the first one or two *gâtrâ*.

It is not unusual to find the same note twice in a *gâtrâ*, e.g. . 6 . 6 . 5 . 6 as the *lâmbâ* version of 356 . 6656 in *gd Godheg sl 6*. This is done repeatedly in the first three *kenongan* of the *lâmbâ* of *gd Karawitan sl 6*, where the *sèlèh* notes of the *dados* are also not respected:

lâmbâ .3.3 .3.3 .3.2 .3.$\hat{1}$

stands for

dados 3565 2126 3565 2321

Gendhing

Overview

The category *gendhing*, in its narrower sense, embraces compositions that vary enormously in length and character, but all have a relatively complicated *skema*. Many *gendhing* require some 25 minutes for performances that do them justice. There are also *gendhing* on twice this scale, as well as some that are rather shorter. The long ones may consist either of long *gongan* or many short *gongan*. *Gendhing*, of which there are several hundred, are therefore substantial pieces that can be compared to symphonies in Western classical music.

To begin breaking the *gendhing* category down into subcategories, one obvious distinction is between soft-style *gendhing*, using vocal parts, and *gendhing bonang*, which are exclusively instrumental. As explained later, the Yogya category of *gendhing soran* does not correspond exactly to *gendhing bonang*: the Yogyanese also give the description *soran* to shorter pieces, such as some *ladrang*, that are performed in a similar style. (A more detailed classification of *gendhing* is needed, and is given later.)

The Austrian pianist Artur Schnabel used to say that there are two kinds of piano recitals: in most of them the first half is boring, and the second half consists of fireworks.[85] A *gendhing* similarly has two main sections, the first of them almost always being calm and reflective, whereas the treatment is usually much livelier in the second section.

After the transition to its second part, a *gendhing bonang* at first gives the impression of following the Schnabel philosophy, because it returns to a mood very similar to the first part. However, things become more exciting later: see **Progress of a gendhing bonang**, p. 80.

In Solonese terminology, the first part of a *gendhing* is called the *mérong*. Within the *mérong* there may be an optional *ngelik* section. Since a *ngelik* section is a vocal form, *gendhing bonang* would not be expected to have them, but they do occur in a few *gendhing bonang*. Yogyanese terminology has no single word that corresponds exactly to *mérong*. The first part of a Yogya-style *gendhing* characteristically has a *lâmbâ–dados* structure (see **Progress of a Yogyanese gendhing soran**, p. 81).

The Solonese term for the second part is *(m)inggah* or *(m)unggah*, corresponding to the Yogyanese *(n)dhawah* —words with opposite meanings, since *minggah* means

85 His recitals were different, he said: both halves were boring.

Relationship of *mérong* and *inggah*

The nature of the relationship between the *mérong* and the *inggah* of a *gendhing* is disputed. Some sources say that the *inggah* section is the real piece, and that the *mérong* is merely an introduction—even implying that any fool can compose a *mérong* for an *inggah*. Others say that the *inggah* section is a simplified version of the *mérong*. Certainly most performances spend more time on the *inggah* than the *mérong*, and the character of *inggah* sections varies much more between one *gendhing* and another. When a *gendhing* is played on a *gamelan sekatèn*, only the *inggah* section is used.

As further evidence in this discussion, it must be pointed out that one kind of compositional activity for Javanese musicians is the creation of new *inggah* for existing *mérong*. Also the *balungan* of the *mérong* section can be relatively irregular, whereas the *inggah* section is most often in *balungan nibani*. *Gendhing* in *pélog* tend to make more use of the *sorogan* notes in the *mérong* than the *inggah*. (However, exceptions can be found among both *gendhing rebab* and *gendhing bonang*; e.g. *gd Pramugari* and *gd Tukung* respectively, both of them in *pathet barang* and making extensive use of 4 in the *inggah*.)

A distinction is made between *minggah kendhang*[86] and *minggah gendhing*. In the latter, the melodic material of the *inggah* is new. The name *minggah kendhang* implies that the melodic material in the *inggah* is the same as in the *mérong*, although reduced to *nibani* form, and the only difference lies in the drumming patterns. *Gendhing* with *minggah kendhang* form the majority. (A *mérong* and a *minggah kendhang* may represent different views of the inner melody. In the *mérong* of *gd Gambirsawit sl 9*, the third *kenongan* ends with *sèlèh* 3, followed by a *gantungan* on 2. In the *inggah*, the 2 is reached by the end of the third *kenongan*, so that the *balungan* line is . 1̇ . 6 . 3 . 2, although versions of the notation with . 1̇ . 6 . 5 . 3 exist.)

When looking at a particular *gendhing* to see which of these two models it follows, it is necessary to check the melodic structure carefully via the *sèlèh* notes. Even if the *mérong* and the *inggah* are of the same length, the first *gongan* of the *inggah* does not necessarily correspond to the first in the *mérong*. An example of this is *gd Téjånåtå pl 5*, with a *minggah kendhang* in which the first, second and third *gongan* correspond respectively to the second, third and first of the *mérong*. It is also necessary to check whether the two parts correspond *gåtrå* by *gåtrå*, in pairs of *gåtrå*, or in a more complex manner.

86 *Minggah kendhang* has another meaning too, referring to an *inggah* section in *ir II* preceding another in *ir III*.

'rise', but *ndhawah* means 'fall'. The *minggah/ndhawah* form differs from that of the first part, and is used exclusively as the second half of a *gendhing*. In place of this special form, some *gendhing* use a *ladrang* or (rarely) a *ketawang* for the second half. Such combinations are identified by *minggah ladrang* or *minggah ketawang* (in Solonese terminology) in their titles.

In contrast to the cyclable *ompak–lik* structures in *ladrang* and *ketawang*, no return to the *mérong* is possible once the *inggah* is entered.

A *gendhing* may in practice have one or more pieces attached to it to form a suite. Pieces in *ladrang* and *ketawang* forms are commonly used as these 'third sections'. In Yogyanese terminology, the word *minggah* indicates a third section of this kind, so that a *gendhing* can then have both *ndhawah* and *minggah* sections.

Soft-style *gendhing* are commonly described as *gendhing rebab*, because the *rebab* is the leading melodic instrument in such pieces, and may supply the *bukå*. In practice a *gendhing rebab* may begin in other ways, as detailed in **Progress of a vocal gendhing**, pp. 78–80, involving optional elements and substitute instruments.

The *padhang–ulihan* structures of *gendhing* vary—Fig. 2.21 is one example—but basically they correspond

P
P | U
.21. 216̣5̣ .... 5̣5̣.6̣ 11.. 11.2 3323 2121̂

P
P | U
.21. 216̣5̣ .... 5̣5̣.6̣ 11.. 11.2 3323 2121̂

P
P | U
.21. 216̣5̣ .... 5̣5̣.6̣ 1̇1̇.2̇ 3̇2̇1̇6 5424 5645̂

U
P | U
.... 55.. 5456 5424 .24. 4565 21.5̣ 6̣12(1)

2.21 *Padhang–ulihan* structure in a *mérong* of *kt 2 ar* form to the scale of the overall composition: the larger forms have longer phrases rather than more short phrases. If the overall structure is analysed as AAAB, for example, the A and B elements vary in size. For example, the first part of the *gendhing bonang* version of *gd Pangrawit kt 8 kp pl 5* from Solo and the *gendhing rebab kt 8 ar* version from Yogya have essentially the same *balungan* contour, but the Yogya version is on twice the scale, so that two *gåtrå* correspond to one *gåtrå* in the Solo version.

Progress of a *gendhing*

The general patterns for the progress of a *gendhing* are described in the display boxes later.

The progress of a specific performance is represented graphically in Fig. 2.22: this is a sequence with *båwå sekar alit Dhandhanggulå pådåsih* leading into *gd Lungit kt 2 kp mg 4 kal ldr Pakumpulan sl 9*.[87] The *gendhing* proper has only a single *gongan* each in its *mérong* and *inggah*, without a *lik* section in the *mérong* and without *andhegan* in the *inggah*. In the attached *ladrang*, the three *gongan* labelled A, B and C are repeated, but after the transition to *ir I* only the first *gongan* is cycled. Various parts of the *skema* were played three times in this particular performance, but there is no special significance in the number three.

Between the rows of time marks, Fig. 2.22 shows the major sections of the sequence, including the positions of the gong and *kenong* strokes.

In Western classical music, the most important speed measure would be the basic tempo in beats per minute, which is often shown at the head of the score as a MM (Maelzel's metronome) figure. A corresponding figure for basic tempo is shown towards the bottom of the diagram here, but it does not represent the way that the Javanese think of the progress of the music. Instead, the speed is viewed in terms of *irådå* and density of decoration.

All the speeds are represented on logarithmic scales, i.e. each doubling of tempo is shown by the same vertical increment. The density of decoration is shown for the *gendèr barung* and *bonang barung*, both of which usually operate at *lampah 4* density in *ir II* (e.g. compare the density of nearly 120 beats/min against a basic tempo of nearly 30 beats/min). These two instruments part company for the first *kenongan* of the *inggah*, because the *bonang barung* continues with *ir II*-type *nibani* patterns at half speed. At the very end of the final *gongan* of the *ladrang*, the *bonang* can, as shown, double its density by returning to *ir II* patterns. Other decorating instruments would play throughout with the same variations of density, but at twice the densities shown.

The scale markings of 60 and 120/min, etc., have been chosen deliberately because some people theorise that the speed of all music relates to a heart rate of 60/min. (No comment on the validity of this theory is implied.) The basic tempi of this performance are in fact entirely normal for *gendhing*: a basic *gendèr* density of just under 120/min in the *mérong*, a slight increase in density during the *inggah*, and an *ir IV* section played considerably faster than half the tempo of the *ir III* sections. The precise densities[88] are respectively 111, 118 and 183/min.

Densities remain high during the *ladrang*: 140.5/min during *ir II*, rising to 160 in *ir I*.

Other points to note in Fig. 2.22 include the brief dips in tempo just before the gong strokes in the *mérong* (and the instant recovery to normal speed thereafter), the complex adjustment of density by the decorating instruments at the transition into the *inggah*, the relative positions of the *ir IV* and *gérongan* sections in the *inggah*, and the use and position of speed-up signals throughout.

The representation in Fig. 2.22 should not be taken too literally, as the transitions are so rapid.

Classification by style

The following classification is not an official one, but makes a rough division according to the main audible features of the pieces. Neither is it complete. Not every piece fits neatly into one group.

- *Gendhing* with a full set of vocal contributions: the *minggah* has *balungan nibani* and is typically performed in *irådå III*, possibly going to *irådå IV*, and contains a *gérongan* in *ir III*, usually only starting more than half-way through it. There may also be a *gérongan* in the *mérong*. The *mérong* may contain a *ngelik*, where again there may be *gérongan*. The piece may have *sindhènan gawan*, but otherwise there will be *sindhènan srambahan* throughout, including during the *gérongan*. Often one or more *andhegan* occur, though usually only in the *minggah*. This relatively large category is the liveliest in style and exploits the resources of the gamelan most completely. It typically uses shorter forms such as *kt 2 kp mg 4* (see **Classification by structure**, p. 81). It includes many of the most often performed pieces, e.g. *gd Gambirsawit* (*sl 9* and

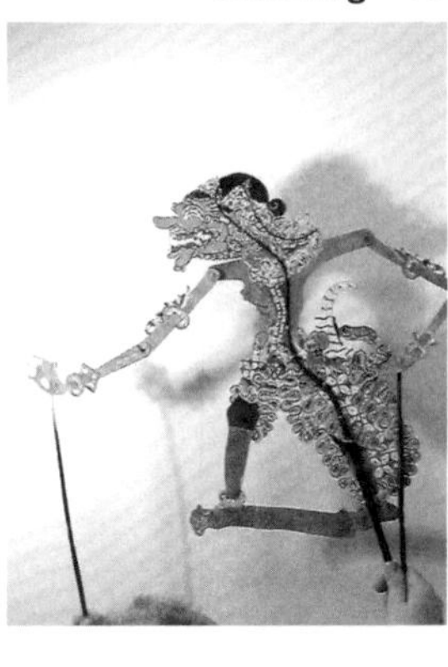

87 Derived from the author's field recording.

88 Subject to error in the tape recording/playback process.

pl 6), *gd Perkututmanggung* (*sl m* and *pl 7*), *gd Randhu kéntir* (*sl m* and *pl 6*), *gd Logondhang pl 5*.

- *Gendhing* with a minimal vocal contribution in the form of *sindhènan srambahan* only, usually without *andhegan*. In the *minggah* the *balungan* may be either *nibani* or *mlaku*. This large category of pieces includes *gendhing* forms longer than *mg kt 4*. It is rather less lively than the first, although the *minggah* is still sometimes in *ir III*. In the most restrained of these pieces, the *minggah* stays in *ir II*. Examples: *gd Mongkok dhélik sl 6*, *gd Elå-elå Kalibeber sl 9*, *gd Såråyudå pl 6*, *gd Miling sl m*. Some, in keeping with their more serious style, are treated almost like *gendhing bonang* and can end in *ir I* with a *seseg*: e.g. *gd Silir Banten pl 7*, *gd Kombangmårå pl 5*, *gd Raranjålå pl 5*.
- *Gendhing* with *bedhayan* chorus, sometimes throughout, and often functioning as part of the accompaniment for a *srimpi* or *bedhåyå* dance. In the sections without a chorus, there is *sindhènan srambahan*. The mixed chorus gives an intense atmosphere appropriate to the sacred dance. This category contains some pieces in *gd ktw* forms and is not large. Examples: *gd ktw Lagu dhempel sl 9*, *gd Téjånåtå pl 5*, *gd Miyanggong pl 6*, *gd Ludiråmadu pl 7*.
- Vocal *gendhing* without a *balungan*, used to accompany *srimpi* or *bedhåyå* dance. They also qualify as *gendhing kemanak*. The melodic line is sung by a *bedhayan* chorus accompanied by soft instruments and punctuating instruments. This is a small category, and several are in the *gd ktw* forms, e.g. *gd ktw Pangkur sl m*,[89] *gd ktw Anglir mendhung pl 7*. In the absence of *balungan* and decorating instruments, the *irâmå* of such pieces is

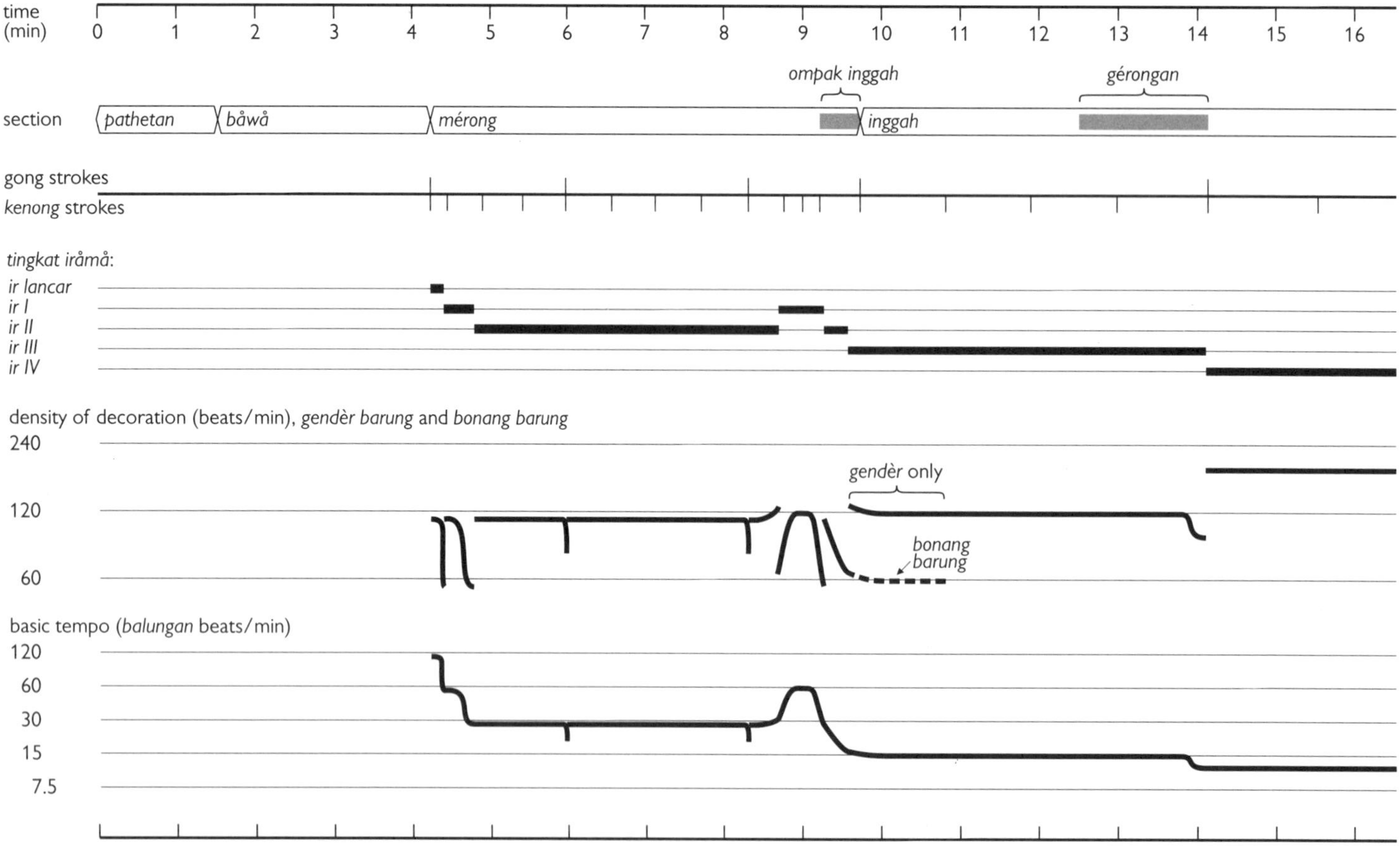

2.22 Progress of a three-part *gendhing* shown in graphical form

89 Not to be confused with *ldr Pangkur*.

unclear: they can be analysed as having either 16-beat *kenongan* (as they are usually notated) performed in *ir II* or 32-beat *kenongan* performed in *ir I*. They are certainly distinct from *ketawang alit*, because they do not use *kempul* and *kempyang*. *Kinanthi* can be treated as a *mérong* in *kt 2 kp* form and performed in this style.

- Classic Solo-style *gendhing bonang*, in which the soft-style instruments other than the *slenthem* do not appear. This is not a large category. Within *laras pélog*, *gendhing bonang* exist in *pathet limå* and *pathet barang*. *Gendhing bonang* in *pélog limå* outnumber all the other *laras–pathet* combinations put together. In *sléndro*, most of the few *gendhing bonang* are in *pathet nem*. *Gd Okrak-okrak* in *sléndro manyurå* is an exception whose origins have been mentioned (p. 57): *gd Bolang-bolang sl m* is another. In the absence of vocal parts or any decorating instruments apart from the *bonang*, much of the interest in these *gendhing* comes from their often unusual phrase contours, mainly in the *mérong*, but the character is usually serious.

  The *balungan* in the *minggah* may be either *nibani* or *mlaku*, although in the latter case it often looks like a *nibani* structure that has had *pancer* notes added.

- Yogya-style *gendhing soran*. In the Yogya tradition a large class of purely instrumental *gendhing*, without soft-style instruments, exists in all *laras–pathet* combinations. The second section has *balungan nibani*, and uses characteristic *garap*. (For further details, see **Progress of a Yogyanese gendhing soran**, p. 81.) These too are sometimes called *gendhing bonang*, and the *bonang* is the melodic leader, but *demung imbal* is the most obvious form of decoration.

➔ p. 81

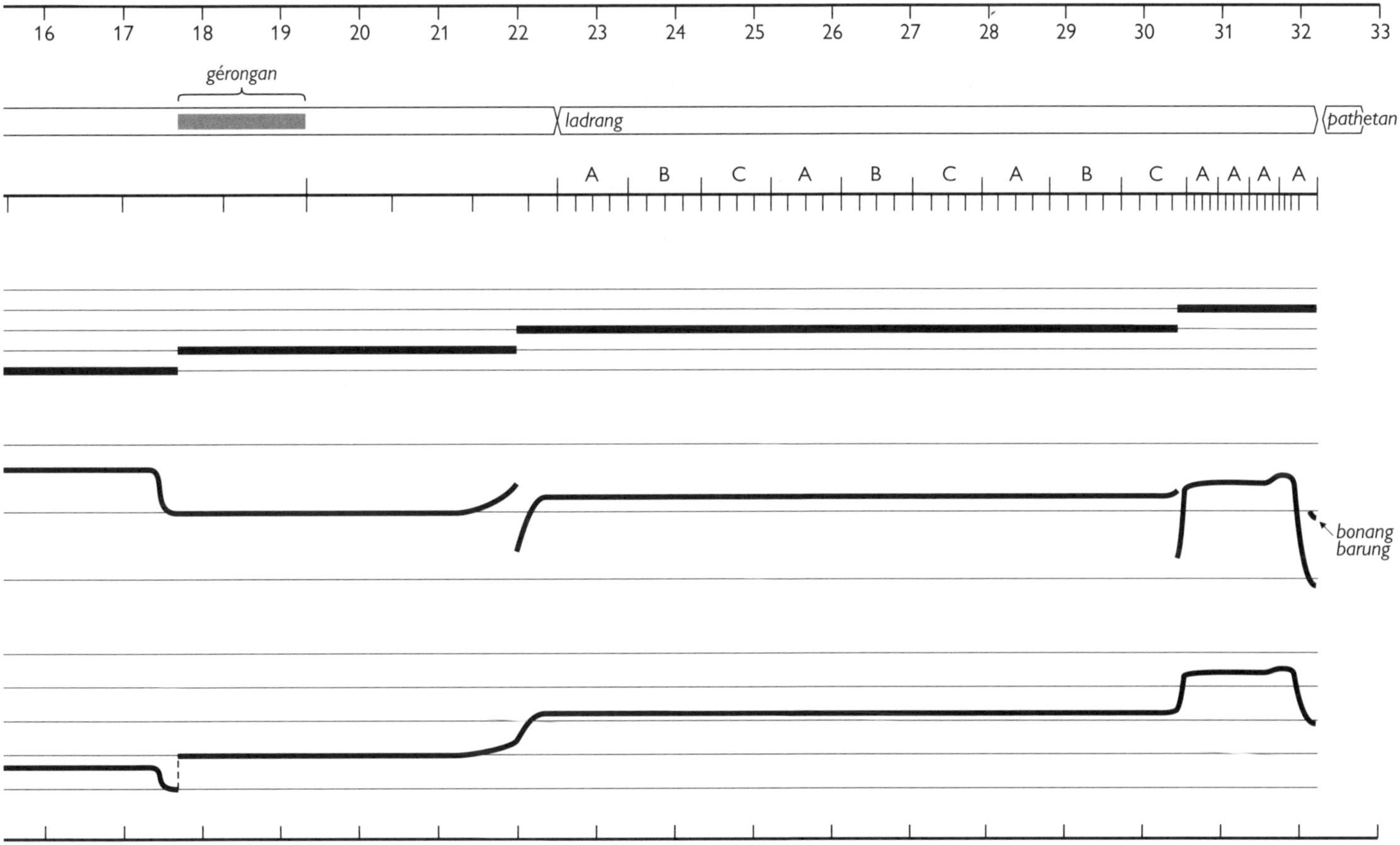

16 17 18 19 20 21 22 23 24 25 26 27 28 29 30 31 32 33

gérongan

ladrang

pathetan

A B C A B C A B C A A A A

bonang barung

Progress of a vocal *gendhing*

Opening

Two optional elements, a *pathetan* and then a *båwå*, begin the sequence for a soft-style *gendhing*. After these, a soft-style *gendhing* normally begins with a *bukå rebab*, the first part of which may be a *pathet*-defining *ådångiyah*. The *gendèr* only gives the *bukå* if for some reason there is no *rebab* present. A *bukå bonang* is possible in a soft-style *gendhing* if neither *rebab* nor *gendèr* is available. Whichever of these melodic leaders supplies the *bukå*, the other instruments do not join in until the *gong bukå*, except sometimes the soft-style decorating instruments.

The home *iråmå* of a *mérong* is *ir II*. Before that *iråmå* is reached, a complex series of speed changes takes place within a few seconds, and players can easily get out of step.

As usual, the speed and rhythm of the *bukå* are at the player's discretion, and only settle down to normal when the *kendhang* enters. In Solonese style, the initial drum-stroke is a *dha*, but its position is not always the same: in *sléndro* the stroke occurs the equivalent of a *gåtrå* before the gong, but in *pélog* it occurs one *gåtrå* earlier. Before this stroke, the *kendhang* may insert a few quiet strokes to encourage the *bukå* player towards the right tempo. Matters are complicated by the use of *sléndro* drumming patterns when a *gendhing* that was originally in *sléndro* (e.g. *gd Kututmanggung*) is played in *pélog*. (Patterns for *kosèk wayangan* are different.) In Yogya style, the initial stroke is not always a *dha*, but always occurs in the earlier position, and sometimes the *kethuk* is struck four beats before the gong. The speed of the drumstrokes leading up to the gong only roughly indicates the required speed after the gong, because it usually drops slightly just before the gong—a minor slow-down compared to those before other gong strokes in the *mérong* (see below).

Mérong

The pace becomes regular immediately after the *gong bukå*. The first few *gåtrå* are played *mbalung* and very strongly by all the melody instruments, and at a speed that corresponds to *iråmå lancar*. In some cases the *balungan* at this point moves twice as fast as the end of the *bukå*, but this is not always shown by the notation.

Moving from *iråmå lancar* to *iråmå dados* means a 4:1 speed reduction, which is usually achieved in two stages. Shortly after the gong there is a steep reduction so that *ir I* is reached by about the middle of the first *kenongan* (for a *gendhing* in *kt 2 kp* form). Typically the speed steadies for a few *gåtrå* and then drops again, reaching *ir II* before the end of the second *kenongan*. For longer forms such as *kt 4 kp*, the speed changes take about the same length of time, but all within the first *kenongan*. At the same time, the *balungan* section reduces its volume level to a normal level for *ir II*.

For the accompaniments of some sacred dances (provided that *ir II* is being used), and sometimes for other serious *gendhing*, the *bonang barung* plays *mipil låmbå* throughout the *mérong*. The *bonang panerus* continues playing at its usual density. In other accompaniments for *srimpi* or *bedhåyå* dances, the *mérong* may be played in *ir I* throughout. In the Solonese style, these dance accompaniments, whether in *ir I* or *ir II*, are played somewhat faster than other *gendhing*. In contrast, Yogyanese dance accompaniments tend to be slower than usual.

Yogya-style *gendhing* usually start with a characteristic *låmbå* section lasting for most of the first *gongan*. Here the melodic line is a simplified version of the usual *balungan*, conforming more or less to the rules of *balungan nibani*. The transition to *ir II* is sometimes only completed towards the end of the *låmbå* section, where the *balungan* becomes *mlaku*. The *låmbå* section is followed by the *dados* section, which has a normal *balungan*.

Once the speed has settled, it remains steady until the end of the *gongan*. In the last *gåtrå* of the *gongan*, the speed relaxes a little, and the gong stroke is slightly delayed. The other instruments delay their gong note too, trying to coincide with the gong stroke, but return to normal speed immediately afterwards, as signalled by a special pattern of drumstrokes (see **Tips & tricks 7**). In *gendhing* with the larger structures (*kt 4 kp*, *kt 2 ar* or larger), a similar but smaller delay may occur at each *kenong* stroke. The delay to the gong stroke is not normal in *bedhåyå*/*srimpi* accompaniments in *ir I*.

A *mérong* can consist of one or more *gongan*, and in most *gendhing* the whole *mérong* can be repeated as often as desired. In Yogya style, only the *dados* section is cycled. During the *mérong*, a transition to a *lik*, if there is one, is signalled in the usual way by the leading melody instrument. The *lik* section ends at the final gong of the *mérong*.

In a vocal *gendhing*, solo *sindhènan* usually starts in the second *kenongan* in the *mérong* and then continues for the rest of the *gendhing*, or until *sindhènan bedhayan* starts. If no *sindhènan gawan* exists for the particular piece, *sindhènan srambahan* will be used. *Sindhènan gawan* starts at whatever point the verse metre dictates, as for *gérongan*.

Progress of a vocal *gendhing* (cont'd)

If there is *gérongan* in the *mérong*, it finishes at a gong, and therefore the starting point depends on the metre; e.g. twelve *gåtrå* before the gong (corresponding to three *kenongan* of *mérong kt 2 kp*) for *kinanthi* metre in *ir II*. *Gérongan* may only occur in the *lik* section, if there is one, or may be used throughout the *mérong*.

During any part of the *gendhing*, although less often during the *mérong*, an *andhegan* may occur.

A mixed *bedhayan* chorus can start in the *mérong*, as early as *sindhènan gawan*, or it may start only in the *inggah*, or even in the 'third section'. It is also possible for the *bedhayan* singing to continue throughout the sequence.

Some *gendhing* have an established exceptional *garap*. The first section of *gd Bondhèt* (in the version known to the Solonese as *Bondhèt Mataram*) can be played in *ir I*, using *kébar*, in both Yogya and Solo traditions. The first parts of certain *gendhing*, e.g. *gd Karawitan*, may be performed in *ir III* throughout, again in both traditions, when they are used as the background to long narrations in *wayang*.

Transition to *inggah*

There may be a special section to be played for the transition, and called *ompak inggah* (Solo) or *pangkat dhawah* (Yogya). The length of this section can be anything from half a *kenongan* to a whole *gongan*. If the *inggah* has *balungan nibani*, the *ompak inggah* will be the same. This means that in many *gendhing* the *balungan* changes from *mlaku* to *nibani* at the *ompak inggah*. For *gendhing* in *kethuk 4* or *8 arang* forms, the *ompak inggah* has *kethuk kerep* or else there is a switch from *arang* to *kerep* during the *ompak inggah*, so that a *kenongan* in the *ompak inggah* is shorter than those in the rest of the *mérong*. The precise location of this transition to *kethuk kerep* varies (especially within the Yogya tradition): see the main text.

To signal the transition to the *inggah* (via the *ompak inggah* section, if any), the *kendhang* causes a speed-up, often as far as *ir I*. The point at which this happens depends on the scale of the *gendhing*, but must of course precede the *ompak inggah* section. For a *gendhing* in *kt 2 kp* form, it typically occurs in the first *kenongan* of the *gongan*, but for larger-scale *gendhing* it happens later.

Once the transition has been signalled and the players have responded, it is not necessary to maintain the speed. The initial *irâmå* of the *inggah* is either *ir II* or *ir III*, so that a speed reduction of 2:1 or 4:1 must be achieved. (If the *inggah* is in *ladrang* form, it may start in *ir I*, so that no change of speed is necessary, although the use of *kébar* means a slight relaxation of tempo.) The new *irâmå*, and all *garap* changes, may be achieved by the time of the gong that ends the *mérong*, or may take a little longer. In some cases this means that a 4:1 reduction of speed is squeezed into one short *kenongan*. There is no pause at the gong. If the goal is *ir III*, the drummer will change to *kendhangan ciblon* or *kosèkan* during the last *kenongan* before the gong, although the *ir III* tempo may not be reached until some point in the first *kenongan* of the *inggah*.

It is possible for a *mérong* with several *gongan* to have more than one exit point, and therefore different *ompak inggah* sections (e.g. *gd Kuwung pl 7*). The point at which the tempo increases determines which exit is taken: the exit point is the next gong after the speed-up.

The speed-up is only necessary as a signal for when to move to the *inggah*. Therefore, if the structure has already been decided, or if there are no options, no speed-up is necessary.

Inggah

The first *kenongan* of the inggah completes, if necessary, the transition to the new *irâmå*. If the goal is *ir III* with *ciblon* drumming, during this first *kenongan* it is common in the Solonese style for the *bonang barung* to play *balungan nibani* patterns, as in the *ompak inggah*, but at half the normal speed. The *bonang panerus* plays at its usual speed. The *bonang barung* often plays a full *sekaran* to the *kenong*, as a signal that it is switching to playing *imbal*.

In a *sléndro* piece whose *inggah* has *balungan nibani*, the *saron* and *demung* play a *pancer* note, typically $\dot{1}$ and typically from the first *kenong* or even the gong, regardless of *irâmå*. *Pancer* notes are less frequently used in *pélog* pieces, although they can be found in many Yogya-style *gendhing*.

In livelier pieces, some or all *saron* and *demung* players may stop playing at the start of the *inggah*, leaving the *slenthem* to carry the *balungan* alone. They are then free to contribute *keplok* or to form (or supplement) the *gérong*.

If there is a *gérongan* for the *inggah*, it will start at such a point that it ends at the final gong. For example, a *gérong* in *kinanthi* form (six lines or *gåtrå* of verse) occupies 1½ *kenongan* of an *inggah* of *kt 4* form played in *ir III*: in other words, one *gåtrå* of verse corresponds to one *gåtrå* of *balungan* in this case. This *gérongan* will therefore start half-way through the third *kenongan*. If there is more than one *gongan* of *inggah*, *gérongan* may be used in each. ➔

Progress of a vocal *gendhing* (cont'd)

There is no established *gérongan* for a section in *ir IV*, although *sindhènan srambahan* and *andhegan* continue.

From *ir III* a transition to *ir IV* can occur at a gong or a *kenong*, after an *andhegan*, or elsewhere. The return to *ir III* may occur whenever convenient, e.g. after an *andhegan* or just before the start of the *gérongan*.

For an *inggah* in *ir III/IV* with *gérongan*, the *bonang* play *imbal* throughout. If the *kendhangan* is *kosèkan* in *ir III*, the *bonang* play *mipil nibani*. A double-density *balungan* played in *ir II* is equivalent in density to *ir I*, so that *kébar* is possible, e.g. in *ldr Loro-loro topèng*, which follows *gd Loro-loro géndhong*. Otherwise for an *inggah* in *ir II* with or without *gérongan*, the *bonang* will play *mipil* in *mlaku* or *nibani* style, according to the type of *balungan*.

Some *gendhing* have major variants in the *inggah*. *Gd Perkukut manggung* has both a *minggah ladrang* and a regular *inggah*, and can use either. One Yogya version of *gd Lambangsari sl m* has the equivalent of a *minggah ladrang* and a regular *minggah*, and can use both. *Gd Elå-elå kalibeber sl 9* has a *minggah* in two sections, one in *ir II* and the other in *ir III*, and alternates between them.

If the *inggah* is in *ladrang* or *ketawang* form, the *garap*, *irâmå* and vocal parts will be those appropriate to the piece. In many pieces it is normal to use a sequence of different *garap* from the available options.

Suwuk

The signals leading to the *suwuk* depend on the *irâmå* and the type of *kendhangan*, and are described in Part 4. Some *gendhing* have a *suwuk gropak* when used in a *wayang* context: otherwise a slow-down is normal. Special *suwuk* sections as described for *gendhing bonang* (right) are not unknown in other *gendhing*. The gong stroke may come only after the last note of a *gérongan* or *sindhènan* (see **... and ending**. p. 35), but the other instruments play their final notes after the gong, as usual.

A *pathetan* may follow.

Third section

If a *ladrang* or *ketawang* is to follow the *inggah*, the *kendhangan* leading up to the gong at the end of the *inggah* includes the usual *suwuk* signals. The tempo changes alone may be sufficient to warn the players of the forthcoming transition, but the *kendhang* may indicate the *bentuk* of the new piece via its characteristic *bukå kendhang* or a variant thereof.

Progress of a *gendhing bonang*

Solo-style *gendhing bonang* have many features in common with vocal *gendhing*, but also some major differences. The *bonang barung* may play one or more out of *ajak-ajak*, *grambyangan* and *ådångiyah* before the *bukå*. (For Yogya-style *garap* in the *ådångiyah*, see p. 143.) The progress of the first half has no unusual points, except that the *balungan* always remains prominent.

The second section maintains the volume level, and normally drops to *ir II* quite soon after it starts; exceptionally it may spend a *gongan* in *ir I* first. Later it becomes louder and faster each time the *minggah* is repeated.

Once this speed-up has started, reaching only a fast *ir II*, the *balungan* may change at the next gong. The changes may only affect detail or they may amount to a wholly new—and usually much shorter—section, labelled *sesegan* or *sabetan*. Even if the basic *minggah* has *balungan nibani*, the *sesegan* section will have *balungan mlaku*, typically with built-in *pancer* notes. A special transition section, called *ompak seseg* or *angkatan seseg*, may lead into the *sesegan*.

Also after the speed-up (and again typically at the next gong), an optional *garap* may begin, in which, if there are two *demung*, one of them plays the *balungan* half a beat late. Two players can do the same on a single *demung*. The players damp their notes only when playing the next note, i.e. a different damping pattern from *saron imbal*. The off-beat player plays any *balungan ngadhal* or *balungan nibani* as written. Otherwise this special *garap* continues until the end: only the note on the final gong stroke is not repeated. The *slenthem* may play the off-beat part.

On each iteration of the *gongan* the tempo increases, ultimately reaching a fast *ir I*. At the maximum speed, the *bonang panerus* part is technically demanding, and the player may resort to simplified patterns.

The approaching *suwuk* is signalled by a slow-down. In a few pieces a special passage—labelled *suwuk(an)* or *ompak suwuk*—replaces the last few *gåtrå*, and the slow-down also signals entry to this passage. From the slow-down almost to the end, the high volume level is maintained, only falling to a moderate level on the final one or two notes: in fact the volume reduction is mainly due to the lengthening gaps between notes.

Gendhing bonang are not preceded or followed by *pathetan*, and are played by themselves, not combined with other pieces to make up suites.

Progress of a Yogyanese *gendhing soran*

The *gendhing* starts with a *bukå bonang*, possibly preceded by an *ådångiyah*. In the last *gåtrå* of the *bukå*, the *bonang barung* plays *gembyangan midak* to the gong note.

Throughout the *låmbå* section, which typically goes at a brisk *ir I* speed, the two *bonang* play *gembyangan midak* at their respective densities (see Part 3 for details of this and other *garap*), and the volume level of the *balungan* remains high. The speed only drops towards the end of the *låmbå* section. At the *dados* section, the *bonang* switch to *mipil låmbå* and then, as the speed falls further to *ir II*, to *mipil rangkep*. All this is completed before the gong.

During the *låmbå* section, the *peking* plays a note on each *balungan* beat in the usual Yogyanese *nikeli* style, i.e. anticipating the notes of the *balungan nibani*. In the *dados* section it doubles its density, now playing eight notes per *gåtrå*, again anticipating the *balungan mlaku* notes.

When *ir II* is reached, the volume level remains fairly high, as in a Solonese *gendhing bonang*. The first part (corresponding to the *mérong* in Solonese terms) is repeated as required, with the usual slight pause before the gong stroke. Then the *kendhang* signals a speed-up to *ir I* in the usual way. The *bonang* switch to *mipil låmbå* when *mipil rangkep* is no longer comfortable. The *peking* plays the same patterns as before, but faster.

The first part of the *gendhing* normally ends in a *pangkat ndhawah* with *balungan nibani*, corresponding to a Solonese *ompak inggah*. In the *pangkat ndhawah* the *bonang* play *gembyangan midak*, at twice the density they used in the *låmbå* section. The *peking* plays four times to each note of *balungan nibani*. The *ndhawah* continues *balungan nibani*.

In the first *kenongan* of the *ndhawah*, the *garap* continues in the same style as during the *pangkat ndhawah*, while the tempo drops to *ir II* level. At the end of that *kenongan*, or at the last *gåtrå* of that *kenongan*, a whole new set of *garap* begins. Up to this point the *saron*, *demung* and *slenthem* have all played the *balungan* as notated. Now the *saron* plays the *balungan* plus the appropriate *pancer* note, and the *slenthem* plays *gemakan*. The *demung* players, typically on two instruments rather than the same one, play a Yogya-style *demung imbal* at one of two speeds. The slower speed is used initially, but after a few *gåtrå* the *imbal* may double in density.

Meanwhile the *bonang* (in the most extreme Yogyanese style) play extended versions of the *mipil nglagu* patterns, but with a lot of *gembyangan*—sometimes a separate *gembyangan* to each *balungan* note. Other players use patterns much closer to Solonese *mipil lumpatan*. The *peking* plays the faster of the *nikeli* styles appropriate for *balungan nibani*, i.e. eight times to each *balungan* note, possibly with simple variations.

After the *kendhang* signals a speed-up, the *demung* halve the density of their patterns when the denser patterns become uncomfortable. When *ir I* is reached, they are then playing just as many notes per second as in *ir II*. If the *demung* were playing lower-density *imbal* patterns, they continue the same patterns but faster. The *saron* continue their previous patterns, but faster. The *peking* changes to playing four times to each *balungan* note, and the *slenthem* may switch to playing *mbandhul*. The *bonang* switch to *ir I* patterns or, when the speed becomes uncomfortably fast, to *gembyangan dados* or *gembyangan midak*. Later, after a further speed-up, the *bonang* start playing *gembyangan cegat* to every second *balungan* note.

The speed increases each time the *gongan* is cycled, but the increases may not be as extreme as in a Solonese *gendhing bonang*. The *garap* described continues throughout, including the final slow-down, until the last *gåtrå*. In the last half-*gåtrå*, both *bonang* play *gembyangan midak* to the gong note.

Gendhing of this kind follow other standard Yogyanese practices: the *bonang panembung* (if available) will play throughout from the *gong bukå* onwards, the *kendhangan* will be the appropriate Yogyanese *kendhangan satunggal*, and *gendhing* in *sléndro* will not use the *kempyang*.

To complicate the classification above, the third section of a *gendhing* may represent a change of character. For example, *gd Lipur Érang-érang pl 6* belongs in the first category above, but it may be followed by *ldr Surung dhayung*: for the latter there is a *bedhayan* chorus that changes the mood. Likewise *gd Laranjålå pl 5* belongs in the second category above, but can be followed by *ktw Barikan*, again with a *bedhayan* chorus.

Classification by structure

In the Surakarta tradition, *gendhing* are classified according to the *kethuk* patterns in the *mérong* and *inggah*—more precisely, according to the number and spacing of the *kethuk* strokes in each *kenongan* of the *mérong* and *inggah*.

In the *mérong* the *kethuk* patterns fall first into two categories: *kethuk kerep* and *kethuk awis/arang* (Fig. 2.23).

Table 2.16
Range of *kenongan* and *gongan* lengths for *mérong*

Kethuk pattern	*Balungan* beats		
	Per *kenongan*	Per *gongan*	
		Gendhing	*Gd ketawang*
Kt 2 kp	16	64	32
Kt 2 ar	32	128	—
Kt 4 kp	32	128	64
Kt 4 ar	64	256	—
Kt 8 kp	64	256	128
Kt 8 ar	128	512	—

Kerep means 'close together', and *kethuk kerep* means a *kethuk* stroke on the last *balungan* beat of the odd-numbered *gåtrå*. Thus *kethuk 2 kerep* means a stroke at the end of the first and third *gåtrå*, or the fourth and twelfth beats of the *kenongan*. *Arang* or *awis* means 'far apart' or 'sparse': a *kethuk* stroke on the last beat of the second, sixth, tenth, … *gåtrå*, or half the density of the *kethuk kerep* structures.

Besides the *kethuk* strokes, the *mérong* uses *kenong* and *gong ageng*, but no other punctuation instruments apart from the special case of *gendhing kemanak*.

kethuk 2 kerep

kethuk 2 arang/awis

kethuk 4 kerep

kethuk 4 arang/awis

kethuk 8 kerep

kethuk 8 arang/awis

2.23 *Kethuk* patterns (per *kenongan*) for *mérong*

Table 2.16 shows the range of standard *mérong* structures actually found. Most *gendhing* have four *kenongan*, giving a range of *gongan* lengths from 64 to 512 *balungan* beats. Some but not all of these variants occur in a smaller class of *gendhing* called *ketawang gendhing*, *gendhing ketawang* or *ketawang ageng*: these, like *ketawang alit*, have only two *kenongan* per *gongan*.

During the *ompak inggah* or *pangkat dhawah*, the *kethuk* pattern may change. In the *kethuk 4 arang* form the *kethuk* pattern normally becomes *kerep* at some point during the transition, so that the last *kenongan*—or even the last one and a half or two *kenongan*—is shorter than the others.[90] In addition, a *salahan* may increase the *kethuk* density, until in the final *gåtrå* before the gong the *kethuk* pattern becomes identical to that in the *inggah*. Some of the resulting patterns, including a range of Yogya variants, are illustrated in Fig. 2.24.

In the *inggah* section, the *kethuk* pattern changes and

kd Cåndrå, Såråyudå, Lålå, etc. (= kt 2 kp)

kt 2 ar

kd Jånggå, Semang kt 4, etc. (= kt 4 kp)

kd Mawur, Mawur Tungkakan (= kt 4 ar)

kd Mawur Tungkakan for gd Wedhikèngser (= kt 4 ar)*

kd Mawur Tungkakan for gd Glendheng (= kt 4 ar)*

kd Semang kt 8 (= kt 8 kp)

kd Pangrawit (= kt 8 ar)

* last two *kenongan* shown

2.24 *Kethuk* patterns preceding *inggah/dhawah* of *gendhing*

90 *Gendhing* showing this change of *kethuk* density are not listed as exceptions in Table 2.17.

Table 2.17
Correspondence between Solo *gendhing* forms and Yogya *kendhangan* for *gendhing*

Solonese *bentuk*	Yogyanese *kendhangan*	
	Sléndro	*Pélog*
Gendhing	Gendhing ageng	
[*Kt 8 ar mg kt 16*][a]	—	*Pangrawit* or *Mawur kt 8* (*kd I*)
Kt 4 ar mg kt 8[b]	*Mawur* (*kd I*)	*Mawur* (*kd I*),[c] *Mawur Tungkakan* (*kd I*)[c]
Kt 2 ar mg kt 4[d]	—	—
Gendhing	Gendhing ageng tengahan	
Kt 8 kp mg kt 16[e]	*Semang [ageng] kt 8* (*kd I*)	*Semang [ageng] kt 8* (*kd I*)
Kt 4 kp mg kt 8[f]	*Jånggå* (*kd I*), *Jånggå låråciblon*[g]	*Semang [alit] kt 4* (*kd I*)
Kt 2 kp mg kt 4[h]	*Cåndrå* (*kd I*), *Majemuk* (*kd I*),[i] *Cåndrå Tungkakan* (*kd I*),[j] *Bandholan* (*kd I*),[k] *Gandrung-gandrung* (*kd II*)	*Såråyudå* (*kd I*), *Majemuk* (*kd I*),[i] *Gandrung-gandrung* (*kd II*)
Gendhing ketawang	Gendhing ageng alit	
Kt 8 kp mg kt 16	—	—
Kt 4 kp mg ldr[l]	—	—
Kt 2 kp mg ldr[m]	*Lålå* (*kd I*),[n] *Lålå Gandrung-gandrung* (*kd II*)	*Lålå* (*kd I*),[n] *Lålå Gandrung-gandrung* (*kd II*)

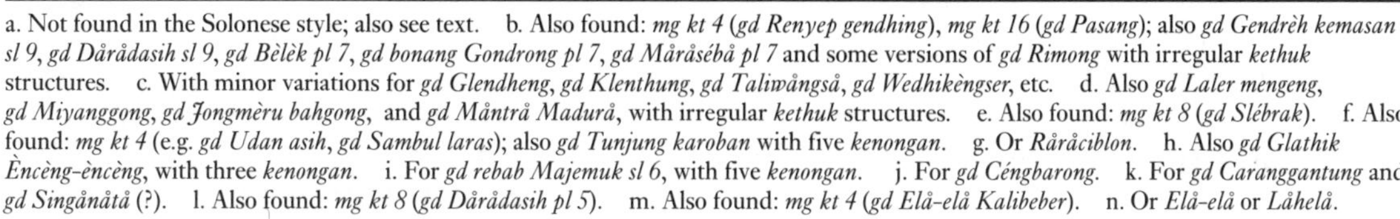

a. Not found in the Solonese style; also see text. b. Also found: *mg kt 4* (*gd Renyep gendhing*), *mg kt 16* (*gd Pasang*); also *gd Gendrèh kemasan sl 9*, *gd Dårådasih sl 9*, *gd Bèlèk pl 7*, *gd bonang Gondrong pl 7*, *gd Måråsébå pl 7* and some versions of *gd Rimong* with irregular *kethuk* structures. c. With minor variations for *gd Glendheng*, *gd Klenthung*, *gd Taliwångså*, *gd Wedhikèngser*, etc. d. Also *gd Laler mengeng*, *gd Miyanggong*, *gd Jongmèru bahgong*, and *gd Måntrå Madurå*, with irregular *kethuk* structures. e. Also found: *mg kt 8* (*gd Slébrak*). f. Also found: *mg kt 4* (e.g. *gd Udan asih*, *gd Sambul laras*); also *gd Tunjung karoban* with five *kenongan*. g. Or *Råråciblon*. h. Also *gd Glathik Èncèng-èncèng*, with three *kenongan*. i. For *gd rebab Majemuk sl 6*, with five *kenongan*. j. For *gd Céngbarong*. k. For *gd Caranggantung* and *gd Singånåtå* (?). l. Also found: *mg kt 8* (*gd Dårådasih pl 5*). m. Also found: *mg kt 4* (*gd Elå-elå Kalibeber*). n. Or *Elå-elå* or *Låhelå*.

the *kempyang* is added (in Yogya, for *pélog* pieces only). The relationship between the *kethuk* and *kempyang* is exactly the same as for *ladrang* and *ketawang*, although without *kempul*, e.g. a *kenongan*

```
 - + -     - + -     - + -     - + - ^
. . . .   . . . .   . . . .   . . . .
```

which is described as a *kethuk 4* structure. This *kethuk* pattern in the *inggah* is separately specified in the description of the *gendhing*. If the gamelan has an *engkuk-kemong*, it is only used in the *minggah*.

The *inggah* form is unique to *gendhing*. Most forms of *mérong* (the exception being the *kt 8 kp* form) can alternatively be followed by a *ladrang*, and after some types of *mérong*—the *gendhing ketawang* forms—a *ladrang* is the norm not the exception. Much less frequently a *ketawang* is used as the second section of the *gendhing*.

The two halves of the *gendhing* are not necessarily of the same length. Most often the Solonese description gives the *inggah* as having twice as many *kethuk* strokes as the *mérong*. If the *mérong* is of *kethuk kerep* form, then the *inggah* is of the same length. If the *mérong* is of *kt 4 ar* form, then an *inggah* of *kt 8* form is only half as long.

The Yogya tradition classifies *gendhing* according to their *kendhangan*, not their *kethuk* patterns (Table 2.17): for example, *gd Gambirsawit sl 9 kd Cåndrå*. Each type of *kendhangan* is named after a reference *gendhing* that uses the particular *kendhangan*. However, the range of *kethuk* patterns is broadly the same as in Solonese *gendhing*. Not every *bentuk* is found in both traditions. In the Yogya tradition the *kethuk 2 arang* form is missing, although one source shows how *kendhangan Mawur* can be adapted for it. On the other hand, the *kethuk 8 arang* form is known in

Yogya, but apparently only for one specific piece, *gd rebab Pangrawit pl 5*, which possibly has the same abbreviated *ompak inggah* as the *kethuk 4 arang* form.[91] The Yogya tradition also has fewer variants in the *gendhing ketawang* class. Table 2.17 also lists many of the *gendhing* with irregular or exceptional structures in both traditions.

The sub-headings for the Yogya half of the table—*gendhing ageng*, *gendhing ageng tengahan* and *gendhing alit*—represent only one of several methods of classifying *bentuk*. Sometimes *ageng* and *alit* refer to the overall scale of the form, sometimes to the *kethuk* density, and sometimes to the number of *kenongan* per *gongan*. There is no standard classification system.

Irregularities in structures

A given *gendhing* can be assigned different *kethuk* structures by different sources—and this is inevitable for some pieces, since the Yogya tradition lacks several of the Solonese *bentuk*. Thus *gd Kaduk manis sl 6* is *kt 4 kp mg 8* in one source, *kt 2 ar mg 8* in another, but the *kenongan* has the same length in both cases. In another case the correspondence is less close: the first part of *gd Randhat sl m* is a single *gongan* of *kt 2 ar* form in one source, but two *gongan* of *gt ktw kt 4 kp* form in another. Here the *kenongan* is again of the same length, the *gongan* is not, but the overall length is still the same.

There are even cases where a *gendhing* is irregular according to one source, but regular according to another. Thus *gd Laler mengeng sl 9* in Solonese sources has three *kenongan* of *kt 2 ar* form, followed by one of *kt 2 kp* form—i.e. half as long. As the *kt 2 ar* form is not used in Yogya, it is no surprise that the Yogyanese version has *kenongan* of *kt 4 kp* form. The repetition of one phrase, amounting to half a *kenongan*, in the latter version makes the final *kenongan* regular.

Exceptionally, the *kempyang* may enter early, before the end of the *mérong*.

Table 2.17 mainly shows irregularities in the first half of the *gendhing*. A few *gendhing* such as *gd rebab Majemuk kt 2 kp mg 4 sl 6* are irregular in both halves. A few also are only irregular in the *inggah*: *gd Hånårågå pl 6* and *gd Loro-loro géndhong sl m* both have regular *kt 2 kp* structures in the *mérong*, and *minggah ladrang*, respectively *ldr Angkruk* with five *kenongan* and *ldr Loro-loro topèng* with three *kenongan*. *Srundèng gosong*, the standard *inggah* for *gd Rujak sentul pl 6*, is even more irregular. It has four *kenongan* with two, two, two and three *kethuk* strokes—a pattern that does not conform to any standard *minggah* structure—and is treated as a double-density *ladrang*.

The special drumming patterns needed for the irregular *gendhing* are known as *kendhangan pamijèn*.

Irâmå and *garap*

Typical *irâmå* and *garap* used with the main categories of *gendhing* are explained in **Progress of a vocal gendhing**, pp. 78–80, **Progress of a gendhing bonang**, p. 80, and **Progress of a Yogyanese gendhing soran**, p. 81.

Table 2.17 correctly suggests that there are different *kendhangan* for *sléndro* and *pélog* in the Yogya style. This is true for Solonese drumming styles too, even though they are not given different names. However, *sléndro kendhangan* styles are used for *gendhing* played in *pélog* if they were originally in *sléndro*, such as *gd Gambirsawit pl 6* or *gd Perkututmanggung pl 7*.

As the table indicates, some structures have more than one *kendhangan* option. In addition to the standard styles of *kendhangan* shown, some *gendhing* are played in *wayang* style with *kosèk wayangan*.

Garap for *wayang* may include *imbal* on *saron* and/or *demung*, and even *suwuk gropak*. *Inggah* sections as well as *ladrang* can be played with *pinjalan*, as in the *gd Téjånåtå – ldr Sembåwå – ldr Playon pl 5* sequence. In the Yogya court tradition, the trumpets that feature in *gati* may also make an appearance in the associated *gendhing* of the *iringan tari*. These types of *garap* can be considered standard, although they are not used on every *gendhing*.

Besides the *gendhing* mentioned under **Progress of a vocal gendhing**, others can have *garap* that is more or less individual. In performances of *gd Lambangsari sl m*, with its alternative *inggah* sections, sometimes the last half-*kenongan* of the *ladrang* version is played at half the expected speed, and the last half-*kenongan* of the regular *inggah* section at twice the expected speed.

Gendhing Gambirsawit sl 9 in Yogya style can have a *ndhawah* section with *balungan mlaku*, played with *mipil* on the *bonang*, before progressing to the more familiar *balungan nibani* version that is played in *ir III* with *bonang imbal*. The same piece can have an independent section called *Kébar Sumedhangan* inserted towards the end of the *mérong*, with complete disregard for the normal structure of the *gendhing*.

The performance of *minggah Kinanthi* as if it were the

[91] A degree of mystery surrounds this piece. One source gives notation for *kendhangan Pangrawit*, with a shortened *ompak inggah* (Fig. 2.24), but not *balungan* notation for the piece. Another source gives a *balungan* notation for the piece, clearly in *kt 8 ar mg 16* form and with an unshortened *ompak inggah*, but uses the description *kendhangan Mawur tungkakan*, which is normally associated, as Table 2.17 shows, with a *kt 4 ar mg 8* form. The performance practice is also unknown to various experts; it is therefore unclear whether the first half really is played in *ir II*, with 16 minutes between gong strokes, as shown in Table 2.14. In the Solo version of the piece, a *gendhing bonang*, the *mérong* appears to have the same melodic structure but on half the timescale (*kt 8 kp*).

mérong of a *gendhing kemanak* has already been mentioned. The same *minggah* section is also played as a *mérong* in more conventional style, with *ldr Kembang pépé* as its *inggah*. When *Kinanthi* is used in its regular role as an *inggah* section in *ir III* following *gd Lobong kt 2 kp sl m*, a special section is often inserted into it. Although the latter is essentially an instrumental piece with *andhegan*, resembling an additional *gongan* of *inggah*, it is referred to as *andhegan Puspanjånå*.

Minggah Kinanthi also exemplifies another element occasionally found in *gendhing*: a *balungan* that changes according to *iråmå*, while keeping the same density (in contrast to the examples of *ladrang* with a double-density version for *ir III/IV*). The *balungan* for *ir II* is

. 1 . 6̣   . 1 . 6̣   . 2̇ . 1̇   . 3 . 2̂
. 3 . 1   . 2 . 6̣   . 2̇ . 1̇   . 3 . 2̂
. 3 . 1   . 2 . 6̣   . 3 . 2   . 3 . 1̂
. 2 . 1   . 2 . 3   . 1 . 2   . 1 . (6)

whereas in *ir III/IV*, with *andhegan* indicated, it becomes

. 1 . 6̣   . 1 . 6̣   . 2̇* 1̇   . 3 . 2̂
. 3 . 1   . 2 . 6̣   . 2̇* 1̇   . 3 . 2̂
. 3 . 1   . 2 . 6̣   . 3* 2   . 2 . 1̂
. 2 . 1   . 2 . 1   . 3 . 2   . 1 . (6)

The 2 in the last *gåtrå* of the third *kenongan* would normally be considered incorrect after a *sèlèh* 2, but the *sèlèh* 2 is not heard, because it falls within the *andhegan*. If the *andhegan* is not taken, the original . 3 . 1̂ is used.

Sléndro/pélog variants

In the process of converting pieces from *sléndro* to *pélog*, *balungan* lines may be left unchanged, as typically when the destination is *pélog manyurå*, or only essential changes may be made, as often when converting from *sléndro manyurå* to *pélog barang*. Sometimes the additional *sorogan* notes available in *pélog* are exploited.

The *sléndro* and *pélog* variants of a piece may have different titles: *gd Gendrèh kt 4 kp mg 8* exists in *sléndro manyurå* and *pélog nem*, but the *pélog* version is also known as *gd Sambul cilik*, and *gd Malarsih kt 2 kp mg 4* exists in *sléndro manyurå* and *pélog barang*, but the latter version is also called *gd Prawan pupur*.

It is possible that some *sléndro–pélog* conversions actually occurred in the opposite direction.

Editable forms

Overview

This heading covers a family of *bentuk* that are used extensively in the accompaniment for *wayang* and, to a lesser extent, dance. They are also played in other contexts. They share one particular feature: they have relatively short *gongan* providing several standard exit points in the piece. During *wayang* or dance they can therefore be brought to an end within a few seconds on a signal from the *dhalang* or dance-master/-mistress, who can thus make the accompaniment follow the action closely. The players can hear the signal directly, but it is also delivered in more explicit form by the *kendhang*.

Collectively these *bentuk* are known by the Yogyanese as *gendhing lampah*; the Solonese seem to have no corresponding collective name for them. They have also been described as 'free structures' in contrast to the other *bentuk*.[92] Here they are called the editable forms because of their most important characteristic. There are in fact two possible levels of editing. Normally the *gongan* are left intact, and editing means deciding which exit to take. Occasionally in dance, the *gongan* themselves are shortened, again on signals from the *kendhang*.

Standard pieces in these forms now exist for each *laras–pathet* combination, e.g. *Sampak manyurå*, except possibly in the case of the *kemudå* form. In addition there are named pieces written in the same forms, e.g. *Srepegan Sri martånå*, *Ayak-ayakan Panjang mas*.

All these forms can be performed without vocal parts. *Sampak* is a purely instrumental form, but the other forms can have *sindhènan*, and some pieces in these forms should be considered as basically vocal, e.g. *Ayak-ayakan Pamungkas*, with its mixed chorus, or *lagu dolanan* written in *srepegan* form, such as *Ménthog-ménthog*.[93]

These pieces are drummed on the *kendhang wayangan* in a *wayang* context, and otherwise on the *ciblon*. The use of a *bukå kendhang* is another common feature.

These *bentuk* are also irregular in the sense of having *gongan* of different lengths. They are clearly related in structure: a ratio of one *kempul* stroke, or a substitute gong stroke, per two *kenong* strokes applies throughout the family. *Kethuk* density varies, but some sources show no *kethuk* strokes in the *sampak* and *kemudå* forms. The *kempyang* is not used at all. More generally, these forms have the densest colotomic structures of any *bentuk*.

92 Vetter (1977).

93 For at least part of the piece: *Ménthog-ménthog* is in *ketawang* form according to some sources.

However, there is a certain amount of confusion about the precise differences within the family. One reason for the lack of clarity is inconsistency in notation. Summaries that define each of the forms by the number of *balungan* beats per *kempul* stroke are unhelpful, because they pose the question of what is a *balungan* beat in each case. Confusion also arises because of differences between Solo and Yogya, and even within the Yogya tradition, over the naming of the various *bentuk*.

Table 2.18 presents a summary of the family, showing the basic structural cells out of which the overall *bentuk* are formed. The use of *pin* within the cells follows the way that these *bentuk* are most often notated, but other notation variants will be found. For example, *srepegan* (in the Solonese sense) are commonly notated as *balungan mlaku*, but the similarities with (16-beat) *lancaran* are more obvious if the *balungan* is written in *nibani* form, and this is sometimes done.

The number of cells per *gongan* varies even between the *gongan* of one *bentuk*, as well as between *pathet*. The end of the *gongan* is marked by a *gong suwukan* stroke that replaces the *kempul* stroke. In *sléndro manyurå* the *ayak-ayakan* in *talu* differs in that every cell ends with a *gong suwukan* stroke.

Table 2.18
Structures and nomenclature of editable forms

Structure (not to constant timescale)	Name	
	Solo	Yogya
. 3 . (2)	*ayak-ayakan* (*ir I*, *sl m* in *talu*)	—
. 3 . 2	*ayak-ayakan* (*ir I*, otherwise)	—
3 2 3 (5) 3 1 2 . 6 1 2 (3)	*ayak-ayakan* (*ir II/III*, *sl m* in *talu*)	—
. 3 . 2 . 3 . 5 3 2 3 5 6 5 3 5 6 1 5 6	*ayak-ayakan* (*ir II/III*, otherwise)	*ayak-ayakan* (all *pathet*)
4 2 4 5	*kemudå/kumudå* (*ir I*)	—
4 2 4 5 4 2 4 5	*kemudå/kumudå* (*ir II*)	—
. 6 . 5 . 3 . 2	—	*srepeg(an)/slepeg(an)*
6 5 3 2	*srepeg(an)/slepeg(an)*	(A) *playon/plajaran* (B) *sampak*
2 2 2 2	*sampak*	(A) *sampak* (B) *sampak gårå-gårå*

If the relatively uncommon *kemudå* form and the Yogya version of *srepegan* are ignored, the table shows three levels of density in terms of colotomic structure. Starting from the least dense, the corresponding Solonese names are *ayak-ayakan*, *srepegan* (or occasionally *slepegan*) and *sampak*.

In the Yogya tradition there is no doubt that *ayak-ayakan* is again the least dense form. In the most extreme Yogyanese view, the next step up is known as *playon/plajaran*, and *srepegan* or *slepegan* is only a transitional passage joining *ayak-ayakan* to *playon*. If the term *playon* or *plajaran* is used (version A in the table), the densest form is again called *sampak*. Other sources (version B) use the term *sampak* for the middle-density form, and then the densest is called *sampak gårå-gårå*.

Each of the editable forms may be performed by itself, but they are also played in suites, usually starting with a less dense form and proceeding to a denser one—although sequences can move in either direction. Any of the forms can also be attached to pieces in other *bentuk*; again the editable form typically follows a form with a less dense colotomic structure. A *srepegan* is often played by way of introduction to a *palaran*, and the two forms may alternate. If an editable form is not followed by a piece in another *bentuk*, it finishes with a special *suwuk* passage, usually short, that is added after the chosen final *gongan* to supply the necessary *ulihan*.

A state diagram for transitions between *ayak-ayakan*, *srepegan* and *sampak* is shown as Fig. 2.16.

Ayak-ayak(an)

Besides the confusion already mentioned, yet more arises in the case of the Solonese *ayak-akayan* because its colotomic structure changes with *irâmå* and because the density of the *balungan* in relation to the structure can vary too.

The default *ayak-akayan* for *sléndro manyurå* begins as shown in Fig. 2.25. The initial *irâmå* is *irâmå lancar*, but the tempo slows down almost at once, and *ir I* is reached by the end of the gong 1. Here the colotomic structure changes from one to two *kethuk* strokes per *kenong*. In the next line, the speed falls further, and the last *gåtrå* of the line can be played in *ir II*. After the asterisk the same tempo is maintained until a speed-up that precedes a *suwuk* or a transition to another piece. The description above is what actually happens, but notation sources often label everything from the first gong 1 onwards as being in *ir II*. Depending on context, the tempo may never fall far enough to reach *ir II*.

The well-known closing piece *Ayak-ayakan Pamungkas* in the same *pathet* proceeds in the same way as far as the asterisk. Then the loud-style *balungan* instruments and the *bonang* drop out and the chorus begins. From the doubled timescale of the colotomic structure during the choral section, the theoretically correct interpretation is that the piece now has a double-density *balungan*, played in *ir III*. Nevertheless, notation sources usually describe this section too as being in *ir II*.

Ayak-ayakan that are basically vocal, such as *Pamungkas* and other closing pieces (*Kaloran* and *Umbul dongå*), are played straight through. Vocal *ayak-ayakan* with *sindhènan* can have *andhegan*.

The standard *ayak-ayakan* contain a section that can be cycled; as notated here, it starts at the second full line. Sometimes, as in this case, there is a *lik* section that can be repeated within the overall cycle.

Omitting the *kethuk* strokes after the second full line, *Ayak-ayakan sléndro manyurå* is

(2)
. 3 . (2) . 3 . (2) . 5 . (3) . 2 . (1)
[2 3 2 (1) 2 3 2 (1) 3 5 3 (2)†
3 5 3(2) 5 3 5(6)† 5 3 5(6) 5 3 5(6) to *lik*
5 3 2(3) 6 5 3(2)† → *srepegan*
3 5 3(2) 3 5 3(2) 5 6 5(3) 2 3 2(1)§]

lik 3 5 6(1)
[2 3 2(1) 3 5 3(2) 5 3 5(6)
5 3 5(6) 5 3 5(6) 3 5 6(1)] 6 5 3(2) → # or *srepegan*

with exits possible at the end of any line, using one of two *suwuk* patterns, according to the gong note:

§2 3 2(1) 3 2 1(6) after gong 1
†1 1 2(1) 3 2 1(6) after other gong notes

There are two possible exits leading to the *srepegan*, according to whether the *lik* is played. Instead of 6 5 3 2, the final *gåtrå* before the *srepegan* may be played as . 3 . 2, which has the same density as the opening of the *srepegan*, i.e. on a constant timescale and in the usual notation:

ay²an	. 3 . 2
srep	3 2 3 2 5 3 5 3 2 3 2 1

Some minor variations of this piece occur, e.g. 5 3 2 1 instead of 3 5 6 1 to begin the *lik* section.

In *Ayak-ayakan Pamungkas* the final gong 2 of the vocal section is followed by a return to the beginning of the piece, at the original tempo and with the same *iråmå* changes, and then at the asterisk (Fig. 2.25) the appropriate *suwuk* pattern is added to close the piece in *ir II*.

The structures of *ayak-ayakan* in the other *laras–pathet* combinations are somewhat easier to read, because most *gåtrå* end with a *kempul* stroke, not a gong. *Ayak-ayakan* use all the soft instruments. The *bonang* play *gembyangan* in *iråmå lancar*, typically with Solo-style *nduduk* patterns and an initial lead-in,

ciblon	b . b . b
balungan	(2)
bonang barung	6 1 . 2 / 2

and *mipil* in *ir I* and *ir II*, although with *gembyangan*, *kempyungan* and *nibani* patterns for various *gåtrå*. In *ir III*, *bonang imbal* is used.

Kenong notes must be considered in pairs. The first of the pair agrees with the second, which may or may not coincide with the note in the *balungan*, for the usual reasons (see Part 3). These principles apply equally when the *balungan* is double-density, as in *Pamungkas*: therefore *kenong* 3 would be played for both the *pin* and the final 3 in 3 1 2 . 6 1 2 3. *Kempul* notes too may disagree with the *balungan* for the usual reasons (see Part 3). In the case of *sléndro manyurå*, where the *kempul* are replaced by

Ayak-ayakan sléndro manyurå (Solo)

balungan
(2)
. 3 . (2) . 3 . (2) . 5 . (3) . 2 . (1)
2 3 2 (1) 2 3 2 (1) 3 5 3 (2) *
3 5 3 (2) 5 3 5 (6)

Ayak-ayakan Pamungkas sl m continues after *:

balungan	3 1 2 . 6 1 2 (3)
vokal	. . 3 1 . 2 2 . . . . 6 1 . 2 2 1 3 3
cakepan	*Dhuh Al- lah mu-gi- mu- gi*

2.25 *Ayak-ayakan* structures and *iråmå* changes, shown on a constant timescale

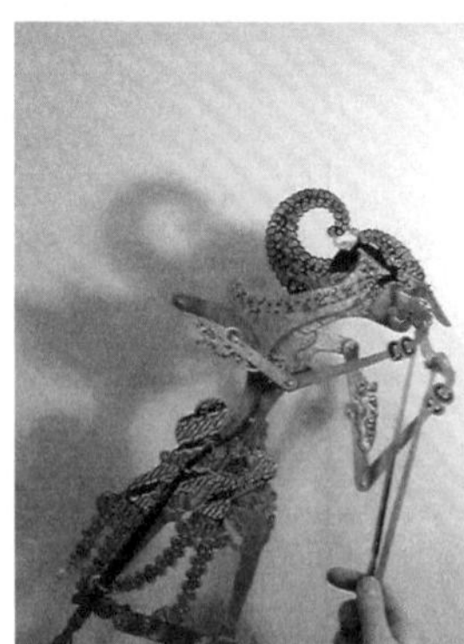

the *gong suwukan*, disagreements are more likely because fewer notes are available from the *gong suwukan*. The final gong stroke may be supplied by the *gong ageng*.

Entry to the *lik* section is signalled by the *rebab*.

Compared with the other editable forms, relatively little editing of *ayak-ayakan* occurs in practice, presumably because in *wayang* contexts they do not accompany fast-moving action.

Kemudå

Sources disagree over the *kemudå* form. There is no doubt that it exists in *pélog limå* and *pélog nem*, and these are probably the best-known versions. Some sources recognise only these versions, while others accept that *kemudå* exists in *pélog barang* and even in *sléndro*. As the structure matches that of one *ayak-ayakan* variant, it is no surprise that the description *ayak-ayakan kemudå* is also found.

One source gives notation for *ayak-ayakan Rangu-rangu pl 7* and again for part of the same piece under the names *srepegan kemudå pl 7* and *srepegan Rangu-rangu pl 7*. The difference in structure between *ayak-ayakan* and *srepegan* would only lie in the ratio of *kethuk* strokes to *kenong* strokes. There are certainly two distinct forms of *kemudå* (Table 2.18); these can be analysed as, in one case, *balungan mlaku* played in *ir I* and, in the other case, double-density *balungan* played in *ir II*.

From all this evidence it remains unclear whether *kemudå* is truly an independent *bentuk*, or simply a label that is attached to a certain small group of pieces that could also be placed in one or more other categories.

Generalisations about the *kemudå* form are dangerous, but *sindhènan* is normally used, and other *garap* can be taken from that of *srepegan* and *ayak-ayakan*.

At least one *langgam*, *Åjå lamis pl 6*, is set in *kemudå* form.[94] This piece has *balungan mlaku* played in *ir III*, with *bonang imbal*.

Srepeg(an)/slepegan, Solo style

The smallest unit of structure in *srepegan* is a four-note cell, commonly called a *gåtrå* as usual.[95] Anything from two to about six *gåtrå* make up a *gongan*. The *srepegan* as a whole consists of a small number of *gongan*, often with an identifiable *lik* section that is played only once or not at all. The *rebab* signals entry to the *lik* section.

The *suwuk* pattern, which is two *gåtrå* in length, may serve all the *gongan*. Alternatively, depending on the *laras* and *pathet*, there may be different patterns for different *gongan*. *Suwuk* patterns can vary from one group to another, so that it is advisable for players to listen to the practice in each group, e.g. to avoid playing 3532 when the rest of the *balungan* players are playing 3632.

A *gåtrå* often has the form *abab* or, especially at the end of a *gongan*, *abcb*. The whole of *srepegan sl 6* is:

```
                       (5)
      [ [  6565  235(3)†
           5353  5235  1̇653  653(2)¶
           3232  356(5)§ ]
lik        2̇1̇2̇1̇  3̇2̇1̇2̇  561̇(6)
           1̇61̇6  2̇3̇2̇1̇  3̇2̇65  323(5) ]
suwuk      †5353  653(2) or ¶3232  363(2)
           or §3235  653(2)
```

94 Another source makes it a *lancaran*.

95 The four-note cell is sometimes notated as two *gåtrå*, which can make the relationship with other *bentuk* clearer.

Gårå-gårå introduction (Yogya)

The opening sequence in *sléndro sångå*

ayak-ayakan

```
                         ...1   ...1   ...(1)
.2.1   .2.1   .2.1   .2.1   ..1.   1121
22.3   123(2) 35.2   356(5) 66.1̇   561̇(6)
1̇61̇.   1̇656   5323   1232   35.2   3565
1̇623   561̇6   1̇623   561̇5   61̇52   532(1)
```

srepegan

```
                     2121   2121   .1.1(1)
2312   356(5) 2356   1̇656   5323   123(2)
3565   3565   6561̇   6561̇   5652   321(6)
1̇51̇6   1̇51̇6   .2.3   .5.3   .2.1   .2.(1)
```

playon

```
                   [ 2121   356(5)
3565   3212   356(5) 3565   612(1)
2132   561̇(6) 561̇6   2353   212(1) ]
```

sampak

```
            [ 2121   356(5) 6565   253(2)
3232   356(5) 6565   232(1) 2121   561̇(6)
1̇61̇6   253(2) 3232   532(1) ]
```

suwuk (from 1) xx 623(5)
(otherwise) xx 356(5)

N.B. As usual in Yogya notation, register dots except for 1̇ are not shown.

Essentially only one *iråmå* is used in *srepegan*, but the tempo can vary over a range. On the same timescale, two *kenongan* of a *lancaran* played in *iråmå lancar* equate to a single four-note cell of the *srepegan*:

lancaran	. 3 . 5 . 6 . 5 . 6 . 5 . 1̇ . (6)
srepegan	3 2 3 2

This may mean that the *srepegan* is in *ir I*, but the question is not very important, and is usually ignored.

The soft instruments and *sindhènan* are used in *srepegan*. The *bonang* may play *imbal* from the start (especially for *wayang*); alternatively they may start by playing *gembyangan cegat* to the *sèlèh* note of the *gåtrå*, later changing to *imbal* at a point chosen by the *bonang barung* player. The *imbal* is followed by a full *sekaran* during the last *gåtrå* of each *gongan*. A pair of *saron* (or a single *saron* with two players) may play *imbal* or *kinthilan*, or one *saron* may play *nyacah* while others continue playing *mbalung* An even stranger combination—a *kinthilan* part on one *saron* and the usual *imbal* part on the other—is also possible. The *peking* may play *nyacah* of its own.

The *kenong* note used throughout the *gåtrå* depends on the *sèlèh* note, subject to the usual rules for the choice of notes (see Part 3). The *kempul* notes too are determined by the *sèlèh* note, but are chosen more freely than in the fixed *bentuk*: notes 3 and 2̇, if available, may be used. In addition, the *kempul* notes may be chosen to indicate high register or a transition to high register.

The *kendhang* may signal a *sirep*, during which the same *garap* continues, and subsequently signal an *udhar*. A specific drum signal causes a *seseg*, during which the *garap* is different: the soft instruments normally drop out, and the *bonang* play *gembyangan cegat*. *Saron imbal* or *kinthilan* is replaced by *mbalung*, but *nyacah* on the *saron* and *peking* may continue. As so often, faster also means louder.

During the *seseg*, *kendhang* signals may take a *srepegan* in any of several directions: to the initial tempo and *garap*, or to another piece—the corresponding *sampak* or *ayak-ayakan*, or a different form such as a *palaran*—or to the *suwuk*. If the *suwuk* is signalled, in the final *gåtrå* of the *gongan*, the first *gåtrå* of the new *gongan* is played, then the appropriate four-beat *suwuk* pattern. There is little or no slow-down at the *suwuk*, and the melody instruments play their last notes more or less with the gong.

The *gong ageng* is not used at all in some performances, e.g. in *wayang*. If used, it may replace certain of the *gong suwukan* strokes, such as the first and last strokes, and those at the end of the overall cycle of *gongan* or the end of the *lik*.[96]

Srepeg(an)/slepeg(an), Yogya style

A Yogya-style *srepegan* is illustrated (opposite) as part of the opening sequence of the *gårå-gårå* in *sl 9*. After the slow-down at the end of the *ayak-ayakan*, the *srepegan* starts at twice the speed, i.e. 2121 takes as long as 21 in the *ayak-ayakan*, and is played without any repeats. At the end of the *srepegan* there is a speed-up, and the *playon* starts at half the speed, i.e. 21 takes as long as . 2 . 1 in the *srepegan*.

The *garap* for the *srepegan* is much the same as for the *ayak-ayakan*. On the *bonang*, besides *mipil* and some stretches of *gembyangan*, one or two *gåtrå* may be played *mbalung*.

The corresponding sequence at the start of *pathet nem* is more complicated, but again involves *srepegan* as a transition passage between *ayak-ayakan* and *playon*.

From its name, *Srepegan Mataram* ought to be a Yogya-style piece, but the Solonese play it too; in structure it is a Solonese *srepegan* (like several others used by the Yogyanese), but its *garap* is in Yogya style.

Playon/plajaran

As can be seen from the display box, the general form of the *playon* is similar to that of a Solonese *srepegan*. *Garap* too is similar, although the *bonang* can play *mipil*, including characteristic Yogya-style details such as *gembyangan sarug* and a *nguthik* pattern for 2353 2121 (= *puthut gelut*). They play *gembyangan cegat* during the *seseg*.

The speed change from the *playon* to the *sampak* is the same as the change from Solonese *srepegan* to *sampak*.

Sampak, Solo style

In the Solonese type of *sampak*, each *gåtrå* of *balungan* consists of the same note played four times (see display box overleaf). When entered from the *srepegan* (from gong 6), the *sampak* represents a halving of speed, i.e. 66 in the *sampak* lasts as long as 561̇6 at the end of the *srepegan*. This means that the time density of the *kenong* and *kempul* strokes stays the same through the transition.

The eight *kenong* notes and four *kempul* notes per *gåtrå* are determined by the rules used for *srepegan*. The

96 In some performances of *srepegan manyurå* as part of *talu*, the *kempul* is replaced by *gong suwukan* at the end of each *gåtrå*, as in *ayak-ayakan manyurå*.

gong ageng is unlikely to replace the *gong suwukan* except on the last stroke.

There is a standard *garap* for the *slenthem*, which plays the note above the *balungan* note, on the preceding half-beat. The pattern may be modified in the last *gåtrå* of the *gongan*, to make a smoother contour, as illustrated for the second *gongan* here:

slenthem

	3 . 3 . 3 . 3 .	5 . 5 . 5 . 5 .	2 . 2 . 2 . 2 .

balungan (and *demung*)

	2 2 2 2	3 3 3 3	1 1 1 (1)
sl	2 . 2 . 2 . 2 .	3 . 3 . 3 . 3 .	5 . 1̇ . 1̇ . 1̇ .
bal	1 1 1 1	2 2 2 2	6 6 6 (6)
sl	1̇ . 1̇ . 1̇ . 1̇ .	5 . 5 . 5 . 5 .	3 . 3 . 3 . 3 .
bal	6 6 6 6	3 3 3 3	2 2 2 (2)

The *peking* and a *saron* may play independent *nyacah*. Alternatively the *peking* may play the combined *slenthem* and *demung* parts. The *bonang* play *gembyangan cegat* to the *sèlèh* notes. The *gendèr* and *gambang* may play until the *seseg*.

For the standard *sampak pl 7* a *saron* counter-melody exists:

balungan

2 2 2 2	3 3 3 3	7 7 7 (7)
7 7 7 7	2 2 2 2	6 6 6 (6)
6 6 6 6	3 3 3 3	2 2 2 (2)

saron

24 .4 34 2	5 6 5 3	6 53 56 7
.3 56 7 .3	56 76 53 2	5 6 7 6
57 .6 .5 6	57 .6 .5 3	56 76 53 2

with corresponding *suwuk* patterns:

from 7: .3 56 53 2
from 6: 56 76 53 2

The *kendhang* can signal a *seseg*, but the *garap* changes less than for the *seseg* in *srepegan*. From the *seseg*, a *suwuk* or a transition to another piece—the corresponding *srepegan* or *ayak-ayakan* or another *bentuk*—may occur. The regular *suwuk* for *sampak* is similar in principle to that of *srepegan*, but on a shorter timescale. On receipt of the *suwuk* signal in the last *gongan*, the *balungan* players play the first two notes of the next *gongan*, then play the *suwuk* note twice—the note 2 for *sl m* and *pl 7*. There is also a special extended *suwuk* from the gong 6 of *sampak sl m*, used to close the *talu* in *wayang*:

666(6) 6666 etc. .2.(2)

although the notes actually played at the end, after a signal on the *kendhang*, will probably be . 5 3(2). This treatment is described as *nitir*. With the standard *suwuk* there is, as in *srepegan*, little or no slow-down. The *nitir* type of *suwuk* is likely to slow down more.

For each *laras–pathet* combination the material of the *ayak-ayakan*, *srepegan* and *sampak* is related. The similarity is most obvious in the case of the *srepegan* and *sampak* in *sléndro manyurå* (below), where the number of *gåtrå* per *gongan* is the same and the *sèlèh* notes match.

Sampak, Yogya style

Sampak of the Solonese type are played in Yogya under the names *sampak* or *sampak gårå-gårå*. The more Yogyanese type of *sampak* can resemble the *playon* in all but its punctuation, with *gåtrå* of the same shape. The *bonang* may play *imbal* until the *seseg*.

Other instrumental forms

Pathet(an)

The *pathetan* is one of the most technically interesting forms within *karawitan*. It consists of phrases highly characteristic of a *pathet*—whence the use of *pathetan* to establish the *pathet* at the start of each act in *wayang*, among other places. The instruments used are mainly the soft-style decorating instruments: *balungan* and *kendhangan* are absent, and punctuating instruments—even the gong—are rarely used.

This is not strictly an instrumental form, because *pathetan* have vocal parts that are sung by the *dhalang* when the form is used as a *sulukan* in *wayang* (see below). However, the vocal parts are absent when a *pathetan* is

Relationship of *srepegan* and *sampak*

srepegan sl m			*sampak sl m*		
		(2)			(2)
3232	5353	232(1)	2222	3333	111(1)
2121	3232	561̇(6)	1111	2222	666(6)
1̇61̇6	5353	653(2)	6666	3333	222(2)

performed as a prelude and/or postlude to a *gendhing*. All the parts follow each other in conventional ways, but do not precisely coincide in time, so that the *sèlèh* principle is less obvious than usual.

Irregular forms

A number of well-established pieces in additional, irregular forms can be heard, but by their nature they do not lend themselves to generalisations. Most are vocal in nature, and are dealt with under the **Vocal forms** heading. Another, used as a *selingan* in certain pieces, is *Kébar Sumedhangan* (essentially in *kt 2 kp* form): see Part 4.

Ceremonial forms

In the repertoire for the various ceremonial gamelan, pieces are mainly in short forms that are unique to the gamelan, resembling most closely those of *lancaran* and *ketawang*. The *gamelan cåråbalèn* repertoire includes pieces called *ladrang*, but, as with all the ceremonial gamelan and their repertoire, the punctuating instruments are not those of regular gamelan—*penonthong*, *kenong* and *gong ageng*, sometimes *kecèr* and *kempul*, but no *kethuk* or *kempyang*. The adoption of the *gangsaran* into the regular repertoire has already been mentioned.

The major exception is the repertoire of the *gamelan sekatèn*, which includes *ladrang* and the *inggah* of *gendhing*, all drawn from the regular stock of gamelan pieces, although performed with different *garap*.

Vocal forms

Various *bentuk* that can be considered as primarily vocal have been mentioned already. In the forms described under this heading, the structure is more clearly the combination of voice plus accompaniment.

In terms of either syllables per second or notes sung per syllable of text, vocal lines move most quickly in *ir I* or *ir lancar*, as illustrated by example (a) in Fig. 2.26. Texts are sung more slowly in *ir II*, especially in the *bedhayan* style. Example (c) includes the standard introductory phrase '*andhé babo*', sung extremely slowly, but the next syllables too are sung slowly, at the rate of only two per *gåtrå*. Example (d), in the usual free rhythm of *sindhènan*, is included for comparison; a *céngkok* suitable for the *gåtrå* . 1̇ 6 5 in the *balungan*, as found at the end of the second line of example (c).

Tembang/sekar

The words and melodies of many of these vocal forms derive from classical Javanese verse. The collective name for the verse forms is *tembang* [*ng*] or *sekar* [*kr*]. Since verse was traditionally sung (unaccompanied) rather than recited, *tembang* or *sekar* is also synonymous with song. Javanese literature has a long and distinguished history, and *sekar* are treated very seriously.

Sekar/tembang metres fall into groups according to their size, from the shortest (*sekar alit/tembang cilik* or

(a) *Lagu dolanan* (*ir I*) . . . . / 6 1̇ . 6 5 / . 2̇ 1̇ . 5 2 / . 5 3 . 2 1
Lum- bung dé- så prå ta- ni på- dhå ma- ka- ryå

(b) *Gérongan* (*ir II*) . . 2̇ 2̇ 2̇ 3̇ 1̇ / . 6 1̇ 2̇ . 1̇ 6 1̇ 6 5 5
Na- li- ka- ni- rå ing da- lu

(c) *Bedhayan* chorus (*ir II*) / . . . 1̇ 1̇
An- dhé
. . 2̇ . 3̇ 2̇ / . 3̇ 1̇ 2̇ 1̇ 6 5
ba- bo
. . 1̇ 2̇ 1̇ 6 / . 6 5 . 6 6
Jang- krik gu- nung

(d) *Sindhènan srambahan* (*ir II*) / 1̇ 1̇ 2̇ 1̇ 6 5 6 6 . 5 4 5 5
ka- lå- på kang maksih mu- dhå

2.26 Examples of singing styles, shown on a constant timescale (with solidus marking *gåtrå* boundary)

mâcâpat) through *sekar tengahan/tembang tengahan* to the largest (*sekar ageng/tembang gedhé*). The structures of the *mâcâpat* metres and some of the *sekar tengahan* and *sekar ageng* metres are described in Appendix 1.

Sekar make a huge contribution to *karawitan*:

- as the origin of instrumental compositions such as *ldr Pangkur*,[97]
- sung as *bâwâ* before *gendhing* or *ladrang*,
- as texts for *palaran/rambangan*,
- as *gérongan* texts in many *bentuk*,
- as *sindhènan* texts in some pieces, in place of *sindhènan srambahan*,
- as texts for *pesindhèn* to sing as extended *andhegan*,
- as texts for *bedhayan* chorus in some pieces,
- as *sulukan* in *wayang*,
- as the main source of the texts sung in popular drama forms (*kethoprak*, *ludruk*) and certain dance-dramas such as *Langendriyâ*.

Fig. 2.27 illustrates the basic version of a *mâcâpat* melody (the first four of the nine lines (*gâtrâ*) of a stanza in *Sinom* metre), plus a more decorated form in which it might be heard in a *bâwâ* or *palaran*. The typical structure of a line is a relatively plain start, often based around a single 'reciting' note (*râtâ*), perhaps preceded by a lead-in (*angkatan*), but followed by a more florid cadence (*sèlèhan*). The melody is in practice subject to considerable variation, as can be seen from three versions of the first line of *sekar ageng Citrâmengeng sl 9*:

2̇3̇ 1̇2̇ 6 1̇653 356 6.1̇.5.6.1̇.2̇
2̇.3̇2̇.1̇ 1̇ . 5 3.2 . 3 5.6.061̇2̇.3̇2̇
2̇.3̇2̇ 1̇.2̇ 6 1̇ 5 2.356.1̇2̇1̇.65.6532
Ri- *sang* *mâ-* *hâ-* *yek-* *ti*

In these examples, the initial notes are the same, and each syllable of the text usually passes through the same notes. The *sèlèh* note too is usually the same. Therefore the contours are essentially the same in each case. (The third example is unusual in finishing an octave lower than the first two.) It seems likely that the differences between these variants are simply the result of particular vocal ornaments (see Part 3), including the very long melisma that ends the third example, becoming frozen into the notation. Vocal ornaments additional to the notes shown are to be expected in performance.

In many of the forms that use these *sekar* texts, the words are sung in free rhythm, but the *pin* in the notation suggest which notes are held longer than others. Also in many such situations, in contrast to a *mâcâpatan* or *kidungan*, the singer benefits from the presence of a *gendèr* to keep him/her in tune by signalling at least the first two or three notes of each line.

The content of these verses is not necessarily ancient. Some of the texts inhabit the same world as the *lakon* of *wayang*. For example, the *Nalikanirâ* text (also called *Kinanthi Semèdi*) relates to the *Ramayana*: the 'great man' (*wong agung*) is Râmâ, here meditating (*semèdi*) amid the monkey army (*bâlâ wanârâ*).

Parabé Sang is an example of a riddle (*wangsalan*), once more demonstrating the Javanese love of wordplay. In this, Smârâbangun is one of the names of the hero Panji: another is Priyâ Wâdâ, hinting at *priyâ* in the third line. Similarly the reference to a fish (*sepat*) in the second

Basic	Decorated
2̇ 2̇ 2̇ 2̇ 2̇ 2̇ 7 65	2̇ 2̇ 2̇ 2̇ 2̇ 2̇ 3̇2̇7 6.5
2 3 5 5 6 7 5 65	2 35 5 5 53 3567 5 76.56.5
7 6 7 5 3 2 2 32	7 65 3 2 2 2 21 1232
2 2 3 2 7̣ 6̣ 7̣6̣ 5̣	2 2 2 2 3 56 327̣ 6̣.5̣

2.27 Basic and decorated versions of *sekar mâcâpat Sinom Logondhang pl 7* (lines 1–4)

Common texts

Nalikanirâ (Kinanthi)

Nalikanirâ ing dalu,	In the night time
wong agung mangsah semèdi,	the great man was engaged in meditation,
sirep kang bâlâ wanârâ,	the monkey army was silent,
sadâyâ wus sami guling,	all had already fallen asleep,
nadyan ari Sudarsânâ,	even Sudarsânâ's younger brother
wus dangu dènirâ guling.	had been asleep for a long time.

Parabé Sang (Salisir, wangsalan)

Parabé Sang Smârâbangun,	His name is the noble Smârâbangun,
sepat dombâ kali Oyâ,	a great fish in the river Oyo,
âjâ dolan lan wong priyâ,	do not play games with men,
Nggeramèh nora prasâjâ.	discourtesy is not straightforward.
Garwâ Sang Sindurâ Prabu,	The wife of the noble King Sindurâ
wicârâ mâwâ karânâ,	speaks with good cause,
âjâ dolan lan wanitâ,	do not play games with women,
tan nyâtâ asring katarkâ.	untruthfulness is often suspect.

97 Sumarsam (1995), p. 205 foll.

line points to *nggeramèh* in the fourth. *Geramèh* is the common name of several species of edible freshwater fish (in English, usually 'gurami'), but *nggeramèh* means 'discourteous'. Moral messages of this kind are still frequently created in the traditional *sekar* metres.

Palaran/rambangan/uran-uran/janturan

Palaran or *rambangan* (its Yogyanese equivalent) typically involves a solo singer of either sex, or a succession of solo singers (often alternating between male and female), singing *mâcâpat* texts accompanied by a much reduced gamelan, in one of two possible *irâmâ*. Sometimes a chorus replaces the solo singers. For the particular *mâcâpat* metres used, see **Appendix 1**: however, the boundary between *mâcâpat* and *sekar tengahan* is somewhat ill-defined, and some texts usually assigned to the latter category are also used. The alternative name *uran-uran* is found for these forms; even *janturan*, although this term is more associated with narration in *wayang*.

To accommodate the different line lengths of the metres, a colotomic 'cell' (*pådå*) is repeated as often as necessary until the end of the line is reached. The cell is related to those of the editable forms—specifically that of a Solo-style *srepegan*:

\+ ^ + ×
. . . .

and in the last cell of the line the *kempul* is sometimes —i.e. at major divisions of the structure—replaced by the *gong suwukan*. 'Line' here corresponds to *gåtrå* as used in the context of *sekar* metres (see **Appendix 1**). The faster *irâmâ* used is described as *irâmâ seseg* or *irâmâ lancar*. The slower may be described as *irâmâ tanggung* or *irâmâ rangkep*, but is effectively *irâmâ lancar rangkep*.

The 'structure' lines in the three examples of Fig. 2.28 show how the *sèlèh* notes, on which the *kenong* and *kempul* notes are based, change during the first line (*gåtrå*, *baris*) of *palaran Pangkur Paripurnå sl 9* in both *irâmâ*. Although these are certainly *sèlèh* notes, they do not always coincide with the notes at the end of the vocal phrases, i.e. at the end of the *baris* or at each *pedhotan* (see **Appendix 1**). The comma in the text line shows the position of the *pedhotan*. The difficulty of remembering or working out these *sèlèh* notes can be judged from the fact that there is often someone in the gamelan signalling numbers to the *kenong* and *kempul* players.

The actual notes played by the *kenong* and *kempul* depend on the usual rules for the *pathet* (see Part 3). The points where the *gong suwukan* replaces the *kempul* are characteristic of the specific *lagu*, not of the basic metre. Thus *Pangkur Paripurnå* has a gong stroke at the end of each of its seven *baris*, whereas *Pangkur Dhudhåkasmaran* has gong strokes in *baris* 2, 3, 5 and 7.

Palaran are usually entered via *srepegan*, sometimes *sampak*. Sequences of *palaran* in different metres, or where *srepegan* alternate with *palaran* in different metres, are common. The *palaran* form has been described as singing texts to a *srepegan*, or alternatively as adjusting a *srepegan* structure to fit a *mâcâpat* text. There is more than one way of fitting the two elements together, as Fig. 2.28 shows: essentially *pådå* are repeated to fit the vocal line—four in the first example, five in the second—implying that the players of the punctuating instruments

Vokal	12 2 2 2 21 1.235. 2 . 3 2 2 . 121 . 6	(*ir lancar*)
Text	*Se- kar pangkur kang wi-, nar- nå*	
Structure	. 2 . 2 . 2 . 2 . 6 . 6 . 6 . (6)	
Vokal	. 1 2 2 2 2 2 1 2 3 . 5 . . 2 2 3 216	(*ir lancar*)
Text	*Se- kar pangkur kang wi-, nar-nå*	
Structure	. 2 . 2 . 2 . 2 . 5 . 5 . 6 . 6 . 6 . (6)	
Vokal	1 2 2 2 2 . 2 1 1. 2 3 5 . 2 . 3 2 2 . 1 2 1 . 6	(*ir rangkep*)
Text	*Se- kar pang-kur kang wi-, nar- nå*	
Structure	. 2 . 2 . 2 . 2 . 6 . 6 . 6 . (6)	

2.28 Examples of vocal lines in *palaran* (*Pangkur Paripurnå, sléndro sångå*), with punctuating instruments shown, on a roughly constant timescale

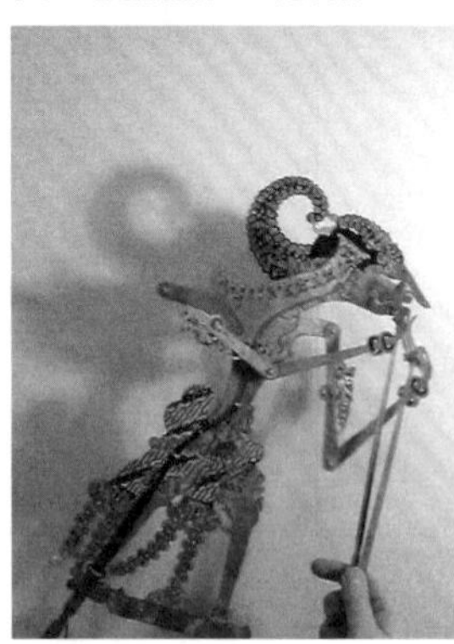

must follow the singer. The *kendhangan* signals when a *kempul* should be replaced by a gong. The second example in Fig. 2.28 inserts a *sèlèh* note 5 in the middle of the *baris* to match the 5 in the vocal line. The third example, like the first, uses four *pådå*, but at a slower tempo.

As indicated by some of the notation, the rhythm of the vocal line is irregular, in much the same way as *sindhènan srambahan* (see Part 3) except that the vocal phrase ends at the gong stroke. The punctuating instruments use regular rhythms, following the *kendhangan*.

The accompaniment consists of *gendèr barung*, *gendèr panerus*, *gambang*, *siter* or *celempung*, *suling*, *keplok*, *kenong*, *kethuk*, *kempul*, *gong suwukan* and *ciblon*, but no *balungan* instruments and no *balungan* line. The *saron* section sometimes plays a pattern (*isèn-isèn balungan*) pointing to an important note at the start of the *palaran*, e.g.[98]

Sèleh note	Patterns (examples)
1	5321
2	.22. 2532
3	.33. 3653; .6.7 .2.3; .3.1 .2.3
5	.55. 51̇65; .5.1 .235; .2.1 .235
6	.5.2 .356; .2.1 .2.6; ?.2.3 .5.6
7	.532 .532 3567; .3.5 .6.7
1̇	.3.5 .6.1̇

These are also possible in the course of a *palaran*, as are additional vocal contributions in the form of both *alok* and *senggakan* (see under **Vocal parts**, p. 230). A *senggakan*, inserted after a gong stroke, usually ends on a note that points to the start of the next line of the *sekar*.

98 *Pathet* is ignored in this listing: not all the phrases shown may be possible in a given *pathet*. These patterns can also be used between sections within a *palaran*.

Andhegan/kèndelan

Andhegan [*ng*] or *kèndelan* [*kr*] are essentially a type of *garap*, but their form deserves mention here.

The simplest *andhegan* consists of a single phrase that the *pesindhèn* chooses from the repertoire of *céngkok srambahan*. It is likely to be one of the more extended and elaborate *céngkok*, e.g. *lampah 8*. Sometimes she sings a whole stanza of *sekar* (typically *måcåpat*). An extended *andhegan* of this kind ends in a metrical phrase, sometimes termed *kusumå*, which leads to the re-entry point (*kenong*, gong, or elsewhere). The *pesindhèn* usually receives the same support from the *gendèr barung* that a male singer receives in a *båwå*.

There are also special long *andhegan*, not conforming to the description above, for certain pieces. A well-known one for *gd Budheng-budheng pl 6* involves the singer switching to speech at one point, after which there is a comic incident. This is an example of an *andhegan gawan*, i.e. an *andhegan* belonging to a specific piece.

Some standard *selingan* bear the name *andhegan*, although they involve the majority of the instrumental players as well as the *pesindhèn*. Examples are to be found in *gd Lobong Kinanthi sl m* (as mentioned above) and *gd Kembang gayam sl m/pl 6*.

Båwå

Texts in any classical metre (**Appendix 1**) may be used as *båwå* before *gendhing*, *langgam* or *ladrang*. Normally this is a solo spot for a male singer, singing strongly in a slow, serious and rhythmically free style. The *gendér barung* may indicate the first notes of each phrase, although some singers do without this support. For some pieces a specific *bawå* with relevant text is normally used, e.g. *bawå S.A. Råråbéntrok* for *gd Gambirsawit*, whereas other *bawå* are used before any pieces in the *pathet* that have the right opening gong note. Some *båwå* include an established *selingan* consisting of a short song (*jineman*) usually sung by all the *pesindhèn*, accompanied by a reduced gamelan—soft-style decorating instruments other than *rebab*, plus punctuating instruments and *kendhang*.

To ensure that the *båwå* ends at the *gong bukå*, the final one or two lines have a regular rhythm—often shown by underlining the text or adding regularly spaced *pin* in the notation. With the *bukå kendhang* and gong note added below, the last two half-lines of *S.A. Citråmengeng sl 9* are

.	.	1	1	5̣	6̣1	12	2
		ka-	*re-*	*nan*	*tyas*	*i-*	*rå*
.	.	6̣1	1	23	2	6̣16̣5̣	
		a-	*lon*	*a-*	*ngan-*	*di-*	*kå*
			b	○	○	○	(5)

or the equivalent of four regular *gåtrå* of *balungan*. It appears that there is no established term for this metrical passage, but it too is sometimes called a *jineman* (cf. under **Sulukan**, p. 95, and **Andhegan**, above). The singer may have to sing up to four notes against one beat of the *kendhangan*, and therefore the end of a *båwå* is usually slower than the end of an instrumental *bukå*. This practice departs from the general pattern for the start of a *gendhing* as described in **Progress of a vocal gendhing**.

The term *båwå suårå* may refer to a short *båwå*, and may be interchangeable with the term *celuk*. Like *båwå sekar*, it appears to be a tautology, since *båwå* normally use *sekar* texts and are always sung.

Sulukan

Sulukan is the collective name for a group of vocal pieces, often translated as 'mood-songs', sung by the *dhalang* during *wayang* performances. They are also (less often) performed as part of some dance suites, where a male singer replaces the *dhalang*. They are accompanied by small groups of soft-style decorating instruments with limited punctuation (Table 2.19). All have the general characteristics of *pathetan* as described under the heading **Other instrumental forms**, p. 90—the freedom of rhythm, and the absence of *balungan* and of the punctuating instruments that have the densest patterns. The texts originate in *sekar*, although some have become corrupted by the passage of time, and no longer make sense.

Pathetan serve to establish the *pathet*, but also to create a calm atmosphere. In *wayang* performances they include *rebab* as well as voice. *Sendhon* represent strong emotion, such as sadness after a death (for which *sendhon Tlutur* is often played). *Ådå-ådå* are short and indicate a tense situation in *wayang*, where *dhodhogan* add to the atmosphere, but are often associated with fight scenes in dance too. The Yogya *kawin* form is somewhat like *ådå-ådå*, but longer, and associated with calmer moods.

Grimingan, being an accompaniment of the *dhalang* on very few instruments—the *gendèr barung* is the only melodic instrument—has some of the characteristics of *sulukan* but is not usually placed in that category.

In some cases the *sulukan* ends with a metrical phrase that leads to the *gong bukå* of a piece, and some soft-style decorating instruments, plus *slenthem* and *kendhang*, join in; again this passage may be called a *jineman*.

Gendhing kemanak

Gendhing kemanak or *gendhing kethuk-kenong* is not a separate *bentuk*: *gendhing ketawang*, *ketawang alit* and *ladrang* can all be placed in this category if they have a vocal line (sung by multiple *pesindhèn* or a *bedhayan* chorus) and use the *kemanak* among the punctuating instruments. These pieces form part of the accompaniment for some *bedhåyå* and *srimpi*. The sole *balungan* instrument, if any, is the *slenthem*.

Jineman

The most frequent usage of the term *jineman*, not to be confused with those found in *båwå* and elsewhere, applies to a repertoire of popular songs in irregular forms, sung by *pesindhèn* with a reduced gamelan. They may be performed by themselves, or attached loosely to other pieces, or in suites such as *jineman Uler kambang – jineman Marikangèn – jineman Mijil*, all in *sl 9*.

Combinations and suites

Some standard ways of combining pieces have been mentioned already; e.g. a *ladrang* and/or a *ketawang* following a *gendhing*, and sequences with *gangsaran* or using *ayak-ayakan*, *srepegan*, *palaran* and *sampak*. Further possible structures are shown in Fig. 3.88. Some standard suites (*talu*) are mentioned under **Wayang kulit**, p. 96. In any sequence, it is normal for all the pieces to be in the same *laras–pathet* combination. If the transition between two pieces is to be seamless, the closing gong note of the first must be the opening gong note of the second, and sometimes the final *gåtrå* of a piece is changed to achieve this.

Non-standard sequences are constructed too, sometimes on the same principles as *talu*, i.e. progressing from less dense to more dense forms. They may also change *pathet* and even *laras*, like *wayang* accompaniments. New compilations of this kind are called *penataan*.

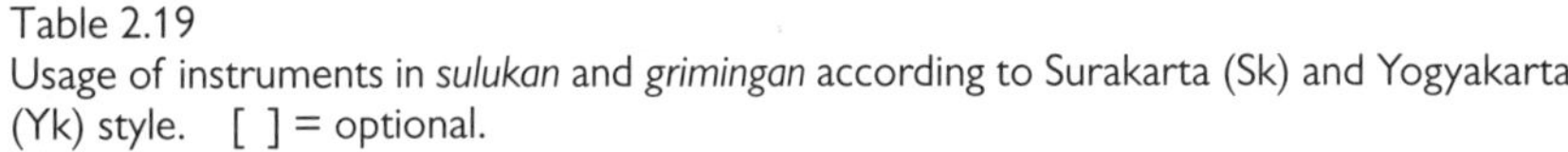

Table 2.19
Usage of instruments in *sulukan* and *grimingan* according to Surakarta (Sk) and Yogyakarta (Yk) style. [ ] = optional.

Instrument	Usage				
	Pathet(an) (Sk), *(le)lagon* (Yk)[a]	*Ådå-ådå*	*Kawin* (Yk only)	*Sendhon*	*Grimingan*
Rebab	Sk, Yk			Yk	
Gendèr barung	Sk, Yk	Sk, Yk	Yk	Sk, Yk	Sk, Yk
Gambang	Sk, Yk			Sk, Yk	
Suling	Sk, Yk			Sk, Yk	
Gong suwukan	Sk, Yk	[Sk], Yk	Yk	Sk, Yk	[Sk]
Kenong	[Sk]	[Sk]		[Sk]	
Kempul	[Sk]	[Sk], Yk	Yk	Sk	[Sk]
Kendhang	[Sk]	[Sk]		[Sk]	[Sk]

a. Also *suluk* (Yk).

Drama and dance

Shadow theatre with flat leather puppets (*wayang kulit*) is the pre-eminent form of theatre in central Java, with the result that other dramatic forms and even dances are always compared with it, and they may borrow some of its elements.

This section provides a very brief introduction to *wayang* and dance, mainly from the player's viewpoint.[99]

Wayang kulit

The general outline of a *wayang* story (*lakon*) is normally as shown opposite, but variations occur: scenes may be added, and even some of the major scenes (*jejer*) may be reduced in length—perhaps to the status of minor scenes (*adegan*)—or deleted altogether. The description here applies mainly to music for *wayang purwå*, i.e. with stories drawn most often from one of the Indian epics (the *Ramayana* or *Mahabharata*). This was traditionally accompanied in *laras sléndro*. Now it is common for pieces in *pélog* to be included, and a few pieces may even switch between *laras* within the melodic line, but *sléndro* is still used most of the time.

The *wayang* falls into three parts played in a rising sequence of *pathet*. These are often called 'acts' in English. A full performance lasts some nine hours, divided only roughly between the *pathet*, starting around 8–9 p.m. The *dhalang* must adjust the timings of the scenes to allow for delays caused by lengthy speeches by and to the sponsors before the performance, and (at the other end) to ensure that he finishes before dawn.[100]

Before the first act, an instrumental *talu* is normally played, although it is sometimes omitted or shortened. In full, its sequence consists of a *gendhing* followed by successively shorter *bentuk*: *ladrang*, *ketawang*, *ayak-ayakan*, *srepegan* and *sampak*. In the Solo tradition, the *talu* is usually in *pathet manyurå*, and one common *talu* consists of *gd Cucur bawuk kt 2 kp mg Paréanom kt 4 – ldr Srikaton – ktw Sukmå ilang – ayak-ayakan – srepegan* (possibly with inserted *palaran*) *– sampak*. The *sampak* has the extended *suwuk* mentioned earlier. These pieces have philosophical significance, and the suite is considered a gift from Ratu Kidul. In the Yogya tradition the *talu* is in *pathet sångå*.

Wayang gedhog, based on stories from the Panji cycle (of Javanese origin), traditionally used a *pélog* accompaniment. A typical *talu* is in *pathet nem*: *gd Gendhiyeng kt 2 kp mg 4 – ldr Sukarsih – ktw Martåpuran – ayak-ayakan kemudå – srepegan pélog nyamat – sampak pélog nyamat*. The final two pieces in *pélog nyamat/manyurå* are notated identically to their *sléndro manyurå* counterparts.

Each act starts with a *pathetan* to establish or confirm the *pathet*. The major scenes begin with a *gendhing*. Much of this is performed in *sirep*—i.e. without loud-style instruments—as background to a narration (*janturan*) by the *dhalang*. For the long narration in the *jejer sapisanan*, the *mérong* of the *gendhing* may be performed in *ir III*. Several *gendhing* are used in this role, depending on the *lakon*, but *gd Karawitan* is the most frequent. When the *dhalang* is about to finish the narration, he signals a transition to *ldr Karawitan*. After this has finished, he starts bringing on the puppets representing the main characters: each is accompanied by a shorter piece reflecting his or her character. For the more *kasar* characters the piece may have *saron imbal* and a *suwuk gropak*.

The *dhalang* advances the action by singing *sulukan* (see **Sulukan** earlier). These may introduce dialogue

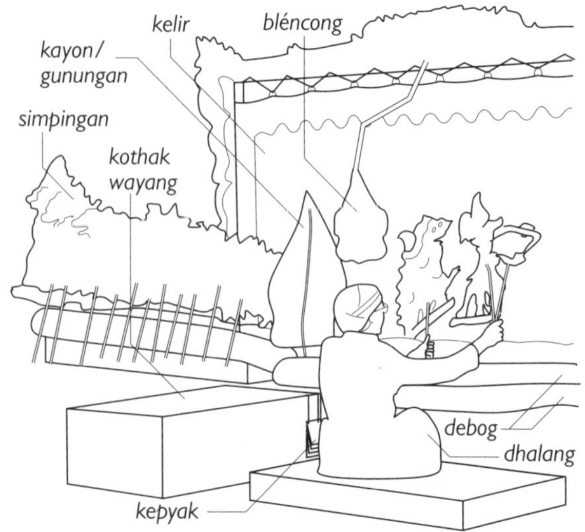

2.29 The *dhalang* in his workplace

99 Numerous books have been published on other aspects of *wayang*, e.g. Keeler (1987 and 1992), Alit Djajasoebrata (1999), Van Ness and Shita Prawirohardjo (1980), Holt (1967). On classical dance, see especially Brakel (1975 and 1995), works cited therein, and other works by the same author.

100 A *dhalang* who gets the timing wrong is described as *kerahinan*, 'caught by the dawn'.

2.30 *Wayang kulit* puppet

(*ginem*) between the characters, or short narrations (*pocapan* or *caritå*, *cariyos*), both of which have a minimal accompaniment in the form of *grimingan* on the *gendèr*.

The other major scenes broadly follow the pattern described for the *jejer sepisanan*. Essentially, the more important scenes imply longer *bentuk*. In specific sections of these scenes, characteristic types of music are used. The *budhalan* is always accompanied by loud, vigorous pieces. The fight sequences are accompanied by *srepegan*, moving to *sampak* for the most intense stages (using Solonese terminology). *Gangsaran* are also used.

Most of these pieces, including the *srepegan*, have vocal parts: *gendhing bonang* are not found. In many performances today, the traditional rules break down during the clown scene within the *gårå-gårå*, and almost anything may be heard. Pieces (including popular songs) may be played at the request of a puppet character or by prior arrangement, and the guest of honour may take a microphone and sing along. The usual *pathet* rules, to say nothing of the progress of the drama, are ignored. *Kraton* performances are more likely to remain 'traditional'.

For many pieces in the accompaniment, the *dhalang* uses verbal cues (*sasmitå*) to indicate which piece he wants,[101] or he may achieve the same result by means of a *bukå celuk*. In pieces with an *ompak–lik* structure, he may need to signal the transition to the *lik*, and will then sing a *kombangan* before the appropriate gong, on the note that the *bonang* would play as *gembyangan* for the same purpose.

An important part of the *dhalang*'s armoury is the wooden *cempålå* (see Table 3.1) which he holds in his left hand and uses to strike the inside of the *kothak wayang* to produce standard signals (*dhodhogan*). He can request *ayak-ayakan*, *srepegan* and *sampak* by *dhodhogan* alone, and the players will respond with the standard piece for the *pathet*. The players therefore have to listen for *dhodhogan* as well as reacting to a range of signals from the *kendhang*. Signals may come via the *kepyak* (Fig. 2.29) instead of the *kothak wayang*. The *dhodhogan* and *kendhangan* signals control other transitions too: to *seseg* sections, in both directions between *srepegan* and *sampak*, into and out of *sirep*, and to the *suwuk*.

Besides the performance practices mentioned above, *wayang* accompaniment has certain other general features. Many pieces are played faster than they would be in a *klenèngan*. Special types of *gendèran* are used in some

Structure of *wayang kulit*

FIRST ACT (*pathet nem*)

- *Jejer sepisanan, jejer parwå* – opening scene, in which the story is introduced; set in the audience hall of the royal palace in the 'home' kingdom
- *Jejer kedhatonan* – set in the inner apartments or the women's quarters (*keputrèn*) of the palace
- *Jejer pasèban njawi* – set outside the palace; includes the assignment of tasks to court officials by the king (*miji punggåwå*), and the departure of the army (*budhalan/jaranan/kapalan* or *jengkar kedhaton*)
- *Adegan perang ampyak* – represents the army battling against all the hostile forces of the forest
- *Jejer sabrangan* – set in the royal palace in the 'foreign' or enemy kingdom; similar to the *jejer sepisanan*, although simpler, but including a *budhalan* for the departure of the foreign army
- *Adegan perang gagal* – an inconclusive clash between the opposing armies

SECOND ACT (*pathet sångå*)

- *Gårå-gårå* – describes a 'disturbance in the realm of nature', paralleling the hero's state of mind; also includes the major appearance of the comic servants (*pånåkawan*), Semar and his adoptive sons Pétruk, Garèng and Bagong
- *Jejer pandhitå, kepandhitan* – the hero seeks enlightenment from a holy man, then sets out on his task (*satriyå lumaksånå*)
- *Perang kembang* – the hero defeats an ogre of the forest (e.g. as in Fig. 2.30)
- *Perang pindho* – an additional battle scene

THIRD ACT (*pathet manyurå*)

- *Jejer manyurå sepisanan* – opening scene
- *Perang tanggung* – the opening (though not conclusive) stage of the closing battle; or the battle may be divided into several shorter scenes
- *Perang amuk-amukan* – the final and more intense stage of the closing battle
- *Tayungan* – the victory dance of the hero (typically Bimå in *Mahabharata* stories, Råmå or Hanuman in *Ramayana* stories)
- *Bojånå åndråwinå* – the feast held by the victors

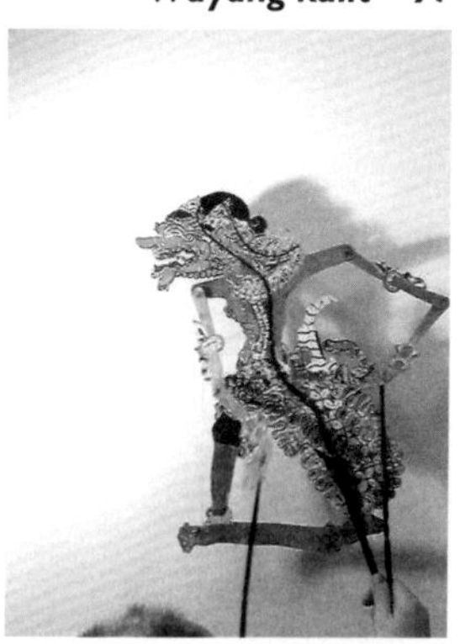

101 Ideally the *sasmitå* are unambiguous, but there are accounts of musicians starting the wrong piece, starting several different pieces, or arguing at length as to which piece the *dhalang* was asking for.

contexts. For some pieces, characteristic *kosèk wayangan* replaces the *kendhangan* that would otherwise be used, e.g. in a *klenèngan*. A wide range of the livelier types of *garap*, such as *saron imbal*, *kinthilan* and *nyacah*, is often heard from the appropriate *balungan* instruments. Individual *dhalang* have their own idiosyncratic performance practices; also favourite compositions, possibly including some specially composed for them.

It is very common for the first act to use pieces that are normally assigned to *pathet manyurå*, e.g. *lnc Béndrong* or *ldr Sigråmangsah*. Otherwise, pieces from the 'correct' *pathet* are used, apart from the exceptional case of the major clown scene. In the Yogya style, some elements at the end of the last act hint at the former existence of a *pathet galong*, higher than *pathet manyurå*.

There are, or have been, many further named styles of *wayang kulit* based on stories from later periods of Indonesian history, extending to the present day: see entries under *wayang* ... in the **Glossary**.

The ensembles used to accompany *wayang kulit* are described on p. 238.

Other forms of drama

Several other forms of *wayang* exist, although they are much less important than *wayang kulit*. Some of them are known to be recent, but there is no certainty about the precise age of the older forms.[102]

These other *wayang* forms again have a *dhalang*. *Wayang golèk*, with three-dimensional wooden puppets (Fig. 2.31), and *wayang klithik*, with flat wooden puppets (Fig. 2.32), are actually more common outside central Java. In *wayang wong* or *wayang orang*, actor-dancers play the same roles as *wayang kulit* puppets but speak and sing too, whereas the *dhalang* supplies the narration and *sulukan*: this form continues to be performed, although with less support than formerly. *Wayang topèng* is another dance-drama form, but with the dancers in masks. *Wayang bèbèr*, in which the *dhalang* delivers the story with the help of a background consisting of a painted scroll that is unrolled during the performance (Fig. 2.33), is thought to be extinct or nearly so.

The 'Ramayana ballet' (Fig. 1.4) is an example of *sendratari*, a modern invention for the tourist trade—essentially *wayang wong* without the narration, which was thought certain to bore *londo* tourists. Other dance-drama forms, *Langendriyå* and *Langen måndrå wanårå*, date from the nineteenth century and are associated with the palaces.

Kethoprak, dating back about 100 years, is the remaining major form of popular drama, not confined to central Java. Originally accompanied by *lesung*-pounding, it has evolved to use a regular gamelan, sometimes with the additional instruments that are now common in *wayang kulit*.

What most of these other forms of drama have in common is a shorter timescale: *kethoprak* can run all night, like traditional *wayang kulit*, but the other forms usually last less than half as long. They still use pieces of the various types mentioned for *wayang kulit*, but not the longer pieces. The same is true when fragments (*pethilan*) of *wayang kulit* are performed.

Classical dances

The general terms for dance are *beksa(n)* [*kr*, *ki*] or *jogèd* [*ng*],[103] and the Indonesian word *tari* is also much used. Dance styles, which are seen in the dance-dramas mentioned above as well as in separate dances, divide broadly into strong male (*gagah*), refined male (*alus*) and female (*putri*) categories, but can be further subdivided. Women regularly dance *alus* roles. Each style is identifiable by a characteristic stance, hand and finger positions, foot positions, and movement styles.[104]

The *bedhåyå* and *srimpi* dances represent the epitome of the *putri* style. They usually take their names from the pieces that accompany them (see box opposite), some of which are *gendhing kemanak*. The *mérong* of the *gendhing* are often played in *ir I*. In addition to the main compositions listed, *ladrang* usually accompany the entry and exit

102 A document dated to 907 AD records the performance of a '*wayang*', but without indicating the nature of the performance. A masked dance form, the predecessor of *wayang wong* and *wayang topèng*, was relatively early.

103 Some sources reserve the term *beksan* for certain categories of dance.

104 For an extensive listing of the movement vocabulary of the Solonese style, see Brakel-Papenhuyzen (1995).

2.31 *Wayang golèk* puppets

2.32 *Wayang klithik* puppets

2.33 *Wayang bèbèr* in Yogyakarta, 1902 (from a photograph believed to be by Kassian Cephas)

of the dancers: however, in the Yogya tradition, suites in *pélog* use the *gati* category instead. The use of trumpets in *gati* may be extended to other parts of the dance accompaniment in Yogya.

Bedhåyå and *srimpi* dances could last well over an hour, but present-day performances are usually much shorter. Other dances are on a lesser timescale, and the accompanying suites are made up of shorter pieces. Some examples of suites for dance accompaniments (*iringan tari*) outside the *bedhåyå* and *srimpi* categories are listed in the display box overleaf: *pathetan*, *ådå-ådå*, other vocal sections and major variations of *garap* peculiar to the suite are not listed.

In the *beksan golèk* subcategory of *putri* dances, a woman is depicted adorning herself. The *bondhan* category, another solo dance, originally represented a mother and her baby. *Gambyong* is a flirtatious dance usually by a solo female dancer.

Although *srimpi* dances are believed to represent battles, the fighting has often become stylised to the point of invisibility. Other types of dance too represent battles. In some that are traditionally danced by men, e.g. *Lawung*

2.34 A *srimpi* rehearsal at SMKI Solo

Bedhåyå and *srimpi* dances

Bedhåyå

Anglirmendhung now danced as *srimpi*
Arjunåwiwåhå *Gd Ranumanggålå pl 6*
Bedhah Mediun
Déwa Ruci
Durådasih *Gd Durådasih*
Éndhol-éndhol *Gd Éndhol-éndhol – ldr Manis – ktw Kaum dhawuk pl 7*
Kabor *Gd Kabor – ldr Gléyong – ktw Sundåwå pl 6*
Ketawang (Solo) related to Bedhåyå Semang
Lahela (Yogya) *Gd Lahela*
Lå-Lå (Solo) *Gd Lå-lå – Gd Gambirsawit – ktw Agung pl 6*
Lambangsari *Gd Lambangsari*
Mangunarjå *Gd Gambirsawit – ldr Utåmå sl 9*
Mantèn
Miyanggong *Gd Miyanggong – ldr Surungdhayung – ktw Sumedhang pl 6*
Pangkur *Gd ktw Pangkur (gd kemanak) – ldr Kembang pépé sl m*
Prabudéwå
Révolusi
Saptå
Sejarah Taman Siswå
Semang (Yogya) related to Bedhåyå Ketawang
Sinom *Gd Sinom – ldr Singå-singå – ldr Sobrang pl 7*
Téjånåtå *Gd Téjånåtå – ldr Sembåwå – ldr Playon pl 5*
Tolu *Gd Tolu – SA Kuswålågitå pl 5*

Srimpi

Anglirmendhung *Gd Anglirmendhung pl 7 (gd kemanak) – ktw Langengitå*
Arjunåmangsah
Gambirsawit *Gd Gambirsawit – ldr Gonjang-ganjing sl 9*
Glondhong Pring *Gd Glondhong pring – ldr Gudhåsih – ktw Sumedhang pl 6*
Irim-irim *Gd Irim-irim – ldr Widanti pl 7*
Lagudhempel *Gd Lagudhempel – ? Mijil dhempel sl 9*
Layu-layu *Gd Layu-layu pl 6*
Lobong *Gd Lobong sl m*
Ludiråmadu *Gd Ludiråmadu – mg Kinanthi – ldr Mijil ludirå pl 7 (gd kemanak)*
Merak Kasimpir
Muncar *Gd Muncar pl 7*
Pandhélori *Gd Pandhélori pl 7*
Renggåwati
Sigråmangsah *Gd Sigråmangsah*
Tamenggitå *Gd Tamenggitå – ldr Winangun pl 7*

ageng (also known as *Trunåjåyå*) and *Båndåyudå*, the fighting is again stylised, and resembles a sort of exercise. This type (*wirèng*), which seems to be represented in carvings at Borobudur, may involve anything from two to sixteen dancers. Another category (*pethilan*) depicts genuine fights such as occur in *wayang*, and is sometimes described as *beksan wayang*. The contest may be between *alus* and *gagah* male characters (e.g. *Sancåyå Kusumåwicitrå*), or in *putri* style, e.g. between two princesses (*Srikandhi Surådewati*).

Male solo dances include the *gandrung* category, representing lovesick heroes, which may also be described as *beksan wayang*. *Gambiranom* and *Gatutkåcå gandrung* are of this type.

The dancers wear masks (*topèng*) in some dances, e.g. *Topèng Klånå*, another *gandrung* dance.

Classical dance is usually accompanied by a *gamelan gedhé* if it is available. Various special features found in *bedhåyå* and *srimpi* accompaniments have been mentioned already, but the accompaniments for the other dance categories show fewer unusual elements.

Other dances

Many other dance forms are found in central Java, some quite local. Any attempt to draw a clear distinction between classical dances and others is a little risky. The *golèk*, *bondhan* and *gambyong* forms are now considered classical dances, but they were originally danced by the disreputable *tlèdhèk*.[105]

105 Brakel-Papenhuyzen (1995).

At the folk dance end of the spectrum are some dances that are performed in trance: traditionally this would have been true of the hobby horse or mask dances known as *kudå képang*, *kudå lumping*, *jathilan* or *ré(y)og*. Other dances (e.g. *slawatan* and related forms) are associated with Islam and/or pre-Islamic religions. There is no standard ensemble or type of accompaniment for these dances, but the ensembles tend to be small and are often itinerant. Among the itinerant groups are some whose instruments—perhaps including small gongs and a *saron*—are hung from a pole carried on the shoulders of two players so that they can be played on the move. The accompaniment may also come from a ghetto blaster rather than a live performing group.

2.35 Dancers from Yogyakarta at the Royal Aquarium, Westminster, in 1882 (after a sketch by Horace Morehen for an unidentified journal: Theatre Museum collection, V&A Images/Victoria and Albert Museum, London)

Examples of dance accompaniments

Båndåyudå *lnc Singånebah – ldr Bimå kurdå – lnc Singånebah pl 7*
Bondhan Sayuk *ayak-ayakan Mangu pl 6 – ldr Énggar-énggar pl 7 – lnc Rambat pl 7*
Gambiranom *lnc Réna-réna – ktw Kinanthi sandhung – srepegan sl 6*
Gambyong Paréanom *ldr Bremårå – kébar Sumedhangan –* (parts of) *gd Gambirsawit pancerånå – kébar Sumedhangan – lnc Sångå pl 6*
Gatutkåcå gandrung *sampak – ktw Kinanthi pawukir – lnc Béndrong – ldr Pucung rubuh – lnc Béndrong – sampak sl m*
Gunungsari *gd Bondhèt – Bondhèt Mataram (as mg) – ldr Bondhèt pl 6*
Menak koncar *ldr Asmarandånå – ldr Asmarandånå as ketawang sl m*
Sancåyå Kusumåwicitrå *ldr Kuwung – srep Rangu-rangu (kemudå) – sampak pl 7*
Sekar pudyastuti *ldr Sri katon Mataram – ldr Mugirahayu sl m*
Srikandhi Surådewati *ldr Sri kuncårå – ktw Kontap – playon – ayak-ayakan – playon pl 6*
Topèng Klånå *lnc Béndrong – gangsaran – ldr Pucung rubuh – lnc Béndrong pl 6*

Review

The preceding pages have described a kind of music that presents a number of problems for a Westerner.

Perhaps the most difficult concept is that of a music that appears to have a 'text'—the *balungan* notation—which however is far from providing all the guidance that the player needs, and must usually be supplemented from other sources. Nor does the part played by any instrument provide the missing information on the 'inner melody' that stands behind the *balungan*. Clearly the music is not unplayable, because the Javanese have managed to keep the tradition alive, and without the help of notation through most of its history. Players in the West

Anatomy of a *gendhing*

gd Pujånggå kt 4 kp mg 8 sl 6

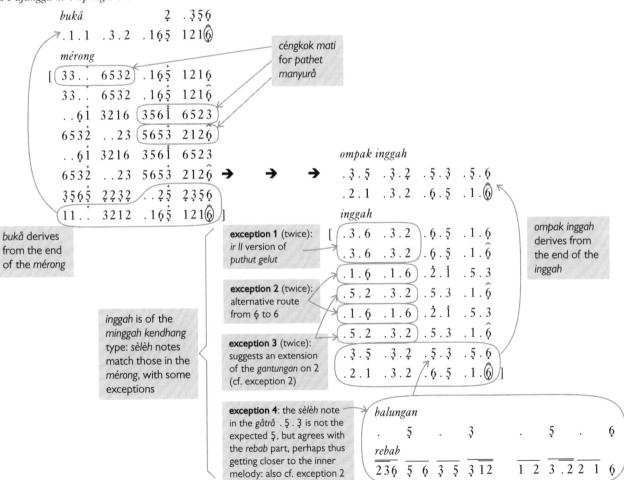

bukå 2̣ .3̣5̣6̣
.1.1 .3.2 .16̣5̣ 1216̣

mérong
[33.. 6532 .16̣5̣ 1216̣
33.. 6532 .16̣5̣ 1216̣
..6̣1̇ 3216 3561̇ 6523
6532̇ ..23 5653̇ 2126̣
..6̣1̇ 3216 3561̇ 6523
6532̇ ..23 5653̇ 2126̣
3̣5̣6̣5̣ 2̣2̣3̣2̣ ..2̣5̣ 2̣3̣5̣6̣
11.. 3212 .16̣5̣ 1216̣]

ompak inggah
.3̣.5̣ .3̣.2̣ .5̣.3̣ .5̣.6̣
.2.1 .3.2 .6̣.5̣ .1.6̣

inggah
[.3.6 .3.2 .6̣.5̣ .1.6̣
.3.6 .3.2 .6̣.5̣ .1.6̣
.1.6̣ .1.6 .2̇.1̇ .5.3
.5.2 .3.2 .5.3 .1.6̣
.1.6̣ .1.6 .2̇.1̇ .5.3
.5.2 .3.2 .5.3 .1.6̣
.3̣.5̣ .3̣.2̣ .5̣.3̣ .5̣.6̣
.2.1 .3.2 .6̣.5̣ .1.6̣]

céngkok mati for *pathet manyurå*

bukå derives from the end of the *mérong*

ompak inggah derives from the end of the *inggah*

inggah is of the *minggah kendhang* type: *sèlèh* notes match those in the *mérong*, with some exceptions

exception 1 (twice): *ir II* version of *puthut gelut*

exception 2 (twice): alternative route from 6̣ to 6

exception 3 (twice): suggests an extension of the *gantungan* on 2 (cf. exception 2)

exception 4: the *sèlèh* note in the *gåtrå* .5̣.3̣ is not the expected 5̣, but agrees with the *rebab* part, perhaps thus getting closer to the inner melody: also cf. exception 2

balungan
. 5̣ . 3̣ . 5̣ . 6̣

rebab
236̣ 5̣ 6̣ 3̣ 5̣ 3̣12 1 2 3.2 2 1 6̣

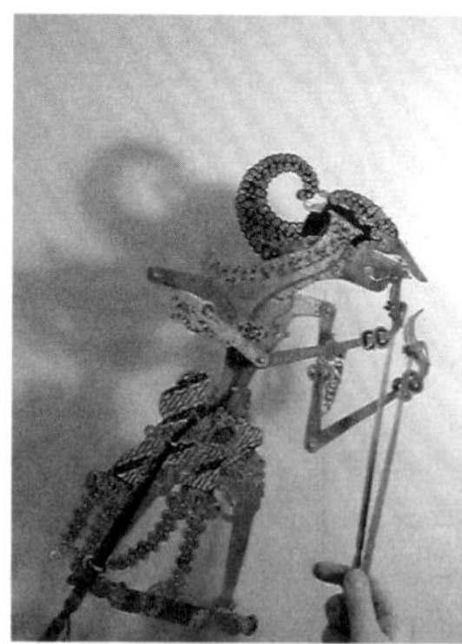

should therefore welcome the situation as a challenge to their musicianship.

The description above of the inner melody 'standing behind' the *balungan* suggests that the relationship and relative status of these two elements are agreed. In fact they are not.[106] It can be argued that the *balungan*, as a realisation of the inner melody, is itself a form of *garap*. Another view is that players deduce an inner melody from the *balungan*, which explains how they can arrive at different inner melodies that then determine their individual *garap*. The discussion of inner melody normally concerns pieces with vocal parts and at least the possibility of a *rebab* part—such pieces forming the bulk of the repertoire. This begs the question of whether inner melody exists in *gendhing bonang*.

An example

A few of the theoretical problems and anomalies that a specific piece can present are illustrated by **Anatomy of a gendhing** on the preceding page. So far as its *pathet* is concerned, the piece is always treated as being in *sléndro nem*, yet three of the four *céngkok mati* of *sléndro manyurå* occur twice each in the *mérong*. In the first *kenongan*, these 'wrong' *céngkok* are at least immediately contradicted by a *céngkok mati* from *sléndro nem*—which recurs as the final phrase of the *mérong*. The *inggah* section, with its *balungan nibani*, provides even less conclusive evidence of *pathet*, thus revealing another weakness of *pathet* analysis methods, including the one described earlier. The *gåtrå* 2̣2̣3̣2̣ in the *mérong* and the corresponding . 3̣ . 2̣ in the *inggah* are strong evidence for *sléndro nem*.

The overall outlines of the piece are clear, with a *minggah kendhang* and an ABBC structure in both halves. In the *rebab* part, the two halves of the *gendhing* are very similar; in fact there is as much difference between the two B *kenongan* as between *mérong* and *inggah*.

Although the *sèlèh* notes in the *inggah* are expected to match those in the *mérong*, there are good reasons for the exceptions. In exception 1, the *puthut gelut* contour in the inner melody is simply represented by its idiomatic versions first for *balungan mlaku* and then for *balungan nibani*. The other exceptions too are about the *mérong* and the *inggah* taking differing views of the inner melody. This is illustrated most strongly by exception 4, in which the *inggah* has a *sèlèh* 3̣ that corresponds to the *rebab* part—which is so often felt to approach the inner melody most closely. In exceptions 2 and 3, it appears that the *inggah* views a *gantungan* (on 6̣ and 2 respectively) as lasting for whole *gåtrå*, whereas in the *mérong* the *balungan* (like the *rebab* part) moves up earlier from the *gantungan* note.

In this piece there is no *gérongan*, and therefore no guidance from that source as to the contour of the inner melody.

Having one of the regular forms, and usually performed as a *klenèngan* piece, this *gendhing* uses *irâmå* in unproblematic ways. Other pieces, especially in the editable forms or when performed for dance or drama, are liable to cause writers to give conflicting explanations of *irâmå*.

From theory into practice

Some players may feel that it is better not to try to analyse pieces, but simply to accept them as presented by their teachers. However, a better understanding of the underlying theory should always result in a better, more idiomatic performance.

When confronted by a new piece in *balungan* notation, players will be aware that the notation is only an approximation to the 'real' piece. Because of the frequent similarities between one piece and another, experienced players are able to apply their existing knowledge of the repertoire to the new piece effectively. This process requires familiarity with the fundamental principles that are valid for any composition. In contrast to the list of fundamental principles of Western classical music, those of *karawitan* can be reduced to three

- contour,
- *sèlèh*, and
- *pathet*

which (like the principles of Western music) are not mutually independent: for example, the correct note for many of the instruments to play at a certain *sèlèh* point depends on *pathet*.

These principles affect what any instrument plays at any point, but to differing degrees. Therefore it is necessary to study the characteristic performance practice of each instrument. This is the purpose of Part 3.

106 Perlman (2004).

Instruments

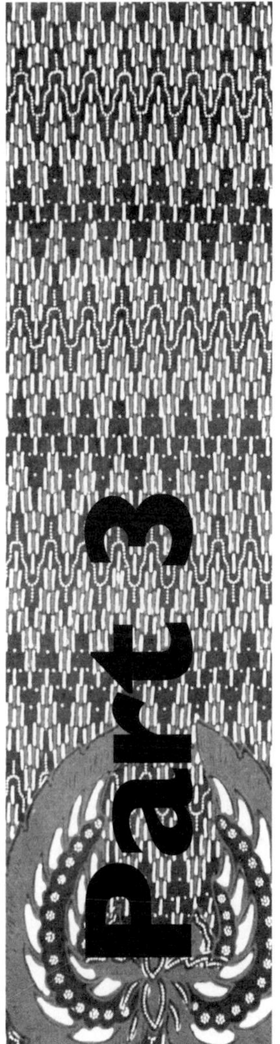

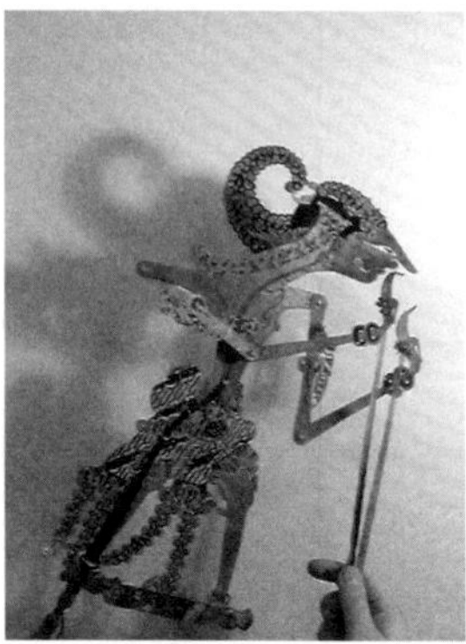

SLÉNDRO — Octave	I				II					III					IV					V					VI					VII		
	2	3	5	6	1	2	3	5	6	1	2	3	5	6	1	2	3	5	6	1	2	3	5	6	1	2	3	5	6	1	2	3
gong ageng [a]	■	■	■	■																												
gong suwukan				○	○	●																										
kempul						○	○	●	●	●	○																					
kenong																○	●	●	●	●	○											
kenong japan [b]													○																			
kethuk															■	■																
engkuk-kemong [c]																			○	○												
kempyang [b]																								□	□							
kemanak																								○	○							
saron panerus/peking																								○	●	●	●	●	●	●		
saron sångå [d]																			○	●	●	●	●	●	●	●	●	○				
saron barung																			○	●	●	●	●	●	●							
saron demung														○	●	●	●	●	●	●												
gendèr panerus													○	○	●	●	●	●	●	●	●	●	●	●	●	●	○	○				
gendèr barung								○	○	●	●	●	●	●	●	●	●	●	●	●	●	○	○									
slenthem									○	●	●	●	●	●	●																	
bonang panerus																				○	●	●	●	●	●	●	●	●	●	●	○	
bonang barung															○	●	●	●	●	●	●	●	●	●	●	○						
bonang panembung [b,e]										○	○	○	○	○	○	○	○	○	○	○	○											
siter peking														○	○	●	●	●	●	●	●	●	●	●	●	●	●					
siter									○	○	●	●	●	●	●	●	●	●	●	●	●	●										
celempung									○	○	●	●	●	●	●	●	●	●	●	●	●	●										
gambang							○	○	○	●	●	●	●	●	●	●	●	●	●	●	●	●	●	●	●	●	●	○	○			
suling																●	●	●	●	●	●	●	●	●	●	●	●	●	●	●		
rebab											●	●	●	●	●	●	●	●	●	●	●	●	●									
sindhèn											●	●	●	●	●	●	●	●	●	●	●	●	●									
wiråswårå							●	●	●	●	●	●	●	●	●	●	●	●														

● ■ normally present   ○ □ sometimes present   ■ □ normally only one out of these

a. The pitch shown may be an overtone about an octave above the fundamental: see note on p. 203.
b. Normally only found in a Yogya-style gamelan. c. The *engkuk* and *kemong* are respectively the higher and the lower of the pair.
d. Normally only one (if any) per gamelan: the compass 6̧ to 3̇ is usual. e. As a Yogya-style instrument, normally in *cacad* form.

3.1 Instrumentation and compass of typical modern gamelan in *sléndro*

PÉLOG	Octave						
	I	II	III	IV	V	VI	VII
	234567	1234567	1234567	1234567	1234567	1234567	1234
gong ageng [a]	■■ ■■						
gong suwukan	○○	○●					
kempul		○○○●●●	●○				
kenong				○●○●●●	●○		
kenong japan [b]			○				
kethuk			■	■			
kempyang [c]					●○		
kemanak					○○		
saron panerus/peking						●●●●●●●	
saron barung					●●●●●●●		
saron demung				●●●●●●●			
gendèr panerus, barang scale			○○●	●● ●●●	●● ●●●	●○ ○	
gendèr panerus, bem scale			○○	●●● ●●	●●● ●●	●●○ ○	
gendèr barung, barang scale		○○●	●● ●●●	●● ●●●	●○ ○		
gendèr barung, bem scale		○○	●●● ●●	●●● ●●	●●○ ○		
slenthem			●●●●●●●				
bonang panerus					●●●●●●●	●●●●●●●	
bonang barung				●●●●●●●	●●●●●●●		
bonang panembung [b]			○○○○○○○	○○○○○○○			
siter peking, barang scale [d]			○○	●● ●●●	●● ●●●	●●	
siter peking, bem scale [d]			○	○●● ●●	●●● ●●	●●●	
siter, barang scale [d]		○○	●● ●●●	●● ●●●	●●		
siter, bem scale [d]		○	○●● ●●	●●● ●●	●●●		
celempung, barang scale [e]		○○	●● ●●●	●● ●●●	●●		
celempung, bem scale [e]		○	○●● ●●	●●● ●●	●●●		
gambang, barang scale [e]		○ ○○●	●● ●●●	●● ●●●	●● ●●●	●● ○○	
gambang, bem scale [e]		○ ○○	●●● ●●	●●● ●●	●●● ●●	●●● ○○	
suling				●●●●●●●	●●●●●●●	●●●●●●	
rebab, pathet nem, barang [f]			●●●●●●	●●●●●●●	●●●●●		
rebab, pathet limå [f]			●●●●●●●	●●●●●●●	●●●●●		
sindhèn			●●●●●●	●●●●●●●	●●●●●		
wiråswårå		●●●●●	●●●●●●●	●●●●●			

a. The pitch shown may be an overtone about an octave above the fundamental: see note on p. 203.
b. Normally only found in a Yogya-style gamelan. c. In a Yogya-style gamelan, traditionally both 6 and 7.
d. Normally one instrument per gamelan, tuned to the *bem* scale or the *barang* scale as required.
e. Either a separate instrument for each scale or one *gambang* serving both scales via the exchange of *wilah*.
f. Normally one instrument per gamelan, tuned for *pathet limå* or *pathet nem/barang* as required.

3.2 Instrumentation and compass of typical modern gamelan in *pélog*. (For symbols, see Fig. 3.1)

Instruments—an overview

Here the instruments are considered individually, and then their combination into various ensembles. With such a wide range of instruments found in gamelan ensembles, there are various ways that they can be grouped and classified.

The layout of Part 3 mainly follows a classification according to the functions of the instruments, expanding on the discussion in Part 2, where the concept of 'stratification' was introduced. First it is worth looking at some other possible classifications.

Tuned vs. untuned instruments

One obvious distinction between different instruments is whether they are tuned to specific notes. In the context of gamelan, this classification does not work very well.

The majority of gamelan instruments are both tuned to specific notes and treated as such. Figs 3.1 and 3.2 cover all the instruments of this type.[1] In addition, the principal drums are tuned towards important notes in the scale. Both heads should give acceptable notes, and there should be a satisfactory interval between them: however, these notes are not very pure, and their absolute pitch is not critical. A few instruments (*kecèr*, *keprak*) produce sounds of definite but impure pitch, but this pitch is not adjustable and is apparently never discussed. Unless the *kepyak* is included, no gamelan instruments are completely untuned.

Organological classification

An organological approach classifies instruments according to how they generate sound. All the major categories of the standard classification[2] are represented in the gamelan: idiophones, chordophones, aerophones and membranophones. One subcategory—directly struck idiophones—accounts for most of the instruments.

The mechanisms of sound production in gamelan instruments are described in **Appendix 4**.

Soft-style and loud-style

As mentioned earlier, the full gamelan of the present day combines two types of ensemble that were originally separate (although the soft-style ensemble did not have a fixed make-up, but acquired instruments over the years). The *slenthem* forms a bridge between the two, as a soft-style instrument that is also a permanent member of a full gamelan and is played in loud-style pieces. The role of the other soft instruments is to decorate or paraphrase.

In practice there are various kinds of gamelan and related ensembles, as discussed later (p. 236 foll.). The *siteran* ensembles count as soft-style, but all the surviving ceremonial ensembles are loud-style.

Classification by construction

One classification often used by the Javanese is by construction. The classification is useful to musicians, since it relates to practical matters such as playing technique, maintenance and tuning. The materials used in instruments are discussed in **Appendix 5**.

The majority of gamelan instruments are of either *wilah(an)* form or *pencon* form.

Wilah instruments

In this class of instruments, the centre of a long bar or *wilah* is struck to produce the note. The Javanese term *wilah* (or *bilah* in Indonesian) will be used here in preference to 'bar' or 'key', both of which words have other musical meanings.

Wilah with various cross-sections are found. Fig. 3.3 shows two broad categories. The plain (*polos* or *lugas*) shapes are found in the *saron* family, all of which are loud-style instruments and need hard beaters. In most modern gamelan, the *blimbingan* shapes are only used on

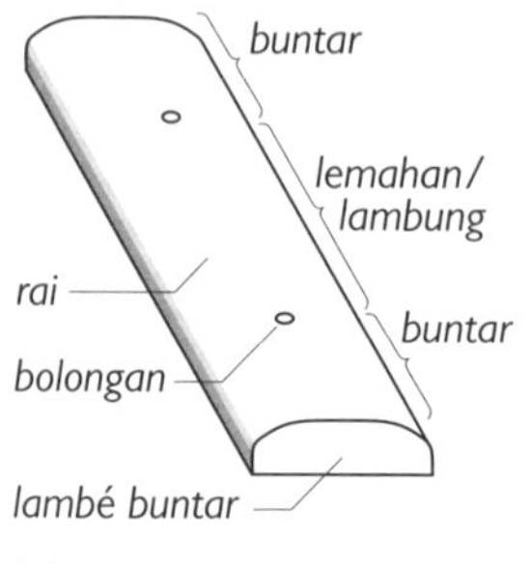

(a) *polos/lugas* shapes

(b) *blimbingan* shapes

3.3 Parts of a *wilah*

1 The pitches shown are based on what appear to be the most reliable measurements, but some sources place certain instruments (usually the gong and *kenong* families) in other octaves. See also pp. 197 and 203n. The Western reference pitch, A = 440 Hz, lies close to notes 5 or 6 in octave IV.

2 Hornbostel and Sachs (1914).

the *gendèr* family all of which are soft-style instruments needing padded beaters. In practice, these *blimbingan* shapes in bronze or brass are thinner than the bronze *polos* shapes. Steel *wilah* of the *polos* shape are also relatively thin.

The shapes can be divided further. The top four profiles in Fig. 3.4 count as *polos*, and the other two as *blimbingan*. Some of these variants are rare in modern gamelan. The same is true of styles for the ends of *wilah*. Generally the *polos* shapes have plain ends, whereas the *blimbingan* shapes have bevelled ends (*paèsan*), but Javanese writers give names to many other variations.

On all *wilah* instruments, the longest *wilah* (= lowest note) is at the left-hand end. The ends of the *wilah* are usually cut so that the whole instrument is tapered (Fig. 3.5).

Pencon instruments

Pencon instruments are those with a roughly hemispherical *pencu*—for which English has several unsatisfactory translations (knob, boss, nipple, dome, pip)—and all are played by striking the *pencu*. Some writers in English simply refer to all such instruments as gongs, but this is not the correct organological description for all the *pencon* instruments: some are classed as **gong-chimes**. The Javanese terms will again be used here for clarity.

Pencon instruments can be further divided according to their shape. First there is a distinction (Fig. 3.7) between the low-profile or squat (*dhempok*) form and the high-profile (*brunjung*) form, steeply sloped like a traditional Javanese roof (see Fig. 1.6). The latter is used for the higher-pitched instruments, or for the higher notes within a set.

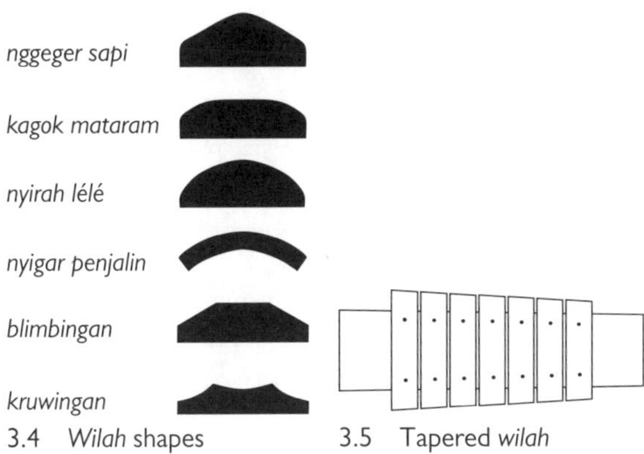

3.4 *Wilah* shapes

3.5 Tapered *wilah*

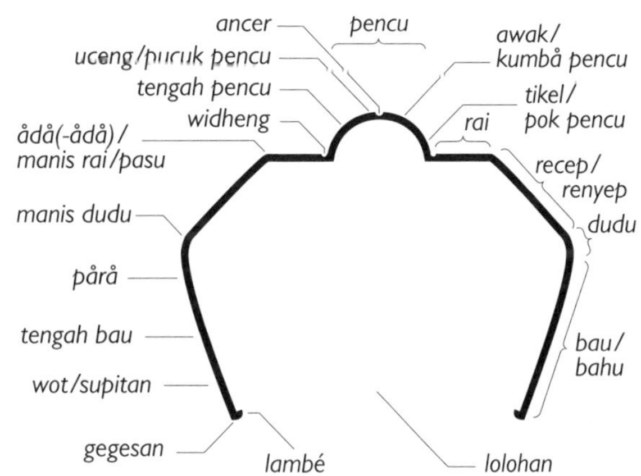

3.6 Parts of a *pencon* instrument

Within each of the two forms, proportions differ from one instrument to another; for example, in the width of the *rai* and the heights of the *pencu* and the *bau*, relative to the diameter. Instruments also differ in details such as the presence or absence of a *widheng* or an *ancer*, and whether the *recep* is concave or flat. There may be a raised ridge around the *widheng*. More will be found under the descriptions of individual instruments.

Fig. 3.6 illustrates the *brunjung* form, but the terminology shown there is applicable to both shapes.

There is also a distinction between *pencon pangkon* and *pencon gandhul*. The former are sometimes called 'sitting gongs' in English, and rest on strings (*pluntur*) strung across wooden frames (*rancakan*). The other instruments, the 'hanging gongs', including all gongs and *kempul*, are suspended from wooden stands (*gayor*) by thick cords (*klanthé*) that pass through small holes in the *bau*. All the other *pencon* instruments in general use are in the first category, except that the *engkuk-kemong* can be found in either form. The *pencon pangkon* instruments are also sometimes called 'kettles' in English, but the average kettle has changed shape considerably since this description was first awarded.

Within the *pencon gandhul*, a further difference in shape can be observed. Most instruments of this type conform to the shape in Fig. 3.8(a), where the *rai* is above the level of the *dudu*, or at least level with it. The *gong ageng* is sometimes made in the *selok* form (Fig. 3.8(b)), where the *rai* is below the *dudu*.

The *kecèr* (Fig. 3.76) is an additional *pencon* instrument outside the categories above.

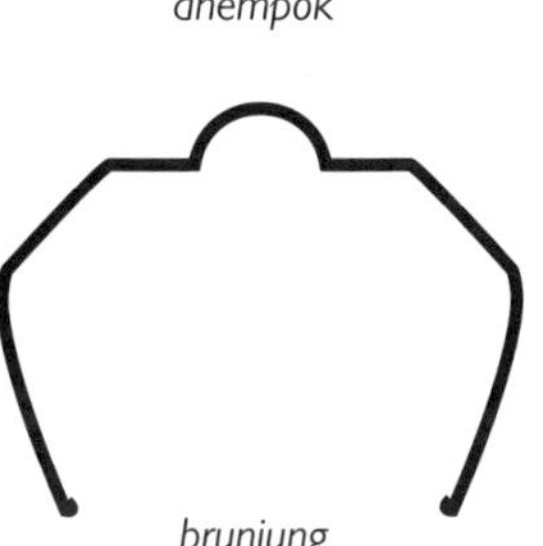

3.7 Pencon forms

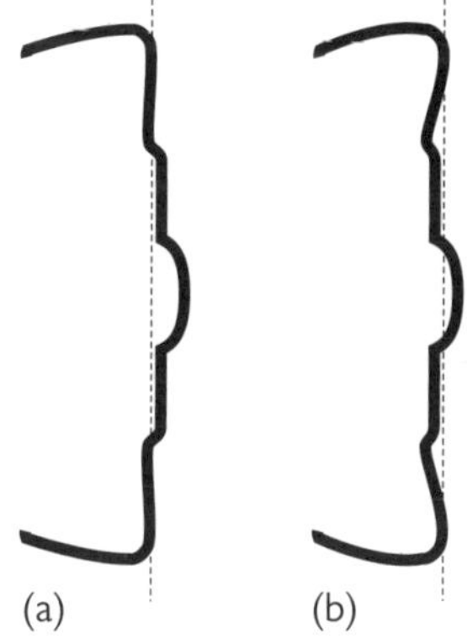

3.8 *Pencon gandhul* forms: (a) general; (b) *gong ageng*

Other instruments

A mixed category of *wilah pencon* instruments exists. These have a *pencu* halfway along the *wilah*. Among the few instruments of this kind, only one is a regular member of modern ensembles: the *gong kemodhong*. The *kenong rèntèng* is a substitute instrument, and the other examples—the *slentho* and related instruments—are obsolete and will rarely be seen outside the royal courts.

The *rebab*, *suling*, *kemanak*, *siter* family and all the drums are discussed under their own headings later.

The text here is based on standard instruments, but non-standard versions can be made, with unusual ranges or tunings, e.g. diatonic tunings or *pélog* scales with all seven degrees present, or with note 4 replacing 3. Also see **Size matters** below. Essentially the makers will supply what customers ask for.

Gamelan have been made where *wilah* replace all the *pencon*, resulting in a smaller, lighter and therefore more easily portable ensemble.

Decoration and finish

Bronze *wilah* instruments are normally filed smooth on top, and less smooth on the underside. Bronze *pencon* instruments are described in terms of which external parts

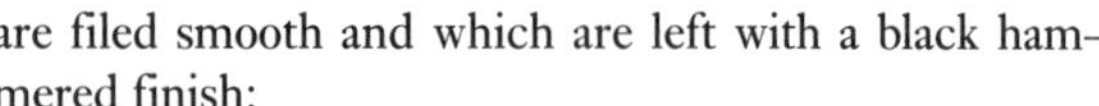

are filed smooth and which are left with a black hammered finish:

Style	Parts filed smooth
Cemengan [*kr*], *ireng* [*ng*]	None
Kembang sepasang	*Pencu*
Padhang rembulan	*Pencu* and *rai*
Bapangan	*Pencu*, *rai* and *recep*
Gilapan	All external parts

Most *pencon* are now made in *gilapan* style, but *gong ageng* and *gong suwukan* can have a range of finishes. The *pencon* instruments in the oldest ceremonial gamelan are *cemengan* throughout.

Frames are often decorated by carving. Standard symbols with traditional meanings occur, and they may be drawn from Hinduism, Buddhism or Islam (Fig. 3.10).

Size matters

Gamelan instruments do not have standard sizes. The laws of physics determine the length of the *suling*, but otherwise the sizes of instruments vary, from the large instruments found in some court gamelan—even larger in old ceremonial gamelan—down to some that are almost toy-sized. Size matters when playing the instruments, and must therefore be considered when purchasing them.

There is a certain amount of status, not necessarily justified, associated with a large *gong ageng*.

In the *saron* section, large instruments containing substantial amounts of metal can produce higher volume, whereas smaller instruments sound unpleasant when hit hard.

When ordering a gamelan that is to be played by small hands, it is possible to specify narrower *wilah* for some instruments, and smaller, lighter *tabuh* for the *balungan* section.

Additional comments on some instruments are to be found below.

The Yogya style

Yogyanese instruments tended to be larger than Solonese instruments, but there is now less difference than formerly, plus extensive trading between the two cities. Playing styles still differ significantly.

The key characteristics of the Yogya playing style can be listed in terms of deviations from Solonese style, as the latter is considered the default. The following list is reproduced, without comment, from a publication of Taman Budaya Yogyakarta, a cultural centre:

- The theme is presented in loud style.
- The *saron* uses *pancer* in some pieces.
- There is *demung imbal* in some pieces.
- The *slenthem* plays in *mbandhul* style.
- The *bonang panembung* plays on the *dhong*.
- The *peking* plays in anticipating style.
- The *bonang* plays in *nglagu* style.
- The *bonang panerus* plays prominently.
- *Gambang* playing contains many 'rolls' (*ngukel*).
- The *suling* line follows the *sindhènan*.
- Some pieces use the *kenong japan*.
- The *kethuk* is not 'rolled' (*nitir*).
- Many *tak* strokes are used in drumming.
- The *bedhug* is used in some pieces.
- *Ketawang* have two *kempul* strokes per *gongan*.
- *Ketawang* allow *ir I*.

(a) Fully carved

(b) Stylised

3.9 Lotus bud finials

The finials in the form of lotus buds and perhaps lotus leaves (Fig. 3.9) that decorate the corners of some frames —for *kenong*, *kethuk*, *kempyang* and *bonang*—are derived mainly from Buddhism. The triangular motifs seen in both Figs 3.9(b) and 3.10 are stylised representations of fire. Certain patterns are stylised versions of Arabic letters or Javanese *aksårå* (**Appendix 3**), so that some instruments may be carrying messages unbeknown to their owner. Customers may also request the use of particular motifs.[3] On the finish of the woodwork, see **Appendix 5**.

Some of the larger frames include detachable sections that make them easier to handle and transport. Gong stands are usually dismountable.

Beaters

For acoustic reasons (see **Appendix 4**) there is a correct beater for each gamelan instrument, with a particular weight and hardness. Other beaters should not be used, and in some cases the wrong beater could damage the instrument.

The generic name *tabuh* covers all beaters, but there are further names for the individual types (Table 3.1).

Playing style: general

Part 3 is based on the assumption that, for each instrument, there are general principles that can be applied to the playing of any *karawitan* composition. In other words, it is not necessary to learn the details of the realisation separately for each piece.

The principle is only valid up to a certain point. Between one piece and another in a given *bentuk*, there can be large differences in the *skema*—i.e. the sequence in which the sections of the piece (if any) are normally performed, the set of *iråmå* normally used and the major vocal and instrumental treatments normally applied. Some pieces have few options; others have many. Also *garap* depends on context: for example, it may change greatly for dance or drama. In spite of these variations, competent players should always be able to apply some more or less appropriate *garap* when they read *balungan* notation and hear the relevant signals from the *kendhang* and from the melodic leader. (If their assumptions prove to be seriously mistaken, they can expect to be corrected.)

Beyond this normal range of *garap*, some pieces—unsurprisingly, some of the most popular and frequently performed—have acquired special *garap* that could not be predicted by the player.

The term for the part played by an instrument is simply the name of the instrument plus *-an*: *gendèran*, etc. The term for the player is made by applying the nasal mutation (p. G-2) to the name of the instrument and adding *pe-/pa-* before it: *penyaron*, *pembonang*, etc.

Rhythm and ensemble

For a player used to playing in a Western ensemble, the experience of playing in an ensemble in Java for the first time can be a major cultural shock. The Javanese approach to ensemble playing is fundamentally different. It could be described as isochronous rather than synchronous: when players play the same number of notes as each other in an given time interval (or twice or four times as many), they may not coincide precisely. Every player has to find a comfortable position within the rhythmic environment presented by the other players. The process by which the players do this has been described as a dialogue (*saraséhan*), although it does not involve words.

It can in any case be difficult for a player to identify the precise location of the beat—for which the *kendhang* is the ultimate authority. Some players deliberately do not play on the beat. Perhaps there is an 'inner rhythm', by analogy with 'inner melody', to which the players try to conform, and the *kendhangan* is only suggesting it.

Other instruments play 'in time' but play so many

3 e.g. an exotic plant called the thistle, on a gamelan destined for Scotland.

3.10 Decoration styles

Table 3.1
Names and uses of beaters for gamelan instruments, etc.

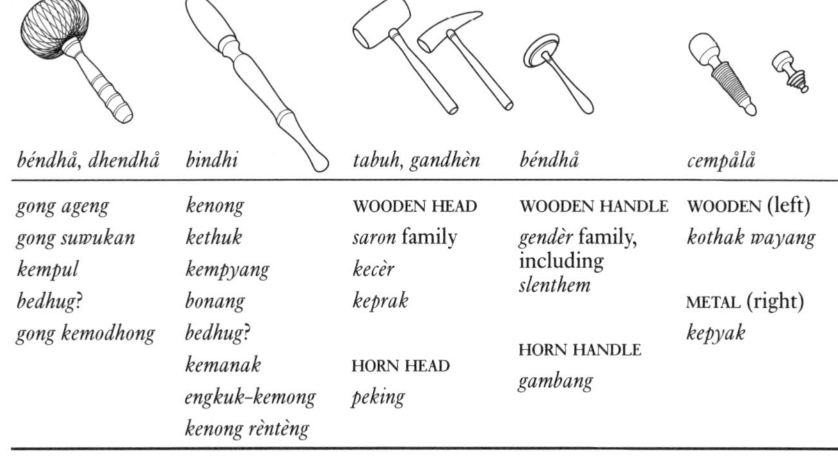

béndhå, dhendhå	*bindhi*	*tabuh, gandhèn*	*béndhå*	*cempålå*
gong ageng	*kenong*	WOODEN HEAD	WOODEN HANDLE	WOODEN (left)
gong suwukan	*kethuk*	*saron* family	*gendèr* family, including *slenthem*	*kothak wayang*
kempul	*kempyang*	*kecèr*		
bedhug?	*bonang*	*keprak*		METAL (right)
gong kemodhong	*bedhug?*			*kepyak*
	kemanak	HORN HEAD	HORN HANDLE	
	engkuk-kemong	*peking*	*gambang*	
	kenong rènteng			

> **Tips & tricks 1**
> **How to get lost**
> There are several easy ways to get lost:
> - by not following the tempo given by the *kendhang*,
> - by not listening out for possible signals that will cause transitions, e.g. to *lik* sections or other pieces, or to different *garap* such as *kébar*—or by not responding to the signals,
> - by playing an instrumental part, e.g. at the start of a new section of a piece, especially at an *irâmâ* change, at twice or half the correct speed,
> - by miscounting the number of occurrences of a repeated element,
> - by not listening to all the information available from other players.

notes that it is difficult for (say) a *balungan* player to identify the *sèlèh* points. The *ciblon* is one such instrument, even when it sticks to regular binary divisions. Therefore the most difficult situation for the other players arises during *ciblon* drumming in *ir III* and *ir IV*, when the *balungan* notes may be seconds apart. The *ciblon* also sometimes complicates the situation by playing triplet cross-rhythms—e.g. three beats against four on the melodic instruments, or even four against three.

Western players are trained to aspire to extreme precision of ensemble, i.e. all playing on the beat. When they apply this approach to *karawitan*, Javanese players quite reasonably criticise them for playing in a stiff or 'wooden' manner. For the Javanese, playing consistently on the beat is only an option, and one that they do not choose to follow much of the time. In fact a sudden transition from their usual apparently relaxed playing style to all playing on the beat can be a very exciting effect.

The missing dimension—volume

The subject of volume in *karawitan* is not much discussed.[4] The music usually proceeds at characteristic volume levels and with characteristic changes of volume at certain points. Faster often means louder. When the soft-style instruments are playing, there is an upper limit to the loudness of the ensemble if the softer instruments such as the *rebab* are not to be drowned out.

The correct balance between the various instruments, called *rampak*, is therefore an ideal, and more than one such balance is possible. For example, when a piece is being played in *ir IV*, the *balungan* should never be prominent and may be almost undetectable. In contrast, during a loud-style *ladrang* played in *ir II*, the *balungan* will always be clear even if the soft-style instruments are playing. See also **Playing a good *balungan***, opposite.

One frequent transition is a sudden drop in volume (*sirep*), which is described under **Multi-instrument *garap***.

The subject of phrasing, i.e. the relative emphasis of the different notes within a melodic line, is barely mentioned in the context of *balungan* playing, or indeed for any other instrument. The reason may be that it is difficult for the player to achieve fine control of volume and tone colour on gamelan instruments, because the various *wilah* or *pencon* of an instrument vary in their response to the beater(s). Variations can also be blamed on the *tabuh* themselves. The evenness of the notes on an individual instrument is therefore much inferior to that expected of most Western instruments.

In spite of these problems, groups of expert players, presumably with practice, do shape phrases carefully. The specific principles that players follow in deciding how to shape a phrase are a non-subject. Perhaps phrasing is learned entirely by example.

For the melody instruments, phrasing does not mean playing louder at structurally important points in order to emphasise them. Instead, the punctuating instruments perform this function.

> **Tips & tricks 2**
> **What to do after getting lost**
> The essential task is to identify a point where one can safely resume playing. There are many such possible points, not all equally easy to identify:
> - a gong, a *kenong*, or an *irâmâ* change, although in some pieces this may mean a long wait,
> - an unusual *gâtrâ*, e.g. a *gâtrâ gantung* in the *balungan*,
> - an *andhegan*,
> - a particular *gérongan* phrase—these being very useful since (with experience) it is possible to predict where the phrase is heading,
> - *sèlèh* notes in the patterns from certain instruments,
> - the last iteration of a repeated element,
> - a specific *kendhangan* pattern—although this requires the most detailed knowledge.

4 Supanggah (1985), writing about '*garap d'intensité*', is an exception.

Balungan instruments

This heading covers four or five different metallophones in a full modern gamelan. They are by no means limited simply to playing the *balungan* exactly as notated. All of them can have, at one time or another, a decorating function. The *saron panerus* almost always plays simple embellishments of the *balungan*. However, in contrast to the decorating instruments, all the regular *balungan* instruments play one note at a time, and a single beater is used.

The *slenthem* is used in both the loud- and soft-style ensembles. Otherwise, all the instruments under this heading belong to the loud-style ensemble.

In *sléndro*, the range of most of these instruments is 6̣123561̇. Yogyanese instruments have traditionally lacked the low 6, but it is now often included on new instruments so that music in all styles can be played on them. If the low 6 is available, the player still has to decide when to use it (see **Tips & tricks 3** and **4**). In *pélog* the compass is 1234567.

Balungan notation usually includes register dots to indicate the octave where the true pitch lies—Yogyanese notation typically does not—and players must fold the notated melody so that it fits within the single octave of the instruments. See **Tips & tricks 4**. If it is necessary to write out the part for an individual *balungan* instrument, the notation always uses the same range of pitches, written 6̣123561̇ or 1234567, even though the various *balungan* instruments cover four different octaves (see Figs 3.1 and 3.2).

Playing a good *balungan*

The *balungan* instruments are often thought of as the easiest of all in the gamelan. In fact they all need to be played carefully, with due attention to timing, volume, and the damping of the notes.

The *saron*, *demung* and *peking* should all play on the beat or slightly behind it, but not ahead of it. The *peking* in particular, because it plays more notes than the other instruments and has a penetrating sound, is quite capable of driving the pace of the whole gamelan if it gets ahead of the beat.

For the *slenthem* the situation is somewhat different: its sound does not have a rapid onset, so that there would be no point in playing ahead of the beat anyway. It is bad style for the *slenthem* to be heard before the other *balungan* instruments. In *ir III* and *ir IV*, some *slenthem* players play well behind the beat.

Volume depends to some extent on the style of the piece but also on the *irâmâ*. Faster basically means louder. Unless a *sirep* is in force, the *balungan* is normally loud in *irâmâ lancar* and *irâmâ tanggung*. The transition from *ir I* to *ir II* is always associated with a major reduction in volume, because the piece is effectively changing from loud

Tips & tricks 3
Interpreting *balungan* (a): using low 6

The simplest advice on the subject of the 6̣ on *sléndro* instruments is to ignore it. However, most players who find a 6̣ on the instrument in front of them will probably want to use it.

Javanese players generally accept the use of the 6̣ when it comes at the end of a falling phrase such as 2126̣, which is very common in *sléndro manyurâ*. Some will use the low 6 in such a phrase only when it comes at important points such as the end of a *gongan*, or at the very end of a piece.

When 6̣ occurs in other positions, its use must be considered carefully, bearing in mind the principle of preserving the contour of the *lagu*. Thus the 6̣ in this passage (*ldr Mugirahayu sl m*) can be played as written

36̣1. 36̣12̂

because it keeps the right contour. The repeated phrase .6̣2 is another that needs the 6̣ if it is available.

In contrast, in the phrase 216̣5̣ (very common as a closing phrase in *sléndro sângâ*) it would be wrong to play the low 6, because it would result in a large leap from a low 6 to a 5 in the octave above at a weak point in the *gâtrâ*. This is one example of a 6 being played high because of the adjacent note.

When leaps are necessary, there is a preference for making them at the end of a *gâtrâ* or another strong point. The mid-point of a *gâtrâ* is stronger than the position between the third and fourth notes of the *gâtrâ*. Leaps are often made between the notes 1 and 6, as in the example 216̣5̣ above.

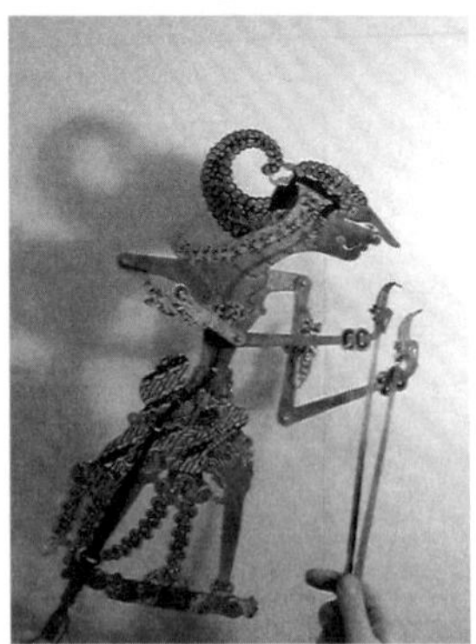

Tips & tricks 4

Interpreting *balungan* (b): placement

This subject is related to **Tips & tricks 3**, but applies to all notes and all *balungan* instruments in *sléndro*.

Balungan notation covers a range of two octaves or more. In the process of transposing the notes into the single octave of the instruments, the *balungan* player can sometimes place the notes in more than one way in *sléndro* because the instruments have 1̇ as well as 1, and may have 6̣ as well as 6. In *pélog*, with a compass consisting only of the notes 1 to 7, there are no such options.

One principle behind the placement of the *balungan* is to preserve the contour of the *lagu* as far as possible. The contour tends to be seen as more important than the octave in which the individual notes of the *gåtrå* lie. Thus 15̣6̣1 and 1̇561̇ will normally both be played as 1̇561̇.

In a *gåtrå* using 1 in the vicinity of 5 and 6, the 1 will almost always represent 1̇ even if for some reason the register dot has been omitted; for example, in 561̇6, 1̇561̇, 1̇656, 6561̇, 61̇65, 1̇653, 3561̇. All these examples will normally be played with 1̇.

In some cases there is no option about the interpretation of the *balungan*. The entire *gåtrå* 3̇2̇12̇ must be transposed down an octave and played as 3212: similarly the *gåtrå* 3̣3̣5̣6̣ must be transposed up and played as 3356, and 5̣3̣16̣ probably played as 531̇6. In other cases the contour is unavoidably altered: for example, 3̇2̇65 must be played as 3265.

Some of the principles mentioned under **Tips & tricks 3** apply more generally; especially the tendency to make a jump between the notes 1 and 6. Thus 3̇2̇16 will be played as 3216 not 321̇6, and certainly not as 3216̣, which would imply the wrong register for the whole *gåtrå*. A similar approach is taken with 2126 1632, which is likely to be played as 2126 1̇632 rather than as 2126̣ 1632.

As always, exceptions occur, usually as a result of the context. Therefore the *balungan* line must be considered as a whole, not *gåtrå* by *gåtrå*. Sometimes the various principles described here conflict, so that different players will disagree about placement.

For example, in *gd bonang Sidåmukti sl 6*, the first *gåtrå* after the *gong bukå* is 6̣12. Considered in isolation, this *gåtrå* asks to be played as written. However, it follows a 5̣ that the *balungan* players must play as 5. On the principle of permitting a jump at the end of a *gåtrå*, there is nothing wrong in going from 5 to 6̣. On the other hand, on the principles of preserving the contour and preferring a jump between notes 1 and 6, it is better to play the 6̣ as 6.

Later in the same piece the two *gåtrå* 216̣5̣ 16̣5̣3̣ occur. How should the second 1 be played? After 6̣5̣, which must be played as 65, the 1 must be played high if the contour is to be retained as far as possible. However, this would suggest incorrectly that the second *gåtrå* was actually 1̇653. Probably most players will play the 1 low.

With Yogyanese notation, which traditionally has no register dots, the player does not have many decisions to make about placement of the *balungan*. If the notation follows extreme Yogyanese practice, with 1̇ in *sléndro* written as 7, and if the instrument has no 6̣, no decisions may be required at all. Sometimes, however, both 1 and 1̇ occur in the notation, and the *balungan* player must then make the usual decisions.

Instruments with more than the usual compass, e.g. *saron wayangan*, offer additional possibilities.

style to soft style. In Yogyanese style, the *balungan* is always rather stronger than in Solonese style, even in the slower *iråmå*, which can include *ir III* in the loud style. The *slenthem* is unable to vary its volume greatly.

The general damping technique for all these instruments is the same: a note should only be damped when the next note is played, maintaining a smooth line—legato playing, in Western musical terminology. The main exception to this rule is the *peking* when playing repeated notes (such as Solonese *nacah låmbå* and *nacah rangkep*): it is only necessary to damp after changing to a new note. (Some players do not do even this, because the sound of the *peking* fades so fast.) If any of the other *balungan* instruments play a note twice in succession, the note is damped just before it is struck for the second time, although not all players observe this rule strictly.

When the gaps between the *balungan* notes are longest, as in *ir III* with a *balungan nibani* or in *ir IV*, the *demung* and *saron* notes fade to inaudibility before the next note, so damping is unnecessary. This lets Javanese players play with one hand only, leaving the other hand free to hold a *kretek* cigarette or a glass of tea.

Beginners often have difficulty at first with the coordination required for the standard playing technique (Fig. 3.17), but this phase soon passes, and thereafter they do not give the matter a second thought. To help in

3.17 Standard use of the *tabuh*

the development of a good damping style, playing one-handed is a useful exercise, because it forces the player to damp only after playing the next note.

Certain playing techniques demand special styles of damping, as explained below.

Saron family

The *saron* family members in regular current use comprise *saron*, *demung*, *peking* and *saron wayangan*. All instruments in the family use the same types of frame (*pangkon, rancakan*). The Solonese frame (Fig. 3.11) has a flat top, whereas on the Yogyanese frame (Fig. 3.12) the scrolled ends rise above the *wilah*. Both of these types of frame are carved from solid wood, and are therefore very heavy even without the weight of the *wilah*. Besides the scrolls (*gelung*), the long sides are usually decorated with carvings. A third form of frame (Fig. 3.13) is assembled from panels: this *kijingan* frame is lighter and costs less, especially if not highly decorated. The name comes from the shape of a traditional Muslim grave (*kijing*, Fig. 3.14).

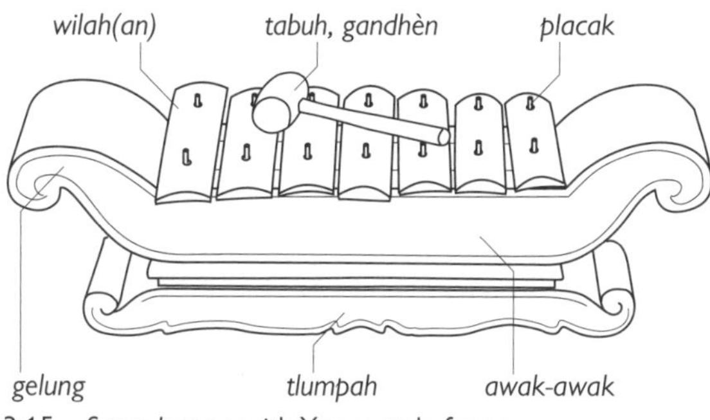

3.15 *Saron barung* with Yogya-style frame

Each *wilah* has two holes that match two pins (*placak*) fixed to the *pangkon*. To prevent unwanted damping or buzzes, the *wilah* should be a loose fit over the pins. The *wilah* sits on a cushion (*tawonan*, *sumpilan*) traditionally made from folded rattan or bamboo, sometimes with a layer of felt on top, and not directly on the *pangkon*. Rubber or foam rubber is a modern substitute material. The cushion serves again to improve the sound quality.

Details of the construction and the terminology used are shown in Figs 3.15 and 3.16.

Basic playing and damping technique

All the *saron* family are played with a beater (mallet, *tabuh*) normally held in the right hand, and notes are then damped with the left hand.

The *tabuh* for the *saron*, *saron wayangan* and *demung* consist of a wooden head on a wooden handle. The flat of the beater head may start out smooth, giving a hard tone quality. During use, the surface becomes rougher and the sound improves as a result. Heads are sometimes made with a grid of grooves on the flats, which speeds up the roughening process.

Even after it has been roughened by use, the flat of the head is considered to produce an unsatisfactory tone quality. The edge of the head is generally preferred, so the head is held at an angle of nearly 45 degrees to the vertical (Fig. 3.17). With a well-worn *tabuh*, it is advisable to experiment to establish which part of the head gives the most pleasant and the most even tone.

Standard *tabuh* are rather heavy for use by children, but smaller and lighter *tabuh* are also available. In the *gamelan sekatèn* the *tabuh* for the *saron* and *demung* may be larger versions of the horn-headed *tabuh* used with the *peking*.

Western players often develop bad habits such as waving the beater in the air, as if to keep time, after playing a note. Javanese players manage to create a wide range of volume levels without ever lifting the beater far from the *wilah*.

Damping the note by simply touching the top of a *wilah* with the hand may be sufficient on the less resonant

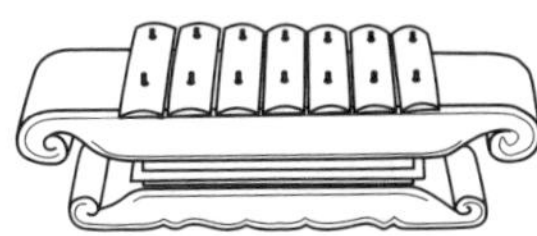

3.11 Solo-style frame

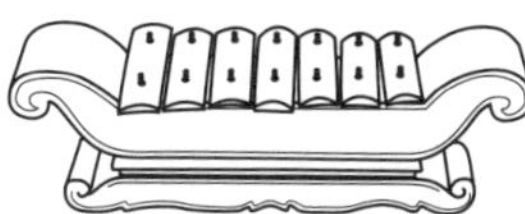

3.12 Yogya-style frame

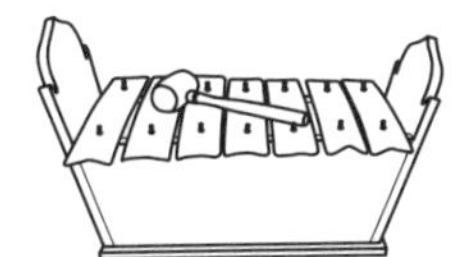

3.13 *Kijingan*-style frame

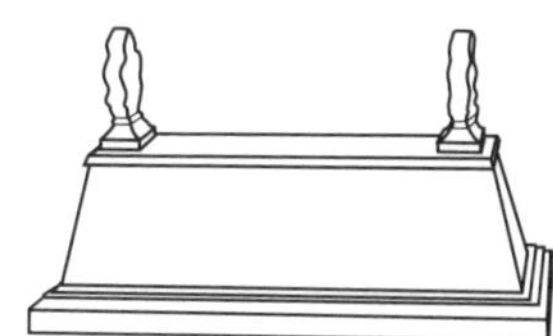

3.14 Muslim grave

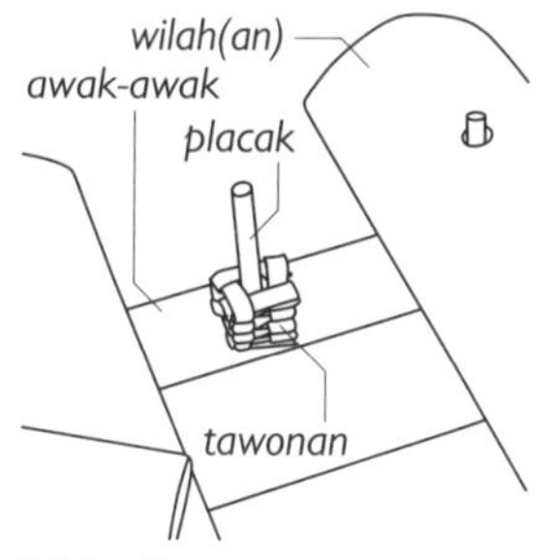

3.16 *Tawonan*

instruments or when the note was not played loudly. At other times the *wilah* must be gripped firmly between the thumb and at least one finger. For differences between the instruments, see below.

Bronze and iron need slightly different playing and damping techniques. Iron *wilah* are thinner than most bronze *wilah*, and do not need to be hit as hard to get the same volume level. Iron also seems to respond more rapidly to the beater. On the other hand, bronze sustains the tone longer, and therefore needs more thorough damping than iron. This effect is especially noticeable on the *demung* because of the amount of metal in the *wilah*.

Saron barung

The *saron barung* is also called *saron ri(n)cik*, but most often simply *saron*.

The *saron* (Fig. 3.15) forms the mainstay of the *balungan* section, and four *saron* (per *laras*) are present in a large gamelan. A few even have eight. In a more modest gamelan, there are usually two. A gamelan bought for educational purposes by a Western school often has extra *saron* to accommodate large classes.

Regular playing style

The regular role of the *saron* is to play the *balungan* as notated, subject to the principles of placement given in **Tips & tricks 1** and **2**. This generalisation applies to all *iråmå*, and to loud and soft playing styles alike. In the slowest *iråmå*, as explained for the *inggah* of *gendhing* (p. 79), the *saron* players may stop playing, and reinforce the singing of the *gérong*. In *ir III* and *ir IV*, the absent *saron* are hardly missed because their sound fades so quickly and because the *balungan* is usually *nibani*.

A number of other standard forms of *garap* can be found in addition, as described below.

Pancer

Pancer notes fill in the gaps in a *balungan nibani*: in other words, the *saron* then plays on the *pin* as well as the written notes. *Pancer* can be regarded as standard *garap* for *balungan nibani* in certain contexts, such as for *ketawang* and the *inggah* of *gendhing*, but mainly in *laras sléndro*. *Pancer* notes are used in *pélog* pieces, but less often. They are part of both Solo and Yogya styles, but the Yogyanese seem to find more use for them.

Although *pancer* notes are an element of *garap*, many *balungan* in both *laras* look like *balungan nibani* that have been filled in with *pancer* notes. Effectively the *pancer* notes have been frozen into the *balungan* notation. (Several examples are to be found among the *sesegan* sections of the *inggah* of Solonese *gendhing bonang*.) In such cases, some of the instruments may play the *garap* appropriate for the original *balungan nibani*.

In *sléndro*, the standard *pancer* note played by the *saron* on a *pin* is 1̇. A 1̇ in the *balungan* is then played as a low 1. Thus (from *ldr Gonjang-ganjing sl 9, lik*)

balungan . 3̇ . 2̇ . 6 . 5 . 1̇ . 6 . 5 . 6

becomes

saron 1̇ 3 1̇ 2 1̇ 6 1̇ 5 1̇ 1 1̇ 6 1̇ 5 1̇ 6

On some old recordings, the *pancer* note is the low 1, although this practice may be associated with the loud style of the piece rather than the age of the recording.

When a *pancer* note other than 1̇ is used, the effect on

Tips & tricks 5
Interpreting *balungan* (c): *gantungan*

A completely empty *gåtrå* does not mean silence from the *balungan* instruments. In accordance with the general principle that a *pin* represents a continuation of the previous note, an empty *gåtrå* is to be interpreted as a *gåtrå gantung* on the note that ended the previous *gåtrå*. For example (*gd Loro-loro géndhong sl m*, *mérong*, start of second *gongan*)

635⑥
. . . . 1̇653 22.3 1232̂

where the last note of the first *gongan* is 6, continuing thoughout the next *gåtrå*. The *saron*, *demung* and *slenthem* typically all play the *gantung* note on the third beat, as if the notation showed

. . 6 . 1̇653 22.3 1232̂

In such situations the notation sometimes shows the note on the third beat, but strictly speaking it is an element of *garap*.

In other cases of *gantungan*, the *balungan* instruments play the *balungan* line as notated. Note the difference in the next *kenongan* of *gd Loro-loro géndhong*

66 . . 1̇653 22.3 1232̂

where the 66 . . at the beginning emphasises that the *gåtrå gantung* is not repeating the final note of the previous *gåtrå*.

the *balungan* is somewhat greater than shown above. For example, the *inggah* of the *gendhing bonang Okrak-okrak sl m* is sometimes written in *balungan nibani* form

. 6 . 5   . 1̇ . 6   . 3 . 2   . 6 . 5̂
. 6 . 5   . 1̇ . 6   . 3 . 2   . 3 . 2̂
. 3 . 2   . 3 . 2   . 3 . 2   . 5 . 6̂
. 5 . 6   . 5 . 6   . 3 . 2   . 6 . ⑤̂

whereas the *balungan mlaku* version is given as

3635 3136 3532 3635̂
3635 3136 3532 3132̂
3132 3132 3132 3536̂
3536 3536 3532 363⑤̂

showing a *pancer* 3 throughout. In the filled-in version, the 3 in the middle of the *gåtrå* . 3 . 2 has been shifted up or down to give 3532 or 3132, and the 1̇ is again played low in the *gåtrå* 3136. The effect is to create *gåtrå* with more normal contours.

In another example, . 3 . 5 . 3 . 2 played as 3235 3632, the 2 in the first *gåtrå* has been chosen in preference to 5 (which would have given 3535). Likewise, the 6 in the second *gåtrå* is preferred to 5—the latter giving a more normal contour, but repeating the end of the previous *gåtrå*.

In *sléndro*, *pancer* 5 is also found. In *pélog*, the *pancer* notes used are 3, 5 and (in *pathet barang*) 7.

It is not impossible for two different *pancer* notes to be used in different parts of a piece: for example, both 5 and 7 in the single *gongan* of *ldr Sumyar pl 7*, so that

. 3 . 2   . 3 . 2̂   . 3 . 2   . 5 . 3̂
. 7 . 6   . 2 . 7̣̂   . 5̣ . 6̣   . 3 . ②

becomes

7̣37̣2 7̣37̣2̂ 7̣37̣2 5653̂
5756 5257̂ 5356 7̣3̣7̣②

When the *saron* players use *pancer* notes, they start playing them at a major structural point—possibly even the *gong bukå*—or at least after the piece has settled at its main *irâmå*. In the case of a *ketawang*, *pancer* may start from the first time the *lik* is played, after which they will continue in the *ompak* as well as the *lik*. In the *inggah* of a *gendhing*, *pancer* notes typically start after the first *kenong*, where various other *garap* changes occur. Once started, *pancer* notes will normally be used until the end of the piece, except that they may stop if the piece speeds up to *irâmå lancar*, e.g. in the course of a *suwuk gropak*.

Nitir

In Solonese style, the *saron* plays nothing for a *pin* on a *dhong* in the *balungan*, simply leaving the previous note to continue. In the Yogyanese treatment called *nitir*, one or more *pin* may be filled in by repeating the previous note:

balungan	5 . 3 .	2365	. . 35
saron	5533	2365	5535

This is only one of several Yogyanese methods of dealing with a *pin*: the others are described below. In Yogyanese notation, the repeated note is often written into the *balungan*. A common Yogyanese version of *lnc Hudan mas* contains examples of this.

Imbal, Solonese style

Saron imbal is an important form of decoration used in some loud-style pieces, and for others in *wayang* style. The principle behind it is that the two players—either at separate instruments, or on opposite sides of one instrument—cooperate to create an interlocking pattern ending at a *sèlèh* note. If the players share an instrument, the advantage is that it is easier for them to stay properly interlocked. The disadvantage is that only one of the players can play on the mid-portion of the *wilah*, and the other player's strokes may cause the *wilah* to jump. If the players compete for the same part of the *wilah*, their *tabuh* will clash, at least in passing. One important feature of *saron imbal* is the style of damping. Each player damps his/her previous note when the other player plays.

The pattern contains runs of consecutive notes; often four notes, either ascending or descending. In terms of number of notes (16) or duration, the length of the pattern is always the same. It covers two *gåtrå* in *irâmå lancar*, one *gåtrå* in *ir I*, and half a *gåtrå* (i.e. with two *sèlèh* points per *gåtrå*) in *ir II*. In Solonese style, *imbal saron* does not seem to be used in *irâmå* slower than *ir II*.

Verbal description of how *saron imbal* works is inevitably long-winded and rather mathematical. The examples below may provide sufficient explanation by themselves. It may also be useful to work out on paper some of the many possible patterns that conform to the principles now described.

The on-beat player, shown as *saron I* in the examples, plays a pattern ending with the *sèlèh* note—the note 2 will be used in the first examples below—and at twice the rate of the *balungan* (in *irâmâ lancar*) or four times the rate (in *ir I*).

All the examples here are for two *gâtrâ* in *irâmâ lancar.* The choice of *balungan nibani* for the examples is irrelevant. The same treatment would be applied to *balungan mlaku* and to any pair of *gâtrâ* with the same final note: the pattern depends only on the *sèlèh* note. The patterns shown for two *gâtrâ* in *irâmâ lancar* would also apply for a single *gâtrâ* in *ir I* with the same final note—i.e. for the *gâtrâ* 3532 in *ir I* for the first examples below.

The players can choose from various patterns, some more difficult than others. In the easiest versions, the on-beat player's pattern starts with the *sèlèh* note twice or four times, then alternates between the *sèlèh* note and the note two above it or two below it. The off-beat player's task is always to play notes adjacent to those chosen by the on-beat player, with the aim of creating a combined pattern containing sequences of consecutive notes.

If the *sèlèh* note is low, as in the first examples below, the other note used by the on-beat player must be above it, i.e. the note 5 in this case, and the off-beat player will probably play the notes above those of the on-beat player. The overall pattern then contains runs of four consecutive notes, 6532. According to whether the on-beat player starts with the *sèlèh* note twice or four times, the results may be

balungan	. 3 . 5	. 3 . 2
saron I	. 2 . 2 . 5 . 2	. 5 . 2 . 5 . 2
saron II	3 . 3 . 6 . 3 .	6 . 3 . 6 . 3 .
combined	32326532	65326532

or

balungan	. 3 . 5	. 3 . 2
saron I	. 2 . 2 . 2 . 2	. 5 . 2 . 5 . 2
saron II	3 . 3 . 3 . 3 .	6 . 3 . 6 . 3 .
combined	32323232	65326532

The off-beat player can also make the pattern as easy as possible by sticking to the same note throughout, between the on-beat player's two notes, so that there are only three different notes involved: this gives a pattern such as

balungan	. 3 . 5	. 3 . 2
saron I	. 2 . 2 . 5 . 2	. 5 . 2 . 5 . 2
saron II	3 . 3 . 3 . 3 .	3 . 3 . 3 . 3 .
combined	32323532	35323532

Conversely, if the *sèlèh* note is high, the other note used by the on-beat player must be low, and the off-beat player will probably choose notes below the on-beat player's notes:

balungan	. 6 . 3	. 5 . 6
saron I	. 6 . 6 . 3 . 6	. 3 . 6 . 3 . 6
saron II	5 . 5 . 2 . 5 .	2 . 5 . 2 . 5 .
combined	56562356	23562356

Again the *sèlèh* note comes at the end of the four-note run, 2356. The off-beat player is not obliged to use these notes. Using the highest possible notes in the off-beat part for the *sèlèh* note 6, the result could be

balungan	. 6 . 3	. 5 . 6
saron I	. 6 . 6 . 3 . 6	. 3 . 6 . 3 . 6
saron II	5 . 5 . 1̇ . 5 .	1̇ . 5 . 1̇ . 5 .
combined	56561̇356	1̇3561̇356

where the *sèlèh* note now comes in the middle of the four-note run.

If the *sèlèh* note is 3 or 5 (in *sléndro*), there are more possibilities for both players. The next set of examples uses *sèlèh* note 5, giving the on-beat player the choice of either 2 or 1̇ as the 'second note'. In the first two examples below, the on-beat player has chosen 2, and a satisfactory overall pattern results if the off-beat player plays 3 and 6 in either order.

balungan	. 6 . 1̇	. 6 . 5
saron I	. 5 . 5 . 2 . 5	. 2 . 5 . 2 . 5
saron II	6 . 6 . 3 . 6 .	3 . 6 . 3 . 6 .
combined	65653265	32653265

or

balungan	. 6 . 1̇	. 6 . 5
saron I	. 5 . 5 . 2 . 5	. 2 . 5 . 2 . 5
saron II	3 . 3 . 6 . 3 .	6 . 3 . 6 . 3 .
combined	35356235	62356235

Off-beat notes 3 and 6 similarly produce good patterns if the on-beat notes are 1̇ and 5:

balungan	. 6 . 1̇	. 6 . 5
saron I	. 5 . 5 . 1̇ . 5	. 1̇ . 5 . 1̇ . 5
saron II	6 . 6 . 3 . 6 .	3 . 6 . 3 . 6 .
combined	6 5 6 5 3 1̇ 6 5	3 1̇ 6 5 3 1̇ 6 5

or

balungan	. 6 . 1̇	. 6 . 5
saron I	. 5 . 5 . 1̇ . 5	. 1̇ . 5 . 1̇ . 5
saron II	3 . 3 . 6 . 3 .	6 . 3 . 6 . 3 .
combined	3 5 3 5 6 1̇ 3 5	6 1̇ 3 5 6 1̇ 3 5

Other choices of off-beat notes may not generate good patterns, depending on which notes the on-beat player chooses: for example

balungan	. 6 . 1̇	. 6 . 5
saron I	. 5 . 5 . 1̇ . 5	. 1̇ . 5 . 1̇ . 5
saron II	3 . 3 . 1 . 3 .	1 . 3 . 1 . 3 .
combined	3 5 3 5 1 1̇ 3 5	1 1̇ 3 5 1 1̇ 3 5

in which the combined pattern contains only short runs, plus several undesirable jumps.

This demonstrates a fundamental problem for the off-beat player, who cannot always know how to respond correctly to the other player: he or she must start first, yet does not know whether the on-beat pattern will start with the *sèlèh* note four times, twice or not at all (see below), nor which other note the on-beat player will choose. In this situation, as in various others in gamelan-playing, the off-beat player has to 'follow from in front'. The reality is that the off-beat player will sometimes guess wrong at the start of the pattern, but must then change in order to respond to whatever the on-beat player does.

The on-beat player can use both of the possible 'second' notes, as in the next two examples. If the same second note is not used twice in succession, runs of five different notes result, as shown by the underlining:

balungan	. 6 . 1̇	. 6 . 5
saron I	. 5 . 5 . 1̇ . 5	. 2 . 5 . 1̇ . 5
saron II	6 . 6 . 3 . 6 .	3 . 6 . 3 . 6 .
combined	6 5 6 5 3 1̇ 6 5	3 2 6 5 3 1̇ 6 5

and

balungan	. 6 . 1̇	. 6 . 5
saron I	. 5 . 5 . 1̇ . 5	. 2 . 5 . 1̇ . 5
saron II	3 . 3 . 6 . 3 .	6 . 3 . 6 . 3 .
combined	3 5 3 5 6 1̇ 3 5	6 2 3 5 6 1̇ 3 5

It is a good idea to leave this trick to the on-beat player. However, if the off-beat player were clairvoyant, even more interesting patterns could be created. As with *demung imbal*, players who regularly play together should be able to achieve more complex patterns.

The examples given so far begin with the on-beat player emphasising the *sèlèh* note by playing it twice or four times. If successive *gåtrå* (or pairs of *gåtrå*, in *ir lancar*) have the same *sèlèh* note, there is no need to emphasise it more than once. Therefore the more complex *imbal* patterns may be used throughout the *gåtrå* (or second *gåtrå*) instead of only at the end: for example

balungan	. 6 . 1̇	. 6 . 5
saron I	. 2 . 5 . 1̇ . 5	. 1̇ . 5 . 2 . 5
saron II	6 . 3 . 6 . 3 .	6 . 3 . 6 . 3 .
combined	6 2 3 5 6 1̇ 3 5	6 1̇ 3 5 6 2 3 5

More advanced players may apply this type of complex *garap* to any *gåtrå*.

From the examples it should be clear that the *sèlèh* note need not be the highest or lowest of the four notes, and that three-, four- and/or five-note runs must occur in the 16-note pattern if the players have chosen the right notes.

A safe rule for the off-beat player is to use the notes on either side of the *sèlèh* note, when possible: the order in which they are used is less important. For a *sèlèh* note at the end of the compass of the *saron*, this option is not available. The highest *sèlèh* notes normally usable are 1̇ in *sléndro*, 6 in *pélog bem*, 7 in *pélog barang*, and the lowest are 6̣ or 1 in *sléndro*, 1 in *pélog bem*, 2 in *pélog barang*.

Simpler *saron imbal* of the following form also occurs:

saron I	. 5 . 5 . 5 . 5	. 2 . 2 . 2 . 2
saron II	6 . 6 . 6 . 6 .	3 . 3 . 3 . 3 .

See also ***Saron wayangan***, p. 133.

Imbal, Yogya style

Yogyanese *saron imbal* is a treatment for pieces in various forms, including loud-style *ladrang* and some of the *gendhing lampah*—specifically *ayak-ayakan* and *playon*,

plus *srepegan* in the narrow Yogyanese sense, i.e. the transition section between these two. It is associated with *kendhangan gembyakan*.

The range of possibilities for Yogyanese *imbal* on the *saron* is actually more limited than on the *demung*, but there are both simple and less simple styles for the *saron*. Compared with Solonese *imbal saron*, there are similarities as well as differences. One similarity is the damping style. The differences include the off-beat player staying closer to the *sèlèh* note, and both players departing further from the *sèlèh* note at the start of their combined pattern than at the end. These are standard features of Yogyanese *imbal demung*, and some *imbal saron*.

The simpler styles involve the on-beat player staying on the *sèlèh* note and the off-beat player staying on the note above it (examples in *ir I*)

balungan	1̇ 6 3 2
saron I	1̇ . 1̇ . 1̇ . 1̇ . 3 . 3 . 3 . 3 .
saron II	. 6 . 6 . 6 . 6 . 2 . 2 . 2 . 2

and the more complex variants are closer to characteristic Solonese *imbal*, including sequences of four different notes

balungan	2 3 5 3
saron I	2 . 5 . 5 . 5 . 5 . 2 . 5 . 5 .
saron II	. 3 . 6 . 3 . 3 . 3 . 3 . 6 . 3

or even five notes:

balungan	3 6 3 2
saron I	2 . 5 . 1̇ . 5 . 3 . 3 . 3 . 3 .
saron II	. 3 . 6 . 6 . 6 . 2 . 5 . 2 . 2

Both styles may be mixed in a single pattern

balungan	5 3 2 3
saron I	5 . 5 . 5 . 5 . 5 . 2 . 5 . 2 .
saron II	. 3 . 3 . 3 . 3 . 1 . 3 . 1 . 3

giving a result that falls within the range of Solonese practice.

Among the common features of the above patterns are the on-beat player always ending on the *sèlèh* note, and the off-beat player always ending on an adjacent note. The on-beat player's penultimate note is either the *sèlèh* note or a note two away from it. These features differ from Yogyanese *imbal demung*.

All these examples match the density of Solonese *imbal saron* and therefore the denser versions of Yogyanese *imbal demung* also. They show two *sèlèh* points per *gåtrå*, although patterns with a *sèlèh* point only on the last note of the *gåtrå* are also found, e.g.

balungan	3 6 3 2
saron I	3 . 3 . 1 . 3 . 6 . 6 . 6 . 3 .
saron II	. 2 . 2 . 2 . 5 . 5 . 5 . 5 . 2

Nyacah

Nyacah are patterns played by a single *saron*, ending on a *sèlèh* note.[5] They are a standard form of *garap* for *srepegan* and *sampak*, but may also be used in other pieces played in *wayang* style. One *saron* may play *nyacah* while a pair of *saron* are playing *imbal*.

A *nyacah* pattern consists of eight notes ending on the *sèlèh* note, and inevitably the pattern must go both up and down. Usually the sequence of notes proceeds stepwise. Jumps are not absolutely forbidden, but are avoided, especially near the *sèlèh* note. It is also possible to repeat a note, but usually only at the beginning of the pattern. Gaps (*pin*) are allowed but seldom occur. There is no obligation for the *nyacah* to coincide with *balungan* notes except at the *sèlèh* note.

An example of *nyacah* patterns for *srepegan sléndro manyurå*:

balungan	3 2	3 2
nyacah	3561̇6532	65353212
balungan	5 3	5 3
nyacah	55535653	23561̇653
balungan	2 3	2 1
nyacah	65352353	23565321

The easiest way to create a *nyacah* sequence is to start with the two notes that it will end with. Taking the *sèlèh* note 2, some possibilities are then:

32323232	32323532
32123532	32126532
32356532	32653212
3261̇6532	
12353212	12123212
12653212	12356532
12323532, etc.	

5 The words *nyacah* and *nacah* are alternative verbal derivatives from *cacah*, and either may be found: it would not be safe to assume that *nyacah* always refers to this style of *garap*, and that *nacah* has other meanings, especially the parts played by the *peking* (see below).

Table 3.2
Nyacah for *srepegan* in *sléndro*

Pathet nem		
26523565	2521265(3)[a]	
56523123	65265235	
22222356[b]	636521 3(2)[c]	
65352132[d]	352652 3(5)	
Pathet sångå		
22221231[e]	51̇52532(1)	
561̇561̇61̇	51̇532532	3521235(6)[f]
1̇651̇561̇6	23525321	352652 3(5)
3̸5232561̇[e]	3̸52325 3(2)[g]	
65352532[h]	352652 3(5)	
Pathet manyurå		
31236532[i]	53252353[j]	6561̇632(1)
561̇56321	31232532[k]	51̇53235(6)[l]
35212356	1̇6563123	636521 3(2)

a. Or 25212653. b. *Sèlèh* note = 3. c. Or 636526̣12.
d. Or 6̣1232352. e. *Sèlèh* note = 5. f. Or 353652 16̣.
g. Or 5̸51̇61̇532. h. Or .6̣1236̣12. i. Or 6̣1213212.
j. Or 6̣26̣12353. k. Or 3216̣1232. l. Or 3563521 6̣.

The next easiest approach is to start on the note above or below the *sèlèh* note, but without then following it with the *sèlèh* note:

35653212	3561̇6532
35321232	35656532
35326532	3561̇3532
3561̇3212	3561̇1232
35356532	35353212

The examples above include some sequences that proceed entirely stepwise, and others with jumps. The *srepegan* example given earlier has some more ambitious patterns. All the patterns shown can be transposed up or down, the limits of the instrument's compass permitting, and the general principles of the examples apply to all other *sèlèh* notes.

Table 3.2 shows a set of 'advanced' examples from one source for *srepegan* in *sléndro*. These include several interesting features:

- the use of 6̣, even in contexts where the *balungan* is around 6 rather than 6̣;
- some use of repetition, and extensive use of jumps;
- the use of *ngencot/neceg* (see next heading);
- patterns not ending on the *sèlèh* note according to the *balungan*, e.g. ending on 6 where 3 would be expected, although other decorating instruments too (including the *bonang*) may play to these alternative *sèlèh* notes.

Ngencot and neceg

These two styles, in which a note is played **while** it is being damped, are considered characteristically Yogyanese, although the Solonese also use them. They offer ways of filling in a *pin* in the *balungan*. In fact the two terms are surrounded by confusion. For some sources, they imply the same *garap*, but *neceg* applies to *ir I* or faster, whereas *ngencot* applies to *ir II*. Other sources give the terms to two different but related forms of *garap*.

There is probably most agreement on the following type of example (this from *ldr Semar Mantu sl m* in *ir II*)

balungan	. 5 5 .	5 3 6 5
saron	. 5 5 3̸3̸	5 3 6 5

where the solidus[6] indicates *ngencot*. Some sources would give the same *garap* for *ir I*, but would then call it *neceg*. Another version of the difference between *neceg* and *ngencot* is as follows

balungan	5 5 . .	5 3 6 5
saron, neceg	5 5 . 3̸3̸	5 3 6 5
saron, ngencot	5 5 . 3̸3̸3̸	5 3 6 5

or

balungan	2 3 2 .	2 3 5 6
saron, neceg	2 3 2 2̸2̸	2 3 5 6
saron, ngencot	2 3 2 2̸2̸2̸	2 3 5 6

and another explanation of *ngencot* is

balungan	. . 5 .
saron, ir I	. 3̸ 5 3̸
saron, ir II	. 3̸3̸5 3̸3̸

It is sometimes said that *ngencot* treatment always applies to the *dhong*, but this is not true, as examples below indicate. In *iråmå lancar*, the doubling of the note results in one note falling on a *dhing*

6 Reminder: although this is standard notation for *ngencot*, it is only one of at least five uses of the solidus in notation.

saron	. 3̸ 3̸ 5	. 3̸ 3̸ 5

and the examples in Table 3.2 include off-beat *ngencot*.

Not every *pin* is filled in with *ngencot*. It can be used when the notes on either side of the *pin* are the same, and for *pin* falling on either the *dhing* or the *dhong*. It is also supposedly not applied to two successive *pin*. However, some sources suggest a *ngencot* treatment for two *pin* (example from *ldr Juru demung pl 6* in *ir II*):

balungan	1 1 . .	1 3 1 2
saron	1 1 1̸ 1̸1̸	1 3 1 2

For those sources who consider *neceg* to differ from *ngencot*, the *neceg* equivalent of the above in *ir I* would be

balungan	1 1 . .	1 3 1 2
saron	1 1 1̸ 1̸	1 3 1 2

The *ngencot* pattern is sometimes thought of as an anapaest, i.e. the damped notes belong with the following note, not the preceding one, as confirmed by examples such as this, in *ir II*:

balungan	6 6 . .	6 6 . 5
saron	6 6 . 6̸6̸	6 6 . 5

(However, this is an oversimplification.) In contrast, *neceg* notes do not always come in pairs, e.g.

balungan	2 6 2 1	. . 1 1
saron	2 6 2 1	1̸ 1̸ 1 1

or

saron	2 6 2 1	1̸ 1 1̸ 1

nor are the notes on either side always the same:

balungan	3 2 1 .	5 6 1 2
saron	3 2 1 1̸1̸	5 6 1 2

The volume level in *ngencot/neceg* is still the normal level for a loud-style *balungan* (reminder: the level does not fall much in *ir II* in the Yogyanese style). Therefore bronze *wilah* need to be grasped firmly in order to achieve sufficient damping: the sound should be completely dead. Before a *ngencot/neceg* note is played, the preceding note must be damped, as usual for any repeated *balungan* note.

Other Yogyanese styles

In *méngkal* or *péngkalan*, some *balungan* notes are displaced, falling on off-beats, e.g.

balungan	5 3 5 .	5 3 5 6
saron	35 .3 .5 .3	.5 3 5 6

The word *péngkalan* refers to a horse kicking out with its hind legs.

The *napas* style of playing follows the same pattern as *neceg*, but the volume level is reduced almost to inaudibility. (*Napas* means 'breath'.)

Another form of decoration is *nyampar*, also called *nyaruk*. This involves bringing in an adjacent note between two *balungan* notes, which must be different, e.g.

balungan	1 2 1 6	5 1̇ 5 2
saron	1 2 1 61̇	561̇ 5 2

where 1̇ is inserted between 6 and 5, and then 6 is inserted between the 5 and 1̇. Often pieces are notated with the *nyampar* notes already included.

Minjal (not to be confused with *pinjalan* in its other senses) is similar to *nyampar*, but applies between two identical *balungan* notes, e.g.

'Exceptional' *garap*

The description in this book covers the most widely used *garap* on the *balungan* instruments, but (as with all other instruments) additional *garap* is also found. The following examples from *wayang* performances illustrate unsurprising extensions of the same principles.

Example 1 (*ir I*)

balungan	3 5 6 5
saron	3 53565

In this example from a *srepegan*, the *saron* changes density in mid-*gåtrå*. In the second half of the *gåtrå*, the relationship between the *saron* part and the *balungan* is the usual relationship between a *balungan mlaku* and a *balungan nibani*.

Example 2 (*ir II*)

balungan	3 2
saron	3 2 1 2
peking	33223322

In this half-*gåtrå* from a *ladrang*, the density ratio between the *peking* part and the *balungan* is the usual Solonese 4:1. The *saron* player, instead of simply playing the *balungan*, has created a part with a density that 'ought' not to be found in a *ladrang*, by expanding the *balungan* in the same way as the first example.

balungan	3 3 2 5
saron	353 2 5

The term *ngracik* indicates a double-density *balungan*. Sources sometimes treat *ngracik* as a form of *garap*, but it is arguably a variant of the *balungan* that simply replaces the 'standard' *balungan* in some situations—especially in *ir III*. As mentioned earlier (p. 26), the *balungan ngracik* sometimes represents the 'real' composition.

In all the styles under this heading, the *garap* may be found written into the *balungan* notation.

Garap for *saron* + other instruments

Various playing styles where one or two *saron* cooperate with other instruments are described under the heading **Multi-instrument *garap*** (p. 231 foll.). These include *kinthilan* and *kébar*.

Demung, *saron demung*

The *demung* (Fig. 3.18) is pitched an octave below the *saron*. In any given gamelan, the *demung* will be larger than the *saron* in all dimensions. However, the *demung* from one gamelan may be the size of the *saron* in another gamelan.

Containing more metal than the *saron*, the *demung* is capable of higher volume and therefore has a specially important role in loud-style pieces. The instrument often functions as a volume control for the other *balungan* instruments, encouraging the *saron* to play loud enough. Its *tabuh* are of the same form as for the *saron*, but larger and heavier.

Normally there is one *demung* for every two *saron* in the gamelan. Therefore a typical gamelan has only one per *laras*, but large gamelan have two or even four. Again, gamelan bought for educational purposes may have additional *demung*.

Regular playing style

The simplest thing to say about the *demung* is that it plays the same part as the *saron*. Very often it does, but it also has its own range of special *garap*. Like the *saron*, it may stop playing in slower *iråmå*.

There are also occasions when the *demung* continues playing the basic *balungan* when the *saron* switch to some form of decoration.

Pancer

Generally the *demung* will do as the *saron* does, playing the same *pancer* notes and in the same places. The *demung* player may also choose to continue playing the *balungan* as written. A major exception to these practices is described below under **Imbal, Yogya style**.

Imbal, Solo style

In *gendhing bonang* in Solonese style, two *demung* or two players on one *demung* often create a characteristic form of decoration. The off-beat player plays the *balungan* half a beat after the on-beat player (cf. *pinjalan*, described under **Multi-instrument *garap***, p. 231 foll.).

This treatment typically starts at the gong after the tempo has increased to a fast *ir II*. It is only applied to *balungan mlaku*: for *balungan nibani* or for *balungan ngadhal*, the off-beat player plays the same as the on-beat player.

Imbal, Yogya style

In traditional Yogyanese style, *imbal demung* is part of the characteristic *garap* for pieces played in the *soran* style. This includes the large category of *soran*-style *gendhing* with *balungan nibani* in the *ndhawah* section. The *garap* is associated with *slenthem gemakan* and *saron pancer*: see **Multi-instrument *garap***. (See also ***Saron barung: pancer***, p. 114, for *garap* in *pélog* pieces.)

Compared with Yogyanese *imbal saron*, there are several differences. In addition, Yogyanese *imbal demung* comes in different levels of density and complexity, as well as versions to suit different *iråmå*.

The notation here designates the off-beat player as *demung I*, which is common but not universal Yogyanese practice. All examples are based on a *balungan nibani*, because this is the most frequent use of *imbal demung*.

The first example is the *imbal låmbå* version for *ir I*, where the pattern consists of only four notes and covers a single *gåtrå*:

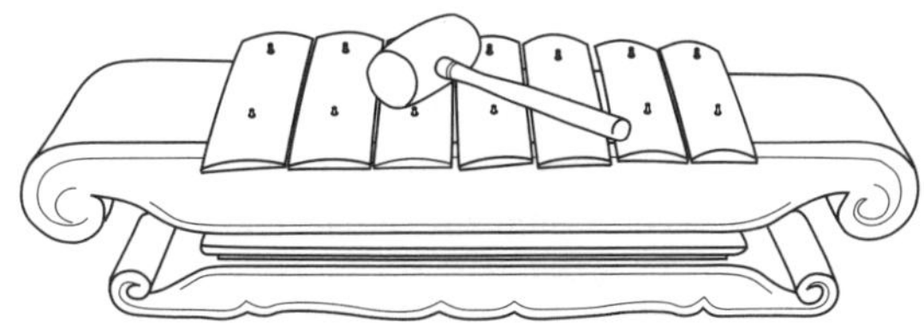

3.18 *Demung* with Solo-style frame

balungan (alternatives)	. 3 . 2
	. 5 . 2
	. 1 . 2
demung I	2 . 2 .
demung II	. 3 . 2

The next example is also for *ir I*, but here there are two *sèlèh* points per *gåtrå*, and twice as many notes:

balungan	. 3 . 2
demung I	3 . 3 . 2 . 2 .
demung II	. 5 . 3 . 3 . 2

The two examples above are the simplest possible, using only the *sèlèh* note and the note above it. (For the usual reason, the 'other' note will sometimes have to be the note below the *sèlèh* note.)

For the slower *iråmå*, longer *imbal* patterns are used, so that the mid-point of the *gåtrå* is also a *sèlèh* point, and more variations are possible. The patterns can be divided in two ways. First, there are two densities: *imbal dados* (lower density) and *imbal rangkep* (higher density). The latter represents the same density as for Solonese *saron imbal*, i.e. a pattern of 16 notes per *gåtrå* in *ir I*, although *imbal* at the lower density seems to be heard more frequently. Second, there are two levels of complexity: *lugu* (plain) and *sekaran*-style.

An example of *imbal dados lugu* in *ir I* or *II* would be

balungan	. 3 . 2
demung I	3 . 3 . 3 . 3 . 2 . 2 . 2 . 2 .
demung II	. 5 . 5 . 5 . 3 . 3 . 3 . 3 . 2

and one possible *imbal dados sekaran* equivalent would be

balungan	. 3 . 2
demung I	3 . 6 . 3 . 3 . 2 . 5 . 2 . 2 .
demung II	. 5 . 1̇ . 5 . 3 . 3 . 6 . 3 . 2

In *ir II*, *imbal dados* is the lower of the two densities normally used, and *imbal rangkep* is also available: Fig. 3.19 shows three examples of the latter. Example (a) is *imbal rangkep lugu*, basically an extension of the *imbal dados lugu* pattern. Example (b) is *imbal rangkep sekaran*, also produced by extending the *dados* version in the same way.

However, the *sekaran* version can include further variations, as shown in example (c). In the first quarter of the *demung I* part, the player has decided to stay on 6 rather than continue alternating between 3 and 6; likewise in the third quarter with the note 5 instead of 2 and 5. The *demung II* part also sticks with one note in some places. Looking in detail at the first quarter of the pattern, if *demung I* stays on 6, it does not inconvenience the *demung II* player, who can still choose between 5 and 1̇. If *demung II* stays on 1̇, then *demung I* must stay on 6 in order to maintain a series of adjacent notes.

The examples in Fig. 3.19 include optional *neceg* on the *demung II* notes that fall on the *pin* of the *balungan*.

In all but one of the preceding examples, there are two *sèlèh* points per *gåtrå* for the *imbal* patterns. The various styles of *imbal demung* have also been classified in another way, according to how long the patterns last. The examples that last for half a *gåtrå* are then classed as *imbal lugu*. Patterns lasting for a whole *gåtrå*, as in this example

balungan	. 3 . 2	. 6 . 5
demung I	2 . 2 . 2 . 2 .	5 . 5 . 5 . 5 .
demung II	. 3 . 3 . 3 . 2	. 6 . 6 . 6 . 5

are called *imbal gåtrå*, and the name *imbal sekaran* is given to more complex patterns lasting for two *gåtrå*, such as the following

balungan	. 3 . 2	. 6 . 5
demung I	2 . 5 . 1̇ . 1̇ .	5 . 1̇ . 5 . 5 .
demung II	. 3 . 6 . 6 . 6	. 3 . 6 . 6 . 5

This classification is obviously incompatible with the first one described above, and it includes lower-density patterns only, corresponding to *imbal dados* in *ir II*.

Another variant is called *imbal ngepok*: this is a way of avoiding repetition in a pattern that covers two identical *gåtrå*:

balungan	. 2 . 1	. 2 . 1
demung I	2 . 2 . 1 . 1 .	1 . 3 . 1 . 1 .
demung II	. 3 . 2 . 2 . 1	. 2 . 2 . 2 . 1

Taking an overview of all these variants, we see that the last note played by **both** players is the *sèlèh* note, and that the off-beat player starts the pattern with the *sèlèh* note. These are the general, though not universal, pattern of Yogyanese *imbal demung*, and represent two differences from *imbal saron*.

A feature of *imbal demung* is that several densities of

Table 3.3
Comparison of types of interlocking *garap* used on *balungan* instruments (Solo and Yogya)

Garap	Notes per *gåtrå*	Used in
Solo		
Saron imbal	8/16/32	*ir lancar/ir I/ir II*
Kinthilan	16	*ir I* and *ir II*
Demung imbal	8	*ir I* and *ir II*
Yogya		
Demung imbal, låmbå	4/8	*ir I/ir II*
Demung imbal, dados	16	*ir I* and *ir II*
Demung imbal, rangkep	32	*ir II*
Saron imbal	16	*ir I*
Kinthilan	16	*ir I*
Solonese *pekingan* for comparison		
Nacah låmbå	8	*ir I*
Nacah rangkep	16	*ir II*

decoration are available for the same *iråmå*—an unusual situation, although not unique. Table 3.3 compares various interlocking styles used on the *balungan* instruments.

Even simpler *imbal demung* patterns are possible, alternating between the *sèlèh* note and an adjacent note, as shown earlier for *imbal saron* in *gendhing lampah*. Again there are *låmbå*-style versions

balungan	. 3 . 2
demung I	1 . 1 . 1 . 1 .
demung II	. 2 . 2 . 2 . 2

as well as a *dados*-style version

balungan	. 3 . 2
demung I	1 . 1 . 1 . 1 . 1 . 1 . 1 . 1 .
demung II	. 2 . 2 . 2 . 2 . 2 . 2 . 2 . 2

For the different types of *imbal* shown above, a variant is also possible in which the on-beat player does not play on the *sèlèh* note: this style is called *pejah*, contrasting with the term *gesang* for the version where the *sèlèh* note is played.

A further and rather surprising variant also occurs, in which the on-beat player plays on the *sèlèh* note, but uses the same note as before. The result is that the note on the *demung* conflicts with the *balungan* at the *sèlèh* point—one of the rare situations where this happens:

balungan	. 3 . 2
demung I	3 . 3 . 3 . 3 . 2 . 2 . 2 . 2 .
demung II	. 5 . 5 . 5 . 5 . 3 . 3 . 3 . 3

Some sources consider this the standard form of Yogyanese *demung imbal*, but performance practice is very varied.

Damping patterns are as for *imbal saron*: i.e. the player damps when the other player hits a new note.

The analysis above shows that *imbal demung* is another situation where a pair of players must listen carefully to each other and respond appropriately. In particular, the off-beat player must detect when the other player is switching between *lugu* and *sekaran* styles, and between different densities (*låmbå*, *dados* and *rangkep*). As one of the sources observes, the results are very dependent on the skills and experience of the players.

Ngencot and neceg

The description of *neceg* and *ngencot* playing on the *saron* applies equally to the *demung*. Usually the *demung* plays *neceg* or *ngencot* wherever the *saron* does. Because of the amount of metal in the *wilah* of a bronze *demung*, a very firm grip is necessary when damping for *ngencot/neceg*.

Garap for demung + other instruments

Various playing styles where the *demung* cooperates with other instruments are described under the heading **Multi-instrument *garap*** (p. 231 foll.).

(a)	*balungan*	. 3 . 2
	demung I	3 . 3 . 3 . 3 . 3 . 3 . 3 . 3 . 2 . 2 . 2 . 2 . 2 . 2 . 2 . 2 .
	demung II	. 5 . 5 . 5 . 5̸ . 5 . 5 . 5 . 3 . 3 . 3 . 3 . 3̸ . 3 . 3 . 3 . 2
(b)	*balungan*	. 3 . 2
	demung I	3 . 6 . 3 . 6 . 3 . 6 . 3 . 3 . 2 . 5 . 2 . 5 . 2 . 5 . 2 . 2 .
	demung II	. 5 . 1̇ . 5 . 1̸̇ . 5 . 1̇ . 5 . 3 . 3 . 6 . 3 . 6̸ . 3 . 6 . 3 . 2
(c)	*balungan*	. 3 . 2
	demung I	3 . 6 . 6 . 6 . 3 . 6 . 3 . 3 . 2 . 5 . 5 . 5 . 2 . 5 . 2 . 2 .
	demung II	. 5 . 1̇ . 1̇ . 1̸̇ . 5 . 5 . 5 . 3 . 3 . 6 . 3 . 6̸ . 3 . 3 . 3 . 2

3.19 Examples of *imbal rangkep lugu* and *imbal rangkep sekaran* for *demung*

Peking, saron panerus

This instrument has two names in regular use. *Peking* is agreed to be a nickname, derived from the name of a small songbird: sources disagree as to which one, and as to whether the origin of the nickname is Yogyanese or Solonese. Besides *saron panerus*, the name *saron peking* is also found.

The *peking* (Fig. 3.20) is pitched an octave above the *saron*, and is built on a smaller scale throughout. There is usually only one *peking* per *laras*, but a few court gamelan have two. It is believed that, in the *peking*'s typical repeating patterns of *xxyy* form (described in more detail below), each pair of notes was originally divided between two instruments.

The *tabuh* of the *peking* usually has a head made of horn (*tanduk*) on a wooden handle, but *tabuh* with hard wooden heads are also found. As with the beaters for the *saron* and *demung*, players use the edge rather than the flat of the head. Notes are damped only when a different note is struck, and sometimes not even then. As most of the *peking* playing styles involve repetitions of notes, the result is that at least half the notes struck are not damped.

The *peking* is one of the instruments where the difference between the characteristic Solonese and Yogyanese styles is most obvious. Having said that, it is important to distinguish between 'typical' and 'characteristic'. Yogyanese *peking* players often play a mixed form of *garap* in soft-style pieces, using characteristically Yogyanese *garap* in *ir I* but something more Solonese in slower *iråmå*. A common feature of both styles is that the *peking* pattern always coincides with the *balungan* note at the *sèlèh* points—i.e. the end of the *gåtrå*, and usually also the mid-point of the *gåtrå* in some *iråmå*. There is not necessarily any coincidence at any other point in the *gåtrå*.

Table 3.4
Solonese *peking* patterns according to *iråmå* and type of *balungan*

Iråmå	*Balungan nibani*	*Balungan mlaku*	Double-density *balungan*	Strokes per *balungan* beat
Ir lancar	*Nacah låmbå*	*Mbalung*	–	1
Ir I	*Nacah rangkep*	*Nacah låmbå*	*Mbalung*	2
Ir II	in this area,	*Nacah rangkep*	*Nacah låmbå*	4
Ir III	*nacah rangkep* patterns		*Nacah rangkep*	8
Ir IV	based on expanding the *balungan*			16

Although the *peking* is classified as a *balungan* instrument, most of the time it contributes simple decoration of the *balungan* line.

Peking: Solo style

In Solonese style, the *peking* plays a continuous line in an even rhythm without gaps. The details of the *garap* vary acording to *iråmå*. Gaps (*pin*) in the *balungan*—whether the regular gaps of *balungan nibani* or irregular ones—must be filled in. The different methods used are described below. The result of the Solonese approach to the *peking* is that the instrument always plays at roughly the same time density, i.e. the same number of notes per second, subject to the usual variations of tempo, and the number of strokes per *balungan* beat is therefore characteristic of the *iråmå*: see Table 3.4.

Because of this strict time relationship in Solonese *pekingan*, the different *iråmå* are often known by the number of *peking* strokes per *balungan* beat, e.g. *iråmå* ¼ for *iråmå dados*.

Mbalung

In a few situations, the *peking* plays the *balungan* as notated. Basically, it plays *mbalung* whenever the tempo is too fast for *nacah låmbå* (see next heading).

This situation arises during the first *kenongan* of a *gendhing* in Solo style, where the *peking* plays *mbalung* until the tempo has dropped to the point where it is comfortable to play *nacah låmbå*. The same can occur when other pieces start unusually fast, e.g. *ldr Moncèr* when played in *wayang* style. It also happens during a *suwuk gropak* (e.g. for a *ladrang*), which may effectively be in *iråmå lancar* or *iråmå gropak*. The *peking* may even be forced to play one note per two *balungan* beats.

In *iråmå lancar*, *lancaran* with either *balungan nibani* or *balungan mlaku* are played *mbalung*. In either case, a *pin* is first filled in according to the usual rule; i.e. it is treated

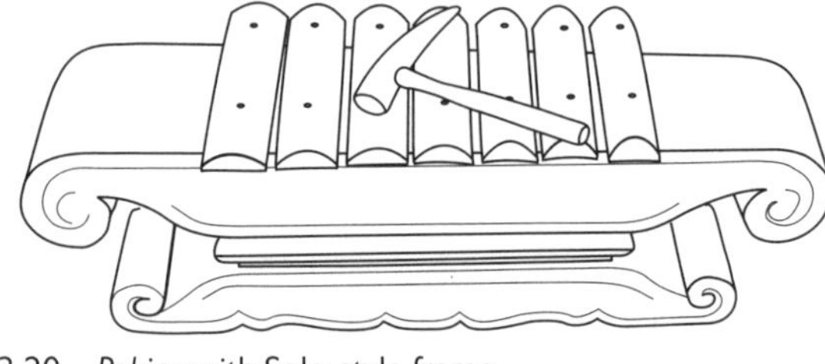

3.20 *Peking* with Solo-style frame

as a repeat of the previous note. As an example, *lnc Kebogiro Glendheng* is basically *mlaku*:

(5̣)

. . 4̣5̣ 4̣5̣4̣5̣ 4̣5̣4̣5̣ . 6̣ . (1)

. 6̣2 . 6̣1 . 6̣ 2 . 6̣1 . 6̣ . (5̣)

and is played by the *peking* in *iråmå lancar* as

(5̣)

5545 4545 4545 5661

1622 6116 2261 1665

A completely empty *gåtrå* can be taken as a *gåtrå gantung* on the previous note, and played with patterns as described below under **Treatment of *gantungan***, p. 128. The same often applies to an empty half-*gåtrå*.

Nacah låmbå

Nacah means 'chop'. It refers to the repetition of the *balungan* note, as if chopping it in two. *Nacah låmbå* or single *nacah* is the standard Solonese treatment for *ir I*. Also the treatment described above for a *balungan nibani* in *iråmå lancar* is effectively *nacah låmbå* too. The basic pattern of *nacah låmbå* means playing the *balungan* note twice; where notated, and again one beat later (in *iråmå lancar*) or half a beat later (in *ir I*). An example in *iråmå lancar* (from *lnc Ricik-ricik sl m*), following gong 6:

balungan	. 3 . 5 . 6 . 5 . 6 . 5 . 1̇ . (6)
peking	6335 5665 5665 51̇1̇6

If the *lancaran* has a *balungan mlaku* as well as a *balungan nibani*, the *peking* may play the *balungan mlaku* instead of giving *nacah låmbå* treatment to the *balungan nibani*.

An example in *ir I*, from *ldr Gléyong pl 6*:

balungan	2 3 2 1 6̣ 5̣ 3̣ 5̣̂
peking	22332211 66553355

As indicated earlier, the *peking* always coincides with the *balungan* on the *sèlèh* note. However, the *nacah låmbå* pattern finishes **after** the *sèlèh* note, and thus the Solonese *garap* for the *peking* (*nacah låmbå* or *nacah rangkep*) is among the few types of decoration that do not end on the *sèlèh* note. Another principle, or at least a strong tendency, is to preserve a smooth contour in the *peking* part.

For a single *gåtrå* in *balungan nibani* form, as well as for a *balungan* that is in *nibani* form throughout, the *peking* uses *nacah rangkep* in *ir I*: see the next heading. Isolated *pin* in the *balungan* imply, as usual, a continuation of the previous note, but require analysis.

Sometimes the obvious *garap* is a *peking* pattern with the same note four times in succession. The situation can occur when a *pin* is filled in but there is no question of a *gantungan*. For example, the second *gåtrå* here is treated as 2356:

balungan	6 5 3 2̆ . 3 5 6̂
peking	66553322 22335566

Some players prefer to avoid playing one note four times, and will therefore change the second pair of the repeated notes, so that it begins as well as ends with the *sèlèh* note (and also breaks the normal rule about playing every note twice):

balungan	6 5 3 2̆ . 3 5 6̂
peking	66553322 32335566

Other players consider this sort of pattern fussy.

When thinking about contours, one sometimes has to choose between a smooth contour in the *peking* part and the contour that most accurately represents the original *balungan*. Sometimes there are good arguments for either approach, and this subject will be revisited below.

Nacah rangkep

Nacah rangkep or double *nacah*, also known as *selang-seling* (= alternating), is the standard Solonese *garap* for *ir II*. The basic principle is to take the two notes *x* and *y* that make up half a *gåtrå*, and play an eight-note pattern of the form *xxyyxxyy*. Once again the *peking* coincides with the *balungan* note at the *sèlèh* points, which occur at the mid-point of the *gåtrå* as well as at the end, and again the pattern finishes just after the *sèlèh* point:

balungan	2 3 2 1
peking	2233223322112211

In accordance with the principle of keeping a smooth contour, the *peking* line tends to avoid making large jumps twice. If a large jump occurs within the half-*gåtrå*, the second half of the eight-note pattern often uses a note adjacent to the *sèlèh* note in place of the expected note. Intervals of a *kempyung* or larger count as large jumps, such as the the interval 26 when realising the cadential phrase 2126̣

balungan 2 1 2 6̣

peking 2 2 1 1 2 2 1 1 2 2 6 6 5 5 6 6

as do jumps from 2 or 3 up to 7. Jumps in the opposite direction, such as from 6 to 2 or 1, may be handled in the same way: 6 6 2 2 3 3 2 2 or 6 6 1 1 2 2 1 1.

If the *balungan* goes into double density in *ir II*, whether for short or long stretches, the *peking* plays *nacah lâmbâ*. Each note in the double-density part of the *balungan* is played twice. The following example (from *ldr Dirâdâmetâ sl 6*, starting after a gong 2) also includes a *pin* that has been filled in by assuming a repetition of the previous note:

balungan . . 2 3

peking 3 3 2 2 3 3 2 2 3 2 3 3 2 2 3 3

balungan 5 6 1̇ . 6 1̇ 5 6

peking 5 5 6 6 1̇ 1̇ 1̇ 1̇ 6 6 1̇ 1̇ 5 5 6 6

balungan 1 2 . 3

peking 1 1 2 2 1 1 2 2 3 2 3 3 2 2 3 3

The sequence 1̇ 1̇ 1̇ 1̇ could also be played as 1̇ 6 1̇ 1̇. The example again uses optional patterns that avoid playing a note four times in succession in the middle of the *gâtrâ*.

A change of *irâmâ* between *ir I* and *ir II* means a transition from *nacah lâmbâ* to *nacah rangkep*. Sometimes players have difficulty with these transitions. The problem seems to be that the *irâmâ* and the *peking* patterns change at slightly different points (Fig. 3.21). In other words, the *irâmâ* changes to *ir II*, requiring *nacah rangkep* timing, before the first pattern (for 2 3 2 1, in *nacah lâmbâ* timing) has finished. A similar situation arises at the transition in the opposite direction, from *ir II* to *ir I*, and likewise at other changes of *irâmâ*.

For double-density *balungan* in *ir III*, the *peking* plays *nacah rangkep* patterns based on each pair of *balungan* notes:

balungan

2 3 2 1 3 2 1 6̣

peking

2 2 3 3 2 2 3 3 2 2 1 1 2 2 1 1 3 3 2 2 3 3 2 2 1 1 6 6 5 5 6 6

For *balungan nibani* in *ir II*, and for the other combinations of *irâmâ* and *balungan* type not yet covered (see Table 3.4), the *balungan* is commonly expanded in some way so that *nacah rangkep* patterns will then fill out the *gâtrâ*. However, there are also less ambitious players who deal with *ir III* and *ir IV* by simply filling the space with repetitions of the *nacah rangkep* pattern that they would use in *ir II*.

To take one example, the case of *balungan nibani* in *ir II*, there are three basic methods. The simplest is to play the same pattern that would be used in *ir I*, but twice over:

balungan . 3 . 5

treated as 3 5 3 5

peking 3 3 5 5 3 3 5 5 3 3 5 5 3 3 5 5

This is not a particularly sophisticated treatment, and more interesting patterns result if the two notes of the *gâtrâ* are first expanded to four. Of the two approaches to this, the simpler one effectively treats each half-*gâtrâ* (of form . *x*) as if it were *gantung x*. For the previous example, this could give

balungan . 3 . 5

treated as 5 3 6 5

peking 5 5 3 3 5 5 3 3 6 6 5 5 6 6 5 5

The note below the 3 could be used instead:

2 2 3 3 2 2 3 3 6 6 5 5 6 6 5 5

Ir I to ir II

balungan — *irâmâ* changes here

2 3 2 1 6̣ 5̣ 3̣ 5̣

peking

2 2 3 3 2 2 1 1 6 6 5 5 6 6 5 5 3 3 5 5 3 3 5 5

pattern changes here

Ir II to ir I

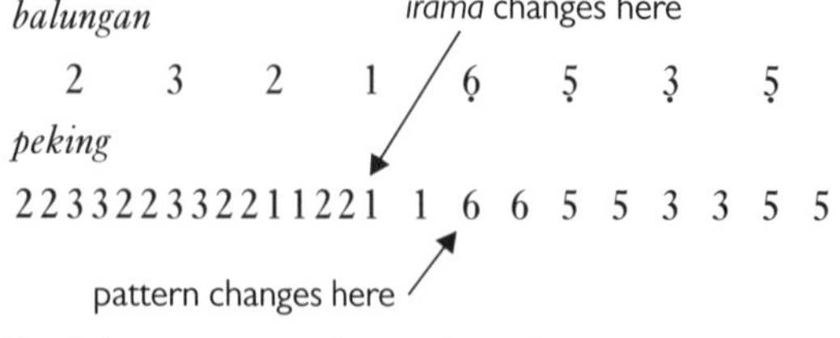

3.21 *Peking* transitions from *ir I* to *ir II* and vice versa

The other approach to expanding the *balungan*, and perhaps the most frequent, is basically the general one given earlier (p. 31). Some attention is given to the direction suggested by the *gåtrå*. Thus . 3 . 5 has an upward direction, so it would typically be expanded to 3565, which has the same upward characteristic:

balungan	.	3	.	5
treated as	3	5	6	5
peking	3355335566556655			

There is no obligation for the resulting pattern to coincide with the *sèlèh* point in the middle of the *gåtrå*: in fact, in a typical *gåtrå* of *nibani* form, the note at the mid-point is adjacent to the final *sèlèh* note, and this guarantees that a *nacah rangkep* pattern of the form shown above will not coincide with the *balungan* at mid-*gåtrå*.

When the two notes of the *gåtrå* are not adjacent, patterns with other structures may be used, but they will still reflect the direction of the *balungan*. For example,

2233223322112211

would be an obvious realisation of the *gåtrå* . 3 . 1, but it could also be played as

3311331122112211

Sometimes a player does not use the same four-note pattern twice, but instead uses two different patterns that are both considered suitable, as in the *ktw Puspåwarnå* examples below.

While the direction of the *balungan* within the *gåtrå* is important, the player may also take account of several other factors when choosing how to expand the *balungan*. For example, if the previous *gåtrå* ended high, the *gåtrå* . 3 . 5 could be expanded as 6535, and so make a smoother contour for the *peking* line. This could be one example of having to choose between giving the *peking* part a smooth contour and preserving the original contour of the *balungan*. The player might also decide to avoid starting the *nacah* pattern with the *sèlèh* note of the previous *gåtrå*.

The *peking* pattern can also move in one direction rather than going up as well as down: thus the pattern 5533553322112211 might be used for . 3 . 1, especially after a *gåtrå* ending above 5.

The limited compass of the *peking* sets bounds on the ways in which a *gåtrå* of *balungan nibani* can be expanded. For the note 1̇ in *sléndro*, there is no higher adjacent note available, so that the *sèlèh* note 1̇ must be approached from below, e.g. to expand . 6 . 1̇ as

66556655661̇1̇661̇1̇

A *gåtrå* that lies entirely high must be transposed down, e.g. treating . 2̇ . 1̇ as if it were . 2 . 1.

Peking players will also spot the standard cadential patterns in the *balungan*, and expand them in a suitable manner. Thus the *gåtrå* . 2 . 6̣ and . 1 . 6̣ in *sléndro manyurå*, especially at an important structural point such as a gong, may stand for the cadence 3216̣, and that is how they might then be expanded, rather than by patterns that might look more obvious, such as 1216̣ or 2126̣. Similarly, . 6̣ . 5̣ may be expanded as 216̣5̣ rather than 16̣3̣5̣.

As an example of the range of *garap* that a player may apply, the following variations were recorded for the two *gåtrå* . 3 . 2 . 1 . 6̣ in the same performance of *ktw Puspåwarnå* (doubling of notes is not shown):[7]

23231212 3121561̇6
23231212 31215656
32321212 16561̇61̇6
32323232 16561̇61̇6
32323232 1656561̇6
35353232 31215656
53532132 3121261̇6
53535232 31215656
53535232 3121561̇6
53535252 31215656

In these examples, the player can be seen using combinations of the principles described above, and there are further combinations that he might have used but did not (e.g. 3232 or 1212 to start the second *gåtrå*). He did not necessarily follow the same principles in both *gåtrå*.

For *balungan nibani* in *ir I*, the *peking* plays *nacah rangkep* patterns based on the two notes of each *gåtrå*:

balungan	. 2 . 1	. 6̣ . 5̣
peking	22112211	66556655

or may play *nacah låmbå* based on an expansion of the *balungan*, as described for *ir II*:

22332211 66553355

7 Sutton (1982).

Treatment of *gantungan*

Special treatment is given to a *gåtrå gantung* or to a longer or shorter *gantungan*. The *peking* then typically plays a pattern using two adjacent notes, the first usually being the note above the *sèlèh* note. In *iråmå lancar* there is a *sèlèh* point at the end of the *gåtrå*, so the *gåtrå* 22. . could be played in any *pathet* as 3322. In *ir I* the same *gåtrå* could be played as 33223322.

Some players think it is important for the *peking* to indicate the *gantungan*: the pattern 33223322 does not, because it could also represent *balungan* .3.2. They will achieve this by first playing the *sèlèh* note four times, e.g. (in *ir I*) 22223322 for this example.

If the *balungan* notation does not clearly indicate the *gantungan* (see p. 30), the treatment will normally be different. For example, if a *gåtrå* is of the form 6356, but is known from other evidence to be *gantung* 6, the *peking* will stick to the notes as notated rather than playing a *gantung* 6 pattern.

The treatment of a *gantungan* must respect the scale and *pathet*, as usual. For a *gantungan* on 6, the adjacent note must be 5 in *pélog bem*. For *sléndro* there is a choice of 5 or 1̇, and for *pélog barang* a choice of 5 or 7, e.g. in *ir I*:

pélog bem	55665566
pélog barang	55665566 or 77667766
sléndro	55665566 or 1̇1̇661̇1̇66

In *pélog nem*, for example, more generally the note 7 should normally be used in a *peking* pattern only if it is present in the *balungan* line. Thus the 7 in the penultimate *gåtrå* of the *ompak* of *ldr Gléyong* can be played, but the *gåtrå gantung* that starts the *ngelik* should use only 5 and 6:

balungan	7 6 5 4̆	2 1 2 ⑥
	. 6 6 6	
peking	77665544	22112266
	55665566	

However, it is not unknown for 7 to be used in *pélog limå / nem* if there is a 7 in an adjacent *gåtrå*. This is illustrated later for the related *pinjalan* technique (see **Multi-instrument *garap***, p. 231 foll.).

To continue with *ldr Gléyong*, the fifth *gåtrå* starts with a full *gåtrå gantung* on the note 2

balungan	2 2 . .̆	2 3 5 6̂
peking	33223322	22335566

whereas in the third *gåtrå* of the *ngelik* the *gantungan* covers the first half of the second *gåtrå*

balungan	5 3 2 3̂	. 3 5 6̆
peking	55332233	22335566
or	55332233	55335566

since the *pin* represents a continuation of the 3 in the previous *gåtrå*.

A *pin* on the *dhong* of a *gåtrå* creates a half-*gåtrå* of *gantungan*. For example, in 356. or .56. the *sèlèh* note is effectively 6, and the half-*gåtrå* will be treated as a *gantungan* on that note. The *peking* will play a pattern that must end on the 6, but may start with an adjacent note, subject to the usual *pathet* rules. Thus in *ir I* a pattern 6666 is always possible, or 1̇1̇66 in *sléndro*, or 7766 in *pélog barang*, or 5566 in any *pathet*. Similarly, in a *gåtrå* of the form *xy*. ., the two *pin* represent a *gantungan* on the note *y*.

In a pattern for a full *gåtrå gantung*, more than one adjacent note can be brought in if the *pathet* allows. Thus in the previous example for *balungan* 22. ., the adjacent note 1 could be used instead of or as well as 3:

33221122 or 11223322 or 11221122

However, the patterns starting with 1 are less likely in this example, because the last note of the previous *gåtrå* is 5, so that a 3 at the beginning of the pattern produces a smoother contour. In *pélog barang*, the note 1 is not native to the *pathet*, so the patterns with note 1 could not be used in the absence of another good reason to use it.

For a *gantungan* that lasts a half or full *gåtrå*, the treatment in *ir II* follows that in *ir I*, but there are more ways of introducing two different adjacent notes (where the *pathet* permits):

balungan	2 2 . .
peking	3322332233223322
or	3322332211221122
or	3322332211223322
or	3322332233221122

or, to signal the *gantungan* more clearly

2222332211223322 etc.

It is not possible to identify *gantungan* in *balungan nibani* just by looking at the *balungan* notation. However, the player might know, for example, that the *gåtrå* .2.1

represented *gantung* 1 in the vocal line. He/she might then stay as close as possible to the *sèlèh* note and play

peking 2211221122112211

to indicate the *gantung* 1, rather than expand the *gåtrå* into a pattern such as 2321

peking 2233223322112211

although there is no obligation to maintain the *nacah rangkep* patterns throughout, so a player wanting to signal the *gantungan* more clearly could use a pattern such as

peking 1111221122112211

For the previous example of a half-*gåtrå* of *gantungan* on note 6, the pattern in *ir II* might be 66665566 or 65665566, etc.

Another possible approach for *gåtrå gantung* departs from the general principles given above. In this, the pattern starts with a repetition of the *sèlèh* note and then continues with a run up or down to the *sèlèh* note. Such treatments are given particularly to notes 2 or 6 in *sléndro manyurå* or to notes 1 or 5 in *pélog limå/nem*: in other words, to *sèlèh* notes that are particularly important in the *pathet*, e.g.

peking 2211221155332211

peking 6666556622335566

Advanced *garap*

Some players will choose to respond to what is going on elsewhere in the gamelan. As a general principle, it is always useful for a player to be familiar with the parts played by other instruments. For the *peking*, the principle becomes more important towards the bottom left-hand corner of Table 3.4. For example, the *inggah* of a soft-style *gendhing* may spend a lot of time in *ir III* and *ir IV*, with the *rebab* as the leading melodic instrument. Ideally the *peking* player will pay special attention to the *rebab* melody—as representing the closest approximation to the inner melody—when deciding how to expand the *balungan*.

Fig. 3.22 shows an example of a *pekingan* that follows a *rebaban*. (The *pekingan* and the *rebaban* come from different sources, and the latter[8] gives alternatives in some places: the version shown for the last two *gåtrå* applies to the *suwuk*.) The *peking* part responds to the *gantungan* from the first halves of the second, eleventh and thirteenth *gåtrå*. It also suggests short *gantungan* elsewhere, but these do not correspond to anything in the *rebaban*. In the fourth and fourteenth *gåtrå*, the *peking* reflects the fact that the *rebab* rises to 5 within the *gåtrå* . 2 . 1 (= *puthut gelut*), and there are several other similar hints. Nevertheless, the *peking* part still coincides with the final note of each *gåtrå* in the *balungan* rather than following the *rebab* slavishly.

To create a corresponding *peking* part for *ir IV*, the pattern for each quarter-*gåtrå* could be played twice, following the principle given earlier.

Nyacah, other special *garap*

The *peking* may play *nyacah* in *srepegan* and *sampak*, using exactly the same type of pattern as the *saron* (see p. 118). These are places where the *saron* may play *imbal* or *nyacah*, or one *saron* may play *nyacah* and the other(s) *imbal*. If a *saron* is playing *nyacah*, the *peking* will deliberately play different patterns from the *saron*.

In *langgam*, two players may play *imbal* patterns of the *saron imbal* type on the *peking* (two *sèlèh* points per *gåtrå*).

Peking: Yogya style

For two reasons, it would not be possible to create a table corresponding to Table 3.4 for the Yogyanese *peking* styles. First, there are far more *garap* variants in use. Second, the *peking* can play patterns with different densities, so that there is no characteristic number of strokes per *balungan* beat for each *iråmå*.

Nikeli

Tabuhan nikeli, best-known of the characteristic Yogyanese styles, is equivalent to Solonese *nacah låmbå*, but advanced by one beat of the *peking* part. The relationship in terms of *balungan* beats varies, as illustrated below.

Balungan nibani

The first example is for the *låmbå* section at the beginning of a piece, where the Yogyanese *peking* part is a full *balungan* beat ahead of the Solonese:

balungan	. 7 . 3	. 7 . 2
peking	7 7 3 3	7 7 2 2

The same treatment may be used in *ir I* for pieces that have *balungan nibani* throughout, but a higher-density version is also available

peking 77773333 77772222

8 From Djumadi, *Titilaras Rebaban untuk SMKI Negeri Surakarta*, SMKI Surakarta, 1983.

9 'Solonese' patterns in faster *irâmâ* too can be heard even on Brunet's recordings from the *kraton Yogya*, which have sometimes been represented as a definitive document of the traditional Yogya style.

and is used during the characteristic *balungan nibani* of the *pangkat dhawah* (= *ompak inggah*) of a *gendhing*.

In some *balungan nibani* sections in *sléndro* (and sometimes in *pélog* too), the standard *saron* treatment adds *pancer* notes. The *peking* may then play a *nikeli* pattern that takes account of the *pancer*:

balungan	. 3 . 2	. 1 . 6
peking	1̇1̇331̇1̇22	1̇1̇111̇1̇66

The first pattern given under this heading (7733 for *balungan* . 7 . 3) has half the density of Solonese *peking* patterns for *balungan nibani*. If the same type of pattern is used for *ir II*, and even more so for *ir III*, the *peking* part is extremely sparse. One alternative approach in slower *irâmâ* is to play the *balungan* notes four times or even eight times instead of twice:

balungan	. 3 . 2
peking (*ir II/III*)	3 3 3 3 2 2 2 2

peking (*ir II/III/IV*)	3333333322222222

but simple variations also occur, especially in the second half of the *gâtrâ*, e.g.

peking (*ir II/III/IV*)	3333333322222332

as well as a long *selang-seling* sequence

peking (*ir IV*)
33223322332233223322332233223322

or the *sèlèh* note played eight times

peking (*ir III*)	2 2 2 2 2 2 2 2

all for the same *gâtrâ* and all ending at the same point.

However, Yogyanese players very often pursue a more radical tactic and simply play Solonese-style patterns in the slower *irâmâ*, especially in soft-style pieces.[9] It is entirely normal to hear Yogyanese-style *nikeli* patterns, ending on the *balungan* notes, give way to Solonese patterns, finishing after the *balungan* note, when a piece enters *ir II*.

balungan	. 6̣ . 5̣	. 1 . 6̣
rebab	2 . 1 2 2 32 1 6̣ 2 21 12 1 2 21 6̣ 5̣6̣1	. 1 1 . 1 . 1 1 . 1 . 2 2 23 21 6̣
treat as	1 2 1 6̣ 2 1 6 5	1 1 2 1 3 2 1 6̣
peking	11221122116655662211221166556655	11112211221122113322332211665566

balungan	. 1 . 6̣	. 2 . 1̂
rebab	232 2 1 1 2 16̣5̣ 6̣12 2 23 21 6̣12	5 561̇ 5 6 1̇61̇ 1̇6 1̇5 2 1 1 2 1
treat as	2 5 2 1 3 2 1 6̣	2 2 3 2 5 3 2 1
peking	22552255221122113322332211665566	22223322332233225533553322112211

balungan	. 2 . 1	. 2 . 6̣
rebab	2 1 232 2 . 2 2 1 1 2 1 2	5 561̇ 2̇ 6 1̇61̇ 1̇6 1̇5 2 23 21 6̣
treat as	2 1 3 2 5 3 2 1	5 6 1 2 3 2 1 6̣
peking	22112211332233225533553322112211	55665566112211223322332211665566

balungan	. 1 . 6̣	. 2 . 1̂
rebab	232 2 1 1 2 1 5̣ 6̣ 1 2 1 121 6̣12	. 2 3 . 5 . 5 5 . 6 . 2 2 1 1 2 1
treat as	2 5 2 1 3 2 1 6̣	2 2 3 2 5 3 2 1
peking	22552255221122113322332211665566	22223322332233225533553322112211

3.22 *Pekingan* for *inggah* of *gd Gambirsawit sl 9* in *ir III*, showing relationship with *rebaban*

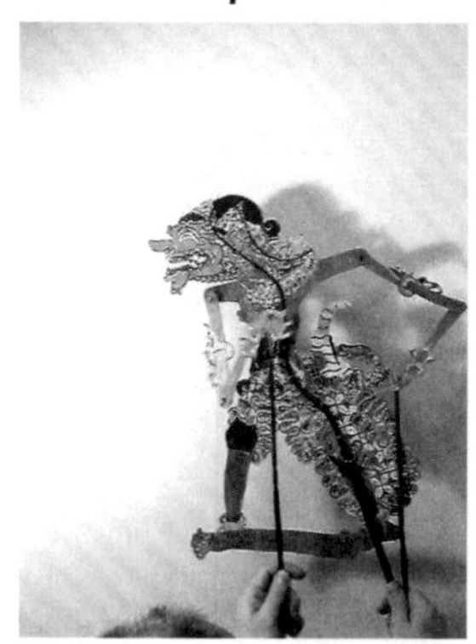

Balungan mlaku

An example for a *balungan mlaku* in *ir I*

balungan	2 1 2 3	2 1 2 6
peking	22112233	22112266

has the form of *nacah lâmbâ*, but is half a *balungan* beat early relative to the Solonese style. This pattern can be played in *ir II* and even *ir III*, giving densities respectively half and a quarter that of Solonese *nacah rangkep.* However, in *ir II* a higher-density pattern, sometimes given the name *nglagu*, is also found. It is equivalent to Solonese *nacah rangkep* advanced by a quarter of a *balungan* beat:

balungan	2 1 2 3
peking	2211221122332233

This pattern can also be used in *ir III*, where again its density is back to half that of Solonese *nacah rangkep.*

Yogyanese players tend to keep the patterns simple: a repeated note in the *balungan* is typically played four times, e.g. *balungan* 2235 as 22223355.

Pin in a *balungan* that is basically *mlaku* can be dealt with in more than one way. Firstly, the *peking* can simply leave a gap:

balungan	6 5 3 2	. 3 5 6
peking	66553322	. . 335566

Alternatively, for the same example it can play the *pin* as a continuation of the previous *balungan* note

balungan	6 5 3 2	. 3 5 6
peking	66553322	22335566

i.e. as if applying a *nikeli* pattern to a *balungan* played *nitir*, or it can repeat the half-*gâtrâ*, with its combination of *pin* + note:

balungan	6 5 3 2	. 3 5 6
peking	66553322	. 3 . 35566

balungan	. 2 . 1	. 6 . 5
rebab	2 1 2 232 2 . 2 2 1 1 2 3 5	.51̇ 1̇ 61̇6 6 1̇ 561̇ 2̇ 61̇65 6 1̇
treat as	2 1 3 2 5 3 2 1	5 5 1̇ 6 2̇ 1̇ 6 5
peking	22112211332233225533553322112211	555566551̇1̇6655662211221166556655

balungan	. 1̇ . 6	. 3 . 2̂
rebab	. 1̇ 1̇.1̇ . 1̇ 1̇.1̇ . 6 5 6 61̇6 6 1̇	5 6 1̇61̇ 5 323 235 5 2 56.
treat as	1̇ 1̇ 2̇ 1̇ 3̇ 2̇ 1̇ 6	2̇ 1̇ 5 3 6 5 3 2
peking	11112211221122113322332211665566	22112211553355336655665533223322

balungan	. 3 . 5	. 2 . 1
rebab	. 6 6.6 . 6 661̇ 561̇ 2̇ 61̇6 5	. 5 561̇ 5 6 1̇61̇ 1̇6 1̇5 2 1 1 2 1 2
treat as	6 6 5 6 2 1 6 5	6 5 3 2 5 3 2 1
peking	66665566556655662211221166556655	66556655332233225533553322112211

balungan	. 2 . 1	. 6̣ . (5̂)
rebab	2 1 232 2 . 2 2 1 1 2 1	232 2 1 121 6̣ 2 21 12 12 26̣1 2 6̣ 5̣
treat as	2 1 3 2 5 3 2 1	3 2 1 6̣ 2 1 6̣ 5̣
peking	22112211332233225533553322112211	33223322116655662211221166556655

3.22 (cont'd)

If the *pin* is on a *dhong* rather than a *dhing*, the *peking* can then play a pattern of the opposite shape:

balungan	5 6 7 .	3 2 7 6
peking	55667.7.	33227766

Again, Yogyanese players may use Solonese *garap* for *balungan mlaku* in slower *irâmâ* (*ir II* or slower).

Double-density *balungan*

If the *balungan* is double-density, which normally only happens in *ir II* or slower *irâmâ*, the *nikeli* pattern is never denser than the pattern that the Solonese would use:

balungan	2 3 2 1 6 1 2 3
peking	2233221166112233

Once again, players may use Solonese *garap* for slower *irâmâ* (*ir II* or slower).

Ngencot, neceg, napas and *nitir*

When the *saron* plays *ngencot* or *neceg*, the *peking* may respond in various ways, three of which are illustrated in this table:

balungan	2 5 2 .	2 5 2 3
saron, nitir	2 5 2 2	2 5 2 3
saron, neceg	2 5 2 2̸	2 5 2 3
saron, ngencot	2 5 2 2̸2̸	2 5 2 3
peking (1)	225522..	22552233
peking (2)	22552222	22552233
peking (3)	2255222̸2̸	22552233

It may simply play one of the normal parts for a *balungan* with a *pin*, labelled *peking* (1) or (2). Alternatively, the *peking* can modify version (2) with a *neceg* stroke, as in *peking* (3).

If there are two *pin* in the *balungan* line, the *peking* can respond in various ways, including *ngencot* of its own: see Fig. 3.23.

balungan	. 5 . 3	. 5 3 2
saron, ngencot	5̸ 5̸ 5 3̸ 3̸ 3	5̸ 5̸ 5 3 2
peking (1)	..55....55..33..	33..335533223322
peking (2)	5555555555553333	3355335533223322
peking (3)	5̸5̸555̸5̸555̸5̸553̸3̸33	3355335533223322

3.23 *Peking* treatment of *balungan* with *ngencot* (additional examples)

If the *peking* is playing a *nglagu*-type pattern, the *ngencot* or *neceg* notes may be repeated as part of the pattern. Fig. 3.23 shows three *nglagu* variants corresponding to those in the previous example. (The examples follow a gong 5.)

The same *garap* variants on the *peking* are applicable whether the *saron* is playing *ngencot*, *neceg*, *napas* or *nitir*.

Nyampar and *nyarug*

The *peking* can handle *nyampar* or *nyarug* notes in various ways. It may play a *nikeli* pattern for the basic unadorned *balungan*, or it may play the *nyampar* or *nyarug* area *mbalung* and the rest *nikeli*. Either approach gives a *peking* part with an even density. Alternatively, in *ir II* or slower *irâmâ*, every note in the expanded *balungan* may be doubled. All these possibilities are illustrated in Fig. 3.25.

Méngkal

A *balungan* that has been expanded into *méngkal* form on the *saron* can then be played by the *peking* in any of the styles suitable for a *balungan* with *pin*:

balungan, basic	3 . 6 5
saron, méngkal	3 . 2 . 3 . 6 5
peking (1)	33..22..33..6655
peking (2)	333̸3222̸2333̸36655
peking (3)	3333222233336655

Imbal

The *peking* may respond to *imbal* on the *demung*, although in some versions the notes that it plays may follow more closely what is happening on the *saron*. The result may be called *imbal peking*, but the *garap* only involves one instrument.

An example in *ir I* has a pattern with the same density as a standard *nikeli* pattern, and is based on the notes played by the two *demung* (in an *imbal lugu* version) but with a slightly different sequence:

balungan	. 5 . 3
demung I	5 . 5 . 3 . 3 .
demung II	. 6 . 5 . 5 . 3
peking	5 5 6 5 3 3 5 3

A higher-density *imbal* is possible in *ir I* (cf. Solonese *saron imbal*), and the following example again has *imbal lugu* on the *demung*:

balungan	. 5 . 3
demung I	5 . 5 . 5 . 5 . 3 . 3 . 3 . 3 .
demung II	. 6 . 6 . 6 . 5 . 5 . 5 . 5 . 3
peking	5566556533553353

These patterns can be used in *ir II* also, but as would be expected, the density can be doubled for *ir II* and *III*. This example has *imbal demung lugu* again:

balungan
. 5 . 3

demung I
5 . 5 . 5 . 5 . 5 . 5 . 5 . 5 . 3 . 3 . 3 . 3 . 3 . 3 . 3 . 3 .

demung II
. 6 . 6 . 6 . 6 . 6 . 6 . 6 . 5 . 5 . 5 . 5 . 5 . 5 . 5 . 5 . 3

peking
55665566556655653355335533553353

It is also possible to ignore the *imbal demung* and use patterns based on the combination of *balungan* + *pancer*, as previously described, the same pattern applying to *ir I*, *II* or *III*. For the above *gåtrå* the *peking* pattern would then be 1̇1̇551̇1̇551̇1̇331̇1̇33.

True *imbal peking* would be the result of two instruments playing interlocking patterns together. This is only possible on the few gamelan that still have two instruments (but cf. **Nyacah, other special garap**, p. 129).

Saron wayangan

The *saron wayangan* (Fig. 3.24) is essentially a *saron barung* with additional *wilah* to extend its range upwards. The most usual range is from 6̣ to 3̇. The extended compass allows more interesting *nyacah* patterns. With two players, it can also contribute *saron imbal* over a wider range than is possible on *saron barung*.

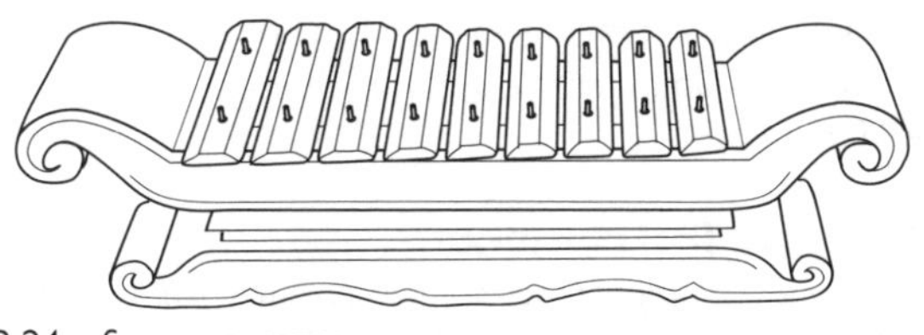

3.24 *Saron wayangan*

The nine *wilah* are responsible for the alternative name *saron sångå*.

As its name implies, the *saron wayangan* is an essential part of the ensemble that accompanies *wayang kulit*. Only one of these instruments was used in the traditional *gamelan wayangan*. In a *gamelan gedhé* there will again usually only be one *saron wayangan*, if any.

Although there is no reason why a *pélog* version of the instrument should not be made, it seems to be found only in the *sléndro* gamelan that are used in the accompaniment for *wayang kulit purwå*.

Fig. 3.24 shows *wilah* of the *blimbingan* form, but other forms are also found.

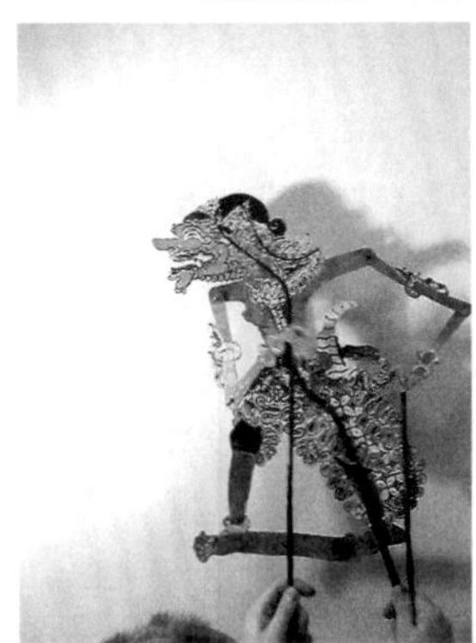

Slenthem

The remaining *balungan* instrument is unique in more than one way. The *slenthem* (Fig. 3.26) is the only soft-style *balungan* instrument and the only one that belongs to the *gendèr* family: in fact its traditional Yogyanese name, still sometimes used today, is *gendèr panembung*. It is also occasionally called *slenthem gantung*.

For construction details, see **Gendèr family**, p. 188. Compared with the *gendèr barung* and *gendèr panerus*, the *slenthem* has wider *wilah* and there is one *placak* per *wilah* instead of per two *wilah*. Each *wilah* has its own tube resonator of circular or flattened circular cross-section.

The *wilah* of the *slenthem* are usually at least as wide as those of the *demung*, although instruments with narrower *wilah* are also made. The diameter of the single beater is in proportion to the width of the *wilah*, i.e. much larger than those of the *gendèr*, although of the same form.

Thanks to its resonators, the *slenthem* is the only instrument able to sustain the *balungan* line in the slower

balungan, basic	1 2 1 6	5 1̇ 5 2
balungan, *nyampar*	1 2 1 6	1̇ 5 6 1̇ 5 2
ir I		
peking (1)	1 1 2 2 1 1 6 6	1̇ 5 6 1̇ 5 5 2 2
peking (2)	1 1 2 2 1 1 6 6	5 5 1̇ 1̇ 5 5 2 2
ir II		
peking (3)	1 1 2 2 1 1 6 6	1̇ 5 6 1̇ 5 5 2 2
peking (4)	1 1 2 2 1 1 6 6	1̇1̇55661̇1̇ 5 5 2 2

3.25 *Peking* treatment of *balungan nyampar*

irâmâ (*ir II* and slower), so it does not stop playing in *ir III* or *ir IV* if/when the *saron* and *demung* fall silent.

The *slenthem* is pitched an octave below the *demung*, and its range is 1 to 7 in *pélog*—all seven notes (cf. *gendèr barung* and *gendèr panerus*)—and $\underset{\cdot}{6}$ to $\dot{1}$ in *sléndro*. Some Yogyanese instruments do not have the $\underset{\cdot}{6}$.

Regular playing style

The fundamental role of the *slenthem* is to play the *balungan* as notated. There are various situations where the *slenthem* continues playing the *balungan* 'straight' but the other *balungan* instruments depart from it.

The general underlying principle is that the *slenthem* plays the plainest version of the *balungan* if there is any choice. In accordance with this principle, the *slenthem* does not play *pancer* when other *balungan* instruments do. In certain pieces all the other instruments realise the *balungan* as notated, but the *slenthem* plays a simplified or 'abstracted' version of it.

The *slenthem* also participates in some simple variations and decorations. Notes are damped as on the *saron* family, although less pressure is needed.

Gemakan and *mbandhul*

Gemakan is a form of *garap* used for *balungan nibani* in *ir II* and slower *irâmâ*. Instead of playing the *balungan* as notated, the *slenthem* plays on the three half-beats that precede each *balungan* note:

balungan	. 5 . 3
slenthem	5 5 5 . 3 3 3 .

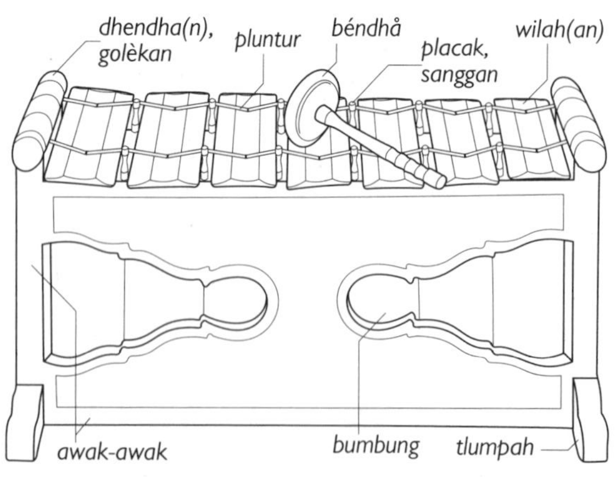

3.26 *Slenthem*

This is a characteristic Yogyanese *garap*, although the Solonese use it too, and it is not possible to specify the limits of its use. (The technique is also sometimes called *ngenyut*, and the term *gemakan* is also used to mean other things.)

The corresponding *garap* for *ir I* is called *mbandhul*, but this is confined to Yogyanese practice and a more limited range of contexts:

balungan	. 5 . 3
slenthem	5 . 5 . 3 . 3 .

Garap for *slenthem* + other instruments

The *slenthem* cooperates with other instruments in various ways. For example, *gemakan* and *mbandhul* form part of a specific treatment for Yogyanese *gendhing soran* (see **Progress of a Yogyanese *gendhing soran***, p. 81).

Interaction between the *slenthem* and *demung* is standard in specific situations, e.g. in the *sampak* form (see ***Sampak***, p. 90). Although the instruments create interlocking patterns, the term *imbal* is not always used.

Another important form of *garap* in which the *slenthem* participates is usually called *pinjalan*.

Details of the above are given under **Multi-instrument *garap***, p. 231.

Other instruments

A few Western instruments retain a regular place in the gamelan of the *kraton Yogya*.

In the Yogyanese *gati* form (see ***Gati***), the trumpet functions as a *balungan* instrument. Compared with conventional *balungan* instruments, it has the advantage of a range wider than an octave, and can therefore represent the *balungan* more accurately. Clarinets and trombones were also used in *gati*, but possibly no longer.

An interesting 'might-have-been' is a specially made *sléndro/pélog* vibraphone that Jaap Kunst gave to the Mangkunegaran palace for use with *Kyai Kanyut Mèsem*. Although the musicians and the prince were enthusiastic about it, the instrument was not taken into use: the player had to stand up to play it, and this conflicted with Javanese tradition.

Obsolete instruments

The *gambang gângsâ* (Fig. 3.27) is a bronze *wilah* instrument of two or more octaves, played with two beaters.

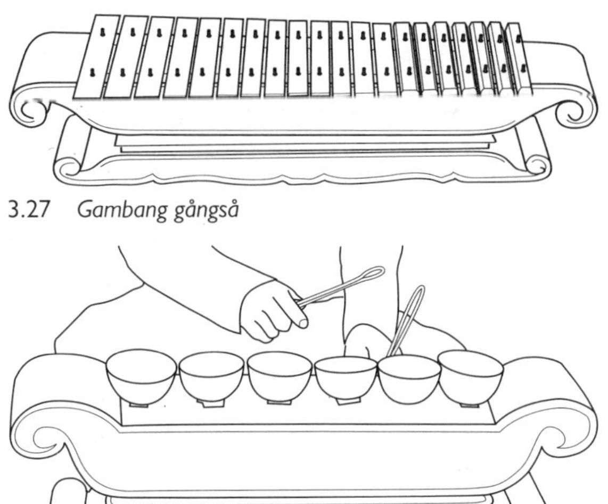

3.27 *Gambang gångså*

3.28 *Celuring*

The *wilah* are similar to those of the *saron* family but narrower, and in shape the instrument is a long *saron*. At the upper end of the instrument illustrated, the form of the *wilah* is closer to *blimbingan*. Hard wooden beaters are used, although their shape is more like that of *gambang (kayu)* beaters; i.e. thin discs, but smaller and without padding. The instrument is now almost confined to a few court gamelan, of the conventional *gamelan gedhé* type as well as the ceremonial *gamelan kodhok ngorèk*. As in regular *balungan* instruments, the *pélog* version has all seven notes. The performance practice of the *gambang gångså* is largely forgotten. In some pieces for the *gamelan kodhok ngorèk* it plays in alternating octaves, like a *saron* alternating with a *peking*, the lower note falling on the beat and the higher note on the following half-beat. It is not clear whether this was the general playing style. From the structure of the beaters, the obvious deduction is that no attempt was made to damp notes after they were played.

A few *celuring* (Fig. 3.28) exist in court gamelan. They are single-octave instruments in which metal cups replace the *wilah*, and are used instead of *peking*. The beaters are bent metal rods.

In a few gamelan, mainly confined to the royal courts, the normal *slenthem* is replaced by instruments with *wilah pencon*. They go by various names (*slentho*, *saron demung ageng*, *saron slenthem*, etc.) and exist in two distinct forms, with either tube resonators (Fig. 3.29) or a trough resonator (Fig. 3.30). The beater is of *bindhi* form, similar in size to that of the *kenong*.

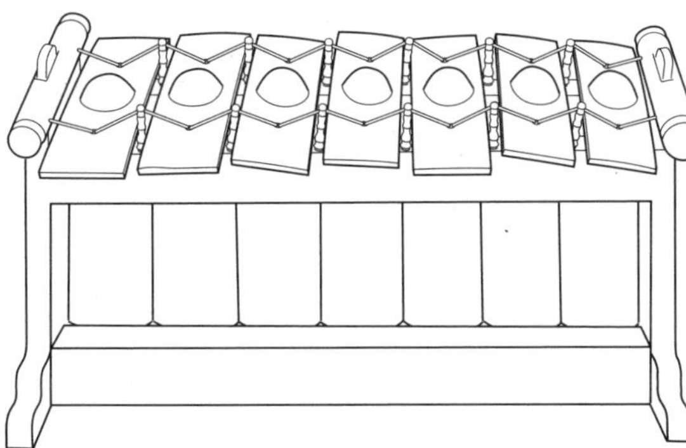

3.29 *Slentho* with tube resonators

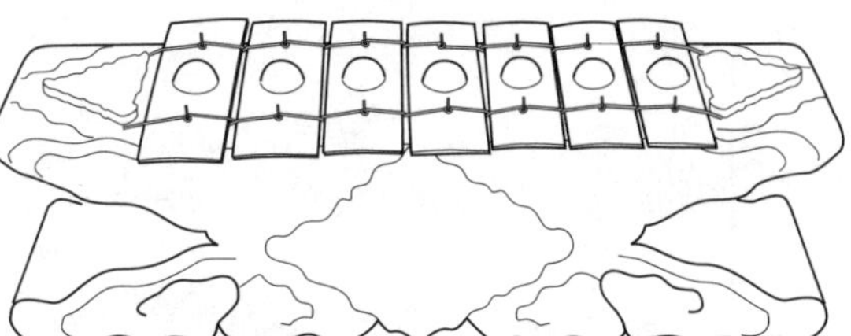

3.30 *Slentho* with trough resonator

Decorating instruments—introduction

The gamelan instruments whose function is considered to be wholly or mainly elaboration, decoration, embellishment or paraphrasing (listed in Table 3.5 and shown in Fig. 3.31) are collectively described in various ways, such as *instrumen rerenggå* (literally 'decorating instruments'), *panerusan*[10] or *isèn-isèn* ('filling-in').

They are also known as *instrumen garap*, which implies that they are the only instruments that 'work out' the *balungan* or the 'inner melody' of a composition. As described earlier, every instrument in the '*balungan* section' in fact has a decorating function, closely based on the *balungan*, at one time or another. Conversely the *bonang panembung*, although belonging to the *bonang* family, has an extremely simple part and actually plays only the *balungan* or, in many situations, even less. And, at a more basic level, every instrument in the gamelan can be seen as executing its own *garap* for the inner melody.

Among the decorating instruments, only the *bonang barung* and *bonang panerus* cooperate in a form of joint *garap*. Otherwise all the instruments operate independently. However, informal interaction can occur if a player executes a *wilet* that another player likes and imitates.

10 Some writers apply this term only to the soft-style decorating instruments.

11 Martopangrawit's typescript collection of *céngkok* for *gendèr* runs to hundreds of pages, without giving detailed advice on how *céngkok* should be chosen, and without covering special *garap* applicable to *wayang* accompaniment, for example.

3.31 Decorating instruments at the *Purå Pakualaman*

The process of realisation means making choices between many possibilities. Out of those possibilities, no two players or teachers are going to agree precisely as to which are acceptable and which are not.

The word 'pattern' here often corresponds directly to *wilet* or *céngkok*. (This applies to the *bonang* family as well as the soft-style instruments.) According to one widely accepted interpretation, the difference between the two terms is that the *wilet* is one specific realisation of the *céngkok*, but other explanations will be encountered. Westerners sometimes translate both words by the jazz terms 'riff' or 'lick': readers are left to decide how appropriate these are.

The *bonang* family is dealt with at length here because of its extensive range of *garap*. Only the general principles of *garap* for the soft-style instruments are covered. For the *gendèr barung* in particular, anything approaching a complete presentation of its functions and its *céngkok* would demand an excessive amount of space.[11]

The *garap* for the *gendèr panerus*, although different from that of the *gendèr barung*, is based on some of its principles: however, its role is much less important. The *gambang* and *celempung/siter* would need less space, but mainly because (frankly) their status is again far lower, and less attention is paid to their parts. The same could be said of the *suling*, in spite of the creativity shown by some players.

Although the term *céngkok* is used in connection with the *rebab* part, the role of the *rebab* is rather different

Table 3.5
Decorating or elaborating instruments

Loud-style	Soft-style
Bonang barung and *bonang panerus*[a]	*Rebab*
	Gendèr barung
Bonang panembung	*Gendèr panerus*
	Gambang
	Celempung, siter, siter peking[a]
	Suling

a. Treated together here

from that of the other 'decorating' instruments, as suggested in Part 2—and justifies the description 'paraphrasing' instead.

Some writers treat the soft-style instruments differently from the *bonang* family. The term *instrumen mukå* ('front-row instrument'), like *panerusan*, seems to be reserved for soft-style instruments such as *rebab*, *gendèr* and *gambang*, and does describe their usual location along the front edge of the gamelan. (The *bonang* typically have a less prominent position.)

Sometimes the terms *wilet* and *céngkok* are only applied to what the soft-style instruments play. Nevertheless, *bonang* players have exactly the same responsibility to realise a composition in a way that is appropriate to the type of piece, the *laras*, *pathet*, *irâmå* and general playing style (including the regional context). However, much of the *garap* for the *bonang* does not depart far from the *balungan* line.

Between the soft-style instruments there are large variations in the style of elaboration, which can be summarised as follows. The *rebab* line is continuous: its contour generally resembles that of the *balungan*, although not in detail, and not in rhythm: essentially the *rebab* part is more complex. The *suling* usually plays relatively short stock phrases to the more important *sèlèh* points. The *gambang*, the *siter* family and both the *gendèr* play continuously, generally coinciding with the *balungan* at the end of the *gåtrå*: in their patterns they also take into account the previous *sèlèh* note. The decorating instruments therefore do not treat gaps in the *balungan* as rests.

Depending on *irâmå*, patterns may terminate at midpoints of *gåtrå*. Such points are sometimes called half-*sèlèh* points.

To complete the picture, the characteristics of vocal parts too must be taken into account: solo *sindhènan* often has features in common with the *suling* part, whereas *gérongan* is much more regular.

Within its characteristic *garap*, each decorating instrument usually has many variants to choose from for a given *gåtrå*, and it is considered good style for players to vary the *garap*, i.e. not necessarily realising a *gåtrå* the same way twice. This even applies to the *bonang barung* and *bonang panerus* within limits.

For most instruments, elaboration means playing more than one note per beat of the *balungan* line. The term **density** refers to the number of notes on the decorating instrument either per second or per *balungan* beat. A ratio of four notes per *balungan* beat, for example, is described as *lampah* 4 (or *laku* 4 [*ng*]). The fastest rate of articulation used by an instrument is sometimes called the **density referent**.

In *irâmå lancar* the *bonang* do not play *mipil*, and the other decorating instruments rarely play. The density relationships for other contexts are summarised in Table 3.6. A table of this kind is only possible because the instruments tend to play at characteristic densities.

However, the table oversimplifies the situation: there is not necessarily a note on every beat of the instrument's part, and beats on some instruments (especially *gendèr barung* and *bonang barung*) are often subdivided. Also, decorating parts can include triplet rhythms, mostly in the form of three notes played across four normal beats, or four across three. The problem with the use of any term such as 'beat' or 'density referent' is to know whether it refers to the basic density of the pattern for the instrument and *irâmå*, as listed in Table 3.6, or to the subdivided beats. This ambiguity is not soluble by using a Javanese term, because Javanese seems not to have one: *keteg* can refer not only to the beats of the part played by an individual instrument, e.g. the *bonang barung*, but also to those of the *balungan* line.

The roles of the *rebab* and the *suling* cannot be fitted into the table. The density of *rebaban* varies, and the *wilet* played by the *suling* are far too free in their rhythms to be characterised in this way.

Table 3.6
Density of decoration vs. *irâmå*

Irâmå	*Bonang barung* (in *mipil*), *peking* [a]	*Bonang panerus* (in *mipil*)	*Bonang barung* + *bonang panerus* (in *imbal*), composite pattern [b]	*Gendèr barung*, basic density	*Gendèr panerus*, *siter*, *celempung*, *siter peking*, *gambang*
Lancar	–	–	*lampah* 2	(*lampah* 1)	(*lampah* 2)
I	*lampah* 2	*lampah* 4	*lampah* 4	*lampah* 2	*lampah* 4
II	*lampah* 2[c]/4	*lampah* 8	*lampah* 8	*lampah* 4	*lampah* 8
III	*lampah* 4[d]/8[e]	*lampah* 16[f]	*lampah* 16	*lampah* 8[g]	*lampah* 16
IV	*lampah* 16[h]	–[h]	*lampah* 32	*lampah* 16[g]	*lampah* 32

a. In Solo style; for Yogya style, see text. b. Also for *sekaran* on either *bonang*, and for *salah gumun* treatment in *langgam*; also for *klénangan*, although this can be at twice the density shown. c. For *mipil låmbå* on *bonang barung*. d. For half-speed *mipil nibani* on *bonang barung*. e. *Peking*, also possible Yogya-style *garap* for *balungan nibani* on *bonang barung*. f. Possible Yogya-style *garap* for *balungan nibani* on *bonang panerus*. g. Often notated at twice this density: see text. h. Both *bonang* play *imbal*.

Bonang family

The instruments of the *bonang* family (Fig. 3.32) consist of a wooden frame (*rancakan*) like a bedstead, with cords (*pluntur*) supporting bronze or iron pots (*pencon*). The end-panels (*tawingan*) vary in height, and the high ones are often detachable. In any style, they are often heavily carved and decorated.

Some *bonang* pots do not produce a satisfactory sound unless the cavity of the pot is blocked off by a cardboard disc (or traditionally a sheet of paper or even a large leaf). Such pots are described as *bonang nggodhong*, and the cardboard discs are an essential part of the instrument.

The family consists of three sizes of instrument. Most important is the *bonang barung*. Pitched an octave higher, and with slightly smaller pots, is the *bonang panerus*. Some Yogyanese gamelan also have a *bonang panembung*, larger than the *bonang barung* and pitched an octave lower. In practice the sizes of the pots vary somewhat: those on a *bonang barung* may be no larger than the pots of a *bonang panerus* in another gamelan. The instruments found in the *gamelan sekatèn* are larger still, as are instruments of similar construction found in other old ceremonial gamelan (see p. 239).

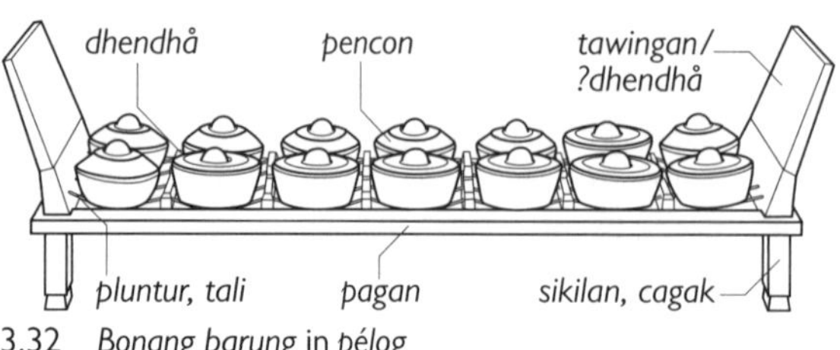

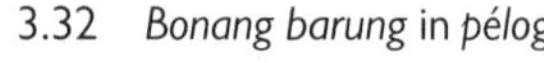
3.32 *Bonang barung* in *pélog*

6	5	3	2	1̇	2̇
1	2̣	3̣	5̣	6̣	1̣

(a) Standard *bonang*

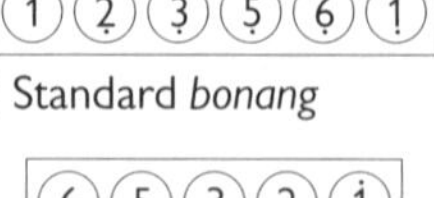

6	5	3	2	1̇
1	2̣	3̣	5̣	6̣

(b) *Bonang cacad*

3.33 Arrangements of *bonang* pots for *sléndro*

3.34 *Bonang panerus* of *cacad* form

3.35 *Bonang barung* in *sléndro*: the player's view

The *sléndro* versions of the *bonang barung* and *bonang panerus* usually have 12 pots (Fig. 3.33(a)), and the *pélog* versions in each size have 14. The instruments are always arranged as two rows of pots covering roughly two octaves. (Similar instruments in other parts of Indonesia have one or three rows, and not always straight rows.)

In Yogya, all sizes of *bonang* in *sléndro* traditionally have only ten pots (Figs 3.33(b), 3.34), and such instruments are sometimes referred to as *bonang cacad* or 'defective *bonang*'. The missing 2̇ causes few problems, but certain complications arise from the absence of the 1̣: see below.

The upper and lower octaves of the instrument are sometimes referred to as 'male' (*lanangan/jaler*) and 'female' (*setrèn/wédokan*) respectively. The shapes of the pots are different: *brunjung* for the higher octave and *dhempok* for the lower (Fig. 3.35).

At first sight, the positions of the pots do not seem logical. In practice the arrangement does make certain characteristic types of pattern easier to play. It is impossible to know whether the patterns were chosen because of the pot positions or vice versa.

For *pélog* the positions of the pots, at least in Solonese practice, depend on the *pathet* (Fig. 3.36). Inner positions go to the notes that are native to the *pathet* (Figs 3.36(a),(b)). The 1̣ is normally placed at the back. The note 7 may be brought in (Fig. 3.36(c)) for some pieces in *pathet nem* where the 1̣ is not needed but the 7 is common, e.g. *ldr Gléyong*. Similarly for pieces in *pathet limå*,

4	6	5	3	2	1̣	7
7̣	1	2̣	3̣	5̣	6̣	4̣

(a) *Bem* scale

4	6	5	3	2	7	1̣
1	7̣	2̣	3̣	5̣	6̣	4̣

(b) *Barang* scale

4	6	5	3	2	7	1̣
7̣	1	2̣	3̣	5̣	6̣	4̣

(c) Optional for *bem* scale

4	6	5	3	2	1	7
7̣	1̣	2̣	3̣	5̣	6̣	4̣

(d) Optional for *pathet limå*

3.36 Arrangements of *bonang* pots for *pélog*

where the 1̣ is frequently used, it may sometimes be more convenient to have that pot on the front row (Fig. 3.36(d)): examples might include several *gendhing bonang*, such as *gd Babar layar.*

Other arrangements of the pots can be found. In Yogyanese practice, the layout of the pots in *pélog* is very variable. There is a general preference for having all the low-octave pots at the front, but the positions of pots 1, 4 and 7 often differ from the standard Solonese positions: see Fig. 3.37.

Too much should not be made of pot positions: expert players simply play the pots where they find them.

With a range of about two octaves, the instruments can cover the most of the range of the *balungan*:

sléndro	*balungan*	2̣3̣5̣6̣12356 1̇2̇3̇5̇
	bonang	[1̣]2̣3̣5̣6̣12356 1̇[2̇]
pélog	*balungan*	1̣2̣3̣4̣5̣6̣7̣1234567 1̇2̇3̇4̇5̇
	bonang	1̣2̣3̣4̣5̣6̣7̣1234567

The characteristic styles of *garap* for the *bonang barung* and *bonang panerus* are closely related, so that they can be considered together. Their *garap* is particularly varied. It falls into three broad categories—*gembyangan*, *mipil* and *imbal*—that are associated in a complex manner with different types of composition, different *irâmâ* and different types of *balungan* (see Table 3.7 and Table 3.8), and are further connected with different styles of *kendhangan*. Besides *gembyangan*, *mipil* and *imbal*, the *bonang barung* and *bonang panerus* play 'straight' *balungan* (*mbalung*) in certain limited circumstances.

The role of the *bonang panembung* is rather different, and its range of *garap* extremely limited.

Playing technique

Each *bonang* is played with a pair of turned wooden beaters (*bindhi*), whose 'business end' is wrapped in red cotton or other fibre. The beaters used on the *bonang barung* are usually larger than those used on the *bonang panerus.* The *bonang panembung* needs even larger beaters, similar in size to those for the *kenong.*

If the player is lucky, the pair of beaters will be straight, and well matched for size and weight and for the resilience of the fibre wrapping. If the beaters are not well matched, it can be difficult to generate an even sound, although in any case the pots vary in their response to the beaters.

The beaters can be held in various ways, not necessarily near the end. If players hold the beaters too far towards the head, they may not be able to reach the pots in the corners of the instrument, especially in *pélog.* There are also two distinct grips—underhand and overhand. In the underhand grip, any force required comes from the thumb rather than a finger. One teacher compares the stick technique to holding a fishing rod, and thus implies a reasonably light grip. A relaxed grasp makes it easier to play rapid figuration. As usual, the correct technique is the one that produces the right sound, and is best acquired by imitation.

Some writers suggest that certain pots are played with one hand rather than the other, but this does not reflect the reality of playing the *bonang panerus* or fast patterns on the *bonang barung*, e.g. in *sekaran.*

Ideally the player should damp the previous note when playing a new note. Damping is feasible during *gembyangan cegat*, between *imbal* notes and often for *mipil* in *bonang barung* parts, especially at the end of the *mipil* pattern. It is rather less practical on the *bonang panerus* and during *sekaran* on either *bonang.*

What players should not do is play the pots 'dead'—i.e. hold the beater in contact with the pot after striking it, as when playing the *kethuk* in faster *irâmâ*. This is a frequent error among beginners.

When players damp notes during *mipil*, they sometimes make the damping audible, so that a new note is immediately preceded by a dead-sounding repetition of the previous one. This practice, particularly common among Yogyanese players, is described in more detail later.

Some players seem to cultivate a technique of half-damping notes to change the sound quality, especially at the transition into the *inggah* of a *gendhing.*

Bonang notation

Some Yogyanese notation for the *bonang* uses two lines separated by a rule, and the *setrèn* notes are then written below the rule

. . 2 . . . 2 . . . .
61 . . 61 . 1561 . 5616

corresponding to the way that the pots are usually arranged. Register dots are then unnecessary.

Other writers use the two lines in the same way as for *gendèr* and *gambang* notation; upper and lower lines

3.37 Some arrangements of *bonang* pots for *pélog*, Yogya style

indicate the right-hand and left-hand parts respectively. The notes of the *bonang* family are generally notated as shown in Fig. 3.33, etc., but some writers show the upper octave as $\dot{1}$, $\dot{2}$, $\dot{3}$, etc., and the lower octave as 1, 2, 3, etc. This book follows the more common practice.

In the examples here, single-line notation is used as far as possible. Two notes played simultaneously are written with the higher one above the lower one: there is no suggestion (in contrast to *gendèr* notation) as to which hand plays which note. To simplify notation, two notes an octave apart that are played together (= *gembyangan*) are often written as a cipher with a solidus

$$\not{3} = \frac{3}{\underset{\cdot}{3}}$$

but confusingly the solidus can sometimes represent a *kempyung* or *gembyung* on the *bonang* (see below). These are of course only two of the various uses of the solidus in notation. Occasionally the solidus can even mean that a *bonang* pot is struck and immediately damped, giving the same type of dead sound as *ngencot* or *neceg* on the *saron*. To avoid misinterpretation, any use of the solidus in the notation of *bonang* parts here is specifically explained.

Table 3.7
Solonese *garap* on *bonang barung* according to *irâmâ* and *balungan* type

Irâmâ	*Balungan* type		
	nibani	*mlaku*	double-density
Ir lancar	*gembyangan cegat* OR *imbal* + *sekaran*	*gembyangan cegat* OR *imbal* + *sekaran*	—
Ir I	*mipil nibani lâmbâ* + *gembyangan lâmbâ* or *dados* + *nduduk gembyang* or *tunggal* + *kempyung* + *gembyung* OR half-speed *gembyangan cegat* OR *imbal* + *sekaran*	*mipil lâmbâ* + *gembyangan lâmbâ* or *dados* + *nduduk gembyang* or *tunggal* + *kempyung* + *gembyung* OR *imbal* + *sekaran*	*mbalung* OR *imbal* + *sekaran*
Ir II	*mipil nibani rangkep* + *gembyangan dados* or *rangkep* + *nduduk gembyang* or *tunggal* + *kempyung* + *gembyung* OR *imbal* + *sekaran*	*mipil rangkep*[a] + *gembyangan dados* or *rangkep* + *nduduk gembyang* or *tunggal* + *kempyung* + *gembyung* OR *imbal* + *sekaran*	*mipil lâmbâ* + *gembyangan dados* or *rangkep* + *nduduk gembyang* or *tunggal* + *kempyung* + *gembyung* OR *imbal* + *sekaran*
Ir III	half-speed *mipil nibani*[b] OR *imbal* + *sekaran*	half-speed *mipil nibani*[b] OR *imbal* + *sekaran*	half-speed *mipil nibani*[b] OR *imbal* + *sekaran*
Ir IV	*imbal* + *sekaran*	*imbal* + *sekaran*	*imbal* + *sekaran*

a. Exceptionally, *mipil lâmbâ*. b. At transitions into *imbal*, during *kosèk wayangan*, and at *suwuk*.

Bonang barung and *bonang panerus*

The *bonang barung* is the melodic leader of the loud-style gamelan ensemble. Leadership comprises, as usual, the tasks of playing the *bukâ* and sometimes signalling the transitions between sections of a piece.

When a full gamelan (as opposed to a *gamelan gadhon*) plays a soft-style piece, the *bonang barung* still plays a full part, but does not lead. Instead, the player responds to

Marking-up notation for the *bonang*

Players find it useful to mark up *balungan* notation with symbols to indicate *garap* for the *bonang*—more specifically, for places where *mipil* is the basic style, because *mipil* is often replaced by various other *garap*. For the Yogyanese style, with its even wider range of *garap* and the need to indicate the register in which notes should be played, more symbols are needed.

The underscore that indicates *gembyangan* may be applied to anything from a single note to the whole *gâtrâ*. It is interpreted as a *gembyangan* on the last note underlined: if any other note should be played instead, its number is written in.

Solonese style

These symbols seem to be widely used.

Gembyangan	$\underline{55}$
Kempyung/gembyung[a]	$\underline{\underline{\underset{\cdot}{5}\underset{\cdot}{3}}}$
Cadential patterns[b]	$1\underset{\cdot}{6}\underset{\cdot}{3}\underset{\cdot}{5}$ (wavy underline)
Straight *mipil*[c]	$\smile{53}$

Yogyanese style

The following is one possible set of mark-up.

Straight *mipil* in upper octave	$\frown{23}$
Straight *mipil* in lower octave	$\smile{56}$
Straight *mipil* moving from upper to lower octave	16
Straight *mipil* moving from lower to upper octave	61
Gembyangan lâmbâ/dados/rangkep	$\underline{3\,.}$
Gembyangan sarug	$\lfloor\underline{53}$
Kempyung/gembyung	$\lfloor\underline{32}\rfloor$

a. Perhaps not a standard symbol. b. Also other special patterns, e.g. any *nibani* pattern in a *mlaku* context. c. *Mipil* is considered the default *garap* and is therefore not usually marked.

signals from the *rebab* or *gendèr*. When the *rebab* or *gendèr* plays the *bukå*, the *bonang barung* joins in at the *gong bukå*. This is also the point where the *bonang panerus* and *bonang panembung* (if any) normally start playing.

When the *bonang barung* is leading the ensemble, its part often provides so much information to the other players that they can deduce the correct *balungan* line (but see **Signalling the *balungan***, p. 168). The *bonang barung* player is one of the few in the ensemble who are expected to know the repertoire thoroughly. In this situation the other players should follow the implied *balungan*, even if the *bonang barung* player makes mistakes.

The *bonang panerus* has a far lower status than the *bonang barung*, and this is reflected in the amounts that professional players are paid. It is often said that people pay very little attention to what the *bonang panerus* is playing.

Another indication of relative status is that, in the standard rotation in a gamelan class, students play the *bonang panerus* before the *bonang barung*. Notwithstanding this, many players find the *bonang panerus* harder to play, for two reasons: it plays more notes, and they are more often off-beat. This density difference is another example of the principle that the instruments that play at the highest density are considered least important.

Even though one *bonang* technique, *imbal*, involves both instruments, *bonang barung* players will still embark on *imbal* in the absence of the *bonang panerus*. In general, the *bonang barung* will play when there is no player for the *bonang panerus*, whereas the converse is not true.

Solo vs. Yogya

It is with the *bonang*—the entire family—that the differences between the characteristic Solonese and Yogyanese styles are most obvious. There is little difference in *imbal*, but Yogyanese and Solonese styles of *gembyangan* and *mipil* differ markedly. Essentially, Yogyanese practice shows much more variety.

In fact the whole approach to the *bonang* is different in the Yogyanese style. The low octave is regarded as home territory, and any move into the higher octave is something of an excursion. Yogyanese notation does not usually include register dots, so that the *bonang* player must, in addition to all other aspects of *garap*, make choices even about the octave in which to play. Needless to say, not all players make the same choices in a given situation.

A further difference in Yogyanese *bonang* style relates to rhythm. Solonese players play *mipil* patterns on the beat. Yogyanese players often do the same but, especially in *ir II*, *bonang barung* players in Yogya also employ certain characteristic patterns that sit on half-beats, as well as other, subtler rhythmic variations that defy notation.

Finally, another obvious general comment about volume levels can be made. In loud-style pieces, the Yogyanese play louder than the Solonese do, in *ir II* or *ir III* as well as *ir I* or *ir lancar*, and this applies just as much to the *bonang* as to the *balungan* instruments. Also the *bonang panerus* is relatively prominent in the Yogya style.

Solonese and Yogyanese styles of *garap* for the *bonang barung* are summarised in Table 3.7 and Table 3.8. These tables do not cover *balungan* of quadruple or higher density, which can also occur in short stretches: if the *gåtrå* in question are not realised with *imbal* and *sekaran*, the *bonang* are most likely to play higher-density stretches *mbalung* or with *gembyangan* to the relevant *sèlèh* note. They also exclude the special *garap* for *langgam*, *ompak klénangan* and *gangsaran*, which are dealt with towards the end of the *bonang* section.

Table 3.8
Yogyanese *garap* on *bonang barung* according to *irâmå* and *balungan* type

Irâmå	*Balungan* type		
	nibani	*mlaku*	double-density
Ir lancar	*gembyangan cegat* + *gembyangan midak* [a] OR *imbal* + *sekaran*	*gembyangan cegat* + *gembyangan midak* [a] OR *imbal* + *sekaran*	—
Ir I	*mipil nglagu* + *nguthik* + *ngrambat* + *gembyangan* + *kempyung* + *gembyung* + *gembyangan midak* [a,b,c] OR *imbal* + *sekaran* OR *gembyangan cegat*	*mipil lâmbâ* + *mipil nglagu* + *nguthik* + *ngrambat* + *gembyangan* + *kempyung* + *gembyung* + *gembyangan midak* [a,b,c] OR *imbal* + *sekaran* OR *gembyangan cegat*	*mbalung* + *gembyangan midak* [a] OR *imbal* + *sekaran*
Ir II	*mipil nglagu* + *nguthik* + *ngrambat* + *gembyangan* + *kempyung* + *gembyung* + *gembyangan midak* [a,b] OR *imbal* + *sekaran*	*mipil rangkep* + *mipil nglagu* + *nguthik* + *ngrambat* + *gembyangan* + *kempyung* + *gembyung* + *gembyangan midak* [a,b] OR *imbal* + *sekaran*	*mipil lâmbâ* + *mipil nglagu* + *nguthik* + *ngrambat* + *gembyangan* + *kempyung* + *gembyung* + *gembyangan midak* [a,b] OR *imbal* + *sekaran*
Ir III	extended *mipil nglagu* OR *imbal* + *sekaran*	*mipil nglagu* OR *imbal* + *sekaran*	*mipil rangkep* + ?*mipil nglagu* OR *imbal* + *sekaran*
Ir IV	*imbal* + *sekaran*	*imbal* + *sekaran*	*imbal* + *sekaran*

a. Before final gong. b. During *lâmbâ*, at transitions into *dhawah*, and before *gong bukå*. c. During *seseg*.

Before the *bukå*

Even before the *bukå*, the *bonang barung* may make other contributions. There is a simple attention-getting pattern (*ajak-ajak*) that can be played by the *bonang*, serving the same purpose as the tapping on the *kendhang* (p. 222):

6̣6̣ . 6̣ 6̣ or 6̣6̣ . 6̣ or simply 6̣ 6̣

Next, there is also a *grambyangan* pattern available for the *bonang barung*—or rather a set of *grambyangan*, indicating either the *laras* alone or *laras* plus *pathet*, and in both short and long forms.

The simplest *grambyangan* (*grambyangan jugag*) is written identically in *sléndro* or *pélog*, for example

                         5̣
6̣ . 5̣5̣2̣ or . . 6̣5̣ 5̣5̣5̣2̣

although what is actually played is closer to

                        5̣
6̣ . 5̣5̣5̣2̣5̣ or 6̣ . 5̣5̣5̣2̣ 2̣

This indicates the *laras* via the interval 5̣–6̣, which is the most characteristic one in the scale. If the interval approximates to a semitone, the *laras* must be *pélog*: a larger interval means *sléndro*. (The notation above is only approximate: the rhythms should be imitated from actual performances.)

Two examples of the full *grambyangan* (*grambyangan wantah*) are (as notated)

2353652 6̣ . 5̣5̣2̣

and

           5̣   5̣
. . 6̣5̣ 5̣5̣5̣2̣ . 235 36 . 532 . . 6̣5̣ 5̣5̣5̣2̣

Another version of the *grambyangan jugag* is

216̣5̣6̣6̣ . .
    2̣2̣

with 7 replacing 1 in *pélog barang*. This version contains more information, revealing the *pathet* as well as the *laras*. To show *pathet* even more clearly, further variants may be used, e.g.

pélog limå (as played)

short:
                        3̣
6̣ . 5̣5̣ . 3̣5̣ . 3̣ . 3̣ 1̣

or
                   5̣
6̣ . 3̣ . 3̣5̣5̣2̣4̣4̣ . 1̣

long:
                                    5̣
6̣6̣ . 5̣3̣ . 5̣5̣2̣3̣ . 1̣1̣2̣3̣5̣5̣5̣ . 1̣

sléndro nem, pélog nem	216̣5̣6̣6̣ . . 2̣2̣
sléndro sångå	216̣5̣5̣5̣ . . 2̣2̣
sléndro manyurå	3216̣6̣6̣ . . 3̣3̣
pélog barang	27̣6̣5̣6̣6̣ . . or 327̣6̣ etc. 2̣2̣

The final two *kempyung/gembyung* may be spaced:

6̣ . 6̣ . or 6̣ . 6̣ . etc.
2̣ 2̣   3̣ 3̣

After the *grambyangan*, the *bonang barung* may play an *ådångiyah* for some pieces. The notation of the *bukå* for a *gendhing bonang* often includes a section that is actually an *ådångiyah*, the same one serving a group of *gendhing* in that *laras* and *pathet*. For example, the *bukå* for *gendhing bonang Babar layar pl 5* may be written (with the addition of register dots where needed)

5̣ . 5̣312 . 5̣ . 5̣312 . 3 . 3 . 2 . 16̣5̣4̣6̣4̣5̣6̣(1)

or

5̣5̣3 . 12 . 5̣ 5̣5̣3 . 12 . 5̣
. 3 . 3 . 321 6̣5̣4̣6̣4̣5̣6̣(1)

or

5̣ . 5̣3 . 3 . . 1235̣ . 5̣ . . 5̣ . 5̣3 . 3 . . 1235̣
. 5̣ . . . 3 . 3 . 321 6̣5̣4̣6̣ 4̣5̣6̣(1)

whereas the *bukå* for *gd bonang Gondrong pl 5* is given as

5̣5̣3 . 12 . 5̣ . 3 . 3 5̣5̣3 . 12 . 5̣
. 56 7656 . 654 24 . 2 4565 242(1)

The part that is common to the two *gendhing* is clearly the repeated phrase 5̣ . 5̣312 . 5̣, with some uncertainty as to whether 5̣ at the end of the phrase is present or, if present, is repeated. The beginning of a well-known recording of *gd bonang Babar layar pl 5* sounds more like

5̣ . 5̣5̣5̣3 . 3 . 312 . 35̣ . 5̣
5̣ . 5̣5̣5̣3 . 3 . 312 . 35̣
. 3 . 3 . 321 . 6̣5̣4̣6̣ 4̣5̣6̣(1)

In other words, the final 5̣ is present both times, and

repeated the first time round. In some performances the 5̣ is emphasised at this point:

5̣ .5̣5̣5̣3 .3.312 .35̣ .5̣5̣5̣5̣ (5 above the last note)

Most of the *gendhing bonang* in *pélog limå* in the Solonese repertoire use the above *ådångiyah*, but a few use one notated as

...1̣ .2̣3̣5̣ ...1̣ .2̣3̣5̣

and played, for example, as

5̣ 5̣ 5̣ 5̣ 5̣
1̣.1̣..2̣3̣5̣.5̣5̣.5̣.. 1̣.1̣..2̣3̣5̣

This execution emphasises the 5̣ at the mid-point.

For *gendhing bonang* in *pélog barang*, the *ådångiyah* are often notated as

(to 6̣) 3.27̣ 27̣.6̣ 3.27̣ 27̣.6̣

(to 5̣) 2 .2.2 .7̣6̣5̣ .2 .2.2 .7̣6̣5̣

the latter being played, for example, as

2.27̣2..7̣6̣.5̣..5̣..2.27̣2..7̣6̣.5̣

These examples are referred to as *ådångiyah* 5̣ or 6̣, from the final note. The choice of the *ådångiyah* seems to be based more on the notes that start the *bukå* and less on the gong notes of the particular piece.

The notation examples above reflect the relatively free rhythm of the *ådångiyah* and *bukå*, which cannot be divided neatly into regular four-note *gåtrå*.

The *ådångiyah* basically consists of a phrase played twice. In Yogyanese style, the closing note (the 5̣ at the end of the *pélog limå* examples above) is repeated on both the first and the second playings of the phrase, and the repeat may be accompanied by the *saron* and *demung*. At this point the *kendhang* has not entered, so that the other players receive no guidance on the rhythm. Therefore the *saron* and *demung* players do not coincide precisely with each other or with the note on the *bonang*, and the *bonang* may even be the last to play the note: the effect is similar to the non-coincident notes that follow a final gong—and to a feature of the *racikan* of pieces in the *sekatèn* repertoire, which may well be its origin.

Bukå bonang

When the *bukå* proper begins, the rhythm can be a little free, and the tempo different from the normal one for the piece. However, it is the job of the *kendhang* player, not the *bonang* player, to set the tempo. Therefore it is entirely acceptable for the *bonang* to start the *bukå* noticeably fast, and be pulled down to the right speed by the *kendhang*. Nevertheless there is a certain amount of tacit negotiation between the players: the *bonang barung* player must **accept** the tempo given by the *kendhang*.

The notated *bukå* is basically played as written (i.e. *mbalung*) but is subject to some elements of *garap*. Occasionally there is a change of register in the *bukå*, and the *bonang* may then use a *gembyang* (see below) to signal the change. For example, the *bukå* of *gd Loro-loro géndhong sl m* is written

.12.13 3216̣ .653 212(6̣)

but if the *rebab* is not available, the *bonang* may play

.12.13 3216̣ 6653 212(6̣)
6̣ (below 66)

Alternatively, this *bukå* may be played just as written.

A *gembyang* may also serve to mark the first one or two notes of the *bukå*. If the *bukå* starts at the bottom limit of the *pathet*, a *kempyung* may be used instead:

6̣ etc.
2̣3̣5̣6̣ 1216̣

The rhythm of the notated *bukå* is sometimes distorted slightly (*nyaruk* or *sarugan*). For example, the start of the *bukå* for *ldr Wilujeng sl m*

1 3 2 6̣ 1 2 3

is sometimes played as

1 3 2 .6̣1 2 3

and *lnc Kebogiro pl 7*

bukå 5̣ 6̣ 7̣ 2 7̣ 3 7̣ 2 7̣ 6̣ 7̣ (5̣)

as 5̣ ..6̣7̣ 2 7̣ 3 7̣ 2 5/5̣ . 5/5̣ .

The different ways of notating the *sarugan* in these examples correctly suggest that the rhythm is somewhat irregular.

The final *gåtrå* of the *bukå* of *ladrang* and *ketawang* is also often the subject of a standard decorative *garap*. In the *sléndro manyurå* the *gåtrå* is frequently written . 126̣, 2126̣, . 1 . 6̣ or 3216̣ but is played

215̣ 6̣1(6̣) or .15̣ 6̣1(6̣)

In *pélog barang*, the *gåtrå* appears as 27̣5̣6̣, . 7̣ . 6̣ or

. 7̣ 5̣ 6̣, and the same *garap* is used, with 7̣ replacing 1. For *sléndro sångå* and often *pélog limå/nem*, the corresponding final *gåtrå* is notated as . 6̣ . 5̣, . 1 6̣ 5̣, 1 6̣ 3̣ 5̣ or 2 1 6̣ 5̣, and is played as

1 6̣ 3̣ 5̣ 6̣ (5)   or   . 6̣ 3̣ 5̣ 6̣ (5)

Yogyanese players sometimes play the *bukå* of *ladrang* or *ketawang* the same way as the Solonese do, complete with the decoration shown above. Much more often they use a characteristic *garap* for the last *gåtrå* of the *bukå* of all *bentuk* larger than *lancaran*. In this they play *gembyangan midak* to the gong note (see **Gembyang(an): 1**). It is also quite common to find the last *gåtrå* notated in a particular way that acts as a reminder of the *gembyangan midak* treatment; for example

5 5 . (5)

which is played

5/5̣ 5̣ 5/5̣ 5̣

Mbalung

The *mbalung* playing of most of the *bukå* by the *bonang barung* has been mentioned. Both *bonang* play *mbalung* in a few other situations:

- at the start of a *gendhing*, following the *gong bukå*, and for a few other pieces with similarly fast starts,
- during a *suwuk gropak*, if necessary,
- briefly during a transition from *ir I* to *iråmå lancar*—in a *lancaran*, for example—and sometimes other transitions,
- sometimes for short stretches of double-density or quadruple-density *balungan*.

Gembyang(an): 1

Gembyangan means 'in octaves', i.e. as two notes an octave apart, played at the same time. For convenience, the same heading is also used for several related techniques that do not involve octaves.

Several different types of *gembyangan* are used on the *bonang*, each connected more or less strongly with certain contexts. Under the present heading are those types mainly associated with *iråmå lancar* (although they are sometimes found in *ir I*), with *bukå*, and with the *srepegan* and *sampak* forms (using Solonese terminology). For the other types, see **Gembyang(an): 2**, p. 158.

Gembyangan cegat/nyegat

This type of *gembyangan* is also known as *gembyangan pinjal/minjal* or, because of its use in *lancaran* (in *iråmå lancar*), as *gembyangan lancaran*. For the *bonang barung*, it consists of the *sèlèh* note of the *gåtrå* played in octaves on the off-beats. It is shown here with the corresponding standard Solonese *bonang panerus* part, in *iråmå lancar*:

balungan   . 5 . 6   . 5 . 3

bonang barung   6/6̣ . 6/6̣ .   3/3̣ . 3/3̣ .

bonang panerus   . . 6/6̣ . . 6/6̣ . 6/6̣   . . 3/3̣ . . 3/3̣ . 3/3̣

The Yogyanese also use this *garap*, but they have further options for the *bonang panerus* part

bonang panerus (1)   6/6̣ 6/6̣ 6/6̣   3/3̣ 3/3̣ 3/3̣

(where the pattern has a triplet rhythm—three notes in the time of four—and the end of the pattern coincides with the *sèlèh* note) and

bonang panerus (2)   6/6̣ . . 6/6̣ . . 6/6̣ .   3/3̣ . . 3/3̣ . . 3/3̣ .

bonang panerus (3)   6/6̣ . 6/6̣ . 6/6̣ . 6/6̣ .   3/3̣ . 3/3̣ . 3/3̣ . 3/3̣ .

bonang panerus (4)   6̣ 6 6̣ 6 6̣ 6 6̣ 6   3̣ 3 3̣ 3 3̣ 3 3̣ 3

among others, and it is not possible to specify the limits of use for each of these.[12]

In both Solo and Yogya styles, the last *gåtrå* of the *bukå bonang* of a *lancaran* uses *gembyangan cegat*, thus anticipating the *garap* of the piece proper. For an exception to this, see under **Gembyang(an): 2**.

Besides its use for *lancaran* in *iråmå lancar*, the treatment is also applied to *srepegan* (as the term is used in Solo)

balungan   5 3 2 3

bonang barung   3/3̣ . 3/3̣ . 3/3̣ . 3/3̣ .

and *sampak*:

balungan   6 6 6 6

bonang barung   6/6̣ . 6/6̣ . 6/6̣ . 6/6̣ .

There are various ways in which a *srepegan* may be

[12] This area of *garap* is a good example of the hazards of trying to set geographical limits to performance practice. Examples (1) and (4) are often thought of as 'Yogyanese' but can also be found far to the east and west of that city.

played, but typically the *bonang* players switch to *imbal* as soon after the start of a *srepegan* as convenient, but they resume *gembyangan cegat* when the *kendhang* signals a *seseg*. If the *srepegan* is followed by a *sampak*, they continue with *gembyangan cegat*.

If a *lancaran* makes a transition from *irâmâ lancar* to *ir I*, normally both *bonang* start playing *mipil* (see below). If the *balungan* is *nibani* in *irâmâ lancar*, typically it is replaced by a *mlaku* version in slower *irâmâ*. Exceptionally, in some contexts the players continue with *gembyangan* in *ir I*, simply playing *irâmâ lancar* patterns at half speed.

While the notes of *gembyangan cegat* are normally taken from the last note of each *gâtrâ*, this does not always apply. In a *lancaran*, the *kenong* and the *bonang* may play either this note or the final note of every second *gâtrâ*. (The *kenong* and *bonang* do not necessarily agree.) The choice of note on these instruments can also serve as a signal for a change of register, e.g. in a piece that contains a *ngelik* section, such as *lnc Rénâ-rénâ sl 6*

balungan	. 3 . 2̂	. 3 . 5̂	. 6 . 5̂	. 3 . (2)
kenong/bonang notes	2	5	5	2
balungan	. 3 . 2̂	. 3 . 5̂	. 2 . 3̂	. 5 . (6)
kenong/bonang notes	2	5	6	6
balungan	. 1̇ . 6̂	. 3 . 2̂	. 3 . 2̂	. 1̇ . (6)
kenong/bonang notes	6	2	2	6
balungan	. 1̇ . 6̂	. 3 . 2̂	. 3 . 2̂	. 1̇ . (6)
kenong/bonang notes	6	2	2	6
balungan	. 2̇ . 3̇̂	. 2̇ . 1̇̂	. 6 . 5̂	. 3 . (2)
kenong/bonang notes	1	1	5	2

where the last three *gongan* constitute the *ngelik*, and the transition into it is signalled by the two *gâtrâ* of the note 6 on *kenong* and *bonang* in the second *gongan*. In the first half of the final *gongan*, another *kenong/bonang* signal, on note 1, indicates the high register of the *céngkok* 2̇ 3̇ 2̇ 1̇.

The *kempul* may use similar signals in *srepegan*, e.g. *srepegan manyurâ* (p. 210), but probably not the *bonang*:

balungan	3232	5353	232(1)
kenong/bonang notes	2	3	1̇
balungan	2121	3232	561̇(6)
kenong/bonang notes	1̇	2	6
balungan	1̇61̇6	5353	653(2)
kenong/bonang notes	6	3	2

In *lancaran*, relatively little account is otherwise taken of the register of the *balungan* when choosing the notes to be played on the *bonang*. (However, see under **Kempyung(an) and gembyung(an)**, p. 166.) If the *bonang* has 1̣, a 1 in the *balungan* should be played as 1̣ plus 1, and the combination of 1 plus 1̇ should be reserved for a 1̇ in the *balungan*. On a *bonang cacat* this choice does not exist.

In Yogyanese style, *gembyangan cegat* can also be found in *ir I* when the tempo is fast, e.g. close to the end of a piece with a *suwuk gropak*, as well as more generally in loud-style *gendhing* and *ladrang* (see **Progress of a Yogyanese gendhing soran**, p. 81):

balungan	6 1̇ 6 5	2 1 2 (6)
bonang barung	1̇/1 . 1̇/1 . 5/5̣ . 5/5̣ .	6/6̣ 6/6̣ 6̣ 6̣

In this example, the final *gâtrâ* uses *gembyangan midak*: see the next heading.

> **Tips & tricks 6**
> **A good *gembyangan cegat* rhythm**
> Many players have difficulty learning the right rhythm for the *gembyangan cegat* part on the *bonang panerus*, the main problem being the timing of the first note. In contrast to most patterns, it does not help much to think forwards from the start of the pattern to the *sèlèh* note or backwards from the *sèlèh* note. Instead, the *bonang panerus* player must listen to the first note from the *bonang barung*, and play on the next half-beat. Playing this first note too late is a very common mistake. The composite pattern for the two *bonang* resembles the 'tiddle-om-pom-pom' rhythm of some well-known hornpipe dances.
>
> | | | | | | | | | |
> |---|---|---|---|---|---|---|---|---|
> | *balungan* (example) | | . | | 1 | | . | | 6̣ |
> | *bonang barung* | | 6/6̣ | | . | | 6/6̣ | | . |
> | *bonang panerus* | . | . | 6/6̣ | . | . | 6/6̣ | . | 6/6̣ |
> | | | ti- | ddle | om | | pom | | pom |

Gembyangan midak/pidak

A characteristic Yogyanese form of *gembyangan* is regularly used at specific places. *Gembyangan midak* or *pidak* consists of a note in the low octave followed by a *gembyangan* on the same note. This pattern is repeated according to the context, as explained below.

In general, the Yogyanese *bonang* style has a strong tendency to use some form of *gembyangan* in the *gåtrå* leading up to each gong, at least in the shorter *bentuk*. (For some exceptions, see under **Gembyang(an): 2**, p. 158.) One such place is the *gåtrå* ending with the *gong bukå*. With the exception of *lancaran*, *gembyangan midak* is in fact the standard Yogyanese *garap* for the end of a *bukå bonang* in any *bentuk* that has a *bukå bonang*. The pattern used there covers four beats of the *bonang barung* part (the *bonang panerus* not being involved at this point):

```
(end of) bukå    1̇ 6 5 3    2 1 2 (6)
bonang barung    1̇ 6 5 3      6   6
                            6̣ 6̣ 6̣ 6̣
```

At the final gong of a piece, the *bonang barung* plays a similar four-beat pattern based on the final gong note, regardless of *irâmâ*. In *irâmâ lancar* and at the end of the *bukå*, the pattern covers a *gåtrå* of *balungan*. At a *suwuk* in *ir I* the pattern covers half a *gåtrå*, and the *bonang panerus* plays the pattern twice in the same time:

```
balungan           2   1   6   (5)
bonang barung      2 1 6̣ .   5   5
                           5̣ 5̣ 5̣ 5̣
bonang panerus     216̣.216̣. 5 5 5 5
                           5̣5̣5̣5̣5̣5̣5̣5̣
```

(The first half of this *gåtrå* uses *mipil*: see the next heading.) If the *gåtrå* leading to the gong is being realised with *gembyangan* anyway (see **Gembyang(an): 2**, p. 158), the type of *gembyangan* changes half-way through, e.g.

```
balungan           .   6   .   (5)
bonang barung        5       5   5
                   5̣ 5̣ 5̣ . 5̣ 5̣ 5̣ 5̣
bonang panerus     5 5     5 5 5 5
                   5̣5̣5̣.5̣5̣..5̣5̣5̣5̣5̣5̣5̣5̣
```

Following the same principle of replacing the last four beats of the *bonang barung* part or eight beats of the *bonang panerus* part, the following are possible realisations of the same *gåtrå* in *ir II*. (The first three-quarters of the *gåtrå* are in *mipil*: see the next heading.)

bonang barung

```
2 1 6̣ . 2 1 6̣ 1 6̣ 5̣ 3̣ .   5   5
                          5̣ 5̣ 5̣ 5̣
```

bonang panerus

```
216̣.216̣.216̣.216̣16̣5̣3̣.6̣5̣3̣. 5 5 5 5
                           5̣5̣5̣5̣5̣5̣5̣5̣
```

The *gembyang midak* patterns are also used in the characteristic *lâmbâ* section that follows the *gong bukå* in *ladrang* and *gendhing*: they are used for each *gåtrå* until the speed drops and the *dados* section begins. Both instruments play separate patterns for each half-*gåtrå*:

```
balungan           . 3 . 2     . 6 . 5
bonang barung        3   2       6   5
                   3̣ 3̣ 2̣ 2̣     6̣ 6̣ 5̣ 5̣
bonang panerus     3 3 2 2     6 6 5 5
                   3̣3̣3̣3̣2̣2̣2̣2̣    6̣6̣6̣6̣5̣5̣5̣5̣
```

By definition, a *lâmbâ* section has *balungan nibani*. Note that the *bonang barung* plays the *gembyangan midak* during the *lâmbâ* section at the same density as in the *gåtrå* before the *gong bukå*:

balungan

```
. 3 . 2   . 3 . 2   . 3 . 6   . 3 . 2
```

bonang barung

```
  3   2     3   2     3   6     3   2
3̣ 3̣ 2̣ 2̣   3̣ 3̣ 2̣ 2̣   3̣ 3̣ 6̣ 6̣   3̣ 3̣ 2̣ 2̣
```

and the *bonang panerus* at twice this density.

Gembyangan midak is an option for *balungan nibani* when it occurs at certain other transitions, but is not standard *garap* for pieces with *balungan nibani* throughout.

Balungan nibani during the *pangkat dhawah* (the transition from the *dados* section into the *dhawah*) of a Yogyanese *gendhing* also receives *gembyangan midak* treatment, but at twice the density shown above:

```
balungan           . 3 . 2     . 6 . 5
bonang barung      3 3 2 2     6 6 5 5
                   3̣3̣3̣3̣2̣2̣2̣2̣    6̣6̣6̣6̣5̣5̣5̣5̣
```

The *bonang panerus* again plays at twice the density of the *bonang barung*.

When the *dhawah* is going into *ir III*, the Yogyanese

prefer to make the transition into *bonang imbal* as early as possible, e.g. at the gong at the end of the *pangkat dhawah*, with the result that the *gembyangan midak* stops at the gong. The Solonese, using *mipil nibani* patterns (see next heading) during the *ompak inggah*, may make the transition at the same point, or may continue *nibani* patterns at half speed until the transition into *imbal bonang*, typically at the first *kenong* of the *inggah*.

Mipil

Mipil or *pipilan* refers to taking something little by little; for example, stripping corn from a cob. To the *bonang* player, *mipil* means taking the *balungan* notes two at a time, i.e. a half-*gåtrå*, and making a pattern out of them. (The alternative name *mlampah* is also found.) *Mipil* is the standard *garap* in *ir I* and *ir II* when the *bonang* are not playing *imbal*. It takes very different forms depending on whether the *balungan* is *nibani* or *mlaku*, and according to the choice of the Solo style or the Yogya style.

Standard *mipil* patterns are usually interspersed with stretches of *gembyangan*, *kempyungan* and *gembyungan* (see **Gembyang(an): 2**, p. 158). There are special *mipil* treatments for the standard cadential phrases of several *pathet* (see **Cadential patterns**, p. 157), as well as for some named *céngkok*. In addition, certain pieces (or parts of them) have unique *garap*.

Balungan mlaku: Solo style

Mipil patterns for the notes *x* and *y* forming a half-*gåtrå* are shown in Table 3.9. The table is strictly a starting point. Solonese *bonang* players often follow the principle 'less is more'. Therefore they consider the basic patterns somewhat unrefined, and prefer to use sparser patterns. A fast tempo may also result in the player omitting the first or last note, or sometimes even more, of a pattern.

The patterns listed under *ir I* are classed as *mipil låmbå* or single *mipil*: these are *lampah* 2 for the *bonang barung*, *lampah* 4 for *bonang panerus*. The *ir II* patterns are called *mipil rangkep* or double *mipil*: these are *lampah* 4 for the *bonang barung*, and *lampah* 8 for *bonang panerus*.

It is common in the *mérong* of a *gendhing* accompanying a *bedhåyå* or *srimpi* dance for the *bonang barung* player to use half-speed *mipil låmbå* patterns in *ir II*. The same practice may occur with any *gendhing* considered particularly refined: this is a very subjective matter, so the use of *mipil låmbå* instead of *mipil rangkep* depends on the player. If the *bonang barung* player chooses *mipil låmbå*, the patterns used may be the fuller ones (*xyxy* rather than *xyx.*). The *bonang panerus* still plays its usual *mipil rangkep*, so that the density ratio between the two instruments is 4:1 instead of the usual 2:1.

Special treatment is necessary when the *balungan* is not in the regular rhythm of *balungan mlaku*. In some cases, irregularities are ignored: for example, isolated off-beat notes as in *gd Loro-loro géndhong sl m*

$\overline{.12}$ $\overline{.13}$ 3 2 1 6̣

which is played as if it were

1 2 1 3   3 2 1 6̣

i.e. 1 2 1 3 as (*bonang barung*, *ir II*)

. 1 2 1 . . 2 1 . . 1 3 1 . . 3 1 .

Frequently, *mipil* treatment of isolated patches of *balungan ngadhal* is still based on taking pairs of *balungan* notes, although it is not always obvious which notes make up the pair. One simple example

balungan

2   3   5 $\overline{6\ \dot{1}}$ $\overline{5\ 6}$ 1̇   5   2

may be easier to interpret if rewritten

. 2 . 3 . 5 . 6   1̇ 5 6 1̇ . 5 . 2

because the note 6 is then clearly the end of the first *gåtrå*. This suggests that the first *gåtrå* is played normally, and only the notes 1̇ 5 6 1̇ need special treatment. These four

Table 3.9
Basic *mipil* styles

	Ir I	*Ir II*
Bonang barung		
Basic pattern	*xyxy*	*xyxyxyxy*
Yogya version	*xyxy* or *xyx* .	*xyx* . *xyxy*
Solo version	*xyxy* or *xyx* .	*xyx* . *xyx* .
Solo version, more refined		*xyx* . . *yx* . or sometimes . *yx* . . *yx* .
Bonang panerus		
Basic pattern	*xyxyxyxy*	*xyxyxyxyxyxyxyxy*
Yogya version	*xyx* . *xyxy*	*xyx* . *xyx* . *xyx* . *xyxy*
Solo version	*xyx* . *xyx* .	*xyx* . *xyx* . *xyx* . *xyx* .
Solo version for *seseg*	. *yx* . . *yx* .	. *yx* . . *yx* . . *yx* . . *yx* .

notes form two pairs, and each pair is played by the *bonang barung* with *mipil låmbå* in *ir II*, resulting in

232..32.565..65. 1̇51̇.61̇6.525..25.

(for example) and the *bonang panerus* plays twice as many notes as the *bonang barung*, giving

1̇51̇.1̇51̇.61̇6.61̇6.525.525.525.525.

for the second *gåtrå*. In *ir I* the *bonang barung* plays such passages *mbalung*, resulting in

2 3 2 . 5 6 5 .   1̇ 5 6 1̇ 5 2 5 .

for the two *gåtrå*, and the *bonang panerus* plays *mipil låmbå* in the usual style of the *bonang barung*:

232.232.565.565. 1̇51̇.61̇6.525.525.

When considering how to realise passages of this kind, it may be helpful to mark up the *balungan* line with curves as used for phrase marks in Western musical notation. Each curve should end on the stronger of a pair of notes. In the following *kenongan* from the *lik* of *ldr Pakumpulan sl 9* (which is played in *ir II*)

66 . 6 5 3 2 3   5 6 1 2 1 6̣ 5̣

the first two *balungan* beats have 6 and a *pin*, which represent a short *gantungan*, so that they need realisation with *gembyangan* (see under **Gembyang(an): 2**, p. 158). The other beats and half-beats can be linked by curves as shown, which indicate the note pairs that should form the *mipil* patterns, but the last four notes suggest a low 5 cadential pattern (see **Cadential patterns**, p. 157).

For isolated *balungan ngadhal* starting on a *dhing* of the *gåtrå*, such as 65621, various interpretations are possible. The *sèlèh* note in each half of the *gåtrå* must be respected. Thus standard *mipil* is an obvious treatment for the notes 56 in the first half of the *gåtrå*: the uncertainty is mainly about the opening of the *gåtrå*. The first note may be given a *mipil* treatment, using the second note too

656.565.212..12. (*bonang barung*, *ir II*)

or it may be played as a *gembyang* (**Gembyang(an): 2** again)

6.565.212..12. (*bonang barung*, *ir II*)
6̣6̣6̣

Alternatively, the *ngadhal* part may be ignored altogether, by treating it as the nearest *mlaku* equivalent—in this case, 5621. This is the most likely solution in *ir I*.

When the *balungan* includes a sequence of off-beat notes or other irregularities, it may be realised with *gembyangan* rather than *mipil*: see *ldr Diràdåmetå* in Part 4 and examples under **Gembyang(an): 2**.

Some specific patterns in the *balungan* are classified as *pin mundur* (see below) and given characteristic treatments. The *garap* used by the *bonang* may reflect the previous *gåtrå*. For example, a *pin* as the first note of the *gåtrå* continues the preceding *sèlèh* note, as usual, but players may thin down the *mipil* pattern to avoid overemphasising the note: thus . 6 following *sèlèh* 5 implies a half-*gåtrå* 56, and may be played as .65..65. (*bonang barung*, *ir II*). The same treatment may be given to the notes *xy* after a *gåtrå gantung* on *x*: for example, in the two *gåtrå* 55.. 561̇2̇, where the second *gåtrå* may start with

.65..65.

The *gåtrå* 65621 following a *sèlèh* 5 may also start as .65..65. (*bonang barung*, *ir II*). In other words, the initial 6 is disregarded, as described earlier.

Particular *gåtrå* that are notated as *balungan mlaku* may be played, by convention, as if they were *nibani*: see **Cadential patterns** and **Other special *garap***, p. 168.

As a general principle, *mipil* is used when the two notes of the half-*gåtrå* are close in pitch, but will tend to be replaced by another treatment if the two notes are far apart. For example, *mipil* is the normal treatment if the two notes make intervals of up to a *gembyung*, e.g. for 12, 13, 15, 21, 31 or 51. For intervals of a *kempyung* or more, one of the treatments described under **Gembyang(an): 2** is more likely: for example, a *gembyangan* pattern to the *sèlèh* note. If the *gåtrå* ends high, e.g. 2126, and the *balungan* continues in a high register, it is considered as a *gåtrå dhélik* and its second half will again have a *gembyangan* treatment.

Treatments for notes towards the bottom limit of the *pathet* are described under **Kempyung(an) and gembyung(an)**, p. 166. Notes at the top end of the *pathet* are not necessarily within the range of the *bonang* at all, so need special consideration. In a *gåtrå* where the first half is out of range, such as 3̇2̇65, the high notes may be transposed down an octave, so that the whole *gåtrå* can be given a conventional *mipil* treatment.

A *gåtrå* whose second half is out of range, such as 562̇1̇, may be treated like any *gåtrå dhélik*; i.e. the high half may be played with *gembyangan* to the *sèlèh* note. Alternatively, such a *gåtrå* may be played with *gembyangan* throughout, as is often done with a *gåtrå* that is high throughout, e.g. 3̇2̇1̇2̇. *Gembyangan* can therefore be a signal of high register or a switch to high register. However, some players will feel that an all-*gembyangan* treatment over-emphasises the *sèlèh* note and is untrue to the contour.

When realising contours like these, it may be helpful to consider the adjacent *gåtrå*. For the two *gåtrå* 1̇2̇1̇6 5312 in *pélog* (e.g. in *gd Lipur érang-érang pl 6*) the treatment adopted for the first *gåtrå* should preferably end with the note 6 rather than 6̣, in order to link neatly to the 5 in the next *gåtrå*. Some players will solve the problem by playing the whole *gåtrå* as *gembyang* 6. Others will try to preserve the contour. In *pélog*, the first half of the *gåtrå* can only be played as 12. Even if the *bonang* had the 1̇, it would be bad style to make a jump at the mid-point and play the second half as *mipil* 1̇6. Another possibility is to play *mipil* on 16, but *mipil* on such a widely separated pair of notes is unusual. This *gåtrå* is in fact a good place to use *gembyangan* in the second half, but with a simple lead-in:

            6   6
121 . . 21 . 16̣6̣ . 6̣6̣ . .

so making a neat transition into the following 5.

For the same two *gåtrå* in *sléndro*, a 12-pot *bonang* would have the high 2, theoretically allowing various other treatments. In practice many players ignore the 2̇ pot, or only use it when playing *gembyang*.

Pin mundur

The term *pin mundur* can be translated as 'delayed *pin*' or 'backwards *pin*', and refers to *pin* that occur on the *dhong* of the *gåtrå*, in contrast to *balungan nibani*, where the *pin* fall on the *dhing*.

There are in fact two distinct forms of *garap* associated with *pin mundur*. A single *pin mundur* in the *gåtrå*, as in 561̇ . or 3 . 32, results in the *bonang* playing half the *gåtrå* as *gembyangan*—for 1̇ and 3 respectively in these two examples. Depending on the note, *kempyung* or *gembyung* may replace the *gembyangan*, as usual: see **Gembyang(an): 2**.

When the *gåtrå* has the form *.xy.*, special *garap* is often used by the Solonese. If *.xy.* follows the *sèlèh* note *y*, the pattern for the *bonang barung* is *.xy..xy.* in *ir I* and *.xy..xy..xy..xy.* in *ir II*. (The *bonang panerus* plays the same patterns twice over.) These interpretations of the *balungan* are a little unexpected, because the *sèlèh* note of the *gåtrå* is apparently *y*, but the pattern *.xy.* played on the *balungan* points to a *sèlèh* note *x*. In *ldr Bimå kurda pl 7*, . 3̣5̣ . after 5̣ is played in *ir I* as

. 3̣ 5̣ . . 3̣ 5̣ .

If *.xy.* follows any other *sèlèh* note, the same *garap* may be used, but the obvious *garap* is often considered more suitable: i.e. a *gembyang* (or *kempyung* or *gembyung*) in the second half of the *gåtrå*, preceded by a half-*gåtrå* of *mipil* on the appropriate notes: thus in *ldr Bimå kurda pl 7* again, . 5̣3̣ . after 6̣ is played in *ir I* as

                6̣   6̣
6̣ 5̣ 6̣ 5̣ 3̣ . 3̣ .

In both of these cases the typical Yogyanese treatment is a *gembyangan* in each half-*gåtrå*. This is one example of a Yogyanese tendency to treat *.x* in the *balungan* as *gantung x* rather than treat the *pin* as a continuation of the previous note. (See under the next heading and p. 162.)

Gåtrå of the form *yxy.* may be treated as if written *yxyx*; for example, 434 . in *gd bonang Tukung pl 7*.

The repeated three-note pattern . 6̣2 is also given *pin mundur* treatment. For two *gåtrå* filled with this pattern, following a *sèlèh* 2, i.e. *xxx*2 . 6̣2 . 6̣2 . 6̣, the *bonang barung* will play per *gåtrå* in *ir II*

. 6̣ 2 . . 6̣ 2 . . 6̣ 2 . . 6̣ 2 .

or a similar pattern, including patterns with groups of three notes

2 6̣ 2 . 6̣ 2 . 6̣ 2 . 6̣ 2 . 6̣ 2 .

related to those described under **Nduduk gembyang**, p. 162. The *bonang panerus* will play similar patterns at twice the speed:

. 6̣2 . . 6̣2 . . 6̣2 . . 6̣2 . . 6̣2 . . 6̣2 . . 6̣2 . . 6̣2 .

In the Yogya style the pattern may be considered as belonging in the low octave, suggesting patterns such as

. 2̣ 6̣ . . 2̣ 6̣ . etc.

Balungan mlaku: Yogya style

Yogyanese style in realising *balungan mlaku* differs notably from Solonese practice in four respects, which are illustrated in more detail below:

- the lower octave is used more extensively than in Solonese style: this principle can best be demonstrated by a worked example covering *kempyungan* and *gembyangan* as well as *mipil*: see p. 169,

- the *mipil* patterns are by no means restricted to the *balungan* notes: the Solo-style patterns are also played, and are sometimes called *baku* (= basic), and the wider-ranging patterns are then described as *nglagu*,
- characteristic rhythms and minor distortions of the regular beat are used in addition to the plainer Solo-style patterns,
- the style of damping described below (p. 152) is frequently used.

The Yogya *mipil* style has some effect in *ir I*, but comes into full flower in *ir II*. It also applies to loud-style pieces with *balungan nibani* in *ir III*. (In *ir III* and *IV*, *imbal* is usual, as in Solonese style.)

Yogyanese players play *mipil* less than Solonese players in comparable contexts. There are two reasons for this. One is their practice of using various kinds of *gembyangan* where the Solonese would continue with *mipil*:

- *gembyangan midak* in the *pangkat dhawah*,
- *gembyangan cegat* as an option in fast *ir I*,
- often some form of *gembyangan* in the *gåtrå* before each gong.

In addition, because of the Yogyanese tendency to realise the *balungan* in the low octave, more opportunities arise for *kempyungan* and *gembyungan* (see below under **Gembyang(an): 2**, p. 158).

The principles of *mipil nglagu* can be illustrated for the *bonang barung* playing the half-*gåtrå* 5 3 in *ir II*. The basic *mipil baku* pattern would be 5 3 5 . 5 3 5 3: i.e. starting with the 5 and ending with the 3. The direction of the contour is essentially downwards, and the most characteristic Yogyanese pattern involves an 'undershoot' in that direction, using note 2 in addition to 5 3. Each half of the pattern can then use either the basic two notes or those two plus the undershoot note. Patterns of the form 5 3 2 . 5 3 2 3 are very characteristic, but several others are possible. Also common are patterns in which the second half starts with the *sèlèh* note played twice, e.g. 5 3 5 . 3 3 5 3. Notes may be played on all eight beats. The following are some further examples for the same half-*gåtrå*:

5 3 2 . 3 3 5 3   5 3 5 . 3 3 2 3
5 3 2 . 3 3 2 3   5 3 5 . 5 3 2 3
5 3 2 . 2 3 5 3   5 3 5 . 2 3 2 3
5 2 3 5 2 3 5 3   5 3 2 5 3 2 5 3
5 3 2 5 2 3 5 3   5 3 5 . 2 3 5 3

All the above still start with the 5 and end with the 3, because anything else would theoretically be wrong. The pattern will normally end with the 3, but more adventurous players will not necessarily start with the 5: for example, they might play 3 5 6 . 5 3 2 3. Thus in a half-*gåtrå* that has an overall falling contour, the player is actually using patterns that rise as well as fall. Strictly speaking, patterns of this kind do not accurately represent the contour of the *balungan*.

In the realisation of a half-*gåtrå* that has a rising contour, an overshoot note above the *sèlèh* note may be used: thus the half-*gåtrå* 3 5 would use the note 6, giving patterns such as 3 5 6 . 3 5 6 5, and so on.

The examples above realise the half-*gåtrå* by using three different notes rather than two. Patterns with even more than three notes occur, e.g. 5 3 2 1 2 3 5 3 for the half-*gåtrå* 5 3. As there are twice as many notes in the patterns for the *bonang panerus*, they offer more opportunity to use complex patterns.

The examples shown are for *ir II*. In *ir I*, players generally stick to patterns containing only two notes, but three-note patterns with overshoot or undershoot also occur on the *bonang barung*. The half-*gåtrå* 6 5 when realised in the lower octave is especially likely to result in a pattern such as 6̣ 5̣ 3̣ 5̣, which recalls Solonese use of *mipil nibani* patterns in a similar situation (see **Cadential patterns**, p. 157). Rhythmic variants such as $\underset{\cdot}{6}\,\underset{\cdot}{5}\,\overline{\underset{\cdot}{3}\,\underset{\cdot}{5}}$. are also found in Yogyanese practice.

Yogyanese players often follow standard Solonese practice when interpreting a single *pin* that falls on the *dhing* of a *gåtrå*, e.g. in . 3 5 6, and treat the *pin* as a continuation of the previous note. Sometimes they take a different view. The first half of this *gåtrå* has the form of *balungan nibani*, and may be given a characteristic Yogyanese treatment for *balungan nibani* as described below, i.e. the notes . 3 are played with *gembyangan* 3. It is not possible to specify which of the two possible treatments is used when.

In a departure from general Yogyanese practice for *balungan mlaku*, players often observe a rule that 6̣ should not be approached from the 2 above it. The *bonang barung* then plays 2 6̣ as (for example) 5̣ 6̣ 1 6̣ in *ir I* or 5̣ 6̣ 1 . 5̣ 6̣ 1 6̣ in *ir II*, and the corresponding patterns for the *bonang panerus* are 5̣ 6̣ 1 . 5̣ 6̣ 1 6̣ in *ir I*, and 5̣ 6̣ 1 . 5̣ 6̣ 1 . 5̣ 6̣ 1 . 5̣ 6̣ 1 6̣ in *ir II*. Yogyanese players may also approach the 5̣ in 1 5̣ and 7̣ 5̣ from below in the same way, and treat 3 7̣ as 2 7̣. Thus the *bonang barung* may play

3756 as 27̣2 . 6̣7̣27̣5̣6̣7̣ . 5̣6̣7̣6̣ (*ir II*)

1615 as 16̣16̣3̣5̣3̣5̣ (*ir I*)

The half-*gåtrå* 21 often receives a slightly unexpected *garap*—indeed, it could almost be considered the standard Yogyanese treatment:

1121 (*ir I*)

212 . 1121 (*ir II*)

The *gåtrå* 2121 may be treated as a whole instead of as two halves, and played (for example)

212 . 1121 (*ir I*)

212 . 212 . 212 . 1121 (*ir II*)

There are some important characteristic rhythms that Yogyanese players use in *mipil* on the *bonang barung*. One affects the first half of the eight-note pattern: the third note is delayed by half a beat, e.g.

5 3 $\overline{.2}$. 5 3 2 3

instead of the basic

5 3 2 . 5 3 2 3

The variant rhythm is not used every time, but mixed in with *gåtrå* using the standard rhythm. The same is true of another variant, often combined with it, in which the fifth note in the eight-note pattern is pulled forward by nearly half a beat:

5 3 $\overline{.2}$ $\overline{.5}$. 3 2 3

The first note in the eight-note pattern can be played early in exactly the same way. (This notation is the best that can be provided, but is not fully accurate: the precise rhythms can only be acquired by listening carefully to actual performances.)

The fifth note of the eight-note pattern, in its variant rhythm, is often repeated, giving an effect called *geter* (= tremble). This treatment is applied to a half-pattern of the form *xxyx*. For the example just given (changing to *xxyx* = 3323), the *geter* version might be notated

5 3 $\overline{.2}$ $\overline{.3}$ 3 3 2 3

The notation suggests that the second note of the *geter* is exactly on the fifth beat of the pattern, but normally it arrives fractionally early. The notation often used by Yogyanese writers for such a half-*gåtrå*, 532 . $\overline{33}$323, indicates that the first note of the *geter* sits squarely on the beat, but this definitely does not describe the reality.

Other small rhythmic variations can be heard. Altogether, the rhythms of the *bonang barung* in Yogyanese practice are very subtle: the instrument so often plays slightly off the beat in *mipil* that the other players in the gamelan are well advised to follow only the notes of the *bonang barung*, never its rhythms.

The *bonang panerus*, by contrast, plays on the beat. Its patterns can be either *baku* or *nglagu*, but without the rhythmic irregularities. Patterns for *ir I* can be identical to those used by the *bonang barung* in *ir II*, e.g.

235 . 2353

In *ir II* the characteristic *nglagu* patterns for the *bonang panerus* often consist of three identical four-note groups and a different final group, e.g.

235 . 235 . 235 . 2353

In patterns of this type, the *bonang panerus* may reverse the direction of the final group, e.g.

235 . 235 . 235 . 5323

In addition to the examples just given, the *ir II* patterns can also consist of two identical groups and then something different.

These patterns can use four different notes rather than three, i.e. they can 'overshoot' or 'undershoot' by two notes rather than one, or they can 'overshoot' **and** 'undershoot' by one note. Patterns with four different notes are possible in *ir I*, though less frequent.

Some examples are now given to illustrate all these principles: for the half-*gåtrå* 6̣1

(*ir I*) 6̣16̣ . 6̣16̣1

(*ir I*) 6̣16̣5̣6̣16̣1

(*ir I*) 6̣12 . 1121

(*ir II*) 6̣12 . 6̣12 . 6̣12 . 216̣1

(*ir II*) 6̣12 . 6̣12 . 6̣123216̣1

(*ir II*) 6̣12 . 6̣12 . 6̣16̣5̣6̣5̣6̣1

(*ir II*) 6̣12 . 6̣12 . 6̣16̣5̣6̣121

(*ir II*) 6̣16̣ . 6̣16̣ . 6̣16̣5̣3̣5̣6̣1

and for 21

(*ir I*) 212 . 1121

(*ir I*) 2 1 6̣ 5̣ 6̣ 5̣ 6̣ 1

(*ir II*) 2 1 2 . 2 1 2 . 2 1 6̣ 5̣ 6̣ 1 2 1

(*ir II*) 2 1 6̣ . 2 1 6̣ . 2 1 6̣ 1 6̣ 1 2 1

and for 1 3

(*ir I*) 1 3 1 . 3 3 5 3

(*ir I*) 1 3 1 . 1 3 5 3

(*ir II*) 1 3 1 . 1 3 1 . 1 3 1 . 1 3 5 3

(*ir II*) 1 3 1 . 1 3 1 . 1 3 5 . 2 3 5 3

The *ir I* patterns might be used in *ir II* on the *bonang barung*.

On both *bonang* in Yogyanese style, the general approach to the various possible intervals in the half-*gåtrå* of the *balungan* is similar but not identical to that described for the Solonese style. Larger intervals (of a *kempyung* or larger) in the *balungan* are liable to be interpreted in whichever way produces the smaller interval on the *bonang*. For example, 1 6 in the *balungan* will be taken as 1 6̣ and played accordingly

bonang barung, *ir II* 1 6̣ 5̣ . 1 6̣ 5̣ 6̣ or 5̣ 6̣ 1 . 5̣ 6̣ 1 6̣

whereas 2 6 may be taken less literally

bonang panerus, *ir I* 3̣ 6̣ 3̣ . 6̣ 6̣ 1 6̣

Bonang barung players often damp selected notes rather obviously, especially in loud-style pieces. This can be done before either a *dhing* or a *dhong*, but not on both sides of the same note, e.g.

3 . 3̸ 2 3 5 or 3 2 . 2̸ 3 5

but not 3 . 3̸ 2 . 2̸ 3 5

where the solidus is used to show that the pot is struck and immediately damped. Once again the notation is not precise, and the rhythm should be copied from performances. *Bonang panerus* players use much less damping in *mipil*, but one typical practice is obvious damping on every fourth note of a pattern, e.g.

5̣ 6̣ 1 1̸ 5̣ 6̣ 1 1̸ 5̣ 6̣ 1 1̸ 5̣ 6̣ 1 1̸ 2 1 2 2̸ 2 1 2 2̸ 2 1 2 2̸ 2 1 2 2̸

in *ir II*, where the solidus has the same meaning as above.

Certain contours and named *céngkok* may receive special treatment in place of standard *mipil*, as explained below under **Yogyanese styles: *nguthik*** and **Yogyanese styles: *ngrambat***, p. 158.

With all these *garap* options to choose from, individuals' playing styles can differ markedly. *Mipil nglagu* (especially the patterns using four different notes), audible damping, off-beat rhythms and *geter* are more or less optional: some players use them frequently, and others barely at all. To some extent, these aspects of Yogyanese style should be regarded as ornaments that do not occur in every possible place, just as an opera singer does not execute a trill or a *messa di voce* on every note. On the other hand, the less often they are used, the less Yogyanese is the resulting sound.

Balungan nibani: Solo style

For *gåtrå* in *nibani* form, there is a large repertoire of standard *garap*, sometimes called *mipil nibani* or *mipil lumpatan*, in *ir I* and *ir II*. Table 3.10 shows a selection from the many patterns in use. A larger collection is available via the associated website.

A *lancaran* that has a *balungan nibani* generally switches to a *balungan mlaku* if played in a slower *irâmâ*.

In *ir III*, the patterns played depend on the style of drumming. During the *inggah* of a soft-style *gendhing* with *gérongan*, *ir III* is the usual *irâmâ*, with optional excursions into *ir IV*: *ciblon* drumming is normal, implying *imbal* on the *bonang*. The transition between *mipil* and *imbal* is described in **Progress of a vocal gendhing** (p. 79).

Some forms of *ciblon* drumming do not signal *imbal*: *kébar* drumming in dance and *wayang* means *imbal*, as does *kiprahan* drumming in dance. In the absence of a *kendhang wayangan* (which is mainly found in gamelan used to accompany *wayang*), *kosèk alus* drumming may use the *ciblon* or even *kendhang gendhing*. *Mipil nibani* patterns are then played on the *bonang*, even in *ir III*.

All the reasons for using *gembyangan*, *kempyungan* or *gembyungan* in place of standard *mipil* patterns remain valid when the *balungan* is *nibani*. In practice, the patterns shown in Table 3.10 are therefore interspersed with *gembyangan* and other patterns. The patterns listed cover a whole *gåtrå*. In *ir II* the patterns can usually be divided into two halves, and the various possible first halves can often be combined with any of the second halves, as the table suggests. This description applies to the *ir I* patterns too, but to a lesser degree. *Bonang panerus* patterns show two distinct styles: some have a sort of reversal of direction at the end, and others do not.

Table 3.10 lists the *mipil nibani* patterns in the order of *sèlèh* notes, starting with the lowest. At the low end, notes 1̣ to 3̣, the patterns listed include a selection from the standard *kempyung* and *gembyung* patterns for these notes: any such pattern shown under **Gembyang(an): 2**, p. 158, can be used. For *sèlèh* notes from 5 upwards, *gembyang* patterns of various kinds are increasingly the normal treatment, especially where the *gåtrå* has a rising shape: either a single *gembyang* is used for the whole *gåtrå*, or separate *gembyang* for each half of the *gåtrå*.

If half of the *gåtrå* is played as a *gembyangan* or *kempyungan/gembyungan* for the usual reasons, then the other half of the *gåtrå* is realised with the appropriate half of a pattern from Table 3.10. For example, the *gåtrå* . 1̣ . 5̣ could be played (*bonang barung*, *ir II*) as

   5̣ 5̣
1̣ 5̣ 1̣ 1̣ . 1̣ . . . 5̣ . 5̣ 5̣ 3̣ . 5̣

Also compare the . 5̣ . 2̣ pattern shown in the table, where a *kempyungan* pattern fills the second half-*gåtrå*.

Therefore, for *balungan* notes towards the extremes of the compass, patterns tend to correspond to two separate half-*gåtrå*.

Of the available patterns for each *gåtrå*, usually some permit smoother transitions from the previous *gåtrå*. For example, the pattern played for . 2 . 1 following a *sèlèh* note below 2 (e.g. 5̣, 6̣ or 1) will typically be one of those starting with 6̣—but there is no obligation to use such a pattern. Similar variant openings are available in several other families of patterns, as the larger collection shows.

The end of the pattern may also take into account the next *gåtrå*: for example, the patterns chosen for . 2 . 1 followed by a *gåtrå gantung* on 5 may incorporate a standard lead-in into the *gembyangan* 5 (see **Gembyang(an): 2**). Again this is only one of many ways of realising the two *gåtrå*:

2 1 2 . 2 1 2 . 2 1 2 . 2 1 6̣ 1   5 . . 5 . . 5 . . 5 . . 5 . . 5
                                  5̣   5̣   5̣   5̣   5̣   5̣

There is further relevant information under **Other special *garap***, p. 168.

In *mipil* for *balungan mlaku*, the pattern *xyx*. implies that the final note, if played, would be *y*. In the *mipil nibani* patterns, the same principle often applies, but many of them include the *sèlèh* note before the end of the pattern and not on the final beat, as in

. 2 . 1 1 2 . . . 3 . 1 1 3 . .

for . 2 . 3 in the *balungan*.

Mipil nibani patterns vary in their density. The one just given belongs to a category of sparse patterns for *ir II* that contain scarcely more notes than *ir I* patterns, and appear closely related to them, e.g.

ir I pattern, half speed	2 1 2 . 3 1 3 .
ir II pattern	. 2 . 1 1 2 . . . 3 . 1 1 3 . .

Using this type of pattern is rather similar to using *mipil låmbå* for *balungan mlaku* in *ir II*.

Players naturally have their favourite patterns. Some opt for the sparser patterns, as Solonese players often do when playing *mipil* for *balungan mlaku*. Some have a strong preference for not playing anything on the *sèlèh* note itself. Others prefer patterns where there is a *pin* on the penultimate beat; 3 1 3 . 2 1 . 2, etc.

Patterns are shown in Table 3.10 for *ir I* and *ir II* and for both *bonang*. The *bonang panerus* patterns are more regular and more repetitive than those for the *bonang barung*, and can therefore be shown in a shorthand form. Patterns shown in square brackets are repeated, in the usual rhythm, as often as necessary to fill the space. Where two patterns are shown in brackets, the first is used in the first half of the *gåtrå*, and the second in the second half of the *gåtrå*. The bracketed patterns of three notes are another way of notating one of the standard *gembyangan* styles: see under **Gembyang(an): 2**.

Table 3.10 does not include notes 4 or 7, but the usual substitution rules apply: 7 can replace 1, and 4 substitutes for 5 in *pélog barang* or 3 otherwise. For example, patterns shown for . 2 . 1 can be made to apply to . 2 . 7̣ in *pélog barang* by changing the note 1 throughout. In *pélog barang* the *gåtrå* . 4 . 2 might be played as

2 4 3 2 2 4 . . 2 4 2 . 3 4 . .

on the basis of the pattern shown for . 5 . 2 in the table. In *pélog limå*, the *gåtrå* . 6̣ . 5̣ might be played as

1 6̣ 5̣ 4̣ 4̣ 6̣ . . 4̣ 6̣ 4̣ 5̣ 5̣ 6̣ . 5̣

if there was evidence of the note 4 in the vocal line, or perhaps in the previous *gåtrå*, using a pattern shown for . 6̣ . 5̣ but replacing note 3 throughout the pattern.

Balungan nibani: Yogya style

Several of the situations where Solonese players use *mipil nibani* patterns do not exist in characteristic Yogyanese practice:

- during the *ompak inggah/pangkat dhawah* of a *gendhing*, because the Yogyanese use *gembyangan midak*,

Table 3.10
Bonang patterns for *balungan nibani*, Solonese style

Balungan	*Bonang barung*			*Bonang panerus*
	Ir I	*Ir II*		*Ir I* and *II* (‡ *Ir II* only)
.2.1	151.151.	2626.6.. 2 2	1515.5.. 1 1	[262.][151.] [626.][515.]
.3.1	151.151.	3636.6.. 3 3	1515.5.. 1 1	[363.][151.] [636.][515.]
.3.2	6.6.6.6. 3 3 2 2	3636.6.. 3 3	2626.6.. 2 2	[363.][262.] [636.][626.]
.5.2	252.6.6. 2 2	253225..	2626.6.. 2 2	[5..][262.] [5..][626.]
.2.3	525.3353.	2626.6.. 2 2	3636.6.. 3 3	[262.][363.] [626.][636.]
.5.3	525.3353.	.5.225..	252.3353	[5..][363.] [5..][636.]
.6.3	636.6.6. 3 3	.6.336..	3636.6.. 3 3	[.56.]636.636.
.3.5	656.5535	535663.. .6.556..	636.5535 .5.553.5	[656.][535.]5535 ‡[656.]353.353.
.6.5	636.5535 363.5535	.6.336.. .6.336..	363.55$\overline{35}$.[13] .5.553.5	[636.][535.]5535 ‡[636.]353.353.
.1.5	616.5535 161.535.	.1.661.. 161.161.	616.5535 161.5565	[161.]5535 [161.]5565
.1.6	515.6616	.1.551..	515.6616	[151.]6616
.2.6	151.6616	21.551..	515661.6	[515.]6616
.5.6	215.6616	51.551..	.6.661.6	‡[515.]161.161.
.2.1	212.2121 612.1121	212.212. .2.112..	212.2121 21612121	[212.]2121 [212.]1121
.3.1	313.2121 313.1121	313.313. 6123313.	313.1121 212.1121	[313.]2121 [313.]1121
.1.2	313.2212	313.313.	313.2212	[313.]2212
.3.2	61232212	312331..	313.21.2	[313.]2232
.5.2	535.212.	.5.335..	212.2212	[535.]2212
.2.3	212.313.	212.212.	313.313.	[212.][313.]
.5.3	525.3353	.5.225..	252.3353	[525.]3353
.2.5	252.5..5 5 5	2..2..2. 2 2 2	.5..5..5 5 5 5	[2..][5..] 2 5

13 The notation $\overline{35}$ represents audible damping of the note 5, which happens to be a frequent practice in patterns for 5.

Table 3.10 (cont'd)

Balungan	*Bonang barung*			*Bonang panerus*
	Ir I	*Ir II*		*Ir I* and *II* (‡ *Ir II* only)
.3.5	636.5535	.6.556..	656.5535	
	363.5..5 5̣ 5̣	3..3..3. 3̣ 3̣ 3̣	.5..5..5 5̣ 5̣ 5̣	[3..][5..] 3̣ 5̣
.6.5	636.5535	.6.336..	363.5535	[636.]5535
and other patterns for .6̣.5̣, transposed up an octave, also (depending on piece): treat second half of *gåtrå* as *gembyang* 5, e.g.				
	636.5..5 5̣ 5̣	.6.336..	5̣5̣5.5̣5.. 5̣ 5̣	[636.][5..] 5̣
or both halves of *gåtrå* as separate *gembyang*, e.g.				
		6..6..6. 6̣ 6̣ 6̣	.5..5..5 5̣ 5̣ 5̣	[6..][5..] 6̣ 5̣
or whole *gåtrå* as *gembyang* 5, using standard patterns				
.1.6	212.6..6 6̣ 6̣	212.212.	216̣6̣6.6̣6 6̣ 6̣	[212.]21[6..] 6̣
.3.6	363.6..6 6̣ 6̣			
or both halves of *gåtrå* as separate *gembyang*, or whole *gåtrå* as *gembyang* 6, using standard patterns				
.5.6	1̇51̇.661̇6	.1̇.551̇..	.6.661̇.6	‡[51̇5.]1̇61̇.1̇61̇.
	or both halves of *gåtrå* as separate *gembyang*, or whole *gåtrå* as *gembyang* 6, using standard patterns			
.1̇.6	both halves of *gåtrå* as separate *gembyang*, or whole *gåtrå* as *gembyang* 6, using standard patterns			
.2̇.6	both halves of *gåtrå* as separate *gembyang*, or whole *gåtrå* as *gembyang* 6, using standard patterns			
.6.1̇	both halves of *gåtrå* as separate *gembyang*, or whole *gåtrå* as *gembyang* 1, using standard patterns			
.2̇.1̇	both halves of *gåtrå* as separate *gembyang*, or whole *gåtrå* as *gembyang* 1, using standard patterns or patterns for .2.1			
.3̇.2̇	patterns for .3.2, or both halves of *gåtrå* as separate *gembyang*, or whole *gåtrå* as *gembyang* 2, using standard patterns			

- during the first *kenongan* of the *inggah/dhawah* of a *gendhing*, because the Yogyanese prefer to make the transition into *imbal* at the end of the *pangkat dhawah*,
- when a piece is played in *ir III* with *kosèk alus* drumming rather than *ciblon*, because *kosèk alus* is not a characteristic Yogyanese *garap*,
- in various pieces with a *balungan nibani*, because the Yogyanese version of the piece has a *balungan mlaku*.

The characteristic Yogyanese patterns for *balungan nibani* are based on replacing every *pin* with the note above or below the note that follows the *pin*, then playing *mipil nglagu* on the resulting filled-in *balungan*. (The process of filling in the *balungan* is similar to that used by the *peking* in realising *balungan nibani* in Solonese style: compare with **Rules of *balungan nibani*** in Part 2, p. 31.) For example, in the half-*gåtrå* .2 the *pin* may be replaced with either 1 or 3, giving 12 or 32, and the corresponding *nglagu* patterns could be 123.1232 or 321.3212 respectively (*bonang barung*, *ir II*).

The two halves of the *gåtrå* may be considered separately. In the first half the *bonang* may use one of these *nglagu* patterns; alternatively it may play the second note of the *gåtrå* as a *gembyangan*, even if there is no other reason to do so. The second half of the *gåtrå* uses a *nglagu* pattern. Some possible alternative interpretations of the *gåtrå* .2.1 on the *bonang barung* in *ir II*:

321.32126̣12.6̣121

123.2232216̣.216̣1

Gangsaran

For most instruments, *gangsaran* involves only one note. The *bonang barung* enjoys a range of *garap*, which is used in both *sléndro* and *pélog*:

balungan

2 2̂ 2̆ 2̂ 2̆ 2̂ 2̆ (2̂)

bonang barung (alternatives)

. 2/2̣ . 2/2̣ . 2/2̣ . 2/2̣

. 6̣/2̣ . 6̣/2̣ . 6̣/2̣ . 6̣/2̣

. 6̣/2̣ 5̣/3̣ 6̣/2̣ 5̣/3̣ 6̣/2̣ 5̣/3̣ 6̣/2̣

. . . 6̣/2̣ . 3̣ 5̣ 6̣/2̣ . 3̣ 5̣ 6̣/2̣ . 3̣ 5̣ 6̣/2̣

of which the last two are perhaps heard most often. The following variants (from the *kraton Yogya*) are examples of *salahan* to signal the *gong ageng* and thus the end of a multi-*gongan* cycle.

. . . 6̣/2̣ . 3̣ 5̣ 6̣/2̣ . 3̣ 5̣ . 6̣/2̣ 3̣ 5̣ 6̣/2̣

. . . 6̣/2̣ . 3̣ 5̣ 6̣/2̣ . 3̣ 5̣ . 5̣ 3̣ 5̣ 6̣/2̣

The *garap* above corresponds more or less to the part played by the *gambyong* in *gangsaran* as heard on the *gamelan cåråbalèn*.

The *bonang panerus* plays either some form of ostinato on the middle 2, alternating the two hands because of the speed, or *gembyangan cegat*.

bonang panerus (alternatives)

22222222222222222222222222222222

2 2 2 2 2 2 2 2 2 2 2 2 2 2 2 2

. 2 2 . 2 . 2 2 2 . 2 2 2 . 2 2

2/2̣ . 2/2̣ . 2/2̣ . 2/2̣ .

of which the second is a form of *nitir*, and the third is called *rijalan*. None of these variants corresponds to a part played by an instrument in the *gamelan cåråbalèn*, although some are similar to the part played by the *rijal* in the *gamelan kodhok ngorèk*.

As an alternative to all the above, the two *bonang* may play an interlocking pattern borrowed from the parts played by the *klénang* and *kenut* for various pieces for the *gamelan cåråbalèn*: see ***Klénangan***, p. 181, where details of appropriate *salahan* are also given.

123.3212216̣.216̣1

2 2
2̣2̣2̣.2̣2̣..212.1121

2 2
2̣2̣2̣.2̣2̣..216̣5̣6̣121

2 2
2̣2̣2̣.2̣2̣..6̣12.6̣121

321.3212216̣5̣6̣121

6̣123321221 2 5̣6̣121

The last of these is the most extreme in style, using four different notes in each half of the *gåtrå*.

In *ir III* the spaces in the *balungan nibani* last twice as long as in *ir II*. If the *bonang* player uses *mipil* at such points, keeping the density of the *nglagu* patterns unchanged, they must contain twice as many notes: this is a sort of super-*nglagu*, which may incorporate *nguthik*-style patterns. Basically, the player must treat the second and fourth beats of the *gåtrå* as *sèlèh* notes and find suitable long patterns to end on them. The first half of the *gåtrå* may again be played as *gembyangan*. Either half-*gåtrå* may use a pattern of the *nguthik* type (see below). Examples of alternative treatments for the same *gåtrå* as above:

2 2 2 2
2̣2̣2̣.2̣2̣..2̣2̣2̣.2̣2̣.. 216̣.5̣5̣3̣5̣6̣12.6̣121

or

2 2 2 2
2̣2̣2̣.2̣2̣..2̣2̣2̣.2̣2̣.. 535.535.216̣5̣6̣121

or

235.5323321 6̣1232 216̣.5̣5̣3̣5̣6̣12.1121

and for the *gåtrå* .6̣.5̣:

5̣15̣6̣1232 16̣5̣15̣6̣16̣ 212.21216̣5̣3̣.5̣5̣5̣3̣5̣

or

212.11215̣6̣1.6̣6̣6̣16̣ etc.

and for .6.5:

5 5 5 5
5̣5̣5̣.5̣5̣..561̇.661̇6 212.21216̣5̣5̣.5̣5̣..

or

6 6
6̣6̣6̣.6̣6̣..561̇.661̇6 653.5535353.55535

To summarise these different approaches to *mipil nibani* patterns:

- the Solonese patterns tend to take two notes and rock between them,
- the Yogyanese patterns use more different notes, and the motion within the pattern resembles the normal stepwise movement of a *balungan*—this can be seen as an extended form of *mipil nglagu*,
- this difference parallels the difference between *mipil baku* and *mipil nglagu*, i.e. the respective Solonese and Yogyanese treatments for *balungan mlaku*.

Cadential patterns

In Solonese style, one of the regular exceptions to the use of normal *mipil* occurs with the standard cadential phrase in certain *pathet*. In *sléndro manyurå* and sometimes *pélog nem*, the phrase notated in the *balungan* is . 1 2 6̣, 2 1 2 6̣, . 2 . 6̣, . 1 . 6̣ or 3 2 1 6̣. The pattern actually used when this phrase occurs (in certain contexts: see below) is described as a 'low 6' pattern, and is taken from the *mipil nibani* repertoire (Table 3.10)—specifically, from those listed for the *gåtrå* . 1 . 6̣, . 2 . 6̣ or . 5̣ . 6̣. On the *bonang barung* it may be, in *ir I* or *ir II* respectively

2 1 5̣ . 6̣ 6̣ 1 6̣ or 2 1 . 5̣ 5̣ 1 . . 5̣ 1 5̣ . 6̣ 6̣ 1 6̣

(for example) or, on the *bonang panerus*, respectively

2 1 5̣ . 5̣ 1 5̣ . 5̣ 1 5̣ . 6̣ 6̣ 1 6̣

or

2 1 5̣ . 5̣ 1 5̣ . 5̣ 1 5̣ . 5̣ 1 5̣ . 5̣ 1 5̣ . 5̣ 1 5̣ . 5̣ 1 5̣ . 6̣ 6̣ 1 6̣

or any of the related patterns for the same *gåtrå* listed in thc collection.

Patterns beginning with 2 can be regarded as inaccurate representations of the *gåtrå* 3 2 1 6̣. Some players will therefore use standard *mipil* for the 3 2, and then a *mipil nibani* pattern for the second half of the *gåtrå*: e.g. 3 2 3 . . 2 3 . 2 1 5̣ . 6̣ 6̣ 1 6̣ (*bonang barung, ir II*). Another possibility, using *nibani* patterns in both halves:

3 1 3 . 2 1 . 2 5̣ 1 5̣ 1 . 6̣ 1 . 6̣

In *pélog barang*, the equivalent *gåtrå* appears as 2 7̣ 5̣ 6̣, . 2 . 6̣, . 7̣ . 6̣ or . 7̣ 5̣ 6̣, and the patterns given above can be played with 7̣ replacing 1.

For *sléndro sångå* and often *pélog limå / nem*, the corresponding phrase is notated as . 6̣ . 5̣, . 1 6̣ 5̣, 1 6̣ 3̣ 5̣ or 2 1 6̣ 5̣. Suitable *mipil nibani* patterns are described as 'low 5' patterns. They include, for *bonang barung*, in *ir I* or *ir II* respectively

6̣ 3̣ 6̣ . 5̣ 5̣ 3̣ 5̣ or . 6̣ . 3̣ 3̣ 6̣ . . 6̣ 3̣ 6̣ . 5̣ 5̣ 3̣ 5̣

or, on *bonang panerus*, respectively

6̣ 3̣ 6̣ . 6̣ 3̣ 6̣ . 6̣ 3̣ 6̣ . 5̣ 5̣ 3̣ 5̣

or

6̣ 3̣ 6̣ . 6̣ 3̣ 6̣ . 6̣ 3̣ 6̣ . 6̣ 3̣ 6̣ . 6̣ 3̣ 6̣ . 6̣ 3̣ 6̣ . 6̣ 3̣ 6̣ . 5̣ 5̣ 3̣ 5̣

as well as related patterns starting with 1 or 2.

In *pélog limå* or *nem*, the cadential phrase can be 1 6 4̣ 5̣, and the note 4 will then replace 3 in one of the standard patterns, e.g.

1 6̣ . 4̣ 4̣ 6̣ . . 4̣ 6̣ 4̣ . 5̣ 5̣ 6̣ 5̣ or with final 4̣ 5̣

Sometimes a low 6 or low 5 pattern is only needed for the second half of the *gåtrå*. In this case, the patterns are simplified. In *ir II*, a pattern indicated above for *ir I* will be used, or a related pattern such as . 6̣ 3̣ 6̣ . . 5̣ 6̣ 5̣. In *ir I*, patterns such as 6̣ 6̣ 1 6̣ or 5̣ 6̣ 1 6̣ are used for low 6, or 6̣ 5̣ 3̣ 5̣ for low 5.

Patterns as shown are standard Solonese *garap* when the cadential phrase occurs at the end of a *gongan*. When the phrase occurs elsewhere in a piece, many players will use the *mipil nibani* pattern: the more important its position, in structural terms, the more likely that a *mipil nibani* pattern will be used. Many players will also use such a *mipil nibani* pattern when the same phrase occurs in another *pathet*, e.g. the phrase 2 1 2 6̣ in *sléndro sångå*, even though it is not a cadential phrase in that *pathet*.

The *mipil nibani* patterns as a group are not characteristic Yogyanese *garap*. When playing in the most characteristic Yogya style, Yogyanese players therefore do not normally use them to realise the cadential phrases, although they do have their own methods. Phrases such as 2 1 2 6̣ are covered by the rule mentioned earlier that 6̣ should not be approached from the 2 above it. The whole cadential *gåtrå* 2 1 2 6̣ or its alternatives can be played on the *bonang barung* as (for example)

2 1 2 . 5̣ 6̣ 1 6̣ (*ir I*) or

2 1 2 . 1 1 2 1 5̣ 6̣ 1 . 5̣ 6̣ 1 6̣ (*ir II*)

and corresponding patterns on the *bonang panerus*.

There are no special *mipil nibani* patterns for the cadential phrase in *sléndro nem* (6 5 3 2). If the phrase is set in the low octave, *kempyungan* will typically be played for the 3̣ 2̣ in either Solonese or Yogyanese style.

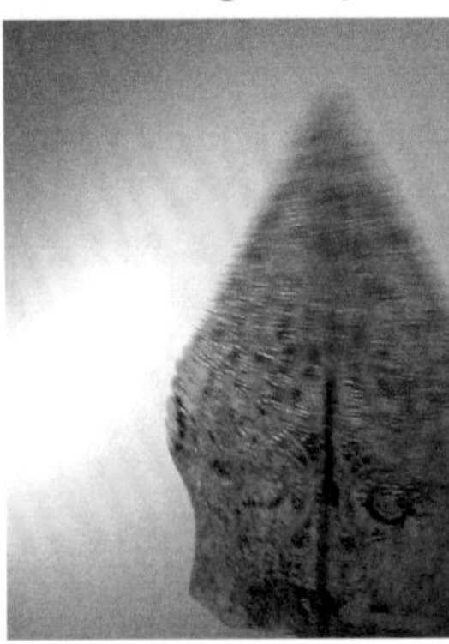

Yogyanese styles: *nguthik*

Nguthik is a specific Yogyanese *garap* for the *céngkok* called *puthut gelut*, and an element of the *nglagu* patterns used for *balungan nibani* (p. 153). Its basic shape is a jump from the lower to the upper octave, achieved via a *gembyangan*, followed by *mipil nglagu*.

Puthut gelut takes many forms, depending on *irâmâ* and *pathet*. In *sléndro manyurâ* it can be notated in the *balungan* as, for example:

balungan, ir I	3	3	.	.	6	5	3	2
balungan, ir I	3	5	6	5	3	2	3	2
balungan, ir I	.	3	.	5	.	3	.	2
balungan, ir II		3		5		3		2
balungan, ir II		6		5		3		2
balungan, ir II		.		3		.		2

The patterns below therefore cover two *gâtrâ* in *ir I* or one *gâtrâ* in *ir II*:

bonang barung (alternatives)

3 6 3 5 6 5 3 2 1 6̣ 1 2 3 2
3̣ 3̣ 3̣

3 6 3 5 6 5 3 2 3 1 2 6̣ 1 2
3̣ 3̣ 3̣

3 6 3 5 6 5 3 2 1 . 3 2 1 2
3̣ 3̣ 3̣

In *sléndro sângâ* the whole pattern is transposed down one note, e.g. for 2 3 2 1 in *ir I* (alternatives)

2 5 2 3 5 3 2 1 6̣ 5̣ 6̣ 1 2 1
2̣ 2̣ 2̣

2 5 2 3 5 3 2 1 6̣ 5̣ 1 5̣ 6̣ 1
2̣ 2̣ 2̣

2 3 5 3 5 3 2 1 6̣ 5̣ 2 5̣ 6̣ 1
2̣ 2̣ 2̣

In the *bonang panerus* version, most of the pattern is in *nglagu* form, e.g. (alternatives, *sléndro manyurâ* version)

3 6 3 5 6 . 3 5 6 . 3 5 6 5 3 2 1 1 6̣ 6̣ 5̣ 6̣ 1 2 3 . 1 2 3 2
3̣ 3̣ 3̣

3 6 3 5 6 . 3 5 6 . 3 5 6 5 3 2 1 1 6̣ 6̣ 5̣ 6̣ 1 2 3 . 3 2 3 2
3̣ 3̣ 3̣

3 6 3 5 6 . 3 5 6 . 3 5 6 5 3 2 1 . 3 2 1 6̣ 1 2 3 . 2 6̣ 1 2
3̣ 3̣ 3̣

As would be expected, the *sléndro manyurâ* version applies also to *sléndro nem* (generally), to *pélog nem* with gong 6 and, with 7̣ replacing 1, to *pélog barang*; the *sléndro sângâ* version also applies to *pélog limâ* and *pélog nem* with gong 5.

These special patterns for *puthut gelut* are more likely to be used when the *céngkok* occurs at a structurally important point, e.g. leading up to a *kenong* or a gong. The alternative *garap* is normal Yogya-style *gembyangan* and *mipil* as suggested by the *balungan* line.

Yogyanese styles: *ngrambat*

The word *ngrambat* describes a vine climbing up a pole; a good description of the contour of this Yogyanese *garap*. It is applied to a *gâtrâ* ending with note 5, or possibly lower, in order to smooth the transition up to 1̇ (or 7 in *pélog barang*) at the start of the next *gâtrâ*. Its name relates to the *céngkok* called *rambatan* on the *gendèr*. The first half of the *gâtrâ* is typically played with *gembyangan* 5 (see below), and the last four notes are 2 3 5 6. Examples in *ir I* and *ir II*, the second using *gembyangan sarug*:

balungan 5 6 5 3 1̇ 6 5 6

ir I 5 . 2 3 5 6 1̇ 6 1̇ . 5 6 1̇ 6
5̣ 5̣ 5̣

ir II
5 5 . . 5 3 5 . 2 3 5 6 1̇ 6 1̇ . 5 6 1̇ 6 5 6 5 . 6 6 6 5 6
5̣ 5̣ 5̣ . 5̣ 5̣

or

5 5 5 . 2 3 5 6 etc.
5̣ 5̣ 5̣ . 5̣ 5̣ . . 5̣ 5̣ 5̣

The same treatments would be given to the *gâtrâ* 5 2 3 5, which is one that the Yogyanese would typically play with *gembyangan* if the next *gâtrâ* did not begin with 1̇. (The *gâtrâ* 5 6 5 3 would not normally be played with *gembyangan*.)

The term *ngrambat* too suffers a certain amount of confusion. In form it is a transitive verb. Some sources use the intransitive verb *mrambat* for this *garap*, and apply *ngrambat* to something else.

Gembyang(an): 2

This heading covers *gembyangan* and certain closely related techniques used in a *mipil* context, i.e. generally for *ir I* and *ir II* and sometimes in *ir III*, and occasionally elsewhere. The *gembyangan* depends only on the *sèlèh* note, and the contour of the *gåtrå* is irrelevant.

These techniques represent a relatively simple approach to the realisation of *gantungan*, compared with the other decorating instruments. The same patterns are applied, in shorter versions, to half-*gåtrå* of *balungan kembar* and sometimes *balungan pin mundur* forms, as well as to *gåtrå dhélik*.

Gembyangan patterns on the *bonang* do not simply describe the shape of the inner melody, but serve a specific purpose of signalling a change of register; most often from low to high, although the opposite change is sometimes signalled in the same way. Usually a whole *gåtrå* is played with *gembyangan* in order to indicate that the next *gåtrå* is in a high register. In a *gåtrå dhélik*—literally a 'low–high' *gåtrå*—the low-to-high transition occurs within the *gåtrå*. A *gåtrå dhélik* is not always notated in the same way: for example, in *ldr Pangkur sl 9*, the second *gåtrå* in the *ir I/II* version may be written as 2165 or 216̣5̣, but in either case the second half is played with *gembyangan* because the next *gåtrå* is high.

Table 3.11
Some contexts for *gembyangan* on *bonang*

Balungan	*Gembyang* note	Duration of *gembyangan*
*xyz*5	5	whole of second *gåtrå*
*xyz*5 . . 5 .	5	whole of second *gåtrå*
2 2 . .	2	whole *gåtrå*
6 3 5 6	6	whole *gåtrå*
. 3 . 6	3 then 6	both halves of *gåtrå*
3 3 5 3	3	whole *gåtrå*, or first half only
3 3 5 6	3	first half of *gåtrå*
3̇ 2̇ 1̇ 2̇	2	whole *gåtrå*
. 3 3 .	3	whole *gåtrå*
. 5 6 .	6	second half of *gåtrå*
. 3 5 2	3	first half of *gåtrå* (Yogyanese style)
2 1 6 5	5	second half of *gåtrå*, or whole *gåtrå*
2 1 6̣ 5̣	5	second half of *gåtrå*, or whole *gåtrå*
2 3 2 .	2	second half of *gåtrå*
*xyz*6 . . 5 1̇	6	first half of second *gåtrå*

Long or short versions of the *gembyangan* patterns may also be applied to whole *gåtrå* or half-*gåtrå* that lies too high to allow normal *mipil* patterns, e.g. 2̇ 3̇ 2̇ 1̇, but sometimes the high notes are transposed down an octave and played with *mipil*.

In addition, the *bonang* play *gembyangan* patterns as *ngelik* transition signals. When the *gendèr* or *rebab* is the melodic leader, both *bonang* still play these signals—typically for a whole *gåtrå*, although they do not always start at the beginning of the *gåtrå*. Thus a *gembyangan* 6 is a normal *ngelik* signal for any of these *gåtrå*:

3 2 1 ⑥   2 1 2 ⑥   1 2 1 ⑥
3 3 5 ⑥   . 1 . ⑥   . 1 2 ⑥

Table 3.11 shows examples of possible positions for these categories of *gembyangan*, and Table 3.12 summarises the notes used in *gembyangan* patterns.

While the word *gembyang(an)* refers to octaves, this heading conveniently covers also several styles of *garap* that are not in octaves. The numerous variants are now described. Unfortunately, the usage of the terminology is particularly inconsistent.

Gembyangan låmbå, dados and *rangkep*

These are the most basic form of *gembyangan*, used in both Solonese and Yogyanese styles. They can be described as the default *garap* for the Yogyanese. In Solonese style they are also correct, but players tend to prefer one of the *nduduk* variants described under the next headings.

Taking the half-*gåtrå* 3 3 as an example, the following variants are generally known as *gembyangan låmbå*:

bonang barung (ir I) $\underset{\cdot}{3}\ \underset{\cdot}{3}\ \frac{3}{\underset{\cdot}{3}}\ .$

bonang panerus (ir I) $\underset{\cdot}{3}\,\frac{3}{\underset{\cdot}{3}}\,.\,\frac{3}{\underset{\cdot}{3}}\,.\,.$

If the *gembyangan* lasts for the whole *gåtrå*, e.g. for 3 3 . . in the *balungan*, basically the patterns above are repeated. The pattern for the *bonang barung* is not repeated exactly, but instead follows the principles of the *bonang panerus* pattern above, i.e. (*ir I*, alternatives)

$\underset{\cdot}{3}\ \underset{\cdot}{3}\ \frac{3}{\underset{\cdot}{3}}\ .\qquad \underset{\cdot}{3}\ \frac{3}{\underset{\cdot}{3}}\ .\ .$

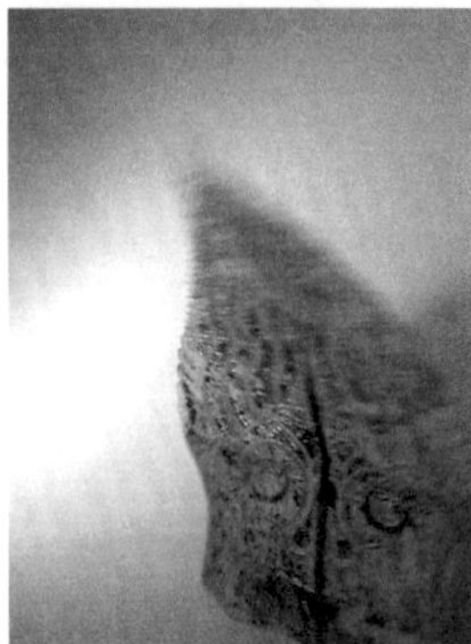

    3   3
3̣ 3̣ 3̣ .   . 3̣ . .

The patterns for *ir II* are variously known as *gembyangan dados* or *gembyangan rangkep.* Their length is exactly double that of the *ir I* patterns, and they can be guessed from the patterns just given. Taking the same example of half-*gåtrå* 3 3 in the *balungan*

bonang barung (ir II)

    3   3
3̣ 3̣ 3̣ . 3̣ 3̣ . .

bonang panerus (ir II)

  3 3   3 3
3̣3̣3̣ . 3̣3̣ . . 3̣3̣3̣ . 3̣3̣ . .

and the patterns can be repeated exactly to fill out a whole *gåtrå.*

For *gåtrå dhélik*, the *gembyangan* patterns may only be used in the second half of the *gåtrå*, the first half being realised with *mipil*, possibly of the *lumpatan* type. For example, the *gåtrå* 2 1 6̣ 5̣ would otherwise be played with *mipil lumpatan* because it is a low 5 pattern. When this *gåtrå* is functioning as a *gåtrå dhélik*, it may be played

ir I

      5
2 1 6̣ . 5̣ 5̣ 5̣ .

ir II

             5   5
2 1 . 6̣ 6̣ 1 . . 6̣ 1 5̣ 5̣ 5̣ . 5̣ 5̣

or

ir II

           5   5   5
2 1 . 6̣ 6̣ 1 . . 5̣ . . 5̣ . . 5̣ .

although straight *mipil* in the first half is equally 'correct'.

Besides the possible positions for *gembyangan* already given, long sequences of off-beat *balungan* notes may be realised in this way. In the following extract from the *lik* of *ldr Pakumpulan sl 9* (played in *ir II*)

                          1̂
. 6 . 5 . 6 . 5   . 6 . 5 6 (1)

each *pin* is, as usual, treated as a continuation of the preceding note, and a *gembyangan* is played on that note. The last 56 is given *mipil* treatment, followed by another *gembyangan* on 1 to the gong:

    1   6   5   6
1̣ 1̣ 1̣ . 6̣ 6̣ 6̣ . 5̣ 5̣ 5̣ . 6̣ 6̣ 6̣ .

    5   6   1̇
5̣ 5̣ 5̣ . 6̣ 6̣ 6̣ . 5 6 5 . 1 1 1 .

In Solonese style, this type of *gembyangan* is properly confined to notes in the middle or upper octaves of the *balungan*, and single-note (*tunggal*) alternatives replace *gembyangan* patterns when the *sèlèh* note is in the lower octave. For the notes 1̣, 2̣ and often 3̣ and 4̣, other *garap* is usual (see **Kempyung(an) and gembyung(an)**, p. 166), so the *tunggal* patterns mainly apply to notes 5̣, 6̣ and 7̣, e.g.

7̣ 7̣ 7̣ . 7̣ 7̣ . .

or the first half of this pattern, or this pattern twice, as necessary. The example is for the *bonang barung*, and must be played twice on the *bonang panerus.*

Otherwise these types of *gembyangan* can be applied to any note in the range of the *balungan*. For *balungan* note 1, the *gembyangan* should use notes 1̣ and 1, because the use of notes 1 and 1̇ would indicate a *balungan* note 1̇. In *pélog* or on a *bonang cacad* in *sléndro* this option is not available. Logically a *gantungan* on 1 should be played with *tunggal* 1 on a *bonang cacad*. Table 3.12 summarises.

In Yogyanese style, *gembyangan* patterns are used regardless of the register of the *sèlèh* note. The following

Table 3.12
Notes used in Solo-style '*gembyangan*' vs sèlèh note

Sèlèh note	*Sléndro*		*Pélog*
	regular form	*cacad* form	
2̇	2 + 2̇	2	2
1̇	1 + 1̇	1 + 1̇	1, or 1̣ + 1
7	—	—	7̣ + 7
6	6̣ + 6	6̣ + 6	6̣ + 6
5	5̣ + 5	5̣ + 5	5̣ + 5
4	—	—	4̣ + 4
3	3̣ + 3	3̣ + 3	3̣ + 3
2	2̣ + 2	2̣ + 2	2̣ + 2
1	1̣ + 1, 1 + 1̇	1, 1 + 1̇	1̣ + 1
7̣	—	—	7̣
6̣	6̣, or 6̣ + 6	6̣, or 6̣ + 6	6̣, or 6̣ + 6
5̣	5̣	5̣	5̣
4̣	—	—	4̣
3̣	—[a]	—[a]	—[a]
2̣	—[a]	—[a]	—[a]
1̣	—	—	—[a]

a. *Kempyungan* or *gembyungan* normally used.

pattern is usable on both *bonang barung* and *bonang panerus*, at the appropriate density, repeated as often as necessary:

    3   3
3̣ 3̣ 3̣ . 3̣ 3̣ . .

Bonang barung players may also apply the characteristic Yogyanese rhythmic variations as described for *mipil*, such as the fractional advancing of the first or fifth notes of an eight-note pattern. Whereas fractional delays (of about half a beat) can be applied to the third note of the eight-note group in *mipil*, here delays of the same amount may be applied to the *gembyang* proper, i.e. to the two notes played an octave apart, e.g.

     3   3
3̣ 3̣ . 3̣ . 3̣ . 3̣ . .

The previous remarks about listening to actual performances apply again.

The *bonang panerus* in the Yogya style may also use patterns incorporating *gembyangan cegat* rhythms, e.g.

  3 3 3
3̣ 3̣ 3̣ . 3̣ . 3̣ .

which may be played once, twice or more according to the *irâmâ* and how much of the *gâtrâ* is to be covered. Patterns with the *gembyangan cegat* rhythm throughout are also usable on the *bonang panerus* (*ir I*), e.g.

balungan	5 3 2 .
bonang panerus	535 . 53532 . 2 . 2 . 2 . (with 2̣ under each of the last four 2s)

or continued throughout a whole *gâtrâ*.

When a *gembyangan* is played for the note 6 and the pattern is approached from the note 1 or higher, there is a standard variant of the *gembyangan* pattern that incorporates a lead-in to give a smoother contour. The variant covers (as a minimum) eight beats, so it can be used for a whole *gâtrâ* in *ir I* on the *bonang barung*, or for a half-*gâtrâ* on the *bonang panerus* and/or in *ir II*. The 8-beat pattern is, for example,

        6   6
2 1 6̣ 6̣ 6̣ . 6̣ 6̣

and is played by both *bonang* at their respective densities, by both Solonese and Yogyanese players. Such treatments can be given to either 6̣ or 6 in the *balungan*. As an example of the latter, the phrase 6532 . 356 can be realised on the *bonang barung* in *ir I* with the 8-beat pattern above covering the second *gâtrâ*, i.e.

                    6   6
6 5 6 . 3 2 3 . 2 1 6̣ 6̣ 6̣ . 6̣ 6̣

In *ir II* the . 3 could be played with *mipil* for 2 3 and the 8-beat pattern above for the 5 6, i.e.

                        6   6
2 3 2 . . 3 2 . 2 1 6̣ 6̣ 6̣ . 6̣ 6̣

Tips & tricks 7
Recovery after the gong in a *gendhing*

In the *mérong* of a *gendhing* played in *ir II*, it is easy to go wrong at the return to normal speed after the delayed gong stroke. Javanese players will manage to delay the final note of the *gongan* by just the right amount, so that it falls very close to the gong stroke. *Londo* players will probably only play the final note after hearing the gong. The *kendhangan* can only resume after this final note has been heard.

The usual *kendhangan* creates two key reference points during the *gâtrâ* that follows the gong. The four *kendhang* strokes after the gong (three *tong* strokes and one *ket*: see p. 218 foll.) represent an immediate return to normal speed. As they are also an exception to the usual fill-in pattern, it is easy to identify them. The last of them coincides with the first *balungan* note, and therefore most players can use it to orient themselves. A further cross-check is available at the last note of the *gâtrâ*, where the *kendhangan* often has a *dha* stroke.

kendhangan	∘∘k∘	kkk∘	kkk∘	kkkb
balungan notes	.	.	.	.
bonang barung:				
for *balungan mlaku*	212.	.12.	232.	.32.
for *balungan nibani*	6̣123	31..	313.	2212
for *pin mundur*	.76̣.	.76̣.	.76̣.	.76̣.
for *gantungan* (1)	5̣5̣5̣. (5 above third)	5̣5̣.. (5 above second)	5̣5̣5̣. (5 above third)	5̣5̣.. (5 above second)
for *gantungan* (2)	5̣..5̣ (5 above each)	..5̣. (5 above)	.5̣.. (5 above)	5̣..5̣ (5 above each)
peking	6221	1221	1223	3223

The *bonang panerus* player plays two notes to every *kendhang* stroke (and should re-enter before the first stroke shown above) but can still use the same reference points.

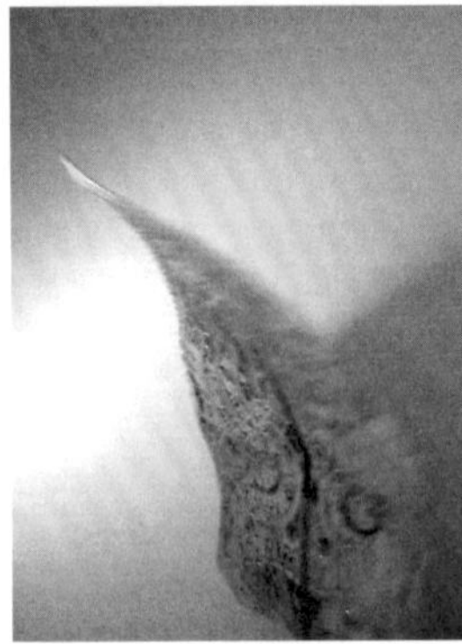

or a *gembyangan* might be played for the whole of the second *gåtrå*.

Longer versions of this pattern are more often based on patterns of three beats as used for *nduduk gembyang* (see under the next heading). Yogyanese players use the lead-in but follow it with 'straighter' *gembyangan* patterns, e.g.

$$2\ 1\ \underset{\cdot}{6}\ .\ \underset{\cdot}{6}\ \frac{6}{\underset{\cdot}{6}}\ .\ .\ \underset{\cdot}{6}\ \underset{\cdot}{6}\ \frac{6}{\underset{\cdot}{6}}\ .\ \underset{\cdot}{6}\ \frac{6}{\underset{\cdot}{6}}\ .\ .$$

Alongside the Solonese patterns for $\underset{\cdot}{6}$ or 6, the corresponding pattern for notes $\underset{\cdot}{5}$ or 5 is

$$\underset{\cdot}{6}\ 1\ \underset{\cdot}{5}\ \underset{\cdot}{5}\ \frac{5}{\underset{\cdot}{5}}\ .\ \underset{\cdot}{5}\ \frac{5}{\underset{\cdot}{5}}$$

(plus the same range of variants as given for note 6) but special patterns for other *sèlèh* notes are perhaps less often used. The following is available for *sèlèh* 3, using *nduduk*-style patterns

$$1\ 2\ \frac{3}{\underset{\cdot}{3}}\ .\ .\ \frac{3}{\underset{\cdot}{3}}\ .\ .\ \text{etc.}$$

or

$$\underset{\cdot}{6}\ 1\ 2\ \frac{3}{\underset{\cdot}{3}}\ .\ .\ \frac{3}{\underset{\cdot}{3}}\ .\ \text{etc.}$$

or

$$\underset{\cdot}{6}\ \underset{\cdot}{6}\ 1\ 2\ \frac{3}{\underset{\cdot}{3}}\ .\ .\ \frac{3}{\underset{\cdot}{3}}\ \text{etc.}$$

and similarly for *sèlèh* 2

$$\underset{\cdot}{6}\ 1\ \frac{2}{\underset{\cdot}{2}}\ .\ .\ \frac{2}{\underset{\cdot}{2}}\ .\ .\ \text{etc.}$$

and similarly for *sèlèh* 1

$$\underset{\cdot}{5}\ \underset{\cdot}{6}\ \frac{1}{\underset{\cdot}{1}}\ .\ .\ \frac{1}{\underset{\cdot}{1}}\ .\ .\ \text{etc.}$$

or

$$\underset{\cdot}{5}\ \underset{\cdot}{6}\ \frac{\dot{1}}{1}\ .\ .\ \frac{\dot{1}}{1}\ .\ .\ \text{etc.}$$

In Yogyanese style, the lead-in 2 1 can be added to a *gembyangan cegat* pattern for the *bonang panerus* to make a hybrid form of pattern, e.g.

$$2\,1\,\frac{6}{\underset{\cdot}{6}}\,.\,\frac{6}{\underset{\cdot}{6}}\,.\,\frac{6}{\underset{\cdot}{6}}\,.\qquad \underset{\cdot}{6}\,\underset{\cdot}{6}\,\frac{6}{\underset{\cdot}{6}}\,.\,\frac{6}{\underset{\cdot}{6}}\,.\,\frac{6}{\underset{\cdot}{6}}\,.$$

or only the first half of this pattern. The second half of the pattern can be played twice more to fill a *gåtrå* in *ir II*.

The Yogyanese and Solonese differ in the range of contexts where they will use *gembyangan*. The Yogyanese will treat a *gåtrå* with an initial *pin* in various ways: the principle given previously, of filling a *pin* with the previous note and playing *mipil* on the resulting pair of notes, is not always observed. One possibility is a quarter-*gåtrå* of *gembyangan* before the *mipil*, e.g. following *sèlèh* 5

balungan

$$.\qquad 6\qquad 3\qquad 5$$

bonang, ir II

$$.\ .\ \frac{5}{\underset{\cdot}{5}}\ .\ 5\ 6\ 5\ .\ 3\ 5\ 3\ .\ 3\ 5\ 3\ 5$$

and another is separate *gembyangan* for the two notes

$$.\ .\ \frac{5}{\underset{\cdot}{5}}\ .\ .\ \frac{6}{\underset{\cdot}{6}}\ .\ .\ 3\ 5\ 3\ .\ 3\ 5\ 3\ 5$$

and yet another is a half-*gåtrå* of *gembyangan*:

$$.\ .\ \frac{6}{\underset{\cdot}{6}}\ .\ .\ \frac{6}{\underset{\cdot}{6}}\ .\ .\ 3\ 5\ 3\ .\ 3\ 5\ 3\ 5$$

The *nduduk* rhythm of the *gembyangan* in the above examples is discussed under the next heading. (In the 'standard' treatment of this *gåtrå*, the *bonang* would play *mipil* on notes 5 6.)

More generally, Yogyanese treatments include the possibility of separate *gembyangan* to each note of a *balungan*. A *gåtrå* of the *xyzx* form, to which the Yogyanese will typically give a *gembyangan* treatment, may have a mixture of *gembyangan* to different notes, e.g. to 6 3 5 6

$$\underset{\cdot}{6}\ \underset{\cdot}{6}\ \frac{6}{\underset{\cdot}{6}}\ .\ \underset{\cdot}{3}\ \underset{\cdot}{3}\ \frac{3}{\underset{\cdot}{3}}\ .\ \underset{\cdot}{5}\ \underset{\cdot}{6}\ \frac{6}{\underset{\cdot}{6}}\ .\ \underset{\cdot}{6}\ \frac{6}{\underset{\cdot}{6}}\ .\ .$$

(using a *gembyangan sarug*: see below) or

$$\underset{\cdot}{6}\ \underset{\cdot}{6}\ \frac{6}{\underset{\cdot}{6}}\ .\ \underset{\cdot}{3}\ \underset{\cdot}{3}\ \frac{3}{\underset{\cdot}{3}}\ .\ 2\ 1\ \underset{\cdot}{6}\ \underset{\cdot}{6}\ \frac{6}{\underset{\cdot}{6}}\ .\ \underset{\cdot}{6}\ \frac{6}{\underset{\cdot}{6}}$$

As so often, it is not possible to set limits on when each treatment might be chosen.

Nduduk gembyang

As an alternative to the forms of *gembyangan* just described, there is a pattern using *gembyangan* in groups of three beats. The *bonang panerus* plays at twice the speed of the *bonang barung*. These are **not** triplet patterns: the notes sit squarely on the normal beats for the instruments. Patterns of this type are characteristically

Solonese, and are considered more refined than the 'straighter' patterns under the previous heading. Some Yogyanese players use the *nduduk gembyang* patterns too.

Just to increase the confusion, some sources give the name *nduduk gembyang* to the *gembyangan lâmbâ/dados/rangkep* patterns.

The 4-beat form of *nduduk gembyang*, which covers a half-*gâtrâ* in *ir I* on the *bonang barung*, is (for example)

```
6     6
6̣ . . 6̣
```

or, depending on context,

```
    6               6
. . 6̣ .     or    . 6̣ . .
```

and the 8-beat version, for a full *gâtrâ* in *ir I* or a half-*gâtrâ* in *ir II*,

```
6     6     6
6̣ . . 6̣ . . 6̣ .
```

or

```
    6     6
6̣ 6̣ 6̣ . . 6̣ . .
```

and the 16-beat version, for a full *gâtrâ* in *ir II*,

```
6     6     6     6     6     6
6̣ . . 6̣ . . 6̣ . . 6̣ . . 6̣ . . 6̣
```

or

```
    6     6     6     6     6
6̣ 6̣ 6̣ . . 6̣ . . 6̣ . . 6̣ . . 6̣ .
```

These patterns can start with the lead-ins mentioned under the previous heading, e.g. (alternatives)

```
        6     6
2 1 6̣ 6̣ 6̣ . 6̣ 6̣

    6     6
2 1 6̣ . . 6̣ . .

        6     6     6     6
2 1 6̣ 6̣ 6̣ . 6̣ 6̣ . 6̣ 6̣ . 6̣ 6̣ . .

    6     6     6     6     6
2 1 6̣ . . 6̣ . . 6̣ . . 6̣ . . 6̣ .
```

and with a simpler lead-in

```
1 6 . . 6 . . 6
  6̣     6̣     6̣
```

As a general principle, the *bonang panerus* simply plays the same patterns but at twice the density, with the same range of options for lead-ins, e.g. for *ir I* (alternatives)

```
6  6  6  6  6  6
6̣..6̣..6̣..6̣..6̣..6̣

  6  6  6  6  6
6̣6̣6̣..6̣..6̣..6̣..6̣.

   6  6  6  6
216̣6̣..6̣..6̣..6̣..

  6  6  6  6  6
216̣..6̣..6̣..6̣..6̣.
```

and for *ir II* (alternatives)

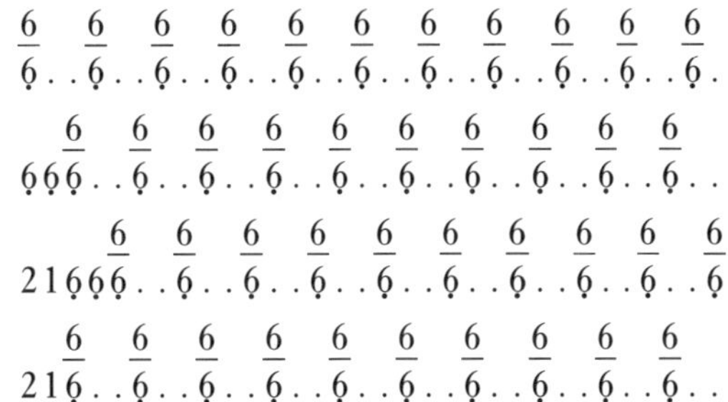

```
6  6  6  6  6  6  6  6  6  6  6
6̣..6̣..6̣..6̣..6̣..6̣..6̣..6̣..6̣..6̣..6̣.

  6  6  6  6  6  6  6  6  6  6
6̣6̣6̣..6̣..6̣..6̣..6̣..6̣..6̣..6̣..6̣..6̣..

   6  6  6  6  6  6  6  6  6  6
216̣6̣..6̣..6̣..6̣..6̣..6̣..6̣..6̣..6̣..6̣

  6  6  6  6  6  6  6  6  6  6
216̣..6̣..6̣..6̣..6̣..6̣..6̣..6̣..6̣..6̣..
```

as well as a denser pattern

```
 3  3  3  3  3  3  3  3  3  3  3
3̣3̣.3̣3̣.3̣3̣.3̣3̣.3̣3̣.3̣3̣.3̣3̣.3̣3̣.3̣3̣.3̣3̣.3̣3̣
```

or half these patterns for a half-*gâtrâ*.

When the *gâtrâ* needs different *gembyangan* in its two halves, the rhythm may continue unbroken, e.g.

```
3     3     3     6     6     6
3̣ . . 3̣ . . 3̣ . . 6̣ . . 6̣ . . 6̣
```

or its equivalent for the *bonang panerus*, or the two halves may be independent, e.g. for . 4 . 6 (alternatives):

```
    4     4                 6     6
4̣ 4̣ 4̣ . 4̣ 4̣ . . 2 1 6̣ 6̣ 6̣ . 6̣ 6̣

4     4     4               6     6
4̣ . . 4̣ . . 4̣ . 2 1 6̣ 6̣ 6̣ . 6̣ 6̣
```

The patterns shown above start at the beginning of the *gâtrâ*. *Nduduk* patterns without lead-ins need not start there, e.g. if the previous *gâtrâ* ends with the same note:

```
balungan        2 3 5 6      . . 6 5
bonang barung   232.5656     ..6.6565
                               6̣
```

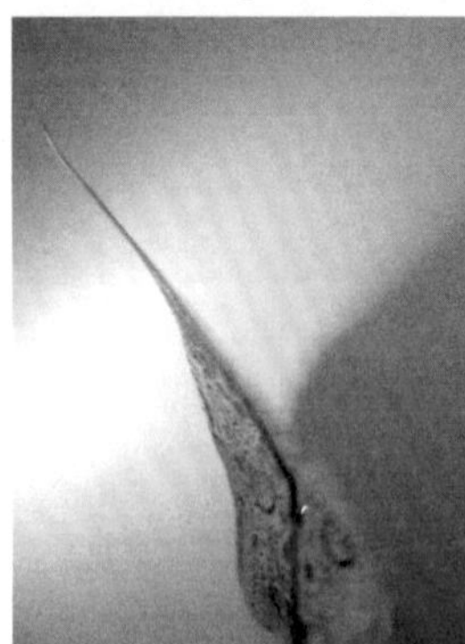

balungan 2 3 5 6 . . 6 6
bonang barung 232.5656 ..6..6..
6̣ 6̣

With nothing played on the *sèlèh* note of the first *gåtrå*, the pattern could be

bonang barung 232.565. 6..6..6.
6̣ 6̣ 6̣

See **Other special *garap***, p. 168, for related examples.

In the most advanced versions of the *nduduk* patterns, they are combined in the same *gåtrå* with *mipil*. In a particular piece, the *gåtrå* 2121 (for example) might be played with *gembyangan* throughout, or the *gembyangan* might be restricted to the last quarter, half or three-quarters of the *gåtrå*, for example on the *bonang barung*:

(last quarter only, *ir II)*

2 1 2 . . 2 1 . 2 1 2 . 1 . . 1
1̣ 1̣

(second half only, *ir I* then *ir II*)

2 1 2 . 1 . . 1
1̣ 1̣

2 1 2 . . 1 2 . 1 . . 1 . . 1 .
1̣ 1̣ 1̣

(last three-quarters only, *ir I* then *ir II*)

2 1 . . 1 . . 1
1̣ 1̣ 1̣

2 1 2 . 1 . . 1 . . 1 . . 1 . .
1̣ 1̣ 1̣ 1̣

A *gåtrå* might end with *gembyangan* as an early warning of a *gantungan* on the same note in the following *gåtrå*.

It is in fact quite common for a *gantungan* to continue across more than one *gåtrå*: in *gendhing*, many examples can be found of 2½ or even 3 *gåtrå* of *gantungan*. The question arises of how each *gåtrå* should begin on the *bonang*: should the pattern of three continue from the previous *gåtrå*, or should a new pattern be started? Perhaps it is not surprising that the former option is normal, since it results in a smoother overall pattern, and these patterns are used for their elegance. For example, for the two *gåtrå* 33. . 3356:

3 . . 3 . . 3 . . 3 . . 3 . . 3
3̣ 3̣ 3̣ 3̣ 3̣ 3̣

. . 3 . . 3 . . 5 6 5 . . 6 5 .
3̣ 3̣

More examples, in which the two half-*gåtrå* are different, for *ir II*

balungan 5 6 7 6
bonang
5 6 5 . . 6 5 . 7 6 7 . 6 . . 6
6̣ 6̣

and

balungan 1 2 1 6̣
bonang
1 2 1 . . 2 1 . 2 1 6 . . 6 . .
6̣ 6̣

and

balungan
5̣ 6̣ 1 2 . 2 3 5
bonang
5̣6̣5̣..6̣5̣.121.2..2 ..2..2..353..53.
2̣ 2̣ 2̣ 2̣

and for *ir I*:

balungan 1 2 3 2 . 2 1 6̣
bonang 121.2..2 ..2.16̣1.
2̣ 2̣ 2̣

When the *bonang barung* needs *nduduk gembyang* patterns during half-speed *mipil låmbå*, it will play patterns of the above types, but at half speed. For example, taking the *gåtrå* 33. . 3356 again:

. 3 . . . . . 3 . . . . . 3 . .
3̣ 3̣ 3̣

. . . 3 . . . . . 5 . 6 . 5 . 6
3̣

which can also be written

3 . . 3 . . 3 .
3̣ 3̣ 3̣

. 3 . . 5 6 5 6
3̣

Nduduk patterns may also be used in place of 'straight' *gembyangan* in passages of off-beat *balungan*, and an example is included under the next heading.

Nduduk tunggal

In Solonese style, the *nduduk gembyang* patterns are often replaced for notes in the lower octave (also sometimes 1) by *nduduk tunggal* (single *nduduk*), except when a change of register is being signalled.

For a full *gåtrå*, the *tunggal* patterns are, for example,

balungan 5̣ 5̣ . .

bonang barung (*ir I*)

5̣ . . 5̣ . . 5̣ .

bonang panerus (*ir I*)/*bonang barung* (*ir II*)

5̣ . . 5̣ . . 5̣ . . 5̣ . . 5̣ . . 5̣

bonang panerus (*ir II*)

5̣ . . 5̣ . . 5̣ . . 5̣ . . 5̣ . . 5̣ . . 5̣ . . 5̣ . . 5̣ . . 5̣ . . 5̣ .

and for a half-*gåtrå* the first half of the above patterns is used.

As regards all the variant patterns that may be needed, such as those continuing across *gåtrå* boundaries and during half-speed *mipil låmbå*, the earlier comments about *nduduk gembyang* patterns apply equally to *nduduk tunggal* patterns. For example, the two *gåtrå* 3̣3̣ . . 3̣3̣5̣6̣ may be played by the *bonang barung* in *ir II* as

3̣ . . 3̣ . . 3̣ . . 3̣ . . 3̣ . . 3̣
. . 3̣ . . 3̣ . . 5̣ 6̣ 5̣ . . 6̣ 5̣ .

and 3̣5̣3̣5̣ . . 5̣ . may be played in *mipil låmbå* as

3̣ 5̣ 3̣ . . 5̣ 3̣ .
5̣ . . 5̣ . . 5̣ .

or

3̣ 5̣ 3̣ . 3̣ 5̣ 3̣ 5̣
. . 5̣ . . 5̣ . .

In an awkward stretch of off-beat *balungan* from *gendhing bonang Babar layar pl 5*

$\overline{32}$ 3 $\overline{21}$ $\overline{.6̣}$ $\overline{.5̣}$ $\overline{.4̣}$ $\overline{.2̣}$ $\overline{.4̣}$ $\overline{.2̣}$ 4̣ 6̣ 5̣

a sequence of short *nduduk tunggal* patterns may be used for one realisation of the second and third *gåtrå*

6̣ . . 6̣ 5̣ . . 5̣ 4̣ . . 4̣ 2̣ . . 2̣
4̣ . . 4̣ 2̣ 4̣ 2̣ . 6̣ 5̣ 6̣ . . 5̣ 6̣ .

although there are other possibilities.

Balungan in the lower octave will be realised with *gembyangan* rather than *tunggal* patterns if a register shift must be signalled, as in *ktw Mijil wigaringtyas pl 6*:

```
balungan          5̣    5̣    .    6
bonang barung     5 . . 5 . . 5 .  6 5 . . 6 5 .
                  5̣     5̣     5̣
```

In Yogya style, patterns of this kind are unlikely, for two reasons: first, the Yogyanese prefer the 'straight' patterns; second, they tend to play *gembyangan* for *sèlèh* notes anywhere in the range of the *balungan*.

Gembyangan sarug

Gembyangan sarug (sometimes known as *gembyangan sekaran*) is a characteristic Yogyanese *garap*, in which a normal *gembyangan låmbå* or *dados* is preceded by an adjacent note or notes. Therefore it relates to the lead-ins described earlier (which the Solonese apparently do not name). However, *gembyangan sarug* can be made out of any notes, and are used very freely. They are especially frequent when the *gåtrå* leading up to a gong is realised with a *gembyangan*—as very often in Yogya style.

In both *ir I* and *ir II*, a single *gembyangan sarug* may cover the whole *gåtrå*, or the *gåtrå* may be divided between two *gembyangan sarug*. Thus the *gåtrå* 5 3 5 6 may be played as (*bonang barung*, *ir I*)

```
    3       6
5̣ 3̣ 3̣ . 5̣ 6̣ 6̣ .
```

or

```
    6   6
5̣ 6̣ 6̣ . 6̣ 6̣ . .
```

and corresponding patterns in *ir II*, such as

```
    3   3         6   6
5̣ 3̣ 3̣ . 3̣ 3̣ . . 5̣ 6̣ 6̣ . 6̣ 6̣ . .
```

Bonang barung players may apply the characteristic Yogyanese rhythmic variations as described earlier for *mipil* and for other *gembyangan* variants.

The notes chosen for the *sarug* may come straight from the *balungan*: the first note of the *sarug* is typically the first note of the *gåtrå*, and then other notes are inserted if necessary to lead to the *sèlèh* note. However, this rule is not absolute. If the *balungan* is *nibani*, notes for the *sarug* may be based on expanding the *balungan* in the usual way. Examples:

```
balungan          6     2     3     5
bonang barung                     5
(a)           2̣  3̣  5̣  .  5̣  5̣  .  .
```

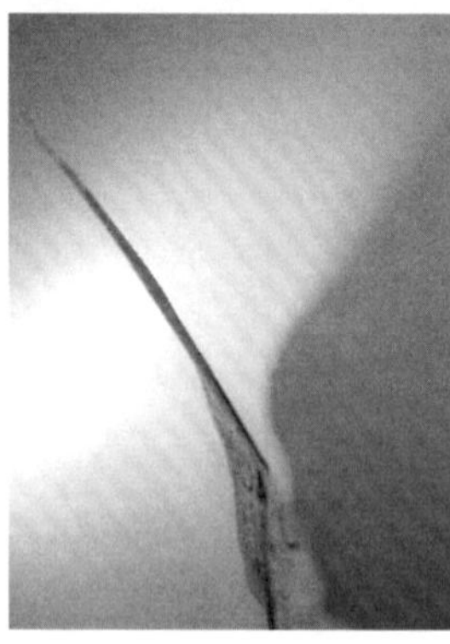

bonang barung
(b)
```
                5     5
2̣ 3̣ 5̣ 5̣ 5̣ . 5̣ 5̣
```

balungan . 3 . ②

bonang barung
(a)
```
            2
5̣ 3̣ 2̣ . 2̣ 2̣ . .
```

bonang barung
(b)
```
            2     2
5̣ 3̣ 2̣ 2̣ 2̣ . 2̣ 2̣
```

Compare a non-*sarug* version:

bonang barung
(c)
```
              2
5̣ 3̣ 5̣ 3̣ 2̣ 2̣ 2̣ .
```

balungan 2 7̣ 6 .

bonang barung (*ir II*)
```
                       6     6
2 7̣ 2 . 7̣ 7̣ 2 7̣ 5̣ 6̣ 6̣ . 6̣ 6̣ . .
```

The equivalent patterns for the *bonang panerus* have the *sarug* pattern only once, e.g. for *ir I*

```
 5  5      5  5
2̣3̣5̣.5̣5̣..5̣5̣5̣.5̣5̣..
```

or

```
 5 5 5     5 5 5
2̣3̣5̣.5̣.5̣.5̣5̣5̣.5̣.5̣.
```

The *sarug* may actually begin in the first half of the *gåtrå*, e.g. in *ir II*

```
             5  5     5  5     5  5
2̣3̣5̣.2̣3̣5̣.23̣5̣.5̣5̣..5̣5̣5̣.5̣5̣..5̣5̣5̣.5̣5̣..
```

or, for the *gåtrå* 5352 in *ir I*,

```
  2     2 2
5̣3̣2̣.2̣2̣..2̣2̣2̣.2̣2̣..
```

alongside a version in which the pattern starts with *mipil*:

```
      2   2 2
5̣3̣5̣3̣2̣2̣2̣.2̣2̣2̣.2̣2̣..
```

Kempyung(an) and *gembyung(an)*

For *sèlèh* notes at the bottom limit of the *pathet*, the regular *mipil* patterns are replaced by another standard form of *garap* in both Solo and Yogya styles.

Different players do not always agree as to which notes should be given this treatment. For *sléndro*, and for *pélog nem* (gong 6) and *barang*, there is no doubt that 2̣ is the lowest note, and many players will normally play *kempyung* for this note, i.e. a 6̣ in addition to the 2̣. Some players will also play either *kempyung* or *gembyung* for 3̣, i.e. respectively a 1 or a 6̣ in addition to the 3̣. (The combination of 1 with 3̣ is characteristic of *sléndro manyurå*, and 7 with 3 corresponds in *pélog barang*.) For *pélog limå* the lowest note in the *pathet* is 1̣, and players may play *kempyung* or *gembyung* for 2̣ as well as 1̣. The corresponding half-*gåtrå* of *balungan nibani* (. 1̣, . 2̣ and . 3̣) receive the same treatments.

Many players will use *kempyung/gembyung* only when the *sèlèh* note is approached from above. This would mean that in the *gåtrå* 2̣3̣5̣3̣ or 5̣3̣2̣3̣ the 2̣3̣ was played with standard *mipil*. In other cases, a *gembyung* may be played for 3̣ but no *kempyung* for 2̣. One reason for not using a *kempyung/gembyung* pattern is that the low note (1̣, 2̣ or 3̣) obviously does not end the phrase. For example, in the cross-rhythms of this *balungan* fragment

5̣3̣2̣5̣ 3̣2̣5̣3̣ 2̣5̣2̣3̣ 5̣6̣5̣3̣

mipil is more likely for the 5̣3̣ at the end of the second *gåtrå*, which is clearly in the middle of a phrase.

Basically the words *kempyung* and *gembyung* describe the sizes of intervals. The usage of the words in the context of *bonangan* as just given is compatible with the general usage. Unfortunately there are some sources that use the terms differently: *kempyung* is used to refer to the combination of 6̣ with either 3̣ or 2̣, and *gembyung* for other combinations, some of which are more often found as part of *sekaran* in the context of *imbal*:

```
2   2   1
6̣   5̣   5̣
```

The following example shows standard treatment of *sèlèh* notes 3̣ and 2̣ in *ir I*.

balungan 5̣ 3̣ 5̣ 2̣

bonang barung
```
6̣ . 6̣ . 6̣ . 6̣ .
3̣   3̣   2̣   2̣
```

bonang panerus 6̣3̣6̣.6̣3̣6̣.6̣2̣6̣.6̣2̣6̣.

Thus the *bonang barung* plays the *kempyung* or *gembyung* in *gembyangan cegat* rhythm, while the *bonang panerus* usually plays standard *mipil* with the same two notes. Another variant for *sèlèh* 3̣ on the *bonang barung* is

```
5̣ 1 1 .     or     6̣ 1 1 .
    3̣                  3̣
```

In *ir II* the *bonang panerus* simply repeats the patterns given above, but the *bonang barung* plays something rather different. Several variants are found for the latter, including both *kempyung* and *gembyung* for 3̣:

```
balungan          5̣         3̣         5̣          2̣
bonang barung (alternatives)
            6̣    6̣                6̣    6̣
      3̣ 6̣ 3̣ 3̣ .  3̣ . . 2̣ 6̣ 2̣ 2̣ .  2̣ . .
            6̣    6̣                6̣    6̣
      3̣ 6̣6̣3̣ 3̣ .  3̣ . . 2̣ 6̣6̣2̣ 2̣ .  2̣ . .
            6̣    6̣                6̣    6̣
      5̣ 6̣ 3̣ 3̣ .  3̣ . . 5̣ 6̣ 2̣ 2̣ .  2̣ . .
                 6̣                     6̣
      3̣ 6̣ 3̣ 3̣ .  3̣ . . 2̣ 6̣ 2̣ 2̣ .  2̣ . .
            6̣    6̣                6̣    6̣
      2̣ 6̣ 3̣ 3̣ .  3̣ . . 2̣ 6̣ 2̣6̣ . 2̣ .  2̣ . .
            1    1
      5̣ 1 5̣ 3̣ .  3̣ . . etc.
            1    1
      6̣ 1 5̣ 3̣ .  3̣ . . etc.
            1    1
      5̣ 115̣ 3̣ .  3̣ . . etc
bonang panerus
    6̣3̣6̣ . 6̣3̣6̣ . 6̣3̣6̣ . 6̣3̣6̣ . 6̣2̣6̣ . 6̣2̣6̣ . 6̣2̣6̣ . 6̣2̣6̣ .
or
    6̣ . . 6̣ . . 6̣ . . 6̣ . . 6̣ . . 6̣ . . 6̣ . . 6̣ . . 6̣ . . 6̣ . . 6̣ .
    3̣     3̣     3̣     3̣     3̣     3̣     2̣     2̣     2̣     2̣     2̣
```

For the *bonang barung* patterns, the initial note may take account of the note that ends the previous *gåtrå*, but it is not possible to give a more precise rule.

In *pélog limå* the bottom limit of the *pathet* is 1̣, and a *kempyung* for this note is normal, but players may not necessarily play *kempyung* for 2̣ or *gembyung* for 3̣. (In any case, *gåtrå* with *sèlèh* 3̣ are rare in *pélog limå* and *sléndro sångå*.) An example in *ir II*:

```
balungan                         2̣           1̣
bonang barung                    5̣    5̣
                         1̣ 5̣ 1̣ 1̣ .  1̣ . .
bonang panerus           5̣1̣5̣ . 5̣1̣5̣ . 5̣1̣5̣ . 5̣1̣5̣ .
```

In *sléndro sångå*, which is supposedly parallel to *pélog limå*, the lowest note in practice is 2̣, so that the situation is as for the other *pathet* in *sléndro*. Thus the absence of 1̣ on a *bonang cacad* causes no problem.

The *bonang barung* may also use the *nduduk* rhythm for a half-*gåtrå* in *ir I*, e.g. for 5̣3̣5̣6̣:

```
6̣      6̣
3̣ . .  3̣ 5̣ 6̣ 5̣ .
```

Similarly, *kempyung* or *gembyung* patterns may be played throughout a *gåtrå gantung* in the low register, e.g. for 2̣2̣3̣2̣ (representing a *gantung* 2̣) in *ir II*:

```
6̣ . . 6̣ . . 6̣ . . 6̣ . . 6̣ . . 6̣
2̣     2̣     2̣     2̣     2̣     2̣
```

It is considered good style when playing the 'chords' of *kempyung* or *gembyung* to play the lower note slightly ahead of the higher one in *ir II*. The lower note falls on the beat. Sometimes the delay between the two notes is such that the result could more accurately be notated:

```
2̣6̣ . . 2̣6̣ . . 2̣6̣ . . 2̣6̣ . . 2̣6̣ . . 2̣6̣ .      or
2̣6̣6̣2̣2̣6̣ . . 2̣6̣ . .  etc.
```

While these patterns are used in both Yogyanese and Solonese styles, the Yogyanese *kraton* style includes a variation in which the 'chords' are re-struck to produce a 'rolled' sound.

Instead of these special *kempyung* and *gembyung* patterns, it is also not unknown for the *bonang barung* to play *mipil*, using the two notes of the *kempyung* or *gembyung*. The preceding example for 1̣ could therefore also be played 1̣5̣1̣ . 1̣5̣1̣ .

The patterns 6̣3̣6̣ . and 6̣2̣6̣ . imply, as usual, a *sèlèh* note of 3̣ or 2̣ respectively. Sometimes the *bonang panerus* echoes the *bonang barung* and plays the two notes in the opposite order, i.e. 3̣6̣3̣ . or 2̣6̣2̣ . Such patterns are arguably 'wrong' because they point towards a different *sèlèh* note.

Kempyung and *gembyung* are standard *garap* for *gantungan* on the lowest notes of the *pathet*, i.e. in places where higher notes would be played with *gembyangan* or *nduduk tunggal*. Similarly, *kempyung* and *gembyung* patterns may be used by the Yogyanese for these notes in the last *gåtrå* of a *gongan*, where they would use *gembyangan* for higher notes. When a low-to-high transition is being signalled, however, *gembyangan* patterns are usual even if the *balungan* notation has the notes 1̣, 2̣ or 3̣.

Notes in the upper octave occasionally receive

gembyungan treatment: this is common for the half-*gåtrå* 41 (*pélog bem*) or 42 (*pélog barang*) in *ir I* or *ir II*:

ir I 4.4.
1 1

ir II 141.4.4.
1 1

Some players will use *kempyung* or *gembyung* instead of *gembyangan cegat* in *lancaran*, even for the *gåtrå* before the *gong bukå*. Such patterns imply that the player is certain that the *balungan* lies in the low register. In these cases the *bonang panerus* too will play the *kempyung* or *gembyung*, and each instrument will use the rhythm of its usual *gembyangan cegat* pattern. The following example is from a Yogyanese version of *lnc Réná-réná sl 6*

bukå	2 3 5	. 3 6 5	. 3 . (2)
bonang	2̣ 3̣ 5̣	. 3̣ 6̣ 5̣	6̣/2̣ . 6̣/2̣ .

balungan	. 3 . 2	. 3 . 5
bonang barung	6̣/2̣ . 6̣/2̣ .	5/5̣ . 5/5̣ .
bonang panerus	. . 6̣/2̣ . . 6̣/2̣ . 6̣/2̣	. . 5/5̣ . . 5/5̣ . 5/5̣

where the original Yogyanese *balungan* notation does not acknowledge the low register. The opening 2̣ of the *bukå* may also be played as a *kempyung*.

Other special *garap*

Special *garap* is associated with certain named *céngkok* and some pieces—not surprisingly, pieces that are played very often.

Puthut gelut (for example, 33. . 6532 in *sléndro manyurå*) is a common *céngkok* that receives a range of special *garap* in Solonese style. (For Yogyanese *garap*, see **Yogyanese styles: *nguthik***, p. 158.) When its first half is written as 33. ., the obvious realisation is with *gembyang* 3, but variations on the standard *garap* are not unusual. In *ldr Wilujeng* (and other pieces) the preceding *gåtrå* is 212 6̣ or similar, and the expected standard cadential pattern for that *gåtrå* can be modified by a transitional pattern pointing to or actually including the 3 of the *gembyangan*, and thus not coinciding with the *sèlèh* note 6, e.g. (alternatives, *bonang barung, ir II*):

215̣5̣1. . 5̣15̣. 6̣12. 3/3̣ . . 3/3̣ . . 3/3̣ . etc.

21. 5̣5̣1. . 5̣15̣. 6̣123/3̣ . . 3/3̣ . . 3/3̣ . . etc.

21. 5̣5̣1. . 5̣15̣. 6̣6̣12 3/3̣ . . 3/3̣ . . 3/3̣ . etc.

211̣5̣15̣5̣1. . 5̣15̣. 6̣12. etc.[14]

The other decorating instruments usually play to a 6 at the mid-point of this *céngkok*, and the *bonang* may do the same, regardless of the *garap* in the preceding *gåtrå*. The second half of the long *gembyangan* 3 may then be replaced by a long or short *gembyangan* 6, with variant *garap* also in the following *gåtrå*, e.g. (alternatives):

3/3̣ . . 3/3̣ . . 3/3̣ . . 6/6̣ . . 6/6̣ . . 6/6̣ .636. . 565323. . 23.

. . 3/3̣ . . 3/3̣ . . 3/3̣ . . 3/3̣ 216̣6/6̣ 656. . 565323. 323.

3/3̣ . . 3/3̣ . . 3/3̣ . . 3/3̣ . . 216̣6/6̣ etc.

3/3̣ . . 3/3̣ . . 3/3̣ . 216̣6̣6/6̣ . 6̣6/6̣ etc.

If *puthut gelut* is written 3323 6532, the first *gåtrå* may be realised as *gembyangan* followed by *mipil* on 23.

Another named *céngkok* that receives non-standard Solonese treatment is *kacaryan*. This appears in *balungan* lines as 6523 or . 5 . 3 in *sléndro manyurå*. It is regularly

Signalling the *balungan*

There are limits to the concept that the *bonang barung* can signal the *balungan* notes to the other players. In any case, *gembyangan cegat* and *imbal* give no indications of the *balungan* contour. *Mipil* gives useful information for most of the time, but is not conclusive: e.g. the *bonang* pattern .65. .65. in *ir I* could represent 5656 or .656 or .65. or 565. in the *balungan*.

The *bonang* uses the same patterns for several versions of the standard cadential phrases, and uses the same *gembyangan* patterns for *gåtrå gantung*, *gåtrå dhélik* and *lik* transitions, even though these may be written quite differently in the *balungan* notation. As indicated earlier, the *bonang* sometimes signal *gantungan* early, which is helpful to the other players.

14 The overscore represents three notes in the time of two.

played with a *nibani* pattern for . 5 . 3 even when written in *mlaku* form.

Puthut gelut and *kacaryan* are transposed down by a note for *pathet sångå*, and their *garap* is then a note lower than shown above. Corresponding changes apply in *pélog*. Some players consider that named *céngkok* of this kind are the province of the soft-style decorating instruments, so that it is inappropriate for the *bonang* to play any special patterns for them.

The popular *bubaran Hudan mas pl 7* is often played with variant *garap*. As the piece is sometimes thought of as being Yogyanese in character, Yogya-style *gembyangan* in the last *gåtrå* of the *gongan* are not unexpected. A stretch of *mipil* of a distinctly *nglagu* character is also found in the final *gongan*:

balungan	2 7̣ 6̣ 5̣ 6̣ 7̣ 6̣ ⑤
bonang barung	. 2 7̣ 2 7̣ 6̣ 5̣ 3̣ 5̣ 6̣ 7̣ 2 7̣ 6̣ 5̣ 6̣ 5̣

The well-known *lnc Kebogiro pl 7*

A	. 6 . 5	. 3 . 2	. 3 . 2	. 6 . (5)	× II
B	. 6 . 5	. 6 . 7	. 6 . 7	. 6 . (5)	× II
C	. 7 . 6	. 3 . 2	. 3 . 2	. 6 . ⑤	

includes special *garap* at the ends of *gongan* B and C in *iråmå lancar*. The final *gåtrå* are played as respectively 2 2 7̣ 6̣ 5̣ and 6̣ 3̣ 6̣ 5̣.

Worked example: analysis of a *balungan* in Yogya style

This is an example of working out the *garap* for the *bonang barung* without the aid of register dots. As a *bubaran*, this piece would normally be played only in *ir I*.

Bubaran Runtung sl 9

bukå	535. 2356 1653 216⑤
balungan	[6365 6365 6365 613(2)
	5352 5352 5352 535(6)
	5326 5326 5326 535(2)
	535. 2356 1653 216⑤]

At the end, the cadential phrase in *sléndro sångå* is 2 1 6̣ 5̣, so this is the obvious interpretation of the final *gåtrå*. The preceding *gåtrå* should be placed high, i.e. 1̇653, so that the 3 is adjacent to the following 2. Similarly the second *gåtrå* of the last *gongan* should be played in the upper octave. All these *gåtrå* ask to be played with standard *mipil*, except that some form of *gembyangan*, e.g. *gembyangan sarug*, is normal Yogyanese treatment in the final *gåtrå*:

5
2121 6̣ 5̣ 5̣ .

The same three *gåtrå* in the *bukå* can be placed in the same octaves, except for the standard *gembyangan midak* treatment in the final *gåtrå*. The first *gåtrå* of the *bukå* can also be played high. However, the *bukå* need not be treated like the same phrase in the body of the piece, so the first three *gåtrå* of the *bukå* might be played low, and the pitch of *gembyangan midak* is ambiguous anyway.

With the *bukå* ending on 5̣, it is logical for the first *gåtrå* of the piece proper to be placed in the low octave as 6̣ 3̣ 6̣ 5̣. The 6̣ 3̣ can be played with standard *mipil* or with *gembyungan*. The 6̣ 5̣ will be played with *mipil*, but perhaps in a variant: 6̣ 5̣ 3̣ 5̣. In the last *gåtrå* the 61 should obviously be taken as 6̣ 1. The 32 can be given either *kempyungan* or *gembyangan* treatment:

6̣ 6̣   2
2̣ . 2̣ .   or   2̣ 2̣ 2̣ .

The second *gongan* must continue in the low octave, giving the possibility of *gembyungan* for the 5̣ 3̣, and the certainty of *kempyungan* for 5̣ 2̣. In the last *gåtrå* the 56 should again be given a *gembyangan* treatment, perhaps with the *sarug* variant. The first half of the *gåtrå* can then have straight *mipil* or another *gembyangan sarug*:

6   3   6
5̣ 3̣ 5̣ 3̣ 5̣ 6̣ 6̣ .   or   5̣ 3̣ 3̣ . 5̣ 6̣ 6̣ .

The third *gongan* too remains low. Perhaps because of the unusual phrase 26, the preceding 53 is likely to be played with straight *mipil*. The 26 may (exceptionally) be treated as if it were x2̣ and given a *kempyungan* treatment, or else played as *gembyangan* 6 in a sort of *sarug* variant:

6̣ 6̣   6
2̣ . 2̣ .   or   2̣ 6̣ 2̣ .   or   2̣ 6̣ 6̣ .

The last *gåtrå* again is likely to receive a *gembyangan sarug* treatment, although 53 could be played with *mipil*:

2   2   3   2   2
5̣ 3̣ 2̣ 2̣ 2̣ . 2̣ 2̣   or   5̣ 3̣ 3̣ . 2̣ 2̣ . .   or   5̣ 3̣ 5̣ 3̣ 2̣ 2̣ 2̣ .

This *gåtrå* is basically low, but most of the final *gongan* is high, as described earlier, so that a low-to-high transition must be signalled by a *gembyangan* in the first *gåtrå* of the last *gongan*. The whole *gåtrå* could be played with a *gembyangan* 5 for this purpose, but it is sufficient to play *gembyangan* in the second half:

5
5̣ 3̣ 5̣ 3̣ 5̣ 5̣ 5̣ .

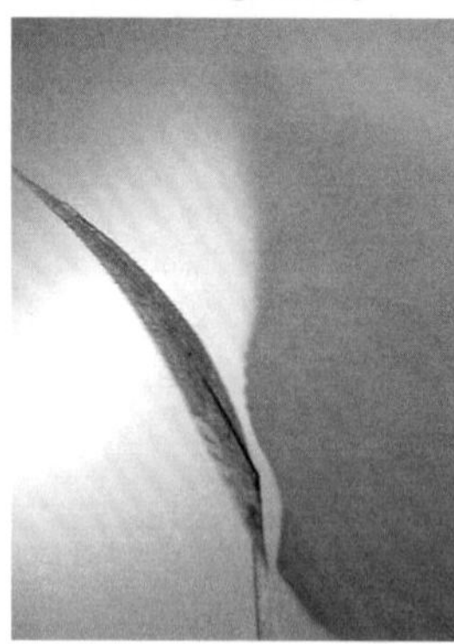

Imbal

Imbal is based on the *bonang panerus* and *bonang barung* playing alternate notes in patterns of four adjacent notes. The four-note cycles are repeated in blocks of various lengths according to need: the examples here show four cycles. Usually the rhythm is completely even and on the beat. Stretches of *imbal* are normally broken up with *sekaran* ([*kr*]; also *kembangan* [*ng*]) played on the *bonang barung* and sometimes on the *bonang panerus* too (see ***Imbal* and *sekaran***, p. 173).

The *bonang barung* typically plays the lower of its notes first and then the higher, but this is not an absolute rule. If it uses the notes 1 and 3 in its upper octave, the *bonang panerus* must use notes in its lower octave in order to create a pattern of adjacent notes:

bonang panerus 2̣ . 5̣ . 2̣ . 5̣ . 2̣ . 5̣ . 2̣ . 5̣ .
bonang barung . 1 . 3 . 1 . 3 . 1 . 3 . 1 . 3

The *bonang panerus* player has the choice of the order of its two notes—in spite of being the less important of the two *bonang*. In the example above, the direction of the pattern is downwards: 5321. If the *bonang panerus* player chooses the other way, a pattern with an upward direction (1235) results:

bonang panerus 5̣ . 2̣ . 5̣ . 2̣ . 5̣ . 2̣ . 5̣ . 2̣ .
bonang barung . 1 . 3 . 1 . 3 . 1 . 3 . 1 . 3

Some players have a preference for one direction (usually the downward direction), but if they change direction they will normally not do so within a *gåtrå*. There are several other options open to the *bonang panerus* player, such as playing its two notes simultaneously as a *gembyung*

bonang panerus 5̣ . 5̣ . 5̣ . 5̣ . 5̣ . 5̣ . 5̣ . 5̣ .
2̣   2̣   2̣   2̣   2̣   2̣   2̣   2̣
bonang barung . 1 . 3 . 1 . 3 . 1 . 3 . 1 . 3

or playing only the note that fits in between the two *bonang barung* notes

bonang panerus 2̣ . 2̣ . 2̣ . 2̣ . 2̣ . 2̣ . 2̣ . 2̣ .
bonang barung . 1 . 3 . 1 . 3 . 1 . 3 . 1 . 3

or even playing this note in octaves (*gembyang*):

bonang panerus 2 . 2 . 2 . 2 . 2 . 2 . 2 . 2 .
2̣   2̣   2̣   2̣   2̣   2̣   2̣   2̣
bonang barung . 1 . 3 . 1 . 3 . 1 . 3 . 1 . 3

It is also possible for the *bonang barung* to depart from the regularity of these patterns, and change direction in the middle of a sequence, e.g.

bonang panerus [5̣ . 2̣ . 5̣ . 2̣ .]5̣ . 2̣ . 5̣ . 2̣ .
bonang barung [. 3 . 1 . 3 . .]. 1 . 3 . 1 . 3

or

bonang panerus [5̣ . 2̣ . 5̣ . 2̣ .]5̣ . 2̣ . 5̣ . 2̣ .
bonang barung [. 3 . 1 . 3 . 1]. 1 . 3 . 1 . 3

or

bonang panerus [5̣ . 2̣ . 5̣ . 2̣ .]5̣ . 2̣ . 5̣ . 2̣ .
bonang barung [. 3 . 1 . 3 . .]31 . 3 . 1 . 3

In longer stretches of *imbal* in this style, the patterns within the square brackets are repeated to fill the space.

Choosing *imbal* notes

The notes used in the *imbal* patterns depend to a greater or lesser degree on the *sèlèh* note. (As to which points should be treated as *sèlèh* points, see ***Imbal* and *sekaran*.**) Several different basic philosophies for choosing *imbal* notes can be identified, ranging from the crude to the very sophisticated, and more than one of them may enter into a player's thinking when approaching a particular piece. There is little agreement between sources.

In addition to these various approaches, the player should take into account the line played by the *rebab*, or perhaps those of the *gendèr* or the *pesindhèn*, as indications of the true inner melody.

- In the crudest approach, the same *imbal* notes are used regardless of *pathet*, except for the obvious replacement of 1 by 7 in *pélog barang*, e.g.

  bonang panerus
  2̣ . 5̣ . 2̣ . 5̣ . 2̣ . 5̣ . 2̣ . 5̣ . 2̣ . 5̣ . 2̣ . 5̣ . 2̣ . 5̣ . 2̣ . 5̣ .
  bonang barung
  . 1 . 3 . 1 . 3 . 1 . 3 . 1 . 3 + *sekaran*

  or

  bonang panerus
  2̣ . 5̣ . 2̣ . 5̣ . 2̣ . 5̣ . 2̣ . 5̣ . 2̣ . 5̣ . 2̣ . 5̣ . 2̣ . 5̣ . 2̣ . 5̣ .
  bonang barung
  . 1 . 3 . 1 . 3 . 6 . 3 . 6 . 3 . 1 . 3 . 1 . 3 + half-*sekaran*

  With either 1 and 3 or 3 and 6 on the *bonang barung*, the notes 2̣ and 5̣ on the *bonang panerus* form sets of adjacent notes.

- Generally players take some account of *pathet*. There is a default choice of *imbal* notes for each *pathet*, and some players will use no others. If they use more than one pair of *imbal* notes in the same *pathet*, the following choices remain the default:

Pathet	*Bonang barung*	*Bonang panerus*
Sléndro manyurå, *sléndro nem*, *pélog nem* (gong 6)	1 and 3	2̣ and 5̣
Pélog barang	7̣ and 3	2̣ and 5̣
Sléndro sångå, *pélog limå*, *pélog nem* (gong 5)	6̣ and 2	1̣ and 3̣

The treatment in *pélog nem* follows that for either *sléndro manyurå* or *sléndro sångå*, according to whether the orientation is towards gong 6 or 5 respectively.

- The next step is to choose *imbal* notes according to both the *pathet* and the relative pitch of the *sèlèh* note within its compass. For example, in *sléndro manyurå* the default *imbal* notes may be applied when the *sèlèh* note is anything up to about 5, i.e. for the entire lower octave and half the middle octave. For *sèlèh* notes 5 and higher, the *imbal* notes may change to 3 and 6. The table above is then expanded to the following

Pathet	*Bonang barung*	*Bonang panerus*
Sléndro manyurå, *sléndro nem*, *pélog nem* (gong 6)	LOW: 1 and 3 HIGH: 3 and 6	LOW: 2̣ and 5̣ HIGH: 5̣ and 1
Pélog barang	LOW: 7̣ and 3 HIGH: 3 and 6	LOW: 2̣ and 5̣ HIGH: 5̣ and 7̣
Sléndro sångå, *pélog limå*, *pélog nem* (gong 5)	LOW: 6̣ and 2 HIGH: 2 and 5 HIGHEST: 5 and 1̇	LOW: 1̣ and 3̣ HIGH: 3̣ and 6̣ HIGHEST: 6̣ and 2

with the same comments as before about the treatment in *pélog nem*.

A set of notes including 2̇ on the *bonang barung* is theoretically possible, but is rarely used.

- The *imbal* notes on the stronger beats may also be chosen according to whether they form harmonious combinations with the *sèlèh* note: for example, the *bonang barung* may use the notes 2 and 5 for *sèlèh* 5. Alternatively the choice may be determined by 'harmony' with the *balungan* notes that occur during the *imbal*. Players may choose to confine this method to *pélog*, since it is generally accepted that any pair of notes in *sléndro* sound satisfactory together.

- Perhaps the most advanced approach to choosing *imbal* notes takes account of the *pathet* again, but in a different way. The *pathet* assigned to the composition is ignored: rather, the *pathet* **orientation** of the *sèlèh* note is the determining factor.

  The most important notes in *sléndro manyurå* are 2 and 6 in any octave, as discussed earlier. Under this approach, the *bonang barung* player chooses *imbal* notes 1 and 3, the default pair for *sléndro manyurå*, when either a 2 or a 6 is the *sèlèh* note. Similarly *sléndro sångå*, *pélog limå* and *pélog nem* with gong 5 are oriented towards the notes 1 and 5: therefore either a 1 or a 5 in any octave as *sèlèh* note causes the player to use 6̣ and 2 for the *imbal* notes. The remaining possible *sèlèh* note is 3, and this is ambiguous in its *pathet* orientation. Probably it will be realised with *imbal* notes 1 and 3 —both on the basis of 'harmony', as discussed in the previous item, and because 3 is the 'avoided note' in *sléndro sångå*, and often also in *pélog limå* and *pélog nem* with gong 5. This approach is particularly likely in *sléndro nem* and *pélog nem*, often called 'mixed' *pathet*.

  As shown below, the choice of *sekaran* for the *bonang* is also normally dependent on *pathet* to a greater or lesser degree. Therefore, in a logical extension of this approach to choosing *imbal* notes, the *sekaran* too may be chosen according to the *pathet* orientation of the *sèlèh* note, rather than the nominal *pathet* of the piece.

- Some sources simply give lists that assign *imbal* notes to each *sèlèh* note, usually appearing to use a mixture of principles, although they do not necessarily take account of the register of the *sèlèh* note. The tables overleaf, derived in this way, introduce additional factors. (The *bonang panerus* notes are on the upper line, the *bonang barung* notes below.) In the smaller table—with the more unusual suggestions—the composite pattern for *sèlèh* 4 ends on the 4, which may reduce the discordance of this note, and the *bonang barung* plays its higher note first, in a break with the usual practice. Both tables suggest *gembyang* 2 on the *bonang panerus* for a surprising number of positions.

Under any of the above philosophies, notes outside the regular *pélog* scales are treated in the usual way. Thus

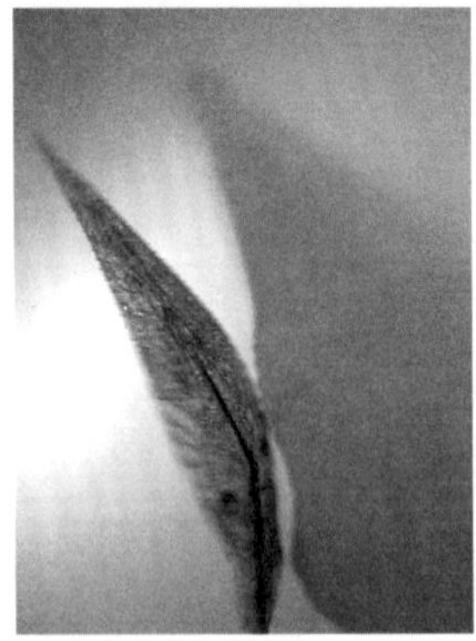

the note 4 may be used in *imbal* patterns if it is present in the *balungan* line of the *gåtrå*, especially in *pélog limå* and *nem*. However, this principle is not always followed, so that clashes can occur between 4 in the *balungan* line and 3 or 5 in the *imbal*. The table at the right even shows the use of 4 in a pattern for *sèlèh* 6 without regard for the presence or absence of 4 in the *gåtrå*. *Imbal* notes are assigned to *sèlèh* 4 in *pélog limå / nem* or *pélog barang* as if it were 3 or 5 respectively. *Sèlèh* 1 in *pélog barang* or 7 in *pélog limå / nem* is likely to be seen as an indicator of a temporary change of *pathet*, as suggested under **Pathet**, p. 57.

Whichever philosophy is followed, special problems arise when *bonang cacad* are attempting the 6̣ 1 2 3 pattern in *sléndro sångå*. Theoretically the pattern is

bonang panerus	1̣ . 3̣ . 1̣ . 3̣ . 1̣ . 3̣ . 1̣ . 3̣ .
bonang barung	. 6̣ . 2 . 6̣ . 2 . 6̣ . 2 . 6̣ . 2

but the *bonang panerus* does not have the 1̣. A variety of solutions to the problem can be found:

- In the crudest approach, the *bonang panerus* simply plays 1 instead of 1̣, so that the four-note pattern no longer consists of adjacent notes. This happens.
- The *bonang panerus* player may leave the *imbal* pattern entirely to the *bonang barung*. The full 6̣ 1 2 3 pattern is difficult to play, but a pattern using three notes is much more practical:

bonang barung	1 6̣ 1 2 1 6̣ 1 2 1 6̣ 1 2 1 6̣ 1 2

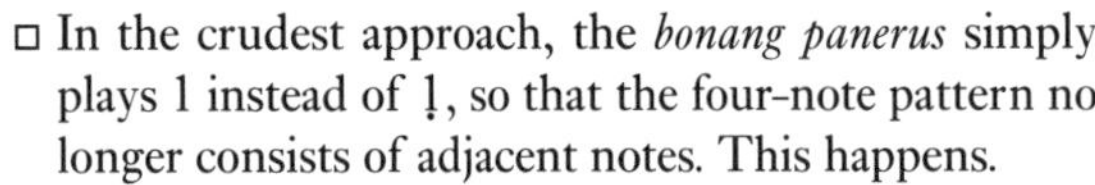

3.38 Sharing the 1 pot

Sèlèh note	*Imbal* notes	*Pathet*	
2̣, 5̣, 6̣, 1, 2, 5, 6, 1̇, 2̇, 3̇,[a] also 3̣ in *sl 9*	1̣ . 3̣ . . 6̣ . 2	*Sl 6, sl 9*	*Pl 5, pl 6*
3̣, 6̣, 1, 2, 3, 6, 1̇, 2̇, 3̣, also 2̣ and 5̣ in *sl m*	2̣ . 5̣ . or 2̣ . 2̣ .[b] . 1 . 3 . 1 . 3	*Sl 6, sl m*	*Pl 5, pl 6*
3̣, 5̣, 6̣, 7̣, 2, 3, 5, 6, 7, 2̇	2̣ . 5̣ . . 7̣ . 3	—	*Pl 7*
2, 5, 6[a]	3̣ . 6̣ . 2 . 5	*Sl 6, sl 9*	*Pl 5, pl 6*
5, 6	2̣ . 5̣ . . 3 . 6	*Sl 9*	
3, 6, also 3̣, 5̣, 6̣, 5 in *sl m*	5̣ . 1 .[c] or 2̣ . 5̣ . . 3 . 6 . 3 . 6	Any *sléndro*	Any *pélog*
1̇	6̣ . 2 . . 5 . 1̇	*Sl 9*	*Pl 5, pl 6*
4, 6	5̣ . 1 . . 4 . 6	—	*Pl 5, pl 6*

a. *Sl 9* only. b. Optionally *gembyang* 2. c. Change 1̇ to 7, 1 to 7̣ for *pl 7*.

Sèlèh note	*Sl 6*	*Sl 9*	*Sl m*	*Pl 5,6*	*Pl 7*
7	—	—	—	3̣ . 6̣ . . 5 . 7	3̣ . 6̣ . . 5 . 7
6	2̣ . 5̣ . . 3 . 6	2̣ . 5̣ . . 3 . 6?	5̣ . 1 . . 3 . 6	2̣ . 5̣ . . 4 . 6	2̣ . 3̣ . . 5 . 6?
5	3̣ . 6̣ . 2 . 5	1̣ . 3̣ . 6̣ . 2	3̣ . 6̣ . 2 . 5?	1̣ . 3̣ . 6̣ . 2	3̣ . 6̣ . 2 . 5?
4	—	—	—	5̣ . 2̣ . . 6 . 4	3̣ . 6̣ . 2 . 4?
3	2̣ . 5̣ . . 1 . 3	2̣ . 5̣ . . 1 . 3	2̣ . 2̣ .[a] . 1 . 3	2̣ . 2̣ .[a] . 1 . 3	2̣ . 2̣ .[a] . 7̣ . 3
2	6̣ . 3̣ . . 5 . 2	1̣ . 3̣ . 6̣ . 2	2̣ . 2̣ . . 1 . 3	2̣ . 2̣ .[a] . 1 . 3	2̣ . 2̣ .[a] . 7̣ . 3
1	3̣ . 6̣ . . 5 . 1̇	1̣ . 3̣ . 6̣ . 2	2̣ . 2̣ .[a] . 1 . 3	1̣ . 3̣ . 6̣ . 2	1̣ . 3̣ . . 6̣ . 2

a. *Gembyang* 2 on *bonang panerus*

- If the two *bonang* are adjacent and suitably oriented, the *bonang panerus* player can lean over and borrow the 1 pot of the *bonang barung* (see Fig. 3.38). The *bonang panerus* player risks getting in the way of the other player's *sekaran*.

  Even if the two *bonang* are on the opposite sides of a square, the *bonang panerus* player may be able to reach the pot by stretching behind him. However, in Yogyanese gamelan the *bonang* are often too far apart to allow this.
- There is also an alternative pattern for the *bonang panerus* part that avoids the 1̣:

bonang panerus	. . 3̣ 2̣ . . 3̣ 2̣ . . 3̣ 2̣ . . 3̣ 2̣
bonang barung	. 6̣ . 2 . 6̣ . 2 . 6̣ . 2 . 6̣ . 2

  The result is known as *imbal kodhokan* or frog-style *imbal*.
- A solution that belongs in the 'incredible but true' category has occurred when the *bonang panerus* player was absent: the *demung* player contributed the missing 1̣ by playing his 1̇, creating a composite pattern 1 6̣ 1 2 1 6̣ 1 2, etc.
- Finally, if the gamelan has a *bonang panembung*, its 1̇ pot can be borrowed as a 1̣ pot for the *bonang panerus*. The 1 from an *engkuk-kemong* can be used in the same way, although it would be unusual for a gamelan to have the combination of (Yogyanese) *bonang cacad* and (more Solonese?) *engkuk-kemong*.

Imbal and *sekaran*

Imbal on the *bonang* does not continue uninterrupted for long stretches. Instead it is broken up by *sekaran* or *kembangan*, which are special patterns leading up to and emphasising the *sèlèh* note. There are characteristic *sekaran* for each *pathet*. In practice, many *sekaran* serve more than one *pathet*. *Sekaran* come in various lengths. The standard length (here called a 'full *sekaran*') replaces four cycles of *imbal*. *Sekaran* longer than this are most likely to be used before a gong, especially in *ir IV*.

Table 3.13 contains a selection of *sekaran* listed by *laras*, *pathet*, length and then roughly in order of first note. A much larger collection is available on the associated website. There are of course endless possibilities, even if one does not go as far as the distinguished player who was known for borrowing TV advertising jingles as *sekaran*. Examination of the table shows certain family resemblances. For example, some *sekaran* listed for *sléndro manyurå* are simply transposed down a note for use in *sléndro sångå*, so that . 6̣ . 3̣ . 6̣ . 1 . 2 . 6̣16̣12 and all its relatives become . 5̣ . 2̣ . 5̣ . 6̣ . 1 . 5̣6̣5̣6̣1, etc.

In the interests of clarity, the full *sekaran* are notated as 16-beat rather than 8-beat patterns, and so on for the other lengths, i.e.

. 5̣16̣ . 5̣ . 2 . 216̣1235

rather than

5̣16̣ 5̣ 2 21 6̣1 23 5

A few *sekaran* include triplet rhythms—as elsewhere, usually three notes against four normal beats—but players often apply slightly irregular rhythms to *sekaran* for the *bonang barung*, including delays to the *sèlèh* note. These rhythms must be acquired by listening.

Sekaran often fall into two halves, and various first halves can be combined with various second halves. For example, the full collection shows some 20 *sekaran* for *sèlèh* 2 in *sl m* that start . 6̣ . 3̣ . 6̣ . 1, often with quite minor differences in the second half. Then there are another nine first halves, not all with major differences, any of which can be combined with any of the 20 second halves to make 180 more *sekaran*.

Sekaran are not often needed for the note 4. In principle, the usual rules can be used to derive suitable *sekaran* from those for notes 3 or 5 by changing the relevant notes to 4. In practice, simple *gembyangan* as shown in the table for *pelog limå* are commonly used in the other *pathet* too.

Sekaran for 7 in *pélog limå/nem* or 1 in *pélog barang* are theoretically impossible, because the occurrence of these notes as *sèlèh* notes should indicate a change of *pathet*.

The note 4 is not likely to be used in *sekaran* for other *sèlèh* notes unless the 4 is present in the *balungan* or a vocal line—either in the same *gåtrå* or at least nearby. Bolder players may ignore this principle.

No *sekaran* are listed for *sléndro nem*, because the *sekaran* as well as the *imbal* notes for *sléndro nem* are normally borrowed from *sléndro manyurå* or *sléndro sångå*.

The register of the *sèlèh* note may be taken into account when choosing *sekaran*. When the *sekaran* is to be followed by high *imbal* notes, it may be more convenient to use a *sekaran* that ends in the upper octave. Thus, for example, the *sekaran* . 5̣16̣ . 5̣ . 2 . 216̣1235 forms a good lead-in for *imbal* notes 3 and 6 on the *bonang barung*.

In those *sekaran* that incorporate *gembyangan* 1, the combination of two notes should be chosen to correspond to the register of the *sèlèh* note, as with *gembyangan* treatment in general. (The table shows only one option in each case.) If the *sèlèh* note is 1 rather than 1̇, the *gembyangan* should therefore be of the form

. 1 . 1 . 1 . . etc.
 1̣ 1̣ 1̣

even though 1̣ is not within the *balungan* range in *sléndro*. On a *bonang cacad* there is of course no option.

While the most basic pattern is a half-and-half split with *imbal* followed by *sekaran*, there is no absolute rule saying that a *gåtrå* must always begin with *imbal*. It is possible, although less common, for a half-*gåtrå* or more of *imbal* to follow a half-*gåtrå* or more of *sekaran*. If the *gåtrå* is *gantung*, the *bonang* may play all of it, or the first half, as a *sekaran* that is largely *gembyangan*—the various such *sekaran* for the note 1 being used frequently for this purpose: also see **Other signals** below, p. 180.

Fig. 3.39 shows examples of how *imbal* and *sekaran* fit together, although it does not by any means exhaust the possibilities. The first example is for a *lancaran*, in which there is only one *sèlèh* point per *gongan* (as far as the *bonang* are concerned, when playing *imbal*). In the standard treatment, as shown, the *bonang* play four cycles of *imbal* followed by a full *sekaran*—to the note 2 in this case.

The numbers at the bottom of the diagram are a method by which *bonang* players or others can try to keep their place amid the long stretches of decoration in *ir III* and (especially) *ir IV*. It is most convenient to ➔ p. 178

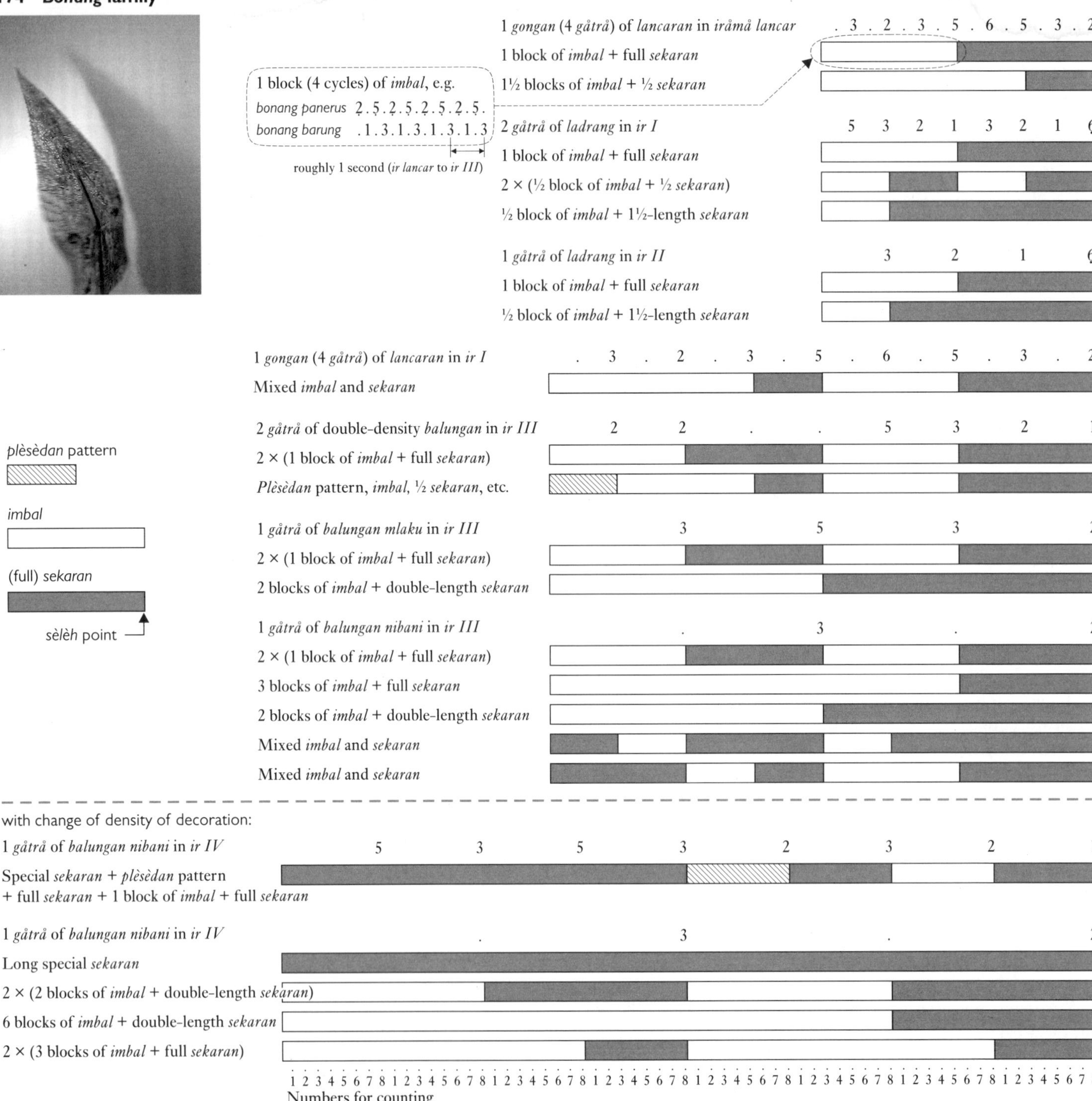

3.39 Examples of structures and relationships of *imbal* and *sekaran* on *bonang*

Table 3.13
Sekaran for *bonang barung*

Sléndro manyurå

Sèlèh 1

35353561
.1.1.1..   11.1.1..
 1 1 1   11 1 1
.1.1.1..   .3.53561
 1 1 1
.1.1.1..   .53.3561
 1 1 1
.1.1.1..   .1.1.1..   .6.2.6..   .3.5.6.1
 1 1 1   1 1 1

Sèlèh 2

.2161612
.3.5.6.1   .216.1.2
.3.5.6.1   .2161612
.356.1.2   .3561612
.6.3.6.1   .2.6.1.2
.6.3.6.1   .2235612
.6.3.6.1   .6165322
.3.2.1.6   .3.6.1.2   .3.6.1.2

Sèlèh 3

.1.61653
 3
.1.5.1..
 3   3
.1.5.1..   .1.51653
 3   3   3
.3561612   .2161653
5151.51.   5151.51.
   3 3   3 3
5151.51.   51535123
   3 3
.2.3.5.6   .1.2.6.5   .6.2.5.3

Sèlèh 5

.1.61615
 5
.6121615
.1.6.1..   .1.61615
 5   5   5
.1.61612   .2161615
 5
.1.5.1.2   .216.1.5
.5.6.1.2   .3.5.216   .5.61615

Sèlèh 6

.1666166
2166.6.6
  66 6 6
.2.3.5.2   .3.21516
.3.5.2.1   .3.21516
.3561612   .2151516
.5.6.2.1   .3.21516
.6.6.6..   .3561216
 6 6 6
.3.5.6.1   .2.3.5.2   .3.21516
...3...1   .2.3....   .6.5.2.1   .3.21516

Sléndro sångå

Sèlèh 1

.525.6.1
.5.2.5.6   .1.52561
.5.2.5.6   .1656561
.2.1.6.5   .656.5.6   .1.56561

Sèlèh 2

.6532322
       2
.165.3.2   .6.5.3.2
.2.3.5.6   .1.5.3.2
.6.6.6..   .6.6.6..
 2 3 2   2 3 2
.6.36.61   .6.35612
.2.1.6.5   .2.3.5.6   .1.2.3.2
also as for *sléndro manyurå*

Sèlèh 3

.3.51653
.1.5.1..   .1.5.1..
 3   3   3   3
565662..   56566253
also as for *sléndro manyurå*

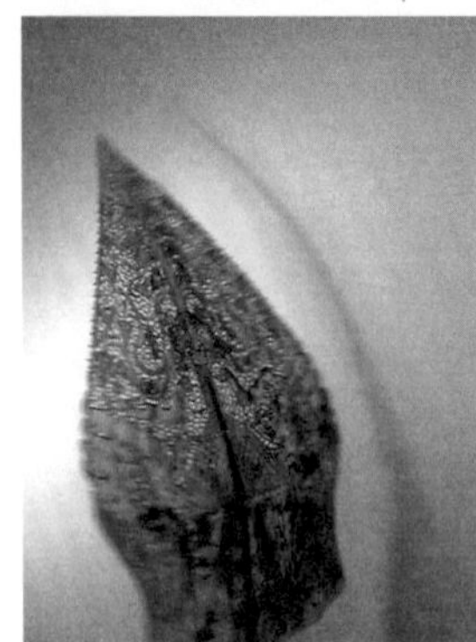

Table 3.13 (cont'd)

Sèlèh 5

. 1 . 6 . 1 . .
  5   5

5 1 5 6 1 2 3 5

. 1 . 6 . 1 . 2   . 2 1 6 5 6 1 5
  5

. 1 . 6 . 1 . .   . 1 . 6 . 1 . .
  5   5   5   5

. 5 . 6 . 1 . 2   . 3 . 1 . 6 . 5

. 6 1 6 . 1 . 6   . 1 . 6 5 3 . 5

. 5 . 6 . 1 . 2   . 3 . 5 . 2 1 6   . 5 . 6 1 6 1 5

also as for *sléndro manyurå*

Sèlèh 6

. 3 5 6 1 2 1 6

. 6 . 6 . 6 . .   . 6 . 2 . 5 . 6

. 6 . 6 . 6 . .   . 6 . 6 . 6 . .
  6   6   6   6   6   6

. 6 . 6 . 6 . .   . 5 1 2 1 5 1 6

also as for *sléndro manyurå*

Sléndro nem

See text

Pélog limå

Sèlèh 1

. 1 . 5 6 5 6 1

5 . 5 . 5 . 5 .
1   1   1   1

6 5 4 2 1 5 1 1

. 1 . 1 . 1 . .   6 5 4 2 1 5 1 1
  1   1   1   1

. 5 . 5 . 5 . .   6 5 4 2 1 5 1 1
  1   1   1   1

and as for *pélog nem*

Sèlèh 2

. 6 . 3 . 6 . .   . 6 . 3 6 5 3 2
  2   2   2

and as for *sléndro manyurå*

Sèlèh 3

. 1 . 5 . 6 . .   . 1 . 5 6 . 1 3

and as for *pélog nem*

Sèlèh 4

. 4 . 4 . 4 . .   . 4 . 4 . 4 . .
  4   4   4   4   4   4

also see text

Sèlèh 5

. 3 5 6 . 1 . 2   2 . 1 6 . 1 . 5

. 6 5 4 4 . 6 5 4   . 2 4 5 4 6 4 5

and as for *pélog nem*

Sèlèh 6

. 4 5 6 5 4 5 6

. 5 1 6 1 5 1 6

2 1 6 6 6 1 6 6   . 4 5 6 5 4 5 6

Sèlèh 7

See text

Pélog nem

Sèlèh 1

6 5 4 2 1 5 1 5
              1

. 1 . 1 . 1 . .   6 5 4 2 1 5 1 5
  1   1   1   1

. 1 . 1 . 1 . .   6 5 4 2 4 5 6 1
  1   1   1

. 2 . 3 . 5 . 6   . 1 . 5 . 6 . 1

and as for *pélog limå*

Sèlèh 2

. 2 1 6 . 1 . 2

. 2 1 6 1 6 1 2

. 3 . 2 . 1 . 6   . . 6 3 . 6 . 1   . 2 . 3 . 5 . 2

. 3 . 2 . 1 . 6   . . 6 3 . 6 . 1   . 6 . 3 2 6 2 2

also as for *sléndro manyurå*

Sèlèh 3

. 1 5 3 5 1 5 3

. 2 5 3 . 2 5 3

. 6 1 6 . 5 . 3

. 1 2 3 . 1 . 3   3 . 2 1 6 1 2 3

. 1 . 5 . 3 . .   . 1 . 5 1 6 5 3
  3   3

Table 3.13 (cont'd)

.3561612 .2161653
also as for *sléndro manyurå*

Sèlèh 4
as for *pélog limå*

Sèlèh 5
.1.61615
5
.1.6.1.2 .2165615
5
.1.6.1.. .1.61615
5 5 5
.356.1.2 .216.1.5
.5.6.1.2 .4565465
.5.6.1.2 .1.3.1.2 .2161615
also as for *sléndro manyurå*

Sèlèh 6
.5121516
61666166
2166.6.6 .4565456
.3561612 .3561216
.5.6.1.2 .3.215.6
.2.1.6.3 ..35.2.1 .3.21516
also as for *sléndro manyurå*

Sèlèh 7
See text

Pélog barang

Sèlèh 1
See text

Sèlèh 2
32765322
.6.3.6.7 .276532.
.3.2.7.6 .636.7.2 .3.67672
also as for *sléndro manyurå*, with 7 replacing 1

Sèlèh 3
7 7
33.333..
67232653
.3.5.3.. .3.57653
.7.5.7.. .7.57653
3 3 3
.2.3.5.6 .7.2.6.5 .7.67653
also as for *sléndro manyurå*, with 7 replacing 1

Sèlèh 4
See text

Sèlèh 5
.2765675
27656235
.5.6.7.2 .2765675
.6.3.5.6 .532.7.5
.7.6.7.. .7.67675
5 5 5
.7.6.7.. .7.67235
5 5 5
also as for *sléndro manyurå*, with 7 replacing 1

Sèlèh 6
27666766
.3567276
37356766
.2.3.4.2 .3.27576
.3.5.6.7 .3.27576
.3.5.6.7 .2.3.4.2 .3.27576
also as for *sléndro manyurå*, with 7 replacing 1

Sèlèh 7
35673567
.535.6.7
....3567 3567
.53.3567 67232567
.6727675 3.353567
.7.7.7.. .53.3567
7 7 7
.7.7.7.. .653.567
7 7 7
also as for *sléndro manyurå*, with 7 replacing 1

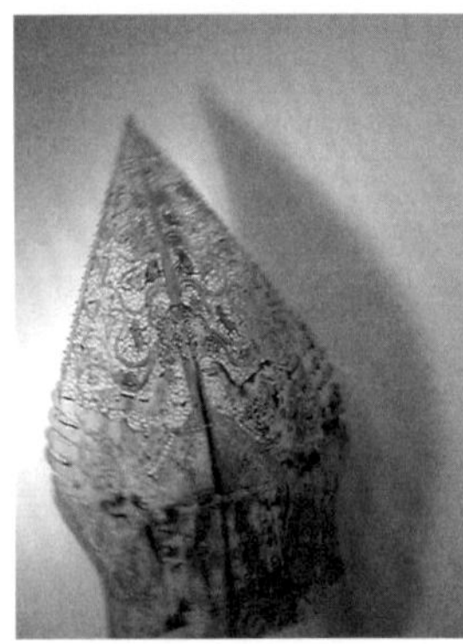

count in cycles of eight, and not only because numbers up to 8 in English are mainly monosyllabic.

Inevitably players differ greatly in their use of *imbal* and *sekaran*. Variations include the length of the *sekaran*, how many different *sekaran* are used for the same *sèlèh* note, and how much of the time is spent in *sekaran*. One expert Javanese player's comment on a large collection of *sekaran* was that none of them was 'wrong', but nevertheless he preferred patterns that he thought agreed best with whatever the *gendèr barung* was playing. Other players take less account of the other instruments.

Sometimes a *gåtrå* or a whole *céngkok* is treated as a unit, using a long *imbal/sekaran* combination such as those shown in Table 3.14. (A larger selection is again available on the website.) The table includes several treatments with a notably vocal character. Some of these patterns originated in *senggakan* or other vocal parts, e.g. from *kethoprak*. For example, in the *ir IV* treatment of *ayu kuning*, the first half uses a phrase to which the words *janji sabar* … are sung. To allow such patterns to be heard clearly, it may be best to omit *imbal* altogether within the *céngkok*, as illustrated in the first half of the first example (but not everywhere else). The *ir III* version of *ayu kuning* is rather different, with four half-*sekaran* to the first four notes of the *balungan*. There are different possible treatments of *puthut gelut*: the *bonang* may play a *sekaran* either to the characteristic mid-point note of the *céngkok* (i.e. 6 in *pathet manyurå* or 5 in *pathet sångå*) or to whatever note is written in the *balungan*.

The patterns in Table 3.14 can be adapted to *pélog* and to other *pathet* by the usual rules. The treatment shown for *puthut gelut* in *sléndro sångå* is also applied to . 2 . 1 in *sléndro manyurå*, and this particular *garap* requires a *kendhang* signal.

Table 3.14
Long *sekaran* and *sekaran* for named *céngkok*. (*Balungan* line is shaded.)

Sléndro manyurå

for 5353 2321 in *ldr Asmarandånå*, double density in *ir IV*

	5		3		5		3
. . . .	. 5̣ . 5̣ . 3̣ . 5̣	. . . 3̣ . 6̣ . .	. 5̣ . 3̣ . 2̣ . 3̣	. . . .	. 5̣ . 5̣ . 3̣ . 5̣	. . . 3̣ . 6̣ . .	. 5̣ . 3̣ . 2̣ . 3̣
	2		3		2		1
. 1 6̣ 2̣ 2	. 1 6̣ 2̣ 2	. 6̣ . 1 . 2 . 3	. 2 . 6̣ . 5̣ . 3̣	. 1 . 3 . 1 . 3	. 1 . 3 . 1 . 3	. 1 . 1 . 1 . .	. 1 . 1 . 1 . .
						1̣ 1̣ 1̣	1̣ 1̣ 1̣

for 61̇3̇2̇ 6321, double density in *ir III*, = *ayu kuning*

6	1̇	3̇	2̇	6	3	2	1
. 6̣ 1 2 1 5̣ 1 6̣	. 5̣ 3̣ . 3̣ 5̣ 6̣ 1	. 3 2 1 6̣ 1 2 3	. 2 1 6̣ . 1 . 2	6̣ 1 2 3 . 3 . .	6̣ 1 2 3 . 3 . .	1 1 . 1 . 1 . .	. 3̣ . 5̣ 3̣ 5̣ 6̣ 1
						1̣ 1̣ 1̣ 1̣	

for 61̇3̇2̇ 6321, double density in *ir IV*, = *ayu kuning*

	6		1̇		3̇		2̇
. . . .	. 6̣ . 2 . 1 . 6̣	. . . . . 2 . 3	. 2 . 6̣ . 2 . 1	. . . 1 . 6̣ . 1	. 6̣ . 1 . 2 . 3	. . . . . 2 . 1	. 2 . 3 . 5 . 2
	6		3		2		1
. . . . . 5 . 3	. 5 . 3	. 6̣ . 1 . 2 . 3	. 2 . 6̣ . 5̣ . 3̣	6̣ 1 2 3 . 1 . 3	. 1 . 3 . 1 . 3	. 1 . 1 . 1 . .	. 3̣ . 5̣ . 6̣ . 1
5̣ 3̣	5̣ 3̣					1̣ 1̣ 1̣	

Sléndro sångå

for 25̣21 or . 2 . 1 in *ir III*, = *puthut gelut*

	2		5̣		2		1
. 6̣ . 2 . 6̣ . 2	. . . 2 . . . 1	. . . 5̣ . . . 2̣	. . . 3̣ . . . 5̣	. . . . . 2̣ 3̣ 5̣	. . . 1 6̣ 5̣ . .	. 5̣ . 2̣ . 5̣ . 6̣	. 1 . 5̣ . 6̣ . 1

for 2132 5321 (double density in *ir III*), = *dhebyang-dhebyung*

2	1	3	2	5	3	2	1
. 2 . 6̣ . 2 . .	. 2 . 6̣ . 2 . .	. 6̣ . 2 . 6̣ . 2	. 2̣ 3̣ . 3̣ 2̣ 3̣ 5̣	. 2 . 5 . 2 . 5	. 2 . 1 . 6̣ . 5̣	. 5̣ . 2̣ . 5̣ . 6̣	. 1 . 5̣ 6̣ 5̣ 6̣ 1

In *ir III* and *ir IV* the mid-point of a *gåtrå* is usually a *sèlèh* point (and for this purpose, eight beats of double-density *balungan* count as one *gåtrå*). However, Fig. 3.39 shows examples where no *sekaran* is played to the mid-point. There is a good reason for this. Many compositions where *imbal* is used—for example, the *inggah* of *gendhing*—have *balungan nibani*. (The relevant examples in Fig. 3.39 show this.) The note at the mid-point of the *gåtrå* must conform to the rules of *balungan nibani* (p. 31). However, it does not necessarily correspond to a note in the inner melody, as reflected in the *rebaban*, *gérongan* or *sindhènan*. If the note at the mid-point in the *balungan* is either absent or unimportant in the inner melody, the *bonang* player may prefer not to emphasise it by playing a *sekaran* to it, or may play a different *sekaran*. This is another illustration of the principle that it is always helpful to know as much as possible about the parts played by the other instruments.

The *bonang barung* may follow its *sekaran* with a special transition into the next *imbal* notes: for example, if the *sekaran* is to any note up to about 2, the first cycle of . 1 . 3 after it may be replaced by 6̣ 1 2 3.

Table 3.15 records two teachers' realisations of a very well-known piece, the *ompak* of *ldr Pangkur sl 9* as played in *ir III*. In nearly half the *gåtrå* the two teachers' realisations are the same. Elsewhere, teacher A uses a range of special patterns, suggesting a more detailed response to the peculiarities of the piece. In the *lik* of this piece, however, teacher B points out that the note 3, the avoided note in the *pathet*, twice occurs at the mid-point of a *gåtrå*, and insists that no *sekaran* should be played to those points in *ir IV*: teacher A makes no such rule. For the record, at least one of the teachers gave a slightly different realisation on another occasion.

When the *bonang barung* plays a *sekaran*, there are three possibilities for the *bonang panerus*:

- □ It may continue playing *imbal*, regardless of the fact that a four-note *imbal* cycle no longer results: some players prefer to do this because they think *sekaran* unnecessary or inappropriate on the *bonang panerus*

  bonang barung

  . 1 . 3 . 1 . 3 . 1 . 3 . 1 . 3   . 6̣ . 3̣ . 6̣ . 1 . 2̣ . 3̣ 5̣ 6̣ 1 2

  bonang panerus

  2̣ . 5̣ . 2̣ . 5̣ . 2̣ . 5̣ . 2̣ . 5̣ .   2̣ . 5̣ . 2̣ . 5̣ . 2̣ . 5̣ . 2̣ . 5̣ .

- □ It may play notes intended to fit with the *sekaran* that the *bonang barung* is playing (although the player can only guess what that will be):

  bonang barung

  . 1 . 3 . 1 . 3 . 1 . 3 . 1 . 3   . 2 1 6̣ . 1 . 2 . 2 1 6̣ 1 6̣ 1 2

  bonang panerus

  2̣ . 5̣ . 2̣ . 5̣ . 2̣ . 5̣ . 2̣ . 5̣ .   3 . 3 . 3 . 3 . 3 . 3 . 3 . 3 .

  3̣ 3̣ 3̣ 3̣ 3̣ 3̣ 3̣ 3̣

For this option, the default part for the *bonang panerus* is a series of off-beat *gembyang* on the note above the *sèlèh* note, but most players choose something more amibitious. The use of *gembyang* 2 on the *bonang panerus* against *gembyang* 1 on the *bonang barung* (or another *sekaran* containing many *gembyang* 1) is very

Table 3.15
Alternative realisations of *ldr Pangkur sl 9, ir III (ompak)*, on *bonang barung*

Gåtrå	Teacher A	Teacher B
. 2 . 1	*Imbal* 6̣–2, full *sekaran* to 1	*Imbal* 6̣–2, full *sekaran* to 1
. 2 . 6̣	*Imbal* 6̣–2, full *sekaran* to 6	*Imbal* 6̣–2, full *sekaran* to 6
. 2 . 1	*Imbal* 6̣–2, full *sekaran* to 1	*Imbal* 6̣–2, full *sekaran* to 1
. 6̣ . 5̣	*Imbal* 6̣–2, full *sekaran* to 5	*Imbal* 6̣–2, full *sekaran* to 5
6 6 . .	Half-*sekaran* to 6, *imbal* 3-6, half-*sekaran* to 6	*Imbal* 3-6, full *sekaran* to 6
5 5 6 1̇	*Imbal* 2–5, full *sekaran* to 1	*Imbal* 6̣–2, full *sekaran* to 1
2̇ 1̇ 5 2	*Imbal* 5–1̇, full *sekaran* to 2	*Imbal* 6̣–2, full *sekaran* to 2
. 1 . 6̣	*Imbal* 6̣–2, full *sekaran* to 6	*Imbal* 6̣–2, full *sekaran* to 6
. . 3 2	First half of *puthut gelut*: *plèsèdan* pattern for 2, *imbal* 2–5, half-*sekaran* to 5	(Would use *plèsèdan* pattern for 2 in *pathet manyurå*, and for 1 in *pathet sångå*) *imbal* 6̣–2, full *sekaran* to 2
5 3 2 1	Second half of *puthut gelut*: two cycles of *imbal* 2–5, 1½-length *sekaran* to 1	*Imbal* 6̣–2, full *sekaran* to 1
2 1 3 2	First half of *dhebyang-dhebyung*: six cycles of variant *imbal* using 6̣–2, half-*sekaran* to 2 (see Table 3.14)	*Imbal* 6̣–2, full *sekaran* to 2
5 3 2 1	Second half of *dhebyang-dhebyung*: two cycles of *imbal* 2–5, 1½-length *sekaran* to 1	*Imbal* 2–5, full *sekaran* to 1
5 6 2̇ 1̇	First half of *ayu kuning*: two cycles of *imbal* 2–5, half-*sekaran* to 6, full *sekaran* to 1	*Imbal* 2–5, full *sekaran* to 1
5 2 1 6̣	Second half of *ayu kuning*: *imbal* 6̣–2, full *sekaran* to 6	*Imbal* 6̣–2, full *sekaran* to 6
. 2 . 1	*Imbal* 6̣–2, full *sekaran* to 1	*Imbal* 6̣–2, full *sekaran* to 1
. 6̣ . 5̣	*Imbal* 6̣–2, full *sekaran* to 5	*Imbal* 6̣–2, full *sekaran* to 5

Table 3.16
Sekaran for bonang panerus

Sèlèh 1

2.2.2.2. 2̣ 2̣ 2̣ 2̣	6̣32135̣6̣1
2.2.2.2. 2̣ 2̣ 2̣ 2̣	6̣1233221
2.2.2.2. 2̣ 2̣ 2̣ 2̣	21233221 2̣
2.2.2.2. 2̣ 2̣ 2̣ 2̣	2.2.2.2. 2̣ 2̣ 2̣ 2̣
.12̣35̣6̣12	.5321.21
.5̣6̣1215̣2̣.	.5̣6̣1215̣1̣. for *sl 9*
5̣6̣12216̣	5̣1525̣.5̣. 1̇ 1̇
.6̣1216̣5̣6̣	3̣.35̣35̣6̣1
.6̣1216̣5̣6̣	3̣.6̣5̣35̣6̣1
16̣5̣2̣5̣6̣16̣	6̣16̣5̣2̣5̣6̣1 for *sl 9*
11 15̣5̣	5̣2̣2̣2̣32̣1. for *sl 9* [15]
11 15̣5̣	.5̣6̣5̣32̣1̣. for *sl 9* [16]

Sèlèh 2

..2̣35̣6̣12	3216̣5̣32̣2
..2̣35̣6̣12	3216̣5̣32̣.
2̣35̣6̣16̣12	1216̣5̣32̣2
216̣35̣6̣16̣	6̣16̣36̣.6̣. 2̣ 2̣
3̣6̣1216̣3̣.	3̣6̣1216̣2̣.
3.3.3.3. 3̣ 3̣ 3̣ 3̣	3.3.3.3. 3̣ 3̣ 3̣ 3̣
3322116̣6̣	5̣5̣16̣5̣3̣2̣6̣
6̣1235353	216̣12.12
6̣1235353	216̣3̣6̣16̣2̣
6̣.6̣5̣6̣.6̣1	6̣.6̣5̣6̣5̣3̣2̣ for *sl 9*
6̣.6̣5̣6̣.6̣1	6̣.6̣5̣6̣.6̣2̣ for *sl 9*
6̣.6̣5̣6̣.6̣1	6̣.6̣5̣6̣15̣2̣ for *sl 9*
.123.6̣12	2 2 .15̣3̣2̣.2̣.
.123.6̣12	.16̣12.12

Sèlèh 3

1.16̣1.12	1.16̣1.5̣3̣
1.16̣1.12	1.16̣16̣5̣3̣
1.13̣5̣6̣12	6̣12316̣5̣3̣
3̣6̣3̣5̣3̣6̣12	326̣5̣6̣2̣5̣3̣
5̣6̣1216̣5̣6̣	2̣3̣5̣6̣16̣5̣3̣
5.5.5.5. 5̣ 5̣ 5̣ 5̣	5.5.5.5. 5̣ 5̣ 5̣ 5̣
.6̣.1216̣.	.6̣.13.3. 3̣ 3̣
.6̣1216̣5̣6̣	2̣3̣5̣6̣5̣3̣2̣3̣
.6̣1216̣5̣6̣	2̣3̣5̣6̣16̣5̣3̣
.6̣1216̣5̣6̣	3̣.3̣5̣16̣5̣3̣
6̣1216̣123	.216̣16̣5̣3̣
.123.6̣123	3 3 .16̣5̣3̣.3̣.

Sèlèh 5

.15̣6̣16̣12	1216̣5̣2̣3̣5̣
.15̣6̣16̣12	3216̣5̣2̣3̣5̣
2̣.5̣.2̣.5̣.	2̣.5̣.2̣.5̣.
.3̣5̣6̣16̣12	1216̣5̣6̣15̣
.3̣5̣6̣16̣12	3216̣5̣6̣15̣
5̣15̣6̣16̣12	1216̣5̣6̣15̣
5̣2̣5̣6̣16̣12	16̣5̣3̣5̣2̣3̣5̣
6.6.6.6. 6̣ 6̣ 6̣ 6̣	6.6.6.6. 6̣ 6̣ 6̣ 6̣

Sèlèh 6

1̇.1̇.1̇.1̇. 1 1 1 1	1̇.1̇.1̇.1̇. 1 1 1 1
216̣6̣6̣16̣.	3̣13̣5̣6̣16̣.
3̣5̣6̣12123	23216̣16̣6̣
3̣5̣6̣12123	23216̣16̣.
3̣6̣3̣5̣6̣161	3216̣5̣3̣2̣6̣
66553322	216̣3̣5̣6̣16̣
6̣3̣6̣12123	53216̣5̣3̣6̣

frequent in *sléndro manyurå* or *nem* (or in *pélog barang*, with 1 replaced by 7). The combination can be transposed down for *sléndro sångå*, so that the *bonang panerus* plays *gembyang* 1 against *gembyang* 6 on the *bonang barung.*

- It may play a *sekaran* of its own, from a repertoire much smaller than the repertoire available to the *bonang barung*, resulting in (for example)

  bonang barung

  .1.3.1.3.1.3.1.3 216̣3̣.6̣.1.216̣16̣12

  bonang panerus

  2̣.5̣.2̣.5̣.2̣.5̣.2̣.5̣. 2̣3̣5̣6̣16̣12121 6̣5̣3̣2̣2

Table 3.16 gives a selection of *sekaran* for the *bonang panerus.* These tend to contain more notes than the average for the *bonang barung*, but the difference is not large. They also have a greater tendency to start and finish on off-beats.

Other signals

In the context of *imbal* and *sekaran*, a further type of signal is sometimes used by the *bonang barung.* It is a pattern equal in length to a half-*sekaran.* Just like a *sekaran*, it points to a particular note, namely the next *sèlèh* note. In contrast to usual practice with *sekaran*, however, such patterns are used at the start of the *gåtrå* and then followed by *imbal.* They may be described as *plèsèdan* patterns by analogy with the signals given by the *kenong*, for example.

The treatment is frequently applied to a *gåtrå gantung*, although it serves more generally to signal an important note or an important transition. *Sèlèh* note 2 is the most

15 For *sl 9*. Each overscore represents three notes in the time of four.

16 For *sl 9*. Each overscore represents three notes in the time of four.

common object of this treatment, but patterns exist for other *sèlèh* notes too. They can be notated as follows

sèlèh 2: . 1 6̣ 2̣ 2 . 1 6̣ 2̣ 2 or . 6̣ 1 2̣ 2 . 6̣ 1 2̣ 2
 or . 3̣ 2̣ 2 . 3̣ 2̣ 2
sèlèh 5: . 6̣ 1 5̣ 5 . 6̣ 1 5̣ 5
sèlèh 6: . 2 1 6̣ 6 . 2 1 6̣ 6
sèlèh 1: . 6̣ 5̣ 1̣ 1 . 6̣ 5̣ 1̣ 1 or . 5̣ 2̣ 1̣ 1 . 5̣ 2̣ 1̣ 1

but the notation is not fully accurate. Taking as an example the first pattern given for *sèlèh* 2, the first three notes . 1 6̣ 2̣ are each played fractionally ahead of the beat, leaving a distinct gap before the note 2. This treatment has the effect of emphasising the final 2.

If one of these patterns is repeated, the result equates to a full-length *sekaran*, and examples will be found in the *sekaran* collection or Table 3.13. The note 1 can of course be replaced throughout by 7̣ to suit *pélog barang*. Of the patterns given above, that for *sèlèh* 1 is not usable on a *bonang cacad*.

The patterns shown are used in most *irâmâ*. In *ir IV* the pattern may be padded out:

. 1 6̣ 2̣ 2 . . . . . 1 6̣ 2̣ 2 . . . . etc.

Other patterns can be used in the same way for signalling at the start of a *gâtrâ*. For *sèlèh* 3, not covered in the list above, patterns such as the following are possible:

 1 1
. 6̣ 1 5̣ 3̣ . 5̣ 3̣ . . 6̣ 1 2 3 . 1 . 3

This is a combination of a standard half-*sekaran* and one cycle of *imbal*, linked by a post-*sekaran* transition, so that the note 3 is strongly emphasised throughout.

Single-instrument *imbal*

Imbal by definition involves two instruments, so what happens if the *bonang panerus* player fails to turn up, or just falls asleep?

The *bonang barung* player normally plays the instrument's usual part, although the easy composite pattern 1 6̣ 1 2 1 6̣ 1 2 etc. is another option when the regular pattern would be . 6̣ . 2, or the player might invent another pattern of similar character, or one consisting of only two adjacent notes.

Although *imbal* is clearly a form of cooperation between two *bonang*, it is entirely normal for the *bonang barung* player to proceed as if the other player does not exist, and it is up to the *bonang panerus* player to fit in. When the *bonang barung* plays something like this

6̣ 1 2 3 . 1 . 3 3 6 . 3 . 1 . 3 6̣ 1 2 3 3 1 . 3 . 2 1 6̣ 1 6̣ 1 2

leaving very few gaps for the *bonang panerus* to fill in, the second instrument hardly seems necessary.

Klénangan

An *imbal* treatment for the *bonang barung* and *bonang panerus* has been borrowed from the ceremonial *gamelan cârâbalèn*, where the lower and upper parts are taken by two instruments respectively called *kenut* and *klénang*.

The *imbal* differs from the versions described up to this point in that pairs of notes alternate rather than single notes. The treatment is sometimes applied to the *ompak* of *ktw Subâkastâwâ* and to other *ketawang* with the same *balungan* in the *ompak*, but it can also be used in other contexts and other *pathet*. The remaining elements of this *ompak klénangan* are described under **Multi-instrument *garap***, p. 231.

The *bonang* parts for each *kenongan* of the *ompak* of *ktw Subâkastâwâ* are

balungan
. 1 . 6̣
bonang panerus
. . 1̣ 2̣ . . 1̣ 2̣ . . 1̣ 2̣ . . 1̣ 2̣ . . 1̣ 2̣ . . 1̣ 2̣ . . 1̣ 2̣ . . 1̣ 2̣
bonang barung
5̣ 6̣ . . 5̣ 6̣ . . 5̣ 6̣ . . 5̣ 6̣ . . 5̣ 6̣ . . 5̣ 6̣ . . 5̣ 6̣ . . 5̣ 6̣ . .

balungan
. 1 . 5̣̂
bonang panerus
. . 1̣ 2̣ . . 1̣ 2̣ . . 1̣ 2̣ . . 1̣ 2̣ . . 1̣ 2̣ . . 1̣ 2̣ . . 1̣ . 1̣ . 1̣ .
bonang barung
5̣ 6̣ . . 5̣ 6̣ . . 5̣ 6̣ . . 5̣ 6̣ . . 5̣ 6̣ . . 5̣ 6̣ . . 5̣ 6̣ . 6̣ . 6̣ . 5̣

The pattern shown above ends with a *salahan* leading to the *sèlèh* note 5. In the compositions for the *gamelan cârâbalèn*, a different *salahan* is used

bonang panerus
. . 1̣ 2̣ . . 1̣ 2̣ . . 1̣ 2̣ . . 1̣ 2̣ . . 1̣ 2̣ . . 1̣ 2̣ . . 1̣ . 1̣ . 1̣ .
bonang barung
5̣ 6̣ . . 5̣ 6̣ . . 5̣ 6̣ . . 5̣ 6̣ . . 5̣ 6̣ . . 5̣ 6̣ . . 5̣ 6̣ . 6̣ . 6̣ . 2

or

bonang panerus

. . 2̣1̣ . . 2̣1̣ . . 2̣1̣ . . 2̣1̣ . . 2̣1̣ . . 2̣1̣ . . 1̣ . 1̣ . 1̣2̣

bonang barung

6̣5̣ . . 6̣5̣ . . 6̣5̣ . . 6̣5̣ . . 6̣5̣ . . 6̣5̣ . . 5̣6̣ . 6̣ . 6̣ . .

even though the *sèlèh* note is again 5.

The *klénangan* patterns are also one option for the *bonang* in a *gangsaran*. (In this *bentuk*, not all the other elements of *ompak klénangan* are used.)

The *gamelan cåråbalèn* has a *pélog* tuning,[17] so that the *klénang* notes shown above are within the range of the *bonang panerus*. A *sléndro* equivalent is not possible on a *bonang cacad* because of the 1̣. A full range of *sèlèh* notes can be accommodated by the following set of patterns, none of which cause problems on a *bonang cacad*:

for sèlèh 2, 3 or 6

bonang panerus	. . 5̣6̣ . . 5̣6̣ . . 5̣6̣ . . 5̣6̣
bonang barung	23 . . 23 . . 23 . . 23 . .

or

bonang panerus	. . 3̣2̣ . . 3̣2̣ . . 3̣2̣ . . 3̣2̣
bonang barung	65 . . 65 . . 65 . . 65 . .

Tips & tricks 8
Easy *sekaran*

For the beginner, there are two tasks when learning to play *sekaran* on the *bonang*: firstly remembering which notes to play, and secondly playing them in the right place. The learning process can be eased by starting with the simplest possible *sekaran*. *Sekaran* can be simple in various ways: the use of repetition, contours that are easier to play, and a low time density.

The plainest type of *sekaran* for the *bonang barung* uses sequences of *gembyangan* to the *sèlèh* note, as illustrated by several *sekaran* for *sèlèh* 1 in Table 3.13. Playing the equivalent patterns for other *sèlèh* notes is equally easy. This type of pattern serves to reinforce the idea of the *sekaran* indicating a particular *sèlèh* note.

The next step beyond this is a full *sekaran* of more varied shape but with notes only on the on-beats, i.e. eight notes in the whole *sekaran*.

Players wanting to make things simpler can also choose *sekaran* consisting of two identical halves, or *sekaran* that involve particularly easy hand movements.

for sèlèh 1 or 5

bonang panerus	. . 3̣5̣ . . 3̣5̣ . . 3̣5̣ . . 3̣5̣
bonang barung	12 . . 12 . . 12 . . 12 . .

or

bonang panerus	5̣3̣ . . 5̣3̣ . . 5̣3̣ . . 5̣3̣ . .
bonang barung	. . 21 . . 21 . . 21 . . 21

Those sources that prefer to relate the patterns to *pathet* may prefer the notes 56 on *bonang barung* and 1̣2̣ on *bonang panerus* for both *sl 9* and *pl 6*, and raise the patterns by one note for *sl m* and *pl 7*, of course changing 1 to 7 for the latter.

'Salah gumun'

A special interlocking *garap* on the two *bonang*—yet another form of *imbal*—is often used in *langgam*. There seems to be no established name for this treatment. *Salah gumun* is an alternative name for *gembyung*, and simply describes the size of the intervals used.

When *langgam* are played on a gamelan, the role of this *garap* is to imitate the interlocking patterns played in *kroncong* by two high-pitched plucked lutes (ukulele or similar instruments) which in combination are called *cak-cuk*. The *bonang barung* plays a series of *gembyung* in which one note (not necessarily the higher one, as in the examples below) coincides with the *sèlèh* note, and the *bonang panerus* plays *gembyung* one note higher and twice as frequently, on the off-beats:

balungan

1̇ 2̇ 6 1̇

bonang panerus

2/6̣ . 2/6̣ . 2/6̣ . 2/6̣ . 2/6̣ . 2/6̣ . 2/6̣ . 2/6̣ .

bonang barung

. . . 1̇/5 . . . 1̇/5 . . . 1̇/5 . . . 1̇/5

The *langgam* form is essentially the same as *ketawang*, and its 'home' *iråmå* is *ir II*. *Rangkep* episodes, i.e. at about two-thirds the speed of *ir II*, are also common in *langgam*. The '*salah gumun*' treatment continues at the same time density, as far as possible. With the addition of a *salahan* that the *bonang barung* may use on the last eight beats in either *iråmå*, the same *gåtrå* in *ir II rangkep* may be played as

17 The pots of the *kenut* and *klénang* are larger than those of the *bonang* in regular gamelan, and their absolute pitch is lower.

bonang panerus

2 . 2 . 2 . 2 . 2 . 2 . 2 . 2 . 2 . 2 . 2 . 2 . 2 . 2 . 2 . 2 .
6̣ 6̣ 6̣ 6̣ 6̣ 6̣ 6̣ 6̣ 6̣ 6̣ 6̣ 6̣ 6̣ 6̣ 6̣ 6̣

bonang barung

. . . 1̇ . . . 1̇ . . . 1̇ . . . 1̇ . . . 1̇ . . . 1̇ . 1̇ . 1̇ . 1̇ . 1̇
5 5 5 5 5 5 5 5 5 5

Alternatively, against the same *bonang panerus* part, the *bonang barung* may play its notes two beats earlier, and must then use a different *salahan*. This version is illustrated for *ir II rangkep*:

. 1̇ . . . 1̇ . . . 1̇ . . . 1̇ . . . 1̇ . . . 1̇ . . 1̇ . . 1̇ . . 1̇ .
5 5 5 5 5 5 5 5 5

Although the examples show a single pattern being played for the whole *gåtrå*, separate patterns may be played to each half of the *gåtrå*. Few rules seem to govern this *garap*, but the following notes are possible choices

Sèlèh note	*Bonang barung*	*Bonang panerus*
2̇	6 and 2̇, 2 and 5	1 and 3, 3̣ and 6̣
1̇	5 and 1̇	6̣ and 2
6	3 and 6	5̣ and 1
5	2 and 5	3̣ and 6̣
3	1 and 3, 3 and 6	2̣ and 5̣, 5̣ and 1
2	6̣ and 2 (2 and 5)	1̣ and 3̣ (3̣ and 6̣)
1	1 and 3	2 and 5

where the notes in parentheses are for *bonang cacad*, and 7 replaces 1 in *pélog barang* as usual.

Bonang panembung

The *bonang panembung* is the lowest-pitched member of the family. It is only a regular part of Yogyanese gamelan, and is now rare. As would be expected of a Yogyanese instrument, the *sléndro* version usually has only ten pots.

3.40 *Bonang panembung*

The example shown in Fig. 3.40 is an exception, from a gamelan in Solo. The beaters are a pair of *bindhi* similar in size to those used on the *kenong*, or *kethuk* and *kempyang*.

The part played by the instrument is easily described. If the *balungan* is already in *nibani* form, no working-out is necessary: the instrument simply plays *gembyang* on the notes of the *balungan nibani*. If the *balungan* is in another form, a *nibani* version must be derived from it, using the rules given earlier (p. 31).

Since the instrument always plays in octaves, the range of notes available is effectively reduced to a single octave. The note 2 is treated as adjacent to either 7 or 1; likewise the note 6. The *bonang panembung* can therefore play . 2 . 7 regardless of whether the final note in the *gåtrå* is 7 or 7̣, but may play . 6 . 7; similarly it can play . 2 . 1 to suit 1̣, 1 or 1̇ in the *balungan*, but may also play . 6 . 1. The 12-pot *sléndro* instrument seen in Fig. 3.40 offers some additional possibilities.

The two notes of the *gembyang* may be played together or slightly separated in time, the lower note being played fractionally earlier, and the upper note falling on the beat. The instrument plays the same part in all *iråmå*.

Soft-style decorating instruments

Rebab

Role

The *rebab*—organologically a two-stringed bowed lute—is the melodic leader of the gamelan ensemble in vocal compositions (which are the majority), and *rebab* players are expected to know the repertoire intimately. In a management sense too, the head of an ensemble is often a *rebab* player.

The tonal quality of the *rebab*, when played properly, has the misfortune to resemble the sound produced by novice violinists. As a result, for many *londo* the instrument is an acquired taste that they acquire late if ever. (A visit to Java will usually convince them of the importance of the instrument.) The thin, penetrating, vocal but not loud sound of the *rebab* is in fact exactly what is needed to cut through the texture of the gamelan.

18 Although the instruments using ivory were said to sound better.

Besides the general functions of any melodic leader instrument, signalling *pathet* via *senggrèngan* and *ådå-ngiyah* as well as giving *bukå* and *ngelik* transition signals, the *rebab* has the specific role of guiding the *pesindhèn*—both to keep them up to pitch and to signal when they should switch to *céngkok miring*. The compass of the *rebab* matches that of the female voice, going as high as 5̇.

In *pélog limå* the strings are tuned to 1̣ and 5̣, i.e. a *kempyung* apart. In all other *pathet* they are tuned to 2̣ and 6̣. A gamelan often has separate *rebab* for *sléndro* and *pélog*, distinguishable by the use of different materials (formerly including ivory) for the neck but not in any functional way.[18]

The *rebab* probably reached Java around the time when Islam arrived, but the precise route and date of its entry into the gamelan are unknown.

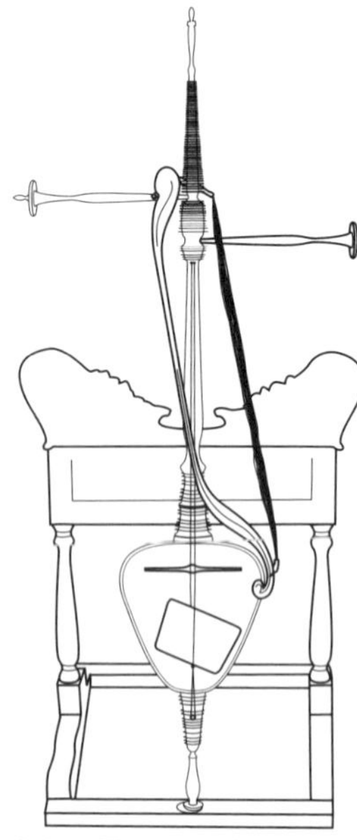

3.41 Traditional stand (*plangkan*) for *rebab*

Construction

The parts of the *rebab* are named in Fig. 3.43. The instrument is mainly of wooden construction, although the 'body' (*menthak*) has in the past been made from a coconut shell. The front of the *menthak* is covered with a thin, fragile skin (*babat*) made from the innards of a water buffalo. The back of the *menthak* is covered by a loose cloth (*dodot*) decorated with gold thread (as in Fig. 3.43), fringes or sequins, for example. Hidden inside the body, a wooden or metal piece (*deder*) separates the *popor ndhuwur* from the *popor ngisor*. Rather than a single piece of wood, several detachable pieces are fitted together to form the length of the instrument. This arrangement allows the *rebab* to be reduced to a manageable size and put in a wooden case to be carried around.

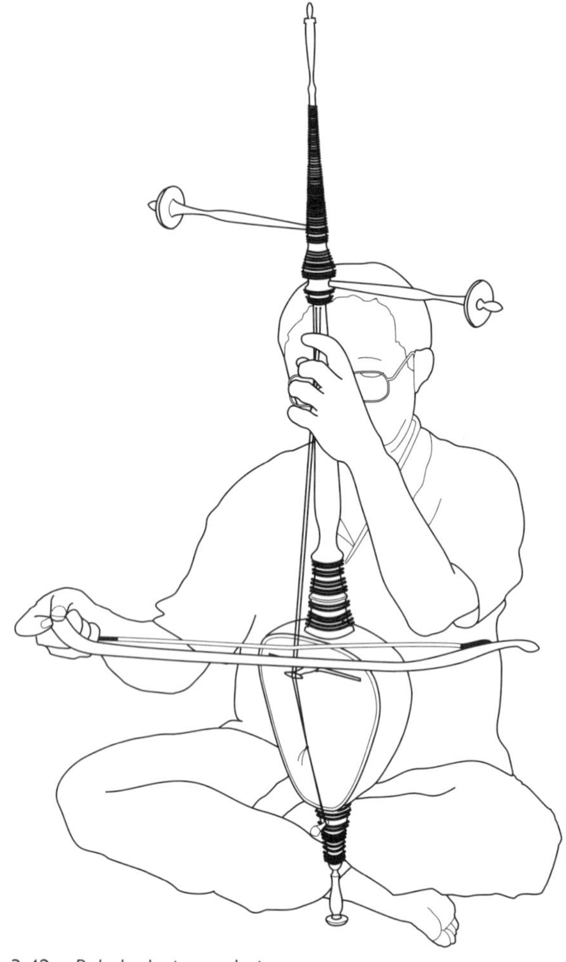

3.42 *Rebab* playing technique

The strings are of brass—strictly one string, since a single length of wire is looped around the *cakilan* at the lower end. At the top end, the strings pass through two small holes (*bremårå*) at the top of the *watangan* and are threaded through the ends of long tuning pegs (*mangol*) that are then inserted into the *irah-irahan*. The playing lengths of the two strings are the same, so that the difference in pitch is due to tension alone. To tune the strings, the *mangol* are grasped by their narrow part—never the *kupingan*, which are purely decorative. By convention, the two *mangol* are turned in opposite directions as viewed from the *kupingan* end. As the two strings are not independent, tuning one can affect the other, and it is difficult to fix the *mangol* in place without changing the tuning. One Westerner has proposed a radical solution to the tuning problems: see **Appendix 5**.

The bridge (*srenten*) is loose and the player places it on the *babat* when first tensioning the strings. The position of the *srenten* can therefore vary slightly, which affects the tuning. Changes to the tension in the string as the instrument is played can cause the *srenten* to fall over. Since so many parts of the instrument are loose, tuning can also be affected if the player changes the pressure on the instrument in almost any way. For these reasons, the *rebab* has been described as conspiring to be unplayable.

Below the *srenten*, the strings are damped in order to avoid unwanted sounds. In Java this is achieved by inserting a fragment of banana leaf between the strings. In the West a piece of tissue paper or cloth serves instead.

The horsehair of the bow is tensioned by part of the right hand (Figs 3.42 and 3.43). As with the instruments of the violin family, players apply rosin to the bow hairs to ensure the right degree of friction with the strings.

If not simply hung on the wall, the *rebab* is usually kept on a stand when not in use. Fig. 3.41 shows a traditional design. The *någå*-based design seen in Fig. 3.44 is popular among *londo* players.

Playing technique

Fig. 3.42 illustrates all the key features of good playing posture:

- the upright position of the instrument, with the top even pointing slightly away from the player,
- a very relaxed left arm and hand posture,
- the left thumb opposite the middle finger, not the index finger,
- the strings stopped by being pulled towards the *watangan*, but nowhere near making contact with it,

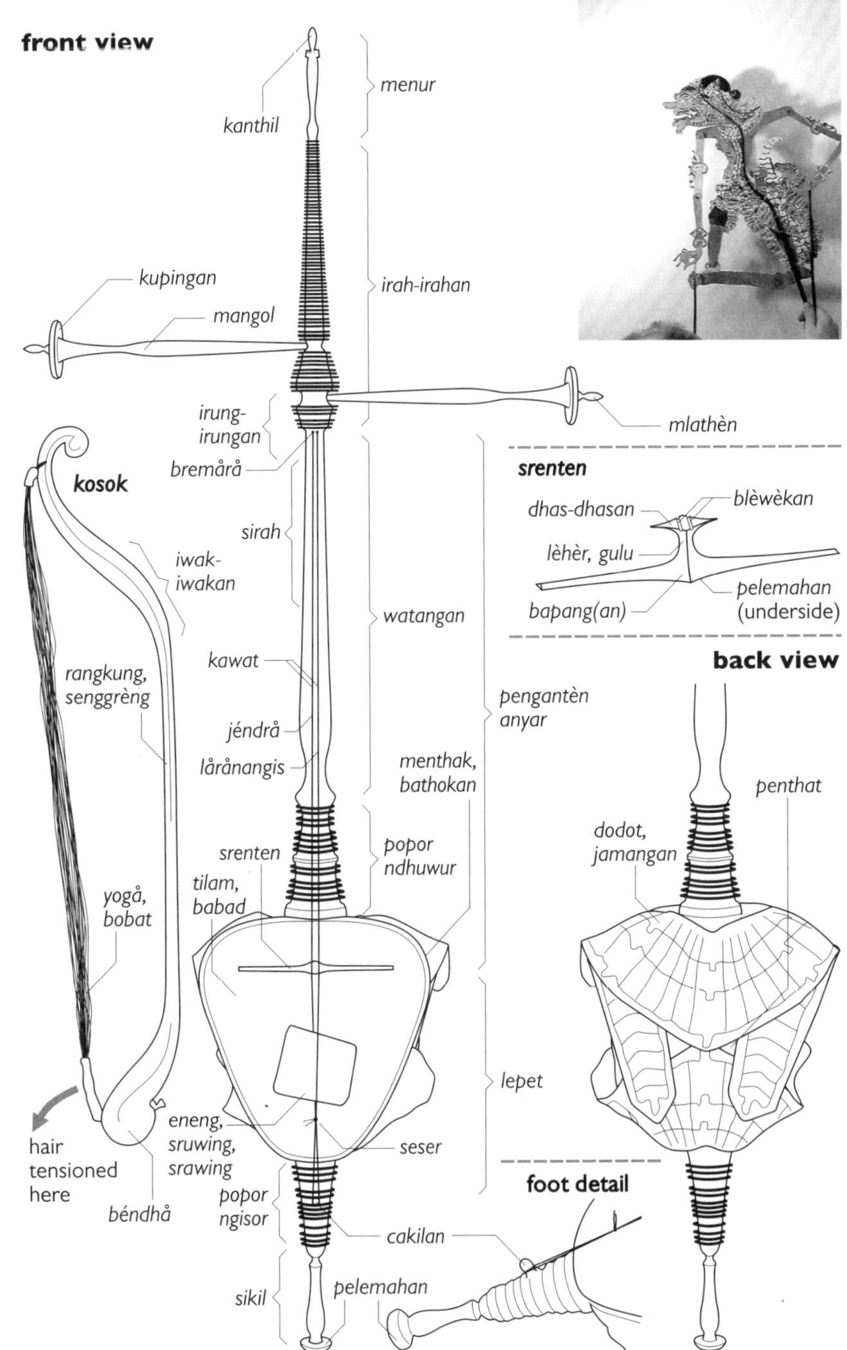

3.43 *Rebab* and *kosok*

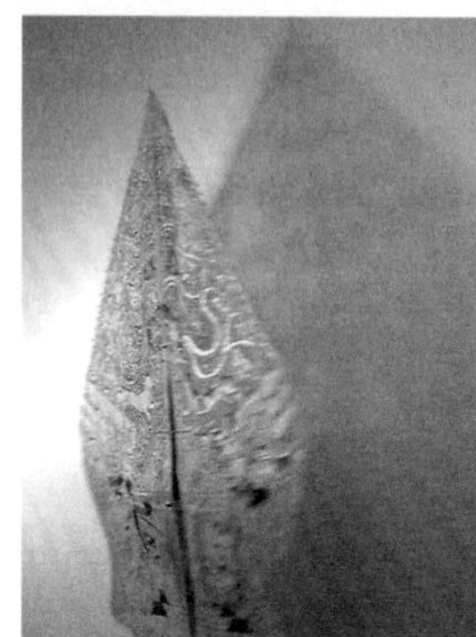

- the instrument rotated by the left hand to determine which string is bowed, instead of the angle of the bow changing (most notes being played on the higher-pitched string, as shown),
- the bow moving parallel to the player's body,
- the bow position only slightly above the *menthak*,
- the 'underhand' bow grip, as for the double bass and the viol family.

As with the violin family, specific left-hand positions (Fig. 3.45) are recognised for the *rebab*, and referred to by Roman numerals that may be written over the notes. Positions I, III and V are used in *sléndro manyurå*; I, II and IV in *sléndro sångå*; all five in *sléndro nem*. The corresponding information for *pélog* can be deduced from the diagram. Fingerings are represented in notation by letter symbols written under the notes (Fig. 3.46, which also shows the names for the fingers). 'Up-bow' strokes (to the left, towards the instrument) and 'down-bow' strokes (to the right, away from the instrument) are shown above the notes as forward slash and backslash respectively.

Strings		Left-hand positions				
Lower	Upper	I	II	III	IV	V
2̣	6̣					
3̣	1	a				
5̣	2	b	a			
6̣	3	c	b	a		
	5	d	c	b	a	
	6	d	d	c	b	a
	1̇		d	d	c	b
	2̇			d	d	c
	3̇				d	d
	5̇					d

watangan

to srenten ↓

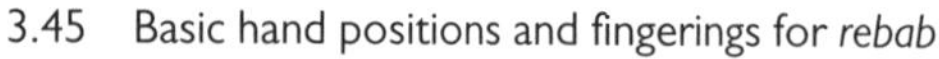

3.45 Basic hand positions and fingerings for *rebab*

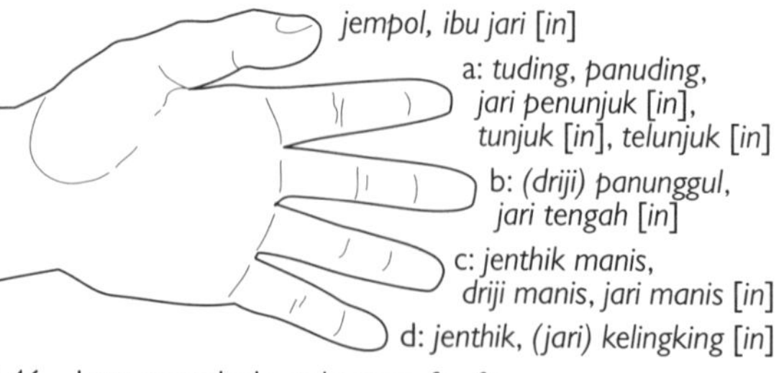

3.46 Letter symbols and names for fingers

3.44 Någå-style stand for *rebab*

The volume level of the *rebab* has only a limited range, but there are still differences of playing style; in particular, the amount of vibrato varies between players.

Garap

In the light of previous remarks about the relationship between the *rebab* part and the inner melody, there is a paradox to be considered. *Céngkok* are supposedly played by decorating instruments as ways of realising the inner melody. If the *rebaban* is very close to the inner melody, can the *rebab* be said to play *céngkok*? The answer depends on how one defines *céngkok*. There is no doubt that the *rebab* has characteristic ways of realising common melodic formulae, as illustrated in Table 3.17 for two named *céngkok* as well as for what might be called a functional pattern, to low 6.

As on other instruments, the realisations of a *céngkok* on the *rebab* take account of the previous and following *gåtrå*, and the degree of variation between one *wilet* and another is consistent with standard practices on other instruments. These points are clear for the low 6 pattern. A version of *puthut gelut* is included in the table to show the presence of 6 in the first half of the *céngkok*: the usual

Table 3.17
Examples of *céngkok* for *rebab* (*sl m*)

'Low 6' pattern

ir II 1 2 1 6̣ 2 1 6̣
ir II 1 2 1 . 6̣ 2 1 . 6̣
ir II 1 2 3 2 16̣21 6̣
ir II 332 2 1 121 6̣
ir II 1 2 1 2 26̣1 1 2 (to *gantung* 2)
ir III 123 6̣ 1 1 2 2 12 1 2 1 . 6̣ 2 1 6̣
ir III 123 216̣ 6̣12 23 12 1 2 1 . 6̣ 2 1 6̣

Ayu kuning (double-density *balungan* 61̇3̇2̇ 6321)

ir III 356 1̇ 2̇ 6 1̇ 2̇ 1̇2̇ 1̇2̇6 3 1 2 1
ir III 6 1̇ 2̇ 6 1̇ 2̇ 1̇2̇ 2̇1̇6 3 1 2 1

Puthut gelut (*balungan* 33 . . 6532)

ir II . 3 566 . 6 6 . 6 . 3 1 2 232 3

balungan mlaku representations of this *céngkok* place the 6 later if they include it at all.

Table 3.18 shows how the realisation of a *céngkok* can vary between *irâmâ*. The variations include the *rebab* 'undershooting' and 'overshooting' the *balungan* notes in the slower *irâmâ*, whereas the versions for *ir I* and *ir II* are very plain. Ornaments—describable as trills—are part of regular *rebab* style but are not shown. The first example in Table 3.18 begins with the most basic bowing style (*kosokan mbalung*), with one note per stroke. *Kosokan milah*, with more than one note per stroke, is seen later in the *gâtrâ*. The special technique of playing 6̣ on the open string together with 2̣ (or 5̣ with 1̣) is called *kosokan ngrecek*, and many other bowing styles have names.

The *rebab* signals the transition to a *lik* section by means of a clear shift of register, although not necessarily with a *céngkok* suggesting a *gantungan* (cf. *bonang* style) even if there is one at the start of the *lik*. For example, the two *gâtrâ* before the *lik* in *ldr Wilujeng sl m* and the first of the *lik* may be played as

```
2 3  1 2  2 3  56 61̇    6  1̇2̇  3̇     1̇2̇  1̇  ⑥
 . 6  6 . 6  .  6  6 . 6
```

where the 5 and 6 are the first evidence that the *ompak* is not going to be repeated. Signals for *lik* transitions may occur earlier or later than this point. In this example, the *rebab* does not pre-announce the *gantungan*.

Fig. 3.47 illustrates graphically[19] a typical relationship between *rebaban* and *balungan*, again using *gd Pujânggâ kt 4 kp mg 8 sl 6* as the example (see the end of Part 2, p. 101). The diagram includes *rebaban* for both occurrences of a phrase of four *gâtrâ*, and for the corresponding places in the *mérong* and *inggah*, although the resulting four lines cannot always be distinguished. The *rebaban* can be described as both undershooting and overshooting the

Table 3.18
Variation of a *céngkok* according to *irâmâ*

ir I (*balungan* 3 5 3 2)
```
/    \    /    \
3    3    3 2  2
```
ir II (*balungan* 3 5 3 2)
```
\ /  \    /    \
123  3    232  2
```
ir III (*balungan* . 3 . 2)
```
\ /  \ /   \ /    \ /  \ /  \     /   \
2 3  5 51̇  6 21  6̣ 6̣  123  3    232  2
```
ir IV (*balungan* . 3 . 2)
```
 /  \   /   \    /     \    /    \
. 1  2   3   5    5 1̇   6    2 1   6̣
/   \     /   \    /    \      /    \
6̣   1 2   3   3    3 2  2 16̣   1 2  2
```

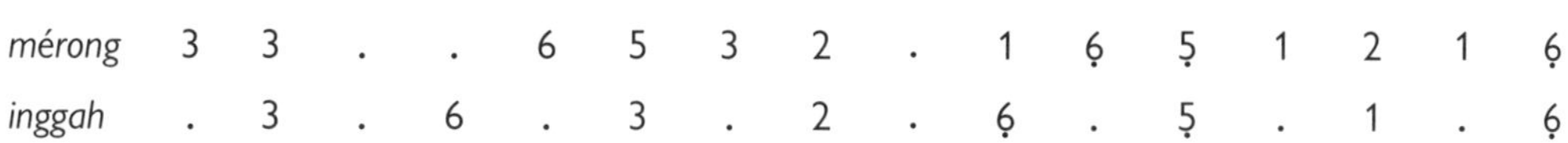

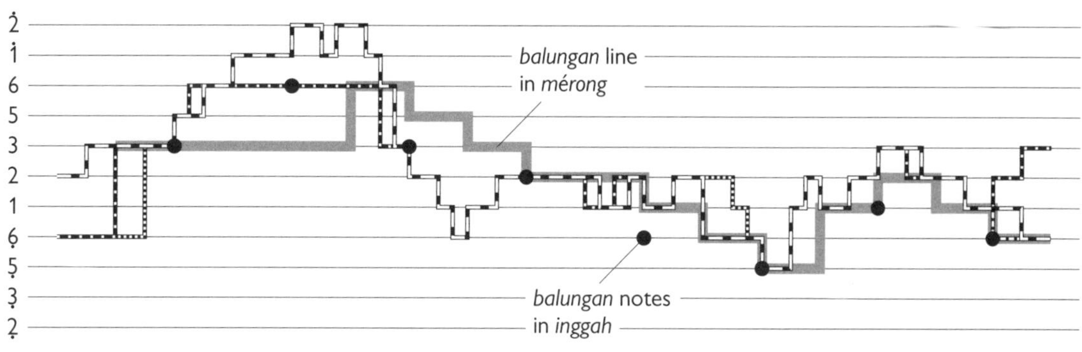

3.47 Example of relationship between *rebaban* and *balungan*

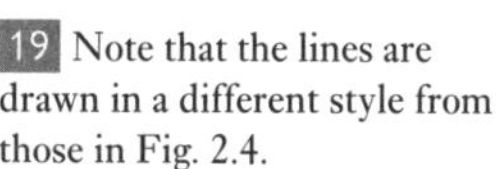

19 Note that the lines are drawn in a different style from those in Fig. 2.4.

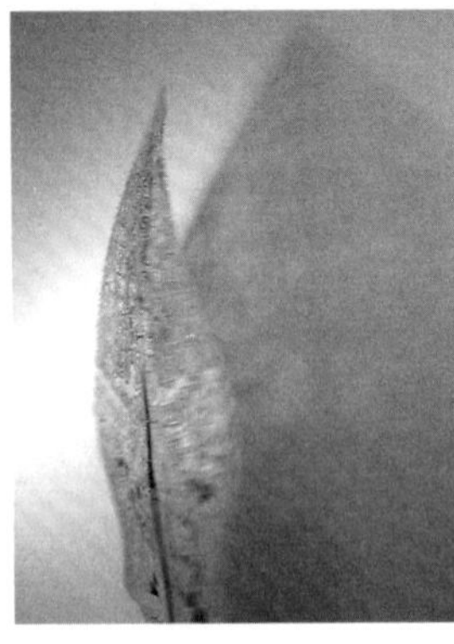

balungan contour, and often as anticipating it. In a few places the various *rebab* lines and the two versions of the *balungan* coincide. Rarely does the *rebaban* trail behind the *balungan*. Fig. 3.47 is a crude example of how the *balungan* represents but simplifies the inner melody, as suggested by the *rebaban*. In the absence of notation for the inner melody—or even of agreement as to what it is in any specific composition—this is about as far as one can go in making general statements about its relationship with the *rebab* part.

Gendèr family

Two members of the *gendèr* family are multi-octave metallophones that function as decorating instruments. The *gendèr barung* and, an octave higher, the *gendèr panerus* are regularly present in modern gamelan. It has been plausibly suggested that the *gendèr panerus* was a later addition, intended to partner the *gendèr barung* as the *bonang panerus* partners the *bonang barung*. However, unlike the two *bonang*, these two *gendèr* never cooperate in a form of joint *garap*. The name *gendèr* by itself implies the *gendèr barung*, which is much the more important of the pair, although (as usual) it tends to play at lower density.

The two instruments have the same form (Figs 3.48 and 3.49), differing only in size. Their compass is also usually the same: the most common compass now, as illustrated, is from 6̤ to 3̇. Older instruments often had fewer notes at one or both ends,[20] and a few modern instruments extend down to 5̤ or up to 5̇.

In *pélog* there are separate instruments for the *bem* and *barang* scales, each with only the basic five notes of its scale. Therefore a double gamelan contains three instruments of each size, all having five notes per octave.

Construction

The *wilah* of the *gendèr* are attached to cords, or strictly one long cord (*pluntur*), suspended between two end-pieces (*dhendhå*) that are attached to a long frame. The *pluntur* are supported at every second *wilah* by *placak/sanggan*, which may or may not be slotted to allow the insertion of the *pluntur*. Besides the form seen in Figs 3.48 and 3.49 (also for the *slenthem* in Fig. 3.26), end-pieces in *kijingan* style are also found. A few instruments in court gamelan have high end-pieces with scrolls (*gelung*); a style more often seen on Balinese instruments.

Bronze is preferred for the *wilah*, but brass is also in common use. Each *wilah* has its own tube resonator, formerly made of bamboo, held loosely in the frame. The *bumbungan* now more often use sheet metal, and their cross-section need not be circular: typically the form could be described as a flattened circle.

The lowest-pitched of these resonators have their tops blocked by *tumbengan*, allowing a shorter length of pipe to be used (see **Pipe resonators** in **Appendix 4**). Before this technique was used, the long pipes made for a rather tall instrument. For the higher-pitched notes, bamboo lengths were cut with nodes in the right places to give the required resonant frequencies. In metal pipes, equivalent nodes are created by inserting metal discs. On tuning methods for all types of resonators, see **Appendix 5**.

Details of the underside of the *wilah* are shown in Fig. 3.50. The reason why it is not practical to switch *wilah* between the *bem* and *barang* scales in the course of a performance can be seen in the complicated method of attaching the *wilah* to the *pluntur* with slivers of wood or bamboo (*sindik*, etc.).

The instruments are played with pairs of beaters (Fig. 3.51) that have a padded ring (*blebet*) encircling a wooden head (*béndhå*). Both their length and the diameter of the *béndhå* are in proportion to the width of the *wilah*: it is said that the length of the handle (*garan*) should span

20 Martopangrawit's collection of *céngkok* for the *gendèr barung* includes variants for instruments without the 3̇.

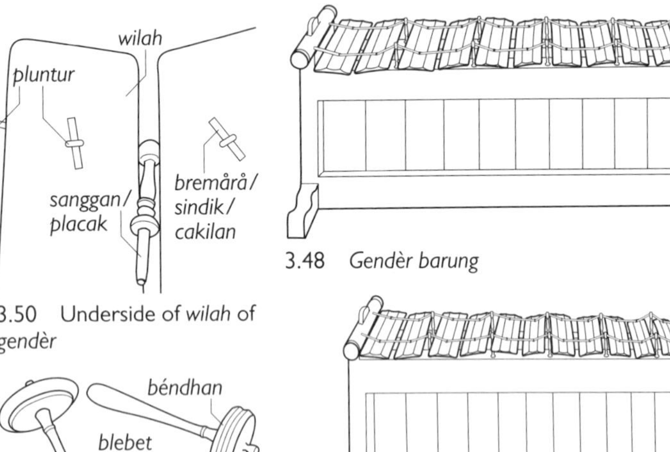

3.50 Underside of *wilah* of gendèr

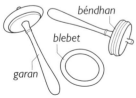

3.48 *Gendèr barung*

3.51 *Gendèr* beater

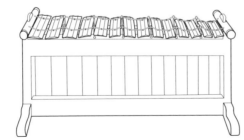

3.49 *Gendèr panerus*

three *wilah*. These considerations relate to the playing and damping techniques.

Playing technique

The playing techniques for both *gendèr* are essentially the same. Each beater is held between the forefinger and middle finger (Fig. 3.52), but other fingers too contribute to the grip during the complex movements of the hands. The player seen in Fig. 3.52 has small hands, whereas another player's index fingers, if fully extended, would touch the heads of the beaters—as would be the situation on the smaller beaters of the *gendèr panerus*.

Damping of notes is a more complex matter on the *gendèr* than on any other instrument—a result of the form usually taken by its *garap*, where the playing of two notes at once is a regular practice (although much less frequent on the *gendèr panerus*), but also of the density of the *céngkok*. Often the damping follows standard practice on the *balungan* instruments, where each new note implies the damping of one previous note (and no more). At other times, two or more notes may be damped at once, e.g. because at the first possible opportunity to damp the earlier note there was no time or else a hand was not in a suitable position. Examples are given under ***Garap*** below.

In Fig. 3.53 the player's right hand is in a position that allows him to damp a note with the heel of the hand. Fig. 3.54 shows various other possible damping techniques. In Fig. 3.54(a) one adjacent note is damped by the left hand. In Fig. 3.54(b) the left hand damps two adjacent notes on the other side. Both these techniques are allowed for either hand, and can be extended to additional notes by the use of the wrist as well as the fingers. Fig. 3.54(c) shows the outstretched thumb damping a note: teachers allow only the right hand to use this technique. The neutral positions of the two hands are somewhat different in practice, as suggested by Fig. 3.53: these relate to the different widths of the *wilah* handled by the two hands.

The perceived elegance of the hand movements, and the resulting attitude to women *gendèr* players, has been mentioned already (p. 16). Aesthetic considerations apart, the movements can also be predicted to be, of all those associated with gamelan playing, among the most likely to cause repetitive strain injury problems.

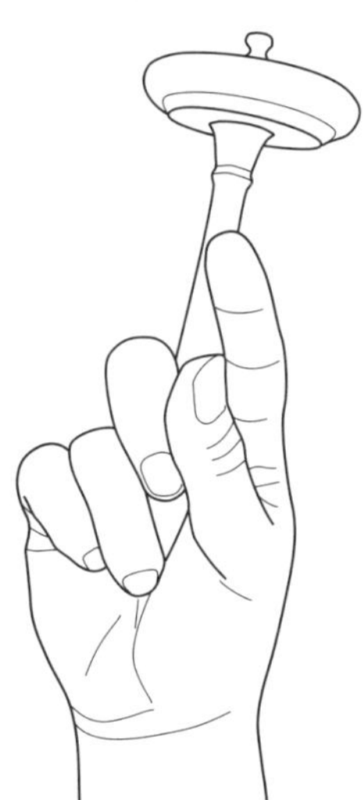

3.52 *Gendèr* beater grip

Gendèr barung

Role

The *gendèr barung* has multiple roles besides decoration. It may give *grambyangan*, provides the *bukå* for specific pieces such as *ktw Subåkaståwå*, and generally acts as the melodic leader of the soft-style ensemble if the *rebab* is absent. It has a special position in *wayang* accompaniment by virtue of the fact that it is hardly ever silent: it

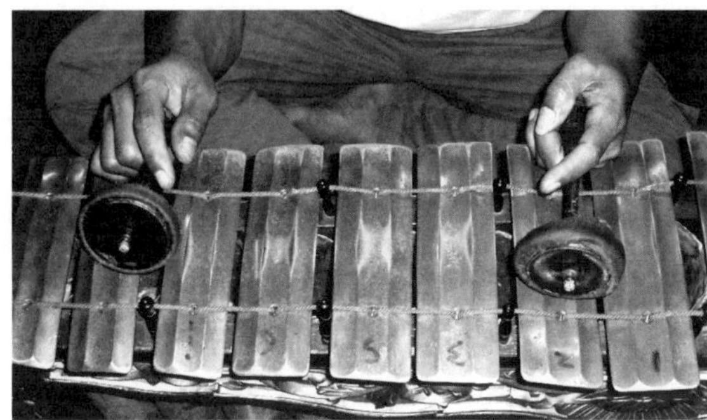

3.53 *Gendèr* playing technique

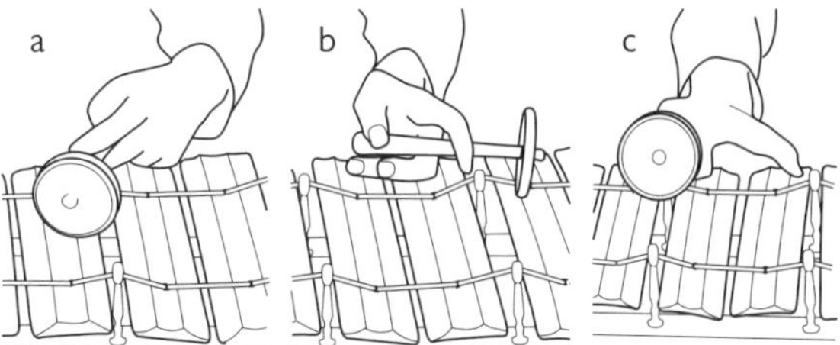

3.54 Further *gendèr* damping techniques

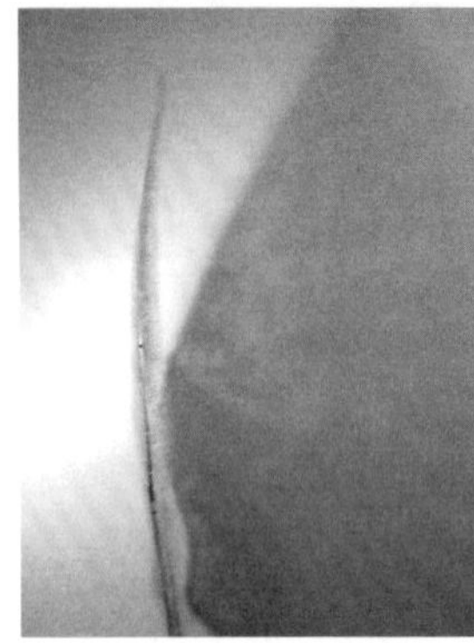

plays not only in instrumental pieces but also in the *sulukan* and *grimingan*. It also supports the singer discreetly in *båwå* and *andhegan* in all performing situations.

In addition, the *gendèr barung* acts as a role model for other decorating instruments; in particular the *gendèr panerus*, *gambang* and *celempung* or *siter*, although it can sometimes influence the *bonang* too. The patterns played by the *gendèr panerus*, *celempung* or *siter*, and (allowing for octave doubling) the *gambang* take a similar form to some of those played by the *gendèr barung*, to the extent that a player might use patterns with basically the same contours for all these instruments without raising many eyebrows. In the case of both *bonang*, although more for the *bonang barung*, it is largely in their *sekaran* that the influence of the *gendèr* is felt.

In common with the other soft-style decorating instruments, the *gendèr barung* may play in all *iråmå* for vocal pieces. It sometimes even enters before the *gong bukå*. It is less likely to play in *ir I* than in slower *iråmå*, but regularly plays during *kébar* and in the editable forms.

Garap

The description here applies mainly to the forms of playing that are regularly heard in *klenèngan*, in which differences between the Solo and Yogya styles are not usually obvious. *Wayang* accompaniment entails additional *garap* styles, showing greater variation between Yogya and Solo. Each city even shows differences between traditional male and female styles of *gendèr* playing for *wayang*.

When formal education in *karawitan* began, teachers used to teach students one *céngkok* per *sèlèh* note, taking *pathet* into account. This approach simplified the student's task, but is no longer considered adequate: the choice of a *céngkok* should be based on the previous *sèlèh* note and other factors as well as the destination. Many of the *céngkok* have names (e.g. as in Table 3.19). Teaching methods vary: some teachers teach the *céngkok* by name, but others do not. Also teachers differ in other ways: some teach realisations of complete pieces, but without giving the necessary explanation of how to adapt the *garap* to other pieces.

Gendèran is notated on two lines separated by a rule, with the right-hand part above. Notes are usually spaced out in order to accommodate occasional half-duration notes, which may or may not be indicated by overscores. *Céngkok* are often divided up to make them easier to read; typically into blocks that correspond to the separate notes of the *balungan*. Examples here deliberately use various styles of notation.

Céngkok are available for *iråmå* from *ir I* to *ir IV*. The following examples are for the first *gåtrå* of *ldr Asmarandånå sl m*; i.e. for 2 1 2 6̣ (or 2 3 2 1 3 2 1 6̣ at double density in *ir III* and *IV*) following *sèlèh* 6̣ at the *gong bukå*:

ir I

5 6	5 1̇	5 6	1̇ 6
1 5̣	6̣ 5̣	6̣ 1	2 6̣

ir II

5 6 5 .	5 6 5 1̇	5 6 5 1̇	5 6 1̇ 6
. . 5̣ 6̣	1 5̣ 6̣ 3̣	. 5̣ 3̣ 5̣	6̣ 1 2 6̣

ir III

. 5 . 6 . 5 . 3	. 6 . 5 . 6 . 3	. 6 . 5 . 6 . 1̇	. 6 . 5 . 6 . 1̇
. . 2 1 6̣ 1 2 .	. . 6̣ 5̣ 3̣ . 3̣ .	. . 6̣ 5̣ 3̣ 5̣ 6̣ .	1 . 6̣ 2 1 6̣ 2 1
. . . 5 . 6 . 1̇	. 5 . 6 . 1̇ . 6	. 5 . 3 . 5 . 1̇	. 5 . 6 . 1̇ . 6
. 2 3 . 3 . 3 .	3 2 1 2 . 2 1 2	. 1 . 6̣ . 5̣ . 3̣	. 5̣ . 5̣ 6̣ 3̣ 5̣ 6̣

ir IV

. 5 . 6 . 5 . 3	. 1̇ . 6 . . . 3	. 1̇ . 6 . . . 3	. 6 . 5 . 6 . 3
. . 1 2 6̣ 1 2 .	6̣ 1 2 1 6̣ 1 2 .	6̣ 1 2 1 6̣ 1 2 .	6̣ . 6̣ 5̣ 3̣ . 3̣ .
. 6 . 5 . 6 . 1̇	. 6 . 1̇ . 6 . 3	. 6 . 5 . 6 . 1̇	. 6 . 5 . 6 . 1̇
6̣ . 5̣ 6̣ 3̣ 5̣ 6̣ .	2 . 1 2 6̣ 1 2 .	6̣ . 5̣ 6̣ 3̣ 5̣ 6̣ .	1 . 6̣ 2 1 6̣ 2 1
. . . 5 . 6 . 1̇	. . . 6 . . . 1̇	. . . 6 . . . 1̇	. 5 . 6 . 1̇ . 6
. 2 3 . 3 . 3 .	3 2 1 2 6̣ 1 2 .	3 2 1 2 6̣ 1 2 .	3 2 1 2 . 2 1 2
. 5 . 3 . 5 . 3	. 5 . 6 . 5 . 1̇	. 5 . 6 . 5 . 1̇	. 5 . 6 . 1̇ . 6
. 1 . 6̣ . 5̣ . 6̣	. 1 . 5̣ . 6̣ . 3̣	. . . 5̣ . 3̣ . 5̣	. 6̣ . 1 6̣ 2 1 6̣

These examples illustrate various general features of many *céngkok* for the *gendèr barung*. Most of the time there are clearly two 'voices', of which the lower responds to the shape of the inner melody or the *balungan*. If the *céngkok* has a vocal origin (see Part 2), it is the lower part that contains the vocal element. Most of the upper parts in the examples given have a common style, dividing into four-note blocks of the form ABAC—a pattern sometimes called *munggangan* after the ceremonial *gamelan munggang* (but also compare the use of *pancer* notes by some *balungan* instruments). The ABAC pattern is not necessarily played in an even rhythm: it may be distorted by a half-beat delay to one or more notes, e.g. $6\ \overline{.\,5\,6}\ \dot{1}$ (see below), or notes may be omitted from the pattern.

Besides their names, *céngkok* are distinguished by their length. Of the set of examples above, the first two

Table 3.19
Abbreviations for names of céngkok for gendèr

Initial letter(s)			
aj	*åjå ngono*	kk	*kuthuk kuning*
ak	*ayu kuning*	nd	*nduduk*
ay	*ayo-ayo*	ob	*ora butuh*
dl, dlb	*duololo besar*	pg	*puthut gelut*
dlk, dlc	*dualolo kecil*	pip	*pipilan*
dd, db	*dhebyang-dhebyung*	pl	*plèsèdan*
ee	*elå-elå*	ps	*puthut semèdi*
g, gt	*gantung*	ram	*rambatan*
gdk	*gendhuk kuning*	ru	*rujak-rujakan*
jk	*jarik/jarit kawung*	s	*sèlèh*
jw	*jawåtå*	tin	*tinandur*
kac, kc	*kacaryan*	tum, tm	*tumurun*
Optional final letter (= ending of *céngkok*)			
g, b, gb	*gembyang*	k, p, kp	*kempyung*

are both variants of *kuthuk kuning gembyang*, described as *lampah* 2 and *lampah* 4 (using the terminology of Table 3.6). *Céngkok* can contain half-duration notes, as in some of the examples below, and the notation on p. 193 for *ldr Wilujeng sl m*[21] even includes a few quarter-duration notes. When these higher-density passages become more frequent, as in the *ir III* and *ir IV* examples above, the *céngkok* are written with extra *pin* and classified as *lampah* 8—strictly speaking, only a difference of notation.[22]

Also seen in the *ir IV* example is a different style of *céngkok*, called *pipilan*, in which the two hands divide a single melodic line between them. A longer example of the style can be seen in a 'special *céngkok*', *puthut semèdi* (the second half of *puthut gelut*) to *sèlèh* 2 from 6̣ in *sl m*:

. 1̇ . . 6 1̇ 2̇ 3̇   2̇ . 3̇ 2̇ . 1̇ . .   1̇ . 1̇ . . 1̇ . 6   3 . 3 . 5 3 5 6
3 . 3 5 . . . .   . 1̇ . . 6 . 6 3   . 6 . 3 5 . 5 .   . 2 . 6̣ 1 . 1 2

This example is typical in having two-note 'chords' only at the end.

As might be expected, *céngkok* are subject to much variation in practice. The following examples, selected from a wide range of sources, are mostly versions of *tumurun*, but the first two are *kuthuk kuning gembyang*. All are for *ir II* and a *sèlèh* 6̣ following a *sèlèh* 2 in *sléndro manyurå*, with 1 at the mid-point of the *gåtrå*, e.g. for . 1 2 6̣ or . 1 . 6̣:

5 6 5 .   5 6 5 1̇   5 6 5 1̇   5 6 1̇ 6
. . 5̣ 6̣   1 . 1 .   . 5̣ 3̣ 5̣   6̣ 1 2 6̣

5 6 5 .   5 6 5 1̇   5 6 5 1̇   5 6 1̇ 6
. . 5̣ 6̣   1 5̣ 6̣ 3̣   . 5̣ 3̣ 5̣   6̣ 1 2 6̣

5 3 5 3   5 6 5 1̇   5 6 5 1̇   5 6 1̇ 6
1 6̣ 5̣ 6̣   1 5̣ 6̣ 3̣   . 5̣ 3̣ 5̣   6̣ 1 2 6̣

5 3 5 1̇   5 6 5 1̇   5 6 5 1̇   5 3 5 6
1 6̣ 1 .   5̣ . 5̣ 3̣   . 5̣ 3̣ 5̣   6̣ 6̣ 6̣ 6̣

5 3 5 .3   5 6 5 1̇   5 6 1̇ .   1̇ 2̇ 1̇ 6
.1 6̣ 1 .   . 5̣ 6̣5̣3̣   . 5̣ 3̣ 5̣   6̣ 1 2 6̣

5 1̇ 5 .   5 6 5 3   5 1̇ 5 .   5 6 1̇ 6
. 1 .6̣ 5̣   3̣ 5̣ 3̣2̣3̣   . 1 . 5̣   6̣ 3̣5̣ .5̣6̣

5 .3 5 1̇   5 6 5 3   5 6 5 1̇   5 6 1̇ 6
.1 6̣ 1 .   . 5̣ 6̣5̣3̣   . 5̣ 3̣ 5̣   6̣ 1 21 6̣

5 3 5 .3   5 6 5 1̇   . 6 . 1̇   . 6 1̇ 6
. . .1 6̣   1 5̣ 6̣ 3̣   . 5̣ 3̣ 5̣   6̣ 3̣ 5̣ 6̣

5 6 5 3   56 .56 1̇   5 6 5 1̇   5 6 1̇ 6
.1 26̣ 12 .   . 3 321   . 5̣ 3̣ 5̣   6̣ 16̣ 21 6̣

5 3 5 .3   5 6 5 1̇   5 6 5 1̇   5 6 1̇ 6
. . .1 6̣   1 5̣ 6̣ 3̣   . 1 . 5̣   6̣ 3̣ 5̣ 6̣

Written into some of the above are extra notes (cf. *nyampar* notes on the *saron*) such as an expert player might insert into the basic *céngkok* at will. However, these examples are all still considered to be *lampah* 4.

Triplet rhythms sometimes occur; for example, three notes in the time of two may be played in the middle of this *céngkok* (*lampah* 4, shown in part) instead of the regular version:

1̇ 6 1̇ 2̇1̇ .1̇2̇ 2̇2̇2̇ → 1̇ 6 1̇ 2̇1̇1̇2̇ 2̇2̇2̇
1 6̣ 5̣ 26̣ .52 . .   → 1 6̣ 5̣ 26̣5̣2 . .

The occurrence of 5 at the start of the examples above is significant. The preceding *céngkok* will often be *jarit kawung*, ending with a *kempyung* (6 against the *sèlèh* note 2). The 5 in these examples represents a logical sequel to the 6 at the end of the previous *gåtrå*, and the 1 in the left-hand part of some variants does the same for the preceding 2. For a *sèlèh* 3 in the previous *gåtrå*, the examples above would typically change, although the second half of the *céngkok* could be exactly the same, e.g.

6 5 6 2̇   6 5 6 1̇   5 6 5 1̇   5 6 1̇ 6
2 1 2 .   1 2 3 1   . 5̣ 3̣ 5̣   6̣ 1 2 6̣

which can be interpreted as *dua lolo* followed by *tumurun*, each in *lampah* 2 form.

21 Which can be adapted for *pélog barang* by the usual method of replacing 1 by 7̣, etc.

22 *Lampah* 4 and *lampah* 8 *céngkok* may be described as *gendèran låmbå* and *gendèran rangkep* respectively. The repetitions seen in the left-hand part of *gendèran rangkep* are sometimes called *umbaran*.

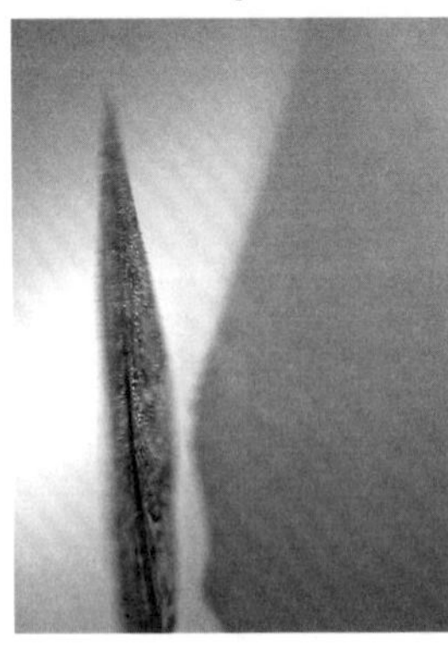

Preceded by a *sèlèh* note that was a long way from 2, the change would be greater. The following is a version of *ayo-ayo* that could be used after a *sèlèh* 2̣

5 6 5 .   5 6 5 2   5 . 5 .   5 . 5 6
. . 2̣ 3̣   5̣ 6̣ 1 .   . 3 2 1   6̣ 1 5̣ 6̣

where the *munggangan* is much the same as for *tumurun*, but the left-hand part starts somewhat lower.

However, this last *céngkok*, as is often the case, does not indicate the register of the inner melody or the *balungan* very clearly. In spite of its two-octave range, the *gendèr* therefore gives less obvious information on the register than the *rebab*, *pesindhèn* and *gambang* do. An example of this can be seen in the complete *gendèran* for *ldr Wilujeng* (opposite), where the last *gåtrå* of the *ompak* is realised with different *céngkok* according to whether the transition to the *ngelik* is taken. *Nduduk* (for the transition) and *tumurun* start, of course, from the same point, but they also both end with a *gembyang* 6̣ + 6. There is surprisingly little difference in pitch between the two *céngkok*, and *tumurun* actually lies higher until the middle of the *céngkok* (in this version). *Nduduk* does then rise one note higher, to 3̇, but this note would not be available on all *gendèr*.

In general these *céngkok* do contain conventional signals that convey, to the expert player, information about the contour of the inner melody—not merely about the *sèlèh* points. The *gendèr* player ideally takes account of the whole contour, choosing a *céngkok* compatible with the *rebab* part at its mid-point and perhaps elsewhere. There are therefore reasons other than simple personal preference for choosing one variant of a *céngkok* over another.

All the examples here confirm that a *céngkok* can end with either a *kempyung* or a *gembyang* interval between the two final notes. *Pathet* characteristics can be seen in this area. A *pin* in the left-hand part represents, as usual, a continuation of the previous note, which becomes part of the closing *kempyung* or *gembyang*. Some *céngkok* exist in high-lying and low-lying variants called respectively *cilik/alit* or *kecil* and *gedhé/ageng* or *besar*.

The great majority of *céngkok* are no longer than the *ir II* examples above. The examples above for *ir III* and *ir IV* therefore contain more than one identifiable *céngkok*. The *ir III* example has *dua lolo ageng* leading to the *sèlèh* 1 of 2 3 2 1, and then *tumurun* to reach the *sèlèh* 6̣ of 3 2 1 6̣. The *ir IV* example uses a stretched version of *dua lolo* to reach 3 at the mid-point of 2 3 2 1, and *jawåtå* for *sèlèh* 1; then a *rangkep* version of *jarit kawung* to the mid-point of 3 2 1 6̣, and *tumurun* to *sèlèh* 6̣.

The *rangkep* or stretched *céngkok* for *ir IV* are made by repeating fragments of a *lampah* 4 or *lampah* 8 *céngkok* to fill out the additional space. This procedure is routine in *céngkok* for the *gendèr panerus*: see below.

As shown opposite, it is also possible for halves of established *céngkok* to be used. A *gåtrå* may be realised with halves of two *céngkok* because of a special situation such as a short *gantungan* (= *balungan kembar*). The first few *gåtrå* of a piece, before the home *iråmå* has been reached, are often realised with unusual *céngkok*.

A large class of *céngkok* exists for realising *gantungan*. The *gåtrå* 3 3 . . in *ldr Wilujeng sl m* is part of the *puthut gelut* contour rather than representing a *gantungan* in the inner melody, and a special *céngkok* (*céngkok khusus*) is used to realise this and the following *gåtrå*. Later, two *gåtrå gantung* 6 in the *lik* are played with (different) *céngkok gantungan*, showing that either hand in the *gendèran* may emphasise the *gantung* note. The short *gantungan* in the penultimate *gåtrå* of the *lik* is realised with a half-length *céngkok gantungan*.

Some special *céngkok*, e.g. those whose names come from a contour in the *balungan* or inner melody rather

6 5 6 3   6 5 6 1̇
. 6̣ 5̣3̣ . 3̣ .   . 6̣ 5̣3̣ 5̣6̣ .

notes damped: 3̣ 6̣ 5̣ ; 3̣

and

. 2̇ . 1̇ . 2̇   . 1̇ 6 5
12 . 6̣ 16̣ 12   . 1 6̣5̣ . 5̣ .

notes damped: 5̣ 6̣ 1 2

and

notes damped: 2̇ 5 6 1̇

. 6 1̇6 . 5   2̇ . 6 1̇ 5
5 . 23 . 2   . 2 6̣1 5̣6̣1

3.55 Damping patterns for selected notes

than their realisation on the *gendèr*, depart from the styles described so far. For one version of *ayu kuning* in *sléndro manyurå*, the first half of the formula (6 1̇ 3̇ 2̇, double density in *ir III*) is realised very sparsely

```
. . . . . . . 6   . . . . . . . 1̇   . . . . . . . 3̇   . . . . . . . 2̇
. . . . . 2 1 6̣   . . . . . 5̣ 6̣ 1   . . . . . 1 2 3   . . . . . 6̣ 1 2
```

and this seems to be the inspiration behind the *bonang* treatment of *ayu kuning* for *ir III* shown in Table 3.14.

Repeated notes, whether on the beat (6̣ 6̣ 6̣ 6̣) or on the half-beat (2̣3̣ .3̣ .3̣ .3̣), are each damped before the next is played, as on *balungan* instruments. The general pattern, of damping the previous note as each new note is

Gendèran for Idr Wilujeng sl m

Bukå

```
balungan  .  1  3  2  6̣  1  2  3
gendèr    .  5  1̇  6  3  5  6  1̇
          .  1  3  2  6̣  1  2  3
          1  1  3  2  .  1  2  (6)
          6  . 6 1̇  6 5 3 5 1̇ 5 6 1̇ 6
          .  1  3  2 1 6̣ 5̣ 3̣ 5̣ 5̣ 6̣ .
```

Ompak

```
ir I      2   1   2   3   2   1   2   6̣
kkk +     2̇ 1̇ 2̇ 1̇ 2̇ 3̇ 2̇ 1̇ 5 3 5 1̇ 5 6 1̇ 6
tumg      2 6̣ 2 1 2 5 6 3 1 6̣ 5̣ 3̣ 5̣ 5̣ 6̣ .
            3   3   .   .
pgg^a     5 1̇ 5 3 5 6 1̇ 6 → *
          3̣ 3̣ 3̣ . 5̣ 5̣ 6̣ .
ir II [ [       2       1       2       3
dl +      2̇ 3̇ .2̇ .1̇2̇ 3̇ 2̇ 1̇ 2̇ 3̇ 2̇ 6 2̇ 3̇ 2̇ 1̇
kkk       2 1 6̣ 2 1 6̣ 2 1 2 3 5 . 2 5 6 3
                2       1       2       6̣
tumg      6 5 6 2̇ 6 5 6 1̇ 5 6 5 1̇ 5 6 1̇ 6
          2 1 2 . 1 2 3 1 . 5̣ 3̣ 5̣ 6̣ 1 2 6̣
                3       3       .       .
pgg^a     5 1̇ 5 3 6 5 6 1̇ 5 6 5 1̇ 5 6 1̇ 6
          3̣ 3̣ 3̣ . . 1 6̣ 3 . 1 . 3 . 1 2 6̣
     *          6       5       3       2
pgk^b     1̇ 2̇ 1̇ 6 1̇ 2̇ 1̇ 3̇ 1̇ 2̇ 1̇ 3̇ 1̇ 2̇ 1̇ 6
          . . 1 2 3 1 2 6̣ . 1 6̣ 1 2 1 6̣1.2
                5       6       5       3
kkk       2 3 2 . 2 3 2 6 2̇ 1̇ 2̇ .1̇2̇ 3̇ 2̇ 1̇
          . . 2 3 5 3 5 . . . .65 3 5 6 3
                2       1       2       6̣
tumg      6 5 6 2̇ 6 5 6 1̇ 5 6 5 1̇ 5 6 1̇ 6
          2 1 2 . 1 2 3 1 . 5̣ 3̣ 5̣ 6̣ 1 2 6̣
                2       1       2       3
dl +      2̇ 3̇ .2̇ .1̇2̇ 3̇ 2̇ 1̇ 2̇ 3̇ 2̇ 6 2̇ 3̇ 2̇ 1̇ → †
kkk       2 1 6̣ 2 1 6̣ 2 1 2 3 5 . 2 5 6 3
```

```
                2       1       2       6̣ ]
tumg      6 5 6 2̇ 6 5 6 1̇ 5 6 5 1̇ 5 6 1̇ 6
          2 1 2 . 1 2 3 1 . 5̣ 3̣ 5̣ 6̣ 1 2 6̣
     †          2̇       1̇       2̇       (6)
ndg       5 6 1̇ 6 1̇ 6 1̇ 2̇ 3̇ . 2̇ . 3̇ 2̇ 1̇ 6
          .21 6̣ . 1 6̣ 1 2 3 1 2 123 2 1 6̣
```

Ngelik

```
                .       .       6       .
gg        1̇ .61̇ 6 .1̇ .61̇ 6 .1̇. 1̇ 2̇ .1̇ .61̇ 6
          . . . 3̣.56̣ 6̣ 6̣ . 3̣ 5̣ 3̣ 5̣ 6̣ 3̣ 5̣ 6̣
                1̇       5       1̇       6
ndg^c     1̇ 1̇ . 2̇ 1̇ .61̇ 2̇ 3̇ . 2̇ . 3̇ 2̇ 1̇ 6
          . 1 6̣ 1 2 3 5 2 3 1 2 123 2 1 6̣
                3       5       6       1̇
dlkg      2̇ 1̇ 2̇ 6 2̇ 3̇ 2̇ 1̇ 6 5 6 2̇ 6 1̇ 2̇ 1̇
          2 2 2 . 6̣ 1 2 3 2 1 2 . .32 1 .
                6       5       3       2
jkk       6 5 6 1̇ 5 6 1̇ 6 1̇ 2̇ 1̇ 3̇ 1̇ 2̇ 1̇ 6
          . 2 6̣ 3 . 1 2 6̣ . 1 6̣ 1 2 1 6̣1.2
                6       6       .       .
gg        . . 1̇ 6 .1̇ .61̇ 6 .1̇ .61̇ 2̇ .1̇ .61̇ 6
          6̣ 6̣ 6̣ 3̣.56̣ 6̣ 6̣ . 3̣ 5̣ 3̣ 5̣ 6̣ 3̣ 5̣ 6̣
                1̇       5̇       1̇       6
ndg^c     1̇ 1̇ . 2̇ 1̇ .61̇ 2̇ 3̇ . 2̇ . 3̇ 2̇ 1̇ 6
          . 1 6̣ 1 2 3 5 2 3 1 2 123 2 1 6̣
                1̇       1̇       3       2
gg +      1̇ . 2̇ 1̇ . . 2̇ 1̇ 6 5 6 1̇ 6 .61̇ 6 → ‡
jkk       3̣ 1 . .6̣1 1 1 . . 2 6̣ 3 .23 5 2
                3       1       2       (6̣) ]
tumg^d    5 3 5 3 5 6 5 1̇ 5 6 5 1̇ 5 6 1̇ 6
          1 6̣ 5̣ 6̣ 1 5̣ 6̣ 3̣ . 5̣ 3̣ 5̣ 6̣ 1 2 6̣
```

a. First half. b. Second half, also = kkk. c. *Nduduk cilik*.
d. For *suwuk*, last notes in left-hand part may be 2̣ 1̣ 6̣

played—or sometimes (by convention) before the next note—is varied when necessary (Fig. 3.55).

These examples also illustrate a more general tendency to damp two or more short-duration notes at once. Occasionally notes are left undamped, but usually only where they 'harmonise' with later notes.

Gendèr panerus

Role

Like the *bonang panerus*, the *gendèr panerus* is not played by itself when its senior partner is not being played.

The absence of the *gendèr panerus* from the instruments that accompany *sulukan* appears to be evidence both for its recent origin and for its relatively low status. While not easy to play, in terms of the number of notes per second, the instrument also does not draw attention to itself.

Although the compass of the *gendèr panerus* matches that of the *gendèr barung*, its lowest notes are rarely used.

Garap

The standard density of *céngkok* for the *gendèr panerus* matches the higher density of those for the *gendèr barung*, and is therefore *lampah 8* in *ir II*. Half-duration notes occur occasionally, but much less often than in *lampah* 4 *céngkok* for the *gendèr barung*.

Notation for the *gendèr panerus* follows the layout of *gendèr barung* notation.

In style the *céngkok* are of the *pipilan* type, with 'chords' usually only at the end of the *céngkok*. Often one element is played three times, then a different element at the end. For example, the following could be played in *sl m* for the *gåtrå* 3 2 1 6̣ after *sèlèh* 1 in *ir II*:

.3...356 .3...356 .3...356 66.53.56
2.212... 2.212... 2.212... ..2..126̣

Because of the repetition of elements, the *céngkok* often does not conform to the contour of the *balungan* or the inner melody, but only to the *sèlèh* note. In addition the *céngkok* may be used for different *sèlèh* notes—2 or 6 in this case, which are a *kempyung* apart.

The repetitions are not always exact, e.g. in this realisation of the same *gåtrå* in *ir III*

.3...356.56.561̇6.3...356535..356
6̣.6̣12...3..3......212......12...

.3...353.561̇6.61̇.3...3565.535.56
2.212...3....32.6̣.6̣12....2...216̣

with effectively two *céngkok*, the second corresponding to the previous example: compare the number of coincidences or *kempyung* relative to the *balungan*.

Simultaneous playing and damping (called *cecegan* or related terms) is a feature of the right-hand parts in *céngkok* for the *gendèr panerus*. The solidus indicates damping in this example:

.1̇.1̸̇.1̸̇.353.6.1̇.6.3.3̸.3561̇6.6̸.1̇2̇6
2.216̣12...216̣.6̣.6̣.6̣12.....532.2.

Otherwise damping follows *gendèr barung* practice.

The various *céngkok* illustrated above could be considered crude by comparison with those for the *gendèr barung*. (All are for *sléndro manyurå*, and are adapted as

Responding to *pathet*

Reminder: the response to *pathet* on all the soft-style decorating instruments is basically as described under ***Pathet*** in Part 2. Many *céngkok* for *sléndro manyurå* go down one note for *pathet sångå*, although some *céngkok* are confined to one *pathet*. Special *céngkok* may be available for *sléndro nem*, although typically only in the lower register.

In *pélog barang*, some players will simply use *céngkok* for *sléndro manyurå*, but a more sophisticated approach is to examine the piece to find out which of the *pathet* in *sléndro* it most closely relates to. In *pélog limå* and *pélog nem* a mixture of *céngkok* for *sléndro manyurå* and *sléndro sångå* is usually needed. *Pélog limå* is more like *sléndro sångå*, and thus less likely to need a mixture.

As neither *gendèr barung* in *pélog* has the note 4, *sèlèh* 4 must be treated as 3 or 5, according to the scale. The same applies to the *gendèr panerus*, *gambang* and *siter* family.

Sèlèh 7 in *pélog bem* and *sèlèh* 1 in *pélog barang* oblige the player to decide whether to switch to the other *pélog* instrument or (for the *gambang* only) to switch the *wilah*. Especially for the *siter* family in this situation, unless there is an instrument available already tuned to the other *pélog* scale, the player must either stop playing if a change of *pathet* has clearly occurred, or else play a normal *céngkok* to a different *sèlèh* note.

The *suling* and *rebab* both have greater freedom to follow the *balungan* or inner melody closely.

usual for other *pathet*.) These *céngkok* are treated as generic, and do not go by the names applied to *céngkok* for the *gendèr barung*. However, a *céngkok* may borrow the name of a *céngkok* for the *gendèr barung* that has the equivalent function, without copying its shape: for example, a *céngkok* ending on 2 in *sl m* may be called *jarit kawung*. There are also special-purpose *céngkok*: for signalling a *lik* transition, for *gantungan*, and for certain named contours such as *puthut gelut*.

Gambang

Construction

The *gambang* is a xylophone. The qualifier *kayu* (= wood) can normally be omitted because the *gambang gångså* is such a rarity. A typical range exceeds three octaves, equivalent to the combination of the *gendèr barung* and the *gendèr panerus*, possibly with additional notes above and/or below, e.g. from 6̣ to 5̈.

The *wilah* of the *gambang* are mounted on a wooden frame of *kijingan* form (Fig. 3.56), which functions as an untuned trough resonator. The *wilah* are retained by thick wire *placak*, but the details differ slightly from those on the other *wilah* instruments: one end of each *wilah* is threaded over a *placak*, but the other end sits between two *placak* (Fig. 3.57).

Various species of timber are or have been used for the *wilah* (see **Appendix 5**). On the effect of atmospheric conditions on the tuning of the instrument, see **Appendix 4**. As the same material is used for all the *wilah*, inevitably the tonal quality at the extreme ends of the range is noticeably inferior (see **Appendix 4** again)—especially at the top end, where the cross-section of the *wilah* becomes nearly square, giving very little resonance.

Like the *gendèr* and *siter* families, the *gambang* has five notes per octave (Figs 3.1 and 3.2). As the *wilah* can be swapped so easily, it is not essential to have separate instruments for the *pélog bem* and *pélog barang* scales, so *gambang* in *pélog* are usually supplied with interchangeable *wilah* for 7 and 1. Some gamelan do have two instruments in *pélog*.

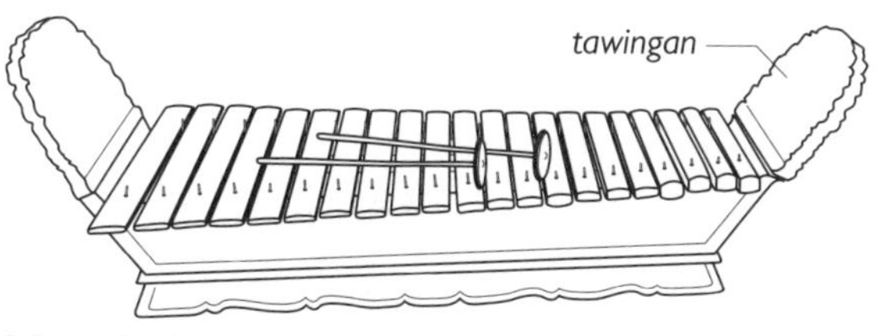

3.56 *Gambang kayu*

Role

The *gambang* has lower status than the *rebab* and *gendèr*, but is a member of the select group of instruments that play in *sulukan*. With its extended range, the *gambang* is better able than the *gendèr* to indicate the true pitch of the inner melody.

The instrument may be played in *ir I*, particularly in *kébar* and in the editable forms, and is regularly used in the slower *iråmå*. There is also a long-established tradition of players using the *gambang* for solo practice.

Playing technique

The *gambang* is played with a pair of beaters (*béndhå*). The wooden head is surrounded by a small thickness of padding, and the handle consists of a long thin piece of horn, whose flexibility ensures that the head bounces immediately off the *wilah*.

Because the sound from the *wilah* fades so rapidly, damping of the notes is unnecessary. The playing technique is therefore relatively easy, apart from the speed at which the instrument plays. The unequal spacing of the *wilah* (closer and closer together towards the top end) represents a minor complication that affects the usual *garap* style, as described below.

Garap

The standard density of *céngkok* for the *gambang* matches that of the *gendèr panerus* and *siter*, i.e. the higher density of those for the *gendèr barung*, equivalent to *lampah 8* in *ir II*. Notation is as for the *gendèr*.

In the most frequently used style of *garap*, streams of notes an octave apart are played. This is known as *toyå mili/banyu mili* (= running water). Repeated notes are fairly frequent, and present no problems to play.

Two examples follow for the 'special *céngkok*' *puthut gelut* in *sl m* in *ir II*, both of which strongly emphasise the 3 in the first half of the *céngkok*, although they end on 6 at the mid-point (as for the other soft-style decorating instruments).

```
       3           3           .           .
333561̇2̇3̇  3̇3̇3̇5̇6̇1̈2̈3̈  2̈1̈2̈3̈2̈1̈2̈3̈  3̈3̈2̈1̈6̇6̇6̇6̇
3̣3̣3̣5̣6̣123  333561̇2̇3̇  2̇1̇2̇3̇2̇1̇2̇3̇  3̇3̇2̇1̇6666
```

placak
bantalan
béndhå
wilah

3.57 *Gambang* details

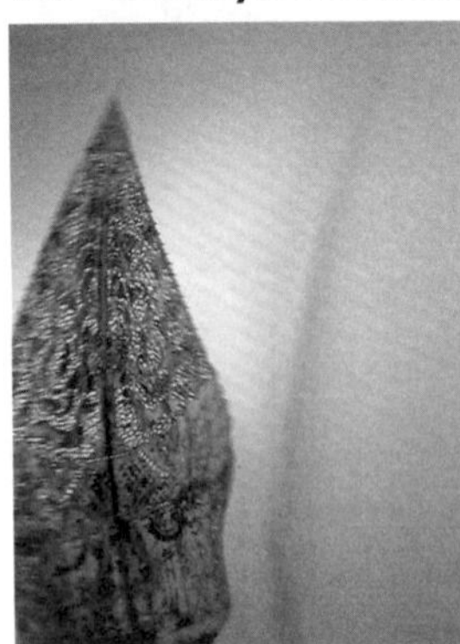

6 5 3 2

5̇3̇5̇6̇1̈6̇5̇6̇ 5̇3̇5̇6̇1̈6̇5̇6̇ 6̇3̇6̇5̇3̇2̇1̇6 61̇61̇2̇2̇2̇2̇

53561̇656 53561̇656 63653216̣ 6̣16̣12222

or (without the *balungan*)

6̣16̣12323 21.3.123 563561̇2̇3̇ 3̇5̇2̇1̇62̇1̇6

6̤1̣6̤1̣2̣3̣2̣3̣ 2̣1̣6̤1̣6̤1̣2̣3̣ 5̣6̣3̣5̣6̣123 35216̣216̣

2̇1̇2̇3̇2̇3̇5̇2̇ 61̇653216̣ 6̣16̣12356 61̇532312

21232352 6̣16̣5̣3̣2̣1̣6̤ 6̤1̣6̤1̣2̣3̣5̣6̣ 6̣15̣3̣2̣3̣1̣2̣

The left- and right-hand parts can be identical, as shown in the first example. There are also common types of variation in both pitch and time, which players are expected to use, although the rules as to when and where to use them are as elusive as ever.

As regards pitch, the left-hand or right-hand part may miss a note (as seen in the second example above), or the two parts may be separated by an octave plus a *kempyung* or a *gembyung* rather than an octave. As regards timing, the right-hand part may include triplet patterns or quick double strikes (these latter sometimes being called *geter*). Some of these variations are illustrated in another example for *puthut gelut* in *ir II*, here spaced out for clarity:

2̇ 3̇3̇ . 2̇ 3̇3̇ . 2̇ 3̇   2̇ 1̇1̇ . 5̇5̇ . 1̇ 2̇ 3̇

2 3 1 2 3 1 2 3   2 1 6̣ 1 6̣ 1 2 3

3̇ 5̇ 6̇ 1̈ 6̇ 1̈ 2̈ 3̈   3̈ 2̈ 1̈ 2̈ 6̇6̇ . 5̇ 6̇

3 5 6 1̇ 6 1̇ 2̇ 3̇   3̇ 2̇ 1̇ 2̇ 6 3 5 6

3̈ 3̈ 3̈ 3̈ 2̈ 1̈ 3̈ 2̈   6̇ 6̇ 2̈ 1̈ 6̇6̇ . 5̇ 6̇

3̇ 3̇ 3̇ 3̇ 2̇ 1̇ 3̇ 2̇   6 6 2̇ 1̇ 6 3 5 6

6̇ 3̇ 6̇ 5̇ 3̇ 2̇ 1̇ 6   6 1̇1̇ . 1̇ 2̇2̇ . 1̇ 2̇2̇

6 3 6 5 3 2 1 6̣   6̣ 1 6̣ 1 2 6̣ 1 2

Another version of the same *céngkok* in *ir I*

62̇63̇ 3̇3̇3̇3̇ 2̇1̇61̇ 61̇2̇3̇ 5̇3̇5̇6̇ 3̇5̇6̇5̇ 5̇6̇5̇3̇ 2̇61̇2̇

6̣26̣3 3333 216̣1 6̣123 5356 3565 5653 26̣12

does not reflect the 6 at the mid-point.

Apart from the repeated notes and the octave doubling, *céngkok* for the *gambang* still resemble *pipilan*-style *céngkok* for both *gendèr*. As with the *gendèr panerus*, there are generic rather than named *céngkok* for each *sèlèh* note, with variants that take into account the previous *sèlèh* note, and the *céngkok* are usually given in *sl m* form, for conversion to other *pathet* in the usual way.

Special *céngkok* are available for a similar range of named contours; also for *gantungan*, such as this for *gantung* 6 in *sl m*

. 55 . 66 . 55 . 66

1 6̣ 1 6̣ 1 6̣ 1 6̣

which can be repeated as necessary to fill the space. As in the earlier example, a double strike is followed by a *pin*.

Siter family

Construction

The *siter* is organologically a zither, from which it takes its name.[23] The family consists of several members but a rather larger number of names. There are certainly instruments in the family separated in pitch by at least an octave. It seems unlikely that the range is any wider, because that would place the lowest instrument below the *slenthem* octave. What follows is an attempt to make sense of the apparent confusion. (See also under ***Siteran* ensembles**.)

So far as the *gamelan gedhé* or *gamelan gadhon* is concerned, the lowest-pitched member of the family is the *c(e)lempung* (Fig. 3.58)—an instrument of somewhat

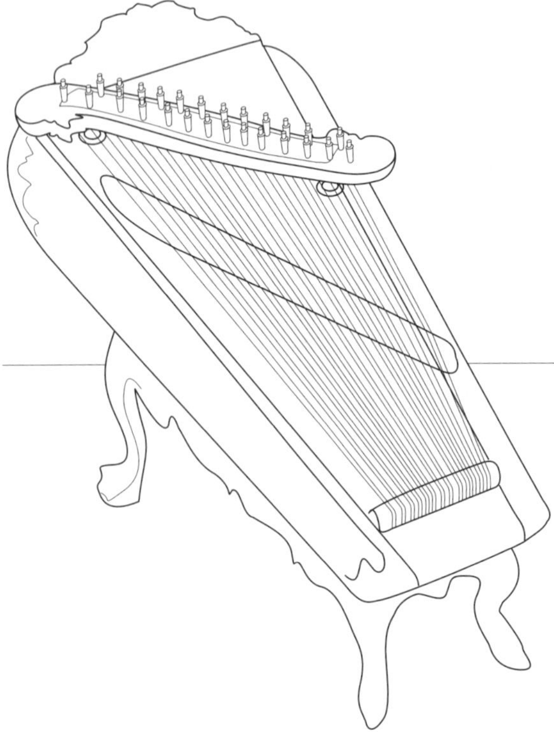

3.58 *Celempung*

23 And has a different etymology from the Indian *sitar*, which is organologically not a zither.

baroque design. It may be significant that the *celempung* is thought to have been introduced into the gamelan in the eighteenth century, i.e. well into the colonial era: European influence seems likely. Court gamelan possess this instrument.[24] Some gamelan have an alternative instrument of the same pitch but with a simpler construction —essentially a rectangular box—which is referred to here as the *siter* without any qualifier.

The *siter peking* (Fig. 3.59) is another instrument of simple construction, pitched an octave above the *siter* and *celempung*. It is most often seen in double-sided or turn-over (*wolak-walik*) form, with *sléndro* and *pélog* on opposite sides. Its size makes it a convenient instrument to carry around for use with gamelan that do not possess any other form of *siter*.

The descriptions above agree with the information in Figs 3.1 and 3.2, but sources disagree about the octave in which the *siter* family is pitched.

These instruments have anything from 11 to 14 notes, each served by a pair of steel strings (see **Strings** in **Appendix 5**). The typical range is from about 2̣ to 3̇. In practice, not every string is necessarily present, because the lowest strings are rarely used. As with the *gendèr* and *gambang*, there are only five notes per octave, so the *pélog* instrument must be re-tuned to switch between the *bem* and *barang* scales.

As one of the highest-pitched of the gamelan instruments, the *siter peking* provides an interesting but extreme demonstration of the principles of Javanese spread tuning: to Western ears it can sound very sharp. One source says that only the notes 2 and 6 need to be tuned to the rest of the gamelan.

It is also suggested that the pair of strings should be tuned slightly apart, creating the same sort of beat-notes that characterise Balinese ensembles. Apart from the special case of the *gong kemodhong*, this is the only regular current use of the technique in central Java.

In *siteran* and *cokèkan* ensembles additional types of instrument are found, possibly having a wider range. The names *siter barung* or *siter besar*, and probably also *siter dårå*, indicate an instrument basically the same as the *siter* as defined above. However, the lower strings may be single rather than double, and used to carry the *balungan* rather than for decoration. The name *siter panerus* should mean the same as *siter peking*: if there is any difference between these two, it is unclear, but instruments with both names are reportedly present in some ensembles. In addition, some *siteran* or *cokèkan* ensembles have (or formerly had) a *slenthem kawat* or *slenthem siter*, which is a single-octave *siter* of *slenthem* pitch, used to play the *balungan*. In *siteran* and *cokèkan* ensembles it is particularly likely that the *siter* instruments will be home-made.

All the instruments of the family contrast with Sundanese zithers (*kecapi*), which are larger, single-strung but with a wider compass, and played from the long side.

Role

Although a member of the *siter* family is usually present in Indonesian recordings, and these instruments are always very audible, their status is still low. They are most likely to be used in lighter vocal pieces. The remarks above about the absence of the *gendèr panerus* from *sulukan* apply equally to the *siter* family.

The information offered here relates to the use of these instruments in regular *gamelan gedhé* and *gamelan gadhon*.

Playing technique

The *siter* family is played from the end of the instrument, and the strings are angled upwards to make this easier —by about 30 degrees for the *celempung*, and a little less on the other instruments. The strings are normally plucked with the thumbnails (which the player must therefore maintain at the right length) or nail extensions, but the use of a plectrum is not unknown.

The positions of the two hands are different (Fig. 3.60). Most fingers of the right hand are under the strings, whereas the left hand is entirely above the strings. Any convenient finger may be used to damp the strings.

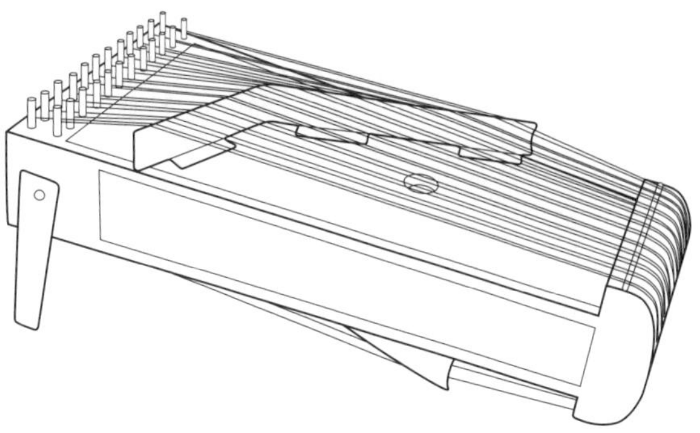

3.59 *Siter peking*

24 This is the only zither mentioned in Kunst (1973), which suggests that the *siter* and *siter peking*, together with their *garap*, are twentieth-century innovations.

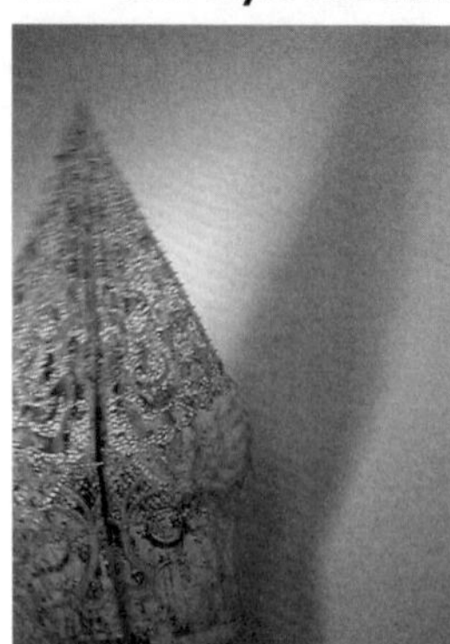

Garap

Discussion of *garap* for the siter family is complicated by the existence of a tradition of *siter* playing outside regular gamelan. (See **Siteran ensembles**.)

In character, the *garap* actually heard on the *siter peking* in *gamelan gedhé* or *gamelan gadhon* is very similar to that of the *gendèr panerus*. There is disagreement as to whether the *celempung* or *siter* uses the same *garap*, or something more closely related to the *gendèr barung*, or something different again.[25] Notation is as for the *gendèr*.

The *pipilan* type of *céngkok*, where the two hands divide a single line between them, is sometimes called *ngracik*. There are also *céngkok* that look similar, but where the notes in the left-hand part are an octave below those that would give a continuous line: this style is called *imbal* or *pinjalan*. In the latter style, notes alternate between the two hands, so that the damping patterns differ from those in the *pipilan* style.

An example such as the following, for 3532 in *sl m* (double density in *ir III* or *balungan mlaku* in *ir II*),

. 3 . . . 3 5 6 . 3̇ . 1̇ . 1̇ . 6 . 3 5 6 . 1̇ . 6 . 3̇ . 1̇ . 3̇ . 2̇
2 . 6̣ 1 2 . . . 2 . 2 1 6̣ . 6̣ . 2 . . . 5 . 5 . 5 . 5 3 2 . 2 .

has both *ngracik* and *imbal* characteristics in places.

In another standard technique called *cecekan*,[26] found only in the right-hand part, the string is damped immediately after it is plucked, e.g.

1̷̇ 1̷̇ . 1̇ . 3̇ . 3̷̇ 3̷̇ 3̇ . 1̇ . 1̇ . 6 . 1̇ 2̇ 3̇ . 3̇ . 3̷̇ 3̷̇ 3̇ . 1̇ . 3̇ . 2̇
2 . 2 . 2 . 2 . 2 . 2 . 6̣ . 6̣ . 6̣ 1 2 . 2 . 2 . 2 . 6̣ . 2 . 2 .

In another technique, called *larutan*, the thumbnail is drawn across several adjacent strings rather than plucking them separately.

Céngkok may *sèlèh* on every *balungan* note, or only at the end of the *gåtrå*. As on the *gendèr panerus*, the *céngkok* tend to be generic, but sometimes they are given names familiar from the *gendèr barung*. Again there are *céngkok gantungan*, e.g. this for *gantung* 6

1̇ . 1̇ . 1̇ . 1̇ 6 1̇ . 1̇ . 1̇ . 1̇ 6 1̇ . 1̇ . 1̇ . 1̇ 6 . 1̇ . 1̇ . 1̇ . 6
. 2 1 6̣ . 6̣ . . . 2 1 6̣ . 6̣ . . . 2 1 6̣ . 6̣ . . 6̣ . 2 1 6̣ . 6̣ .

and 'special *céngkok*' for some long *balungan* contours.

Sources that believe in different *garap* for the *siter peking* and *celempung* prefer *pipilan*-style *céngkok* for the former and *imbal*-style *céngkok* for the latter.

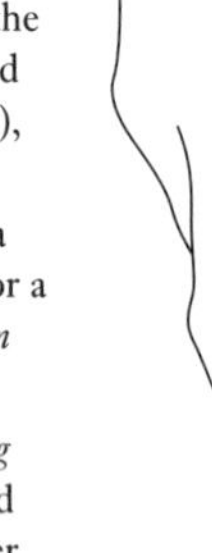

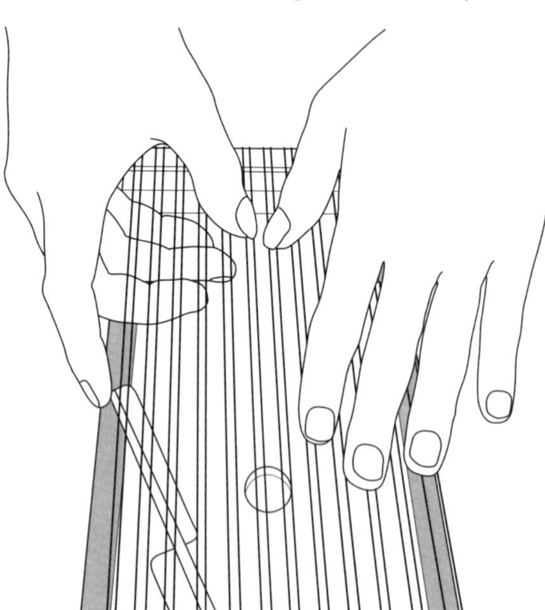

3.60 *Siter* playing technique demonstrated on *siter peking*

Suling

Construction

The *suling* is a simple keyless end-blown flute made from a thin-walled bamboo tube.[27] The bamboo is cut so that the tube is blocked by a natural node (*ros*) at one end, and a notch is cut in the *ros* and the adjacent part of the tube (Fig. 3.62) to form the sharpened edge (*irung-irungan*) against which the player's breath is directed. A strip of rattan or bamboo is tied to make a ring (*suh*) around the end of the tube, forming a duct to direct the air. The *suling* can therefore be classed as a duct flute, ring flute or fipple flute (the *ros* acting as the fipple). The *suh* is not permanently attached to the bamboo tube, and a string tied around the tube guards against its loss.

The variants of the instrument in current use (Fig. 3.63) have four holes (*sléndro*) or five holes (*pélog*). In Yogya a six-hole instrument was traditional for *pélog* (as it remains in Sunda), and such instruments can still be found—and made on request. The lowest notes for these variants (i.e. the notes formed when all the finger-holes are closed) are respectively 2̣, 1̣ and 3̣.[28]

The diameter of the *suling* may be slightly smaller at the *ros* end, but the taper is not usually obvious.

The length of the *suling* depends on the tuning of the gamelan for which it is designed. Among the *suling* in

25 For a more detailed analysis of the principles underlying the *céngkok* of the *siter* family (and other decorating instruments), see Sutton (1993).

26 Or *cecegan*. The term is a variant of *ceceg/neceg*, used for a similar technique on the *saron* and *demung*, etc.

27 This section on the *suling* in all its variants has benefited from consultations with Roger Vetter, Joan Suyenaga, Nikhil Dally and (particularly) Andrew Timar. The conclusions are the author's.

28 Kunst (1973) describes a six-hole *pélog* instrument with 1 as the lowest note, but this type of instrument does not seem to be current.

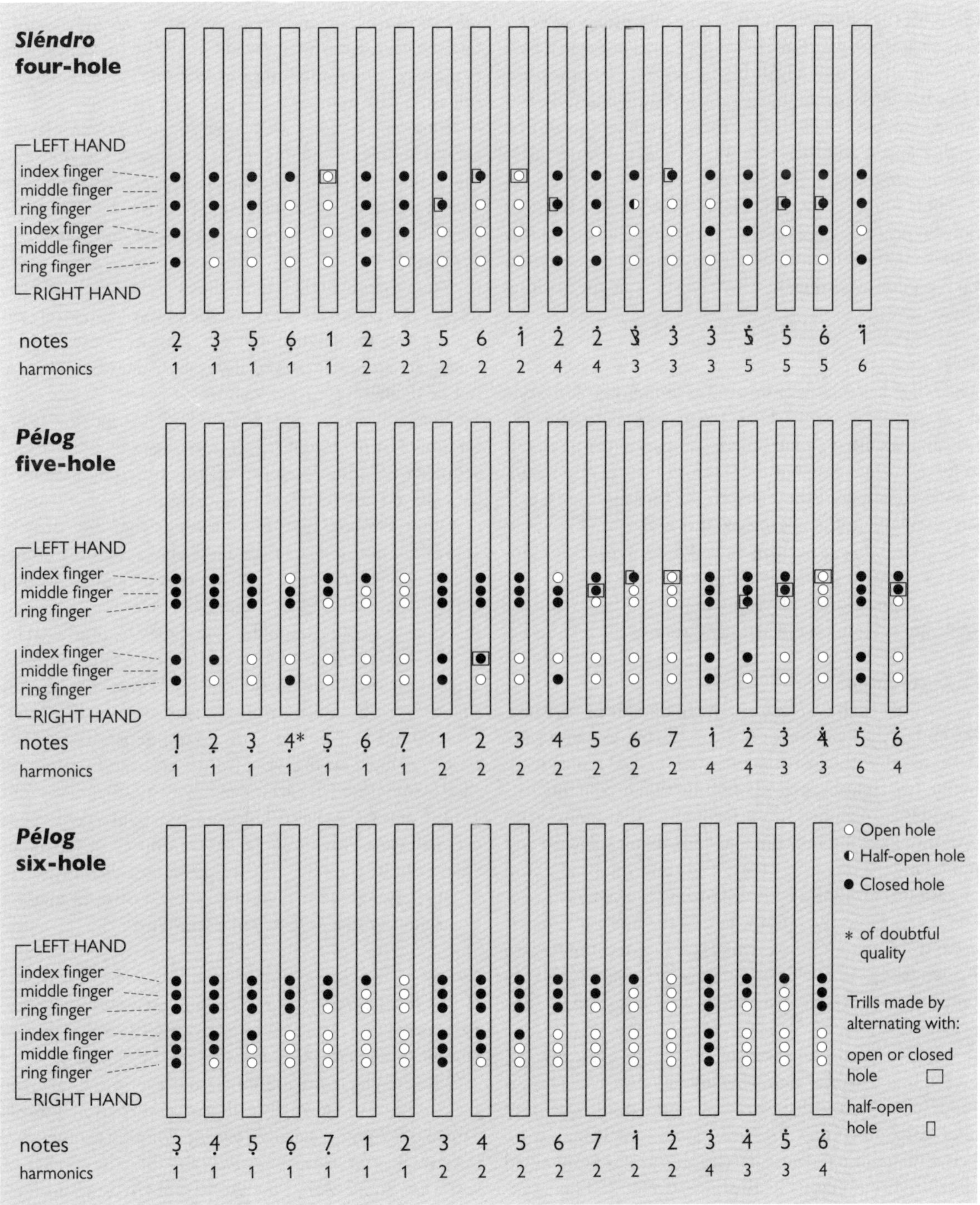

Sléndro four-hole

LEFT HAND: index finger, middle finger, ring finger
RIGHT HAND: index finger, middle finger, ring finger

notes	2	3	5	6	1	2	3	5	6	1	2	2	3	3	3	5	5	6	1
harmonics	1	1	1	1	1	2	2	2	2	2	4	4	3	3	3	5	5	5	6

Pélog five-hole

LEFT HAND: index finger, middle finger, ring finger
RIGHT HAND: index finger, middle finger, ring finger

notes	1	2	3	4*	5	6	7	1	2	3	4	5	6	7	1	2	3	4	5	6
harmonics	1	1	1	1	1	1	1	2	2	2	2	2	2	2	4	4	3	3	6	4

Pélog six-hole

LEFT HAND: index finger, middle finger, ring finger
RIGHT HAND: index finger, middle finger, ring finger

notes	3	4	5	6	7	1	2	3	4	5	6	7	1	2	3	4	5	6
harmonics	1	1	1	1	1	1	1	2	2	2	2	2	2	2	4	3	3	4

○ Open hole
◐ Half-open hole
● Closed hole

* of doubtful quality

Trills made by alternating with:
open or closed hole □
half-open hole ▯

3.61 Fingering for *suling*

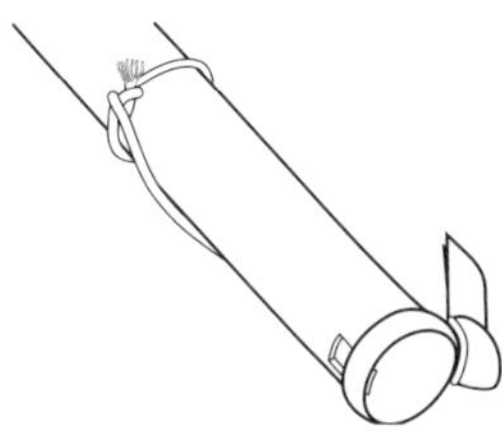

3.62 Mouthpiece of *suling*

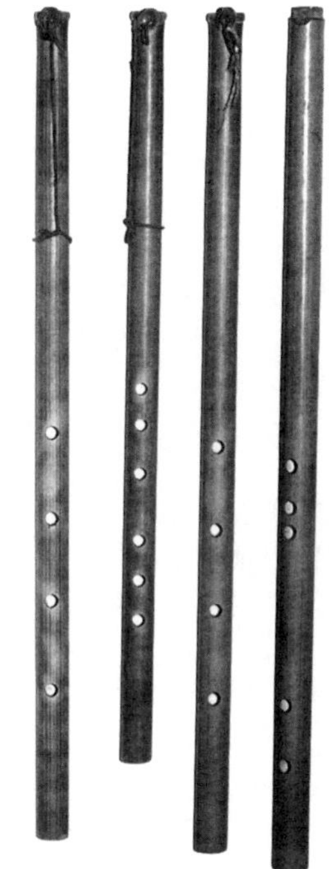

3.63 A selection of *suling* in both *laras*

Fig. 3.63, the four-hole and five-hole instruments belong to a *tumbuk nem* gamelan. In such a gamelan the *sléndro* 2 will typically be only a little higher in pitch than the *pélog* 1 (see Fig. 2.9), so that the *suling* are of similar length. In a typical *tumbuk limå* gamelan these two notes would be further apart, and therefore the two *suling* would differ more in length.

Some sources[29] say that the six-hole *pélog* instrument can also produce a *sléndro* scale with *miring* notes, but this is an oversimplification, because the *miring* notes should vary in pitch according to which *miring* scale they belong to (see ***Laras***).

Role

The *suling* has relatively low status among the soft-style decorating instruments, but some players take it more seriously than others. One source compared its role to salt in food, i.e. bringing out the flavour of the composition. Another compared the *suling* to the birds in the trees,[30] suggesting that it is not missed if it is absent. The presence of the *suling* is perhaps valued most in *pathetan* and, more generally, in *gadhon* performances.

The *suling* is often played by someone whose main responsibility is another instrument, such as the *gong ageng*.

Playing technique

As the duct of the *suling* is on the underside of the tube, the end of the instrument rests on the player's lower lip. All variants of the instrument are supported underneath by the two thumbs, placed opposite the middle fingers.

Notes are obtained by the techniques that are usual on unimproved wind instruments,[31] involving standard and non-standard fingerings (Fig. 3.61) and the production of various harmonics by overblowing. In the bottom octave, i.e. as far as the point where all the holes are uncovered, the notes are fundamentals (= first harmonics: see **Appendix 4**). All the higher notes are overblown, and the range up to $\dot{1}$ exploits harmonics up to the sixth (= fifth overtone).

Besides the useful range of notes (less than two octaves), Fig. 3.61 also shows the lowest notes available, although they have little power and are not used. There are alternative fingerings for some notes, which may work better than those shown: for example, a 6 may be obtained as a third harmonic, using the fingering for $\underset{.}{2}$. This situation is inevitable because of the variations between one *suling* and another, and because every gamelan has a different *embat*. Even with the aid of all the tricks available to players, a *suling* made for use with one gamelan may be unusable with another.

Some *miring* notes are shown for *sléndro*, but players should be able to find fingerings for others. The note 4 in the highest octave on the five-hole *pélog* instrument is shown as flat, i.e. as having a 'vocal' 4 pitch: how far this is from the 4 on the other instruments will again depend on the gamelan.

Notes much higher than those shown can be produced, but are rarely used. As the player cannot rely on hitting the right harmonic every time, some 'wrong notes' are a regular part of *suling* style, and may or may not be deliberate.

Normally each note is tongued, i.e. the air flow is interrupted by the tongue to produce the note. In notation, sequences of notes produced without tonguing are joined by a curved line (slur) or by underlining.

Other symbols have the meanings that are usual in *kepatihan*, but *sulingan* uses additional symbols to indicate ornaments. A wavy line over or after a note means a trill—or an effect that could sometimes be described more accurately as a wobble. These may be produced by briefly opening or closing one of the holes, or by flexing a finger joint or rolling the finger while it is in contact with the *suling*. The holes involved are shown in Fig. 3.61. (Sometimes half-holing is necessary, depending on the *suling*.) A line curving away from a note (and written either below it or after it) means that the fingers are slid away from the covered holes—a procedure sometimes called *usapan*—giving a final note of unpredictable pitch. A straight line joining two notes means a slide or portamento between them. A comma or an apostrophe marks a break similar to a *pedhotan* in a vocal line.

Garap

Garap for the *suling* has several similarities to *sindhènan*. Players may be criticised for following the *sindhènan* too closely—and *pesindhèn* for imitating the *suling*.

The regular contributions from the *suling* take the form of phrases (normally called *céngkok*) played towards a major *sèlèh* point, usually a *kenong*. These are sometimes described as *sulingan srambahan*, and, like the *céngkok* of *sindhènan srambahan*, they are free in rhythm and normally end after the *sèlèh* point. A *céngkok* is characterised

29 e.g. Kunst (1973).

30 Not perhaps a helpful simile when, thanks to massive habitat destruction and the Javanese love of caged birds, most of the bird population of central Java seems to be behind bars.

31 i.e. those without keys such as are seen on Boehm system flutes and other standard modern instruments of the Western symphony orchestra.

Table 3.20
Examples of *céngkok* for *suling*

Sléndro manyurå

Céngkok srambahan for *sèlèh* 2

3̇ 3̇ 3̇2̇1̇ 3̇ 5̇ 2̇ (also for *sl 9*)

3̇ 3̇ 3̇2̇1̇ 3̇ 5̇ 2̇ 3̇1̇2̇, 6 6 653 6 1̇ 5 (65)32

Céngkok srambahan for *sèlèh* 6̣

3̇ 3̇ 3̇2̇1̇ 3̇ 5̇ 2̇ 3̇1̇2̇, 6 6 6

Céngkok srambahan for *sèlèh* 6

3̇ 3̇ 3̇2̇1̇ 3̇ 5̇ 6̇ 5̇ 1̇ 6̇

Selitan/kombangan for *gantungan* 6

3̇5̇6̇.5̇6̇

3̇5̇6̇.3̇6̇.3̇6̇

3̇6̇.3̇6̇.3̇6̇.6̇5̇6̇

Kombangan for *gantungan* 2

62̇.62̇.62̇

Sléndro sångå

Céngkok srambahan for *sèlèh* 5̣

6 5 3 6 5 (6 5 6 5)

2̇ 2̇ 2̇.1̇ 3̇5̇ 2̇, 6 6 6 .5 3 61̇ 5

5 6 1̇ 2̇1̇ 2̇.1̇ 3̇5̇ 2̇, 6 6 6 .5 3 61̇ 5, (61̇ 5)

Céngkok srambahan for *sèlèh* 5

1̇ 6 2̇ 1̇ 3̇ 2̇ 3̇ 5̇ 3̇ 5̇ 6̇ 5̇

Céngkok khusus for *puthut gelut* (*balungan* 22 . . 2321), *ir II*

. 2̇ 2̇ 2̇ . 2̇ 1̇ 6 2̇ 3̇ 2̇ 3̇ 5̇ 2̇ . . 3̇ 2̇ 1̇

by its *sèlèh* note and its length: there are longer and shorter *céngkok*.

Shorter *céngkok* are also used at other points earlier in the *kenongan*, roughly corresponding to the positions of *isèn-isèn* in *sindhènan*. These short *céngkok* typically start after the first note of a *gåtrå*.

Special-purpose patterns also exist. *Selitan* or *selingan* are signals to indicate high register or a transition to a high register, and may therefore be used at any point in a *kenongan*, as necessary: for example, in *ldr Wilujeng sl m* the last *gåtrå* before the *ngelik* and the first *gåtrå* of the *ngelik* will both use a *selitan* for 6. *Kombangan* are similar *céngkok* used to mark *gantungan* at any point.

There are also specific *céngkok* for named contours such as *ayu kuning* and *puthut gelut*.

Because of the irregular rhythms of *céngkok*, it is essential to learn them by listening, but the examples shown in Table 3.20 should give an idea of the style. Optional elements are in parentheses. Features illustrated in the table include:

- different *céngkok* for *sèlèh* notes an octave apart, although some *céngkok* are used for two octaves,
- common initial phrases for *céngkok* with different *sèlèh* notes,
- repeated elements in *céngkok* for *gantungan*,
- the use of notes up to 1̇ in *sléndro*,
- variations in length and complexity, requiring the longer examples to start earlier.

No *céngkok* for *sléndro nem* are shown. On other instruments, special *céngkok* for *sléndro nem* only exist for the low register, but the *suling* effectively does not have a low register.

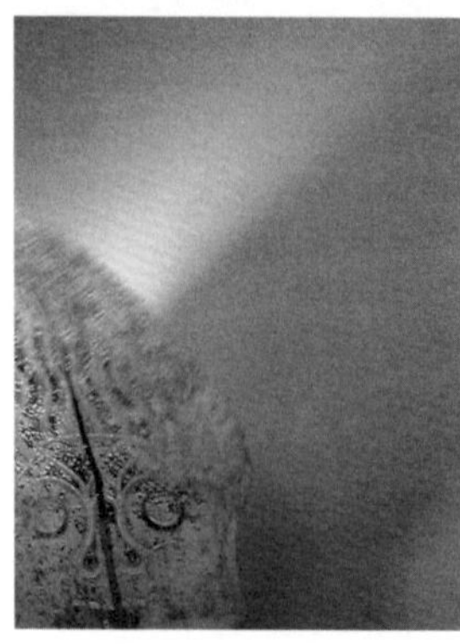

Punctuating instruments

As explained in Part 2, each *bentuk* is characterised by its own pattern of strokes on the punctuating (colotomic, time-marking, phrase-marking, phrase-making, inter-punctuating, accentuating) instruments. The usage of these instruments in a *gamelan gedhé* is summarised in Table 3.21.

In performances by other types of ensemble, the punctuation may be much more sparse. For example, the *gadhon* ensemble will have gong strokes as a minimum—although typically the *gong kemodhong* substitutes for the *gong ageng*—but may use no other punctuating instruments. In *siteran* ensembles too, the gong (in this case a *gong bumbung*) is the only punctuating instrument. The instruments with the densest patterns are those most likely to be omitted, and also those whose parts are most subject to variation and disagreement.

Most of the punctuating instruments have onomatopoeic names.

Gong ageng

The *gong ageng* has a special status among all the gamelan instruments. It is regarded as the unique repository of the spirit of the gamelan. Sometimes the *gong ageng* has a name, which may also be assumed by the gamelan as a whole. When the gamelan is honoured by gifts of food or flowers, they are placed beside the *gong ageng*. The formal inauguration of a new gamelan is marked by the striking of the *gong ageng*, preferably by an old and respected person.

As the iconic gamelan instrument (although its early history is unclear—see **Origins of *karawitan*** in Part 2, p. 24) the *gong ageng* is familiar enough not to need description. Size varies. The tendency is for larger gongs to give lower-pitched notes, but the correlation is not absolute. Rich purchasers in the West sometimes insist on a *gong ageng* of 1 metre diameter, and on a low pitch. Neither of these characteristics actually guarantees a high-quality instrument.

Some of the status of the *gong ageng* must be due to its cost. The price of all gongs increases with size. That of the *gong ageng*—at least for bronze—is disproportionate to its size in comparison with the other hanging gongs. The high cost is due to the technical difficulties and uncertainties of the manufacturing process, as well as to the amount of raw material in the instrument. Because of the cost of bronze instruments, the iron alternative is attractive: iron instruments with a satisfactory sound are now available, although they are not as robust as bronze, and can go out of tune if mistreated.

On the methods of supporting all types of gongs, see **Gong stands**. These methods are illustrated in Fig. 3.64, where the relative sizes of *gong ageng* and other *pencon gandhul* can also be seen.

The beater used with the *gong ageng* has a heavy wooden head surrounded by a thick layer of padding. This beater produces less satisfactory sounds with the *gong suwukan* and *kempul*. In emergency, the side of a clenched fist is an excellent substitute for the usual beater: again it does not work so well on the other *pencon gandhul*. The *gong ageng* is never damped.

The pitch of the *gong ageng* lies in the range from 2 to 6, not excluding 4 in *pélog*, but is always the lowest pitch of any instrument in the gamelan. A *gong ageng* pitched at 6 is now likely to be regarded as too high, as it may conflict with the lowest-pitched *gong suwukan*. In a double

Table 3.21
Usage of punctuating instruments vs. *bentuk*

Bentuk	*Gong ageng*	*Gong suwukan*	*Kenong*	*Kempul*	*Kethuk*	*Kempyang*[a]
Gangsaran	×[b]	×	×	×	×	
Lancaran/bubaran	×[b]	×	×	×	×	
Ketawang/langgam	×		×	×	×	×
Ladrang	×		×	×	×	×
Gendhing/gendhing ketawang						
— *mérong*	×		×		×	
— *inggah*[c]	×		×		×	×
Ayak-ayakan	×[d]	×	×	×	×	
Srepegan/playon	×[d]	×	×	×	×	
Sampak	×[d]	×	×	×	×	

a. For Yogya style, in *pélog* only. b. At end of overall cycle; otherwise *gong suwukan*. c. For *minggah ladrang* or *minggah ketawang*, standard instruments for the *bentuk* are used. d. Possibly at end.

gamelan there is usually a separate *gong ageng* per *laras*, and they have different pitches. The pitch is in fact so far from those of the main melodic instruments that the tuning relative to the rest of the gamelan is not critical.[32]

Single gamelan in the palaces may also have two gongs (often tuned to 5 and 6), so that there is a general question as to which gong should be used when. Gongs seem not to be pitched consistently higher or lower in one *laras* than the other. Indeed, if a double gamelan has two *gong ageng*, each of them may not be regarded as assigned to one *laras* or the other: instead, the *pathet* of the piece may determine the choice of the gong. Thus a gong tuned to 5 may serve pieces in *pélog limå* or *sléndro sångå*, whereas a gong tuned to 6 may serve pieces in most other *pathet*, and any pieces with gong 6. In a single gamelan too, the gong will be chosen to provide the best 'harmony' with the gong note. Only one gong will be used in a piece.

An *ombak* or beat-note is an essential feature of any *gong ageng*. Compared with gongs in other parts of Indonesia, the central Javanese *gong ageng* has a relatively slow *ombak*. The Javanese themselves refer not only to the pitch or frequency of the *ombak* but also to the **number** of audible beats.

The musical function of the *gong ageng* is always as the most important phrase-marker, whence the term *gongan* for the stretch of music that it marks off, but in various contexts it is replaced by the *gong suwukan*: see ***Gong suwukan* and *siyem***, p. 204. In *lancaran/bubaran* and *gangsaran*, the *gong ageng* is only heard as *gong bukå* and at the end of the overall cycle. The relationship of the gong strokes to the rest of the punctuation has been described in Part 2. On the timing of gong strokes, see **... and finishing**, p. 35, and **Progress of a vocal *gendhing*** in Part 2, p. 78; also **Delaying the strokes**, p. 206.

Gong kemodhong

The *gong kemodhong* or *gong kemådhå* is a substitute instrument, used in place of the *gong ageng*. In structure it is a *wilah pencon* instrument, with two *wilah* tuned to slightly sharp and slightly flat versions of the same note.[33] Effectively the instrument is a very short *gendèr*, and the methods of supporting the *wilah* are similar to those on

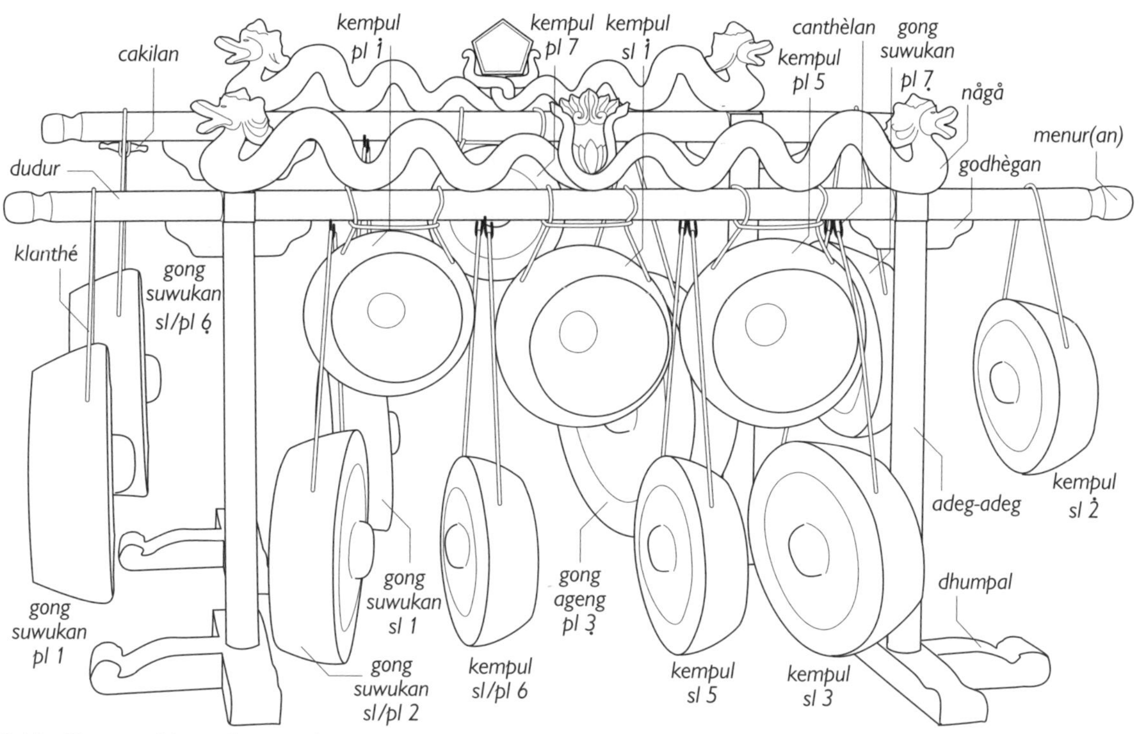

3.64 Gongs and *kempul* on stands

32 Various sources including Kunst (1973) indicate that the pitches of the *gong ageng* and *gong suwukan* are separated by a full octave or more. Figs 3.1 and 3.2 are based (with less than total confidence) on other sources that place these two types of gong close together in pitch, as well as on the implausibility of the pitch of the *gong ageng* being an octave lower than shown (implying a pitch around 20 to 30 Hz, near the lower limit of the audible range). Such disagreements about the numbers may be due to the difficulty, even with current technology, of measuring very low pitches, probably complicated by the presence of the *ombak*. Various measuring techniques are liable to measure overtones of a note rather than the fundamental. Although most gamelan instruments have no harmonic overtones, the *gong ageng* is an exception, if the explanation of the *ombak* given in Appendix 4 is correct: some measurements of the *gong ageng* may therefore be recording a strong second harmonic or similar overtone, not the fundamental.

33 Not, as sometimes suggested, two adjacent notes, e.g. 3 and 5, because the resulting *ombak* would be much too fast.

the *gendèr*. The average of the two pitches lies within the range of *gong ageng*, and the difference between the two pitches creates the required *ombak*.

There are two distinct styles of construction, but always with at least one ceramic pot that functions as a Helmholtz resonator (see **Appendix 4**) for the *wilah*. In the instrument shown in Fig. 3.65, the two *wilah* share a single resonator hidden inside a wooden box (*plangkan*, *grobogan*). (For the internal details, see Fig. A9 in **Appendix 4**.) *Gong kemodhong* with a separate resonator for each *wilah* (Fig. 3.66) are also made, but have the disadvantage that they cannot be played single-handed.

Because of the effect of the resonator(s), the sound of the *gong kemodhong* is relatively pure, lacking the subtle spectrum of overtones that characterises the *gong ageng* (and distinguishes the best examples from the rest).

Preferably the two *wilah* are struck at the same time, but a satisfactory sound (including the *ombak*) still results if the *wilah* are struck in quick succession. Sometimes, to substitute for the *gong suwukan*, only one of the two *wilah* is struck.The beaters used may be much smaller than those of the *gong ageng*, and they have much less padding.

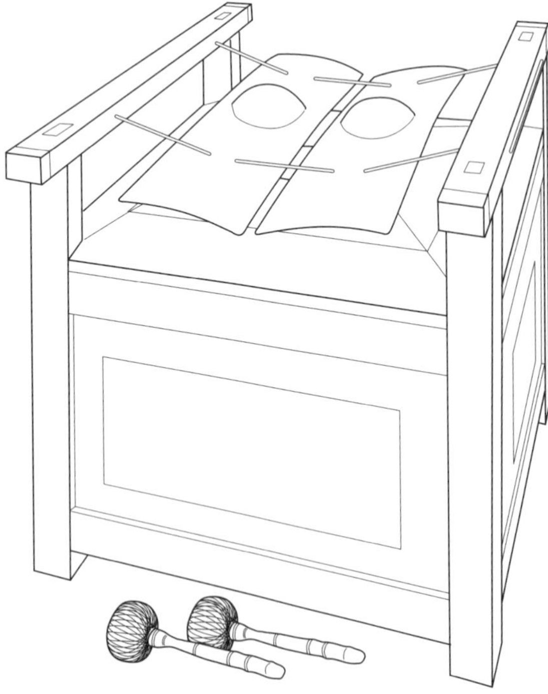

3.65 *Gong kemodhong*

The *gong kemodhong* is often present in *gadhon* ensembles, serving both *laras*. It may be played by someone who is also responsible for one of the other instruments, such as the *slenthem*. (The instrument shown in Fig. 3.65 is, at 64 cm, inconveniently tall for this purpose.) *Siteran* or *cokèkan* ensembles (see below) sometimes have a *gong kemodhong* rather than a *gong bumbung*, and the instrument may then have metal fixtures that allow two people to carry it on a horizontal pole between them.

Gong bumbung

The *gong bumbung* or *gong bambu* is another substitute instrument, replacing the *gong ageng* in many itinerant ensembles (see **Siteran ensembles**, p. 238). It consists of two bamboo tubes (Fig. 3.67), a longer one inside a shorter one, the overall length being typically something under one metre.

The player treats the *gong bumbung* like a brass instrument, i.e. it is a lip-reed instrument. Blowing into the smaller tube creates a surprisingly deep sound. Compared with the *gong ageng* and *gong kemodhong*, the *gong bumbung* differs in that the sound stops instantly instead of dying away gradually.

When used in *siteran* ensembles, the *gong bumbung* is normally played by the *kendhang* player or a *siter* player, and is placed on a stand so that the player only has to turn aside slightly to reach it.

Gong suwukan and siyem

After the *gong ageng*, the next hanging gong in size can have one of two names; *gong suwuk(an)* or *siyem*. There are multiple explanations of the difference (if any) between the two:

- The *siyem* is a type of *gong suwukan* with a wide *bau*;
- The *siyem*, unlike the *gong suwukan*, is cast and not forged.[34] It has been further asserted that the *siyem* is therefore an idiophone instrument (in contrast to the other gongs and *kempul*, which were said to have membranophone characteristics, because the sound-producing parts of their structures were in tension);[35]
- The *siyem* is smaller than the *gong suwukan*, although this would tend to contradict the next suggestion;
- The *siyem* is a low-pitched *gong suwukan*, e.g. tuned to 6̦; or
- The two names are entirely interchangeable.

34 Kunst (1973).

35 Suryabrata (1987). Presumably he meant the *pencu*, *rai* and *recep*, as it is not possible for the entire structure to be in tension. It seems doubtful that he would have had access to the measuring instruments necessary to ascertain the state of the metal.

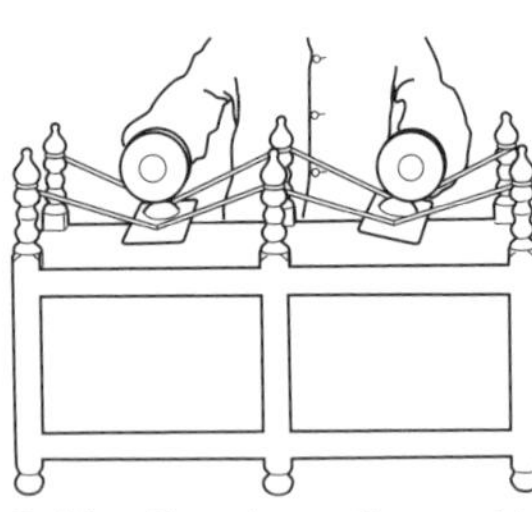

3.66 *Gong kemodhong* with two resonators

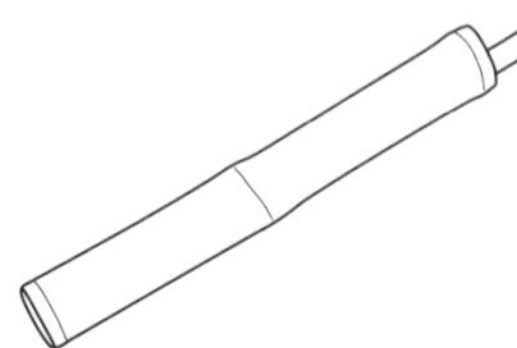

3.67 *Gong bumbung*

These instruments will be referred to here as *gong suwukan*, with no further comment on the competing explanations.

Details of the construction and playing technique for the *gong suwukan* are generally as for the *gong ageng*. In the absence of a special medium-sized beater for the *gong suwukan*, the *gong ageng* or *kempul* beater may be used.

Opinions differ as to whether an *ombak* is desirable or essential in *gong suwukan*. There is most support for the idea that the lowest-pitched *gong suwukan*, particularly the 6̣, should have an *ombak*.

If a gamelan has a single *gong suwukan*, it will be tuned to 2, which is compatible with all *pathet*. In a *tumbuk nem* gamelan, it may be possible for a single *gong suwukan* 2 to be shared between the two *laras*. If there are more *gong suwukan* than this, as is usual for modern gamelan, they are normally tuned to 6̣ and 1 in each *laras*, plus 7̣ for *pélog*. Again, depending on the *embat* of the gamelan, further sharing between the *laras* may be possible; the *sléndro* 1 serving also for 7̣ or 1 in *pélog*. It would seem unreasonable for a *pélog* gamelan to have a *gong suwukan* 1 without a corresponding 7̣, but such a situation has occurred. The use of the register dots here clarifies the relationship between the various *gong suwukan*: all are higher in pitch than the *gong ageng*. It can be safely assumed that a gamelan will not have a *gong suwukan* 6̣ if its *gong ageng* is tuned to 6, because their pitches would sound the same.

Gong stands

The *gong ageng* and other *pencon gandhul* are hung from a stand (*gayor*), but the exact arrangements vary.

The cords (*klanthé*) of the gongs are used in various ways. They may simply be hung from a hook (*canthèlan*) fixed to the horizontal pole, or else hung on one of the ends (*dudur*) of the pole. Alternatively the *klanthé* may be split, with one half ending in in a loop and the other in a toggle (*cakilan*).

In modern gamelan it is common for the *gong ageng*, *gong suwukan* (singular or plural) and *kempul* for one *laras* to be on a single long stand, and for one player to look after all of them. For various reasons—such as limited space or the need to share a single *gong ageng* between both *laras*—the most commonly used gongs and *kempul* from both *laras* may be combined, as shown in Fig. 3.64. In old court gamelan, two *gong ageng* often occupy a small *gayor*, and the other *pencon gandhul* are placed on a separate *gayor*, with the result that at least two players are needed. If there is an extensive set of *gong suwukan*, requiring a separate *gayor* (not necessarily near the others), a third player may be required.

The name *gong suwukan* implies that the instrument is associated with the ends of pieces, but in fact it is the *gong ageng* that is heard at the end of any type of piece that uses both types of gong. The name is supposed to relate to the use of the instrument in *wayang* accompaniment, where the gong may be heard at the end of *sulukan* as well as in pieces in the editable forms. Elsewhere, the *gong suwukan* replaces most of the *gong ageng* strokes in those situations where the strokes occur close together; i.e. *lancaran*/*bubaran*, *gangsaran* and any usage of the editable forms outside *wayang*: cf. ***Gong ageng***. Thus the *gong suwukan* is heard in two out of the three *gongan* of *lnc Singånebah*, for example. The *gong suwukan* is only damped when it is substituting for the *kempul*, i.e. in *gobyog* or *talu*.

Apart from its function as a punctuating instrument, the *gong suwukan* is also occasionally used to emphasise isolated notes in the *balungan*, especially in the *inggah* of *gendhing*. This is a standard feature of certain pieces (e.g. *ldr Loro-loro topèng*, used as the *inggah* of *gd Loro-loro géndhong sl m*), but also can occur in others on a signal from the *kendhang*.[36] Also see ***Gobyog(an)***, p. 234.

If there are several *gong suwukan* available, the choice of which to play at a given point will depend to some extent on *pathet*. Another principle, of preferring *kempyung* or *gembyung* intervals if there is no *gong suwukan* to match the *sèlèh* note, also applies; however, it cannot be put into practice if the gamelan has a limited set of *gong suwukan*.

With a full set of *gong suwukan* (6̣, 7̣, 1 and 2 *pélog* and 6̣, 1 and 2 *sléndro*), the likely choices are

Sèlèh note	*Gong suwukan*
1	1
2	2
3	7̣ for *pl 7*, 1 otherwise, especially in *sl m*; possibly 2 in *sl 6*; possibly 6̣
4	(treat as 3 or 5 according to *pathet*)
5	2; possibly 1 in *sl 9* or *pl 5*
6	6̣, possibly 2
7	7̣

although another note might be preferred, dependent on the context.

36 This *garap* is sometimes called *gong salahan*.

Delaying the strokes

The punctuating instruments are not always struck on the beat. The *kethuk* and the others that are played more frequently than the *kethuk* (i.e. *kempyang, engkuk-kemong, kemanak*) are always played on the beat, but strokes on the *kenong, kempul* and all types of gongs may be delayed under certain conditions.

In *ir I* and faster *irâmå*, all the punctuating instruments are normally played on the beat, or with at most a minimal delay. However, a *kenong plèsèdan* stroke is delayed. In *ir II* and slower *irâmå*, a delay similar to this is applied to the *kenong, kempul* and gong strokes. The delay may be slightly longer in the slowest *irâmå*.

Regardless of the above, the *kenong japan* is always on the beat, and other punctuating strokes too may be on the beat—one or more reasons may apply in a particular case:

- when *gong suwukan* and (less often) *kempul* or *kenong* strokes are used as decoration rather than punctuation, e.g. those in *ldr Loro-loro topèng* and *ktw Kasatriyan*, and the *gong suwukan* strokes that are inserted on a signal from the *kendhang*,
- during *kébar* or *gobyog* treatments,
- in dance (apart from *kenong plèsèdan*), because the strokes are reference points for dancers' movements,
- when it is the style of the group, e.g. as often at the Mangkunegaran palace, where only *kenong plèsèdan* strokes may be delayed,
- during an *irâmå* transition from *ir I* to *ir II*,
- on a *pin* in the *balungan*,
- in the Yogya style for *kempul* strokes, according to some, although *kenong* strokes may be delayed.

The correct amount of delay is difficult to define.[37] It is only a small fraction of a second, and Western players who have not heard enough Javanese performances are liable to overdo it. Delays are not cumulative: i.e. if a *kenong plèsèdan* stroke is delayed in *ir I*, it is not given any additional delay in *ir II*.

The information above does not apply to certain other regular delays: the longer delay to the final gong stroke of a piece, and the delay to the *gong ageng* stroke at the end of the *mérong* of any *gendhing* and to the *kenong* strokes in the *mérong* of the longer *gendhing* forms.

37 One Javanese teacher compared it to the time between the water buffalo excreting and the ordure hitting the ground. Given the long journey to find the nearest water buffalo, the author has not yet managed to make an objective measurement of this interval.

Kenong

Construction

The *kenong* is a large bronze or iron *pencon pangkon* of *brunjung* form. When necessary, this regular form of *kenong* is called *kenong jaler* or *kenong lanang(an)* to distinguish it from the *kenong japan* (see below).

Historically there was only a single *kenong* in the gamelan, tuned to 5. The next development was the addition of a *kenong* 6, said to be linked to *wayang* performance. In modern gamelan, the *kenong* is used in sets (Fig. 3.68) matching all or most of the notes of the *laras*. The set may constitute an open octave, the Yogyanese being said to prefer the range 3 to $\dot{2}$ as against the range 2 to $\dot{1}$ at Solo. A closed octave ranging from 2 to $\dot{2}$ can be considered a complete set.

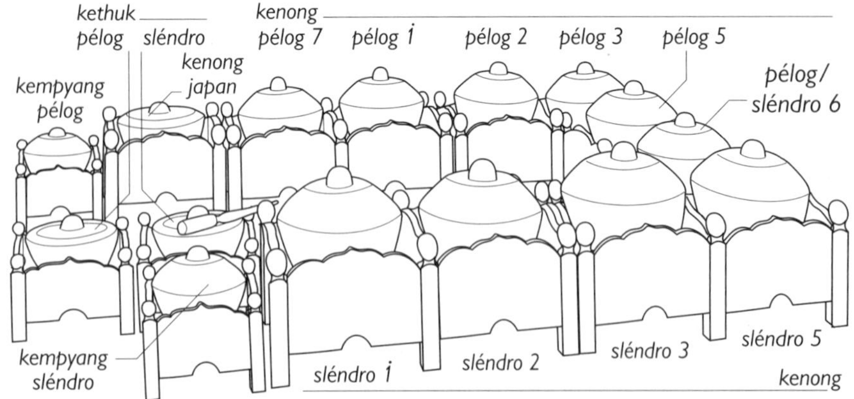

3.68 Set of *kenong* with *kethuk* and *kempyang*

A *pélog* gamelan normally has *kenong* 7 and $\dot{1}$ but not 4. In a double gamelan with *tumbuk nem*, the *sléndro* 5 can often be used as as *pélog* 4, but this is not the standard *garap*: see **Garap** below. As with other punctuating instruments, a single *kenong* may be shared between the two *laras* for the *tumbuk* note(s) of a double gamelan—e.g. for 6 in Fig. 3.68.

A minimum set of *kenong* would include 5, 6 and 7 in *pélog*; 5, 6 and $\dot{1}$ in *sléndro*. As described below, the note 1 is often played as 5.

The single *kenong* pots of early gamelan were placed in square open *rancak(an)*, in which the pot was supported by strings (*pluntur, tali*) running diagonally between the corners of the frame. With the larger numbers of *kenong* pots now in use, the *rancakan* are typically made to house two or more pots side by side.

The beaters for the *kenong* are *bindhi* larger than those used on the *bonang barung*. For convenience in playing certain *bentuk* where the *kenong* strokes are close together, especially *srepegan/playon* and *sampak*, two beaters are necessary.

Role

The *kenong* (which is present in the oldest surviving ceremonial gamelan) is second in importance after the *gong ageng* among the punctuating instruments. A stretch of music marked off by *kenong* strokes is a *kenongan*, and the gong and *kenong* are the only instruments that give their names to structural elements in this way.[38]

In addition to its function as a punctuating instrument, the *kenong* occasionally reinforces the *balungan* note. This is a feature of certain pieces such as *ldr Loro-loro topèng*, the *inggah* of *gd Loro-loro géndhong sl m*, but the practice is much less common than the equivalent on the *gong suwukan* and *kempul*.

Playing technique

There is little to be said about playing technique for the *kenong*, except that different damping practices are necessary for different *bentuk*. In *ketawang*, *ladrang* and longer forms, *kenong* notes are not damped. In most situations where the *kenong* strokes are close together, i.e. in *lancaran/bubaran*, *srepegan/playon*, *ayak-ayakan* and *palaran*, *kenong* notes should be damped (with either the hand or the beater) midway between *kenong* strokes. In *sampak* the *kenong* is damped only at the change to a new note, as shown by the arrows below:

```
                damp 2      damp 3      damp 1
                  ↓           ↓           ↓
             ^^^^^^^^^^^^^^^^^^^^^^^^^^^^^^^^^
balungan      2 2 2 2  3 3 3 3  1̇ 1̇ 1̇ 1̇
kenong notes 2———————  3———————  1̇———————
```

On delays relative to the *balungan*, see **Delaying the strokes**. On the complications that result from a single player handling other instruments as well as the *kenong*, see **Kethuk**, p. 210, and ***Kempyang***, p. 211.

Garap

Even if the gamelan has a full set of *kenong*, the notes used depend to some extent on *pathet*, as shown in the table below. In *sléndro*, a middle 1 is played as 5 in *sl 9*, giving a *kempyung* interval, and only a high 1 is played as 1̇: the same applies in *pl 5* (where 1̣ is also played as 5) and typically in *pl 6*. In *sl m* the 1 in either register is played as 1̇.

Sèlèh note	*Kenong* note	
	Sl m	*Sl 9, pl 5/6*
1̣, 1	1	5
2̣, 2	2	2
3̣, 3, 3̇	3	3
5̣, 5	5	5
6̣, 6	6	6
1̇	1̇	1̇
2̇	2̇ or 2	2̇ or 2

For a limited set of *kenong* pots—only 5, 6 and 7 *pélog* and 5, 6 and 1̇ in *sléndro*—the choice of *kenong* note will be determined more strongly by *pathet*:

Sèlèh note	*Kenong* note			
	Sl m	*Pl 7*	*Sl 9*	*Pl 5/6*
1̣, 1	1̇	—	5	5
2̣, 2, 2̇	6	6	6	6
3̣, 3, 3̇	6	6	6	6
5̣, 5	5	5	5	5
6̣, 6	6	6	6	6
7̣, 7	—	7	—	7
1̇	1̇	—	1̇	5

A *sèlèh* 4 in *pl 7* is unlikely. The notes given in the tables are the default notes, and there are several situations in which they are ignored (assuming that there are alternative *kenong* notes available), quite apart from the changes that result from a limited range of *kenong* pots. When the *kenong* note coincides with the *balungan* note, this is called *kenong(an) mbalung*, *kenong(an) ancer* or *kenong(an) tunggal råså*. A *kenong* note a *kempyung* above the *balungan* note, as shown above for 1̣ or 1 in *sl 9*, is called *kenong(an) kempyungan* or *kenong(an) adu manis*. A *kenong* note a *gembyung* above the *balungan* note, as shown in the second table above for 3̣, 3 or 3̇, is called *kenong(an) gembyungan* or *kenong(an) salah gumun*.

A *gantungan* in the *balungan* or the inner melody is regularly signalled by an immediately preceding *kenong*: this is known as *kenong(an) plèsèdan*.[39] Since *gantungan* most often start in odd-numbered *gåtrå*, and *kenong* strokes occur at the ends of even-numbered *gåtrå*, this is a

38 The term *kempulan* may be found, referring to the four-note unit (eight notes if double-density) ending with a *kempul* stroke in *ayak-ayakan*. This unit is more often referred to as a *gåtrå*. In *sl m* the unit ends with a *gong suwukan* and should then be called a *gongan*.

39 Teachers usually give the literal meaning of the root *plèsèd* as 'slip', 'slide', but it can also mean 'miss the mark', 'pun' or 'hint'. The term *kenong(an) plèsèdan* may be given also to anticipations of vocal lines, here called *kenong pinatut*.

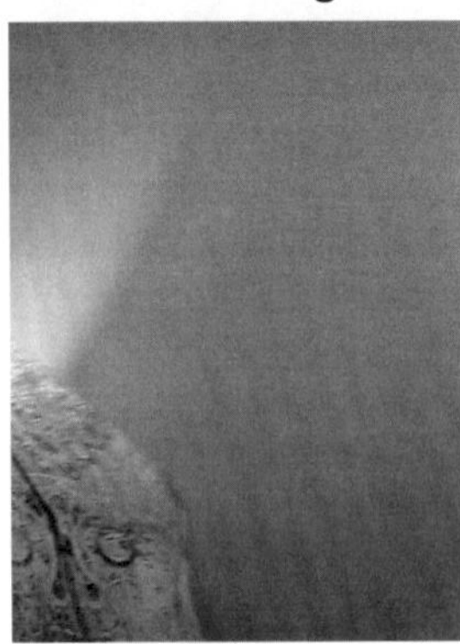

frequent situation. The *sindhènan* or another vocal line may also cause a *kenong* note to be changed, which is sometimes called *kenong(an) p(in)atut*. Both of these practices are illustrated in the *ompak* of *ldr Wilujeng pl 7*, at the first and second *kenong* strokes respectively

2 7̣ 2 3   2 7̣ 5̣ 6̣̂^{3} 3 3 . .   6 5 3 2̂^{5}
5 6 5 3   2 7̣ 5̣ 6̣̂   2 7̣ 2 3   2 7̣ 5̣ 6̣̂

where the *kenong* 5 anticipates the *sindhènan*. The *kenong plèsèdan* stroke is normally delayed even in the faster *irâmâ* (see **Delaying the strokes**).

In structures of AAAB form, the *kenong* note may also be changed deliberately at the end of the third *kenongan* A to anticipate the first note in the B *kenongan*:

. 3 . 1   . 3 . 2̂   . 3 . 1   . 3 . 2̂
. 3 . 1   . 3 . 2̂^{6} . 6̣ . 5̣   . 1 . (6)̂

This practice, emphasising the change in the *balungan* (and helping players who have miscounted the repetitions), may be called *kenong(an) tuturan*.

The *kenong* is also sometimes used to signal a high register or a move to a high register. This has been illustrated in connection with the *bonangan* for a *lancaran* (p. 145). In the same connection, the possible use of pairs of *kenong* notes in *lancaran* was mentioned, and the regular use of the same *kenong* note throughout a *gâtrâ* of (Solo-style) *srepegan*. In (Solo-style) *sampak* the principle is extended to eight strokes per *gâtrâ*, as shown above. The Yogya equivalents of Solonese *srepegan* and *sampak* (Table 2.18) work on similar principles.

Garap called *kenong banggèn*, *kenong sungsun* or *kenong goyang (sungsun)*, where some *kenong* strokes are repeated twice more, is known for certain *ladrang*, e.g. *ldr Sobrang pl 7* and *ldr Surung dhayung pl 6*, the latter being shown here, with *kenong* 2 in each position marked

. . 5 6   1 2 3 2̂   . ^2 1̂ 6   5 6 1 2̂
. ^2 3̂ 5   . 6 4 5   6 6 2 1   3 2 6 5

but these pieces are also played with standard *garap*.

A few pieces have special *garap* on the *kenong*. In the well-known double-density three-*kenongan ldr Loro-loro topèng*, used as the *inggah* of *gd Loro-loro géndhong sl m*

3 5 6 1̇   6 5 3 2   2 2 1 6̣   3 5 3 2̂
2 2 2 3   5 6 5 3̆   5 2 5 3   2̇ 3̇ 2̇ 1̂
2̇ 6 2̇ 1̇   3̇ 2̇ 6 5̆   3 3 . 5   6 3 5 (6)̂

the sequences of 2 in two places are given additional *kenong* (and *gong suwukan*) strokes

in *ir II*, *kébar*:

3 5 6 1̇ 6 5 3 (2)̂ 2̂ (2)̂ 1 6̣ 3 5 3 (2)̂
2̂ (2)̂ 2 3 etc.

in *ir III/IV*:

3 5 6 1̇ 6 5 3 (2)̂^(2)̂^(2)̂ 1 6̣ 3 5 3 (2)̂^
(2)̂^(2)̂ 2 3 etc.

This *garap* has variants; for example, some versions of the *balungan* have 2 2 2 6̣ instead of 2 2 1 6̣, allowing an additional *kenong* stroke on the fourth 2 of the sequences (at least in *ir II*). Also see **Ompak klénangan**, p. 234.

Kenong japan

The *kenong japan*[40] or *kenong jepang* (Fig. 3.68) is a large *pencon* instrument of *dhempok* form, resembling an oversized *kethuk* rather than the other *kenong*, and found only in Yogya-style gamelan. It is tuned to 5̣, in the octave below the other *kenong*, and is sometimes described as a 'female' *kenong* (*kenong setrèn*). There is a separate *kenong japan* for each *laras*.

The *kenong japan* is confined to *lancaran/bubaran* and *gangsaran*, to *ketawang* and *ladrang* in the loud style, and to accompaniments for pieces in *tayuban* style. In those contexts, the traditional Yogya style requires all *kenong* strokes to use the instrument: the *kenong japan* is never mixed with the other *kenong*. The strokes are not delayed relative to the *balungan* beats.

If a *kenong japan* is present in a gamelan, it is played by the same player who handles the other *kenong* (and possibly the *kethuk* and other punctuating instruments). The standard *kenong* beater can be used.

Kenong rèntèng

The *kenong rèntèng* is a substitute instrument of *slentho* form made in bronze, brass or iron, offering a substantial cost saving over a set of separate *kenong* pots (even in iron). The notes can be whatever the customer wants, but the example in Fig. 3.69 is a *pélog* instrument with the notes 3, 5, 6, 7, 1̇ and 2̇.

The beaters used on the *kenong rèntèng* are similar to those used on normal *kenong*, or perhaps slightly harder. The tone quality and volume of the *kenong rèntèng* are both satisfactory, but do not provide a perfect match for

40 No connection with Japan has been established.

the regular *kenong*. Because of the resonators, the sound dies away more slowly than on regular *kenong*.

Kempul

Construction

The *kempul* is the next smaller *pencon gandhul* after the *gong suwukan* (Fig. 3.64).

This is another instrument that has acquired more notes over the centuries. The earliest gamelan have only a single *kempul*, tuned to 5 or 6, if they have one at all. A fully equipped modern gamelan has *kempul* 3, 5, 6, 1̇ and 2̇ in *sléndro*; 3, 5, 6, 7, 1̇ and 2̇ in *pélog*. Because the pattern of usage differs from that of the *kenong*, the 3 and 2̇ are relatively rarely needed, and are arguably optional. A *kempul* 4 in *pélog* is unlikely to be found, and in a *tumbuk nem* gamelan a *kempul* 5 *sléndro* may be able to substitute for it anyway.

Role

The *kempul* has a less important punctuating role than the *kenong*, and is not used in all *bentuk*. *Gendhing* (in the narrower sense) do not use it in either the *mérong* or the *inggah*. The *kempul* could be described as subdividing the *kenongan*, but in several *bentuk* (Fig. 2.18) it is missing from the first *kenongan* of the *gongan*.

Besides its use as a punctuating instrument, the *kempul* reinforces the *balungan* notes as a form of decoration in certain pieces. For example, in the *ngelik* of *ktw Kasatriyan sl 9* a sequence of *kempul* and *gong suwukan* is used

6 5 2̇ 1̇   3̇ 2̇ 6 5̂   . . 1̇ 6 5 (2)   1 6̣ 3̣ ⑤

where the *gong suwukan* stroke replaces the usual *kempul* stroke.

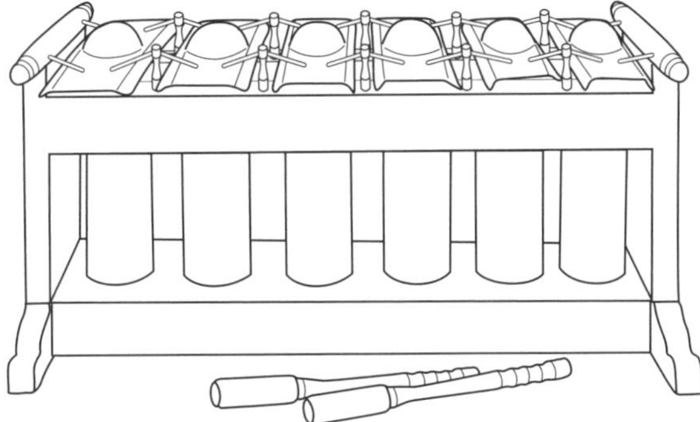

3.69 *Kenong rèntèng*

On the additional *kempul* strokes for *ompak klénangan*, see under **Multi-instrument *garap***, p. 231.

Playing technique

The *kempul* is played with a smaller version of the *béndhå* used on the gongs.

Like the *kenong*, the *kempul* is only damped (with the hand and/or the beater) when the strokes are close together, i.e. in *lancaran/bubaran*, at least some of the editable forms—*srepegan* and *sampak*—and possibly *palaran* and *ayak-ayakan*. Damping is also normal between the additional *kempul* strokes that may be used in *kébar* (see under **Multi-instrument *garap***, p. 231) and those used for decorative purposes, as illustrated above. Damping usually happens midway between the *kempul* strokes. However, in all the contexts mentioned, the *kempul* stroke immediately before a *gong ageng* or *gong suwukan* need only be damped after the gong stroke.

On delays relative to the *balungan*, see **Delaying the strokes**.

Garap

The choice of note is slightly more *pathet*-dependent for the *kempul* than for the *kenong*. The default notes are 6 for *pathet manyurå* and 5 for *pathet sångå*, but further considerations enter the picture when a complete table of *kempul* notes vs. *sèlèh* notes is attempted. *Garap* in *pélog* follows that in *sléndro* in the usual way, and careful players will take account of the character of pieces in *pl 7* rather than simply use the notes shown below.

Sèlèh note	*Kempul* note			
	Sl m	*Pl 7*	*Sl 9*	*Pl 5/6*
1̣, 1	1̇	—	5	5
2̣, 2	6	6	5 or 6	5 or 6
3̣, 3, 3̇	6	6	6	6
4̣, 4	—	?	—	6
5̣, 5	5	5	5	5
6̣, 6	6	6	6	6
7̣, 7	—	7	—	7
1̇	1̇	—	1̇	1̇
2̇	2̇ or 2	2̇ or 2	2̇ or 2	2̇ or 2

The occurrence of a *sèlèh* 4 in *pl 7* is unlikely. The table does not include the use of *kempul* 3. In practice it is used

for *sèlèh* 3̣ or 3 in the editable forms, and in lighter pieces that might be played for *wayang*. The *kempul* 2̇, if present, is likely to be treated similarly.

Terminology for some of the *garap* follows that of the *kenong*: *kempul mbalung*, *kempul ancer* or *kempul tunggal råså* for a *kempul* note that matches the *balungan* note; *kempul kempyungan* or *kempul adu manis* for a note a *kempyung* above the *balungan* note; *kempul salah gumun* (or sometimes *kempul adu manis*) for a note a *gembyung* above the *balungan* note; *kempul pinatut* for a note anticipating a note in a vocal line.

Kempul plèsèdan also occur, but much less often than *kenong plèsèdan*, because the *kempul* stroke comes at the end of an odd-numbered *gåtrå*. However, as one example, a *gåtrå* felt to be strongly oriented to 5, e.g. 3 5 6 5, at the end of the *gongan* in a *ladrang* or a *ketawang* might be a good reason to choose *kempul* 5 at the end of the preceding *gåtrå*, regardless of the *balungan* note and with or without evidence that 3 5 6 5 represented a *gantungan*.

Like the *kenong*, the *kempul* can signal a high register or a move to a high register.

The following example, for *srepegan manyurå*, illustrates several of the principles just mentioned

balungan	3 2 3 2	5 3 5 3	2̇ 3̇ 2̇ (1̇)
kenong notes	2	3	1̇
kempul notes	6	1̇	1̇
balungan	2̇ 1̇ 2̇ 1̇	3 2 3 2	5 6 1̇ (6)
kenong notes	1̇	2 or 2̇	6
kempul notes	1̇	6 or 2̇	6
balungan	1̇ 6 1̇ 6	5 3 5 3	6 5 3 (2)
kenong notes	6	3	2
kempul notes	6	6 or 3	2

mérong kt x ar

mérong kt x kp

inggah, ladrang, ketawang

lancaran

3.70 Relationship between *kethuk* and *kenong* strokes and *balungan*

and this pattern of *kenong* and *kempul* notes would apply equally in *sampak manyurå*, which has the same *sèlèh* notes.

Garap called *kempul susun/sungsun* is used for some *ladrang*, e.g. when played in *tayuban* style in the Yogya tradition: this means repetition of the *kempul* stroke on the next *balungan* beat. This may be applied only to the regular three *kempul* strokes per *gongan*, but otherwise looks very similar to the more familiar extra *kempul* strokes that may be used in *kébar* (see **Kébar**, p. 231).

In a *palaran*, the *kenong* and *kempul* notes in a given 'cell' are not necessarily the same. The *kempul* player must interpret any hand signals accordingly. For example, a hand signal for 2 will be taken by the *kenong* player as meaning 2, but the *kempul* player will usually interpret it as requesting a *kempul* 6.

Kethuk

Construction

The *kethuk* is a small *pencon pangkon* of *dhempok* form, made of bronze, brass or iron. It is usually supported in a small *rancakan* of its own (Fig. 3.68), smaller than those of the *kenong* but of the same style, or it may share a small double *rancakan* with a *kempyang*.

There is a separate *kethuk* for each *laras*. The tuning is not absolutely standard: 2 in *sléndro* and the 6̣ just below it in *pélog* are typical, but the adjacent 1 in *sléndro* and 2 in *pélog* are also found. The pitches are at the bottom end of the *kenong* range.

The name of the *kethuk* is significant in itself. Among the onomatopoeic names of the punctuating instruments, *kethuk* is unusual in ending with a stop consonant. As in the names of drumstrokes, the stop consonant indicates a 'dead' sound. The practical significance of this is explained under **Playing technique** below.

Role

The *kethuk* provides the densest patterns among the punctuating instruments that are used across the full range of *bentuk*. It is also an important method of classifying *gendhing* in the narrower sense—at least in the Solo tradition, although the Yogyanese too sometimes refer to *kethuk* structures in this connection.

Fig. 3.70 shows how the pattern of the *kethuk* strokes remains constant across a wide range of *bentuk* and timescales, regardless of the presence of *kempyang* strokes.

(*Kempul* strokes are not shown.) Longer *mérong* forms would require the extension of the patterns to the left.

Playing technique

In the most basic technique, the *kethuk* is struck on the beat, then the beater is held in contact with the *pencu* afterwards, to damp the sound immediately.

In the slower *iråmå*—*ir II* and below—the single stroke on the *kethuk* is replaced by a series of strokes that create a 'rolled' sound lasting for one second or even longer. From the graphical examples below

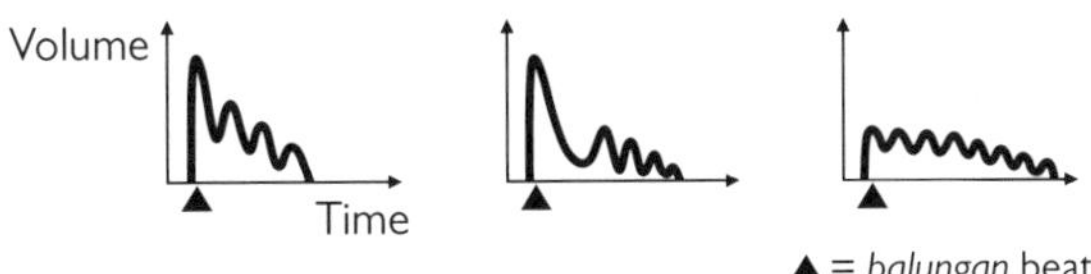

it can be seen that in each case the effect is to soften and spread the sound. This is a characteristically Solonese technique, traditionally not used by the Yogyanese.

In the loud style in *ir I*, there are additional possibilities: a quick double stroke, with the second stroke also damping the sound; or a single stroke left to ring very briefly before it is damped.

The beater may be identical to the *kenong* beater, or slightly smaller. A player who is responsible for the *kethuk* as well as the *kenong* may use the same beater for both instruments.

Garap

Standard *kethuk* positions are shown in Fig. 2.18, Fig. 2.23 and Table 2.18. Standard changes found in *ompak inggah/pangkat dhawah* are shown in Fig. 2.24: these may be called *kethuk salahan*.

The other usage of the term *kethuk salahan* is for optional variant punctuation patterns that signal the approach of a gong in smaller *bentuk*. In a *ketawang* such as *Puspåwarnå*, the final *gongan* may use this pattern in *ir II* (not showing the *kempyang* strokes, which are as usual):

. 2 . 3   . 2 . 1   . 3 . 2   . 1 . (6)

The pattern can be described as inserting extra *kethuk* strokes on either side of the final *kempul*. It can also be used in a *ladrang*—again, before the last gong of an overall cycle, in either *ir I* or *ir II*.

Kethuk salahan are also used in the *inggah* of *gendhing*, e.g. in a *gendhing bonang* of *mg kt 8* form, again from the Yogya tradition so without *kempyang* (part of the final *kenongan*):

3 6 3 5   3 6 3 2   3 6 3 2   3 6 3 (5)

Another is known as *kethuk banggèn*:

. . . . (.)

Double strokes called *kethuk susun/sungsun* are used in Yogya for *ladrang* performed in the *tayuban* style in *ir II*, e.g. *ldr Rujak jeruk sl m* (double density):

. 5 . 2   . 5 . 3   . 5 . 6   . 5 . 2
. 5 . 2   . 5 . 3   . 5 . 6   . 5 . 2
6 3 5 6   . 1 3 2   5 3 2 1   6 5 2 3
6 5 2 .   2 3 5 6   1 6 5 3   6 5 3 (2)

Another similar type of *garap* may be used in Yogya for loud-style *ladrang* in *ir II*, but with three equally spaced strokes instead of the usual one, i.e. per *gåtrå*:

. . . .

With some of the *kethuk* strokes only a quarter-beat away from *kempyang* positions, this *garap* may only be feasible in *sléndro*, where there are no *kempyang* in the Yogya style. The example is from *ldr Sigråmangsah sl m*:

3 5 6 1   3 2 1 6   3 5 6 1   3 2 1 6
3 5 2 3   1 2 1 6   3 2 6 3   6 5 3 (2)

Kempyang

Construction

The *kempyang* consists of either one or two small *pencon pangkon* of *brunjung* form in bronze, brass or iron.

In the Solo tradition the *kempyang* is a usually a single pot tuned to 1 in *sléndro* or 6 in *pélog*. A few gamelan have two pots, both tuned to 6.[41] Yogyanese gamelan have no *kempyang* in *sléndro*, but two pots tuned to 6 and 7 in *pélog*.

A single *kempyang* is usually supported in a *rancakan* of its own. Pairs of *kempyang* may be placed in a double *rancakan* of the same style (Fig. 3.71), or in a miniature version of the *rancakan* used for *bonang*.

41 It is not clear whether these are (or should be) deliberately tuned off in order to generate beats.

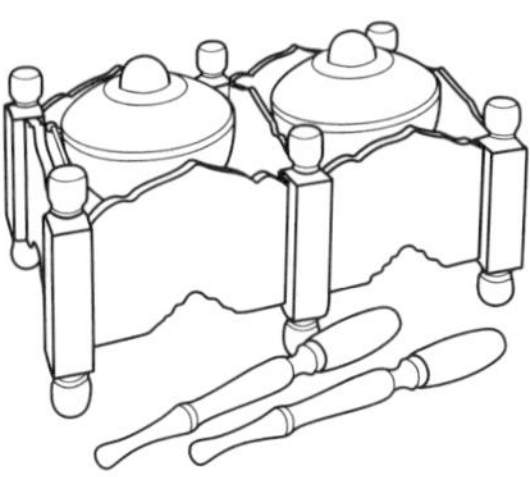
3.71 Two-pot *kempyang*

Role

The role of the *kempyang* is a little surprising, since it is absent from so many *bentuk*. Also, in those *bentuk* where it is used—*ladrang*, *ketawang*, *inggah* and possibly *bubaran*—it often plays simultaneously with a *pancer* note from the *balungan* section. If the *pancer* note is the same as the

kempyang note, which is often the case, the *kempyang* only reinforces the *pancer*: otherwise, as will often occur in *pélog*, the two notes will conflict twice per *gåtrå*.

Playing technique

The *kempyang* is never damped. In the Yogya style the two pots are played simultaneously, which means that the player needs two beaters: this makes it even less practical for the same player to deal with the *kenong* too. From the layout of some gamelan (e.g. *Kyahi Kaduk manis*, pictured on p. 236) it is clear that a separate player is there responsible solely for the *kethuk* and *kempyang*, even when the *kempyang* has only a single pot. (The *engkuk-kemong* may possibly replace the *kempyang* in *sléndro*, but this does not change the situation.)

The frequent use of the note 7 when the *kempyang* is played in pieces in *pélog bem* comes as a surprise, and some musicians have been sufficiently disturbed by it to call for the safer note 5 instead. Nevertheless the combination of 6 and 7 remains the standard in Yogya.

Garap

The regular usages of the *kempyang* have been described in Part 2 under **Gendhing: classification by structure**, p. 83, and (for shorter *bentuk*) in Fig. 2.18 and Table 2.18. In addition the Yogya style allows the *kempyang* to be inserted between the other punctuating strokes in *bubaran* (not *lancaran*), i.e. 16 *kempyang* strokes per *gongan*.

Kethuk salahan do not seem to involve changing the positions of the *kempyang*, but it would be no surprise to find an exception.

42 Not all sources agree on the assignment of the names.

43 e.g. Supanggah (2002) says the *engkuk-kemong* is not found in Yogya, but the present author knows of several there.

44 At the Pakualaman and elsewhere, confirmed on occasions some six years apart.

Engkuk-kemong

The *engkuk-kemong* is a pair of small *pencon* of *dhempok* form (slightly larger than the *kethuk*) in bronze, brass or iron, which may be found either as *pencon pangkon* on a *rancakan* or as *pencon gandhul* on a small *gayor* of their own (Fig. 3.72). The instrument is only found in *sléndro*, and the pots are tuned to 1 and 6̣—the *engkuk* and the *kemong* respectively.[42] A single beater of the *kethuk* or *kenong* type is used, and the player may look after the *kethuk* and *kempyang* as well. Both notes are played on the beat and may be damped.

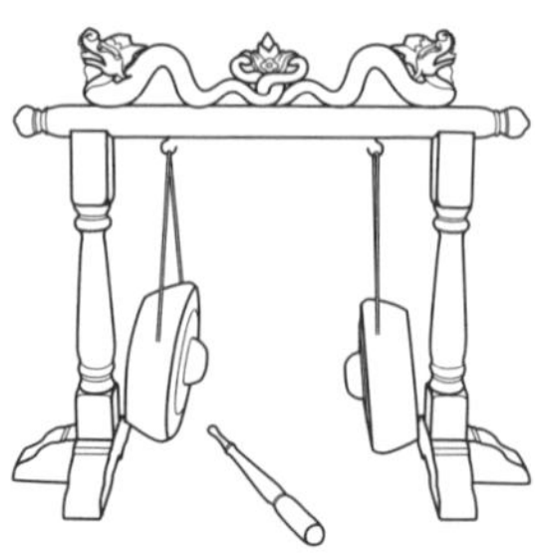

3.72. *Engkuk-kemong*

It is unclear whether the *engkuk-kemong* is more widely used in Solo or in Yogya: it appears to be rare in both cities,[43] and there is no agreement on its *garap*, nor on the types of piece where it is played. More than one source has the *engkuk* and *kemong* simply substituting for the *kempyang* and *kethuk*, respectively. The *garap* described here was recorded relatively recently:[44] the example below, with the *engkuk* and *kemong* represented by e and k respectively (as there seem to be no established symbols for this instrument), is the first *kenongan* of a *ladrang* that has a double-density *balungan* in *ir III*.

```
          e k e     e k e
ir II     2 1̇ 2 6̣   2 1̇ 2 3̂

          e k e     e k e
ir III    2 3 2 1̇   3 2 1 6̣

          e k e     e k e
          2 3 2 1̇   6̣ 1 2 3̂
```

In the *ir II* version, the *kethuk* is surprisingly struck at the same time as the *kemong* (and the usual 'rolled' *kethuk* strokes may be used). The two examples together show an *engkuk-kemong* pattern whose density relative to the *kethuk* changes with *irâmå*—an anomalous situation. *Kethuk salahan* may still be heard when the *engkuk-kemong* is used.

Kemanak

The *kemanak* (Fig. 3.73) is always described as resembling a banana. It may be made in any of the usual metals. The shape varies, especially in the area where it is held (*bèngkok* and *kawetan*). The instrument is used in pairs typically tuned to two notes close together: the lower is around 6, and the upper in the vicinity of 7 or 1̇ (*sléndro* or *pélog*). As the tuning is evidently not considered critical, the same pair is used for both *laras*. Not all gamelan have the *kemanak*, but they are essential to the performance of some *bedhåyå* and *srimpi*.

As playing the *kemanak* is a two-handed task, two players are needed. The beater is of the *bonang* type, and

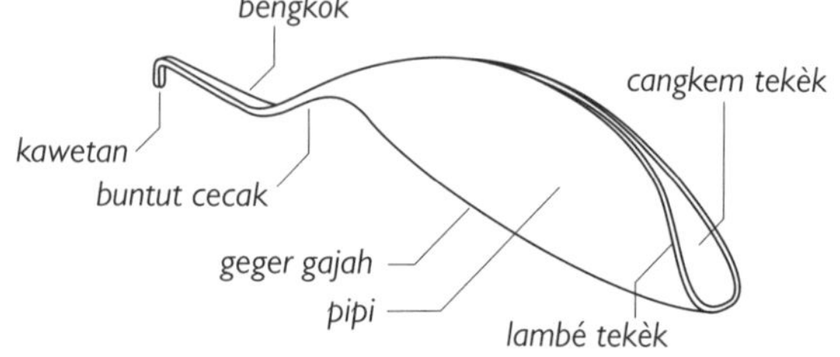

3.73 Parts of a *kemanak*

therefore it is convenient for the *bonang* players to play the *kemanak*: the *bonang* are never played in *gendhing kemanak*. The method of playing the *kemanak* is shown in Fig. 3.74, and has three stages, numbered in the diagram. First the instrument, held in front of the player, is struck by the beater. Then the player moves the *kemanak* in an arc past his left ear, as if to throw it over his shoulder (stage 2). Towards the end of this movement, the player damps the instrument with his thumb (stage 3).

The reason for moving the *kemanak* in this way at stage 2 is obscure. For the player the result is a small but perceptible rise in the pitch of the sound, due to the Doppler effect, as the *kemanak* approaches his ear. The frequency shift can be calculated as little more than 0.5 per cent, but this is just sufficient for the ear to detect. For anyone else nearby, listening from a different angle, the Doppler shift will be much less, and therefore usually undetectable.

The basic pattern of *kemanak* strokes follows that of other punctuating instruments (writing the notes as 6 and 7)

kemanak 7 6 7 .
[*balungan*, *ir II*] . .

but usually the 6 is struck and immediately damped, i.e. played *ceceg* (as shown by the solidus in Fig. 3.77), to close this pattern. Also there is normally some kind of *salahan* to the gong, which may be as simple as not damping one of the *ceceg* notes. The word *balungan* is placed in brackets because many *gendhing kemanak* are purely vocal and have no *balungan*.

The other punctuation in *gendhing kemanak* is *kethuk*, *kenong* and gong: the *kempyang* is not used even if the basic *bentuk* is *ladrang* or *ketawang (alit)*.

Kecèr

The *kecèr* is a pair of small cymbals, or often two pairs (Fig. 3.75), where the lower cymbal is attached to a *pangkon* of the *saron* type and the other is loose but tied to it by a cord. Two shapes are found (Fig. 3.76): circular (*kecèr kambali*) and eight-sided (*kecèr bintang*). *Kecèr* are used in *wayang kulit* accompaniment, but as the *dhalang* wishes, and at no fixed places.

Other types of cymbals called *kecèr* or *rojèh* are found in ceremonial gamelan—sometimes only a single cymbal played with a *gandhèn*.

Substitute instruments

A few other substitutions occasionally occur. When a gamelan is played in the back of a truck, as sometimes happens at festivals, a bass guitar may replace a set of *kempul*.

The *gong bumbung*, a substitute instrument, may itself be replaced by someone blowing across the top of a bottle. This is called a *gong gendul*.

Dhalang may prefer Western-style cymbals to the more delicate sound of the *kecèr*.

Other instruments

The instrumentation of the ceremonial gamelan is described under **Ensembles**, p. 239 foll. Various additional types of hanging gong are found there, some of them without *pencu*: *campur*, *penonthong*, *béri*, *bendhé*.

A few ceremonial gamelan have a 'bell-tree' (*byong*, *gentorag*, *krompyong*, *kroncong*, *sekar/kembang delimå*).

Keplok

Keplok is rhythmic clapping, usually divided between an on-beat part and an off-beat part. The combined density of the two parts in *ir IV* corresponds to *lampah* 32. *Keplok* is an essential part of the texture of *iråmå rangkep* (including *ir II rangkep*), and helps to keep the other players in rhythm. It is often provided by *balungan* players who have stopped playing during *ir IV*. *Keplok* is an equally important element of *kébar*, *kiprahan* sections of dance suites, and *palaran*.

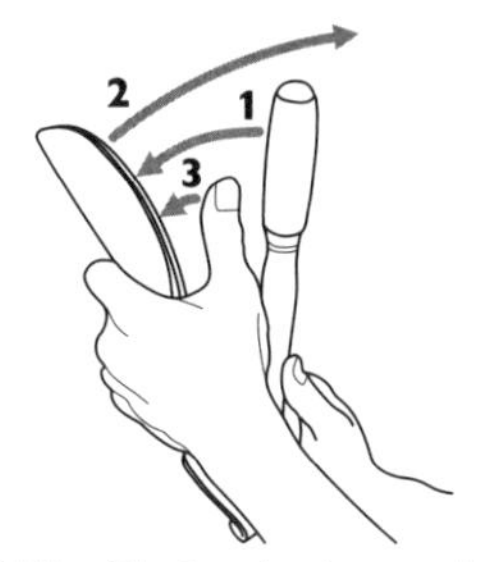

3.74 Playing the *kemanak*

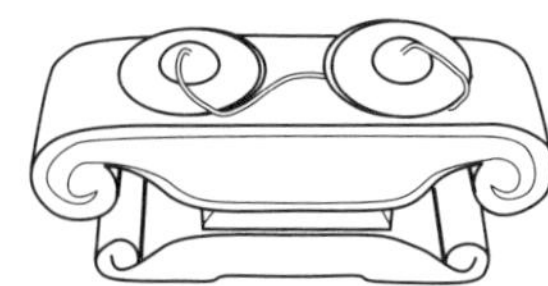

3.75 Kecèr

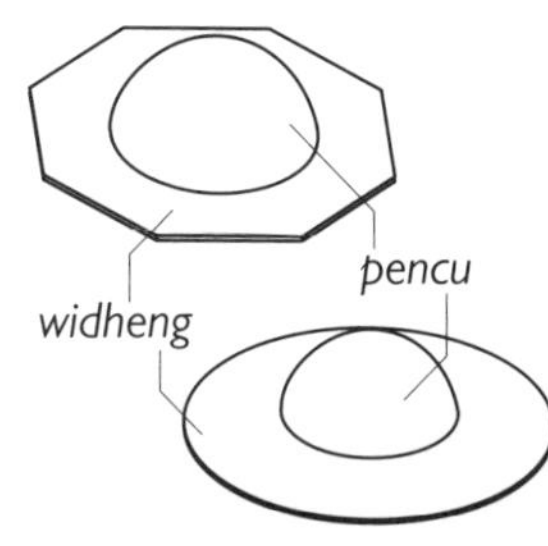

3.76 Parts of a *kecèr*

kemanak 7 6 7 6̸ 7 6 7 6̸ 7 6 7 6̸ 7 6 7 6̸ 7 6 7 6̸ 7 6 7 6̸ 7 6 7 6 7 6 7 6̸
[*balungan*] . . . . (.)
alternative *salahan* for *kemanak* 7 6 7 6̸ 7 6 7 6̸ 7 6 7 6̸7676 7 .
alternative *salahan* for *kemanak* 7 6 7 6̸ 7 6 7 6̸ 7 6 7 6̸7.76 7 .

3.77 *Kemanak* pattern in a 16-beat *ketawang* in *ir II*

Drums

General

Construction

Most drums (Fig. 3.78) used in the gamelan have a common structure, and the differences are only in size and to some extent in shape. According to the general pattern, the heads (*tébokan*, *wengkon*) of the *kendhang* are held on to the body (*ploncon*) by straps (*janget*) made from rawhide. The skin of the drumhead is wrapped round a wooden or bamboo hoop (*blengker*), and is pierced to allow the *janget* to pass through. The straps run zig-zag between the heads, acting only on the *blengker*, not directly on the skins.

Solonese drums traditionally use goatskin for the drumheads. Yogyanese drums traditionally use water-buffalo skin, and some Solonese players prefer this material for its greater weight and 'punch'.

The drum bodies have traditionally been made from *nångkå* (jackfruit) wood. In recent years the makers have had difficulty obtaining suitable supplies of timber. One reason given is that larger trees are less productive of fruit, and therefore get cut down before they reach the right size for the drum-makers. This situation has had two consequences. First, drums have been made from poor-quality timber, with very uneven grain leading to splits in the body. Second, other timbers such as teak and *munggur* (see **Appendix 5**) are replacing *nångkå*.

The cavity inside most drums is basically cylindrical, but the internal structure may create more than one tuned resonator. Fig. 3.79 shows a shallow cavity (*rau*) behind the large head.[45]

Externally, most modern drums are barrel-shaped, i.e. roughly cylindrical but tapering towards each end. They are also asymmetrical, with one head larger than the other. The larger head produces a lower-pitched sound and is usually played with the right hand. A few players reverse the drums, not necessarily because they are left-handed.

The larger drums are provided with a handle, rather loosely attached to the body. Where the handle meets the body it is surrounded by a decorative plate (*manggisan*).

The body of a *kendhang* is often extensively decorated by carving (Fig. 3.80) and subsequent painting. If not painted, the drum is usually waxed or varnished.

Tuning

On the drums constructed as described above, rawhide rings (*suh*) are moved along the straps to adjust the tension in the heads. The tuning process must give not only the right note but also the right sound. Since the tuning straps affect both heads, it can be difficult to achieve this

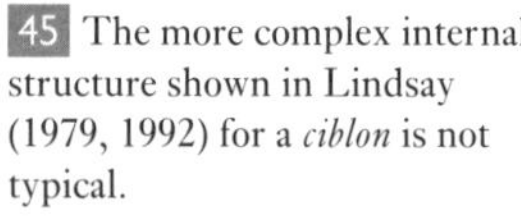

45 The more complex internal structure shown in Lindsay (1979, 1992) for a *ciblon* is not typical.

3.79 Interior of a *ciblon* (large head)

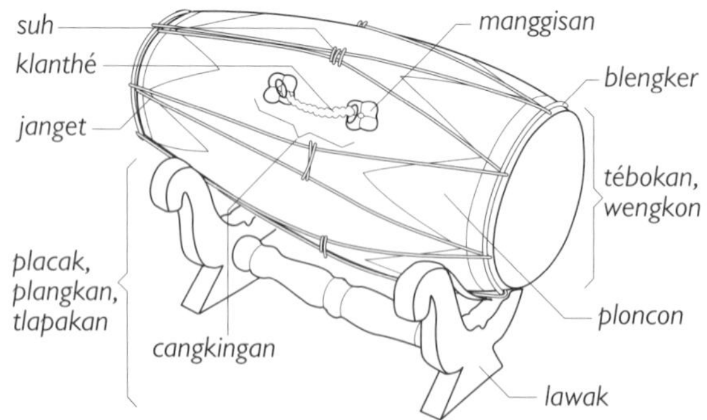

3.78 Parts of a *kendhang*

3.80 Carving a *bedhug* in *munggur* wood

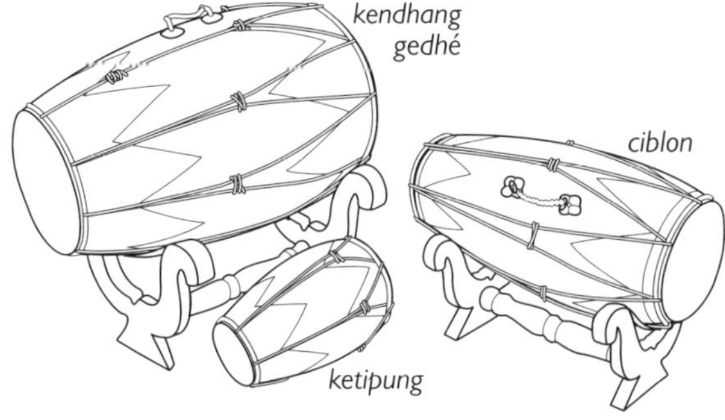

3.81 Layout for a set of *kendhang*

aim, especially when the atmospheric humidity is too high or too low. Drums have bad days. They need to be retired when they no longer have any good days.

Arrangements for playing

Most of the drums sit on stands (*tlapakan*). In a typical arrangement (Fig. 3.81), the drums are laid out so that the player turns his/her whole body through 90 degrees (to left or right) in order to play the *ciblon*. After switching to the *ciblon*, the player may still play occasional *dha* strokes on the *kendhang gedhé*.

The *ketipung* is often placed on the player's lap to be played. It may be placed on the ground, but this means that the player's hand must move further between the heads of the *kendhang ageng* and *ketipung*. The other *kendhang* normally remain on their stands.

Unlike drums in other parts of Indonesia, the main drums in central Java are played with bare hands. To avoid extraneous noises, players must remove rings or bracelets before playing.

Individual drums

Kendhang ageng

The *kendhang ageng* [*kr*] or *kendhang gedhé* [*ng*] is the largest of the drums regularly used in the gamelan. It is used either by itself or in combination with the *ketipung* or *penunthung*. Because it may be used on its own for drumming at least the first part of a *gendhing*, this drum is also sometimes known as *kendhang gendhing*. Another name occasionally found is *kendhang bedhugan*.

The large head of the *kendhang ageng* is tuned roughly to the note 2, or possibly to 1 for *pélog limå*. The small head is tuned roughly a *kempyung* higher.

When the *kendhang ageng* is used by itself, its patterns are referred to as *kendhang(an) siji* [*ng*] or *kendhang(an) satunggal* [*kr*], abbreviated to *kd I*.

Ketipung

The *ketipung* is the smallest of the *kendhang*. It is not usually played on its own.

The large head of the *ketipung* is tuned roughly to the note 6, or perhaps to 5 for *pélog limå*. The small head is tuned about a *kempyung* higher.

The use of *kendhang ageng* together with *ketipung* is called *kendhang(an) loro* [*ng*] or *kendhang(an) kalih* [*kr*], or *kendang dua* in Indonesian, all abbreviated to *kd II*. In this type of *kendhangan*, the *kendhang ageng* provides the *dha* stroke, and the other strokes come from the *ketipung*.

Penunthung

The *penunthung* is another small drum, slightly larger than the *ketipung*, found in some ceremonial gamelan. In a normal *gamelan gedhé* its role is taken by the *ketipung*, and the rest of the description here applies to the *ketipung* when used in this way.

The role of the *penunthung* in the ceremonial gamelan is to contribute two strokes per *gåtrå* as follows

balungan	5 3 5 6
penunthung	. p p .

The name *penunthung* can be interpreted as 'the thing that goes "*thun-thung*"'. Sometimes, mainly in *gendhing* of a more serious character, including *gendhing bonang*, this pattern of strokes is imitated by a second drummer, alongside the player on the *kendhang ageng* who is supplying the standard *kd I* patterns. For *ir II* the pattern is

balungan	5 3 5 6
penunthung/ketipung	. p p . . p p .

Curiously, it is the *penunthung* player who has the responsibility for signalling speed changes and transitions. Otherwise the *penunthung* patterns continue unchanged, except that they often include a *salahan* to signal the gong stroke, e.g. (*ir II*, *mérong*, *kethuk 2 kp*)

. p p $\overset{+}{.}$. p p .
. p p $\overset{+}{.}$ p . p p $\widehat{(.)}$

and for a corresponding *minggah kethuk 4*

. p p $\overset{+}{.}$. p p . . p p $\overset{+}{.}$. p p .

. p p . . p p .p .p .p .p .pp p p (.)

The combination of *kendhang ageng* with *penunthung* is still regarded as *kendhangan satunggal*. It is also possible for a single player to look after both drums, by angling the *penunthung/ketipung* so that its head is close to the larger head of the *kendhang ageng*.

Ciblon

The *kendhang ciblon*, commonly referred to simply as *ciblon*, is used on its own in certain contexts. It is associated with dance, but also in general with the livelier forms of *garap*. In *klenèngan*, the *ciblon* is often played for most of the time, because it is used during *irâmâ III/IV* sections in the *inggah* of *gendhing*, and often during the vocal sections of other shorter pieces.

The *ciblon* is intermediate in size between the *ketipung* and *kendhang ageng*. The Yogyanese sometimes use the name *kendhang batangan*[46] instead, and the external shape of the drum can be somewhat different; either a cylinder or a truncated cone. These alternative shapes are common among older drums.[47]

46 The significance of the description *batangan* is unclear. The word *bathang* can refer to various cylindrical objects (and its Indonesian equivalent *batang* has that meaning), but *batang* in Javanese can mean 'guess', 'puzzle' or 'riddle'.

47 Including drums in ceremonial gamelan: see Fig. 3.99.

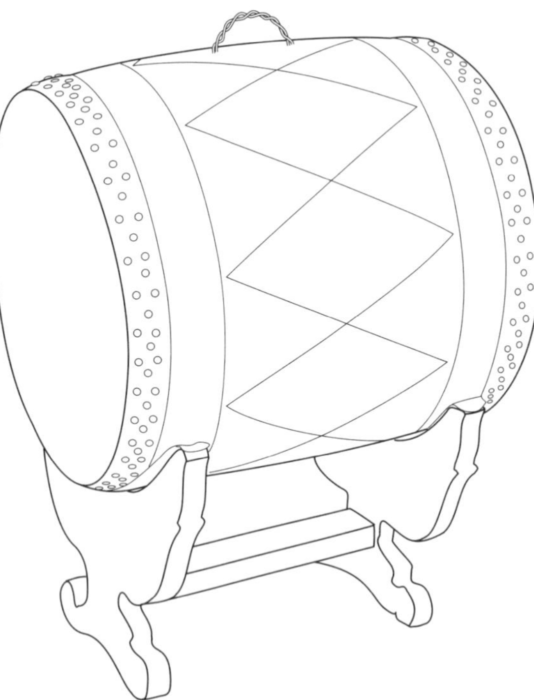

3.82 *Bedhug* on a stand

3.83 Large *bedhug* at the *kraton Yogya*, with a frame about 2 m high

The tuning of the *ciblon* is not standardised. Often the two heads are tuned towards roughly the same notes as the *kendhang gedhé*, but in a higher octave.

Because of the strong association between *irâmâ wilet* and *ciblon* drumming, sources of notation sometimes apply the label '*irâmâ ciblon*' to the double-density version of the *balungan* used in *ir III*. (However, *kosèkan* drumming can also be used in *ir III*: the difference between this and *ciblon* drumming is that the latter implies *bonang imbal* and other *garap* differences.) A Yogyanese term often used for *ciblon* drumming is *kendhangan gembyakan*, the latter word meaning 'enjoyment' or 'pleasure'.

Kendhang wayangan

The *kendhang wayangan* or *kendhang sabet* is essentially a slightly larger version of the *ciblon*, offering a greater weight of sound for the accompaniment of *wayang*. There is a particular type of *kendhangan*—called *kosèk wayangan* or simply *kosèkan*—associated with it. If a gamelan does not possess a *kendhang wayangan*, its repertoire is played on a *ciblon* and/or *kendhang gedhé* instead.

Bedhug

The *bedhug* (Fig. 3.82), sometimes known as *teteg*, is the odd one out among the drums in the gamelan, for various reasons. Its heads are pegged to the body and their tensions therefore cannot be adjusted. Its shape is symmetrical, in contrast to most other drums. The *bedhug* differs too in sometimes being suspended from above in a frame (*jâgrâ*, Fig. 3.83) or a *gayor* rather than sitting on a stand. It is also the only drum (apart from those of the ceremonial gamelan) struck with a beater rather than with the bare hand. The beater can take various forms, e.g. a long wooden stick with an unpadded spherical wooden head of about 40–50 mm diameter, or a smaller version of the *béndhâ* used with the *kempul*, or a fatter version of the beaters used with the *kenong*.

For the *bedhug* found in the *kraton* and in mosques, it is probably a case of the larger, the better. Certainly some very large instruments are to be seen (for example, Fig. 3.83). The *bedhug* that are used in regular gamelan are rather smaller, but their size and shape vary. They are typically similar in length to the *kendhang ageng* but larger in diameter.

The *bedhug* has a very limited role outside ceremonial gamelan, and is therefore absent from most gamelan. It is

Kendhang notation

A separate notation system is used for *kendhangan*. In fact several systems have been used and are still used, but the one described here is the most widely taught. The symbols indicate the sounds, and therefore apply to all drums, ignoring the differences in the way the strokes are produced.

The symbols are basically taken from the alphabet, although some of them actually go back to earlier notation schemes: the P and b symbols were originally ♀ and ♁, representing the small and large heads respectively. Another element from earlier schemes is the filling-in of a symbol as one way to indicate a damped stroke. A stroke through the symbol is also used to indicate damping.

Like *kepatihan*, *kendhang* notation can vary, sometimes because of the limitations of the writing/printing method used. *Ket* is sometimes indicated by a vertical bar |, but this is liable to confusion with lower-case l, depending on the typeface used. Also not all writers are careful to distinguish between *lang* and *lung*, both of which may be written with upper-case or lower-case l. Here a cursive lower-case ℓ is preferred for *lung*, and k for *ket*. The *tak* stroke can be found written with upper- or lower-case t or a plus sign. Many writers use the same symbol for *tok* and *tong*.

The *dhelang* and *thulung* strokes are written as two separate symbols joined by an overscore, which makes their rhythm clear. The other combination strokes, including those where the heads are not struck simultaneously, are written with single symbols.

The apparent inconsistencies in the table below (the same symbol for *dhak* and *dhlak*, similar symbols for *dhlong* and *dhong*, and the *tong* symbol sometimes used for *tok*) reflect the way in which *ciblon* drumming varies from player to player: an individual player may consistently play *dhlak* rather than *dhak*, for example, so that no confusion arises in practice.

Notation for *kendhangan* is usually divided into units corresponding to four, eight or sixteen beats (very roughly 2, 4 or 8 seconds, respectively), which are often underlined. These blocks of notation, as for other instruments, may end at the *sèlèh* note or the following half-beat. Since the *kendhang* player controls tempo, symbols are available to show changes of *iråmå* and tempo. When the *iråmå* changes down, the *gåtrå* containing the transition may be marked by double underlining. A speed-up is shown by a right-pointing arrow under the *gåtrå*, and a slow-down by a left-pointing arrow. The dot (*pin*) and the overscore have the same meanings as in *kepatihan*.

Symbols

đ, ◖	*dhak*	ȸ	*d(h)lang*	ℓ	*lung*	P	*thung/dhung*
d	*(n)d(h)ang*	b°	*d(h)long*	t, T, +	*tak*	P (filled)	*thut*
b	*dhe/d(h)en/bem/ d(h)un/dha(h)*	B°	*dhong*	ŧ, P̶	*t(h)lang*	3, ●	*tok*[a]
		ƀ, ▶	*d(h)ut*	ṗ	*t(h)lok*	o	*tong*
b̄L	*d(h)elang*	h	*hen/hun*	p°	*t(h)long*		
ƀ, ▶	*d(h)et*	k	*ket*	P̶ℓ	*t(h)lung*		
◖	*d(h)lak*	L	*lang*	P̄ℓ	*thulung/dhulung*	a. Also often written o	

less uncommon in Yogya than in Solo. It was chosen in place of the *keprak* to direct the 'Ramayana ballet' at Prambanan. In the *gamelan sekatèn* it functions as a punctuating instrument equivalent to the *kempul*, and not as a time-keeper. As a member of a regular *gamelan gedhé* it contributes only one type of very loud stroke, instead of or in addition to the *dha* stroke on the *kendhang ageng*. The *bedhug* is arguably essential to the character of pieces in the *gati* form (see p. 72). If used in other *kendhangan* (where it is optional) it imparts a Yogyanese feel.

Kendhangan

Methods of producing the various drumstrokes are shown in the next four pages, and the notation system for *kendhangan* is described above. The relationship between the *kendhang* and the rest of the ensemble is described in **Principles of *kendhangan***, p. 222.

A few examples will illustrate the way in which drumstrokes are used to create patterns. More and longer examples are to be found in Part 4.

➔ p. 223

Drumstrokes—general

The diagrams below are for general guidance only. The correct place to strike a drum is whichever place produces the right sound, and students can only learn the strokes by imitation. Because drums differ, it is advisable to try various places in order to identify the best. Among other things, it is always worth rotating the drum and trying different parts of the head. Some strokes are particularly difficult to locate; notably the *thung* on the *ciblon* and *kendhang ageng*. Others become difficult if the *blengker* projects above the drumhead.

The diagrams depict the standard arrangement, where the right hand plays the larger head of the drum, and the left hand plays the smaller head.

The names[48] of the sounds give important information about their quality. Names ending in a vowel or -n, -m or -ng represent bounced, undamped strokes: the hand is not held in contact with the head after the stroke. Names ending in a stop consonant (-t or -k) are damped: the hand does not bounce off the head, but remains in contact with it after the stroke. The *tong* and *tok* strokes are not the same, but not all sources distinguish between them: the difference lies in whether the stroke is damped, not in the particular fingers used.

In the strokes that use, or can use, two or more fingers, the fingers should land together, so that only one sound is heard.

Some strokes use both heads. For details, see Table 3.22, **Combination strokes** and ***Kendhang* notation**.[49] In most of the strokes, the head that is not being struck may be damped with the hand in order to stop it contributing to the sound. The position of the hand is not critical: it can be anywhere that is convenient in relation to the preceding or following stroke. However, for certain strokes—especially *tak*—the damping is essential, whereas for the *thung/dhung* and *lang* strokes the non-struck head must be left free to sound.

Ketipung strokes

RIGHT-HAND STROKES

Thung/dhung is a bounced stroke with the basic pitch of the large head—the deepest of all the *ketipung* strokes. It can be produced in several ways. It is often made with the index finger (**a** below) or the middle finger (**b**), or even both together, near the edge of the drumhead. The finger(s) must be just far enough across the edge of the head, as shown in Fig. 3.84. Alternatively the stroke can be made with the thumb by rotating the hand (**c**), in the same way as for the *hen* stroke on the *ciblon*; in this case the hand is further across the head.

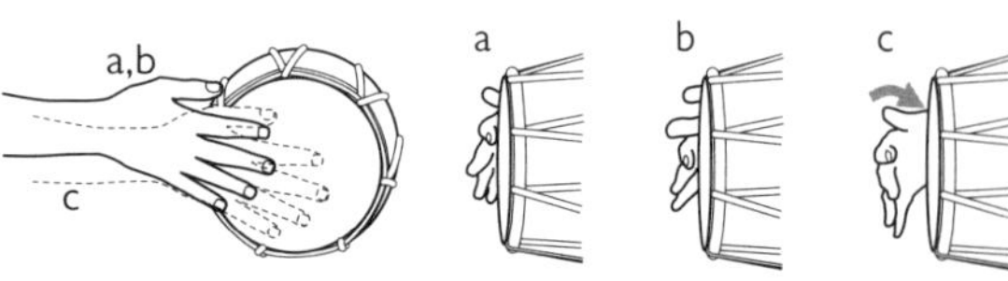

Ket is produced by one or more fingers, which may remain in contact with the head after the stroke. In any case the drumhead is damped by the other fingers, which are held in contact with the head throughout. The diagrams show the index and middle fingers producing the stroke, and the ring finger and little finger resting on the head. In alternative hand positions, such as that shown for the equivalent stroke on the *ciblon*, the thumb and the heel of the hand too damp the head, and the stroke is made by more than two fingers. This is a relatively quiet stroke, used mainly to fill in patterns in *kendhangan kalih*.

LEFT-HAND STROKES

Tak is an unbounced stroke as described for the *ciblon* (see below). Since the head is so small, the spread-out left hand may stretch right across it. *Tak* can be a very loud stroke, and is often used to get the players' attention, e.g. in a *bukå*.

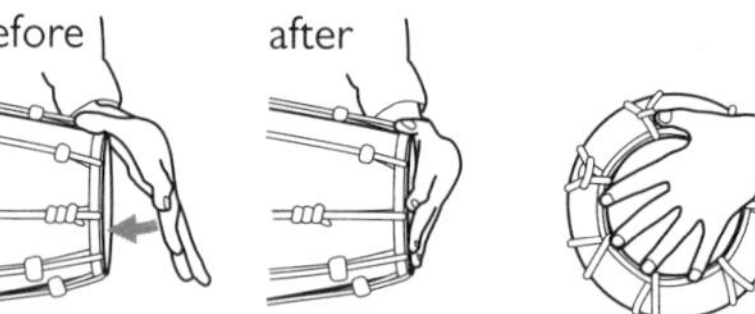

Tong is the highest-pitched stroke on the *ketipung*, produced as a 'rimshot' as described for the *ciblon*, or with one or two fingers elsewhere on the small head. Like *ket*, this stroke has a filling-in role.

The **tok** stroke, a damped equivalent of *tong*, produced as on the *ciblon* (see below), is also possible.

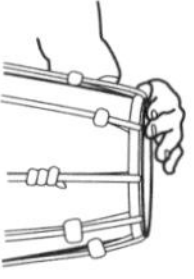

48 Some sources distinguish between the name of a stroke and its sound: e.g. the stroke called *tepak* produces the sound called *tak*. This book follows general practice in using only the names of the sounds. Names are also subject to some variation of spelling, perhaps because of the usual inconsistency over d/dh and t/th (see **Glossary**), or perhaps because the names are onomatopoeic and arbitrary anyway.

49 Other combinations have been given names but are not in common use. Names are also given to sequences of strokes that are better regarded as *céngkok* or *wilet*.

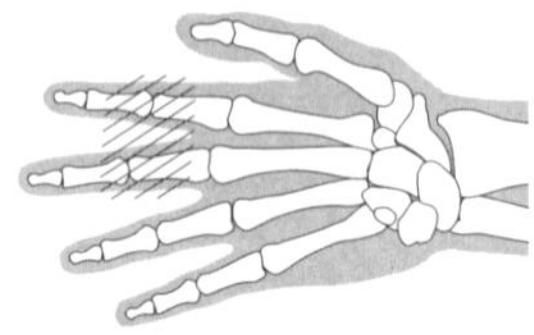

3.84 Contact area for *thung* stroke on *ketipung* (versions a and b)

Kendhang ageng strokes

RIGHT-HAND STROKES

Dha(h)/dhe/d(h)en/bem[50] is a bounced stroke with the deepest pitch of any on the *kendhang ageng*. Contrary to expectation, perhaps, it is not produced by striking the centre of the head. Instead, most of the hand, with the fingers held close together, strikes only the outer part of the head. (The hand can also be higher, e.g. as for *dhet* on the *ciblon*.) The hand contact area is shown in Fig. 3.85, and the hand posture shown in Fig. 3.86 should help. Some practice is necessary to ensure that the *dha* is free from the sound of finger contact. This stroke is sometimes reinforced by playing a *tak* on the small head of the *ketipung*.

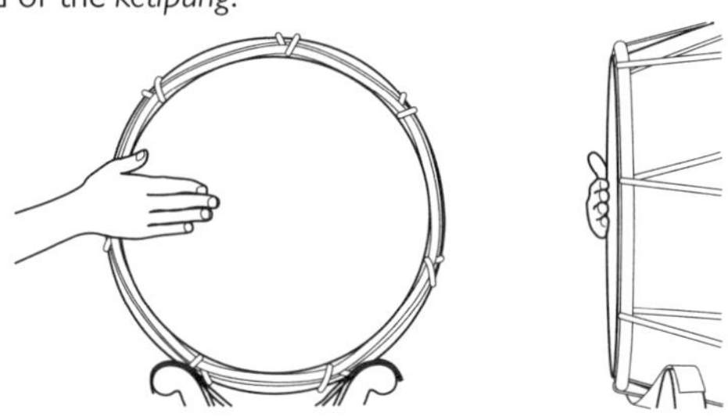

Thung/dhung is, as on the *ciblon*, a stroke near the centre of the large head that causes the small head to resonate: see the description on the next page. The thumb position is near the edge of the head.

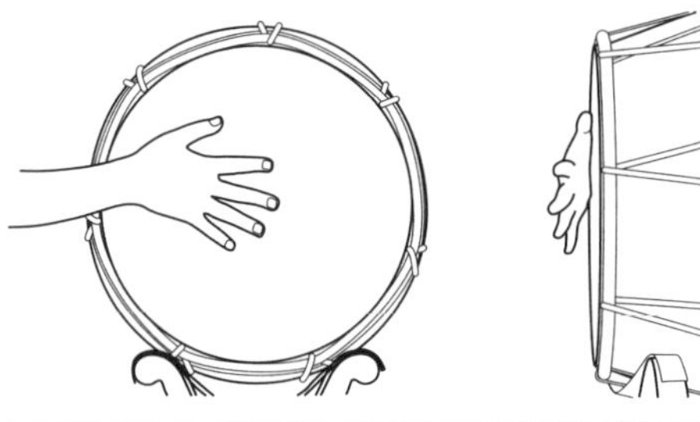

Ket is produced in the same way as on the *ketipung*, with a similar sound and role. The hand position is not critical.

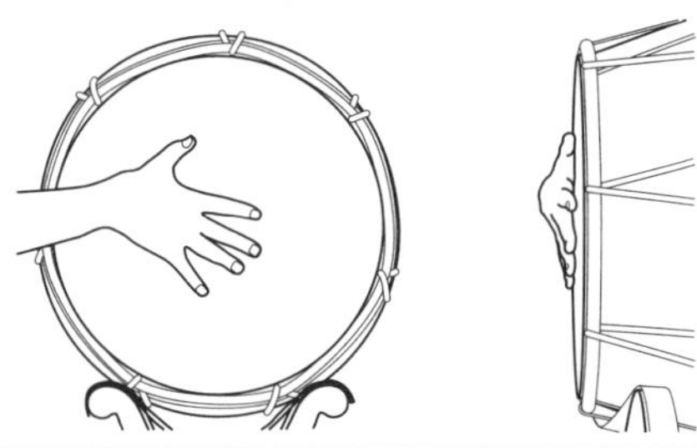

Hen/hun is one of several *ciblon* strokes that may sometimes be played on the *kendhang ageng*. It is played in the same way as on the *ciblon*, with the thumb in the outer area of the drumhead, but not too close to the edge. The pitch is the same as for the *dha*.

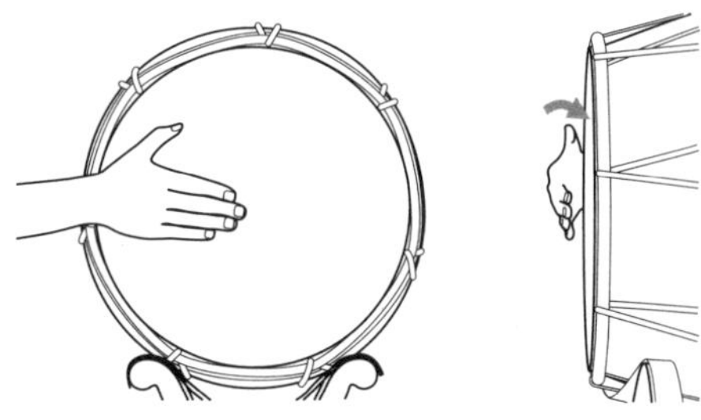

LEFT-HAND STROKES

As on the *ketipung*, ***tong*** is the highest-pitched stroke, played with one or more fingers very close to the edge of the small head. The hand position may be as shown below, or as shown for the *ketipung*. The role of this stroke is as described for the *ketipung*, although its sound is closer to the *ciblon* version.

The ***tok*** stroke, a damped equivalent of *tong*, produced as on the *ciblon* (see below), is also possible.

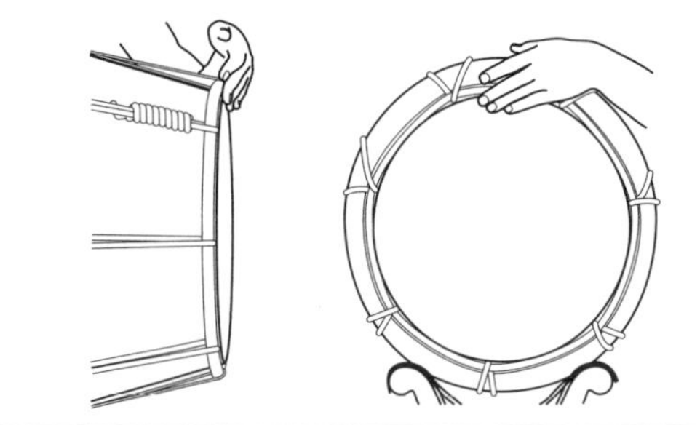

Tak is made in the same way as on the *ciblon* (see below), although its maximum volume and impact on the *kendhang ageng* are not quite as great.

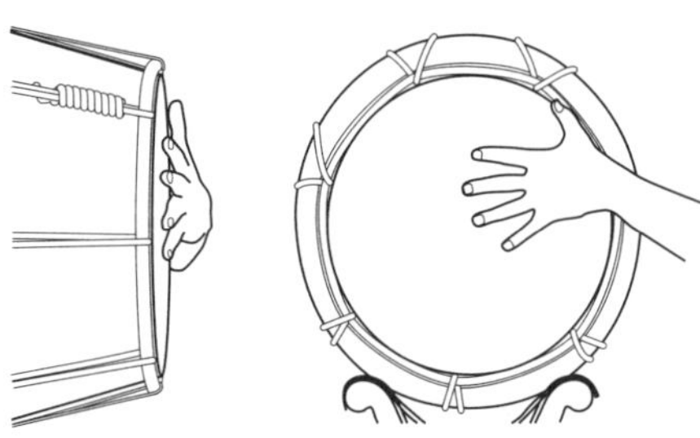

50 The name *dhang* is also found, not to be confused with the different stroke on the *ciblon*.

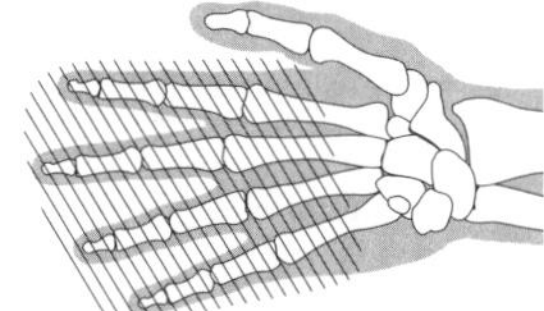

3.85 Contact area for *dha* stroke on *kendhang ageng*

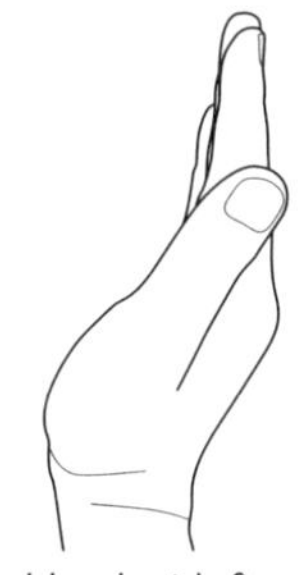

3.86 Hand with fingers flexed for *dha* stroke

Ciblon strokes—right hand

D(h)en/dhe/d(h)un is a bounced stroke made in the same way as *dha(h)/dhe/bem* on the *kendhang ageng*, except that less of the hand covers the head (Fig. 3.87). Various hand positions around the periphery of the drumhead are possible, e.g. the position shown below for *dhet*. Used by itself and as part of

- □ *(n)d(h)ang*
- □ *d(h)lang*
- □ *dhelang*
- □ *d(h)long*
- □ *dhong*

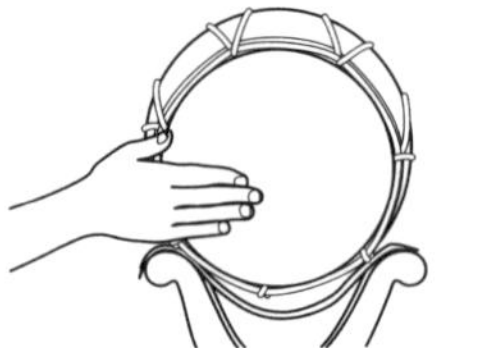

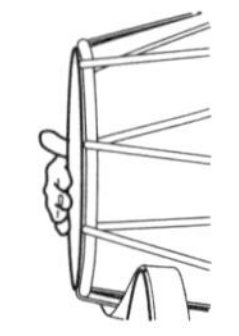

Ket is the same stroke as on the *ketipung* and *kendhang ageng*, and is used in the same ways. As shown, the periphery of the head is damped by the heel of the hand and at least the little finger, and the stroke is made by one or more other fingers. The hand positions described for the other drums can also be used.

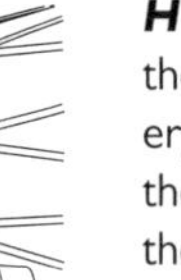

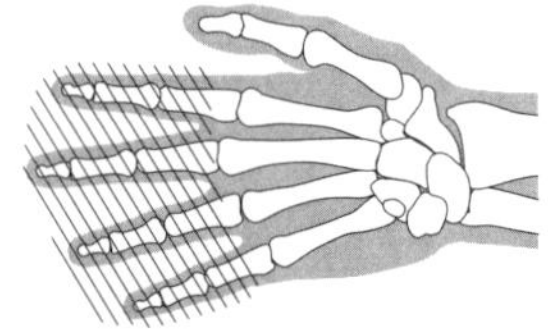

3.87 Contact area for *dhen* stroke on *ciblon*

Thung/dhung is the most difficult stroke on the *ciblon* (and the *kendhang ageng*). It involves striking the large head with four fingers (which may be close together, as for *dhet*) in order to make the small head resonate. The thumb and heel of the hand stay in contact with the edge of the head throughout so that it does not sound. The hand position must be just right to generate the desired sound: clear, free from the sound of finger contact, and matching the *lung* stroke—a good way to acquire *thung* is to imitate the (easier) *lung*. *Thung* is used by itself and as part of

- □ *thulung/dhulung*
- □ *t(h)lung*
- □ *t(h)lang*
- □ *t(h)long*
- □ *t(h)lok*
- □ *thut*

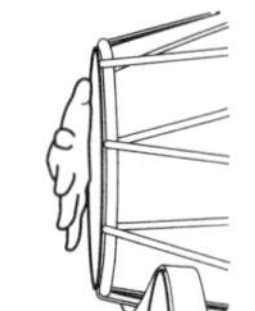

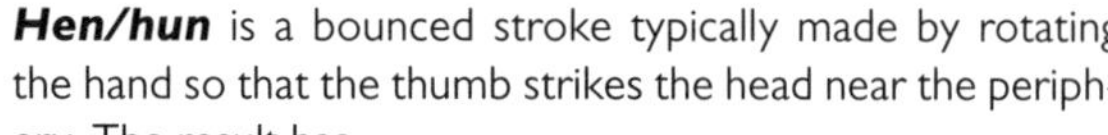

Hen/hun is a bounced stroke typically made by rotating the hand so that the thumb strikes the head near the periphery. The result has the same pitch as the *dhen*, but less weight.

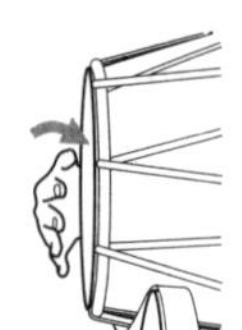

Dhet is the unbounced equivalent of *dhen*: the range of hand positions is the same, but the hand stays in contact with the drumhead after the stroke. Used by itself and as part of

- □ *dhak*
- □ *d(h)lak*

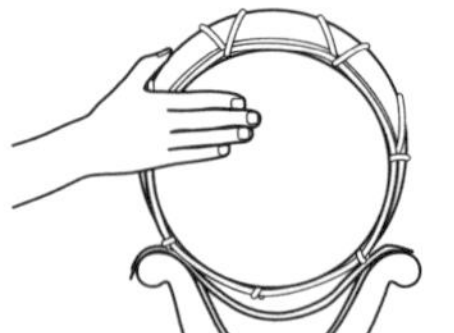

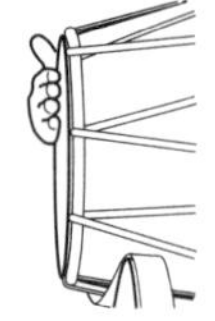

Dhut starts as a *dhet*, then the hand slides across or down the drumhead, producing a rising pitch.

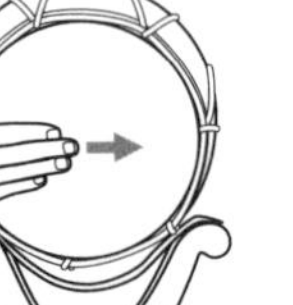

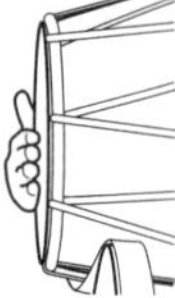

Table 3.22
Summary of drumstrokes, including combination strokes

Right hand	Left hand						
	None	*lung*	*lang*	*tak*	*tong*	*tok*	*dhut*
None	–	*lung*	–	–	*tong*	*tok*	–
dhe/dha(h)/ d(h)en/bem/ d(h)un/dhang[a]	*dhe/dha(h)/ d(h)en/bem/ d(h)un/dhang*[a]	–	*(n)d(h)ang; dhelang;*[b] *d(h)lang*[c]	–	*dhong; d(h)long*[c]	–	–
thung/dhung	*thung/dhung*	*thulung/ dhulung;*[b] *t(h)lung*[c]	*t(h)lang*[c]	–	*t(h)long*[c]	*t(h)lok*[c]	*thut*
hen/hun	*hen/hun*	–	–	–	–	–	–
ket	*ket*	–	–	–	–	–	–
d(h)et	*d(h)et*	–	–	*dhak; d(h)lak*[c]	–	–	–
dhut	*dhut*	–	–	–	–	–	–

a. On *kendhang gedhé* only. b. LH stroke follows RH stroke, in rhythm.

Ciblon strokes—left hand and combinations

LEFT-HAND STROKES

Lang and ***tak*** are made with a spread-out hand. It is often convenient to use the thumb on the rim of the head as a sort of hinge, as shown. The result should be a clear (and possibly very loud) slapping sound, and the impact of the individual fingers should not be heard. *Lang* is bounced, and *tak* is unbounced. These strokes are used only as part of

- □ *(n)d(h)ang*
- □ *d(h)lang*
- □ *dhelang*
- □ *t(h)lang*
- □ *dhak*
- □ *d(h)lak*

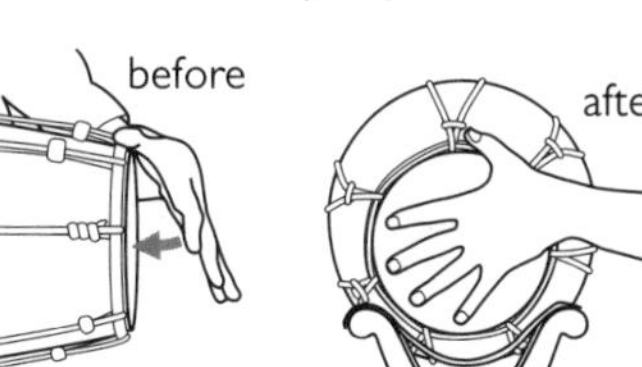

Tong is a bounced 'rimshot' made with one or more fingers close to the edge of the head. The sound should be rather penetrating and should take some of its quality from the wood of the drum body, giving the highest pitch of all the *ciblon* strokes. *Tong* is used by itself and as part of

- □ *d(h)long*
- □ *dhong*
- □ *t(h)long*

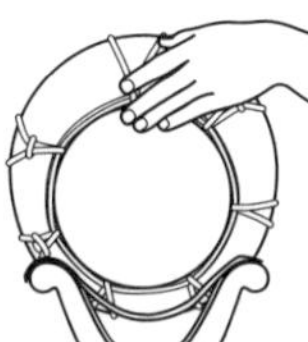

Tok is an unbounced 'rimshot', the damped version of *tong*, made with two or three fingers close to the edge of the head, in the position shown below or as shown for *tong* above. Used by itself and as part of *t(h)lok*.

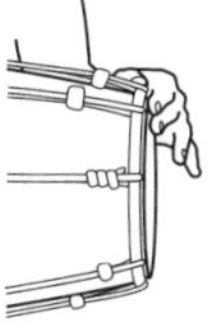
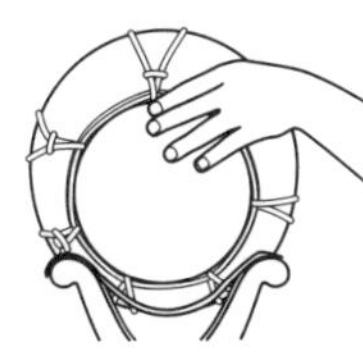

Dhut is produced in the same way as *dhut* on the large head. Used only as part of *thut*.

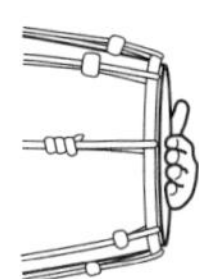
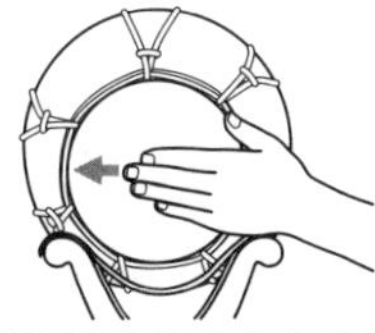

Lung is a bounced stroke made with one finger—index finger, middle finger, or ring finger—near the edge of the head. It therefore corresponds to *thung* on the *ketipung* except that it has the basic pitch of the small head. *Lung* is used by itself and as part of

- □ *thulung*
- □ *t(h)lung*

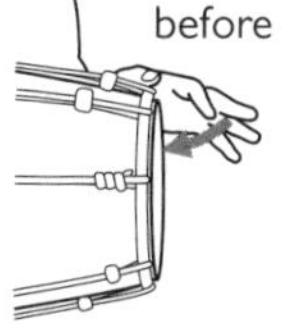

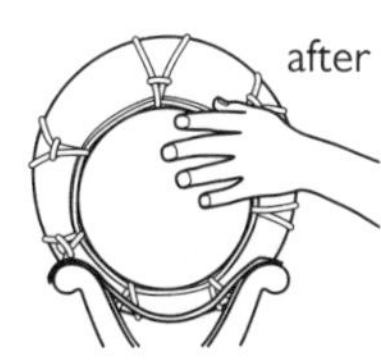

COMBINATION STROKES

Simultaneous

(N)d(h)ang consists of *lang* and *dhen* played simultaneously. This is potentially the loudest of all the *ciblon* strokes.

Dhong consists of *tong* and *dhen* played simultaneously.

Dhak consists of *dhet* and *tak* played simultaneously. This is another loud stroke.

Thut is a rare stroke combining *thung* on the large head with *dhut* on the small head.

Near-simultaneous

In each case the large head is struck first, then the small head immediately afterwards. Because of the characteristics of *ciblon* rhythms, the question of which element should be on the beat is a little academic: however, it is usually the second.

D(h)lang and ***d(h)long*** consist of *dhen* played on the large head, followed respectively by *lang* or *tong* on the small head.

D(h)lak consists of *dhet* followed immediately by *tak*.

T(h)lang, ***t(h)long***, ***t(h)lok*** and ***t(h)lung*** consist of *thung* on the large head followed respectively by *lang*, *tong*, *tok* or *lung* on the small head.

Separate, in rhythm

Two named strokes are in this category. Each consists of two constituent strokes played in rhythm: they are notated with two symbols joined by an overscore, indicating that the combined stroke has the duration of a regular *ciblon* stroke. The first element of the stroke is on the beat

Dhelang consists of *dhen* on the large head followed by *lang* on the small head.

Thulung/dhulung consists of *thung* on the large head followed by *lung* on the small head. The two elements of *thulung* should sound very similar.

Principles of *kendhangan*

The *kendhang* in the ensemble

The role of the *kendhang* player is not identical to that of an orchestral conductor in the West, but overlaps with it. In Javanese terms, the *kendhang* generally functions as the *pamurbå iråmå*. The *kendhang* is responsible for starting some types of piece, i.e. it gives them a *bukå kendhang*. In most cases it

- gets the players' attention before the *bukå* by playing a few quiet *ket* strokes,
- determines the tempo,
- indicates certain changes of *garap*, including some changes of volume level,
- controls transitions between one piece and another, and
- indicates when a piece should end.

The *kendhang* is not always in ultimate control. In *wayang* the *kendhang* player responds to signals from the *dhalang*, and thus conveys the *dhalang*'s wishes to the other gamelan players. In dance, the player is subservient to the dance-master or -mistress if there is one; otherwise he must follow the dancer, who then determines the progress between sections of a dance. The *kendhang* may also play patterns reflecting specific movements by the dancer, e.g. *kris* thrusts. In *wayang* the *kendhangan* may similarly echo the actions of the puppets, especially in battle scenes.

In other contexts too, the *kendhang* does not give the other players all the information that they need. For example, the metrical phrase that ends a *båwå* may be sung more slowly than an instrumental *bukå*—unsurprising, because the singer may be singing up to four notes per beat. In this case the *kendhang* indicates where the other players should enter, but not the speed after the *gong bukå*, and experienced players will know that the speed immediately after the gong should be faster. Likewise, the beginning of a new *gongan* in the *mérong* of a *gendhing* (see **Tips & Tricks 7**) requires the players to listen for the gong stroke as well as the *kendhangan*. In other words, the cohesion of the ensemble still relies on the players' understanding of how these types of transition should be played.

The nature of drum patterns

All *kendhangan* consists of patterns of several different strokes. There is no particular link between the type of stroke and its place in the *gåtrå* or *gongan*: in principle any stroke can occur anywhere.

In *kendhangan I* or *II*, about five different drum strokes are used. The individual strokes can be divided into those that are intended to catch the other players' attention and those that merely fill in the pattern. The *tong*, *tok* and *ket* strokes often perform the latter function. In *kendhangan I* for *gendhing*, the filling-in strokes may be barely audible, or even not played, for most of the time. In this case the filling-in strokes in the *mérong* are only played—or only played obviously—on either side of the gong stroke, in order to control the slow-down before the gong stroke and then to re-establish the normal tempo after the gong.

Compared with *kendhangan I* or *II*, the *ciblon* offers more than twice as many different strokes, and the density of the strokes is often twice as high. For these reasons, *ciblon* drumming is relatively difficult.

Patterns for all types of drumming, like those for melody instruments, normally use a hierarchy of binary divisions. Triplet patterns—as usual, three beats against four standard beats—occur in some contexts. *Salahan* patterns for the last *gongan* of a cycle or an approaching *suwuk* often use cross-rhythms with groups of three beats (not triplets): see Part 4.

The effect of drum patterns

The specific task that the drummer has to perform is exemplified by Figs 2.15, 2.16 and 3.88. Fig. 3.88 shows a possible *skema*—or rather multiple possible *skema*—for a very popular *gendhing*, *gd Randhu kéntir*, which may be performed in either *sléndro* or *pélog*. The diagram shows a *sléndro manyurå* version. The standard *inggah* for the *gendhing* is *ldr Ayun-ayun*. Other pieces included are an optional *lik* (with its own name) for the *inggah*, an inserted *langgam*, and a 'third section' in the form of a *ketawang*. Fig. 3.88 by no means exhausts the possible ways of performing this *gendhing*. Fig, 2.15 shows the *kendhang* controlling changes of *irama* and *garap* within a single *bentuk*, and Fig. 2.16 shows the same for a group of closely related *bentuk*.

For such sequences the task of the drummer is to provide appropriate signals to cause the transitions, and sometimes to select between several possible options; also to choose between *garap* variants, since the *ladrang* can be played in four different *iråmå*, with optional *kébar* in *ir I*. Wherever there is an arrow in the diagram, the *kendhang* player must play an appropriate pattern.

Special *kendhangan* signals can also indicate more local changes of *garap*, including extra *gong suwukan* strokes.

In most *kendhangan*, various elements are essential: a *bukå* to start the piece, signals for changing *iråmå*, methods of speeding up or slowing down, signals for *sirep* and *udhar*, and a *suwuk* to end the piece, or a transition into another *bentuk*. These all relate to performance details where the *kendhang* is in charge. In addition, there may be variant *kendhangan* available for *ngelik* sections, but entry to the *ngelik* is controlled by another instrument.

Kendhangan kalih

For the smaller fixed forms, up to *ladrang*, the *bukå kendhang* in Solonese style starts seven beats before the gong, e.g. for *ladrang*

t t P b   oobPoobP
. . . . (.)

whereas the Yogyanese equivalent starts one beat earlier:

    t   b ktP b   t P t P
or t   t t P b   t P t P
or t   b t P b   t P t P
    .   . . . (.)

The above are three versions of the default Yogya *kendhangan kalih* for *ladrang*, which the Solonese know as '*kendhangan Mataram*', although they modify the *bukå* pattern to something like

t t P b   ktP ktP

Lancaran is typically the first type of *kendhangan* that students learn to play. A description of drumming for Solo-style *lancaran* now follows. The *bukå*

t t P b   o P o P

is followed by a *gongan* with the same pattern throughout, in order to establish a steady tempo

o P o P   o P o P   o P o P   o P o P

and then the next (one or more) *gongan* use the standard pattern, in which *dha* strokes coincide with *kempul*

P P P P   P b P P   P b P P   P b P P

There is a syncopated version of the above:

P P P P   .Pb P P   .Pb P P   .Pb P P

In the final *gongan* of the overall cycle, the standard pattern is replaced by cross-rhythms—as usual, groups of three beats, in this case marked by *dha* strokes—reverting to the standard pattern in the third *gåtrå*:

b P P b   P P b P   P b P P   P b P P

For a speed-up (*seseg*), the last *gongan* of the cycle is modified

b P P b   P P b tP   P P P b   o P o P

or the last *gåtrå* is changed—typically in the last *gongan* of the cycle, although it can happen elsewhere

P b P PP

and the o P o P pattern is often played throughout the next *gongan* in order to steady the new tempo.

The *suwuk* signal, using a *thlang* stroke borrowed from the *ciblon*, occurs at the end of the penultimate *gongan*

P P P P   P b P P   P b P P   P b P t

and the last *gongan* uses a special pattern, during which the tempo drops

    P t P t   P b P t   b P o b   o P o .
or P o P o   P b P o   b P o b   o P P .

As usual in *kendhangan*, there is no stroke on the final beat. A transition to *ir I* can occur during any *gongan*, accompanied by a slow-down:

P P P P   P b P P   .bP.b.Pb   PtPb.P.b

If the *lancaran* is to be followed by a *ladrang*, for example, a transitional passage starts during the final *gongan*, with a slow-down to reach *ir I*:

P t P t   P b P .   t t P b   oobPoobP

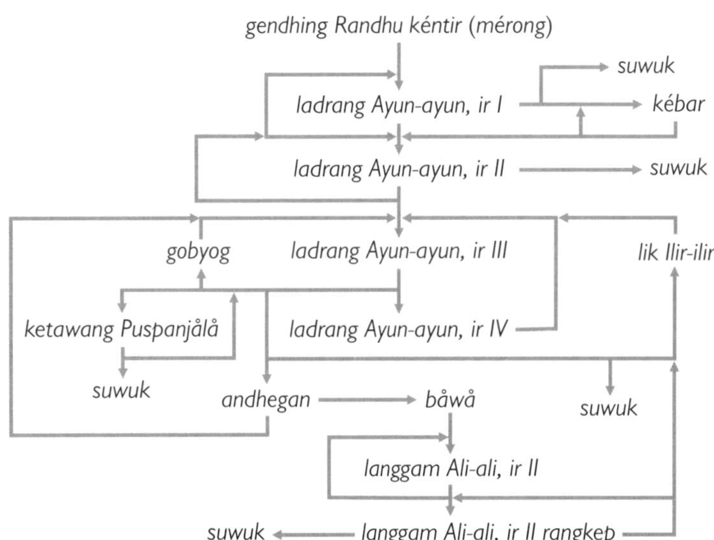

3.88 *Skema* of a sequence, in diagrammatic form

In these *lancaran* patterns the *dha* stroke can optionally be reinforced by a *tak* on the *ketipung*.

Kendhangan satunggal

The larger fixed forms—*gendhing* in the narrower sense—may have *kendhangan satunggal* throughout, but other types of *kendhangan* are used in each half of the *gendhing*: *kosèk wayangan* or occasionally *kébar* in the *mérong*; *kosèk wayangan* or *ciblon* in the *inggah*, as well as all the appropriate types of drumming for *inggah ladrang* or *inggah ketawang*. *Kosèk alus*, also possible in *inggah*, is another type of *kendhangan satunggal*.

For each *gendhing* form there is at least one standard *kendhangan*, with versions for *sléndro* and *pélog*. In the Solonese style, *kendhangan* starts four *balungan* beats before the *gong bukå* for *sléndro*, and four beats earlier for *pélog*.[51] In the Yogya style, *kendhangan* always starts in the earlier position. *Gendhing* transposed from *sléndro* to *pélog* (e.g. *gd Gambirsawit pl 6* or *gd Kututmanggung pl 7*) are drummed with *kendhangan* for *sléndro*.

Kendhangan for each *gendhing* form consists of a characteristic pattern of *thung*, *dha* and *tak* strokes that can be notated quite economically. In addition there are standard patterns of *ket* and *tong* strokes that fill in the gaps in these characteristic patterns, as well as standard patterns to signal the slow-down to the gong, the recovery to normal speed thereafter, and the *suwuk*.

Ciblon drumming

Drumming patterns on the *ciblon* are usually assembled from building blocks to fit the composition. Components are chosen to suit their position in the *bentuk*.

One of the simplest examples is for *srepegan*. The first element is the short *bukå*—this *bentuk* always has a *bukå kendhang*—and different *pathet* have different *bukå*. The following is a simple *bukå* used for *sl m* and *sl 6*:

b . t t (t)

The first *gåtrå* of each *gongan* may use any of a variety of elements, e.g.

t t t t t b t t
or . b . b . b . b
or Pℓ k Pℓ k Pℓ k Pℓ k
or Pℓ kt kP Pℓ kt kP Pℓ kt
or t t b t t b t t b t t b t t b t etc.

In the last item above, the pattern continues across *gåtrå* boundaries. Otherwise these elements can be repeated for the next *gåtrå*, although there are also special patterns (not listed) for *gåtrå* in the middle of a *gongan*. However, the *gåtrå* leading to a gong has a special pattern, of which these are some variants:

Pℓ d t b . thb d
or Pℓ d t b . th Pℓ d
or Pℓ d t .b. th Pℓ d

To indicate a speed-up (*seseg*), a special *gåtrå*-length pattern replaces the standard gong pattern:

ddd d . d d d d
or P d t . ddd d d

The *suwuk* is signalled by another special *gåtrå* leading to the end of the last *gongan*

. d t . b b t k
or . d b . d b t k

and the final two *gåtrå* which may be drummed as

b k t k b k t kP P P P P d ∘ . .
or b k t k b k t k P P P t P b . .

A *sirep* may be signalled by

. d . t .h bd. .

In the case of major structures such as *ladrang* or *inggah* sections in *ir III* or *IV*, the building blocks have names and/or numbers and are divided into *sekaran* and *singgetan*, the latter being associated with main structural points such as the ends of *kenongan* and *gongan*. These blocks are combined according to standard schemes. Fig. 3.89 shows a structure to which each *gongan* of a *ladrang* in *ir III* conforms more or less closely. *Ngaplak seseg* and *gong seseg* patterns are available to signal that the next *gongan* will be the last. In the final *gongan*, special *suwuk* versions of *sekaran* and *singgetan* are played, and element n is followed by a return to *kd I* or *kd II*. The entry of the *ciblon* (*angkatan ciblon*) is not shown in Fig. 3.89, and there are in fact several ways in which the *ladrang* in *ir III* may be entered.

Many *ciblon* drumming patterns, including those used in *ladrang* and *gendhing*, have the names of dance movements to which they are related. *Ciblon* drumming for dance is structured differently, and has even more of these named 'functional' patterns.

51 The *kendhang* player may in practice contribute a few quiet *ket* strokes before the *tak*, to encourage the *bukå* player towards the right tempo.

Ladrang Asmarandånå sl m

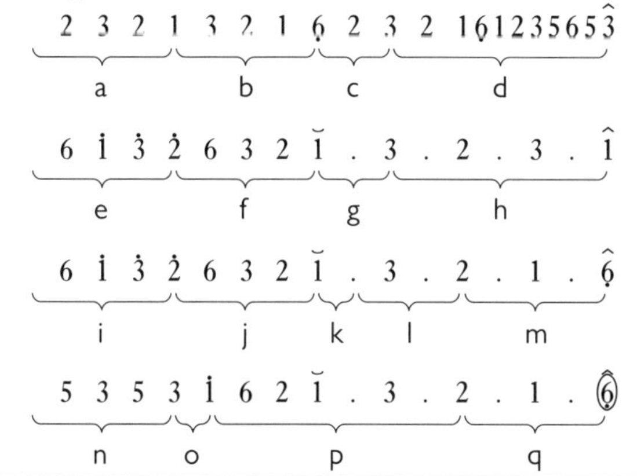

a	Numbered *sekaran*
b	= a, or another numbered *sekaran*
c	First half of a
d	*Kèngser* or *kèngser batangan* (a *singgetan*)
e	= a, or another numbered *sekaran*
f	= b, or another numbered *sekaran*
g	First half of e
h	*Kèngser* or *malik* (a *singgetan*)
i	Numbered *sekaran*
j	Numbered *sekaran*
k	First quarter of i
l	*Magak* (a *singgetan*)
m	*Kawilan* or *wedhi kèngser* (a *singgetan*)
n	= m
o	First quarter of m
p	*Ngaplak* (a *singgetan*)
q	*Gong batangan* or *gong seseg* (a *singgetan*), or a numbered *sekaran*

3.89 *Skema* for *ciblon* drumming in a *ladrang, ir III*

Other rhythm instruments

Tenor drum

In the Yogyanese *gati* form (see ***Gati***), the Western tenor drum supplies an essential part of the *kendhangan*, including rolls played with two drumsticks.

Keprak

The *keprak* (of which a relatively curvaceous example is shown in Fig. 3.90) is a classic wooden slit drum, struck with a wooden beater. It is used by the dance-master or -mistress to signal speed and certain transitions in accompaniments for dance; likewise by the *dhalang* in some dance-drama. Its penetrating sound is easily heard over the sound of a large gamelan.

The *keprak* (confusingly, also sometimes called *kepyak*) is closely related to the *kentongan* (Fig. 3.91) used by *kampung* nightwatchmen to signal to their colleagues: in this function, different patterns of strokes indicate the occurrence of different crimes.

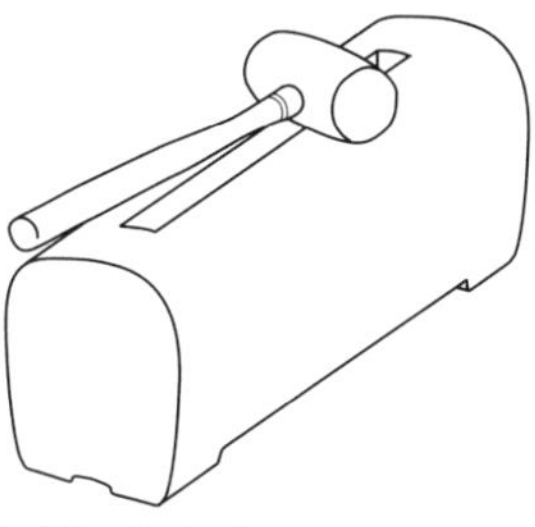

3.90 *Keprak*

Frame drums

Single-headed hand-held frame drums (*rebånå*, *terbang*, etc.) are not normally part of a gamelan. However, they are in common use for accompanying the singing of Islamic texts (*santiswårå*) by small groups that meet in private houses (not mosques). They also feature in other small non-gamelan ensembles.

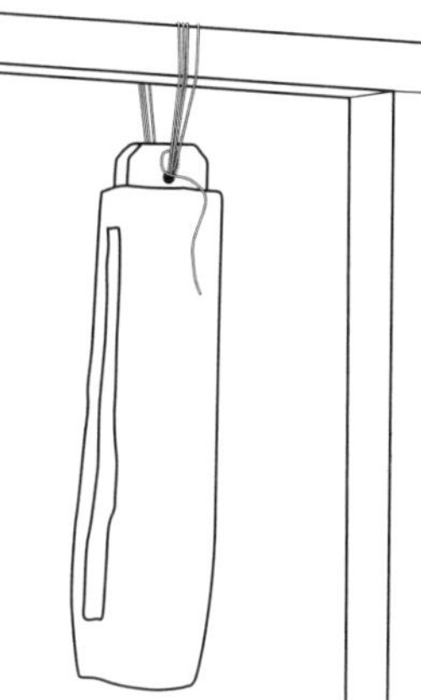

3.91 *Kentongan*

Kepyak

The *kepyak* consists of one or more metal plates hung on the outside of the *kothak wayang*, and struck by a miniature mallet (*cempålå*—the same term as for the mallet used on the *kothak* itself) held between the toes of the *dhalang*'s right foot.

In Yogya the *kepyak* takes the form of a single iron plate backed by a block of wood (Fig. 3.92) and struck by a metal *cempålå* as shown in Table 3.1. The Solonese version consists of three or four bronze plates, of similar size to the Yogya equivalents, struck with a wooden *cempålå*. (The *kepyak* is visible in Fig. 2.29.)

On the signals given by the *kepyak*, see p. 97.

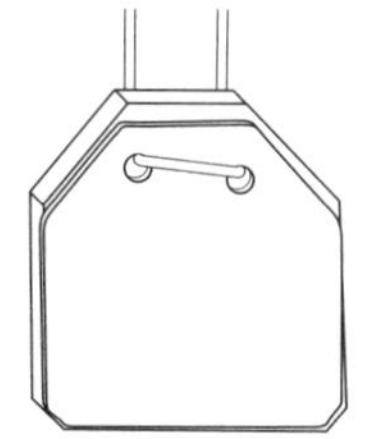

3.92 *Kepyak*

Miscellaneous percussion

One of the many developments in *wayang kulit* in recent years is the addition of Western percussion instruments —anything from a suspended cymbal to an entire drum kit—to the regular ensemble. Typically these instruments add to the non-musical effects that accompany the fight scenes.

Vocal parts

Javanese singing is, like the *rebab*, something of an acquired taste for many Westerners—the female style giving listeners the most difficulties. It is perhaps worth pointing out that these singing styles are cultivated deliberately, and are unrelated to any inherent characteristics of Javanese voices.[52] Like the *rebab*, singing is an essential element of *karawitan*. Western gamelan players who do not participate in the singing and/or who do not have *pesindhèn* singing regularly with them are therefore experiencing the musical culture only partially.

It must be admitted that Javanese singing voices are not 'well-produced' by the standards of Western classical music. Some singers' careers are therefore shorter than they should be. Also there is little or no attempt to smooth the transition between the 'head voice' and the 'chest voice'—a fault by Western standards.

A wide vocal range is expected of singers. To reach the highest notes (up to 5̇) it is necessary to be a tenor or a soprano. Westerners with other, untrained voices may resort to falsetto, but this is not normal practice in *karawitan*. A *dhalang* characterises the *wayang* characters by pitch as well as other vocal features, and must therefore command an even wider range than other singers.

52 As can be confirmed by listening to church choirs in central Java, or to the *cianjuran* vocal style of Sunda. *Cianjuran* or *tembang Sunda* is an intimate indoor style of performance for connoisseurs, where the singers do not have to compete with a gamelan.

balungan	. . 6 . 3 2 1 6̂
vokal	. . . . 6 6 .1̇ 6 . . 1̇ 2̇ .3̇ 1̇ 2̇1̇ 6
cakepan	*Pa- ra- bé Sang Små- rå- bang- un*
balungan	3 5 6 1̆̇ 6 5 3 2̂
vokal	. . . . 3̇ 3̇ 2̇1̇ 6 1̇ 2̇3̇ 1̇6 5 . 5653 2
cakepan	*se- pat dom- bå ka- li O- yå*
balungan	5 6 5 3̆ 6 5 3 2̂
vokal	. . 5 6 .5 5 65 3 . . 36 5 . 5653 2
cakepan	*å- jå do- lan lan wong pri- yå*
balungan	6̣ 1 2 3̆ 5 6 5 (3)
vokal	. . 6̣ 1 .2 2 .3 3 . . 5 6 .5 5 65 3
cakepan	*ngge-ra- mèh no- ra pra- så- jå*

3.93 Example of *gérongan* word setting, *ldr Pujirahayu pl 6* (*ngelik, ir II*)

In spite of the importance of the vocal element of *karawitan*, there is surprisingly little writing on the subject, and especially on male singing style.

Male voices and *gérongan*

If the general beliefs about the development of *karawitan* are correct, male singers (*wiråswårå*) must have participated before female singers, although the nature of their contribution is not clear. Solo singing in *palaran*, *båwå* and *sulukan* has been mentioned in Part 2, but unison male choral singing is more widespread, being found in all the fixed *bentuk* (excluding *gangsaran*). Singers in the male chorus (*gérong*) are also called *penggérong*.

The example in Fig. 3.93 illustrates various features commonly found in *gérongan*: vocal phrases that coincide with the last note in most *gåtrå*; an exception in the second *kenongan*, where a long phrase continues after the first *gåtrå*; entry in a relatively high register, but a lower (and often much less audible) pitch at the final gong; a phrase that reflects a *gantungan* in the inner melody (the first *gåtrå*). Not seen in this example is enjambment, i.e. the continuation of a vocal phrase after the gong, often into a *gåtrå gantung*. An example is to be found in *ktw Subåkaståwå sl 9* in Part 4.

In *ir II* the lines of the *wangsalan* cover two *gåtrå* and two vocal phrases. In an *inggah* in *ir III*, the most frequent relationship is one line (*gåtrå*) of verse per *gåtrå* of *balungan*. In some *gérongan* the final *kenongan* has two versions, the lower one (ending an octave lower) being sung for the *suwuk*.

The example shows the same vocal phrase being used for both occurrences of one *gåtrå* in the *balungan*. In fact phrases are fairly standardised, to the extent that an expert musician can create a suitable *gérongan* for an unfamiliar piece just by looking at the *balungan* notation.

Female voices

The penetrating vocal quality of central Javanese female singers (*pesindhèn*, *waranggånå* or *swåråwati*) and the similar sound of the *rebab* meet the same need—to be heard through the dense texture of the gamelan. It is believed that women first sang with the gamelan in mixed choruses, starting in the nineteenth century. Women sometimes sing in unison in groups, and continue to sing in mixed groups (see **Mixed singing** below). However, the solo singing role is now more important, although historically it has a different origin, as a development of the role of the *tlèdhèk/ronggèng*, who was a singer as well as a dancer. Solo *sindhènan* is heard in all vocal compositions unless there is a mixed chorus throughout, whereas there are many vocal pieces without *gérongan*.

There are, or have been, differences in *pesindhèn* singing style between Solo and Yogya, as well as stylistic changes over the years, but generalisations are risky.[53]

The most frequent vocal contributions by *pesindhèn* take the form of short phrases with words that are entirely unrelated to the piece. The phrases are of two kinds: *sindhènan srambahan* and *abon-abon* (or *isèn-isèn*). *Sindhènan srambahan* (the latter word meaning 'general-purpose') is the more important, being sung at the stronger points in the structure. *Abon-abon* are optional, and are sung at the weaker points.

Sindhènan srambahan phrases vary in length. They can contain different numbers of syllables, and for this purpose are characterised as *lampah x*, where *x* can be 4, 8 or 12 (referring to syllables, not notes or beats). Besides this there may be more than one note per syllable, and the *pesindhèn* sings the whole *céngkok* in very free rhythm, the last note(s) typically being sung after the end of the *gåtrå*. In the example (Fig. 3.94), *céngkok* of *lampah* 8 or 12 form cover anything up to a whole *gåtrå*—occasionally even more—in the *mérong*. (The *gendhing* shown is of Yogya origin, and has a *låmbå* section: this and the *ompak inggah/pangkat dhawah* are omitted.) One long *céngkok* (*lampah* 12) to the gong at the end of the *mérong* is

5 6 1 2 2 2 2 1 161 6 2 3 212 1 1
a- mi- wit- i sindhèn sen-dhon ing pra- dång- gå

as against shorter phrases to the same *sèlèh* note

5 6 1 . 6 5 2 16161 (*lampah* 4)
ki- na- pak-nå

5 6 5 161 5 2 2161 1 (*lampah* 8)
gar-wå ri- sang Da-nan-jå- yå

Plèsèdan are an important subcategory in the repertoire of *sindhènan srambahan*. In these, the *pesindhèn* initially aims at the expected *sèlèh* note, but then continues past the *sèlèh* point and ends on a note corresponding to an important note—often a *gantungan* or a *balungan kembar*—in the following *gåtrå*, e.g.

balungan	5	3	5	6
balungan	1	6	5	3
sindhènan	. 2 32	1 . 26	6 61 65	3 . 5
balungan	2	2	.	.
sindhènan	. 3	2	.	.

For named types of *plèsèdan* used in specific contexts, see under *plèsèdan* in the **Glossary**.

When the *rebab* plays *céngkok miring*, the *pesindhèn* follows suit. The following is an example of a *céngkok miring* that can be transposed up or down for other *sèlèh* notes:

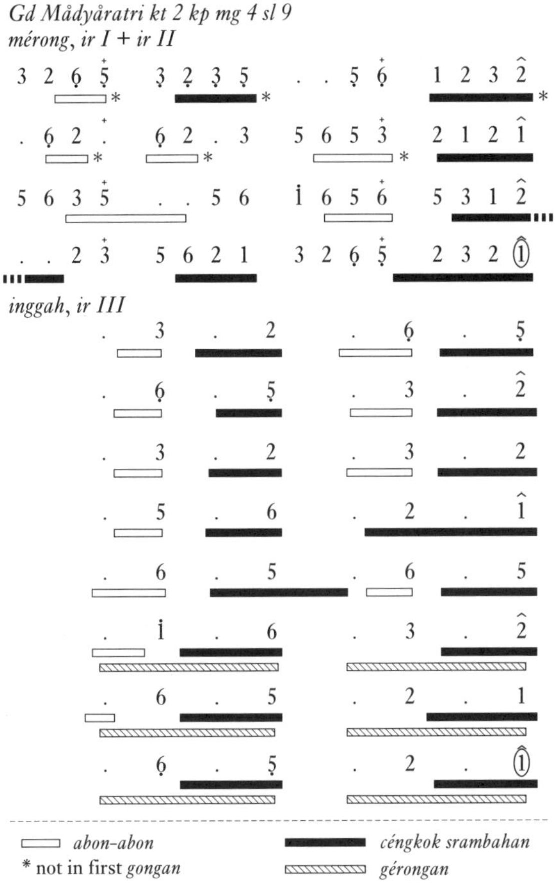

Gd Mådyåratri kt 2 kp mg 4 sl 9
mérong, ir I + ir II

3 2 6 5 3 2 3 5 . . 5 6 1 2 3 2
. 6 2 . 6 2 . 3 5 6 5 3 2 1 2 1
5 6 3 5 . . 5 6 1 6 5 6 5 3 1 2
. . 2 3 5 6 2 1 3 2 6 5 2 3 2 1

inggah, ir III

. 3 . 2 . 6 . 5
. 6 . 5 . 3 . 2
. 3 . 2 . 3 . 2
. 5 . 6 . 2 . 1
. 6 . 5 . 6 . 5
. 1 . 6 . 3 . 2
. 6 . 5 . 2 . 1
. 6 . 5 . 2 . 1

abon-abon — *céngkok srambahan*
* not in first *gongan* — *gérongan*

3.94 Positions of *abon-abon* and *céngkok srambahan*

[53] See Sutton (1991), for example.

Ornaments

Ornaments that are familiar from the vocal styles of other cultures are employed by both female and male singers in Java, but they seem to be another of the 'non-subjects' in *karawitan*.

Singers insert these ornaments at will, and there are no standard positions for them. It seems likely that the ornaments are treated more or less as part of the *céngkok*, so that they ought not to be described in isolation.

It follows from all the above that this is another element of *karawitan* to be learned by listening and imitation. The description here attempts only to give a flavour of these ornaments.

The amount of ornamentation depends on the singer's personal taste, and some singers use very little. For *gérong* and other groups of singers in unison, the inclusion of ornaments is difficult, because the singers must agree on them. Ornaments are heard occasionally in *gérongan*, but again there is the question of what is ornament and what is the basic vocal line. If a certain fragment of *gérongan* is sung variously as

$$3\quad 3\quad \overline{3\,2}\,1 \qquad \text{or} \qquad 3\quad 3\quad \overline{\overline{5}3\,2}\,1$$

is the note 5 an ornament? As the basic contour is probably 3 3 2 1, perhaps the last note 3 in the two examples is also an ornament.

There is no standard notation for ornaments (because student are expected to learn by imitation). Here the additional notes are written as small superscripts. However, it is not safe to divide *céngkok* rigidly into main notes and ornaments. In other words, the emphasis in ornaments differs from that of their counterparts in Western music. It is not even clear whether ornaments should be regarded as **on** a note or **between** notes. The examples below show some patterns of emphasis that actually occur.

The terminology for ornaments is again unstandardised. In some sources, all types are called *gregel*. The term *(e)luk* (literally 'curve', 'arc') sometimes refers to an entire long melisma, such as is used for the *sèlèhan* towards the end of a line (*baris*, *gåtrå*) in *sekar* (see **Vocal forms**). As indicated earlier, the notation for this melisma in a given line can vary significantly between one source and another: perhaps some of the variations count as ornaments. The words *luk* and *gregel* will also be found as terms for **categories** of vocal ornaments, each with several sub-types.

The nearest equivalent Western terms for ornaments are used below. Examples that can be compared with mordents (both upper and lower) are regularly used by solo singers of both sexes. Turns are less frequent. The mordents are sometimes extended to a length where they could be considered short trills, i.e. repeated alternations between two notes, which may then be called *ombak banyu*. Longer trills (possibly more common than the shorter ones in Western classical music) seem to be absent from Javanese practice.

The 'lower mordent' is inserted between a note and the next lower note

(basic pattern) $3^{23}2$
or (extended) $3^{2}3^{23}2$,
also $3^{23}2^{1}2$, which is a turn in Western terms

and the 'upper mordent' is inserted between a note and the next higher note:

$2^{32}3$ or $2^{3232}3$

The 'turn' goes between two notes of the same pitch

(basic pattern) $2^{321}2$,
(in practice) $2^{32}12$ or ${}^{23}2^{1}2$, etc.

but the two main notes may alternatively be separated by only a single note:

$\underline{2^{3}2}$ or $\underline{2^{1}2}$

Ornaments can also fill gaps larger than that between two adjacent notes, e.g. from 6 down to 2:

$\underline{36^{5353}}\ \underline{21}$

The notes of an ornament may belong to the end of one syllable or to the start of the next, as illustrated in various examples here, including the *céngkok miring* example below. Again there seems to be no standard pattern. Ornaments can also be confined to the middle of a syllable

$\underline{\dot{1}^{\dot{2}1\dot{2}}\dot{1}^{6}\dot{1}6}$

but sometimes they clearly anticipate the next syllable:

$\underline{\underset{\cdot}{5}\ \underset{\cdot}{6}^{1}}\ 1$

The amount of vibrato (*?geteran*) used by singers is within the limits found in Western classical music. Some Javanese singers use very little, but the maximum amount that will be heard is less than some Western opera singers regularly use.

The speed of execution of the ornaments is somewhat variable. They can be sung at the same speed as Western singers would use for equivalent ornaments, but can also be much slower, so that the individual notes are heard clearly. In some cases, the notes could be regarded either as vibrato or as an ornament.

6 6 . 2̇ 1̇^6 1̇ 6 5̣ 32.3 ^5̣3 5̣2 3

Pesindhèn are expected to deliver suitable *céngkok* for any piece. Even when the piece is unfamiliar, they should be able to identify upcoming *sèlèh* notes from the contours of the phrases in the *balungan* and elsewhere, using their knowledge of what is characteristic of each *pathet*.[54] They often carry a small book with them, but it is a book of texts, not *céngkok*. When several *pesindhèn* are present, they normally sing as individuals, but their procedure for sharing the work is unclear. Often one singer is clearly senior to the others.

Abon-abon can be as short as two syllables, e.g. the phrase sung against 6̣ 2 in the fifth *gåtrå* of the *mérong* of *gd Mådyåratri*,

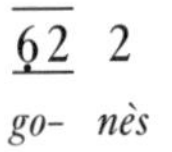

6̣2 2
go- nès

but can also be as long as *céngkok srambahan*, and repetition of the words is relatively frequent (*gonès gonès*, or longer sequences such as *man éman éman éman*).

The words in *abon-abon* are conventional, and in *céngkok srambahan* they can be much the same. *Céngkok srambahan* may also use *wangsalan*: these consist of pairs of lines, in which the first line has four or eight syllables and the second has eight.

Sindhènan gawan is by definition unique to a piece, but in form it still looks like *céngkok srambahan* and possibly *abon-abon*. The words, however, may relate to the piece. As described in Part 2, *pesindhèn* may sing entire stanzas of *sekar* in various contexts.

As indicated in Fig. 3.94, *sindhènan srambahan* begins as *ir II* is reached—just before the second *kenong* in this *gendhing*. It then continues until the end of the piece unless *sindhènan bedhayan* (see **Mixed singing** below) takes over: if the piece goes into *ir IV*, solo *sindhènan* will be the only singing heard there (if *senggakan* are not considered a form of song).

Andhegan

(See also **Notation of structure**, p. 41, and ***Andhegan/kèndelan*** in Part 2, p. 94.) *Andhegan/kèndelan* are a situation where the *pesindhèn* sings unaccompanied—or with at most a limited accompaniment from the *gendèr barung*. They are comparable with vocal cadenzas in Western classical music, although without the emphasis on vocal gymnastics.

Some *andhegan* are unique to a particular piece, and these are typically among the longer examples. Sometimes there are *sèlèh* points in the course of the *andhegan* —corresponding to notes in the *balungan* notation—and the *balungan* instruments play these notes after a special pattern from the *kendhang*, to coincide also with the vocal line.

Andhegan start at specific positions in a given piece (if it has any at all), but always at a relatively weak point in the *kenongan*. An *andhegan* is not necessarily taken every time the passage is played. The length of the *andhegan* in the notation varies; from less than a *gåtrå* to most of a *gongan*. However, the actual duration of the *andhegan* may be shorter or longer than the notation would imply.

The first indication of an imminent *andhegan* is a slow-down, signalled by a special *kendhang* pattern—*andhegan* being associated with *ciblon* drumming. The *penggérong* anticipate the *andhegan* with an *alok*; a rising *yu*. When everything stops, the players wait for a *tak* stroke on the *ciblon* (just as they wait for a final gong stroke at the end of a piece), and only play their final note after hearing the *tak*, accompanied by an *ah* on a falling pitch from the *penggérong*. Sometimes this final note is not the note recorded in the *balungan*. The *pesindhèn* may pause noticeably before actually starting the *andhegan*.

The drummer must be familiar with the *céngkok* that the singer is likely to use, because a *kendhangan* pattern can give the other players information about where to re-enter. Sometimes a particular *céngkok* on the *gendèr barung* (or *bonang barung*) leads to the re-entry, and the *kendhangan* pattern then starts much earlier to signal it, e.g. (from the *inggah ladrang* of *gd Kututmanggung sl m*)

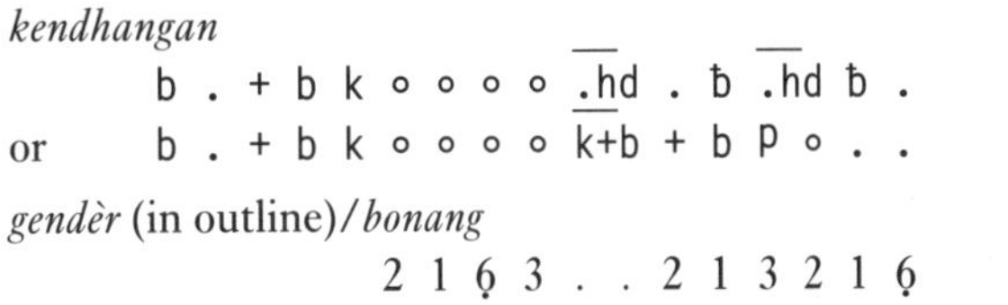

kendhangan

b . + b k o o o o .hd . ƀ .hd ƀ .
or b . + b k o o o o k+b + b P o . .

gendèr (in outline)/*bonang*

2 1 6̣ 3 . . 2 1 3 2 1 6̣

where the other instruments enter at the final 6̣. The *kendhangan* can signal a change from *ir III* to *ir IV* or vice versa at re-entry: a faster tempo means *ir IV*. However, sometimes there is no *kendhangan* before the re-entry, and the players simply resume playing when the *pesindhèn* reaches the *sèlèh* note—in which case no *iråmå* change is possible. All players know the *sèlèh* note.

Altogether *andhegan* cover a wide variety of practice:

54 The level of skill expected can be judged from what is probably urban legend, but no less revealing for that. The story is that a *pesindhèn* arrived late at a *klenèngan* and found that the players had already embarked on a *gendhing*. She sat down and contributed appropriate *céngkok srambahan* all through the remainder of the piece—only to discover at the end that the piece had been a *gendhing bonang*, which did not require her services. Sceptics may wonder why she did not notice that the soft-style decorating instruments were not in use, or how she could have forgotten that sessions often start with a *gendhing bonang*.

there are even names for different types. Of the various elements mentioned here, not all are necessarily present in a particular *andhegan*, so it is safest to learn every *andhegan* individually.

Mixed singing

Mixed (*putrå-putri*, *priyå-putri*) singing is not unusual. This style is usually called *sindhènan bedhayan*, implying a firm link between mixed singing and *bedhåyå* (and *srimpi*) dance accompaniments. However, these two dance forms are dated (in the *Wédhå Pradånggå*) to the fourteenth century, long before women are supposed to have participated in gamelan groups. This style is also used outside dance accompaniment: it is standard in some pieces, optional in others—for example, *ldr Sri katon sl m* has a *bedhayan* chorus alternative as well as the regular *gérongan*—and is often used in conjunction with *pinjalan* on the instruments.

The general character of *sindhènan bedhayan* has been illustrated under **Vocal forms** in Part 2. Vocal contours that would never be heard in *gérongan* can occur in *bedhayan* singing. The men sing an octave below the women.

Antiphonal singing by male and female groups features, for example, in *Tahu tempé*, a *lagu dolanan* in which the two groups sing of the rival virtues of beancurd (*tahu*) and fermented soya beans (*tempé*). In *langgam Petis manis*, the *gérong* interjects comments on what the *pesindhèn* is singing.

Senggakan and *alok*

The members of the *gérong* make other regular vocal contributions in the form of *senggakan* and *alok*. The two terms are not used consistently, but generally *senggakan* are considered to be words that do not belong to the main *gérongan* text, whereas *alok* are isolated nonsense syllables, often with no precise pitch, used to enhance the atmosphere of a performance. For some specific types, see under *senggakan* ... in the **Glossary**.

The phrases *Mugi lestari-o* and *Mugi rahayu-a* sung between the stanzas of the *gérongan* in *ldr Mugirahayu* are certainly *senggakan*. The same description may be given to long strings of nonsense syllables such as

$$. \ \dot{2} \ . \ \dot{1} \ \dot{3} \ \dot{2} \ . \ . \ . \ 5 \ . \ 6 \ \dot{1} \ 5 \ . \ .$$

é- ya- é- o é- ya- é- o

$$. \ \dot{2} \ . \ \dot{1} \ \dot{3} \ \dot{2} \ . \ . \ . \ 6 \ 5 \ . \ \overline{5\dot{1}}\,\overline{6\dot{1}}\,\overline{5\dot{1}} \ 6$$

é- ya- é- o ya- é yaé-o-é yaé-o

as well as to intelligible texts such as

$$. \ . \ . \ . \ 6 \ \dot{2} \ \dot{1} \ 6 \ . \ . \ \dot{2} \ \dot{3} \ \dot{2} \ 6 \ \dot{2} \ \dot{1}$$

jan- ji sa- bar o- ra dhå ka- su- su

$$. \ \dot{1} \ 6 \ \dot{1} \ 6 \ \dot{1} \ \dot{2} \ \dot{3} \ . \ \dot{3} \ \dot{2} \ \dot{3} \ \dot{2} \ \dot{3} \ \dot{5} \ \dot{2}$$

sa-wah-é jembar-jembar pa- ri- né le- mu-le- mu

(or with $\dot{3}\,\dot{1}\,\dot{2}$ at the end). These last two examples, transposed between *laras* and *pathet* as necessary, are inserted into many pieces in *ir IV*. The second (quoted in a *sl m* version) covers the first half of *ayu kuning*: cf. Table 3.14.

Common *alok* include

- □ unpitched *a-é* (sometimes written *hak-é*) inserted so that the *é* coincides with a *kempul* stroke, especially in *kébar*,
- □ sequences of pitched nonsense syllables (*é-o-a-o-é*, etc.),
- □ a rising *yo* or *yu* just before the *kenong* or gong,
- □ repeated *lhå* in triplet patterns on the same note.

More complex patterns occur in some *gendhing* in *srimpi* or *bedhåyå* accompaniments; e.g. falling *yo*, rising *yu*, falling *yo* on the first three beats of each *gåtrå*, with occasional shouts of *woi*.

Some of these are illustrated in Part 4. Together with others, they can also be heard on commercial recordings.

Multi-instrument *garap*

This section covers a variety of performance practices that involve at least three instruments,[55] i.e. where that number of instruments diverge from their 'normal' or default *garap*. Joint *garap* for two instruments—the two *bonang*, as well as for two instruments of the same type or one instrument with two players—has been covered elsewhere.

Sirep

The word *sirep* means 'calm', and indicates a reduction in the volume level—the result of the loud-style instruments either playing quietly or dropping out altogether. A transition to *sirep* is usually signalled by a specific *kendhangan* pattern, and the return to normal volume (*udhar*) is signalled in the same way.

During *wayang*, *sirep* provides a quiet background for narration by the *dhalang*. Long stretches of *sirep* therefore occur in the opening scene, for example, where the story is introduced at length—in this case, with the loud-style instruments silent.

Sirep is widely used in other situations outside *wayang*. For example, a *sirep* and later *udhar* within the final *gongan* form a characteristic part of the *suwuk* in some Yogyanese *soran* pieces, with the loud-style instruments only reducing their volume. In a *ladrang* such as *Sigråmangsah*, the *sirep* occurs at the middle or end of the second *gåtrå*, and the *udhar* at the end of the sixth. This pattern is used for both *suwuk gropak* and regular slow *suwuk*.

In vocal pieces the *sirep* may involve the loud-style instruments dropping out, as in *ayak-ayakan Pamungkas* during *ir III* (i.e. the vocal section). In other pieces, such as many *lagu dolanan* and *langgam*, these instruments will still play, but more quietly. In such pieces the cycled *gongan* (singular or plural) may then alternate between instrumental and vocal realisations, the former being at regular volume and the latter in *sirep* (at least during the actual singing). *Sirep* during *srepegan* has been described in Part 2: see also p. 62 on the use of the *sirep* signal on the *kendhang* in *sampak* for a different purpose.

A brief *sirep* in another specific context is mentioned under the next heading.

Kébar

Kébar, meaning 'display' or 'showing-off', is a lively treatment mainly for *ladrang* (including when used as *inggah*) in *ir I*, or in *ir II* if the *balungan* is double-density. Said to be of village origin, it is now found everywhere.

Kébar involves a slight relaxation of speed, a switch to *imbal bonang*, the addition of *keplok* and *alok*, the optional addition of extra *kempul* strokes, and a full set of decorating instruments, all accompanied by a particular type of *ciblon* drumming. There may be special vocal parts. The optional changes to the *kempul* strokes consist of

- □ an extra stroke at the end of the first *gåtrå*, where there would usually be none,
- □ repetitions (on the next *balungan* beat) of the strokes at the end of the first, third and fifth *gåtrå*,
- □ more complicated patterns at the end of the seventh *gåtrå*, for which there are in fact two variants. In one version, the usual *kempul* note is repeated on the next *balungan* beat and then there is a third stroke 1½ beats later. In the other version, the second stroke occurs 1½ beats after the first, and the third falls on the beat before the gong. In either variant, the *kempul* note played on the third stroke will normally be the gong note, and therefore not necessarily the same as on the first and second strokes.

The principles can be illustrated by *ldr Pangkur sl m*:

3 2 3 1̆ 3̆ 2 1 6 1̇ 6 3 2̆ 5̆ 3 2 1
3 5 3 2̆ 6̆ 5 3 2 5 3 2 1̆ 3̆ 2 ˘ 1 ⑥

or, for the last two *kenongan*,

3 5 3 2̆ 6̆ 5 3 2 5 3 2 1̆ 3 ˘ 2 1̆ ⑥

In this example, the last *kempul* note before the gong is 6, but the preceding two notes are 1̇. In accordance with the usual principles for choosing *kempul* notes in *pathet manyurå*, the other notes here (after the first, third and fifth *gåtrå*, respectively) are 1̇ twice, 6 twice and 6 twice more. In situations where *kempul kempyungan* would be usual, the *kempul* notes are played *mbalung* in *kébar* if the gamelan has the appropriate *kempul*: thus *balungan* 1 in *sl 9* would be played with *kempul* 1̇, not 5. The *kempul* strokes are on the beat during *kébar*.

55 Several of the headings here should be regarded as flexible: players should expect to encounter well-established practices that are given the same names but differ from those described here, which are simply those that have come to the author's notice by one route or another.

The start of *kébar* is signalled by the *kendhang* player switching to the *ciblon* at the third *kenong* of the *ladrang*. There is therefore time for the *kempul* player to start the extra *kempul* strokes by the end of that *gongan*. When the *ladrang* is the *inggah* of a *gendhing*, the *angkatan ciblon* starts in the *mérong* at the corresponding point relative to the gong. The *bonang barung* player can optionally play a full *sekaran* over the last *gåtrå* before the gong, or a half-*sekaran* over the last half-*gåtrå*, and then both *bonang* players start *imbal* after the gong.

To signal the end of *kébar*, the *kendhang* player speeds up slightly towards the end of the *gongan*. There are in fact several ways in which the treatment may end. It is possible to return to a non-*kébar* treatment in *ir I* for one or two *gongan*, after which a gradual slow-down to *ir II* is the usual next step. This is a typically Yogyanese option. A typically Solonese alternative involves a continuation of the faster tempo after the gong, followed by a sudden transition straight from *kébar* to *ir II* at the second *gåtrå* of the *gongan*. The transition to *ir II* may be completed entirely within the *gåtrå*, or may take a little longer. The loud-style *balungan* and decorating instruments, i.e. not the *slenthem*, may observe a *sirep* after the first note of the second *gåtrå* but re-enter at the start of the third *gåtrå*. The *kenong* note at the end of the second *gåtrå* is played.

It is also possible to make a transition from *kébar* straight into *ir III*, the *bonang* playing *imbal* without interruption (see p. 62): normally the transition takes place in the last *gåtrå* of the *gongan*. Similarly it is then possible to make an instant return from *ir III* to *kébar* in *ir I* at the gong.

Some pieces with *kébar* treatment are used as *selingan*; for example, *Kébar Sumedhangan* in both *gd Gambirsawit* and the dance accompaniment for *Gambyong Paréanom*.

Kinthilan, Yogya style

Kinthilan is a lively, not to say noisy, technique for two *saron* or for two players on one *saron*, and used instead of *saron imbal*. In fact, as another form of interlocking pattern, it is sometimes classified as *imbal*. In Yogyanese practice it is typically to be found in loud-style *ladrang* played in *ir I*—a context where the Solonese more often use *kébar* as described above, although the term *kinthilan* is known in Solo too (see below). Similarly, the Yogyanese use *kinthilan* in *playon*, for which the Solonese equivalent is *saron imbal* in *srepegan*.

The word *kinthil* means 'follow', implying that the off-beat player's task is always to play what the on-beat player has just played. To obtain the basic line used by the two *saron*, the density of the *balungan* is doubled in the usual way (see p. 31) without any change of speed. One *saron* (or one player on a shared instrument) plays this part. The other player plays the same part, but delayed by one-quarter of a *balungan* beat. Fig. 3.95 shows an example. The volume level of the *saron* is high.

The density of the combined *saron* parts is four times that of the *balungan*, and thus the same as in *saron imbal*. The two players damp their notes as for a normal *balungan*, i.e. not in the same pattern as for *saron imbal*. If two players are sharing an instrument, only the player of the *saron II* (off-beat) part damps.

During *kinthilan*, the *slenthem* usually plays only on the *dhong*: in other words, if the *balungan* is *mlaku*, the *slenthem* player must invent and play a *nibani* version of it (see p. 31). The *demung* plays the straight *balungan*.

Kinthilan, Solo style

In Solonese practice the term *kinthilan* can cover various interlocking patterns.

When the on-beat player is playing *nyacah* patterns, *kinthilan* means that the off-beat player is expected to imitate them, and this is particularly difficult since the off-beat player can only guess what is coming next: the only certainty is the *sèlèh* note. The combined pattern has the same density as *saron imbal*.

In Solonese style the two players may also play completely independent parts, chosen from various options, still at *saron imbal* speed. In this situation, the off-beat

Balungan, and *demung*	2 3 2 1	6 5 3 2
Double-density version, and *saron I*	2 . 3 . 5 . 3 . 2 . 3 . 2 . 1 .	6 . 5 . 3 . 5 . 3 . 2 . 1 . 2 .
Saron II	. 2 . 3 . 5 . 3 . 2 . 3 . 2 . 1	. 6 . 5 . 3 . 5 . 3 . 2 . 1 . 2
Slenthem	. 2 . 1	. 3 . 2

3.95 *Kinthilan* example, Yogya style

player ‘follows’ the on-beat part in time, but not in the sense of copying it.

A slower version of *kinthilan* is used in *ir II*, e.g. in the *mérong* of *gendhing* as part of *wayang* accompaniments:

balungan	2 1 6̣ 5̣
saron I	2 1 2 1 6 5 6 5
saron II	2 1 2 1 6 5 6 5

These patterns are identical to those played by the *demung* and *slenthem* as part of *pinjalan* (see below).

Pinjalan

With the usual warning about confusion between the terms *pinjalan*, *imbal* and *gemakan*, here this name is given to a form of *garap* involving the *saron*, *demung* and *slenthem*. It is used in *ir II*, and is applied to *ladrang*, including when they are used as *minggah* to *gendhing*, as well as to the *minggah* form itself. The treatment is mainly applied to pieces in *pélog*: *ldr Wilujeng* and *ldr Moncèr* are two exceptions in *sléndro*. *Pinjalan* is one treatment where the *demung* breaks an unwritten rule and plays more notes than the *saron*.

The basic principles are that

- The *demung* plays two notes per *balungan* beat, using patterns that are usually equivalent to *mipil låmbå* on the *bonang barung*, e.g. 2121 for *balungan* 21;
- The *slenthem* plays the same notes on the following half-beat;
- The *saron* plays in one of two ways: either it can play the straight *balungan*, or it can play the *balungan* notes that fall on the strong beats (*dhong*) but play them on the *dhing* too. These two options could be called respectively *pinjalan mbalung* and *pinjalan ngedhongi*. The latter option seems to be more usual;
- The *peking* plays the *demung* and *slenthem* parts, which together amount to a normal pattern for the *peking*.

The last principle is important: *pinjalan* is often described as dividing the *peking* part between the *demung* and *slenthem*. The combined shape of the *demung* and *slenthem* parts mainly follows the usual rules for Solonese *pekingan*, including the handling of *gantungan* and large jumps in the *balungan* line, as well as other details mentioned earlier. If there is a second *demung*, it plays the same part as the *slenthem*.

An example of a single *gåtrå*:

balungan	1 2 1 6̣
demung	1 2 1 2 1 6 5 6
slenthem	1 2 1 2 1 6 5 6
saron (mbalung)	1 2 1 6
saron (ngedhongi)	2 2 6 6
peking	1122112211665566

This example shows the *demung* and *slenthem* following the common *peking* practice of making a large jump (1 6 in this case) only once.

In *pinjalan* the *demung* player, like the *peking* player, has a certain amount of discretion about which notes to use: examples are given below. The *peking* and *demung* players will not necessarily make the same choices. It is the *slenthem* player’s job to repeat whatever notes the *demung* uses.

An example of a three-*gongan ladrang* where *gongan* B and C constitute the *lik* section, *ldr Playon pl 5*:

Balungan

A	.6̣12 16̣4̣5̣̂ 3365 3216̣̂
	5̣6̣12 3212̂ 16̣5̣4̣ 246⑤
B	.542 1245̂ .542 1245̂
	6542 1232̂ 66.7 567⑥
C	.654 2212̂ ..24 5.65̂
	6542 16̣4̣5̣̂ .6̣12 16̣4̣⑤

The basis of the *demung/slenthem* parts, without doubling, is

A	5612 1645 3365 3216
	5612 3212 1654 651 245
B	6542 1245 6542 1245
	6542 1232 5667 5676
C	7654 2212 2224 6565
	6542 1645 5612 1645

or in full, on either *demung* or *slenthem*

56561212 16564545
33336565 32321656 etc.

Some features of the *demung* part are

- a more decorative treatment at the end of *gongan* A, in full 65651245,

- the introduction of the note 7 in *gåtrå* 1 of *gongan* C, because of its presence in the previous *gåtrå*, although the notes 5 6 could equally well be used in place of 7 6,
- pairs of note 2 in *gåtrå* 2 and 3 of *gongan* C, rather than other theoretically possible notes such as 1 2 or 3 2, after a similar example in *gongan* A; on the other hand, *gåtrå* 7 of *gongan* B, another example of *balungan kembar*, is realised with 5 6 rather than 6 6.

If the *balungan* is *nibani*, additional decisions have to be made about which notes to use on the *demung*, and thus the *slenthem* too. The *bonang* may play *gåtrå* or half-*gåtrå* with *gembyangan* for any of the usual reasons. In such situations, the *demung*/*slenthem* notes may stay closer to the *sèlèh* note than might be expected—but the general approach to the selection of notes remains much the same as used by the *peking* in Solonese style. When not playing *gembyangan*, the *bonang* may play standard *mipil* on the notes used by the *demung* and *slenthem*, rather than the usual Solonese *nibani* patterns.

An example of another three-*gongan ladrang* with a *lik* section consisting of *gongan* B and C, *ldr Sukarsih pl 6*:

Balungan

A	. 2 . 1	. 2 . 1	. 3 . 5	. 3 . 2
	. 6 . 5	. 3 . 2	. 5 . 4	. 1 . (6)
B	. 5 . 6	. 5 . 6	. 2 . 1	. 2 . 6
	. 3 . 2	. 3 . 5	. 1 . 6	. 3 . (2)
C	. 3 . 2	. 3 . 5	. 1 . 6	. 3 . 2
	. 6 . 5	. 3 . 2	. 5 . 4	. 2 . (1)

Basis of *demung* and *slenthem* parts:

A	2321	2321	3235	3212
	6535	3212	5654	2156
B	5656	562 356	2321	3256
	3532	3565	12 56	3532
C	3532	3565	12 56	3532
	6535	3212	5654	215 321

More decorative treatments as used in the previous example occur in two places. The underlining shows where the *bonang* play *gembyangan*.

A slightly similar form of *garap* in Yogya style is dealt with under **Peking: Yogya-style** (p. 132).

Ompak klénangan

This treatment is applied to the *ompak* of *ktw Subåkaståwå* and other *ompak* with the same notes, and to a few other pieces. It consists of *klénangan* on the two *bonang* (see p. 181) together with a non-standard punctuation pattern:

. 1 . 6 . 1 . 5 . 1 . 6 . 1 . (5)

Another version is

. 1 . 6 . 1 . 5 . 1 . 6 . 1 . (5)

Neither of these treatments closely matches the patterns of the *gamelan munggang* (see under **Ensembles**, p. 240), although theoretically based on them—and in any case the ceremonial gamelan is rather different from modern gamelan in its instrumentation. The first example above simply consists of additional *kempul* strokes superimposed on the regular *garap* for a *ketawang*.

The *garap*, or the transition to this *garap* from the standard treatment for a *ketawang*, is signalled by special *kendhangan*.

Gobyog(an)

Gobyog is a lively treatment applied to part of a *gongan* of *ladrang*. The following example comes from a Yogya-style performance of *ldr Gonjing miring sl m*. The *ir III* version of the *ladrang* has a double-density *balungan*, and the third *kenongan* is normally played as

1 2 1 3 1 3 1 2 1 2 1 3 1 3 1 2

in which, as usual in Yogya, the *kempyang* is not used. A speed-up towards the end of the preceding *kenongan* signals entry into the *gobyog* treatment, where, instead of the version above, the density of the *balungan* is doubled again and the *kenongan* is treated as four *gongan* of *lancaran*, although with no final *gong ageng*:

1 2 1 2 1 2 1 (3)
1 3 1 3 1 3 1 (2)
1 2 1 2 1 2 1 (3)
1 3 1 3 1 3 1 (2)

This may be easier to interpret if written as *balungan nibani*, with the *kethuk* strokes added, e.g.

. 1 . 2 . 1 . 2 . 1 . 2 . 1 . (3)

for the first phrase/'*gongan*'. Normal *garap* for a *lancaran* applies—*gembyangan cegat* on the *bonang*, *kenong* notes typically in pairs, and the expected notes on the *kempul* and *gong suwukan*. The next *kenongan* reverts to regular *ir III* treatment.

The same performance included a variant treatment of the first *kenongan*, which normally consists of 2321 3216 played twice. (This treatment seems to have no name, and, although different from *gobyog* as described above, is not unrelated.) After a slow-down immediately before the gong, this *kenongan* was played in *ir IV*, with non-standard punctuation again

. 2̂ .̆ 3̂ .̆ 2̂ .̆ 1̂ .̆ 3̂ .̆ 2̂ .̆ 1̂ .̆ (6̂)
. 2̂ .̆ 3̂ .̆ 2̂ .̆ 1̂ .̆ 3̂ .̆ 2̂ .̆ 1̂ .̆ (6̂)

plus *kethuk* strokes on all 16 half-beats of each line above. The *bonang* played *gembyangan cegat* to the *sèlèh* notes (3–1–2–6 in each line), and the *kenong* and *kempul* notes were in pairs, based on the same *sèlèh* notes. A slow-down in the last four beats signalled a return to *ir III*.

Gobyog treatment is also found in Solo. The following is a Solonese treatment of *ldr Ayun-ayun sl m/pl 6*, again applied in *ir III*, but showing a *srepegan* punctuation structure. Starting after the gong, the *balungan* instruments and the extra punctuation play two *gåtrå* at a fast pace, after which there is an *andhegan*, and then the instruments re-enter. This happens twice

2̂ 6̽ 2̂ 6̽ 2̂ 6̽ 2̂ 6̽ … (*andhegan*) … 1̽
5̂ 1̽ 5̂ 1̽ 5̂ 1̽ 2̂ 3̽ … (*andhegan*) … 2̽
6̂ 2̽ 6̂ 2̽ 6̂ 2̽ 5̂ 3

after which there is a return to the regular *balungan* in *ir III*. The first two lines above can be considered as a version of the first *kenongan* of the *ladrang*, and the third line above corresponds to the first quarter of the third *kenongan*: effectively the second *kenongan* disappears.

As *gobyog* is a standard treatment for only a few pieces—and varies between sources—there is not enough evidence to say whether the use of *lancaran* structure in one case and *srepegan* in the other amounts to a general Yogya–Solo difference.

Gobyog is not confined to *ir III*: it also occurs in *ir II* in *ldr Gégot pl 6*.

Solonese *sampak*

The parts played by the *balungan* section in Solo-style *sampak* have already been described in Part 2. They amount to a joint *garap* by at least three instruments if the *peking* plays the combination of the *slenthem* and *demung* parts, but this is only one option. The *peking* may play *nyacah* instead of this part. *Nyacah* on at least one *saron* is also common.

Solonese *gendhing bonang*

As described under **Progress of a *gendhing bonang***, p. 80, the *inggah* section of a *gendhing* may have *demung imbal*, with the off-beat *demung* part also played on the *slenthem*.

This *garap* is applied to *gendhing bonang* in either *laras*, whereas *pinjalan* (another form of *imbal* involving the *demung*, as described above) is normally confined to *pélog*.

Yogyanese *gendhing soran*

As described under **Progress of a Yogyanese *gendhing soran***, p. 81, the *ndhawah* section of a *gendhing soran* involves *demung imbal* (in the usual Yogya style), combined with either *gemakan* or *mbandhul* on the *slenthem*, according to *iråmå*.

Ensembles

The instruments described above are combined to form several distinct types of ensemble, mainly according to the intended function of the gamelan.

Sléndro and *pélog* ensembles

As described in connection with the gongs, *kenong* and *kempul*, some instruments can usually be shared between the two halves of a double gamelan, because most double gamelan have a *tumbuk*. However, it is sometimes convenient in teaching institutions to separate the *sléndro* and *pélog* sections, and then a full set of instruments in each *laras* is desirable.

The drums serve both *laras*. A *rebab* can also do so. The *siter* family instruments can also be tuned for either *laras*. The *kemanak* are not strongly bound to one *laras*. To allow the two halves of a gamelan full independence, two copies of some of these instruments will therefore be necessary.

Gamelan ageng/gedhé

A *gamelan gedhé* (Figs 3.96 and 3.97) is simply a large gamelan, but the term is applied to ensembles capable of tackling most types of gamelan music. It should therefore have full sets of soft-style and loud-style instruments. The substitute instruments such as *gong kemodhong* and *gong bumbung* are unnecessary, and a *gamelan gedhé* will not always have all the instruments found in a gamelan intended only for accompanying *wayang kulit*.

The number of instruments in the *balungan* section varies, but a gamelan with only two *saron*, one *demung* and a *peking* is still a *gamelan gedhé*. The decorating instruments (loud- and soft-style), punctuating instruments and drums are never duplicated.

For dance accompaniment a *gamelan gedhé* is usually necessary. Even if the accompaniment consists largely of *gendhing kemanak*, needing a much reduced ensemble, there are also the entry and exit pieces in the loud style, requiring a full *balungan* section.

Gamelan gadhon

By definition a *gamelan gadhon* is an incomplete ensemble: *gadhon* refers to eating side dishes without rice— rice being the real food, as every Indonesian knows. This may seem surprising, because a *gadhon* ensemble consists of

3.96 A back view of gamelan *Kyahi Kaduk Manis* – *Kyahi Manis Renggå* at the *kraton Solo*

Table 3.23
Make-up of ensembles (examples)

Instrument	*Gamelan gedhé*	*Gamelan bonangan*	For *wayang kulit purwå*		*Gamelan gadhon*	*Siteran* and *cokèkan* ensembles
			Basic	Extended		
Gong ageng	■	■	■	■		
Gong suwukan	■	■	■	■		
Gong kemodhong					■	
Gong bumbung						■
Kempul	■	■	■	■	□	
Kenong	■	■	■	■	□	
Kenong japan	□	■				
Kethuk	■	■	■	■	□	
Engkuk-kemong	□			□		
Kempyang	■	■	□	□	□	
Kemanak	■					
Kecèr	□		■[a]	■[a]		
Saron panerus	■	■	□	■		
Saron (barung)	■	■	□	■		
Saron sångå	□		■	■		
(Saron) demung	■	■	□	■		
Gendèr barung	■		■	■	■	□
Gendèr panerus	■		■	■	■	
Slenthem	■	■[b]	■	■	■	□
Bonang barung	■	■		■		
Bonang panerus	■	■		■		
Bonang panembung	□	□		□		
Siter peking	□		□	□		■[c]
Siter	□		□	□		■[c]
Celempung	■		■	■	■	■[c]
Gambang	■		■	■	■	
Suling	■		□	■	■	
Rebab	■		■	■	■	□
Kendhang ageng	■	■		□	■	
Kendhang ketipung	■	■		□	■	
Kendhang ciblon	■			□	■	■
Kendhang wayangan			■	■[d]		
Bedhug	□	□				

■ Usually present. □ May be present.

a. Also *kepyak*. b. And/or *slentho* in old gamelan. c. At least one of these instruments, but possibly several *siter/celempung* of different sizes and known by other names. d. Also possibly other drums and often a Western-style drum kit.

soft-style instruments with a limited number of punctuating instruments, and therefore demands competent players and has a less obvious appeal to listeners. In other words, this is a connoisseurs' ensemble.

In the instrumentation the *bonang* are missing, and the *slenthem* is the only *balungan* instrument. The complement of punctuating instruments varies, but a gong is the only essential instrument. It may be a *gong kemodhong*, located (for example) so that the *slenthem* player can play the gong notes in *gendhing* or other forms in slow *iråmå*. If there is no *gong suwukan*, one *wilah* of the *gong kemodhong* is played instead, giving a low pitch without an *ombak*.

Ensembles for *wayang*

In the days before electronic amplification, *wayang* was accompanied by a reduced ensemble (the 'basic' ensemble listed in Table 3.23), in either *sléndro* or *pélog* according to the type of *wayang* (see **Dance and drama**, p. 96). The *balungan* section was small—although typically including a *saron wayangan* to allow more varied *imbal* and *nyacah*—and there would be no *bonang*. The description *gamelan wayangan* refers to this instrumentation.

Present-day performances routinely use large ensembles combining *sléndro* and *pélog* plus added Western percussion instruments, and as many *pesindhèn* as money permits. It is reasonable for several singers to share the heavy workload of *sindhènan*.

Miniature ensembles

To meet the need for better portability—allowing an entire gamelan to be transported in a small van—some educational institutions in the West buy special gamelan in which the instruments are reduced in size throughout, and the bulkier *pencon* instruments are replaced by *wilah*-based alternatives. The smaller instruments are also more practical for children to play.

Siteran ensembles

In fact two terms, *siteran* and *cokèkan*, describe these groups. The latter term is said to have Chinese connections: if that is true, present-day ensembles seem to have lost the connections. Opinions differ as to the meanings of the terms. Some sources say that a *gendèr barung* is essential in a *cokèkan* ensemble: others consider the two

3.97 The *sléndro* section of a *gamelan gedhé* (with South Bank Gamelan Players)

terms interchangeable. The term *siteran* is preferred here for the simple reason that the presence of at least one member of the *siter* family is essential.

The basic minimum *siteran* ensemble consists of one *siter*, a *ciblon*, a *gong bumbung* and a *pesindhèn*. That does not mean four people, because it is normal for the *gong bumbung* to be played by the *siter* player or the *ciblon* player—either or both of whom may also sing. Further *pesindhèn* (Fig. 3.98) and instruments may be added. Additional *siter* will usually be of different types (see **Siter family**, p. 196).[56] If the ensemble does not have a *slenthem kawat* for the *balungan*, a normal *slenthem* may be used.

Many *siteran* ensembles are itinerant, going around the restaurants in the evenings and playing for reward. Such ensembles typically use a few easily portable instruments. Other *siteran* groups have permanent homes in hotel lobbies. There is also no clear distinction between *siteran/cokèkan* and *gadhon* ensembles. The term *gadhon* is more likely to be reserved for ensembles that are based on a reduced *gamelan gedhé*, but this usage is not always followed.

These groups may play the same material as regular gamelan ensembles—or at least items with names familiar from *karawitan*—and the singers and players may include established gamelan musicians. It is not clear how independent the *siteran* tradition is, but at least a degree of influence from the villages seems likely. The *siter* instruments typically differ from those used in gamelan, and some of the *garap* is distinctive. The emphasis is firmly on the vocal part(s). The possibility of more than one *siter* in the ensemble raises the question of how they should interact, if at all: in practice, interlocking *garap* occurs between certain of the instruments.

3.98 *Siteran* group

Ceremonial ensembles

The existing gamelan to which the earliest dates are given have ceremonial functions, and differ in their instrumentation from the types of ensemble described in Table 3.23. Each type is exemplified in the palaces of both Solo and Yogya—confirming that they date from before the splits in the Mataram kingdom—and some are or were also to be found in other cities such as Bantèn and Cirebon. The *gamelan sekatèn* are thought to be the most recent of them.

In the Principalities, all these ceremonial gamelan are considered *pusåkå*. Instruments in some of them have metal brackets that allow them to be carried in procession, and some are played while being carried.

The instruments are distinct in some ways from those of modern gamelan: they tend to be larger and (except in the *gamelan sekatèn*) of *cemengan* form; the pitch is lower; the drums are usually of conical shape rather than modified barrel shape; and the range of notes available is limited. The *gamelan sekatèn* is much more like a modern gamelan. Since differences exist between gamelan of the same type, the description below is somewhat simplified.[57] In some cases, the names of the instruments do not agree between the gamelan.

Apart from the *gamelan sekatèn*, the tunings of these gamelan are problematic, as they do not always conform neatly to the *sléndro–pélog* distinction, and are not even

Names of gamelan

The names of gamelan are very often in Old Javanese, which means that they tend to contain Sanskrit roots. They are also particularly likely to be obscure anyway, and to harbour multiple meanings. Also a given word can have different meanings in Old Javanese, modern Javanese and Indonesian—all of which will inevitably be in the minds of the Javanese—and homonyms abound.

It can be important to translate established compound words as compounds, not as their constituent parts. For example: *lebdhå/labdhå* = 'achieve', *jiwå* = 'spirit', 'soul', 'life', but *Lebdhåjiwå* = 'restored to life'. On the other hand, the name *Kanyut mèsem* is a rather artificial compound (= 'carried away by smiles') made from the separate names of two single gamelan *Kanyut* ('carried away', 'drifting') and *Mèsem* ('smiling')

Gamelan names can have the character of nouns, verbs or adjectives.

56 Also see Plate 21 in Lindsay (1979).

57 The longer descriptions in Kunst (1973) do not necessarily agree in every way with the current state of these gamelan.

roughly consistent between the various palaces. Taking into account the low pitch, the few notes and the unusual tunings, the assignment of *kepatihan* numbers to the notes is a little arbitrary.

According to tradition, all the ceremonial gamelan are played as the ruler commands. In practice the occasions include certain rituals occurring at irregular intervals, such as weddings and circumcisions, but very few regular events. The main exception is the use of the *gamelan sekatèn* throughout Sekatèn week (see **Appendix 6**).

Gamelan munggang

With its three basic notes, which also give it the alternative name of *gamelan patigan*, the *gamelan munggang* is often described as primitive, and it is ascribed the earliest date of any gamelan. The main melodic instruments are several sets of three large *bonang*-style *pencon* in two octaves, housed in frames containing either three or six pots, and called *bonang* or *gambyong*.[58] The other instruments are (with reference to Fig. 3.99):

1 *kenong [japan]*: behind the *peneteg ageng*
up to 3 *kècer* or *rojéh*: on the *gayor* at the right
2 *penonthong*: on the *gayor* at the left
2 *gong ageng*
1 large drum (*peneteg ageng*)
1 small drum (*peneteg alit*)

Most *gamelan munggang* have notes that can be treated as *pélog* 1, 6̣ and 5̣: *K.K. Guntur laut* is an exception. The gamelan plays only one piece, with a wide tempo range. It consists of the ostinato pattern 1 6̣ 1 5̣ as heard in the *ompak* of many *ketawang*, including *ktw Subåkaståwå*.

Gamelan kodhok ngorèk

This gamelan takes its name from the croaking of frogs, but the basic melody instruments (*gambyong*/*bonang* and *rijal*) produce only two notes, so the name does an injustice to the skills of Javanese frogs. The instruments are

2 *gambyong* or *bonang*	2 *rijal*
2 *penonthong*	1 *kenong*
2 *gong ageng*	
1 set of *kecèr*	1 *byong*
1 *peneteg ageng*	1 *peneteg alit*
1 *gendèr barung*	1 *gambang gångså*

The *rijal* is a higher-register *bonang*. Both types of *bonang* are arranged as eight *pencon* in a single long row. The tuning of their notes is *pélog* (the *gamelan kodhok ngorèk* in the *kraton Yogya* again being an exception), but the *gendèr* and *gambang gångså* play a counter-melody in *sléndro*. At the *kraton Yogya*, *saron* and *demung* are sometimes used too. The most often heard piece is sometimes called *Dhendhå gedhé*, but another two pieces, *Dhendhå santi* and *Dhendhå sèwu* (or *Pedaringan kebak*), exist.

Gamelan cåråbalèn

The main melodic instruments of the *gamelan cåråbalèn* are again sets of three *bonang*-style *pencon*; one called

3.99 A *gamelan munggang* (*Kyahi Kangjeng Guntur laut* at the *kraton Yogya*)

58 At Solo, one of these sets of three *pencon* is identified as *penitir*, *banggèn* and *kenongan*, corresponding to notes 1, 6̣ and 5̣ respectively.

3.101 *Bonang* of a *gamelan sekatèn* (*Kyahi Någåwilågå*, at the *kraton Yogya*)

gambyong or *bonang*, the other divided into *kenut* and *klénang*. In this case the notes make up a six-note scale of *pélog* type, but one of each set of three notes is not normally used. The full instrumentation is

1 *gambyong* (2 sets of three *pencon*)
1 *kenut* (notes 5, 6) + 1 *klénang* (notes 1̇, 2̇)
1 *gong ageng* — 1 or 2 *kempul*
1 or 2 *kenong [japan]* — 1 or 2 *penonthong*
1 *peneteg ageng* — 1 *peneteg alit*

The repertoire consists of nine pieces, some of which are (sometimes) assigned to regular *bentuk* of *karawitan*:

Gangsaran — *Ladrang Babat kenceng*
Gangsaran Pati — *Ladrang Bali balèn*
Lancaran Glagah kanginan
Lancaran Klumpuk — *Lung gadhung*
Ketawang Pisan(g) Bali — *Tunggul råjå*

Some of these are played in sequences: *Klumpuk – Bali balèn – Klumpuk*; *Glagah kanginan – Babat kenceng – Glagah kanginan*; *Gangsaran – Pisang Bali – Gangsaran*. When *gangsaran* is played on a regular gamelan, the gong, *kempul* and *kenong* parts go to the corresponding instruments, and the *penonthong* part goes to the *kethuk*.

Gamelan sekatèn

Each *kraton* has a pair of *gamelan sekatèn* in *laras pélog*. The origins of the ensembles and the Sekatèn week rituals are obscure, as is the name *sekati/sekatèn* itself (a favourite object of *jarwådhosok*).[59] According to tradition, the gamelan were created as part of the Islamic missionary activities, but (whatever the truth of that) it is now believed that the festival replaces a pre-Islamic one.

For Sekatèn week, these gamelan are carried in procession to a pair of small buildings north and south of the main entrance to the Great Mosque (*Mesjid Ageng*) on the west side of the open space (*Alun-Alun Lor*) north of the *kraton*, and are played there in alternation throughout the day. Because of the amount of metal in these instruments, their maximum volume level is very high, although it is difficult to believe that they were ever heard as far away as legend says. Traditionally the ruler rewards a player who manages to break a *wilah*.

The instrumentation is

1 *bonang* — 1 or 2 *demung*
2 or 4 *saron barung* — 1 or 2 *saron panerus*;
1 *kempyang* — 1 *campur* (Yogya only)
2 *gong ageng* — 1 *bedhug*

At Yogya the *balungan* section has the smaller number of *balungan* instruments. The beaters can be outsize versions of the horn-headed beaters used on the *peking* in regular gamelan, and are said to be lead-weighted.

The *kempyang* has two pots, tuned to 6 and 7 (Yogya) or both to 6 (Solo), and the *campur* is a pair of small hanging gongs with a similar function to the *kempyang* or *kemanak*. The *bedhug* functions as a punctuating instrument equivalent to a *kempul*. Surprisingly, there is no *kenong*.

The *bonang* can be considered as the combination of a single-octave *bonang panembung* and a single-octave *bonang barung* with extra pots (Fig. 3.100). The upper octave functions as the melodic leader and, in the absence of conventional drumming, its player also controls tempo. The *panembung* octave often has two players (Fig. 3.101).[60]

In the Sekatèn week performances the three *pathet* of *pélog* are played in succession. For each *pathet* there is a key piece: *gd Rangkung* in *pl 5*, *gd Rambu* in *pl 6*, *gd Barang miring* in *pl 7*. These three pieces are described as being in *ladrang* form. Each is preceded by a long preamble (*racikan*) on the *bonang barung* in rather free rhythm, punctuated by a few notes on the *bonang panembung* and the *balungan* instruments. *Gd Rangkung* is believed to be the only piece in the whole gamelan repertoire that ends with gong 4. After these pieces, others in *ladrang* form or *gendhing* form are played (but only the *inggah* sections of the latter).

59 After hearing the fifth different explanation, the author stopped counting.

60 This has not always been the practice, as illustrated by an 1888 picture by a local Yogya photographer, showing one player on the *panembung* side of the gamelan that is also seen in Fig. 3.101.

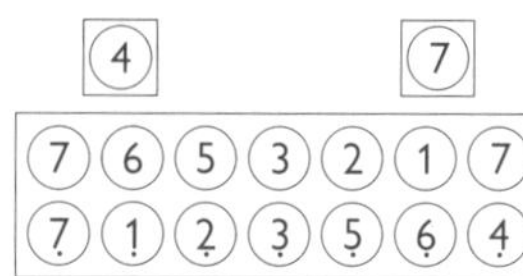

3.100 *Bonang* layout in *gamelan sekatèn*

Review

The preceding sections of Part 3 have tried to give an idea of the responsibilities of a player, not just a set of notes that can be played in specified circumstances.

Reviewing first the relationship between the *balungan* or the inner melody and what individual instruments play, there are clearly differences between certain categories of instruments. When the *balungan* instruments play decoration, they stay (on average) closest to the *balungan*. The soft-style decorating instruments lie at the opposite extreme: they require the most detailed knowledge of basic musical principles and of the individual piece. For this reason it is not practical to learn to play such instruments from the printed page, and they are accordingly more difficult to study than the others.

The *bonang barung* and *bonang panerus* can be placed somewhere between the other two categories, with an extremely wide range of *garap*, which is nevertheless always tied quite closely to the *balungan*. Playing the *kendhang* is difficult in a somewhat different way, because it involves responsibility for controlling the tempo and managing transitions (although the player can in practice get away with many incorrect strokes).

Examples have been given of different ways in which players may realise the same passage. Some *céngkok* can be described as easy, and others as difficult. Performing contexts matter too: playing *lnc Singånebah* in one's first gamelan class is one thing, but playing it as part of the accompaniment to the dance *Båndåyudå* is quite another.

There is also great scope for players to exercise personal taste when playing the more advanced instruments, e.g. taking different decisions as to how often their *céngkok* should coincide with the notes of the *balungan*. Experience with one instrument can, as mentioned already, help when playing another. Good *rebab* and *gendèr* players tend to make good *bonang* players if they choose to play *bonang*.

It would be wrong to suggest that even experienced Javanese musicians always know the right thing to play. There is such a thing as 'busking' a part in a gamelan performance, and even a word for it (*nawur*). The player can sometimes choose patterns that do not strictly fit, but also do not noticeably disturb the performance.[61] This option is only available to players of the decorating instruments. *Balungan* players who forget the *balungan* line have nowhere to hide, and standard Javanese practice in this situation is to pretend to play the instrument without actually making contact between *tabuh* and *wilah*.

Full competence means being able to realise a piece adequately, but also being able to fit successfully into any group regardless of its possibly unfamiliar habits. This competence also includes the ability to recover from disasters of various kinds. There are many pieces where unusual *garap* has become standard, and new pieces are being written all the time, so that even an expert might occasionally need guidance.

Players who study the gamelan with only one teacher do not gain a proper perspective on the performance practice of *karawitan*. They will not know whether the *garap* that they have been taught is in general use or is unique to the teacher, or if it has been deliberately simplified to help students. The widest possible range of teachers and playing experience—with different sorts of material, in different performing contexts (*klenèngan*, dance or *wayang*), in different groups and in different types of group—is always useful. In this way, players also expose themselves to variant versions of well-known compositions, and learn more about which performance practices are unusual.

Several books have included a 'full score' of a passage of music as played by a gamelan.[62] Apart from the fact that this exercise consumes a large quantity of paper in order to convey a useful picture, there is a good reason for not repeating it here: it encourages a 'vertical' view of the musical texture, which is not the Javanese approach.

61 e.g. the *kacang asin* ('salted peanuts') technique on the *siter* family, where the player creates *pathet*-specific ostinato patterns without committing to particular *sèlèh* notes (Sutton, 1993).

62 e.g. Kunst (1973), Malm (1977) and Sorrell (1990), using staff notation with or without modification. Some Indonesian gamelan primers include partial scores in *kepatihan*.

Notation

Contents

Kendhangan

General notes

The examples below are simply a selection of pieces in a variety of *bentuk*, styles, *laras*, *pathet* and *iråmå*, and illustrating a variety of standard *garap* techniques and occasionally some non-standard details. They range from simple pieces that beginners may play in their first classes to some of the 'warhorses' of the repertoire, and include the pieces often described as 'core repertoire'. Otherwise no special claims are made for these examples as being essential, important, outstanding, classic, or anything else. Some have been chosen because they can be heard on commercial recordings, although the performance details given below will not necessarily match those on the recordings.

Punctuating instruments other than the gong are generally shown selectively, e.g. only for the first *gongan* or the first line. Some mark-up for *bonangan* is included. Otherwise these examples are mainly left as exercises for the reader in choosing *garap*, based on the guidance both here and in the main text. The *bukå* is usually shown in its basic form, leaving the reader to decide on matters such as *sarugan*, octave placement and the treatment of the final *gåtrå* if the *bonang* is being used. The layout of the notation is deliberately inconsistent, demonstrating some of the variety of styles that will be found in other sources.

For some pieces, detailed *garap* notes will be added to the associated website.

The material has been typeset for compactness, and should be written out in a more user-friendly form for playing.

Abbreviations

bal, b *balungan* *gér, g* *gérongan* *p.d.* *pangkat dhawah*

Lnc Manyar sèwu sl 6/m

bukå . 1̇ . 6 . 1̇ . 6 . 5 . (3)

ir lancar

A [. 5 . 3 . 5 . 3 . 5 . 3 . 6 . (5)

B . 6 . 5 . 6 . 5 . 6 . 5 . 3 . (2)

C . 3 . 2 . 3 . 2 . 3 . 2 . 1̇ . (6)

D . 1̇ . 6 . 1̇ . 6 . 1̇ . 6 . 5 . (3)]

ir I A [5 2 5 3 5 2 5 3 5 2 5 3 6 3 6 (5)

B 6 3 6 5 6 3 6 5 6 3 6 5 3 1 3 (2)

C 3 1 3 2 3 1 3 2 3 1 3 2 1̇ 5 1̇ (6)

D 1̇ 5 1̇ 6 1̇ 5 1̇ 6 1̇ 5 1̇ 6 5 2 5 (3)]

ir I counter-melody

A [5 23523 5 23523 5 23523 6 3563(5)

B 6 35635 6 35635 6 35635 3 1231(2)

C 3 12312 3 12312 3 12312 1̇ 561̇5(6)

D 1̇ 561̇56 1̇ 561̇56 1̇ 561̇56 5 2352(3)]

ir II + III

A [65323523 65323523 65323523 6653563(5)

B 1̇6535635 1̇6535635 1̇6535635 3321231(2)

C 53212312 53212312 53212312 1̇1̇6561̇5(6)

D 2̇1̇6561̇56 2̇1̇6561̇56 2̇1̇6561̇56 5532352(3)]

Title. *Manyar sèwu* = 1000 weaverbirds.

Skema and **garap**. There are numerous ways of performing this piece. It can be treated as a simple *lancaran* in *ir lancar* with *balungan nibani*, and the first *ir I* version shown can be used as a counter-melody on one or more *saron*. In *ir I* the same version can be played by all or most of the *balungan* section, with the optional counter-melody shown being played by one or more *saron*. In *ir II* or *III*, the punctuation pattern may be changed to that of a *ladrang*, i.e.

65323523 etc.

in which case *gong ageng* is used throughout.

In *ir lancar*, *bonang* play *gembyangan cegat*, with *kenong* notes in pairs. In *ir I* and *II*, *bonang* play *mipil*. In *ir III*: three blocks of *bonang imbal* + full *sekaran* to each *kenongan*; alternatively, 1 block of *imbal* + full *sekaran* to each half-*kenongan*. (1 block of *imbal* = 4 cycles.) For transitions between *irâmå*, typically last *gåtrå* of *gongan* D has the new *garap*: e.g. at transition from *ir lancar* to *ir I*, this *gåtrå* uses *mipil*.

Also played in *pl 7*: *balungan* is basically unchanged, except 3532 for 3132, otherwise 7̣ for 1, 7 for 1̇.

Lnc Singånebah sl 6/m

bukå 5̣ 3 2̣ . 5̣ 3 2̣ . 5 . (3)

A [. 5 . 3 . 5 . 3 . 5 . 3 . 2 . (1)

B . 2 . 1 . 2 . 1 . 2 . 1 . 3 . (2)

C . 3 . 2 . 3 . 2 . 3 . 2 . 5 . (3)]

Counter-melody

A [1̇ 6 5 3 1̇ 6 5 3 1̇ 6 5 3 2 3 2 (1)

B 5 3 2 1 5 3 2 1 5 3 2 1 3 5 3 (2)

C 6 5 3 2 6 5 3 2 6 5 3 2 5 6 5 (3)]

Title. *Singånebah* = pouncing lion.

Skema and **garap**. ABC, *suwuk* usually after C. Counter-melody may be played by one or more *saron* in *ir lancar*, or used as standard *balungan* in *ir I*.

Also played in *pl 7*: see under *Båndåyudå*. Counter-melody for *pl 7*:

A [7 6 5 3 7 6 5 3 7 6 5 3 6 5 6 (7)

B 3 5 6 7 3 5 6 7 3 5 6 7 3 5 3 (2)

C 6 5 3 2 6 5 3 2 6 5 3 2 5 6 5 (3)]

Lnc Kebogiro glendheng pl 5

bukå . 2 . 1 . 2 . 1 . 6̣ . (5)

[. . 4̣ 5̣ 4̣ 5̣ 4̣ 5̣ 4̣ 5̣ 4̣ 5̣ . 6̣ . (1)

. 6̣ 2 . 6̣ 1 . 6̣ 2 . 6̣ 1 . 6̣ . (5)]

Title. This is a half-*kenongan* extracted from the *minggah* of *gd bonang Glendheng pl 5* and re-notated. *Glendheng* = ?grumble. *Kebogiro* is the name of a specific piece, but is also sometimes used a near-synonym for *lancaran*.

Skema and **garap**. Cycled as shown. *Bonang* notes can be 5–5–5–1 in first *gongan*; 1–1–1–5 in second *gongan*. *Kenong* notes can be the same, or in pairs. The irregular rhythms of this piece are liable to reduce inexperienced players to the giggles. A *sléndro* version also exists, and another in *pl 7*.

Bubaran Hudan mas pl 7

bukå 7̣ 7̣ 7̣ 5̣ 6̣ 7̣ 2 2 7̣ 6̣ 5̣ 6̣ 76̣5̣3(5)

[6̣ 5̣ 3 2 6̣ 5̣ 3 2 . 3 2̣ 3 6̣ 5̣ 3 (2)

6̣ 5̣ 3 2 6̣ 5̣ 3 2 . 3 2̣ 3 6̣ 5̣ 3 (2)

7̣ 5̣ 6̣ 7̣ 5̣ 6̣ 7̣ 2 2 7̣ 6̣ 5̣ 6̣ 7̣ 6̣ (5)

7̣ 5̣ 6̣ 7̣ 5̣ 6̣ 7̣ 2 2 7̣ 6̣ 5̣ 6̣ 7̣ 6̣ (5)]

Title. *Hudan mas* = golden rain.

Skema and **garap**. Cycled in *ir I* as shown. *Suwuk* at second gong (using *gong ageng*) or fourth gong: the latter seems to be usual. *Garap* for *bonang* is often more or less Yogyanese, e.g. *gembyangan sarug* to gongs, triplet *gembyangan* or alternating octave *gembyangan* on *bonang panerus* for 7̣5̣6̣7̣, *gembyangan midak* at *gong suwuk*. See main text for variant *garap* to gong 5̣. A Yogya version replaces . 32̣3 with 332̣3. Loud throughout. *Kenong japan* if available. *Kempyang* is sometimes used throughout on off-beats, in which case it should be Yogya-style instrument (notes 6 and 7).

Ktw Puspåwarnå sl m, gaya Solo

bukå 6̣ 6̣ 1 2 3 . 2 . 1 3 3 1 2 . 1 2 (6)

ompak [[. 2 . 3 . 2 . 1 . 3 . 2 . 1 . (6)]

transition to *lik* . 1 . (6)

lik . . 6 . 2̇ 3̇ 2̇ 1̇ 3̇ 2̇ 6 5 1̇ 6 5 (3)

. . 3 2   5 3 2 1   . 3 . 2   . 1 . (6)
. 2 . 3   . 2 . 1   . 3 . 2   . 1 . (6)]

Gérongan

bal   .   .   6   .   2̇   3̇   2̇   1̇
gér   . . . .   3̇ 3̇ .   1̇ 3̇ 2̇ 2̇
kembang   ken-   cur

bal   3̇   2̇   6   5   1̇   6   5   (3)
gér   1̇ .   6 1̇ 2̇ . 3̇   1̇ 2̇ 6   5 . .   6   6 1̇ 2̇   6 1̇ 6 5   3
ka-   car-   yan   a-   nggung   ci-   na-   tur

bal   .   .   3   2   5   3   2   1
gér   . . . . .   6 1̇ 2̇ 2̇ .   3̇ 1̇ 2̇ 6   3 .   3 5 3 2   1
sè-   dhet   kang   sa-   ri-   rå

bal   .   3   .   2   .   1   .   (6)
gér   . . . . .   3 . 5   2 . .   3 5 3   3 .   1 2 1   6̣
gan-   des   ing   wi-   rå-   gå

bal   .   2   .   3   .   2   .   1
gér   . . . . .   2 1 3   3 . .   6̣   2 .   3 5 3 2   1
kè-   wes   yèn   ngan-   di-   kå

bal   .   3   .   2   .   1   .   (6)
gér   . . . . .   3 . 5   2 . .   3 5 3   3 .   1 2 1   6̣
a-   nge-   nga-   nyut   ji-   wå

Title. *Puspåwarnå* = kinds of flowers.
Skema. *Ir I*, changing to *ir II* in the first *gongan*. *Ompak* is played again in *ir II*, followed by *lik*. Because the last *gongan* of the *lik* is the same as the *ompak*, the *ompak* is usually played only once on subsequent iterations. The *suwuk* comes at the end of the *lik*, still in *ir II*.
Also played in *pl 6* (with essentially unchanged *balungan*) and *pl 7* (with expected changes).
Garap. *Bonang* play *mipil lumpatan* for *balungan nibani*, except where *gembyangan* is indicated. *Pesindhèn*, *gérong* and soft-style decorating instruments take part.

Ktw Puspåwarnå sl m, gaya Yogya

Realisation in Yogya loud style.

bukå   6 1 2 3   3 2 1 2   2 1 3 2   6 6 . (6)
[5 2̇ 5 3   5 2̇ 5 1̂   5 3̇ 5 2   5 1̇ 5 (6)
5 2 5 3   5 2 5 1   5 3 5 2   6 3 5 (6)
. 6 1 2   5 3 2 1   3 2 6 5   1 6 5 (3)
6 1 3 2   6 3 2 1   3 5 3 2   3 1 2 (6)
5 2 5 3   5 2 5 1   5 3 5 2   5 1 5 (6)]

Skema. As for the Solonese version, except that *ir II* is reached during the *bukå*, and the repeat of the *ompak* is written into the notation.
Garap. Use *kenong japan* throughout if available. No *kempyang*. *Slenthem* plays *nibani* (as in Solo version) during first two *gongan* and last *gongan*, except for last *gåtrå* of second *gongan*. *Balungan* section uses 1̇ in 1 6 5 3, otherwise 1, and does not use low 6. No soft-style decorating instruments, no vocal parts. *Bonang* (patterns given for *bonang barung*: *bonang panerus* should copy style). *Bonang barung* may play *ajak-ajak* before *bukå*. *Gembyangan midak* at *gong bukå* and *gong suwuk*. First two *gongan* interpreted as being in low octave, i.e. *kempyung/gambyung* patterns: 5 1 as 6̣ 1 2 . 6̣ 1 2 1; 6 3 5 6 as low-octave *mipil* (e.g. 5̣ 3̣ 5̣ . 5̣ 3̣ 2̣ 3̣) followed by *gembyangan sarug* on 5̣ 6̣; 6 as low in 6 1 2 and 6 1 3 2. 6 5 in third *gongan* also low, followed by Yogya-style low 6 pattern (e.g. 5̣ 6̣ 1 . 5̣ 6̣ 1 6̣) and *gembyangan sarug* on 5̣ 3̣. 6 3 2 1 as *gembyangan sarug* on 6̣ 3̣ followed by *nglagu* 2 1 2 5̣ 6̣ 1 2 1. *Nguthik* pattern for 3 5 3 2. *Nglagu* pattern for 3 1, then low 6 pattern or *gembyangan* to gong.
Loud throughout!

Ktw Subåkaståwå sl 9

bukå   . 2 . 1   . 2 . 1   2 2 1 1   . 1 6̣ (5̣)
ompak [[. 1̇ . 6̣   . 1̇ . 5̣   . 1̇ . 6̣   . 1̇ . (5̣)]
transition to *lik*   . 1 . 6̣[5]   . 1 . (5̣)
lik   . 2̇ . 1̇   . 6 . 5   . 2 . 1   . 6̣ . (5̣)
. 2̇ . 1̇   . 6 . 5   . 2 . 1   . 6̣ . (5̣)[1]
. 2 . 1   . 2 . 6̣   . 2 . 1   . 6̣ . (5̣)]

Gérongan

bal   .   2̇   .   1̇   .   6   .   5
gér   . . .   2̇ 2̇   2̇ 3̇ 1̇ . .   2̇ 3̇ 2̇ 2̇ .   6 1̇ 6   5
Na-   li-   ka-   ni-   rå   ing   da-   lu

bal   .   2   .   1   .   6̣   .   5̣
gér   . .   6   1̇   6 5 2 3 2   1 . .   2 3 2 2 .   6̣ 1 6̣   5̣
wong   a-   gung   mang-   sah   se-   mè-   di

bal   .   2̇   .   1̇   .   6   .   5
gér   . . .   2̇ 2̇   2̇ 3̇ 1̇ . .   2̇ 3̇ 2̇ 2̇ .   6 1̇ 6   5
Si-   rep   kang   bå-   lå   wa-   nå   rå

bal   .   2   .   1   .   6̣   .   5̣
gér   . .   6   1̇   6 5 2 3 2   1 . .   2 3 2 2 .   6̣ 1 6̣   5̣
sa-   då-   yå   wus   sa-   mi   gu-   ling

bal   .   2   .   1   .   2   .   6̣
gér   . 6̣ 1 . .   1 1   1 2 1 . .   2 2 .   2   3 2 1 6̣
na-   dyan   A-   ri   Su-   dhar-   så-   nå

bal   .   2   .   1   .   6̣   .   5̣
gér   . . . .   2 2   2 3 1 . .   2 3 2 2 .   6̣ 1 6̣   5̣
wus   da-   ngu   dèn   i-   rå   gu-   ling

Title. *Subåkaståwå* = bestowing honour.
Skema. *Ir I*, changing to *ir II* in the first *gongan*. *Ompak* is played again in *ir II*, followed by *lik*. The *ompak* is often played only once on subsequent iterations. The *suwuk* comes at the end of the *lik*, still in *ir II*.
Garap. Normally has *bukå gendèr*. If *bonang* plays *bukå*, last *gåtrå* has usual low 5 *bukå* pattern. *Bonang* play *mipil lumpatan* for *balungan nibani*, except where *gembyangan* is indicated. Start of last *gongan* of *lik* can also have half-*gåtrå* of *gembyangan* then half-*gåtrå* of *mipil*. *Pancer* 1̇ from start of *lik*. *Pesindhèn*, *gérong* and soft-style decorating instruments take part.
Also performed in *pl 5/6*: no changes to *balungan*.

Gérongan:

gér . . . . 2̇ 2̇ 2̇ 3̇ 1 . . 6 1̇ 2̇ . 1̇ 1̇ 2̇ 1̇ 6 5
gér . . 4 5 6 5 4 6 5 4 2 1 . . 6̣ 1 2 . 1 1 2 1 6̣ 5̣
gér . . . . 2̇ 2̇ 2̇ 3̇ 1 . . 6 1̇ 2̇ . 1̇ 1̇ 2̇ 1̇ 6 5
gér . . 4 5 6 5 4 6 5 4 2 1 . . 6̣ 1 2 . 1 1 2 1 6̣ 5̣
gér . 6̣ 1 . . 1 1 1 2 1 . . 2 2 . 3 1 2 1 6̣
gér . . . . 2 2 2 3 1 . . 6̣ 1 2 . 1 1 2 1 6̣ 5̣

Ktw Barikan pl 5

bukå 2 3 5 3 2 1 5 5 1̇ 6 5 3 2 (1)
ompak [[. 1 2 3 5 3 2 1 5 5 1̇ 6 5 3 2 (1)]
lik 5 5 . . 6 4 6 5 7 6 2 4 2 1 6̣ (5)
1 1 . . 2 3 2 1 5 5 1̇ 6 5 3 2 (1)]

Title. *Barikan* = together.

Skema and garap. *Ir I*, changing to *ir II* in the first *gongan*. *Ompak* twice, then *lik*. *Bedhayan* chorus throughout. Same words each time in *ompak*. *Suwuk* at end of *lik*. Soft-style decorating instruments take part.

Chorus

ompak . 1 2 3 5 3 2 1
. . . . . . 2 . 3 . . 5 3 . 2 . 3 1
Ra- ha- yu- a
5 5 1̇ 6 5 3 2 1
. . . 0 5 5 5 1̇ 6 . . 5 3 . 2 . 3 1
sla- met sla- met sa- lå- mi- nyå
lik 5 5 . . 6 4 6 5
. . . . 5 5 5 6 4 . 5 6 1̇ . 1̇ 2̇ 1̇ 6 5
se- sen- ti si- na- wang ki- dung
7 6 2 4 2 1 6̣ 5̣
. . . . 7 6 2 5 4 5 2 1 1 2 1 6̣ 5̣
Bi- na- rung pra- dång- gå ngra- ngin
1 1 . . 2 3 2 1
6̣ 1 . . 1 1 1 2 1 0 2 3 . 2 . 3 1
gen- dhing ke- ta- wang Ba- ri- kan
5 5 1̇ 6 5 3 2 1
. . . 0 5 5 5 1̇ 6 . . 5 3 . 2 . 3 1
Pa- nu- lak ing pån- cå bå- yå

Ldr Wilujeng sl m

bukå 1 3 2 . 6̣ 1 2 3 1 1 3 2 . 1 2 (6)
ompak [[2 1 2 3 2 1 2 6[3] 3 3 . . 6 5 3 2[5]
5 6 5 3 2 1 2 6̣ 2 1 2 3 2 1 2 (6)]
transition to *lik* 2 1 2 (6)
lik . . 6 . 1̇ 5 1̇ 6 3 5 6 1̇ 6 5 3 2[6]
6 6 . . 1̇ 5 1̇ 6[1] 1̇ 1̇ 3 2 . 1 2 (6)]

Gérongan

bal . . 6 . 1̇ 5 1̇ 6
gér . . . . 6 6 6 1̇ 5 . 6 1̇ 2̇ . 3̇ 1̇ 2̇ 1̇ 6
Pa- rab- é Sang Små- rå- ba- ngun
bal 3 5 6 1̇ 6 5 3 2
gér . . . . 3̇ 3̇ 3̇ 2̇ 1̇ . 2̇ 1̇ 6 5 . 6 3 5 3 2
se- pat dom- bå ka- li O- yå
bal 6 6 . . 1̇ 5 1̇ 6
gér . . . . 6 6 6 1̇ 5 . 6 1̇ 2̇ . 3̇ 1̇ 2̇ 1̇ 6
å- jå do- lan lan wong pri- yå
bal 1̇ 1̇ 3 2 . 1 2 6̣
gér . . 1̇ 2̇ 1̇ 6 3 5 3 2 . . 3 5 3 3 . 1 2 1 6̣
ge- ra- mèh no- ra pra- så- jå

Title. *Wilujeng* = blessing, well. The *ngoko* equivalent, *Slamet*, is sometimes used instead.

Skema. Starts in *ir I*, transition to *ir II* usually in first time through *ompak*. Then *ompak* is repeated, with transition to *lik*. On subsequent iterations, *ompak* twice before *lik*. *Suwuk* at end of *lik*.

Garap. *Pesindhèn*, *gérong* and soft-style decorating instruments take part. If *bonang* gives *bukå*, standard low 6 decoration for last *gåtrå* of *bukå*. In *ir II*, 3 3 . . 6 5 3 2 may be treated as *puthut gelut* by *bonang* as well as other decorating instruments. *Pinjalan* is occasionally used (even in *sléndro* version). Also played in *pl 7* and in a rare *pl 5* version.

Bukå and *balungan* for *pl 7*:

bukå 7̣ 3 2 6̣ 7̣ 2 3 7̣ 7̣ 3 2 . 7̣ 5̣ (6)
ompak 2 7̣ 2 3 2 7̣ 5̣ 6̣ 3 3 . . 6 5 3 2
5 6 5 3 2 7̣ 5̣ 6̣ 2 7̣ 2 3 2 7̣ 5̣ (6)
lik . . 6 . 7 5 7 6 3 5 6 7 6 5 3 2
6 6 . . 7 5 7 6 7 7 3 2 . 7̣ 5̣ (6)

Gérongan

. . . . 6 6 6 7 5 . 6 7 2̇ . 2̇ 3̇ 2̇ 7 6
. . . . 3̇ 3̇ 3̇ 2̇ 7 . 2̇ 3̇ 6 7 5 . 5 6 5 3 2
. . . . 6 6 6 7 5 . 6 7 2̇ . 2̇ 3̇ 2̇ 7 6
. . 5 6 7 6 5 7 6 5 3 2 . . 7̣ 2 3 . 2 2 3 2 7̣ 6̣

Ldr Semar mantu sl m, gaya Yogya

Ladrang in Yogya loud style, using *ir I* and *ir II*

bukå bonang 5 3 6 5 2 1 3 2 6 5 1 6 2 1 2 (6)

ir I

A (× II) [2 1 2 3 2 1 2 6 2 1 2 3 2 1 2 6
2 1 2 3 2 1 2 6[5] 5 5 6 5 6 1̇ 6 (5)
B (× II) 1̇ 6 1̇ 2 1̇ 6 3 5 1̇ 6 1̇ 2 1̇ 6 3 5
1̇ 6 1̇ 2 1̇ 6 3 5[2] 2 3 1 2 3 5 3 (2)
C (× II) 5 3 6 5 2 1 3 2 5 3 6 5 2 1 3 2
5 3 6 5 2 1 3 2[6] 6 5 1̇ 6 2 1 2 (6)]

ir II, ngracik (demung mlampah)

A (× II) [212.2153 212.2156 212.2153 212.2156
212.2153 212.2156[5] 5 5 6 5 6 1̇ 6 (5)

B (× II) 1̇61̇.1̇632 1̇61̇.1̇635 1̇61̇.1̇632 1̇61̇.1̇635
1̇61̇.1̇632 1̇61̇.1̇635[2] 2 3 1 2 3 5 3 (2)

C (× II) 55.5365 22.2132 55.5365 22.2132
55.5365 22.2132[6] 6 5 1̇ 6 2 1 2 (6)]

Title. *Semar mantu* = Semar holds a wedding.

Skema. AABBCC in *ir I*, repeated. Typically in second iteration, transition to *ir II*, then *saron* switch to *ir I* patterns at next gong. Cycle AABBCC in *ir II*. Return to *ir I*, with *saron* switching to *ir I* patterns when *ir II* patterns become uncomfortable. Cycle AABBCC in *ir I*.

Garap. In *ir II*, all *pin* are replaced by *ngencot*, i.e.

212.2153 212.2156 → 2122222153 2122222156
1̇61̇.1̇632 1̇61̇.1̇635 → 1̇61̇1̇1̇1̇632 1̇61̇1̇1̇1̇635
.55.5365 .22.2132 → .5555365 .2222132

Slenthem plays *ir I* version of *balungan*, and *peking* may base its *garap* on *ir I* version of *balungan*.

Bonang. In *bukå*, third *gåtrå* is treated as 6̣ 5̣ 1 6̣, followed by *gembyangan midak* to gong. In A, 2 6 as Yogya-style low 6 pattern; 5 5 6 5 with *gembyang* 5 for whole *gåtrå* in *ir I*, but *gembyang* 5 followed by *mipil* on 6̣ 5̣ in *ir II*; last *gåtrå* played in low octave, with *gembyangan* (standard or *sarug*) in second half. In B, first six *gåtrå* are in low octave, with 1̇ 2 played as *kempyung*; seventh *gåtrå* as *gembyangan*; last half-*gåtrå* of *gongan* uses *gembyangan* (either standard or *sarug*). In C, seventh *gåtrå* is played in the lower octave, or might be *gembyangan* throughout. Last half-*gåtrå* of *gongan* uses *gembyangan*. In *ir I*, *gembyangan cegat* may replace *mipil* if the tempo is fast. *Gembyangan midak* for last half-*gåtrå* to *gong suwuk*.

Kenong japan throughout if available. Otherwise, expected *kenong* notes except *kenong plèsèdan* before seventh *gåtrå* in each *gongan*. No *kempyang*.

Sirep from first *kenong* to third *kenong* of final *gongan*.

Ldr Gléyong pl 6

bukå 2 2 3 5 6 7 6 5 4 2 1 2 (6)
ompak [[2 3 2 1 6̣ 5̣ 3̣ 5̣ 2 3 2 1 6̣ 5̣ 3̣ 5̣[2]
2 2 . . 2 3 5 6 7 6 5 4 2 1 2 (6)]
transition to *lik* 2 1 2 (6)
lik . 6 6 6 5 3 2 3 . 3 5 6 7 6 5 3
6 5 3 2 . 3 5 6 7 6 5 4 2 1 2 (6)]

Gérongan, ir II: Parabé Sang

bal . 6 6 6 5 3 2 3
gér . . . . 6 6 . 6 6 . . 2 3 . 5 5 6 5 3
bal . 3 5 6 7 6 5 3
gér . . . . 5 5 3 6 6 . . 2 3 . 5 5 6 5 3
bal 6 5 3 2 . 3 5 6
gér . . . . 5 5 6 3 2 . . 1̇ 2̇ . 3̇ 1̇ 2̇ 1̇ 6
bal 7 6 5 4 2 1 2 6̣
gér . . 1̇ 2̇ 6 . 5 4 5 4 . 5 6 2 3 1 . 1 2 1 (6̣)
bal 2 3 2 1 6̣ 5̣ 3̣ 5̣
gér . . . . 3̇ 3̇ 2̇ 1̇ 6 1̇ 2̇ 3̇ 1̇ 6 5 . 3 3 5 6 5
bal 2 3 2 1 6̣ 5̣ 3̣ 5̣
gér . . . . 3̇ 3̇ 2̇ 1̇ 6 1̇ 2̇ 3̇ 1̇ 6 5 . 3 3 5 6 5
bal 2 2 . . 2 3 5 6
gér . 3 2 . . 2 2 2 3 1 . 2 1̇ 2̇ . 3̇ 1̇ 2̇ 1̇ 6
bal 7 6 5 4 2 1 2 6̣
gér . . 1̇ 2̇ 6 . 5 4 5 4 . 5 6 2 3 1 . 1 2 1 (6̣)

Second *gongan* uses second stanza: *Garwå Sang Sindurå prabu / wicårå måwå karånå / åjå dolan lan wanitå / tan nyåtå asring katarkå*.

Title. *Gléyong* = swinging.

Skema and **garap**. *Ompak* may be cycled in *ir I* or *ir II*: transition to *ir II* in usual place, *kd II* only. *Lik* is entered in *ir II* after usual signal, typically on second time around *ompak*. *Gérongan* lasts for two *gongan*: second *gongan* may be regarded as a repeat of the *ompak*, as shown, or alternatively be regarded as a modified version, with *balungan* changed (6 5 3 5, not the octave below) and corresponding changes to *garap*. *Suwuk* in *ir II* at end of *gérongan*, or in *ir I* after return from *lik*. *Pinjalan* is possible, starting from beginning of *lik*: in this case, no return to *ir I*.

Bonang. Low 5 pattern possible for 6̣ 5̣ 3̣ 5̣; *gembyangan* possible for . 3 5 6, with lead-in from 2.

Ldr Tirtåkencånå pl 5/6

bukå 1̇ 5 6 1̇ 3̇ 2̇ 1̇ 6 5 4 2 4 5 6 4 (5)
ompak [[2 1 2 6̣ 2 1 6̣ 5̣ 2 1 2 6̣ 2 1 6̣ 5̣
1 5̣ 6̣ 1 3 2 1 6̣ 5̣ 4̣ 2̣ 4̣ 5̣ 6̣ 4̣ (5̣)]
lik (× II) 5 6 1̇ 2̇ 5 6 1̇ 2̇ 5 6 1̇ 2̇ 1̇ 6 5 5 6 1̇ 2̇ 5 6 1̇ 2̇ 5 6 1̇ 2̇ 1̇ 6 5
1̇ 5 6 1̇ 3̇ 2̇ 1̇ 6 5 4 2 4 5 6 4 (5)]

Gérongan: *Parabé Sang*

bal 5 6 1̇ 2̇ 5 6 1̇ 2̇ 5 6 1̇ 2̇ 1̇ 6 5
gér . . 6 1̇ . 2̇ 5 6 1̇ . 2̇ 5 6 1̇ 2̇ 3̇ 1̇ 2̇ 1̇ 6 5
bal 5 6 1̇ 2̇ 5 6 1̇ 2̇ 5 6 1̇ 2̇ 1̇ 6 5
gér . . 6 1̇ . 2̇ 5 6 1̇ . 2̇ 5 6 1̇ 2̇ 3̇ 1̇ 2̇ 1̇ 6 5
bal 1̇ 5 6 1̇ 3̇ 2̇ 1̇ 6
gér . . . . 1̇ 1̇ . 1̇ 2̇ . 3̇ 3̇ 2̇ 1̇ 2̇ . 3̇ 1̇ 2̇ 1̇ 6
bal 5 4 2 4 5 6 4 5
gér . . 5 6 4 . 2 4 5 6 4 . 5 6 1̇ 1̇ 2̇ 1̇ 6 5
gér second time, ends 2 4 5 6 4 . 5 6 2 3 1 . 1 2 1 6̣ 5̣

Title. *Tirtåkencånå* = golden holy water.

Skema and **garap**. *Ompak* may be cycled in *ir I*, but usually goes into *ir II*. *Bonang* plays first and third *gåtrå* as *mipil* 2 1 2 . 6̣ 2 6̣ . , but standard low 6 pattern for whole *gåtrå* in *ir II*. Optional low 5 pattern for second and fourth *gåtrå*. Transition to *lik* in *ir II* is signalled by *angkatan ciblon*, at which point *bonang* also signals via *gembyangan* 5. In *lik* (usually played twice), *bonang* *imbal*: mainly 6 and 2 on *bonang barung*. First *kenongan*: three blocks of *imbal*, then full *sekaran* to 1, ditto for second *kenongan*. In third and fourth *kenongan*, one block of *imbal* and full *sekaran* to each *gåtrå*. *Gåtrå* 6: *imbal* 1 and 3 on *bonang barung*. *Gåtrå* 7: *imbal* 1 and 4 (2 and 5 on *bonang panerus*) then *sekaran* consisting of repeated 4 only (off-beat 5 on *bonang panerus*). Second time around *lik*, *bonang* plays last *gåtrå* as (for example) *gembyang* 5 then short low 5 pattern using note 4 (e.g. 646 . 5545). *Suwuk* usually in *ompak*. *Pesindhèn*, *gérong* and soft-style decorating instruments take part.

Ldr Pangkur sl 9

bukå . 2 . 1   . 2 . 1   2 2 1 1   . 6 . (5)

ir I/II [2 1 2 6   2 1 6 5   6 5 2 1   3 2 1 6
2 3 2 1   5 3 2 1   3 2 1 6   2 1 6 (5)]

ir III/IV

ompak [[. 2 . 1   . 2 . 6   . 2 . 1   . 6 . 5[6]
6 6 . .   5 5 6 1   2 1 5 2   . 1 . 6
. . 3 2   5 3 2 1   2 1 3 2   5 3 2 1[5]
5 6 2 1   5 2 1 6   . 2 . 1   . 6 . (5)]

transition to *lik*   . 2 . 1   2 3 5 6 1 . 2 (1)

lik . . 1 .   3 2 1 2   . . 2 3   5 6 3 5[1]
1 1 . .*   3 2 1 6   2 1 5 3   6 5 3 2
. . 2 3*   5 6 3 5   1 6 5 6   5 3 2 1[5]
5 6 2 1   5 2 1 6   . 2 . 1   . 6 . (5)]

Gérongan, ir I

bal 2 1 2 6 2 1 6 5
gér . 2 2 2 2 1 2 6 3 3 3 3 . 6 1 5
Pang- kur wi- rå- må låm- bå gå- lå- gå- lå cak- rik- é
bal 6 5 2 1 3 2 1 6
gér . 5 6 5 . 5 6 2 1 . 5 5 2 2 1 1 6
sléndro pa- thet- é så- ngå mu- gå da- di sa- rå- nå
bal 2 3 2 1 5 3 2 1
gér . . 2 3 5 . 3 6 5 . 5 3 5 2 3 1
ma- nung- gal la- hir trus ing ba- tin
bal 3 2 1 6 2 1 6 (5)
gér . 1 1 1 . 3 2 1 6 . 2 3 1 . 6 . 5
trus ma- ju tan- på mun- dur pa- tuh lan tang- guh

Gérongan, ir II: *Parabé Sang*

bal 2 1 2 6 2 1 6 5
gér . . . . 2 2 2 1 6 . 1 2 2 3 1 . 2 6 1 6 5
bal 6 5 2 1 3 2 1 6
gér . . . . 5 5 . 6 1 . 2 6 1 5 2 . 2 3 2 1 6
bal 2 3 2 1 5 3 2 1
gér . . . . 5 5 . 6 1 . 2 1 6 5 6 1 6 5 2 3 2 1
bal 3 2 1 6 2 1 6 (5)
gér . . 3 5 2 . 2 3 2 1 6 . 1 2 2 3 1 . 2 6 1 6 5

Gérongan, ir III, after first *kenong*: *Nalikanirå*

bal 6 6 . . 5 5 6 1
gér . . . . 6 6 6 1 6 6 . . 5 5 . 6 6 5 1 1
bal 2 1 5 2 . 1 . 6
gér . . . . 2 1 6 5 2 . . 3 5 . 2 3 2 1 6
bal . . 3 2 5 3 2 1
gér . . . . 5 5 . 6 1 . 2 1 6 5 6 1 6 5 2 3 2 1
bal 2 1 3 2 5 3 2 1
gér . . . . 2 2 2 3 2 2 . . 3 5 . 2 3 2 1
bal 5 6 2 1 5 2 1 6
gér . . 5 6 1 2 2 . 3 1 . 2 6 1 5 2 . 2 3 2 1 6
bal . 2 . 1 . 6 . (5)
gér . . . . 2 2 2 3 1 . . 2 3 2 2 . 6 1 6 5

Title. *Pangkur* = ?mattock, but the piece takes its name from the *mâcâpat* melody on which it is based.

Skema. Wide range of possibilities. May be cycled in *ir I*, or in *ir I kébar*. After transition to *ir II* in usual place, may be cycled in *ir II*. May go to *ir III* with *ciblon* drumming, either from *ir II* or straight from *ir I kébar*. In *ir III*, *ompak* may be cycled by itself, or followed by *lik*. *Suwuk* possible from *ir I*, *ir II*, *ir III* (from *ompak*): in *ir III*, return from *ciblon* to *kd II* after 5 6 2 1. Often followed by other pieces to make suites; e.g. *srepegan* (including *Srepeg Mataram* in Yogya style), *palaran*, *ketawang* or *langgam*.

Garap. See Part 3 for notes on named *céngkok* and *bonang* realisation in *ir III*. Also performed in *sl m* and *pl 7*.

Sléndro manyurå version:

bukå 3 . 2   . 3 . 2   3 3 2 2   . 1 2 (6)
ir I/II 3 2 3 1   3 2 1 6   1 6 3 2   5 3 2 1
3 5 3 2   6 5 3 2   5 3 2 1   3 2 1 (6)

ir III/IV, and *gérongan* for *ir III*:

ompak
bal . 3 . 2 . 3 . 1
bal . 3 . 2 . 1 . 6
bal 1 1 . . 6 6 1 2
gér . . . . 1 1 1 2 1 6 . 6 6 . 1 1 6 2 2
bal 3 2 6 3 . 2 . 1
gér . . . . 2 1 2 6 3 . . 5 6 . 3 5 3 2 1
bal . . 5 3 6 5 3 2
gér . . . . 6 6 . 1 2 1 2 3 2 1 6 1 2 1 6 3 5 3 2
bal 3 2 5 3 6 5 3 2
gér . . . . 3 3 3 5 3 . . 5 6 3 5 3 2
bal 6 1 3 2 6 3 2 1
gér . . 6 1 2 3 3 . 5 2 . 3 1 2 6 3 . 3 5 3 2 1
bal . 3 . 2 . 1 . (6)
gér . . . . 3 3 3 5 2 . . 3 5 3 . 1 2 1 6

transition to *lik*

bal . 3 . 2 . 6 i̇ (2̇)
gér . . . . 6 6 . 6 i̇ 2̇ . 2̇ 2̇ . i̇ i̇ 2̇ 3̇ 2̇
lik, gér . . 2̇ . 5̇ 3̇ 2̇ 3̇
gér . . 3 5 6 i̇ 5 6̂
bal 2̇ 2̇ . . 5̇ 3̇ 2̇ i̇
gér . . 2̇ 2̇ . . 2̇ 3̇ i̇ . 2̇ 3̇ 3̇ . i̇ 3̇ 2̇ i̇
bal 3 2 6 5 i̇ 6 5 3̂
gér . . 6 i̇ 2̇ . 3̇ i̇ 2̇ 6 5 . . 6 6 i̇ 2̇ 6 i̇ 6 5 3
bal . . 3 5 6 i̇ 5 6
gér . . . . 3 3 . 3 5 6 . i̇ 2̇ . 3̇ i̇ 2̇ i̇ 6
bal 3 5 6 i̇ 6 5 3 2̂
gér . . . . 3̇ 3̇ 3̇ 2̇ i̇ . 2̇ i̇ 6 6 i̇ 2̇ i̇ 6 3 5 3 2
bal 6 i̇ 3̇ 2̇ 6 3 2 1
gér . . 6 i̇ 2̇ 3̇ 3̇ . 5̇ 2̇ . 3̇ i̇ 2̇ 6 3 . 3 5 3 2 1
bal . 3 . 2 . 1 . (6)
gér . . . . 3 3 3 5 2 . . 3 5 3 . 1 2 1 6̣

Gérongan for *sl m*:
Ir I: transposed up one note from *sl 9* version, with '*patheté sångå*' replaced by '*pathet manyurå*'. *Ir II*: up one note from *sl 9* version. *Ir III*: see above.
Second stanza of *Nalikanirå* for *lik*: *Kukusing dupå kumelun / ngeningken tyas Sang Apekik / kawengku sagung jajahan / nanging sanget angikibi / Sang Resi Kanékåputrå / kang anjog saking wiyati*
Pl 7 version of the *balungan* is the same apart from replacement of 1 by 7̣, i̇ by 7, and 5̇ 3̇ 2̇ 3̇ in *lik* by 4̇ 3̇ 2̇ 3̇.
Examples of *alok* and *senggakan* in *ir I kébar* (not during *gérongan*), for *sl m*:

bal 3 2 3 1 3 2 1 6̂
vokal 3 5 6 i̇ 2̇ 3̇
sing sa- yuk sing ru- kun-

bal i̇ 6 3 2 5 3 2 i̇̂
vokal 2̇ 3̇ 5̇ 2̇
é

bal 3 5 3 2 6 5 3 2̂
vokal 3̇ 5̇ 2̇
o- é ya

bal 5 3 2 1 3 2 1 (6)
vokal (two voices in alternation, not precisely pitched)
o o o o o o o o o o o o o o o o

bal 3 2 3 1 3 2 1 6̂
vokal *yo*

bal i̇ 6 3 2 5 3 2 i̇̂
vokal 3̇ 5̇ 2̇
o- é

bal 3 5 3 2 6 5 3 2̂
vokal 3̇ 5̇ 2̇
o- é

bal 5 3 2 1 3 2 1 (6)
vokal, not precisely pitched
. lå lå lå lå lå a- é a- é yo

Ldr Dirådåmetå sl 6

bukå . 6̣ 1 . 2 1 6̣ 5̣ i̇ i̇ 2̇ i̇ 3̇ 2̇ i̇ (6)
A . 6 6 . 6 6 5 6̂ i̇ 6 5 3 2 2 3 2̂
6̣ 3̣ 6̣ 5̣ 6̣ 3̣ 6̣ 2̣ 6̣ 3̣ 6̣ 5̣ 6̣ 3̣ 6̣ (2̣)
B [6̣ 3̣ 6̣ 5̣ 6̣ 3̣ 6̣ 2̣ 6̣ 3̣ 6̣ 5̣ 6̣ 3̣ 6̣ 2̣
6̣ 3̣ 6̣ 5̣ 2 3 5 . 2 3 5 3 2 1 2 (6̣)^3
C 3 3 6 5 2 1 2 6̣^{3} 3 3 6 5 2 1 2 6̣
3 3 6 5 2 1 2 6̣^{3} 3 3 6 5^6 3 2 1 (2)
D . . 2 3 5 6 i̇ . 6 i̇ 5 6^2 1 2 . 3^6 5 6 i̇ . 6 i̇ 5 6^2
1 2 . 3^1 5 6 i̇ . 6 5 6 i̇^{6} 6 5 6 1 2^6 . 3 5 (6)
E . 5 i̇ 6 . 5 i̇ 6 . 5 i̇ 6 5 i̇ 6 i̇ 6 5 3^6 2 2 3 2̂
6̣ 3̣ 6̣ 5̣ 6̣ 3̣ 6̣ 2̣ 6̣ 3̣ 6̣ 5̣ 6̣ 3̣ 6̣ (2̣)]
F [6̣ 3̣ 6̣ 5̣ 6̣ 3̣ 6̣ 2̣ 6̣ 3̣ 6̣ 5̣ 6̣ 3̣ 6̣ 2̣
6̣ 3̣ 6̣ 5̣ 6̣ 3̣ 6̣ 2̣ ↘ 6̣ 3̣ 6̣ 5̣ 6̣ 3̣ 6̣ (2̣)]
suwuk gropak . 3̣ . 5̣ . 3̣ . (2̣)

Title. *Dirådåmetå* = raging elephant.
Skema for *wayang*-style performance. Usually has *bukå rebab* unless played as *inggah* to *gd Kocak*. A: *ir I*, going to *ir II*. BCDE cycled in *ir II*. Speed-up in *gongan* B or E causes transition to F. *Suwuk gropak*. Other *skema* are used too.
Garap. *Pesindhèn*, *gérong* and soft-style decorating instruments take part. Vocal parts (not shown) include *miring* notes. If *bukå* is played on *bonang*, last two *gåtrå* are played an octave down, except that gong note can be played as *gembyang*. Low 6 patterns for 2 1 2 6̣ in *gongan* B and C, possibly with variant *garap* at transition to *gembyangan* 3, as for *puthut gelut*. In *ir I* before *suwuk gropak*, *bonang* may play 6̣ 3̣ 6̣ 5̣ 6̣ 3̣ 6̣ 2̣ with *gembyungan* for 6̣ 3̣, and *tunggal* 5̣.
Possible *pekingan* for D:
3322332222332233 5566i̇i̇i̇i̇66i̇i̇5566
1122112222332233 5566i̇i̇i̇i̇66i̇i̇5566
1122112222332233 5566i̇i̇i̇i̇665566i̇i̇
5566556611221122 2233223355665566
For E: 556655i̇i̇666655i̇i̇ 666655i̇i̇6655i̇i̇66 i̇i̇66i̇i̇66 etc.

Ayak-ayakan Pamungkas sl m

(2) . 3̂ . (2) . 3̂ . (2) . 5̂ . (3) . 2̂ . (1)
2 3̂ 2 (1̂) 2 3̂ 2 (1̂) 3 5̂ 3 (2̂)

bal 3̇ 1 2̇ . 6̣ 1 2̇ (3)
gér . . 3 1 . 2 2 . . . . . 6̣ 1 . 2 2 1 3 3
Dhuh Al- lah mu- gi- mu- gi
bal 6 5 6 i̇̂ 6 5 3 (2)
gér . . . . 6 6 . i̇ i̇ . 2̇ i̇ 6 3 . 2 5 3 2
ka- pa- re-ngå pa- ring Rah- mat

bal 3 1 2 .̂ 6̣ 1 2 (3)
gér . . 3 1 . 2 2 . . . . 6̣ 1 . 2 2 1 3 3
dhuh Al- lah les- ta- ri- yå
bal 6 5 6 1̂̇ 6 5 3 (2)
gér . . . . 6 6 . 1̇ 1̇ . 2̇ 1̇ 6 3 . 2 5 3 2
In- do- né- si- a mer- di- kå
bal 6 6 . 1̂̇ 2̇ 3̇ 2̇ (1̇)
gér . . . . 6 6 . 6 1̇ . 2̇ 3̇ 3̇ . 1̇ 3̇ 2̇ 2̇
wa- så- nå wos- ing ma- ngi- dung
bal 3̇ 2̇ 6 3̂ 6 5 3 (2)
gér 1̇ . 6 1̇ 2̇ . 3̇ 1̇ 2̇1̇63 . . 1̇ 2̇ 6 . 5 3 5 3 2
tar- len a- mung a- mu- mu- ji
bal 5 6 5 3̂ 2 3 2 (1)
gér . . . . 3 3 3 5 3 . . 5 6 . 3 5321
mu- gi bång-så In- do- né- sia
bal 6̣ 1 2 3̂ 5 6 1̇ (6)
gér . . . . 6̣ 1 2 2 3 3 5 6 1̇ 2̇ . 3̇ 1̇ 2̇ 1̇ 6
se- puh a- nèm ja- ler ès- tri
bal 3 5 6 .̂ 2̇ 3̇ 2̇ (1̇)
gér . . . . 6 6 . 6 1̇ . 2̇ 3̇ 3̇ . 1̇ 3̇ 2̇ 2̇
mu- gi kar-så a- ma- nung- gal
bal 3̇ 2̇ 6 3̂ 6 5 3 (2)
gér 1̇ . 6 1̇ 2̇ . 3̇ 1̇ 2̇1̇63 . . 1̇ 2̇ 6 . 5 3 5 3 2
gu- mo- long ge- leng- ing kap- ti
suwuk . 3 . (2) . 3 . (2) . 5 . (3) . 2 . (1)
2 3 2 (1) 2 3 2 (1) 3 5 3 (2)
1 1 2 (1) 3 2 1 (6̣)

Title. *Pamungkas* = the last thing.
Skema. Played straight through without repeats: for *iråmå* changes, also see under ***Ayak-ayakan*** in Part 2, and Fig. 2.25. Very common as a closing piece played by itself or attached to the end of a piece with gong 2.
Garap. *Bonang* and *balungan* instruments other than *slenthem* drop out at gong 2 before vocal section, re-entering at gong 2 before *suwuk*. Soft-style decorating instruments continue. *Gong ageng* shown may be replaced by *gong suwukan*.
Bonang: *Nduduk gembyang* until first gong 1, then *mipil* in *ir I* for next two *gåtrå* and in *ir II* for last *gåtrå* before gong 2. At *suwuk*, same *garap*, continuing in *ir II* for final two *gåtrå*. 1121 as *gembyangan* then *mipil*. 3216̣ as two separate *lumpatan* patterns, e.g. 313.2212215̣.6̣1.6̣
Also played in *pl 7*.

Langgam Ngimpi sl 9

By Ki Nartosabdho.
For *balungan* and *sindhènan*, see p. 69.
Text: *Sripat sripit lèmbèhané mrak kesimpir / gandhes luwes wiragané anglamlami / sèdhet singset besus angadi busånå / dhasar ayu maksih kenyå tan kuciwå / tak caketi adhuh mèsem sepet madu / ora sråntå tak gandheng malah gumuyu / katon bungah kenyå kang pindhå hapsari / kuciwåné kabèh mau amung ngimpi.*
Title. *Ngimpi* = dreaming.
Skema. *Bukå celuk* ends, and instruments enter, at end of first *gåtrå* of *lagu*, in *ir II*. *Lagu* and *ompak* together are cycled in *ir II*. At end of first *gåtrå* of *ompak*, optional transition to *ir II rangkep*. *Suwuk* at end of *lagu* in either *iråmå*, but usually in *ir II rangkep*.
Garap. Generally as described under **Langgam** in Part 2. Possible *andhegan* in first *gåtrå* of last *gongan* of *lagu*: 1̇* 2̇ 6 1̇
Senggakan to *kenong* 5 at mid-point of *gongan* in *lagu*:

1 2 3 1 6 5
la- o- la- é lon-tong
or *i- ki wis jam pi- rå*

As often with *langgam* and *lagu dolanan*, this piece is transposed to other *laras*/*pathet* combinations.

Iringan tari Båndåyudå pl 7

A *wirèng* suite using *lnc Singanebah* – *ldr Bimåkurdå* – *lnc Singanebah*.

bukå 5̣ 3̣ 2̣ . 5̣ 3̣ 2̣ . 5 . (3)
A [. 5 . 3 . 5 . 3 . 5 . 3→§ . 6 . (7)
B . 6 . 7 . 6 . 7 . 6 . 7 . 3 . (2)
C . 3 . 2 . 3 . 2 . 3 . 2 . 5 . (3)]
transition to *ladrang* § . 5̣ 6̣ (7̣)
. 7̣ 6̣ 7̣ 2 3 2 7̣ . 7̣ 6̣ 7̣ 2 3 2 7̣
6̣ 7̣ 3 2 . 7̣ 5̣ 6̣ . 5̣ 3 . 2̣ 3 6̣ (5̣)
A . . . 5̣ . 2̣ 3 5̣ . . . 5̣ . 2̣ 3 5̣
. . . 5̣ . 2̣ 3 5̣ . 3 5̣ . 6̣ 7̣ 6̣ (5̣)
B . 7 7 . 7 6 5 6 5 6 7 . 7 6 5 6
5 6 7 . 7 6 5 6 . 5 3 . 2 3 6 (5)
C . 2 2 . 2 3 2 7̣ 6̣ 7̣ 2 . 2 3 2 7̣
6̣ 7̣ 3 2 . 7̣ 5̣ 6̣ . 5̣ 3 . 2̣ 3 6̣ (5̣)
transition to *lancaran*, after A
. 6 . 5̂ . 6̆ . 5̂ . 6̆ . 5̂ . 6̆ . (7̂)

Title. *Båndåyudå* = hand-to-hand fighting. *Bimå kurdå* = angry Bima.
Skema. *Lancaran*, *ir lancar*. Transition to *ladrang* signalled by speed-up then slow-down to *ir I*. In *ladrang*, *gongan* are cycled AABBCC, *ir I* throughout. Return to *lancaran* in *ir lancar* and *suwuk*.
Garap. *Kd II* for *lancaran*, special *ciblon* drumming for *ladrang*. In *lancaran*, *kenong* in pairs, *gembyangan cegat* on *bonang*. Various *kenong plèsèdan* on gong of *ladrang*: A, *plèsèdan* 7 on repeat; B, *plèsèdan* 7 first time, 2 on repeat; C, *plèsèdan* 2 first time.
Bonang: . 5̣6̣7̣ *mbalung*; . 7̣5̣6̣ as standard low 6 pattern; . . . 5̣ as *nduduk tunggal*; . 3 5̣ . with *pin mundur* pattern.

Gd Gambirsawit kt 2 kp mg 4 sl 9

bukå 5̣ 5̣ 6̣ 1 2
. 2 . 2 1 1 2 1 3 2 1 2 . 1 6̣ (5̣)

```
mérong A  . 3̣ 5̣ 2̣    . 3̣ 5̣ 6̣ → †
   [ [  . . . 5̣    2̣ 3̣ 5̣ 6̣ †   2 2 . .    2 3 2 1̂⁵
        . . 3 2    . 1 2 6̣     2 2 . .    2 3 2 1̂⁵ → §
        . . 3 2    . 1̇ 6 5     . . 5 6    1̇ 6 5 3̂²
        2 2 . 3    5 3 2 1     3 5 3 2    . 1 6̣ (5) ]
lik  B  6 6 . .    6 6 . .     2̇ 2̇ . .    2̇ 3̇ 2̇ 1̇
        . . 3̇ 2̇    . 1̇ 2̇ 6     2̇ 2̇ . .    2̇ 3̇ 2̇ 1̂̇
        . . 3̇ 2̇    . 1̇ 6 5     . . 5 6    1̇ 6 5 3̂²
        2 2 . 3    5 3 2 1     3 5 3 2    . 1 6̣ (5) ]
     §  . 2 . 1    . 6̣ . 5̣     . 6̣ . 5̣    . 3 . 2̂⁵
        . 3 . 5    . 2 . 1     . 2 . 1    . 6̣ . (5)
inggah [ . 6̣ . 5̣   . 1 . 6̣     . 1 . 6̣    . 2 . 1̂⁵
        . 2 . 1    . 2 . 6̣     . 1 . 6̣    . 2 . 1̂⁵
        . 2 . 1    . 6 . 5     . 1̇ . 6    . 3 . 2̂⁵
        . 3 . 5    . 2 . 1     . 2 . 1    . 6̣ . 5̣̂ ]
```

Gérongan for *inggah*, *ir III*: *Nalikanirå*

```
bal              .              1              .              6̣
gér  . . 1̇ 1̇ . . 1̇ 2̇ 6 . 1̇ 2̇ 2̇ . 6 2̇ 1̇ 6
bal              .              3              .              2
gér  . . 5 6 1̇ . 2̇ 6 1̇ 5 3 . . 5 5 6 1̇ 5 6 5 3 2
bal              .              3              .              5
gér  . . . . 6 6 6 1̇ 5 6 1̇ 2̇ 2̇ 3̇ 1̇ . 2̇ 6 1̇ 6 5
bal              .              2              .              1
gér  . . . . 2̇ 2̇ 2̇ 1̇ 6 1̇ 2̇ 1̇65 5 6 1̇65 2 3 2 1
bal              .              2              .              1
gér  . . 2̇ 2̇ . . 2̇ 3̇ 3̇ . . 2̇ 2̇ . 1̇ 1̇ 2̇ 3̇ 1̇
bal              .              6̣              .              5̣
gér  . . 6 6 . 1̇ 1̇ 1̇ 2̇ 6 . 1̇ 2̇ 1̇ 6 1̇ . 2̇ 6 1̇ 6 5
```

Title. The title is assumed to be taken from a particular *bathik* pattern. *Gambir* is a climbing plant, *Uncaria gambir*, connected with the betel-chewing cult. *Sawit* is a *bathik* outfit, such as sometimes worn by a bridal pair.

Skema and **garap**. This piece is played in many different ways. A specific *båwå*, *S.A. Råråbéntrok*, is often used. As a *srimpi* accompaniment, the *mérong* is played in *ir I* with *bedhayan* chorus throughout. For *klenèngan* performances, as would be expected, the *mérong* goes into *ir II* and can have *gérongan* in the *lik* section: the *inggah* may be in *ir II* with *bonang* playing *mipil lumpatan* (using details indicated in the notation) or may be in *ir III* and *IV* with *imbal* on the *bonang*. In the latter case, *gérongan* occupies the last 1½ *kenongan*. In *ir III/IV*, *gåtrå* . 3 . 5 may change to . 6 . 5, preceded by *kenong plèsèdan* 6. Named *céngkok* in *inggah*: all pairs of *gåtrå* . 2 . 1 . 2 . 1 are *puthut gelut* followed by *dhebyang-dhebyung*; . 3 . 2 is *kacaryan*. Where there is no *gérongan*, *sindhènan srambahan* is used. Details are otherwise commonly as described in Part 2 for vocal *gendhing*: e.g. the sequence AABA in the *mérong*, with *bonang* playing *mipil lumpatan* in the *ompak inggah* except where *gembyangan* is marked. Further variations are possible in *wayang*. The *inggah* is often followed by *ldr Gonjang-ganjing*. An optional standard *selingan*, *Kébar Sumedhangan*, breaks into the *mérong* and changes its character, involving *ciblon* drumming, a form of slow *imbal* in the *balungan* section, and *imbal* as well as *mipil* on the *bonang*. A common Yogya version also has a *bulungan mlaku* for the *ndhawah*, played with standard *mipil nglagu* on the *bonang*, and this section may be played in addition to the *balungan nibani* version. *Gendhing Gambirsawit* is also well known in a *pl 6* version, *gd Gambirsawit Pancerånå*: this forms part of a dance suite *Gambyong Paréanom*, in which *Kébar Sumedhangan* figures again.
The *inggah* of the *gendhing* is sometimes played as a four-*gongan lancaran*.

Gd Perkututmanggung kt 2 kp mg ldr sl m

```
bukå                                  6 6 1̇     6 5 2 3
           2 1 2 .    2 1 6̣ 5̣    3̣ 3̣ . 5̣    6̣ 1 2 (1)
mérong [   . 1 1 .    1 1 2 3    5 6 5 3    2 1 2 1
           . 1 1 .    1 1 2 3    5 6 5 3    2 1 2 1̂
           3 2 1 2    . 1 2 6    3 5 6 1̇    6 5 2 3̂²
           2 1 2 .    2 1 6̣ 5̣    3̣ 3̣ . 5̣    6̣ 1 2 (1) ]
```

minggah ladrang ir I/II

```
       [   3 2 5 3    6̣ 2 6̣ 1    3 2 5 3    6̣ 2 6̣ 1
           3 2 1 6    5 1̇ 5 6    3 2 5 3    6̣ 2 6̣ (1) ]
```

ldr ir III/IV

```
       [   3 6 3 2*   5 6 5 3    6 1̇ 3̇ 2̇    6 3 2 1̂
           3 6 3 2*   5 6 5 3̆    6 1̇ 3̇ 2̇    6 3 2 1̂
           3 6 3 2*   6 3 5 6̆    3 5 6 1̇    6 5 1̇ 6̂
           3 2 3 2    5 6 5 3̆*   6 1̇ 3̇ 2̇    6 3 2 (1̂) ]
```

Gérongan, ir III: Nalikanirå

```
bal   3     6     3     2     5     6     5     3
bal   6     1̇     3̇     2̇     6     3     2     1̂
bal   3     6     3     2     5     6     5     3
gér   . . . 6 5 6 3 2 . . 5 6 1̇ 2̇ 6 1̇653
bal   6     1̇     3̇     2̇     6     3     2     1̂
gér   . . 6 1̇ 2̇ 3̇ 3̇ . 5̇ 2̇ . 3̇ 1̇2̇6 3 . 3 5321
bal   3     6     3     2     6     3     5     6
gér   . . . . 6 6 6 1̇ 5 . 6 1̇ 2̇ . 3̇ 1̇ 2̇ 1̇ 6
bal   3     5     6     1̇     6     5     1̇     6̂
gér   . . . . 3̇ 3̇ 3̇ 2̇ 1̇ . 2 6 5 . 3 3 5 6 6
bal   3     2     3     2     5     6     5     3
gér   . . 3 2 . 3 . 5 2 . . 5 6 1̇ 2̇ 6 1̇653
bal   6     1̇     3̇     2̇     6     3     2     (1)
gér   . . 6 1̇ 2̇ 3̇ 3̇ . 5̇ 2̇ . 3̇ 1̇2̇63 . 3 5321
```

Title. *Kututmanggung* or *Perkututmanggung* = turtle dove coos.

Skema and **garap**. As usual for vocal *gendhing*. *Sindhènan gawan* in *ladrang*, *ir III*. *Ladrang* also has *gérongan* for *ir I* and *ir II*. *Bonang* may treat 6523 as *kacaryan*. Note many *ayu kuning* in *ldr, ir III*.
An alternative *minggah kendhang* in *kt 4* form may be played in *ir II* with *kd I* or *kosèk wayangan*, *pancer* and *mipil lumpatan* on *bonang*:

. 2 . 1   . 2 . 3   . 5 . 3   . 2 . 1̂
. 2 . 1   . 2 . 3   . 5 . 3   . 2 . 1̂
. 3 . 2   . 1̇ . 6   . 2̇ . 1̇   . 5 . 3
. 2 . 1   . 6̣ . 5̣   . 6̣ . 1   . 2 . (1)

This *gendhing* is also played in *pl 7*:

bukå   6 6 7   6 5 6 3
2 7̣ 2 .   2 7̣ 6̣ 5̣   3̣ 3̣ . 5̣   6̣ 7 2 (7)
mérong [. 7̣ 7̣ .   7̣ 7̣ 2 3   5 6 5 3   2 3 2 7̣
. 7̣ 7̣ .   7̣ 7̣ 2 3   5 6 5 3   2 3 2 7̣̂
3 2 7̣ 2   6 3 5 6   3 5 6 7   6 5 2 3̂²
2 7̣ 2 .   2 7̣ 6̣ 5̣   3̣ 3̣ . 5̣   6̣ 7 2 (7)]

minggah ladrang ir I/II
[3 2 5 3   6̣ 2 6̣ 7̣   3 2 5 3   6̣ 2 6̣ 7̣
3 2 7 6   5 7 5 6   3 2 5 3   6̣ 2 6̣ (7)]

ldr ir III/IV
3 6 3 2   5 6 5 3   6 7 3̇ 2̇   6 3 2 7̂
3 6 3 2   5 6 5 3̆   6 7 3̇ 2̇   6 3 2 7̂
3 6 3 2   6 3 5 6̆   3 5 6 7   6 5 7 6̂
3 2 3 2   5 6 5 3̆   6 7 3̇ 2̇   6 3 2 (7)

Adaptation of the *gérongan* is left as an exercise for the reader.

Gd bonang Babar layar kt 4 kp mg 8 pl 5

bukå (after *grambyangan* and *ådångiyah*)
. 3 . 3   . 3 2 1   . 6̣ 5̣ 4̣ 6̣   4̣ 5̣ 6̣ (1)
mérong A [. . . 1   . 6̣5̣4̣5̣6̣1   . 6̣5̣4̣5̣6̣1   . 6̣5̣4̣5̣6̣1
2 3 1 2   . 1 6̣ 5̣   2 2 . .   5̣ 6̣ 1 2̂
. . . 2   3 5 3 2   3 5 3 2   323 21.
6̣.5̣.4̣.2̣.   4̣.2̣4̣ 6̣ 5̣   2 2 . .   5̣ 6̣ 1 2̂
. . . 2   3 5 3 2   3 5 3 2   323 21.
6̣.5̣.4̣.2̣.   4̣.2̣4̣ 6̣ 5̣   3 3 . .   2 1 2 3̂
. . . 3   6 5 421   5̣ 5̣ . .   5̣ 5̣ . 6̣
1 1 . .   1 1 6̣ 5̣   4̣5̣4̣5̣4̣5̣4̣5̣   4̣5̣4̣5̣ 6̣ (1)
B . . . 1   . 6̣5̣4̣5̣6̣1   . 6̣5̣4̣5̣6̣1   . 6̣5̣4̣5̣6̣1
2 3 . .   6 5 3 2   3 2 1 6̣   5̣ 3 2̣ 3̂
. . . 3   1̣ 2̣ 3̣ 3̣   1̣ 2̣ 3̣ 3̣   6̣ 5̣ 3̣ 5̣
6̣5̣6̣ 5̣ 3   6̣ 5̣ 3̣ 5̣   . 5̣ 3̣ 2̣   5̣ 6̣ 5̣ 3̂
. . . 3   1̣ 2̣ 3̣ 3̣   1̣ 2̣ 3̣ 3̣   6̣ 5̣ 3̣ 5̣
6̣5̣6̣ 5̣ 3   6̣ 5̣ 3̣ 5̣   . 5̣ 3̣ 2̣ →§   5̣ 6̣ 5̣ 3̂
. 4̣ . 2̣   4̣ 5̣ 2 1   4̣ 1 . 2̣   3̣ 5̣ 6̣ 5̂
. . 5 6   7 6 5 4   2 1 6̣ 5̣   4̣5̣4̣5̣ 6̣ (1)]

ompak inggah   § 5̣ 6̣ 5̣ 4̣
. 4̣ . 4̣   . 4̣ . 1   . 1 . 1   . 1 . 5̣
. 1 . 5̣   . 1 . 5̣   . 4̣ 4̣ 6̣   4̣ 5̣ 6̣ (1)
inggah A [. 2 3 3   . 1 2 1   . 2 3 3   . 1 2 1
5̣ 5̣ . .   5̣ 5̣ . 4̣   2̣ 4̣ 5̣ 6̣   . 1 . 6̂
. . 2 1   . 6̣ 2 1   6̣ 5̣ 4̣ 4̣   2̣ 1 2̣ 1
5̣ 5̣ . .   5̣ 5̣ . 4̣   2̣ 4̣ 5̣ 6̣   . 1 . 6̣
. . 2 1   . 6̣ 2 1   6̣ 5̣ 4̣ 4̣   2̣ 1 2̣ 1
2 3 . .   6 5 3 2   3 2 1 6̣   2 1 6̣ 5̂
4̣ 2̣ 1 .   1̣ 2̣ 4̣ 5̣   4̣ 2̣ 1 .   1̣ 2̣ 4̣ 5̣
6̣ 1 . .   1 1 6̣ 5̣   4̣ 2̣ 4̣ 5̣   4̣ 2̣ 4̣ (1)
B . 2 3 3   . 1 2 1   . 2 3 3   . 1 2 1
5̣ 5̣ . .   5̣ 5̣ . 6̣   1 2 1 6̣   5̣ 3 2̣ 3
. 3 5̣ 6̣   5̣ 3 5̣ 6̣   4̣ 4̣ 2̣ 4̣   2̣ 1 2̣ 1
5̣ 5̣ . .   5̣ 5̣ . 6̣   1 2 1 6̣   5̣ 3 2̣ 3
. 3 5̣ 6̣   5̣ 3 5̣ 6̣   4̣ 4̣ 2̣ 4̣   2̣ 1 2̣ 1
2 3 . .   6 5 3 2   3 2 1 6̣   2 1 6̣ 5̂
4̣ 2̣ 1 .   1̣ 2̣ 4̣ 5̣   4̣ 2̣ 1 . →‡   1̣ 2̣ 4̣ 5̣
6̣ 1 . .   1 1 6̣ 5̣   4̣ 2̣ 4̣ 5̣   4̣ 2̣ 4̣ (1)]

ompak seseg   ‡ 1̣ 2̣ 4̣ 5̣
6̣ 1 . 5̣   . 1 . 5̣   . 4̣ 4̣ 6̣   4̣ 5̣ 6̣ (1)
seseg [6̣ 5̣ 4̣ 6̣   4̣ 5̣ 6̣ 1   6̣ 5̣ 4̣ 6̣   4̣ 5̣ 6̣ 1
6̣ 5̣ 4̣ 6̣   4̣ 5̣ 6̣ 1   2 3 2 1   6̣ 5̣ 6̣ 3̂
6̣ 5̣ 6̣ 3   6̣ 5̣ 6̣ 3   6̣ 5̣ 6̣ 3   6̣ 5̣ 3 2̣
5̣ 3 2̣ 5̣   3 2̣ 5̣ 3   2̣ 5̣ 2̣ 3   5̣ 6̣ 5̣ 3̂
6̣ 5̣ 6̣ 3   6̣ 5̣ 6̣ 3   6̣ 5̣ 6̣ 3   6̣ 5̣ 3 2̣
5̣ 3 2̣ 5̣   3 2̣ 5̣ 3   2̣ 5̣ 2̣ 3   5̣ 6̣ 5̣ 4̂
. 4̣ . 4̣   . 4̣ . 1   . 1 . 1→†   . 1 . 5̣
. 1 . 5̣   . 1 . 5̣   . 4̣ 4̣ 6̣   4̣ 5̣ 6̣ (1)]

suwuk   † . 1 . 5̣
. . 2 3   5̣ 5̣ . 3   6̣ 5̣ 3 2̣   . 3 . (5)

Title. *Babar layar* = setting sail.

Skema. As usual for *gendhing bonang*: see main text.

Garap. This piece attracts a variety of special *garap* on *bonang*, of which the following examples are a selection: *bonang barung* parts are given here, but *bonang panerus* parts can be deduced from them. Notation above is written to clarify *gåtrå* boundaries, making it easier to work out *bonang* and *peking* parts, but most notation sources write it differently.

Mérong

Gongan 1 and 2, *gåtrå* 2–4: short *nduduk tunggal* 1, then *mipil*, e.g. 1 . . 1 6̣5̣6̣ . 4̣5̣4̣ . 6̣1 6̣ .

Gongan 1, *gåtrå* 6: low 5 pattern or straight *mipil*.

Gåtrå 8 and 16, second half: ending in *gembyangan*, or *mipil* throughout.

Gåtrå 12 and 20: 2 3 2 . . 3 2 3 3 2 3 . 2 1 . 1 or 2 3 2 . 3 2 . 3 . 3 2 3 2 1 . . 1 or with *gembyangan* 3 in first half.

Gåtrå 13 and 21: e.g. all as short *nduduk tunggal* 6̣ . . 6̣ 5̣ . . 5̣ 4̣ . . 4̣ 2̣ . . 2̣

Gåtrå 14: e.g. 4̣ . . 4̣2̣4̣2̣4̣6̣5̣6̣ . . 5̣6̣ ., or *nduduk tunggal* 2̣ in first half.

Gåtrå 24: similar principles as *gåtrå* 8.

Gåtrå 25–26: e.g. *gembyangan*, possibly replacing last note of pattern with 6, then . 6 3 6 . . 5 6 5 5 4 2 . 1 2 . 1

Gåtrå 30–32: 6̣ 5̣ with regular *mipil* pattern; 4̣ 5̣ as straight *mipil* (4̣ 5̣ 4̣ .), repeated and ending with first half of *gåtrå* 32, or with *nduduk tunggal* 4̣ until first quarter of *gåtrå* 32 followed by *mipil* (4̣ 5̣ 4̣ .), then *mipil* on 6̣ 1 or *mipil* followed by *nduduk tunggal* 1 (cf. *gåtrå* 8, 16, 24).
Gongan 2, *gåtrå* 5–6: e.g. starting with ¼ *gåtrå* of *mipil* then *gembyangan*, possibly replacing last note of pattern with 6 and starting *gåtrå* 6 as *gåtrå* 26 of *gongan* 1. Also possibly straight *mipil* on 23 then *gembyangan* in *gåtrå* 5.
Gåtrå 7: as two separate *mipil lumpatan* patterns (1 2 3 . 2 1 . 2 2 1 5̣ . 6̣ 1 . 6̣ etc.) or regular *mipil*.
Gåtrå 12 and 20: e.g. . 6̣ 3̣ 6̣ . . 5̣ 6̣ 5̣ 3̣ 5̣ 3̣ . 5̣ 3̣ . 5̣
Gåtrå 13 and 21: first half with any suitable pattern given in main text.
Gåtrå 14 and 22: e.g. as *gåtrå* 12 and 20.
Gåtrå 25: *mipil lumpatan* pattern for . 3 . 2 transposed an octave down and with 4 replacing 3.
Gåtrå 32: as in *gongan* 1.
Ompak inggah: straight *gembyangan låmbå* and corresponding *tunggal* patterns may be easier than *nduduk* patterns, to ensure synchronisation with *balungan* section. Second half of last *gåtrå* as *mipil* or as *tunggal* 1.
Inggah
Gongan 1, *gåtrå* 8 and 16: with *mipil lumpatan* pattern or *nduduk tunggal* 6̣.
Gåtrå 9–10 and 17–18: first half of *gåtrå* 9/17 with *nduduk tunggal* 6̣, switching to 2 on last note of pattern, then . 2 6̣ 2 . . 1 2 1; then *gåtrå* 10/18 starts . 6̣ 1 . . 6̣ 1 6̣
Gåtrå 12 and 20: start *kempyungan* pattern with 4̣: 4̣ 5̣ 1̣ etc.
Gåtrå 21: 2̣ 3̣ 2̣ . then *nduduk gembyang* 3,
Gåtrå 23: as *mérong*, *gongan* 2, *gåtrå* 7.
Gåtrå 29: *mipil* 6̣ 1 6̣ . then *nduduk tunggal* 1.
Gongan 2: any *gåtrå* repeated from *gongan* 1 receive same *garap*.
Ompak seseg: same remarks as for *ompak inggah*.
Last *kenongan* of *seseg*, and *suwuk*: even more than for *ompak inggah* and *ompak seseg*, regular *gembyang* patterns may be easier because of the tempo.
Seseg section is also played independently as a four-*gongan ladrang*. There are also other pieces with the same name: a *ladrang* in *sl 9* and a *gendhing* in *pl 7*.

Gd Lipur érang-érang kt 2 kp mg 4 kal ldr Surung dhayung pl 6

bukå 6 . 6 . 6 . 5 6 5
. 5 . 6 . 5 3 2 1 1 3 2 . 1 6̣ (5)

mérong
A [[. 6̣ 5̣ . 5̣ 6̣ 1 2 1 3 1 2 . 1 6̣ 5̣[1]
1̇ 1̇ . . 1̇ 1̇ 2̇ 1̇ 3̇ 2̇ 1̇ 2̇ . 1̇ 6 5
. . 5 . 5 5 . 6 1̇ 2̇ 1̇ 6 5 3 1 2[6]
6 6 . . 6 5 3 2 1 1 3 2 . 1 6̣ (5)]
transition to *lik* . 1 6 (5)[1]
lik B 1̇ 1̇ . . 1̇ 1̇ 2̇ 1̇ 3̇ 2̇ 1̇ 2̇ . 1̇ 6 5
. 6 2̇ 1̇ . . 1̇ . 3̇ 2̇ 1̇ 2̇ . 1̇ 6 5
. . 5 . 5 5 . 6 1̇ 2̇ 1̇ 6 5 3 1 2[6]
6 6 . . 6 5 3 2 1 1 3 2 . 1 6̣ (5)]

ompak inggah
. 6 . 5 . 3 . 2 . 3 . 2 . 6̣ . (5)
minggah [. 6̣ . 5̣ . 3 . 2 . 3 . 2 . 6 . 5
. 2̇ . 1̇ . 2̇ . 1̇ . 3̇ . 2̇ . 6 . 5
. 6 . 5 . 6 . 5 » . 1̇ . 6 . 3 . 2
. 6 . 5 . 3 . 2 . 3 . 2 . 6̣ . (5)]
Transition to *ladrang* C: . 6 5 3 2 (1)
Ladrang:
ompak
[A . . 5̣ 6̣ 1 2 3 2 . 2 1 6̣ 5̣ 6̣ 1 2
. 2 3 5 . 6 4 5 6 5 6 2 1 3 2 6̣ (5)
B . . 5̣ 6̣ 1 2 3 2 . 2 1 6̣ 5̣ 6̣ 1 2
. 2 3 5 . 6 4 5 6 5 6 2 1 . 5 6 (1)
lik C . . 3̇ 2̇ . 1̇ 6 5 1̇ 2̇ 1̇ 6 3 5 3 2[6]
6 6 . . 6 5 4 5 6 5 6 2 1 3 2 6̣ (5)]

Title. *Lipur Érang-érang*: consoled by admonition. *Surung dhayung*: push the oars.
Skema. (Optional) *båwå* to start, e.g. *S.T. Lalijiwå*, *S.A. Ndhadhap manteb*.
Mérong: AABA.
Inggah: In *ir III*, optionally to *ir IV* at gong, then back to *ir III* immediately before *gérongan*, repeat to taste. Speed-up to *ir II*, leading to
Ladrang: enter at *lik* (C); cycle ABC to taste; *suwuk* after A. (*Ldr Sri Sinubå* is also used instead of *Surung dhayung*)
Garap. *Mérong*: *sindhènan srambahan*.
Inggah: *Sindhènan srambahan*, with *gérongan* and *sindhènan kinanthi* starting at symbol ». No *andhegan*.
Ladrang: *Bedhayan* chorus throughout, with *cakepan wangsalan*. *Ir II*, with *pinjalan ngedhongi* throughout.
Gérongan: *Nalikanirå*

bal . 1̇ . 6
gér . . 1̇ 1̇ . . 1̇ 2̇ . 3̇ 1̇ 2̇ . 3̇ 1̇ 2̇ 1̇ 6
bal . 3 . 2
gér . . 1̇ 2̇ . 3̇ 1̇ 2̇ 6 5 3 . . 3 6 5 . 5 6 5 3 2
bal . 6 . 5
gér . . . . 6 6 . 6 1̇ . 2̇ 2̇ 3̇ 1̇ . 1̇ 2̇ 1̇ 6 5
bal . 3 . 2
gér . . . . 3̇ 3̇ 2̇ 1̇ 6 1̇ 2̇ 3̇ 1̇ 6 5 . 5 6 5 3 2
bal . 3 . 2
gér . . 1 2 3 . 2 1 2 1 6̣ . . 3 5 . 5 6 5 3 2
bal . 6̣ . (5)
gér . . 3 5 . 6 2 . 1 6̣ . . 2 3 1 . 1 2 1 6̣ 5̣
Chorus, *ldr Surung dhayung, ir II*
bal . 6 5 3 2 (1)
gér . . . . . 1̇ 1̇
An- dhé

C *bal* . . 3 2 . i̇ 6 5̂
gér . . . . . 2̇ . 3̇ 2̇ . . 3̇ i̇ . 2̇ i̇ 6 5
ba- bo

bal i̇ 2̇ i̇ 6 5 3 1 2̂
gér . . . 0 . i̇ 2̇ i̇ 6 . . . 6 . 5 . 6 6
Jang- krik gu- nung
Mén- då wå nå

bal 6 6 . . 6 5 4 5̂
gér . . . . . 6 i̇ 2̇ . 3 . i̇ . 2̇ i̇ 6 5
pu- put ji- wå
se- so- tyå reng-

bal 6 5 6 2 1 3 2 6̣ ⑤
gér . . . 6 . 2 3 1 . . 2 3 1 . . 2 6̣ 5̣
dhuh ku- su- må
ga- ning kar- nå

bal A . . 5̣ 6̣ 1 2 3 2̂
gér . . . . 0 . . . 1 2 3 2
ba- bo

bal . 2 1 6̣ 5̣ 6̣ 1 2̂
gér . . . . 3 1 2 6̣ 5̣ . . . 3 5 . 6 5 3 2
sir kan- tå- kå
så- på ing- kang

bal . 2 3 5 . 6 4 5̂
gér . . . . . 2 3 5 . . . 6 . 4 5 6 5
yèn tan ning- gal-
pan- tes nge- ngu-

bal 6 5 6 2 1 3 2 6̣ ⑤
gér . . . 6 . 2 3 1 . 2 1 6̣ 5̣
i Ba- dhå- yå
dang Ba- dhå- yå

bal B . . 5̣ 6̣ 1 2 3 2̂
gér . . . . 0 . . . 2 3 2
ba- bo

bal . 2 1 6̣ 5̣ 6̣ 1 2̂
gér . . . . 3 1 2 6̣ 5̣ . . . 3 5 . 6 5 3 2
sir kan- tå- kå

bal . 2 3 5 . 6 4 5̂
gér . . . . 0 . . . .
bal 6 5 6 2 1 . 5 6 ①̂
gér . . . . i̇ i̇
An- dhé

Gd Lintang karahinan sl m kd Cåndrå

Yogya-style *gendhing soran* with *minggah kendhang* (in Solonese terms)

bukå 6 6 1 6 5 3 5 2 3 5 3 6 6 . ⑥̂
lâmbå . 3 . 2̇ . 3 . 2 . 3 . 6̇ . 3 . 2

. 6 . 2̇ . 6 . 2 . 3 . 6̇ . 3 . 2̂
. 6 . 2̇ . 3 . 1 . 3 . 2̇ . 1 . 6̂
3 5 6 1̇ 6 5 3 5 2 3 5 3̇ 2 1 2 ⑥
dados [3 5 3 2̇ . 3 5 2 . 3 5 6̇ 3 5 3 2̂
1 6̣ 1 2̇ . 3 5 2 . 3 5 6̇ 3 5 3 2̂
1 6̣ 1 2̇ 1 1 2 1 3 5 3 2̇ 6 3 5 6̂ §
3 5 6 1̇ 6 5 3 5 2 3 5 3̇ 2 1 2 ⑥̂]
p.d. § . 2 . 1̇ . 6 . 5 . 2 . 3̇ . 1 . ⑥
ndhawah [. 3̇ . 2 . 3̇ . 2 . 3̇ . 6 . 3̇ . 2̂
. 6̇ . 2 . 6̇ . 2 . 3̇ . 6 . 3̇ . 2̂
. 6̇ . 2 . 3̇ . 1 . 3̇ . 2 . 1̇ . 6
. 2̇ . 1 . 6̇ . 5 . 2̇ . 3 . 1̇ . ⑥̂]

Title. *Lintang kara(h)inan* = morning star.
Skema and ***garap***. Generally as described for Yogya-style *gendhing soran*. For specific *garap* principles, see under ***Peking*** and ***Bonang*** in Part 3. No *kempyang*. If *bonang* uses Yogya-style patterns in the *ndhawah*, they can include *nguthik* variants for . 3 . 2, and *gembyangan* in more places than shown (but places marked with *gembyangan* can have *mipil*).

Gd bonang Sidåmukti kt 4 ar mg 8 sl 6

bukå 2 . 2 . 6̣ . 2 . 1
. 3 . 2 . 1 6̣ 5̣ 3̣ 2̣ . 3̣ 5̣ 6̣ 3̣ ⑤
mérong [6̣ 1 2 . 2 1 6̣ 5̣ 1 6̣ 5̣ 3̣ 6̣ 5̣ 3̣ 5̣
6̣ 1 2 . 2 1 6̣ 5̣ 1 6̣ 5̣ 3̣ 6̣ 5̣ 3̣ 5̣
3 3 . . 3 3 5 3 6 5 3 5 3 2 1 2
5 6 5 3 2 1 6̣ 5̣ 3̣ 2̣ . 3̣ 5̣ 6̣ 3̣ 5̣̂
6̣ 1 2 . 2 1 6̣ 5̣ 1 6̣ 5̣ 3̣ 6̣ 5̣ 3̣ 5̣
6̣ 1 2 . 2 1 6̣ 5̣ 1 6̣ 5̣ 3̣ 6̣ 5̣ 3̣ 5̣
3 3 . . 3 3 5 3 6 5 3 5 3 2 1 2
5 6 5 3 2 1 6̣ 5̣ 2 2 . 3 1 2 3 2̂
. . 2 3 6 5 3 2 6 6 . i̇ 6 5 3 5
2 3 5 6 3 5 3 2 6 6 . i̇ 6 5 3 5
2 3 5 6 3 5 3 2 6 6 . i̇ 6 5 3 5
2 3 5 6 5 3 2 1 6̣ 1 3 2 . 1 6̣ 5̣̂[1] → §
1 1 . . 3 2 1 6̣ 3̣ 5̣ 6̣ 5̣ 2̣ 2̣ 3̣ 2̣
5̣ 3̣ 2̣ 5̣ 2̣ 3̣ 5̣ 6̣ 3̣ 5̣ 6̣ 5̣ 2̣ 2̣ 3̣ 2̣
3 3 . . 3 3 5 3 6 5 3 5 3 2 1 2
5 6 5 3 2 1 6̣ 5̣ 3̣ 2̣ . 3̣ 5̣ 6̣ 3̣ ⑤]
ompak inggah
§ . 1 . 6̣̇ . 5̣ . 3̣ . 5̣ . 6̣̇ . 5̣ . 3̣
. 5̣ . 3̣ . 5̣ . 3̣ . 5̣ . 2̇ . 6̣ . ⑤
inggah [. 6̣ . 5̣ . 6̣ . 5̣ . 6̣ . 5̣ . 3 . 2
. 3 . 2 . 3 . 2 . 5 . 3 . 1 . 6̣̂
. 1 . 6̣ . 1 . 6̣ . 3 . 6 . 3 . 2

. 6 . 5   . 3 . 2   . 5 . 3   . 1 . 6 [2]
. 3 . 2   . 3 . 2   . 5 . 6   . 5 . 3
. 5 . 6   . 5 . 3   . 2 . 3   . 6 . 5 → ‡
. 1 . 6   . 5 . 3   . 1 . 6   . 5 . 3
. 5 . 3   . 5 . 3   . 5 . 2   . 6 . (5)]

ompak seseg

‡ 3 6 3 5   3 6 3 2   3 6 3 5   3 6 3 2
3 6 3 5   3 6 3 2   3 5 3 2   3 6 3 (5)

sesegan [3 6 3 5   3 6 3 5   3 6 3 5   2 2 3 2
5 3 2 5   3 2 5 3   2 5 2 3   5 6 5 3
6 5 6 3   6 5 6 3   6 5 6 3   2 2 3 2
5 3 2 5   3 2 5 3   2 5 2 3   5 6 5 3 [1]
1 1 . .   1 1 2 3   5 6 1 6   5 3 2 1
2 3 5 6   1 6 5 3   5 6 5 3   2 1 6 5
3 6 3 5   3 6 3 2   3 6 3 5   3 6 3 2
3 6 3 5   3 6 3 2   3 5 3 2   3 6 3 (5)]

Title. *Sidåmukti* = ?success and comfort in life; also a *bathik* pattern.
Skema and **garap**. As usual for *gendhing bonang*. For *bonang*, *mipil lumpatan* throughout *balungan nibani*. Other usage of *mipil lumpatan* and general usage of *kempyungan* and *gembyangan* are notated from an actual performance, but other usages as described in the main text would also be 'correct'. *Pancer* 1 in *inggah* from end of first *kenongan* until start of *ompak seseg*.

Gd bonang Tukung kt 2 kp mg 4 pl 7

For *grambyangan* and *ådångiyah* to 5 (for *pl 7*), see main text.

bukå . 5 . 5   . 5 . 5   6 7 2 7   6 5 3 (5)

mérong

[6 7 2 7   6 5 3 5   6 7 2 7   6 5 3 5
3 3 . 1   2 3 5 3   . 7 . .   5 6 7 6
. 6 5 3   2 3 5 3   6 7 6 5   3 2 7 2
. 7 . .   5 6 7 2   . 7 . .   5 6 7 6
. 6 5 3   2 3 5 3   6 7 6 5   3 2 7 2
. 7 . .   5 6 7 2   . 7 . .   5 6 7 6 → §
5 4 . 2   4 5 421   4 1 . 2   4 5 6 5
. . 5 .   5 5 . .   6 7 2 7   6 5 3 (5)]

ompak inggah

§ . 7 6 .   6 7 2 3   2 7 6 .   6 7 2 3
4 3 4 .   4 3 4 .   4 3 4 6   4 3 4 (2)

inggah

[4 3 4 6   4 3 4 2   4 3 4 6   4 3 4 2
4 3 4 6   4 3 2 3   . 3 3 3   2 7 5 6
3 5 6 7   6 5 6 3   6 5 3 5   6 5 3 2
5 3 2 5   3 2 5 3   . 3 3 3   2 7 5 6
3 5 6 7   6 5 6 3   6 5 3 5   6 5 3 2
5 3 2 5   3 2 5 3   . 3 3 3   2 7 5 6
. 7 6 .   6 7 2 3   2 7 6 .   6 7 2 3
4 3 4 .   4 3 4 .   4 3 4 6   4 3 4 (2)]

Title. *Tukung* = tailless chicken.
Skema and **garap**. As usual for *gendhing bonang*, except no separate *sesegan* section. For *bonang*, *gembyangan* not *tunggal* patterns for *gantungan* 7 in first three *kenongan*, because of register shift; *gembyangan* to 5676 with optional lead-in from 2; . 7 6 . as *balungan pin mundur*; 45421 on *bonang barung* as 454 . . 54 . 542 . 12 . 1; 434 . as if 4343; 2756 with standard low 6 pattern; 4323 in *ir I* as 72 followed by *gembyang* 3.

Gd Téjånåtå kt 2 kp mg 4 kal ldr Sembåwå dados ldr Playon pl 5

bukå . 3 . 2
1 . 6 5   . 5   . 3 . 2   1 . 6 5
. 3 . 3   . 2 . 1   . 1 . 5   6 1 2 (1) [5]

mérong

A [. 2 3 3   . 1 2 1   . 2 3 3   . 1 2 1 [3]
3 3 . .   3 3 5 3   6 5 3 5   3 2 1 2
. . 2 .   2 2 1 2   3 3 . .   1 2 3 2 [5] → §
1 1 . .   5 6 1 2   1 3 1 2   . 1 6 (5)

B . 6 2 1   . 6 5 .   5 6 2 1   . 6 3 5 [3]
3 3 . .   3 3 5 3   6 5 3 5   3 2 1 2
. . 2 .   2 2 1 2   3 3 . .   1 2 3 2 [5] → §
1 1 . .   5 6 1 2   1 3 1 2   . 1 6 (5)

C . 6 2 1   . 6 5 .   5 6 2 1   . 6 3 5 [1]
(*lik*) 1 1 . .   1 1 2 1   3 2 1 2   . 1 6 5
. . 5 .   5 5 4 5   6 6 . .   4 5 6 5 [4]
4 4 . .   4 2 4 5   4 6 4 5   . 4 2 (1) [5]]

ompak inggah

§ . 3 . 1   . 3 . 2   . 3 . 2   . 6 . (5)

inggah

(B) . 2 . 1   . 2 . 1   . 3 . 2   . 6 . 5 [3]
. 2 . 3   . 5 . 3   . 6 . 5   . 3 . 2
. 3 . 2   . 5 . 3   . 5 . 3   . 1 . 2 [5]
. 3 . 1   . 3 . 2   . 3 . 2   . 6 . (5)

(C) . 2 . 1   . 2 . 1   . 3 . 2   . 6 . 5 [1]
lik . 2 . 1   . 2 . 1   . 3 . 2   . 6 . 5
. 6 . 5   . 4 . 6   . 5 . 6   . 4 . 5 [4]
. 6 . 4   . 6 . 5   . 6 . 5   . 2 . (1) [5]

(A) . 2 . 3   . 2 . 1   . 2 . 3   . 2 . 1 [3]
. 2 . 3   . 5 . 3   . 6 . 5   . 3 . 2
. 3 . 2   . 5 . 3   . 5 . 3   . 1 . 2 [5]
. 3 . 1   . 3 . 2   . 3 . 2   . 3 . (1) [1]

ldr Sembåwå

A, *lik* [. . 3 2 . 1 6 5 1 2 1 6 5 3 5 6
. 6 5 3 6 5 3 5 1 2 1 6 5 3 2 (3)

B . 3 2 3 2 1 2 1 . 1 1 1 2 3 5 3 → ‡
. 3 5 6 7 6 5 3 5 3 2 3 2 1 2 (1)

C . 1 1 1 2 3 2 1 . 1 1 1 2 3 5 3 → ‡
. 3 5 6 7 6 5 3 5 3 2 3 2 1 2 (1)]

transition to *ldr Playon*

‡ . 3 5 6 7 6 5 3 5 3 2 3 1 2 3 (5)

ldr Playon

A [. 5 4 2 1 2 4 5 . 5 4 2 1 2 4 5
6 5 4 2 1 2 3 2 6 6 . 7 5 6 7 (6)

B . 6 5 4 2 2 1 2 . . 2 4 5 . 6 5
6 5 4 2 1 6 4 5 . 6 1 2 1 6 4 (5)

C . 6 1 2 1 6 4 5 3 3 6 5 3 2 1 6
5 6 1 2 3 2 1 2 1 6 5 4 2 4 6 (5)]

Sindhènan bedhayan, after first *kenong*

bal 3 3 . . 3 3 5 3 6 5 3 5 3 2 1 2
g . . . . 0 3 5 6 . . . . 6 . 5 . 6 3 2 1 2
An-dhé A- mar su-

bal . . 2 . 2 2 1 2 3 3 . . 1 2 3 2
g . 2 . . . . . 0 . . . . . . 1 2 3 . . 0 . 3 . 2 . . 1 1 . 2 3 2
di An-dhé A- mar su- di

bal 1 1 . . 5 6 1 2 1 3 1 2 . 1 6 (5)
g . . . 1 . 1 2 1 . . 6 1 2 3 2 . . 3 3 . . 1 2 . . 1 6 . 5
sin- dhèn gen- dhing Té- jå- nå-

B . 6 2 1 . 6 5 . 5 6 2 1 . 6 3 5
g . 5 . . . . 0 . 2 . . 3 1 2 1 6 . 5
tå Té- jå- nå-

bal 3 3 . . 3 3 5 3 6 5 3 5 3 2 1 2
g . 5 . . . . 0 3 5 6 . . . . 6 . 5 . 6 3 2 1 2
tå An-dhé ing ri- ku-

bal . . 2 . 2 2 1 2 3 3 . . 1 2 3 2
g . 2 . . . . . 0 . . . . . . 1 2 3 . . 0 . 3 . 2 . . 1 1 . 2 3 2
lem An-dhé ing ri- ku- lem

bal 1 1 . . 5 6 1 2 1 3 1 2 . 1 6 (5)
g . . . 1 . 1 2 1 . . 6 1 2 3 2 . . 3 3 . . 1 2 . . 1 6 . 5
ke- mis ping ca- tur kang cån-

C . 6 2 1 . 6 5 . 5 6 2 1 . 6 3 5
g . 5 . . . . 0 . . . . 2 . . 3 1 2 1 6 . 5
drå tur kang cån-

(*lik*) 1 1 . . 1 1 2 1 3 2 1 2 . 1 6 5
g . 5 . . . . 0 . . . . 1 1 . . . . . 3 1 2 . . 3 1 . . 6 5
drå An-dhé Ma- di- la-

bal . . 5 . 5 5 4 5 6 6 . . 4 5 6 5
g . 5 . . . . 0 . . . . 4 5 6 . . . . 6 . 5 . . 4 4 . 5 6 5
kir An-dhé Ma- di- la- kir

bal 4 4 . . 4 2 4 5 4 6 4 5 . 4 2 (1)
g . . . 4 . 4 5 4 . . 2 4 . 5 6 5 . . 6 6 . . 4 5 . . 4 2 . . . 1
du- må- dyå É- hé kang war-

A . 2 3 3 . 1 2 1 . 2 3 3 . 1 2 1
g . 1 . . . . 0 . . . . 3 . . 2 3 . . 2 3 1 2 1
så hé kang war-

bal 3 3 . . 3 3 5 3 6 5 3 5 3 2 1 2
g . 1 . . . . 0 . . . . 3 5 6 . . . . 6 . 5 . 6 3 2 1 2
så An-dhé Pra- bu ke-

bal . . 2 . 2 2 1 2 3 3 . . 1 2 3 2
g . 2 . . . . . 0 . . . . . . 1 2 3 . . 0 . 3 . 2 . . 1 1 . 2 3 2
nyå an-dhé Pra- bu ke- nyå

bal 1 1 . . 5 6 1 2 1 3 1 2 . 1 6 (5)
g . . . 1 . 1 2 1 . . 6 1 2 3 2 . . 3 3 . . 1 2 . . 1 6 . 5
ngra- suk bu- så- nå brå mul-

B . 6 2 1 . 6 5 . 5 6 2 1 . 6 3 5
g . 5 . . . . 0 . 2 . . 3 1 2 1 6 . 5
yå na brå mul-

bal 3 3 . . 3 3 5 3 6 5 3 5 3 2 1 2
g . 5 . . . . 0 3 5 6 . . . . 6 . 5 . 6 3 2 1 2
yå An-dhé Ha- ma- ku-

bal . . 2 . 2 2 1 2 3 3 . . 1 2 3 2
g . 2 . . . . . 0 . . . . . . 1 2 3 . . 0 . 3 . 2 . . 1 1 . 2 3 2
thå An-dhé Ha- ma- ku- thå

bal . 3 . 1 . 3 . 2 . 3 . 2 . 6 . (5)
g . . 1 1 . . . 1 . . 6 1 2 3 2 . . 3 3 . 2 1 2 . . 1 6 . 5
je- ja- mang Ki Nå- rå- wis- thå

inggah, starting at (B) (note possible change of timescale)

bal . 2 . 1 . 2 . 1 . 3 . 2 . 6 . 5
g . 2 3 2 3 2 . 1 1 . . 2 2 . . 3 1 . . . . . 3 1 2 . . 3 1 . 2 . 6 5
Ba- bo ba- bo Ra- dèn Nå- rå- wis-

bal . 2 . 3 . 5 . 3 . 6 . 5 . 3 . 2
g . 5 . . . . . . 0 . . . 0 3 5 6 . . . . 6 . 5 . 6 3 2 . 1 . 2
thå an-dhé tan ka- tong-

bal . 3 . 2 . 5 . 3 . 5 . 3 . 1 . 2
g . 2 . . . . . . 0 . . . . 1 2 3 . . . . 3 . 2 . . 1 1 . 2 3 2
tong an-dhé tan ka- tong- tong

bal . 3 . 1 . 3 . 2 . 3 . 2 . 6 . (5)
g . . . 1 . 1 2 1 . . 6 1 . 2 3 2 . . 3 3 . . 1 2 . . 1 6 . . . 5
wa- don lir Nar- Pa- ti Kar- nå

(C) . 2 . 1 . 2 . 1 . 3 . 2 . 6̣ . 5̣
g . 23 23 2.1 1 . . 22 . . 3 1 . . . . . 31 2 . . 3 1 . 2 .6̣5̣
Ba- bo ba- bo Ra- dèn pu- ti Kar-

lik within (C)
bal . 2̇ . 1̇ . 2̇ . 1̇ . 3̇ . 2̇ . 6 . 5̂
g . 5̣ . . . . 0 . . . . 1̇ 1̇ . . . . . 3̇ 1̇ 2̇ . . 3̇ 1̇ . 2̇ 6 5
nå an-dhé Pa- tih Ret-

bal . 6 . 5 . 4 . 6 . 5 . 6 . 4 . 5̂
g . 5 . . . . 0 . . . . 4 56 . . . . 6 . 5 . . 4 4 . 565 5
nå an-dhé Pa- tih Ret- nå

bal . 6 . 4 . 6 . 5 . 6 . 5 . 2 . ①
g . . . 4 . 454 . . 2 4 . 565 . . 66 . . 4 5 . . 4 2 . . . 1
Ge- na- wa- ti pan sa- wån-

(A) . 2 . 3 . 2 . 1 . 2 . 3 . 2 . 1̂
g . 1 . . . . 0 . . . . 3 . . 2 3 . . 23 1 2 1
då pan sa- wån-

bal . 2 . 3 . 5 . 3 . 6 . 5 . 3 . 2̂
g . 1 . . . . 0 . . . . 3 56 . . . . 6 . 5 . 63 2 1 2
då an-dhé Lir su- man-

bal . 3 . 2 . 5 . 3 . 5 . 3 . 1 . 2̂
g . 2 . . . . 0 . . . . 1 23 . . . . 3 . 2 . . 1 1 . 232 2
tri an-dhé lan Su- man- tri

bal . 3 . 1 . 3 . 2 . 3 . 2 . 3̇ . ①
g . . . 1 . 121 . . 6̣ 1 . 232 . . 3 3 . . 1 2 . . . . . 0 1̇ 1̇
lan Pra- bu Har- ju- nå. An-dhé

ldr Sembåwå (note possible change of timescale)

A, *lik* . . 3̇ 2̇ . 1̇ 6 5̂
gér . . . . . 2̇ 3̇ 2̇ . . 3̇ 1̇ . 2̇ 1̇65
Ba- bo

bal 1̇ 2̇ 1̇ 6̆ 5 3 5 6̂
gér . . . . . 1̇ 2̇1̇ 6 . . . 6 . 5 6 6
Le- la drang- an

bal . 6 5 3̆ 6 5 3 5̂
gér . . . . . 5 65 3 . . 6 6 . 55 6 5
dyah ca- tur kang

bal 1̇ 2̇ 1̇ 6̆ 5 3 2 ③
gér . . . . . 1̇ 1̇ 2̇1̇ 6 . . 35 5 . . 65 3
ma- gut yu- då

B . 3 2 3 2 1 2 1̂
gér . . . . 2 3 . 23 1 2 1
Ba-

bal . 1 1 1̆ 2 3 5 3̂
gér . 1 . . . 1 2 3 . . 5 3 . 2 . 3
bo ka- wu- wu-

bal . 3 5 6̆ 7 6 5 3̂
gér . 3 . . . 5 . 66 . . 5 6 . 3565 3
så Ban- jar- an sa-

bal 5 3 2 3̆ 2 1 2 ①
gér . . . . . 2 3 2 1 . 2 16̣ 12 . . 3 1
ri Na- rén- drå

C . 1 1 1 2 3 2 1̂
gér . . . 1 2 1 . . . . . 2 3 2 1
Ba-

bal . 1 1 1̆ 2 3 5 3̂
gér . 1 . . . 1 2 3 . . 5 3 . 2 . 3
bo ka- wu- wu-

bal . 3 5 6̆ 7 6 5 3̂
gér . 3 . . . . 0 . . . . . .
så

5 3 2 3̆ 2 1 2 ①
gér . . . . 1̇ 1̇
An- dhé

A, *lik* . . 3̇ 2̇ . 1̇ 6 5̂
gér . . . . . 2̇ 3̇ 2̇ . . 3̇ 1̇ . 2̇ 1̇65
Ba- bo

bal 1̇ 2̇ 1̇ 6̆ 5 3 5 6̂
gér . . . . . 1̇ 2̇1̇ 6 . . . 6 . 5 6 6
Wus a- ngra- suk

bal . 6 5 3̆ 6 5 3 5̂
gér . . . . . 5 65 3 . . 6 6 . 55 6 5
bu- så- nå ma-

bal 1̇ 2̇ 1̇ 6̆ 5 3 2 ③
gér . . . . 1̇ 1̇ 2̇1̇ 6 . . 35 5 . . 65 3
né- kå war- nå

B . 3 2 3 2 1 2 1̂
gér . . . . . . 2 3 . . 23 1 . 2 . 1
Ba-

bal . 1 1 1̆ 2 3 5 3̂
gér . 1 . . . 1 2 3 . . 5 3 . 2 . 3
bo Ma- ku- thå

bal . 3 5 6̆ 7 6 5 3̂
gér . 3 . . . 5 . 66 . . 5 6 . 3565 3
lan to- pong kar- nå

bal 5 3 2 3̆ 2 1 2 ①
gér . . . . . 2 3 2 1 . 2 16̣ 12 . . 3 1
dé- wang- kå- rå

C . 1 1 1 2 3 2 1̂
gér . . . 1 2 1 . . . . . 2 3 . 2 . 1
Ba-

bal . 1 1 1̆ 2 3 5 3̂
gér . 1 . . . 1 2 3 . . 5 3 . 2 . 3
bo Ma- ku- thå
bal . 3 5 6̆ 7 6 5 3̂
gér . 3 . . . . 0 . . . . . .
lan
bal 5 3 2 3̆ 5 5 6 ⑤
gér 5 5
An- dhé

ldr Playon
A . 5 4 2 1 2 4 5̂
gér . . . . 6 1̇ 1̇ 2̇ 1̇ 6 5
Ba- bo
bal . 5 4 2̆ 1 2 4 5̂
gér . . . . . 5 6 1̇ 1̇ . . 2̇ 2̇ . 1̇ 6 5
Di- pa- ti ing
bal 6 5 4 2̆ 1 2 3 2̂
gér . . . . 5 6 4 5 4 2 2 2 2 . 2 2 1 2 2
Tir- tå ken- cå- nå ma- ngar- så
bal 6 6 . 7̆ 5 6 7 ⑥
gér . . . 6 . 1̇ 2̇ 3̇ 1̇ . . 2̇ 2̇ 1̇ 2̇ 1̇ 6
nå ma- ngar- så
B . 6 5 4 2 2 1 2̂
gér 6 5 4 5 4 2 2 1 2
Ba-
bal . . 2 4̆ 5 . 6 5̂
gér . 2 . . . 2 4 5 . 6 5 . 4 5 6 5
bo Ba- nyak wi- dhé
bal 6 5 4 2̆ 1 6̣ 4̣ 5̣̂
gér . . . . 5 6 4 5 4 2 1 1 1 . 1 2 1 2 6̣ 5̣
lan Ha- ryå Ba- nyak se- på- trå
bal . 6̣ 1 2̆ 1 6̣ 4̣ ⑤
gér . . . 6̣ . 1 2 3 2 . . . 3 1 2 1 6̣ 5̣
nyak se- på- trå
C . 6̣ 1 2 1 6̣ 4̣ 5̣̂
gér . . . . 0 1 2 1 2 1 2 6̣ 5̣
A- dèn a- dèn
bal 3 3 6 5̆ 3 2 1 6̣̂
gér . 6 5 3 . . 6 5 6 5 6 5 3 2 1 2 1 6̣
Ba- nyak wi- dhé
bal 5̣ 6̣ 1 2̆ 3 2 1 2̂
. . . . 0 . . . . . .
bal 1 6̣ 5̣ 4̣̆ 2 4 6 ⑤
gér 5 5
An- dhé

A . 5 4 2 1 2 4 5̂
gér . . . . 6 1̇ 1̇ . 2̇ 1̇ 6 5
Ba- bo
bal . 5 4 2̆ 1 2 4 5̂
gér . . . . . 5 6 1̇ 1̇ . . 2̇ 2̇ . 1̇ 6 5
Ka- pat- ing kang
bal 6 5 4 2̆ 1 2 3 2̂
gér . . . . 5 6 4 5 4 2 2 2 2 . 2 2 1 2 2
Bu- pa- ti ma- ngre- but yu- då
bal 6 6 . 7̆ 5 6 7 ⑥
gér . . . 6 . 1̇ 2̇ 3̇ 1̇ . . 2̇ 2̇ 1̇ 2̇ 1̇ 6
ngre- but yu- då
B . 6 5 4 2 2 1 2̂
gér 6 5 4 5 4 2 2 1 2
Ba-
bal . . 2 4̆ 5 . 6 5̂
gér . 2 . . . 2 4 5 . 6 5 . 4 5 6 5
bo Dyah te- ram- pil
bal 6 5 4 2̆ 1 6̣ 4̣ 5̣̂
gér . . . . 5 6 4 5 4 2 1 1 1 . 1 2 1 2 6̣ 5̣
ka- di pu- tri ing cem- på- lå
bal . 6̣ 1 2̆ 1 6̣ 4̣ ⑤
gér . . . 6̣ . 1 2 3 2 . . . 3 1 2 1 6̣ 5̣
ing cem- på- lå

Title. *Téjånåtå* = royal aura. *Sembåwå* = proper. *Playon* = running.
Skema. Generally as indicated by chorus notation. For *srimpi* accompaniment, *mérong* played in fast *ir I* (about 50 s for *gongan* C); for *klenèngan*, fast *ir II* (about 90 s for *gongan* C). *Mérong* played ABCAB or ABCA; *inggah* BCA in fast *ir II*. Both *ladrang* in similarly fast *ir II*: *Sembåwå* ABCABC or ABCAB, *Playon* ABCAB.
Garap. If *ir II*, *bonang barung* plays *mipil låmbå* in *mérong*. *Pinjalan* from start of *inggah* to end of suite. *Bedhayan* chorus throughout.

Pinjalan: possible *demung* part

minggah

B	23232121	23232121	32321212	65653535
	23235353	56565353	65653535	32321212
	32321212	56565353	53532323	12123232
	31312121	32321212	13131212	65653535
C	23232121	23232121	32321212	65653535
	21212121	23232121	32321212	65653535
	65654545	24245656	56565656	45456565
	64645454	65654545	46464545	21215321
A	21212323	21215321	21212323	21215321
	23235353	56565353	65653535	32321212

```
          32321212 56565353 53532323 12123232
          31312121 32321212 13131212 31315321
```

ladrang Sembåwå

```
A [ 21213232 31316565 12121656 53535656
    56565353 65653535 12121656 53532323
B   53532323 21215321 21212121 23235353
    53535656 76765353 53532323 21215321
C   21212121 23232121 21212121 23235353
    53535656 76765353 53532323 21215321 ]
```

transition to *ldr Playon* 65651245

ladrang Playon

```
A [ 65654242 12124545 65654242 12124545
    65654242 12123232 56566767 56567676
B   76765454 22221212 22222424 65656565
    65654242 16564545 56561212 16564545 suwuk
C   56561212 16564545 33336565 32321656
    56561212 32321212 16565454 65651245 ]
```

Kendhangan

Filling-in strokes for *kendhangan* for *gendhing* are shown separately. *Pin* in other *kendhangan* may also be filled in with *ket* or *tong* strokes.

Kendhangan bubaran (kd II)

```
bukå                                t   t t P b  tPt t b
dados A  PP.P.P.t  PP.P.P.t  PP.P.PbP  PbPb.PbP →‡
      B  tPb.tPb.  tPb.tPb.  tPb.tPbP  PbPbtPbP
suwuk ‡ .tPP.P.b  .tPPbtPb  ttPbttPttPtt  bPttbtPPP.
```

From a Yogya source. A *låmbå* section is available, but is not required in departure pieces such as *Hudan mas*. In *ir I*, *dados* version A may be used throughout, or alternated with B, but *suwuk* usually happens from A.

Kendhangan ketawang (kd II)

```
bukå                      t t P b   . P bPb
ompak       . P b . P . P b   . P . P . b . P
          .P.b.P.b...P.b.P  ..Pb.k.P.kPbP.bP
ir II   [ .k.k.k.k.k.ktP.b  .k.P.k.P.kPbP.bP →‡
          .P.b.P.b...P.b.P  ..Pb.k.P.kPbP.bP ]
seseg   ‡ .P.P.P.bo∘kP.b.P  ∘kPbo∘kP.bo∘ktP.b
suwuk     .t.P.b...P.k.P.b  .k.P.k.t.k.P.k.t
          .k.b.k.P.k.k.k.b  .k.∘.k.Pkkk∘k∘k.
```

Kendhangan ladrang Mataram (kd II)

```
bukå                   t    b t P b   t P t P
ir I  [ .t.P.tP.  tP.b.∘tP  .b.tPP.P  .b.∘tP.b
        .∘tP.b.t  PP.P.b.P↘ .b.∘tP.b  .∘tP.b.P ]
transition to other irâmå   .b.b.P.b  .t.P.t.P
suwuk   .t.P.tP.  tP.b.∘tP  .b.t.PP.P .b.ttP.b
        .ttP.b.t  tP.ttP t  tb.P.t.b  .t.P.P..
```

From a Yogya source for the default *kd II* for *ladrang*. Only the *ir I* sections are shown. Other sources show *ket* strokes in place of *tong*.

Kendhangan ladrang (kd II)

```
bukå                              t t P b   ∘∘bP∘∘bP
ir I   [ ∘∘bP∘∘bP  ∘∘bP∘∘bP  ∘∘bP∘∘bP  ∘∘bP∘∘bP
         ∘∘bP∘∘bP  ∘∘bP∘∘bP  PbP.b.Pb  ∘∘bP∘∘bP ]
transition to ir II
         ∘∘bP∘∘bP  ∘∘bP∘∘bP  ∘∘bP∘∘bP  PbktPbktPb
         .P.b.ktP∘kPb∘k∘t    .P.P.P.b.P.kPb.P
         ∘kPb.Pb.PbP.b.Pb    ...k...PP.Pb.P.b
ir II  [ ...k...k...k...P    .P∘kbP.b...k...k
         ∘kbP∘kbP∘kPbP.bP→‡  ...k...P.b.ktP.b
         .P.b.ktP∘kPb∘k∘t→¶  .P.P.P.b.P.kPb.P
         ∘kPb.Pb.PbP.b.Pb    ...k...PP.Pb.P.b ]
ir II lik .PbP.b.P..Pb.Pb.   PbP.b.Pb.....b.P
         ..Pb.Pb.PP.P.b.P→‡  ...k...P.b.ktP.b
         .P.b.ktP∘kPb∘k∘t    .P.P.P.b.P.kPb.P
         ∘kPb.Pb.PbP.b.Pb    ...k...PP.Pb.P.b
transition to ir I
                          ¶  .P.P.P.b.P.t.b.P
         .∘.b.P.∘.b.∘.P.b    ∘∘bP∘∘bP
suwuk patterns
ir I     ∘∘bP∘∘bP  ∘∘bP∘∘bP  ∘∘bP∘∘bP  .b.P.ttb
         .P.ttb.P  .ttb.P.t  tb.P∘P∘b  .kkPkkk.
ir II                     ‡  .P.b...P.b.ktP.b
         .P.b...P..Pb.k.t    .P.P.P.b.P.ttb.P
         .ttb.P.ttb.P.ttb    kkk∘kkkPkkk∘k∘k.
```

From Solonese sources. Sparse stretches may be filled in, e.g. `...k` as `.k∘k` or `∘∘∘k`, etc. In a *lik* of more than one *gongan*, the second *gongan* may use the *lik* pattern again or revert to the *ompak* pattern.

Kendhangan gd kt 2 kp mg 4, sléndro (kd I)

Basic pattern

```
bukå                          b  ∘ ∘ ∘ (∘)
mérong      . . . b  . . . t  . P . b  . . . b
            P . P .  . P . P  b . P .  . P . .
            . P . b  . . . P  P b P .  . P . b
            P . P .  . P . b  . P . .  b P . (.)
ompak inggah
            . P . b  . . . P  . . . P  . . . b
```

. t . p . b . p . p . b .t.p...(.)
inggah .p. . . .p. . . .p. p b . t p .
. . p . p . . p p . p b . t p .
. . p . p . . p p . . p p . p t
b . b p . b p . p b p . b p . (.)

Additional signals:
After *bukå* o o o b o o o t .o.p.okb .okokok b̂
.p.okpko kokpkkkp
.kkbkkkokkkpkkko kkkokkkpkkkokkko
Regular filling-in pattern: ookokkkokkkokkko
where strokes are replaced by *thung*, *dha* or *tak* from the basic patterns above.
Pattern for slow-down to gong, *mérong*: kkkbkkkpookokok(.)
Recovery after gong: oo.okkkokkkokkkb
Speed-up to *ir I* for transition to *inggah*, following gong
oo.okkkokkkokkkb .k.k.k.k.k.k.k.t
kokp.o.b o o o b
suwuk . tpp p p b . p p . . p b p . b
p . b p ooobopt̄bk ooopooob
.kkokkkokkkokok.

transition from *mérong* to *ladrang*
p . b p . b . p o p
on *kd II* t t p b oobpoob(p)

Kendhangan Cåndrå

Yogya equivalent of *kendhangan satunggal* for *gd kt 2 kp mg 4* in *sléndro*.

bukå t . p . b . p . .
låmbå . p . b . . . p . . p . . p . .
p . p . . p . b . . . p . p . t
b p . b . . . p . p . b . p . p
.b.tpp.p .b.p.p.b .p...p.. .b.p.k..
dados .b.p.p.b ....p .....p.. ...p....
.p...p.. ...p.p.b ...t...p ...p...t → §
.b.p...b.......p .p.b.p.. .bp.p..p
.b.tpp.p .b.p.p.b .p...p.. .b.p.k..
p.d. § .b.p...b ...t...b ...t...p ...t.p.b
.p...b.p ...b...p .b.p...b .t.p.tb.
ndhawah ...b.p.p .t.b...p pp.tbp.b ...t.p.. → ‡
..pp.p.p .p....pp pp.tbp.b ...t.p..
..pp.p.p .p.b...t .p.p.t.p pp.p.p.p
.p...b.p ...b.p.. .b.p...b ...p.tb.

optional for *sesegan*
...b.p.p .t.b...p pp.p.p.b ...t...p → ‡
...p.p.p .p.....p .p.p.p.b ...t.p..
...p.p.t .p.b...t .p.p.t.t .p.p.p.b

.p...b.p ...b.p.. .b.p...b .p.t.t..
suwuk ‡ ..pp.p.p .p....pp pp.pbp.b .t.t.p..
...b.p.b .p.b...t bp.b...p ..ptbp.b
.p...b.p .k.b.p.k ...p...b ..k.k.k.

Ciblonan examples

Examples of named *sekaran* and *singgetan* (see Fig. 3.89)

Sekaran Ia p b pl kt kp o th k pp p p pl kt kp th pl
Sekaran Ib d th bk b d o th k lp kp lt b pl d db .
¼ *Sekaran Ib* then *Kèngser batangan*
d th dk bt kp th pl d bd b th tp lp th b t
Gong batangan oh bd bd .b .d pl bd b bb bk bk .b .p pl bd b

Glossary

This vocabulary is based on the one in Vol. 3 of *Karawitan*, edited by Becker and Feinstein, but is expanded from about 800 entries (here revised in some cases) to over 2400. The new entries include more terms from dance and *wayang*.

The vocabulary originally served to explain the usage of terms in the Indonesian and Javanese sources translated in *Karawitan*. Some of the terms included were of only historical interest. Other terms applied exclusively to Sundanese or Balinese music (although representing only a fraction of the terms needed to deal with those cultures). Non-musical usages of the words were not, and are still not, covered.

Becker and Feinstein did not try to place multiple meanings in any particular order, such as historical order or frequency of use. Because of the works chosen for their collection, it is quite possible that some of the terms or usages are *hapax legomena*. For the present version, an attempt has been made to put the more frequent meanings first.

Etymologies and literal meanings have been added in braces at the ends of some entries. Most of the entries are Javanese words, but some are clearly of Indonesian origin and are marked as [*in*]. In fact there is a constant two-way traffic between the two languages. When speaking or writing Indonesian, musicians use the Javanese terms freely (because Indonesian often has no suitable word of its own), but apply Indonesian grammatical affixes to the words. In some cases, the speaker will not necessarily be sure which language the word belongs to.

Variant spellings are often given here, but readers should still expect to see further variations, especially in older works. The notes below on Javanese orthography may be useful.

Javanese grammar and syntax

Javanese, like Indonesian, is a mildly agglutinative language, i.e. it uses root words by themselves or with one or more affixes (prefixes, infixes and suffixes). Most roots consist of two syllables. The meanings of the affixes and their combinations are too numerous to list. Some examples in use:

- *nglaras* (= to tune) consists of the root *laras* (= tuning) preceded by a prefix that turns it into a transitive verb,
- *pangrebab* (= *rebab* player) has two prefixes, the *pe/pa-* corresponding to the ending '-er' in English,
- *kraton* (= royal palace) derives from *ratu* (= king, queen) and incorporates both the prefix *ke-* and the suffix *-an*.

The infixes *-um-* and *-in-* occur after the initial consonant of a root, e.g. *kambang/kumambang*; *gonjing/ginonjing*. Infixes are rare and somewhat literary: although they have meanings, it is not always necessary to take account of an infix when translating, because the infix is often being used purely to make the words fit the metre. The same applies to the prefix *(h)a-*.

Prefixes in particular make words more difficult to recognise. The *ng-* in *nglaras* is an example of a nasal mutation applied to a root. This mutation varies according the initial letter(s) of the root. It is therefore useful to be able to recognise the standard mutations, as shown in Table G1.

Example of word analysis

Pangajapsih, the name of a *sekar tengahan* metre (see Appendix 1), has four syllables. The *pa-* and the *ng-* suggest a root *kajap*, *ngajap* or *(h)ajap*: any of these would be *ngajap* in mutated form. A dictionary will confirm the existence of *ajap/ajab*, meaning 'hope for'. *Sih* is a common root meaning 'love'.

Javanese has no standard plural form. An 'indefinite plural' for a noun is formed by simply repeating it: e.g. *ricikan-ricikan* = various instruments. However, often only the context shows whether the meaning of the noun is singular or plural, and sometimes it is impossible to be sure which is meant. Singular and plural meanings may even need to be rendered into English with different words.

It is also often difficult to decide which part of speech in English—noun, verb, adverb or adjective—to choose when translating a Javanese word.

English-speakers should note that in Javanese and Indonesian the noun is followed, not preceded, by adjectives and other

qualifier words. A large gamelan is a *gamelan gedhé*. Similarly, when two nouns are juxtaposed, the second may qualify the first: *gambang gångså* = bronze *gambang*. However, sometimes the two nouns have equal status, and a conjunction, idiomatically omitted in Javanese, must be supplied in English: *Gambang Suling* = *gambang* and *suling*.

Speech registers

A notable feature of Javanese is its use of language registers to reflect the relative social status of the speaker and the listener.

The basic speech level is *ngoko* or Low Javanese, used between equals or when addressing a listener of lower status. For a proportion of the vocabulary, including a number of words relevant to *karawitan*, there is an alternative word in the *kråmå* speech register (= High Javanese), which is used when addressing someone of higher status.

Thus a teacher could refer to the *gamelan* (a *ngoko* word), but a student replying to the teacher in Javanese should refer to the *gångså* (the equivalent word in *kråmå*). When using the Indonesian language, in which the Javanese speech registers do not exist, Javanese musicians may use either the *ngoko* or the *kråmå* word, so Western students need to become familiar with both, without necessarily knowing which belongs to which register. This description of the speech registers is simplified. For a fuller picture, readers are referred to grammars of Javanese.[1]

In this work, *ngoko–kråmå* pairs are indicated by [*ng*] and [*kr*]. A few terms from the *kråmå inggil* (*ki*) register and Indonesian (*in*) are also marked. Dictionaries usually list the words under their *ngoko* forms, with cross-references from the items in other speech registers. Here the terms are generally listed under whichever form seems to be more frequent.

Speech registers affect the forms of numerals: see the lists on pp. 38 and A-7. Some other common word pairs:

Ngoko	*Kråmå*	English
gedhé	*ageng*	large
cilik	*alit*	small
kembang	*sekar*	flower
tembang	*sekar*	song
dadi	*dados*	be, become
(m)laku	*(m)lampah*	walk
tibå/nibå	*(n)dhawah*	fall

Additional extra-formal speech levels are used in the *kraton*: *(båså) bagongan* by retainers, and *båså kedhaton* by the ruler and high officials. Words from Old Javanese (*jåwå kunå*) or *kawi* (its literary/poetic vocabulary) often occur in sung texts and in the names of compositions and gamelan.

Pronunciation and spelling

These notes apply only to Javanese as spoken and written in the Principalities.

a

In final open syllables, i.e. when not followed by a consonant, a is usually pronounced /ɒ/. In fact, the only exceptions seem to be the common word *(n)ora* and the less common *(m)boya*.

The same pronunciation applies to a in a penultimate syllable when it is separated from a final -a by a single consonant or certain consonant clusters. For this purpose, c, dh, j, ng, ny and th count as single consonants. The consonant clusters include those ending in r (*gåtrå*, *Cåndrå*, *tåmbrå*, etc.) and those consisting of a single consonant preceded by its 'homorganic' nasal consonant, i.e. the nasal consonant articulated at the same place in the mouth:

låmbå, *påncå*, *gåndå*, *kåndhå*, *jånggå*, *gånjå*,
nångkå, *tåmpå*, *gångså*, *brångtå*, *bråntå*, *pånthå*.

Compare *tanpå*, *jakså*, *astå*, *garwå*, *atmå*, *karyå*. The rules above apply separately to each part of a compound word; thus *måcåpat*, *Måråsånjå*. Note *Asmarandånå* but *Asmårådånå*.

For clarity, syllables with the /ɒ/ quality are normally written with å in this book: this is common practice outside Java, though rare in Javanese sources. One recent dictionary underlines a when it does not have the /ɒ/pronunciation. An a with the /ɒ/ quality may also be written as o in Java—against official policy—leading to possible confusion with o pronounced as /o/. This practice is especially common in proper names. Solo is actually Sålå.

b, d, g and final k

The stop consonants b, d and g in final position are pronounced unvoiced, i.e. as if written p, t or k respectively. For this reason, spellings with voiced and unvoiced final stops coexist: *manteb/mantep*, *pélog/pélok*, *cacad/cacat*, etc.

These three unvoiced stops are pronounced rather weakly in final position, and the -k is reduced to a glottal stop /ʔ/. This rule too applies separately to each part of a compound word, and if the suffix -an is added to a word ending in -k, the k is still pronounced as a glottal stop. For example, the k represents a glottal stop in both places in *ayak-ayakan*.

e, è, é

More than one scheme is in use to distinguish between these three sounds. As an alternative to the scheme with the acute and grave accents, as used here,[2] the 'weak' e (called a *pepet* in Javanese) may be written ê or ĕ: the other two types of e are then written without an accent. Another possibility is to leave *pepet* unmarked but use a macron (ē) to show the other two types.

1 e.g. Robson (1992).

2 And in Robson's grammar (1992), as well as dictionaries such as Herrfurth (1972), Horne (1974), Pigeaud (1994), Robson and Singgih Wibisono (2002) and at least two Javanese–Indonesian dictionaries.

Table G1
Nasal mutations to mark transitive verbs

Monosyllabic roots		
w-	adds	ngu-
others add		nga-/nge-
Polysyllabic roots		
b-	becomes	mb-
c-	becomes	ny- [a]
d-	becomes	nd-
dh-	becomes	ndh-
f-	becomes	m-
g-	becomes	ngg-
h-	becomes	ng-
j-	becomes	nj-
k-	becomes	ng-
l-	becomes	ngl-
m-	remains	m-
n-	remains	n-
ng-	remains	ng-
ny-	remains	ny-
p-	becomes	m-
r-	becomes	ngr-
s-	becomes	ny- [a]
t-	becomes	n-
th-	becomes	n-
w-	becomes	m-
y-	becomes	ngy-
any vowel adds		ng-

a. If the initial consonant is repeated in the middle of the root, a mutated form with n- may also be found:
cacah → *nacah/nyacah*
susul → *nusul/nyusul*

(The é and è pronunciations are two allophones of the same phoneme, called *taling* in Javanese, and can theoretically be distinguished by the context.[3] Also see Appendix 3.)

Some writers follow the official spelling policy and simply write all three vowels with an unmarked e—as for Indonesian, where two qualities of e are not written differently.[4]

All of these schemes can be found in Java and elsewhere, so that students will sometimes have to work out which is in use.

The pronunciation of other vowels also varies according to context, but this is not reflected in the spelling system.

l

The normal l sound of Javanese is a 'light' or 'clear' l, found in English as pronounced in Ireland, also in some positions in some British dialects of English. The 'dark l' /ɫ/ used by most American and Australian English dialects and in some British English occurs in only two Javanese words: *lha* and *lho.*

Vowel variations

The weak e sound often alternates with a, for example in the common prefixes *pe-*, *se-* and *ke-*:

penerus/panerus;
setunggal/satunggal

In some contexts, especially where the next syllable begins with l or r, the vowel may be dropped:

keraton/karaton/kraton; *paringgitan/pringgitan*;
celuring/cluring; *Terunåjåyå/Trunåjåyå*

More generally, any vowel is liable to be replaced by its neighbour in this series:

```
é —— i —— u
è          |
e —— a —— o
```

Consonant variations

The official spelling system (see below) distinguishes the two varieties of d and t in writing, but the Javanese do not consistently follow it, so that dh and th may be written as d and t respectively.[5] Since Indonesian has only one variety of these consonants, it is natural for the Javanese variants not to be distinguished in an Indonesian context. In older material, dh and th are often written ḍ and ṭ: this avoided confusion with the Old Javanese aspirated consonants written as dh and th.

Initial h is often not used, so that *hudan* alternates with *udan*, and so on; also h between two vowels is sometimes dropped, giving pairs such as *bahu/bau.*

The consonant y is optional between i and another vowel, so *siyem* alternates with *siem*, and so on. Similarly, w between u and other vowels is optional (*Puåså/Puwåså*). Alternation of w and u before a vowel occurs: *suårå/swårå.*

Additional consonants are found in loanwords. For words containing sy, pronounced /ʃ/ as in English '*sh*eep', there is always an alternative with s, e.g. *syair/sair.* Words with kh similarly often have an alternative with h. Z has its expected pronunciation. The consonants f and v, which only occur in loanwords, are sometimes pronounced as would be expected, but Indonesians perceive both of them as foreign and often pronounce them like p, and may spell them so. Thus

pilem, filem		= film
Pébruari, Fébruari		= February
tilpun	Dutch *telefoon*	= telephone
vulpen, pulpen	Dutch *vulpen*	= fountain pen

Javanese pronunciation

Letter	IPA symbol	Nearest English equivalent
a	/ɑ/	*a*rm; also see text
	/ɒ/	*a*ll (USA); hot (British)
b	/b/	*b*ed; also see text
c	/tʃ/	*ch*at
d	/d̪/	dental d sound, not found in English; also see text
dh	/ɖ/	retroflex d sound, not found in English
e	/ə/	*a*mid, written
è	/ɛ/	f*e*d
é	/e/	d*ay*, but without the i sound, i.e. é is a pure vowel, not a diphthong
g	/g/	*g*o; also see text
h	/h/	*h*oe
i	/i/	w*i*t
j	/dʒ/	*j*udge
k	/k/	s*k*in; also see text
l	/l/	*l*ight; also see text
m	/m/	*m*y
n	/n/	*n*ot
ng	/ŋ/	si*ng*, si*ng*er; not finger
ny	/nj/	ca*ny*on
o	/o/	n*o*, but without the u sound, i.e. o is a pure vowel, not a diphthong
p	/p/	s*p*an
r	/r/	*r*un
s	/s/	*s*it
t	/t̪/	dental t sound, not found in English
th	/ʈ/	retroflex t sound, not found in English
u	/u/	p*oo*l, p*u*ll
w	/w/	*w*it

Additional consonants occur in loanwords: see under **Consonant variations**. When vowels are juxtaposed (**ao**, **au**), they are pronounced separately, not as diphthongs.

3 The é and è are written for syllables that the Javanese consider open and closed, respectively, subject to some rules of vowel harmony (Robson, 1992).

4 In Indonesian, final e with the /e/ quality often alternates with -ai: *ramai/rame, balai/bale.*

5 The two varieties of t and d are genuinely different phonemes, and minimal pairs can be found.

and a v in a loanword may also be rendered as b, as in *piyul* or *biola*, which are alternative renderings of 'violin'.

The name Yogyakarta itself is an exception to normal spelling practice, because the correct spelling for the way it is actually pronounced would be Jogjakarta. The reasons for the inconsistency are obscure. The name is written in numerous other ways, even in current material.

Stress

Javanese is a syllable-timed language. Syllable stress is weaker than in English, usually falling on the penultimate syllable: if that syllable has a *pepet*, the stress moves to the final syllable, as in *peking*.

Older spelling systems

A new spelling system was introduced in 1972 for Indonesian and Javanese:

tj	became	c
dj	became	j
j	became	y
ch	became	kh (in loanwords)
oe	became	u

Further variations will be found in old material, since the use of the Roman alphabet instead of the Javanese script (*aksårå*, see **Appendix 3**) to write Javanese is a relatively recent development. Kunst, for example, writing in the first half of the twentieth century, used a spelling convention very close to the post-1972 system, except that he used ch for c.

Compound words

There is no consistency in the writing of compound words. This will be obvious from the way that names, including names of pieces, vary. For example:

Langengitå; Langen gitå; Langen Gitå; Langen-gitå

Reduplicated words such as *ådå-ådå* can be found in a shorthand form: *ådå*[2]. This practice is officially deprecated but still universal. The reduplicated element may be followed by a suffix, e.g. *ayak*[2]*an*.

Variant forms

Base forms and forms with the suffix *-an* often alternate, without much difference of meaning: e.g. *gembyang cegatan* beside *gembyangan cegat*.

Alternative forms with and without reduplication of the first syllable are not unusual, e.g.

barangan/babarangan; *lagon/lelagon*

Throughout this work, forms separated by a comma or a solidus are alternatives, and parentheses indicate optional elements, e.g.

peking, *saron panerus* = *peking* or *saron panerus*
sekati/sekatèn = *sekati* or *sekatèn*
ladrang(an) = *ladrang* or *ladrangan*

Names of people and places tend to show more variations of spelling than most words. The writing of å as o is particularly frequent—Solo, Purworejo, Mojokerto—but the two variants may coexist. Personal names, being sacred, have often retained their pre-1972 spellings. For all personal names, the owner's own preference, where known, has been followed; for other names, this work tends to follow whichever form seems to be in general use.

Alphabetical sequence

The sequence of entries in the glossary is strictly alphabetical, ignoring spaces and diacritics. So å is treated as a; é, è and e are treated as being the same letter.

Other indexing sequences are used in other dictionaries, especially those published in Java and more or less influenced by the traditional Javanese script: for example, ny and ng may be treated as single letters, all the è-/é- entries may be separated from the e- entries, d and dh may be indexed as the same letter, or all dh- entries may be separate, and so on.

Abbreviations

Various abbreviations for musical terms are in common use, without much standardisation.

ar *arang*
aw *awis*
ay[2]**an** *ayak-ayakan*
bal *balungan*
bb *bonang barung*
bk *bukå*
bp *bonang panerus*
brg *barang*
bub *bubaran*
cbl *ciblon*
ckp *cakepan*
gd *gendhing*
gdh *gendhing*
gend *gendhing*
gr *gérong(an)*
ir *irâmå*
jin *jineman*
kal *kalajengaken*
kas *kaselingan*
k *kendhang(an)*
kd *kendhang(an)*
kendh *kendhang(an)*
ket *ketawang*
ketw *ketawang*
kn *kenong*
kp *kerep*
kr *kerep*
kt *kethuk*
kth *kethuk*
ktp *ketipung, ketampèn*
ktw *ketawang*
lad *ladrang*
ladr *ladrang*
lan *lancaran*
lanc *lancaran*
lc *lancaran*
lcr *lancaran*
ldr *ladrang*
lgm *langgam*
lik *ngelik*
lnc *lancaran*
lr *laras*
m *manyurå*
man *manyurå*
mg *minggah*
m gr *mulai gérong*
mny *manyurå*
mr *mérong*
my *manyurå*
omp *ompak*
pa *putrå*
pal *palaran*
pi *putri*
pl *pélog*
pt *pathet*
SA *sekar ageng*
sengg *senggakan*
SKar *sarjana karawitan*, = degree in *karawitan*
sl *sléndro*
SM *sekar mâcâpat*
srep *srepegan*
ST *sekar tengahan*
sw *suwuk*
swk *suwuk*
ump *umpak*

Glossary

åbå gestural signals performed in rehearsal or in performance to indicate to other musicians the correct pitch, a drum stroke, or the moment for a stroke on the *kethuk*, *kempul*, *kenong* or *gong*.
åbå-åbå = *åbå*.
abdi dalem a servant in the royal palace.
abon-abon short phrases sung by the *pesindhèn* at unstressed positions within a *gendhing* (cf. *sindhènan srambahan*).
ådå, ådhå?, ådhå-ådhå? = *manis rai*.
ådå-ådå **1** a kind of song of the category *sulukan*, sung by a *dhalang* in a *wayang* performance in order to portray a tense atmosphere (*suasånå tegang*) or a critical situation (*keadaan gawat*), accompanied by *gendèr* and *keprak* (or *kepyak*), sometimes punctuated by *kendhang* and *gong*. **2** see *ådå*.
ådångi(y)ah an introductory phrase to a *gendhing*, preceding the *bukå*, which identifies the *pathet* of the *gendhing* to follow.
adat tradition, custom.
adeg-adeg an upright of a *gayor*.
adegan minor scene in *wayang* (cf. *jejeran*).
adegan gapuran *wayang* scene at the gate of the royal palace.
adu manis = *kempyung* (1).
agal = *gagah*.
ageng [*kr*] → *gedhé* [*ng*]
ageng inggil large-sized, describing *wayang kulit* characters of the large *kasar* type.
agung = *ageng*.
ajak-ajak a short pattern played on the *bonang barung* to attract attention before the start of a piece. {= invitation}
åjå ngono a particular vocal melodic pattern and the way in which it is realised on *rebab, gendèr, gambang, celempung, gendèr panerus* and *suling*.
aksårå **1** a written syllable. **2** a letter of an alphabet. **3** the traditional Javanese script. **4** a character of the traditional Javanese script.
alat bubut lathe, used to create the *widheng* around a *pencu*.
alit [*kr*] → *cilik* [*ng*]
alok short vocal phrases, sometimes of indefinite or indeterminate pitch, inserted within a piece (usually by men) to enhance the mood. Examples: *a-é* (*haké*), *lo-lo-lo*, *woi*, etc. {= shout, yell}
alon slow tempo.
alu pestle used in the *lesung*.
alun-alun an open square north or south of the *kraton*.
alus refined, opposite of *kasar*; term describing a category of male dance roles.
alus impur a subcategory of *alus* roles, e.g. Arjunå, Råmå. {= bent-legged refined}
alus kalang kinantang a subcategory of *alus* roles, e.g. Bismå, Wibisånå.
amardåwå lagu (competence in) singing styles; one of the skills of a *dhalang*.
amardi båså (competence in) the different language registers used by *wayang* characters; one of the skills of a *dhalang*.
ambah-ambahan the octave or register in which a melody is set.
Among Beksů (in full, *Bebadan Among Beksů*) the dance teaching department of *Kridhå Mardåwå*.
ampilan dalem regalia; ceremonial objects showing the owner's status.
ancak framework enabling gamelan instruments to be carried on the shoulders of two or four people.
ancer a small dimple at the centre of a *pencu*.
åndhå see *titilaras åndhå*.
andheg division of lines in traditional verse forms; a group of such lines.
andhegan [*ng*] → *kèndelan* [*kr*] **1** stopping but not ending, with reference to *gendhing* in which the gamelan players stop, the *pesindhèn* sings alone briefly, then the musicians resume playing. **2** = *andheg*.
andhegan ageng a major division in verse forms, corresponding to a whole stanza.
andhegan alit one or more *gåtrå* (2) forming a minor division of a verse form.
andhegan gawan an *andhegan* (1) melody in which the text and its melody are used exclusively with one piece.
andhegan gendhing = *andhegan* (1).
andhegan selingan a fixed song, usually from one of the *sekar* poetic forms, inserted into a piece; the remaining gamelan players wait silently until the song is ended, then continue playing the piece.
anggong *kraton* official with the job of arranging gamelan.
anggrèk, angguk **1** a children's singing and dancing game. **2** a type of *rodat*.
ångkå see *nut ångkå, titilaras kepatihan*.
angkatan **1** beginning. **2** transition. **3** lead-in at beginning of a *gåtrå* (2) of *sekar*.
angkat-angkatan **1** section of a *gendhing* (1). **2** a *gendhing* (1) of two movements.
angkatan ciblon **1** the section of a *gendhing* (1) in which the *ciblon* begins to play; or the transition section between *iråmå II* and *iråmå III*. **2** the part played by the *ciblon* to indicate the transition from *iråmå II* to *iråmå III* (Solo).
angkat(an) dhawah the beginning of the *dhawah (inggah)* section or the transition to the *dhawah (inggah)* section from the *mérong* section of a *gendhing*.
angkat(an) inggah = *angkat dhawah*.
angkat(an) minggah = *angkat dhawah*.
angkat(an) munggah = *angkat dhawah*.
angkatan seseg the transition to, or beginning of, the section of a *gendhing* that is played fast (*seseg*).
angkatan sindhèn the point in a *kenongan* at which the *pesindhèn* begins the vocal melody for a particular musical phrase.
angkatan ungguh = *angkat dhawah*.
angkep = *gembyangan*.
angklung **1** a bamboo idiophone, producing a single note when shaken. **2** see *gamelan angklung*.
angkring = *tracak* (1).
antal slow tempo.

åntåwacånå (competence in) the various speaking styles and pitches of the puppets in a *wayang kulit* performance, differentiated by the *dhalang*.

antep heavy (of voice?).

antup bottom end of *gapit*, pointed to allow insertion into banana trunk.

arah nådå melodic direction.

arang [*ng*] → *awis* [*kr*] refers to one possible spacing of the *kethuk* strokes in the *mérong* of a *gendhing*, as marked by '*kethuk 2 (4, 8) arang (awis)*': cf. *kerep*. {= infrequent, widely spaced}

ASKI (*Akademi Seni Karawitan Indonesia*) university-level arts institute in Solo, later renamed STSI; also similar institute at Padang Panjang, Sumatra.

astånå palace.

ASTI (*Akademi Seni Tari Indonesia*) arts institute founded in Yogya in 1963, followed by branches in Denpasar and Bandung: also see *ISI*, *STSI*.

atéla(h) a short jacket worn as part of *pakaian jåwå*.

ater masuk transition (into).

awak part of a *pencu*.

awak-awak the long side of the *pangkon* of a *saron*, etc.

awicaritå competence in the various *lakon* and the dramaturgy of *wayang*; one of the skills of a *dhalang*.

awis [*kr*] → *arang* [*ng*]

ayak-ayakan one of the formal structures of gamelan *gendhing* (1), the least dense of the 'editable' forms.

ayu kuning a melodic pattern heard in *balungan* lines, realised with special patterns on decorating instruments.

babad **1** the skin covering the *menthak* of a *rebab*. **2** chronicle, document.

babarangan = *barangan*.

babon **1** original (gamelan) from which the tuning of a new instrument or gamelan is copied. **2** see *pathet babon*. {*babu* = mother}

badhåyå = *bedhåyå*.

badhong chest ornament of half-moon form, worn by dancers and *wayang kulit* characters.

Badui a type of *rodat* from the Sleman area.

bahiri = *bèri*.

bahu = *bau*.

bait verse couplet.

baku **1** basic, essential. **2** outline, referring to role of punctuating instruments.

baku swårå tonic.

bali balèn to and fro.

balungan **1** the part played by *slenthem*, *saron demung* and/or *saron barung*. **2** one note or beat of the melody played by *slenthem*, *saron demung* and/or *saron barung*. **3** the melody of a composition as usually notated, with register dots. **4** an underlying melody, which may be realised on the *bonang panembung* (Yogya) or implied by the *gendèr/rebab* (Solo). {= skeleton, frame}

balungan dhawah = *balungan nibani*.

balungan gendhing **1** = *balungan* (3). **2** 'inner melody' of a composition.

balunganing gendhing = *balungan* (3) or *balungan* (4)?

balungan kembar a *balungan* with a repeated note in a half-*gåtrå*, e.g.

3 3 5 6

balungan lampah = *balungan mlaku*.

balungan mlaku **1** stepwise *balungan* (3) in which there are no *pin*. **2** stepwise *balungan* (3) in which there may be *pin*, but not at regular intervals as in *balungan nibani*.

balungan mlampah = *balungan mlaku*.

balungan mulur *balungan* (3) with twice density of *balungan mlaku*. {= extended *balungan*}

balungan narancag a fast-moving *balungan* (3).

balungan ndhawahi **1** = *balungan nibani*. **2** *balungan* (3) as in the following example:

. . . $\hat{6}$. 3 5 $\hat{6}$. 5 3 $\hat{2}$. 3 5 ⑥

balungan ngadhal *balungan* (3) in which each *sabetan* (2) contains two or more notes, for example,

$\overline{25}$ $\overline{35}$ $\overline{23}$ 1

{*ngadhal* = crawl like a lizard}

balungan nggantung *balungan* (3) with no melodic motion, in which a single tone is sustained, e.g. 3 3 . .

balungan ngracik a double-density *balungan* (3), e.g. a *gåtrå* (1) consisting of

2 $\bar{3}$ 2 $\dot{1}$ $\underset{\cdot}{6}$ $\bar{1}$ 2 3

balungan nibani *balungan* (3) characterised by alternating ciphers and *pin*, with the *pin* falling on the *dhing*; e.g.

. 5 . 6

balungan pin mundur *balungan* (3) in which there are *pin* at the accented points, for example,

2 . 1 . or 2 . 2 6 or . 3 5 .

balungan plèsèdan *balungan* (3) in which the melodic line of the *sindhèn*, *kenong* or *rebab* part ends on a pitch that is (first) not the *sèlèh* tone, and (second) usually stressed in the succeeding *gatrå*.

balungan rangkep **1** = *balungan kembar*. **2** double-density *balungan*.

balungan tikel double-density *balungan* (3).

bambu bamboo.

bancak doyok theatrical form using two comedians in masks.

bancik drumstand.

bandholan a lively style of *kendhangan*.

bandhul = *mbandhul*.

banggèn **1** a *bonang*-type instrument in *gamelan monggang*, tuned to 6 and grouped with *kenongan* and *penitir*. **2** a *bonang*-type instrument in *gamelan kodhok ngorèk*. **3** see *kethuk banggèn*, *kenong banggèn*.

bangsal hall.

banjaran sari dance drama at Pura Pakualaman, similar to *langen driya*.

bantalan the cloth strip on which the *wilah* of the *gambang* rest.

banyakan **1** a *slenthem* playing style, = *gemakan* (1). **2** = *pinjalan* (1). {*banyak* = goose}

banyol humour; one of the skills of a *dhalang*.

banyolan jokes, joking.

banyu mili style of *gambang* playing almost entirely in octaves, evenly subdivided in fast, regular pulses involving continuous motion in both hands.

bapang **1** a type of dance in strong male style, e.g. for some members of the Kurawa clan. **2** the wide part of a *srenten*, which rests on the *babat*.

bapangan **1** an instrument of the *pencon* type with only its *pencu*, *rai* and *recep* filed to a smooth finish. **2** = *bapang*.

bårå two pieces of cloth with fringes, hanging on both sides of the waist in *wayang wong* costume.

barang **1** one of the tones of the gamelan; in the *kepatihan* system of notation, *sléndro* tone *barang* = 1, *pélog* tone *barang* = 7. **2** see *pathet barang.*

barang alit = i̇

barangan **1** supporting instrumental parts in the gamelan. **2** the *gamelan bebarangan*. **3** itinerant street musicians.

barang miring **1** a tuning that is neither *sléndro* nor *pélog*, sometimes employed by the *rebab*, *pesindhèn*, other vocal parts and possibly the *suling*; said to approach the scale of *pélog barang*, but is played in the context of *sléndro*. **2** a tuning that is basically *sléndro* but is mixed with *pélog* vocal pitch-levels. **3** the name of a *gendhing* (1), i.e. *Barang Miring.*

barat [*in*] West(ern).

baris [*in*] **1** line of dance. **2** line of *tembang*, *palaran*, etc.; = *gåtrå* (2).

barung description applied to instruments pitched in middle register within a family: see *gendèr barung*, *saron barung*, *bonang barung.*

barungan the melodic phrases played by the upper-octave *bonang* of the *gamelan sekatèn* between the strokes of the *balungan* (on *demung*) and/or the lower-octave *bonang (panembung).*

batangan see *kendhang batangan*, *kengsèr batangan.*

bathik (also *batik* [*in*]) dyed textiles produced with wax resist.

bathok(an) = *menthak.*

bau the 'edge', 'rim', 'flange' or turned-over part of a *pencon* instrument.

båwå **1** a vocal composition, usually sung by a male soloist, and longer than *celuk* (2), used as an introduction to a *gendhing* in place of an instrumental *bukå*: the poetic form may be *sekar ageng*, *sekar tengahan*, or *sekar måcåpat*. **2** voice/singing.

båwå suårå a short vocal melody for introducing a *gendhing*: ?= *celuk* (2).

bebarangan = *barangan.*

bebendé = *bendhé.*

bèbèr **1** see *wayang bèbèr.* **2** see *kendhangan bèbèr.*

bebukå = *bukå.*

bedhåyå **1** the most solemn court dance of the palaces of Solo and Yogya, usually performed only on such special occasions as a royal wedding or the anniversary of the coronation of a king, and involving eight or nine female dancers. **2** a dancer in the *bedhåyå* dance.

bedhayan **1** *bedhåyå*-like. **2** the style of vocal music used to accompany *bedhåyå*. **3** see *sindhènan bedhayan.*

bedhèlan a type of *sanggan.*

bedhol songsong a ceremony at the *kraton Yogya* on 2 *Sawal* and 12 *Mulud*, the occasion for a *wayang* performance. {= removal of the parasols}

bedhug a large pegged drum usually suspended from a framework and played with a padded beater, usually only present in some court and ceremonial gamelan; also used in mosques for summoning the faithful.

bégalan = *perang kembang.*

beksa alus dance in the refined male style, sometimes performed by women as well as men, representing characters such as Arjunå, Kresnå and Laksmånå.

beksa gagah dance in the strong male style, representing characters such as Bimå, Rahwånå and Klånå.

beksa kasar ?

beksa(n) [*ki*, *kr?*] → *jogèd* [*ng*] **1** dance in general. **2** classical dance. **3** dance depicting a fight.

beksan golèk a type of solo female dance (Solo and Yogya), representing a young woman dressing up and applying make-up.

bem **1** one of the tones of the *pélog* scale, *bem* = *panunggul* = 1 (in *kepatihan* notation system). **2** a modal classification that groups together *pélog nem* and *pélog limå* (Yogya). **3** a deep-sounding, right-hand stroke on the *kendhang ageng*. **4** the large head of a *kendhang.*

benang string, yarn.

béndhå **1** beater for the gong, *kempul*, *gendèr* or *gambang*. **2** the bulging part of the *kosok*, where it is held.

bendhé a small thick-walled hanging gong used in archaic ensembles such as the *gamelan sekati/sekatèn* of Yogya.

béndrong(an) rhythmic interlocking patterns produced by several people striking a *lesung.*

béngkok **1** ? type of *bonang*. **2** curved part of the 'handle' of the *kemanak.*

bentuk [*in?*] (one of the) formal structures of compositions in *karawitan.*

béragan a low-pitched *gérongan* line sung high.

bère, ?bèré = *bèri.*

bèri **1** a bossless hanging gong. **2** a pair of cymbals beaten with a hard mallet: also see *rojèh* (2).

be(r)lian a durable timber sometimes used for the *wilah* of the *gambang kayu.*

berpathut lima = *patut lima.*

besalèn a hut containing a forge where instruments are made.

besi [*in*] iron, steel (as material for gamelan instruments).

beskab/beskap a short jacket worn at Solo as part of *pakaian jåwå.*

bibaran = *bubaran.*

bilah(an) [*in*] = *wilah.*

bindi, bindhi beater for the *bonang*, *kethuk*, *kempyang* or *kenong*, also sometimes used on *bedhug.*

binggel bracelets, as part of *wayang wong* costume.

blangkon men's headgear made from permanently wound and sewn *bathik* cloth, part of *pakaian jawa.*

blebet the padded ring around the beaters for the *gendèr* and *slenthem.*

bléncong the oil lamp traditionally used to throw the shadows in *wayang kulit.*

blengker the hoop around the head of a *kendhang.*

bléru unintentional changes in gamelan or vocal tunings; out of tune. {= dissonant, inharmonious, false}

blèwèkan the grooves in the top surface of the *srenten*, where the strings sit.

blilu ta(h)u, bliru ta(h)u to learn to play an instrument by listening and imitating; play by ear.

blimbingan see *wilah blimbingan.*

bobat the horsehair of a *kosok.*

bobokan description of a gong with a particularly wide *rai.*

bojåndå åndråwinå feast scene following the final battle in *wayang.*

bokongan ra(m)pèkan style of *kain/dodot* (1) as worn by dancers and puppets representing troops.

bokongan raton style of *kain/dodot* (1) as worn by dancers and puppets representing royalty.

bolong(an) 1 the holes in a *wilah* for the *pluntur*. 2 the holes in the *bau* of a gong, etc., for the *klanthé*. 3 = *nåwå*.
bonang 1 a rack of ten, twelve or fourteen small, horizontally suspended gongs arranged in two rows. 2 = *bonang barung*. 3 a type of Balinese instrument.
bonangan the part played by the *bonang*.
bonangan nglagu 1 a Yogyanese style of *bonang* playing, departing more from the *balungan* notes than standard *mipil baku*. 2 *mipil* patterns on the *bonang* for *balungan nibani*.
bonang barung the mid-range instrument in the *bonang* family.
bonang cacad/cacat a *bonang* in *sléndro* tuning with only 10 pots, i.e. without 1̣ and 2̇. {*cacad* = deficient}
bonang gedhé (*gedhé* [*ng*] → *ageng* [*kr*]) = *bonang barung*.
bonang ilu a three-pot *bonang*.
bonang klénang an archaic *bonang* found in *gamelan monggang* and *gamelan kodhok ngorèk*: see also *kenut* and *klènang*.
bonang nggodhong a *bonang* pot that needs a leaf or a sheet of paper underneath it to produce a satisfactory sound.
bonang panembung 1 the lowest-pitched and largest instrument in the *bonang* family (Yogya). 2 the lower octave of the *bonang* of the *gamelan sekatèn* (Solo).
bonang panerus the highest-pitched and smallest instrument in the *bonang* family.
bonang penerus = *bonang panerus*.
bondhan type of female solo dance representing a mother with her child.
bondhan kejawan a description of a type of gong, with a narrow *bau*.
branggah see *kris branggah*.
bremårå 1 the two holes in the *watangan* of the *rebab*, into which the strings are threaded. 2 = *cakilan* (1), *sindik*. {= bumblebee}
brunjung with a sloping *recep*, giving a high profile, as in the pots of the upper octave of a *bonang* (cf. *dhempok*).
bubaran 1 one of the formal structures of gamelan *gendhing* (1). 2 a piece, typically in *lancaran*, *bubaran*, *ayak-ayakan* or *ladrang* form, used to signal the end of a performance or event. {*bubar* = disperse}
bubat = *bobat*.
bubukå 1 = *bukå*. 2 see *bubukå gendhing*, *bubukå opaq-opaq*.
bubukå gendhing first *gongan* of a *gendhing* (1), including the *låmbå* (1).
bubukå opaq-opaq (Yogya) = *bukå*.
budhalan [*ng*] *wayang* scene representing the departure of the army (also *jengkar* [*ki*]).
budhalan wadyå sabrang [*ng*] *wayang* scene representing the departure of the foreign army.
budheg dead-sounding. {= deaf}
bukå the opening phrase, or introduction, of a *gendhing*.
bukå celuk a *bukå* that is a solo song: also see *celuk*.
bukå gambang a *bukå* that is played on the gambang.
bukå gendèr a *bukå* that is played on the *gendèr*.
bukå kendhang a *bukå* that is played on the *kendhang*.
bukå opak-opak = *bukå*.
bukå rebab a *bukå* that is played on the *rebab*.
bulu-bulu feathers in a *jamang*.
bumbung(an) 1 a resonator made of bamboo or sheet metal, mounted in the frame of an instrument of the *gendèr* family. 2 see *gamelan bumbung*. 3 see *gong bumbung*.
bunderan the disc of metal from which a *pencon* instrument is formed.
buntal garland worn from the waist by dancers.
buntar 1 the end portion of a *wilah* (of *saron*, *slenthem*, *gendèr*, etc.), which is filed in order to tune the *wilah* upwards. 2 the flat part of the *wilah* of the *gong kemodhong*.
buntut an imitation tail used in a monkey costume.
buntut cecak thin part of *kemanak* close to *béngkok*. {= lizard's tail}
buyung = *kendhil grabah*.
byong a 'Turkish crescent' or bell-tree as found in the archaic *gamelan Kodok Ngorèk* of Yogya and Solo.
byur see *rebab byur*.
cagak a leg of a *rancakan*.
cakepan the words of a vocal part.
Cakil monster with prognathous jaw, a type found in *wayang* and dance.
cakilan 1 a short strip of wood or bamboo used to attach the *wilah* of a *gendèr* or *slenthem* to the *pluntur* (= *bremårå* (2), *sindik*). 2 a wooden toggle used to join the *klanthé* of a gong, etc.
cakil(an) rebab a peg on the *popor ngisor* of the *rebab*, around which the strings are fastened.
calapitå 1 = *kemanak*. 2 = *gambang gångså*.
calong 1 = *jublag*. 2 = *gambang*.
calung an instrument consisting of a set of bamboo tubes supported on a frame, and struck by a beater in the same way as a *saron*.
caluri *suling*.
caluring 1 = *suling*. 2 = *celuring*.
campur punctuating instrument found in *gamelan sekatèn* at Yogyakarta, consisting of two hanging gongs (*bendhé*) and having a similar function to *kethuk* and *kempyang*.
campur sari [*in*] (composition or performance in) a mixture of styles.
Cåndrå see *kendhangan Cåndrå*.
cangkem tekèk ? the slit of the *kemanak*.
cangkingan handle (of a *kendhang*).
cangkriman riddle in verse form.
canthèlan 1 a hook from which gongs or *kempul* are hung on a *gayor*. 2 a post from which the *wilah* of the *gong kemodhong* are suspended.
cårå balèn *balèn* [*ng*] → *wangsul* [*kr*] see *gamelan cåråbalèn*.
cårå njåbå performance style outside the *kraton Yogya*.
cårå njero performance style within the *kraton Yogya*.
cårå wangsul *wangsul* [*kr*] → *balèn* [*ng*]
caritå, critå [*ng*] → *cariyos* [*kr*] narration of the *dhalang* without gamelan accompaniment.
cariyos [*kr*] → *caritå* [*ng*]
caruk 1 a Balinese bamboo *gambang*. 2 a form of interlocking pattern played by melody instruments in Sundanese *gamelan saléndro*, etc., similar to *imbal* in central Javanese playing.
ceceg(an) see *neceg*.
cegatan editing of phrases in *srepegan* or *sampak*: also see *gembyangan cegat*.
cekak brief, abridged.

celåndå (cindhé) (silk) trousers worn under *dodot* by male dancers and *wayang* puppets.

celempung a trapezoidal zither.

celuk **1** the giving of a signal, to call. **2** a short vocal introduction to a *gendhing* in which the text is taken from the same poem as that sung within the *gendhing*; may be sung by a male or a female singer.

celuring **1** small cymbals played by striking one hand-cymbal against a cymbal mounted on a frame: same as Balinese *cèng-cèng*. **2** a small *saron* with metal cups in place of *wilah*, used as a substitute for *saron panerus* in a few gamelan (Yogya).

cemengan [*kr*] → *ireng* [*ng*] description of a bronze instrument of *pencon* type (typically *gong ageng* or *gong suwukan*) that is left black instead of being filed smooth.

cempålå **1** a round wooden knocker (*cempålå kayu*) with which the *dhalang* strikes the puppet box to give signals to the gamelan, to punctuate sentences, and to create tension by fast, repeated knocking. **2** a similar metal knocker (*cempålå besi*) used on the *kepyak* for the same purposes. **3** the wooden mallet used to strike the *keprak* (1).

cempurit rods, made of horn, attached to the arms of a *wayang kulit* puppet.

cèng-cèng two small pairs of Balinese cymbals in which one cymbal of each pair is mounted on a wooden frame.

céngkok, cèngkok **1** melodic pattern or formula, often with a name, played by the *gendèr, rebab, gambang, suling* or *celempung*, etc.; sometimes used interchangeably with *wilet*. **2** *gongan*, melodic pattern of one *gongan* duration. **3** style, such as *céngkok Suråbåyå* or *céngkok Cirebon*. **4** a melodic pattern consisting of two *wilet*, i.e. a *padhang* and *ulihan*. **5** = *kosok*. {both spellings are in widespread use, but *céngkok* is arguably the technically correct one}

céngkok gawan **1** *céngkok* that are exclusive to only one *gendhing*. **2** texts that are exclusive to only one *céngkok* in only one *gendhing*.

céngkok mati fixed *céngkok*, unique to one *pathet*.

céngkok miring *céngkok* using *miring* notes.

céngkok rangkep refers to the partial repetition of patterns within *céngkok* when moving from *irååmå III* (*irååmå wilet*) to *irååmå IV* (*irååmå rangkep*).

cenguk a single exclamation such as *'sooooo'* or *'oooo'* inserted in a piece, usually sung by the *gérong*.

centhé **1** a high-pitched *saron* belonging to a village-style *gamelan barut*. **2** = *saron panerus*.

Chevé refers to the *Galin–Paris–Chevé* system of notation that served as the basis for the *kepatihan* system of notation. {Emile Chevé, 1804–1864}

ciblon **1** = *kendhang ciblon*. **2** see *irååmå ciblon*. **3** the section of a piece where the *ciblon* is used. **4** sounds made by slapping water, which inspired *ciblonan*.

ciblonan the lively style of drumming performed on the *kendhang ciblon*.

cilik [*ng*] → *alit* [*kr*] small.

clempung = *celempung*.

cluring = *celuring*.

cokèk(an) **1** perform (music) in the streets. **2** see *gamelan cokèkan*. **3** = *céngkok*.

colokan see *senggakan colokan*.

colongan curtailment of a phrase, e.g. of a *srepegan* in a dance suite, on a signal from the *kendhang* (cf. *cegatan*).

cunduk hair-ornament worn by dancers and *wayang* puppets.

dadi [*ng*] → *dados* [*kr*]

dados [*kr*] → *dadi* [*ng*] **1** *irååmå dados* = *irååmå II*. **2** the section of a *gendhing* that occurs after the tempo has settled and the *saron* part is *mlaku* (Yogya) **3** to continue with another piece of the same formal structure as the preceding piece.

dågå = *sirah* (2).

damar (Bali) = *bléncong*.

damel [*kr*] → *gawé* [*ng*]

danåwå ogre character in *wayang*.

dangdut, dangdhut style of popular music, with influences from mainland Asia, sometimes played in *karawitan* contexts. {from characteristic drum beats}

dasar = *dhasar*.

dawai [*in*] wire, string.

dåyå swårå dominant and/or subdominant tone.

debog = *gedebog*.

deder a piece of steel or wood about 25 cm long inside the *bathokan* of a *rebab*, joining the upper and lower parts of the instrument.

degung see *gamelan degung*.

demung **1** = *saron demung*. **2** = *slenthem gantung*.

demung ageng (*ageng* [*kr*] → *gedhé* [*ng*]) = *saron demung ageng*.

demung gantung = *slenthem*.

demung lantakan = *saron demung lantakan*.

demung pencon = *saron demung ageng*.

derukan a hole in a gong, *wilah*, etc., for the *klanthé* that suspends it.

dhådhå one of the tones of the gamelan scale. In the *kepatihan* system of notation, *dhådhå* = 3.

dhagelan **1** *wayang kulit* puppets representing servants. **2** see *sekar dhagelan*.

dhalang **1** the puppeteer in a *wayang kulit* performance. **2** the person who sings the *suluk* from the *wayang kulit* repertoire while narrating and commenting upon the action of a *wayang orang* performance. **3** one of the ceremonial objects in the royal palace, having the form of a deer.

dhalang jemblung popular theatrical form from Banyumas, using four actor-singers but no gamelan.

dhasar most important note (in a *pathet*, etc.): cf. *tonika*.

dhas-dhasan the top of the *srenten*, where the strings sit.

dhawah [*kr*] → *tibå* [*ng*] **1** the section of a *gendhing* (2) that follows the *dados* section: also see *inggah*. **2** the second section of a *gendhing* (2), in which the melody (*lagu*) is basically the same as in the *mérong* section: this definition contrasts *dhawah* with *inggah* (2). **3** the second section of a *gendhing* (2), in which the first section has two or four *kethuk* per *kenong* and the second section is in *ladrang* form: see also *inggah ladrang*. **4** = *balungan nibani*. **5** to make a transition from a *båwå* to a *gendhing*. {= fall}

dhawahan the playing of the *saron* and *demung* on stressed notes in the *racikan*.

dhawahi = *nibani*.

dhedheg to hammer from outside (for purposes of tuning).

dhempok having a near-flat *recep*, giving a low profile, as in the pots of the lower octave of a *bonang* (cf. *brunjung*).

dhendhå **1** a beater for the *kempul*, gong or *bendhé*. **2** a cross-rail of the *rancakan* of a bonang. **3** = *dhendhan*. **4** the end-piece of a *rancakan* (e.g. of *bonang*).

dhendhan the round wooden post at each end of a *gendèr* frame that holds the ends of the *pluntur*.

dhendhan kijingan an alternative to the usual *dhendhan*, of gravestone shape.

dhenggung part of the title of some *gendhing bonangan*.

dherodhog, dherudhug *dhodhogan* of pattern .tt t.

dhesthar [*ki*] → *ikat* [*ng*]

dhing **1** the least important pitch-level of a given *pathet*. **2** see *dhing-dhong*.

dhing-dhong **1** the stress system of gamelan *gendhing*; *dhing* = unstressed beat, *dhong* = stressed beat. *Dhong* usually falls on the second and fourth beats of a four-beat unit, i.e.

.	.	.	.
dhing	*dhong*	*dhing*	*dhong*
alit	*alit*	*gedhé*	*gedhé*

2 = *dhong-dhing* (1). {*dhong alit/cilik* = small *dhong*; *dhong gedhé/ageng* = large *dhong*}

dhodhog **1** an instrument similar in shape to the *bedhug*, but with a drumhead on only one end. **2** a box (replacing the *kothak wayang*) on which *dhodhogan* are produced in *wayang wong* performances.

dhodhogan sequence of sounds made by the striking of the *cempålå* against the puppet box or *kepyak* by the *dhalang* during a *wayang kulit* or *wayang wong* performance.

dhodhogan nggantèr long *dhodhogan* in triplet rhythm, e.g. introducing an *ådå-ådå*.

dhog the sound made by striking the puppet box with the *cempålå*.

dhompo description of a piece already played in the other *laras*.

dhong **1** the most important pitch-level of a given *pathet*. **2** see *dhing-dhong*.

dhong dhèng dhung dhang dhing **1** mnemonics for the five tones of a *sléndro* or *pélog* scale. **2** = *pupuh* (1).

dhong-dhing **1** the name for the ordering of the vowel sounds in the last syllable of each line of a *sekar tengahan or sekar mâcâpat*: = *guru-lagu*. **2** = *dhing-dhong*. **3** a kind of Balinese musical notation (*upuh dhong-dhing*). **4** the colotomic structure of a *bentuk*.

dhumpal/dhumpul the feet of a *gayor*.

dhundhung sounds made by the *penunthung* drum.

dhuwung [*kr*] → *keris* [*ng*]

dijuluk a method of raising the pitch of an instrument by filing the *buntar* (for *wilah*-type instruments) or the *pencu* (for *pencon* instruments).

DIY *Daerah Istimewa Yogyakarta*, Special Administrative Region around Yogyakarta.

dodot [*kr, ng*] → *kampuh* [*ki*] **1** royal dress, larger than *kain*, worn by officials and by male dancers and *wayang* puppets in some roles. **2** the cloth cover of the *menthak* of a *rebab*, often highly decorated.

dodot kemben breastcloth worn by *bedhåyå* dancers.

dolanan **1** light songs often accompanied by gamelan. Since the song is primary, *dolanan* played by the gamelan often do not conform to one of the regular formal structures of gamelan *gendhing*. **2** children's songs. {*dolan* = play, game}

dongèng story.

drodhog = *dherodhog*.

druta (låyå) fast tempo.

dudu the periphery of a *pencon* instrument where the *recep* joins the *bau*.

dudur the horizontal rail of a *gayor*.

èblèk protective covering for *wayang* puppets in the *kothak*, made from plaited bamboo and cloth.

édan-édanan male and female clowns.

eluk **1** a vocal ornament; a long melisma. **2** a division of a *gendhing* consisting of two *gatrå*. **3** a category of vocal ornaments. {= arc, curve, wave}

embat **1** the raising or lowering of the pitch of the keys of the gamelan instruments, especially with attention to compatibility with voices; the nuances or 'correction' of a tuning system. **2** a comparison of the smallness or largeness of a particular gamelan tuning, the relative tuning of a gamelan or the intervallic structure of a gamelan.

embat alam natural tuning.

embat buatan an artificial tuning.

embat colongan a tuning in which the interval between two neighbouring tones is made smaller or larger according to the desires of the tuner.

embat kodrat = *embat alam*.

embat laras ati **1** a tuning in which the intervals between the tone *dhådhå* (= 3) and its lower neighbour, and between the tone *dhådhå* and its upper neighbour, are widened. **2** a tuning that is 'energetic' and 'lively'. **3** a tuning that is lower than a basic tuning. **4** a *gong ageng* with a higher pitch and a faster *ombak* (Solo).

embat lugu **1** a tuning lacking a clear sequence of larger and smaller intervals. **2** a 'straightforward' tuning.

embat nglaras ati = *embat laras ati*.

embat nyendari **1** a tuning that is higher than a basic tuning. **2** a tuning in which the interval between the tone *dhadhå* (= 3) and the tone *gulu* (= 2) is made smaller, or a tuning in which the interval between the tone *dhådhå* and the tone *limå* (= 5) or *pélog* (= 4) is made smaller. **3** a tuning that gives rise to an unassuming, soft-spoken mood (*råså*). **4** a tuning that is peaceful.

embat nyenggani a tuning that has the characteristic of *senggani*, or 'sounding together'.

embat nyundari = *embat nyendari*.

embat sundari **1** = *embat nyendari*. **2** a *gong ageng* with a lower pitch and slower *ombak*.

empu expert, e.g. *empu karawitan* (= expert on *karawitan*).

enam alternative spelling for *nem*, meaning pitch 6.

endhas [*ng*] → *sirah* [*kr*] = *pencu*.

éndhong a quiver worn on the back.

enem = *enam*.

eneng a folded fragment of banana leaf placed between the two strings of the *rebab* below the bridge, in order to make the sound purer.

ènèng-ènèng = *klénang*.

enges **1** (of music) pleasant, agreeable. **2** (competence in) conveying emotion in *wayang*; one of the skills of a *dhalang*.

engkuk a small gong paired with the *kemong*, another small gong: see *engkuk-kemong*.

engkuk-kemong the two small gongs, *engkuk* and *kemong*, which may hang vertically or be suspended horizontally, and are referred to as a single instrument (found in Solonese gamelan, in *sléndro* only); they have a punctuating function, alternating strokes as do the more common *kempyang* and *kethuk*. Example:

e k e t e k e . e k e t e k e n

where e = *engkuk*; k = *kemong;* t = *kethuk*; n = *kenong*.

engkyèh a *kendhangan I* style for *inggah* of *gendhing*.

ening = *eneng*.

ènjèr(an) **1** the stage of a dance suite covering the preparations for a battle. **2** a duet in *bedhåyå*.

entol a long pole used as a lever in the manufacture of gongs, etc.

èpèk a leather or velvet belt worn by men as part of *pakaian jåwå* and by male dancers.

epos [*in*] epic.

gabahan = *liyepan*.

gadhon = *gamelan gadhon*.

gagah(an) vigorous; description of *wayang* characters and a male dance style.

gagah impur a style of male dance (Yogya) for strong but refined characters, e.g. Prabu Suyudånå, Patih Udåwå: cf. *alus impur*.

gagah kalang kinantang a style of male dance (Yogya and Solo) for strong aggressive characters, e.g. Sutéja, Indrajit: cf. *alus kalang kinantang*.

gagah kalang kinantang råjå a style of male dance (Yogya) for strong aggressive kings, e.g. Bålådéwå, Rahwånå.

gagah kambeng a style of male dance (Yogya and Solo) for strong, honest, tenacious characters, e.g. Åntåréjå, Åntåsénå.

gagrag style (= *céngkok* (3)).

galing one of the ceremonial objects in a royal palace, having the form of a peacock and symbolising authority.

galong see *pathet galong*.

gambang a xylophone with wooden or bamboo keys suspended over a wooden trough: sometimes used interchangeably with *gambang kayu*.

gambang gångså an obsolete instrument like a *gambang kayu* but with bronze keys, now rarely found outside *kraton* ensembles such as *gamelan kodhok ngorèk*.

gambang kayu a *gambang* with wooden keys.

gambang salukat **1** = *celempung*. **2** = *gambang gangså*.

gambang sorogan a *gambang* in *pélog* with interchangeable *wilah* for notes 1 and 7.

gambelan = *gamelan*.

gambyong **1** a type of female solo dance representing a woman adorning herself. **2** a single-row instrument of *bonang* type in ceremonial gamelan.

gambyongan **1** = *gambyong* (1). **2** ? wooden puppet representing a female dancer.

gamelan [*ng*] → *gångså* [*kr*] generic term for ensemble, usually indicating an ensemble with bossed gongs.

gamelan angklung **1** a Balinese ceremonial gamelan consisting of various metallophones, small gongs and occasionally *angklung*; distinguished from other Balinese gamelan by (usually) a four-toned *sléndro*-type scale system. **2** a Sundanese ensemble consisting of several *angklung* (bamboo idiophone).

gamelan arja a Balinese, seven-toned, *pélog* (*saih pitu*) gamelan, which accompanies the dance-drama *arjå*. The gamelan consists of two *suling*, two drums, cymbals and two *guntang* (single-stringed bamboo zither).

gamelan barong landung a form of Balinese *gamelan semar pegulingan* with a five-toned *pélog* (*patut lima*) tuning.

gamelan barut a gamelan made from steel—the *saron* from sheet metal, and the gongs from oil drums.

gamelan batèl the Balinese *gendèr* quartet to which are added several small, horizontally suspended gongs, cymbals and drums when accompanying either a *wayang kulit* or a dance performance of the *Ramayana* epic.

gamelan bebarangan a small itinerant gamelan; street musicians.

gamelan bonang(an) a gamelan that includes *bonang* and *saron* but does not include *gendèr*, *rebab*, *gambang* or *suling*. Contrasts with *gamelan klenèngan* (1) and *gamelan gedhé*.

gamelan bumbung an ensemble of bamboo instruments from central or East Java.

gamelan cangkem the use of voices to imitate gamelan instruments.

gamelan cåråbalèn a type of archaic gamelan found in the palaces of Solo and Yogya with either four or six tones per octave.

gamelan cåråwangsul = *gamelan cårå balèn*. {*wangsul* [*kr*] → *bali* [*ng*]}

gamelan caruk a Balinese ensemble using *caruk* and *saron*.

gamelan cilik a gamelan using small *wilah*-type instruments made from iron.

gamelan cokèk(an) **1** imprecise term used for small gamelan ensembles in central Java, often interchangeable with *gamelan siteran* or *gamelan gadhon*, but usually indicating an itinerant ensemble (cf. *gamelan gadhon*): instrumentation usually includes one or more *siter*. **2** a small gamelan from the Jakarta area, which accompanies *(wayang) cokèk* (or *Ciokek*) performances of Chinese origin (= dance performances similar to *tayuban*). The instrumentation may include a small *gong*, *kenong*, *kethuk*, *siter* and *kendhang*, plus a *gambang*, *suling* and *rebab*, or a *gendèr* and *slenthem*; other sources list *gong kemodhong* or *gong bumbung*, *kendhang batangan*, *siter* and *slenthem* or *gendèr barung*.

gamelan degung a small Sundanese gamelan, which always includes the instrument *degung* (a row of six, small, horizontally suspended gongs) and is characterised by a five-tone-per-octave tuning, which is best regarded as a variant form of *pélog*.

gamelan demung = *gamelan tembung*.

gamelan gadhon a small gamelan without *saron* or *bonang*, often with *gong kemodhong* in place of *gong ageng*, and often having no other punctuating instruments: sometimes used interchangeably with *gamelan cokèkan*, but usually refers to an ensemble with a fixed location.

gamelan gålå ganjur the same as *gamelan kodok ngorèk*, called *gålå ganjur* when the *gendhing Gålå Ganjur* is played.

gamelan gambang a small, ceremonial, Balinese gamelan of four bamboo xylophones and one or two *saron* with a seven-toned *pélog* (*saih pitu*) tuning.

gamelan gambuh a Balinese ensemble with a *saih pitu* tuning (seven-toned *pélog*), which accompanies the dance-drama *gambuh*. The instrumentation includes several very large *suling, rebab, kendhang*, small horizontal gongs and cymbals.

gamelan gedhé (*gedhé* [*ng*] → *ageng* [*kr*]) a gamelan with a full range of instruments in *sléndro* and *pélog*.

gamelan gendèr a Balinese ensemble with a *sléndro* tuning, consisting of two or four *gendèr*, which accompanies *wayang kulit*.

gamelan génggong a Balinese ensemble consisting of jew's harps (*génggong*).

gamelan gong a large, ceremonial, Balinese gamelan consisting of about twenty-five or more instruments, including a *trompong* (large *bonang*). *Gamelan gong* is a five-toned *pélog* gamelan (*patut limå*) in *selisir* tuning.

gamelan gong gedhé = *gamelan gong.*

gamelan grantang a Balinese ensemble of xylophones with keys made from bamboo tubes.

gamelan gumbeng an ensemble of bamboo instruments from the Banyumas area.

gamelan halus classical types of gamelan in Central and East Java and Madura.

gamelan janger a Balinese gamelan consisting of *gendèr*, *suling*, *terbang* and *kendhang*, which accompanies the dance-drama *janger.*

gamelan jegog a Balinese gamelan based on large bamboo instruments, using a four-note scale.

gamelan jemblung a bamboo gamelan found in the border areas between Sunda and Central Java.

gamelan jengglong ensemble used to accompany *wayang jengglong.*

gamelan jogèd = *gamelan rindhik gegandrungan.*

gamelan kålå ganjur = *gamelan gålå ganjur.*

gamelan kasar folk-style gamelan in Central Java and Madura.

gamelan kebyar a large, Balinese, five-toned *pélog* gamelan (*patut limå*) in *selisir* tuning known for its brilliant style of performance.

gamelan kecapi a Sundanese ensemble consisting of two or three *kecapi* and a *rebab* or *suling.*

gamelan klenèngan **1** a large gamelan ensemble that plays without *saron demung* and *saron peking* or *bonang*, in which the *gong suwukan* or *gong kemodhong* may substitute for the large gong. **2** see *klenèngan*. **3** = *gamelan gedhé.*

gamelan klenyitan = *gamelan klenèngan.*

gamelan kliningan a Sundanese gamelan.

gamelan kodhok ngorèk a type of archaic gamelan found in the palaces of Solo and Yogya, which includes only three tones per octave.

gamelan krumpyung a bamboo gamelan from around Wates (south-west of Yogyakarta).

gamelan lengkap = *gamelan gedhé.* {*lengkap* = complete}

gamelan lokanantå **1** = *gamelan monggang.* **2** a mythical gamelan said to have been created in: (a) *c.* 347 AD, consisting of three gongs (Ranggawarsita, *Kitab Jitapsårå*, n.d.); (b) *c.* 235 AD, consisting of *gong, kendhang, kethuk, kenong and kemanak* (Koesoemadilaga, *Pakem Sastramiroeda*, 1930); (c) *c.* 404 AD, instrumentation as in (b) above (Ranggawarsita, *Puståkå Råjå*, 1884–92); (d) *c.* 245 AD, instrumentation as in (b) above (Warsadiningrat, *Wédhå Pradånggå*).

gamelan lokånåtå = *gamelan lokanantå.*

gamelan luang a small, ceremonial, seven-toned *pélog* (*saih pitu*), Balinese gamelan with *gangsa*, *bonang*, *bedhug* and *gong.*

gamelan mardånggå an ancient war gamelan.

gamelan monggang a type of archaic gamelan found in the palaces of Yogya and Solo, which includes only three tones per octave.

gamelan monggang patalon a *gamelan monggang* played in the palace square; = *gamelan patalon.*

gamelan munggang = *gamelan monggang.*

gamelan pakurmatan ceremonial gamelan, i.e. any of *gamelan cåråbalèn*, *gamelan kodhok ngorèk*, *gamelan munggang*, *gamelan sekatèn.*

gamelan patalon an archaic gamelan, either *gamelan monggang, gamelan kodhok ngorèk* or *gamelan cårå balèn*, which plays in the palace square to honour the ruler when he approaches the field to witness sporting events, or to announce the arrival of important personages.

gamelan patigan = *gamelan monggang.*

gamelan patut lima any Balinese gamelan with five tones per octave (*patut limå*).

gamelan pegambuhan = *gamelan gambuh.*

gamelan pelégongan a Balinese gamelan (*patut lima, selisir* tuning) similar to, but larger than, the *gamelan semar pegulingan.*

gamelan penthung = *gamelan jengglong.*

gamelan pèrèrèt = *gamelan serunèn.*

gamelan piano = *gamelan selap.*

gamelan pramuni a gamelan invented in the twentieth century with instruments in the shape of bamboo cylinders.

gamelan puwi-puwi gamelan including a local form of clarinet (*puwi-puwi*), formerly used by Yogya *kraton* guard.

gamelan rèntèng a small Sundanese village ensemble consisting of a *bonang*, a multi-octave *saron* and one or two hanging gongs.

gamelan rindhik gegandrungan a Balinese gamelan (*patut limå*, low *tembung* tuning) modelled on the *gamelan pelégongan* but consisting of only about a dozen players. The keys of all the instruments are made of bamboo and are suspended over bamboo resonators.

gamelan salundhing an old-fashioned Balinese gamelan, of the seven-toned *pélog* (*saih pitu*) type, with large iron keys resting on trough resonators.

gamelan sebarung = *gamelan sepangkon.*

gamelan sekatèn = *gamelan sekati.*

gamelan sekati a kind of *pélog* gamelan played at the *Sekatèn* festival, characterised by the large size of the instruments and by the strong, powerful style of performance.

gamelan selap gamelan (Sunda) using instruments with extra *wilah* to make available more than one scale, possibly a full diatonic scale.

gamelan selisir **1** any Balinese gamelan of the five-toned *pélog* (*patut lima*) type in a high register (*selisir*). **2** one of the modes of the *saih pitu* (seven-toned *pélog*) tuning system.

gamelan selonding = *gamelan salundhing.*

gamelan semara dana a Balinese gamelan with all seven *saih pitu* notes.

gamelan semar pegulingan a Balinese gamelan smaller than the *gamelan gong* and more delicate in sound. It may be either seven-toned *pélog* (*saih pitu*) or five-toned *pélog* (*patut lima*) in a high tuning (*selisir*).

gamelan sengganèn **1** a small gamelan without bossed gongs, having only *wilah* instruments, with the *kenong, kempul, bonang* and *gong* all in a row: the whole ensemble may be packed into a box. **2** a type of gamelan with iron keys. **3** a type of gamelan with glass keys.

gamelan sepangkon a single set of gamelan instruments, in either the *sléndro* or the *pélog* system.

gamelan seprangkat **1** double gamelan; a set of gamelan instruments in both the *sléndro* and the *pélog* tunings. **2** = *gamelan sepangkon.*

gamelan serancak = *gamelan sepangkon.*

gamelan serunai = *gamelan serunèn*.

gamelan serunèn a small gamelan ensemble possibly with only a *kendhang*, *gong* and *kethuk*, but which must include the double-reed instrument *somprèt* (*serompèt/salomprèt/terompèt/serunai*).

gamelan seton = *gamelan Setu*.

gamelan Setu an archaic gamelan, either *gamelan monggang*, *gamelan kodhok ngorèk* or *gamelan cårå balèn*, which plays for special ceremonies on Saturday (*setu*).

gamelan siteran a small ensemble that includes at least one *siter*; e.g. *rebab*, *suling*, up to four sizes of *celempung/siter*, *ciblon*, *gong kemodhong*.

gamelan smårå pegulingan = *gamelan semar pegulingan*.

gamelan somprèt = *gamelan serunèn*.

gamelan srunèn = *gamelan serunèn*.

gamelan sukati Sundanese term for *gamelan sekati*.

gamelan sunarèn any Balinese gamelan of the *patut limå* type tuned to middle frequencies (*sunaren*).

gamelan talu = *gamelan patalon*.

gamelan tembung any Balinese gamelan of the *patut lima* type tuned to lower frequencies (*tembung*).

gamelan tètèt = *gamelan serunèn*.

gamelan wayangan **1** a *sléndro* gamelan used to accompany *wayang kulit purwå*, consisting of (for example) *rebab*, *gendèr barung*, *gendèr panerus*, *gambang*, *saron wayangan*, *demung*, *slenthem*, *peking*, *kecèr*, *suling*, *kenong* (3 pots), *kethuk*, *kempul* (3 gongs), *gong suwukan*, *gong ageng* and *kendhang wayangan*. **2** a *pélog* gamelan used to accompany *wayang gedhog*.

gancaran **1** fluent, moving quickly. **2** pace, flow. **3** to paraphrase poetry into prose or to read poetry without singing. **4** a *gendhing* (1) such as *Gangsaran* from the *gamelan cårå balèn* repertoire with pitch 2 added and played continuously by the *saron*.

gandhangan = *kidungan*.

gandhèn beater for the *saron* or *demung*.

gandhul **1** to delay, lag behind. **2** see *pencon gandhul*.

gandrung **1** dance representing a lovesick hero. **2** see *kendhangan Gandrung-Gandrung*.

gångså **1** bronze. **2** (*gangsa*) a Balinese gamelan instrument similar to a Javanese *gendèr*. **3** [*kr*] → *gamelan* [*ng*]

gangsaran one of the formal structures of gamelan *gendhing*, involving a one-note ostinato section usually with transitions to and from pieces in other *bentuk*.

ganjur the core (ostinato) section of a *gangsaran*.

gantungan see *gåtrå gantungan* and *balungan nggantung*.

gapit rod, made from horn, split at the top to be attached to a *wayang kulit* puppet.

gårå-gårå opening of the second section of a *wayang* performance, in which the hero retires to the forest to meditate; includes a clown scene. {= turbulence in the realm of nature}

garap(an) **1** way of working or fashioning; specifically the way in which an instrumental part realises the *balungan* or the 'inner melody'. **2** the creation of melodies (*wilet*) on the *gambang*, *gendèr*, *rebab*, or other elaborating instrument.

garebeg any of the three principal religious festivals celebrated at the *kraton*: *Garebeg Maulud/Mulud* (= birthday of Muhammad), *Garebeg Besar* (= *Idul Adha*, *Idul Korban*) and *Garebeg Puasa/Påså* (= *Idul Fitri*, *Lebaran*).

garingan a dance rehearsal without accompaniment.

garo = *kempyang* (4).

garudhå mungkur a decorative motif used in clothing.

gati a piece in *ladrang* form and *laras pélog*, featuring some Western instruments and commonly used as an entry or exit piece in Yogya-style *srimpi* or *bedhåyå* accompaniments.

gåtrå **1** a metrical unit of gamelan *gendhing* (1), consisting of four *sabetan* (or beats), usually manifested as strokes of the *saron*. **2** a single line of verse in a *sekar måcåpat*. {= embryo}

gåtrå dhélik a *gåtrå* in which the melodic line makes a large upward jump. {from *gedhé* = low-pitched, *cilik* = high-pitched}

gåtrå gantung(an) (also see *balungan nggantung*) a *gåtrå* in which the melodic line remains on the same note, shown in *balungan* notation by (for example)

. . . . or 6 6 . . or . . 6 .

{*gantung* = hanging}

gåtrå mlaku see *balungan mlaku*.

gåtrå nibani see *balungan nibani*.

gawan a term used in vocal music to indicate that a particular *céngkok*, *andhegan* or text is restricted in its use; e.g. *andhegan gawan*, *sindhènan gawan*.

gawang dhalang the key players supporting a *dhalang*; the *kendhang* and *gendèr barung* players, perhaps also the *rebab* player.

gawan gendhing texts that are exclusive to only one *gendhing*.

gawé [*ng*] → *damel* [*kr*] the off-beat part in *imbal demung* or *imbal saron* (cf. *ngedhongi*, *nginthil*).

gaya [*in*] style, e.g. regional style (*gaya Yogya*, *gaya Solo*).

gayaman see *kris gayaman*.

gayor **1** the wooden frame for hanging the *kempul*, *gong suwukan* and *gong ageng*. **2** the hook on which the *klanthé* of a gong, *kempul*, etc., is hung.

gebing(an) *wayang kulit* puppet before being given the details that determine its character.

gecul see *gendhing gecul*.

gedebog banana trunk, into which *wayang kulit* puppets are inserted.

gedhé [*ng*] → *ageng* [*kr*] large.

gedhog **1** see *wayang gedhog*. **2** = *dhodhogan*.

gegel joint between upper and lower arm of a *wayang kulit* puppet.

gegelan grooves surrounding the upright of a *gayor*.

geger gajah the back part of a *kemanak*.

gegesan **1** the part of the *bau* adjacent to the *lambé* on a *pencon* instrument. **2** the end of a *wilah* on the *gong kemodhong*.

géjog(an) = *béndrongan*.

gelang bracelet worn by dancers and *wayang* puppets.

gelombang [*in*] = *ombak*.

gelung(an) [*ng, kr*] → *ukel* [*ki*] **1** the carved scrolls on the ends of the frames of the *saron* family; also the same style of carving used on the frames of *gendèr*, *slenthem*, etc., in some *kraton* gamelan. **2** hair curl pointing forward from the back of the head, worn by male dancers and *wayang* puppets. {*gelung* = hair knot, chignon}

gelung bokor hair style worn by female dancers in *wayang wong*.

gelung keling hair bun, worn by *wayang* puppets.

gelung tekuk = *sanggul.*

gemakan **1** *slenthem* playing style in which the instrument plays each note of a *balungan nibani* on the preceding three half-beats. **2** = *pinjalan* (1). **3** the combination of *gemakan* (1) in *ir II* and *mbandhul* in *ir I*.

gembrotan (Yogya) = *cokèkan.*

gembyakan see *kendhang gembyakan.*

gembyang **1** an interval separated by four keys on the *gendèr.* **2** an octave.

gembyangan **1** a *bonang* technique involving octave playing. **2** an octave.

gembyang(an) cegat(an) a type of *gembyangan* playing on *bonang*, falling on the off-beats. {*cegat* = block the way, lie in wait for}

gembyang(an) dados a type of *gembyangan* playing on *bonang*, as in the following example:

balungan 6 6 . .

bonang barung $\underline{6}$ $\underline{6}$

6̣ 6̣ 6̣ . 6̣ 6̣ . .

gembyang(an) låmbå **1** a type of *gembyangan* playing on *bonang*, as in the following example:

balungan 6 6

bonang barung $\underline{6}$

6̣ 6̣ 6̣ .

2 (Yogya) = *gembyangan pidak.*

gembyang(an) lancaran = *gembyangan cegat.*

gembyang(an) midak = *gembyangan pidak.*

gembyang(an) minjal = *gembyangan cegat.*

gembyang(an) nyegat = *gembyangan cegat.*

gembyang(an) nitir **1** a type of *gembyangan* playing on *bonang* in Yogya style, where the *gembyang* notes have a characteristic off-beat pattern. **2** (Yogya) a type of long *gembyangan* on *bonang*, used in a *mipil nglagu* context.

gembyang(an) pidak a type of *gembyangan* playing on *bonang* in Yogya style, where the *gembyang* notes alternate with single notes.

gembyang(an) pinjal = *gembyangan cegat.*

gembyang(an) rangkep a type of *gembyangan* playing on *bonang*, as in the following example:

balungan 6 6

bonang barung $\underline{6}$ $\underline{6}$

6̣ 6̣ 6̣ . 6̣ 6̣ . .

gembyang(an) rangkep nikeli a type of *gembyangan* playing on *bonang*, as in the following example:

balungan 6 6

bonang barung $\underline{6}$ $\underline{6}$ $\underline{6}$ $\underline{6}$

6̣ 6̣ 6̣ . 6̣ 6̣ . . 6̣ 6̣ 6̣ . 6̣ 6̣ . .

gembyang(an) sarug/saruk a type of *gembyangan* playing on *bonang* in Yogya style, where the *gembyang* notes are preceded by one or more adjacent notes. {*sarug* = drag the foot}

gembyang(an) sekaran = *gembyangan sarug.*

gembyangan tunggal (Yogya) = *gembyangan cegat.*

gembyung **1** an interval separated by one key of the *gendèr*, e.g. 2–5. **2** the playing of 6̣ in addition to 2̣ or 3̣ on the *bonang.* **3** the playing of 6̣ in addition to 3̣ on the *bonang* (cf. *kempyung*).

gembyungan = *gembyung* (2).

gendèr **1** an instrument with thin bronze or brass keys, each suspended over a tube resonator. **2** *gendèr barung.*

gendèran **1** technique or style of playing the *gendèr.* **2** an ensemble of *gendèr barung*, *gendèr panerus*, *gambang*, *suling*, *gong kemodhong* and *kendhang.*

gendèran låmbå lower-density playing style for *gendèr barung*, used in *céngkok* of *lampah* 2 and *lampah* 4 form.

gendèran rangkep higher-density playing style for *gendèr barung*, used in *céngkok* of *lampah* 8 form.

gendèr barang a *pélog gendèr* tuned to pitch-levels 2, 3, 5, 6 and 7.

gendèr barung the middle-sized *gendèr*, usually referred to simply as *gendèr.*

gendèr barut simple *gendèr* used in itinerant ensembles (see *ngamèn* (1)).

gendèr bem = *gendèr nem.*

gendèr gedhé (*gedhé* [*ng*] → *ageng* [*kr*]) = *gendèr barung.*

gendèr giying a ten-keyed Balinese *gendèr*, larger than the *gendèr pamadé.*

gendèr kantil the smallest Balinese one-octave *gendèr.*

gendèr nem a *pélog gendèr* tuned to the pitch-levels 1, 2, 3, 5 and 6.

gendèr pamadé a ten-keyed Balinese *gendèr.*

gendèr panembung (Yogya) = *slenthem (gantung).*

gendèr panerus the smallest, highest-pitched *gendèr.*

gendèr penerus = *gendèr panerus.*

gendèr rambat fourteen- or fifteen-keyed *gendèr*, leader of the *gamelan semar pegulingan.*

gendhèng **1** songs accompanied by gamelan. **2** vocal music.

gendhing **1** a generic term for any gamelan composition. **2** the designation of a class of formal structures characterised by relatively greater length (minimum *kethuk 2 kerep*) and the absence of *kempul.* **3** the section of a large piece which follows the *mérong.* **4** tunes that have *irâmå*, for example, *gendhing terbang.* **5** gamelan maker. **6** instrumental music as opposed to vocal music (*gendhèng*). **7** = *kemanak.* **8** = *rebab.* **9** = gamelan.

gendhing ageng (*ageng* [*kr*] → *gedhé* [*ng*]) gamelan pieces with long *gongan* such as those with the formal structures *kethuk 16 kerepan* (*minggah*), *kethuk 8 kerep*, *kethuk 8 awis* (?) and *kethuk 4 awis. Gendhing ageng* are part of a tripartite category, which also includes *gendhing tengahan* and *gendhing alit.* {= large *gendhing*}

gendhing alit (*alit* [*kr*] → *cilik* [*ng*]) gamelan pieces with relatively short *gongan* such as the formal structures *kethuk 2 kerepan* (*ladrang* and *ketawang*) and *kethuk 2 kerep.* {= small *gendhing*}

gendhing bandholan *gendhing* (2) with three or five *kenongan.*

gendhing banyolan *gendhing* (1) in light style with *gembyakan* drumming.

gendhing beksan pieces used for dance accompaniment.

gendhing bonang(an) **1** any *gendhing* (1) in which the introduction is played on the *bonang* and the *gendhing* is played in loud style (Solo): see also *gendhing soran.* **2** *gendhing tengahan* and *gendhing ageng* in which the *bonang* plays the introduction, the *bonang* is the principal melodic instrument, and the *rebab*, *gendèr*, *celempung*, *suling* and *gambang* do not play.

gendhing cilik (*cilik* [*ng*] → *alit* [*kr*]) = *gendhing alit.*

gendhing dhårå = *gendhing tengahan.*

gendhing dolanan see *dolanan.*

gendhing gagah = *gendhing sabetan.*
gendhing gambang *gendhing* in which the *buka* is played on the *gambang.*
gendhing gecul *gendhing* that are light or humorous in character.
gendhing gedhé (*gedhé* [*ng*] → *ageng* [*kr*]) = *gendhing ageng.*
gendhing gendèr *gendhing* in which the *buka* is played on the *gendèr barung.*
gendhing geréjå *gendhing* composed for Christian church services.
gendhing gérong(an) *gendhing* based upon a vocal form and including a *gérong.*
gendhing gobyog pieces of a cheerful character.
gendhing jangkep ? *gendhing* with *inggah kendhang.*
gendhing jejer a piece used to accompany the first scene in a *wayang* performance.
gendhing kadhatonan a piece used to accompany a scene in the royal palace where the king meets his consort.
gendhing kapalan a piece used to accompany a scene of soldiers riding out to battle.
gendhing kemanak vocal pieces played with a few gamelan instruments (*kemanak*, *kethuk*, *kendhang*, *kenong* and *gong*) to accompany *bedhåyå* and *srimpi* dances; not necessarily in *gendhing* (2) form; can also be *ladrang* or *ketawang (alit).*
gendhing kendhang *gendhing* in which the *buka* is played by the *kendhang*, i.e. pieces of the categories *playon, sampak, srepegan, ayak-ayakan, gendhing cårå balèn, gendhing monggang* and *gendhing kodhok ngorèk.*
gendhing ketawang = *ketawang gendhing.*
gendhing kethuk-kenong = *gendhing kemanak.*
gendhing klenèngan pieces typically performed in *klenèngan* sessions.
gendhing lampah(an) (Yogya term) formal structures that can be edited to length on command from the *dhalang* or *kendhangan*, i.e. *ayak-ayakan*, *srepegan*, *kemudå*, *playon*, *sampak.*
gendhing lancaran = *lancaran.*
gendhing lésan vocal pieces accompanied by gamelan.
gendhing mares = *gati.*
gendhing monggangan *gendhing* with the same formal or melodic structure as *gendhing monggang.*
gendhing pakurmatan compositions performed on ceremonial gamelan.
gendhing pamijèn **1** *gendhing* that do not conform to the usual gamelan formal structures, e.g. a *gongan* with only three *kenongan.* **2** *gendhing* in regular formal structure with a non-standard *kendhang* part.
gendhing panembråmå = *panembråmå.*
gendhing parikan = *gendhing tlèdhèk.*
gendhing penutup closing piece.
gendhing prenès *gendhing* that include an *inggah* with *ciblon* drumming and are lighthearted in character.
gendhing rebab *gendhing* in which the *bukå* is played on the *rebab.*
gendhing sabetan loud-style *gendhing.*
gendhing sabrangan **1** a piece used to accompany a scene for a foreign king. **2** = *gati*, *mares.*
gendhing sedhengan = *gendhing tengahan.*
gendhing sekar compositions, e.g. *ketawang*, with melodies derived from traditional *sekar.*
gendhing sindhèn **1** *gendhing* based upon a vocal form in which the *bukå* is sung by the *pesindhèn.* **2** *gendhing* in which the *pesindhèn* has a major role, originally without *gérong.*
gendhing soran a loud-style gamelan piece (Yogya): see also *gendhing bonang.*
gendhing talu *gendhing* that are played before a *wayang kulit* performance.
gendhing tengahan gamelan pieces with *gongan* of medium size such as the formal structures *kethuk 8 kerepan* (*minggah*), *kethuk 4 kerep* and *kethuk 2 awis*: see *gendhing ageng* and *gendhing alit.* {= middle-sized *gendhing*}
gendhing thuthuk **1** gamelan *gendhing* based upon an instrumental idiom as opposed to *gendhing* based upon vocal melodies. **2** gamelan *gendhing* played exclusively by percussive instruments, thus without *rebab* or *suling.* {= struck *gendhing*}
gendhing tlèdhèk(an) **1** a repertoire of *gendhing*, which formerly accompanied the dancing of the *tlèdhèk*, featuring the *sindhèn* melody and often composed of non-standard *gongan* structures. **2** any *gendhing* arranged in the style used for the accompaniment of a *tlèdhèk* dancer, often including *gendhing* with closely spaced and irregular *kempul*, *kethuk* and *kenong* strokes and special *kendhang* patterns.
gendhing wayangan a piece usually used to accompany a *wayang kulit* performance.
gendhuk kuning the name of a *gendèr* melodic pattern.
genjring an instrument similar in shape to a small *terbang*, with attached jingles; = tambourine.
genthå prayer bell.
genthong = *kendhil grabah.*
gentorag rod with small bronze bells attached in concentric circles: also called 'bell-tree' or 'Turkish crescent' (cf. *byong*); found in certain archaic Javanese gamelan (*kodhok ngorèk*) and in some Balinese gamelan (*pelégongan*).
genukan (Yogya term from *pedhalangan*) = *grimingan.*
gerantung a type of drum made from bamboo.
gérong **1** a unison male chorus that sings with a gamelan. **2** a mixed chorus that sings with a gamelan in certain types of piece.
gérongan the part sung by the *gérong.*
gérong mbalung = *gérong milah.*
gérong milah *gérongan* that is nearly identical to the *balungan* melody.
gérong putrå-putri a mixed chorus.
gesang [*kr*] → *urip* [*ng*] **1** a change of gamelan playing style, from soft to loud. **2** description of a type of *imbal demung* with a note played on the *sèlèh* note (cf. *pejah*). {= alive, lively}
geter(an) **1** a type of double stroke on the *bonang* in Yogya-style *mipil.* **2** a (?mainly Yogyanese) *gambang* playing style involving quick repetition of notes. **3** ?vocal vibrato. {= tremble}
gilapan a description of an instrument of the *pencon* type that has been filed smooth all over on the outside.
ginem dialogue delivered by a *dhalang.*
gineman = *pathetan* (1).
gladhi a rehearsal, e.g. for traditional dance.
gladhi resik a dress rehearsal.
glebeg Yogyanese *gambang* playing style involving damping.
gobyog(an) (?mainly Yogya) a replacement section, with a livelier style of *garap*, inserted into certain pieces.

godhagan interval.
godhègan the decorative brackets at the top of the uprights of a *gayor.*
golèk **1** see *beksan golèk*. **2** see *wayang golèk*.
gong **1** a generic term for any kind of vertically or horizontally suspended gong. **2** the largest gong in the gamelan (*gong ageng*). **3** a (Balinese) gamelan that uses a large hanging gong.
gong ageng (*ageng* [*kr*] → *gedhé* [*ng*]) = *gong gedhé*.
gongan a formal structure marked at the end by a stroke on a hanging gong, *gong ageng*, *gong siyem*, or *kempul* (as in *sampak* and *srepegan*).
gong angklung **1** a Balinese *gamelan angklung*. **2** a Javanese *angklung* ensemble. **3** a single bamboo instrument that functions as a gong: also called *gong bumbung*.
gong bambu = *gong bumbung*.
gong bèri an instrument of gong form but without a *pencu*.
gong bukå the gong stroke at the end of the *bukå*.
gong bumbung a wind instrument functioning as a substitute for a *gong ageng*, and consisting of a small bamboo tube inside a large one.
gong dhudhuk = *gong kemodhong*.
gong gedhé (*gedhé* [*ng*] → *ageng* [*kr*]) the largest hanging gong.
gong gendul a *gong bumbung* substitute made from an empty liquor bottle. {*gendul* = bottle}
gong kemådhå = *gong kemodhong*.
gong kemodhå = *gong kemodhong*.
gong kemodhong an instrument with two large keys, often with a raised boss in the centre, suspended over a resonator box, sometimes used as a substitute for the *gong ageng*, e.g. in a *gamelan gadhon*.
gong salahan a gong played where normally no gong is expected, e.g. to reinforce the melodic line.
gong siyem **1** = *gong suwukan*. **2** a type of *gong suwukan*.
gong suwuk(an) **1** a large hanging gong, smaller than *gong ageng*, larger than *kempul*. **2** the final gong stroke of a piece.
gosokan = *kosokan*.
goyang see *kenong goyang*.
grambyangan **1** a melodic unit indicating the *pathet*, played by the *gendèr* or *bonang* to alert the players before the beginning of a piece. **2** a melodic unit indicating the *pathet* played by the *gendèr* to accompany the talking of a *dhalang*. **3** a melodic unit, indicating the *pathet*, played by the *bonang* preceding the *racikan* (opening section) in *gendhing* from the repertoire of *gamelan sekati*. **4** = *grimingan*.
grambyangan jugag short *grambyangan*.
grambyangan wantah long *grambyangan*, the usual or normal form.
grantang **1** bamboo *gambang*. **2** *rebab*.
gregel **1** a vocal ornament of short duration like a Western turn or mordent. **2** generic term for various vocal ornaments.
greget tension, drive, energy.
grimingan a style of rapid, non-metric, *gendèr* playing used in a *wayang kulit* performance to indicate pitch and *pathet* register to the *dhalang* and to create a tense atmosphere.
grit frame drum (*terbang*) struck with a mallet.
grobogan **1** the wooden frame of the *gendèr barung, gendèr panerus* and *slenthem*; also the wooden frame enclosing the resonator of a *gong kemodhong*. **2** a box-like resonator, the wooden frame of the *gambang*.
grompolan ear ornament (?of circular form) worn by dancers.
grontolan **1** = *geter* (2). **2** type of irregular rhythm used in *gendèran*.
gropak see *irâmå gropak*.
grup [*in*] group.
gubahan (thin) part of *gapit* of a *wayang kulit* puppet, where the horn (originally bent double) was straightened out.
gubar **1** bossless gong. **2** medium-sized gong.
guci = *kendhil grabah*.
gulu **1** one of the tones of the gamelan scale, notated 2 in the *kepatihan* system. **2** the narrow part of the *srenten* between the *dhas-dhasan* and the *bapang*. {= neck}
gumbeng see *gamelan gumbeng*.
gunungan **1** = *kayon*. **2** heap of rice distributed at *kraton* festivals. {*gunung* = mountain}
gupek the smaller of the two drums in a Balinese *gamelan gong*.
gurnang an instrument like a *kenong* but suspended by a cord like a *bendhé*, a kind of *penonthong*.
guru **1** the stressed position in gamelan *gendhing* and *kakawin* poetry: alternates with *lagu*, unstressed position. **2** the equivalent of *dhong*, stressed position in *gendhing,* which alternates with *dhing*, unstressed position: see *dhing-dhong*.
guru-lag(h)u **1** the pattern of final syllables of each line in the forms *sekar tengahan* and *sekar mâcåpat*: = *dhong-dhing*. **2** the stress pattern of a line of verse.
guru wilangan the total number of syllables of a line of verse.
gusèn crude, as description of *wayang* characters.
guyon joke.
halus = *alus*.
hésthåkawåcå gendhing the rhythmic pattern of a piece in the context of dance, especially the pattern of *kethuk*, *kenong* and gong in Solonese dance style.
ikat, iket [*ng*] → *dhesthar/udheng* [*ki*] a headcloth worn by men; hand-wound (cf. *blangkon*).
imbal a style of playing in which two identical or similar instruments, or two players on the same instrument, or two hands on one instrument, play interlocking parts forming a single more or less repetitive melodic pattern.
imbal bonang *imbal* playing that is shared between *bonang barung* and *bonang panerus*.
imbal dados the medium-density *imbal demung* pattern, typically used for *irâmå I* and *irâmå II*.
imbal demung *imbal* playing that is shared between two *saron demung* or two players on the same *demung*.
imbal-imbalan = *imbal*.
imbal klénangan a style of *imbal bonang* that is used in *gamelan cårå balèn* and *gangsaran*.
imbal kodhokan **1** a style of *imbal bonang* optionally used by *bonang panerus* of *cacad* form in *sléndro sångå*. **2** *bonang imbal* in which the *bonang barung* part coincides in pitch with the *sèlèh* note.

imbal låmbå the least dense *imbal demung* pattern, typically used for *irâmâ I* and *irâmâ II*.
imbal lugu the simplest style of *imbal demung* (cf. *imbal sekaran*).
imbal ngepok a type of *imbal demung*.
imbal rangkep the densest *imbal demung* pattern, for *irâmâ II*.
imbal saron *imbal* playing that is shared between two *saron* or two players on the same *saron*.
imbal sekaran a more complex version of *imbal demung* (cf. *imbal lugu*).
imbal Surabayan a style of *imbal bonang* popular in East Java (Surabaya).
inggah [*kr*] → *unggah* [*ng*] **1** the section of a *gendhing* that follows a *mérong* and has the form *kethuk* 4 or 8 or 16 *kerepan*: also see *dhawah*, *inggah ketawang* and *inggah ladrang*. **2** the section of a *gendhing* that follows a *mérong* and has a basic melody (*lagu*) that differs from the *mérong*. **3** (Yogya term) indicating a transition to a piece in shorter form (*ladrang* or *ketawang*) after the *ndhawah* section of a *gendhing*.
inggah gendhing **1** an *inggah* section in which the basic melody (*lagu*) differs from the *lagu* of the *mérong*. **2** an *inggah* section that has twice as many *kethuk* per *kenong* as the preceding *mérong*.
inggah-inggahan **1** = *inggah*. **2** an *inggah* section of a *gendhing* that is in *ladrang* or *ketawang* form and consists of an *umpak* and a *ngelik*.
inggah kendhang **1** an *inggah* section of a *gendhing* that has the same basic melody (*lagu*) as the preceding *mérong*. **2** an *inggah* section in which the *saron* melody is an abstraction of the *saron* melody of the *mérong*. **3** an *inggah* section in *ir II* (followed by an *inggah* section in *ir III*).
inggah ketawang(an) an *inggah* section of a *gendhing* that has the formal structure of a *ketawang*.
inggah ladrang(an) an *inggah* section of a *gendhing* that has the formal structure of a *ladrang*.
instrumèn garap elaborating instrument(s).
instrumèn mukå soft-style elaborating instrument(s). {= front-row instrument(s)}
instrumèn rerenggå embellishing instrument(s).
irah-arahan the decorative part of the neck of a *rebab* above the *watangan* and below the *menur*.
irâmâ **1** tempo, also known as *lâyâ*. **2** rhythm. **3** refers to the different tempo relationships within a *gongan* or *gendhing*: *irâmâ* is the expanding and contracting of structural units such as the *gatrâ* and the degree or level at which the *gâtrâ* is subdivided (or filled in). A *gongan* in *irâmâ I* takes approximately half the time to perform as a *gongan* in *irâmâ II*. Each change in *irâmâ* either expands by two the time of the preceding *irâmâ* level (*irâmâ I* to *irâmâ II*) or contracts by one-half the time of the succeeding *irâmâ* level (*irâmâ II* to *irâmâ I*). The degree of subdivision can be measured according to the number of strokes on the *saron panerus* to one *sabetan* (beat) of the *balungan* (in usual Solo style). The table below illustrates this and provides the common terms for the different levels of *irâmâ*: see also *irâmâ gropak*.

Irâmâ level	*Irâmâ* name	*Peking* strokes per *sabetan*	Also called
	gropak	½	*irâmâ* 2/1
½	*lancar*	1	*irâmâ* 1/1
I	*tanggung*	2	*irâmâ* 1/2
II	*dados*	4	*irâmâ* 1/4
III	*wilet*	8	*irâmâ* 1/8
IV	*rangkep*	16	*irâmâ* 1/16

irâmâ ciblon = *irâmâ wilet*.
irâmâ dadi (*dadi* [*ng*] → *dados* [*kr*]) = *irâmâ dados*.
irâmâ dados (*dados* [*kr*] → *dadi* [*ng*]) = *irâmâ II*; see *irâmâ* (3).
irâmâ ditugal = *irâmâ mlumpat*.
irâmâ gropak **1** an *irâmâ* (3) even faster than *irâmâ lancar*. **2** the fastest *irâmâ*.
irâmâ kalih = *irâmâ dados*.
irâmâ kenceng **1** a type of fast drumming used in *irâmâ rangkep*. **2** a fast tempo suitable for accompanying *wayang* and dance (cf. *irâmâ kendho*, *irâmâ sedheng*).
irâmâ kendho a relaxed tempo suitable for *klenèngan* (cf. *irâmâ kenceng*, *irâmâ sedheng*).
irâmâ lâmbâ fast *irâmâ*; = *irâmâ tanggung*.
irâmâ lancar *irâmâ* ½; see *irâmâ* (3). {*lancar* = swift}
irâmâ lancaran = *irâmâ lancar*.
irâmâ mlumpat the skipping over of one of the levels of *irâmâ* (3), e.g. moving from *irâmâ III* to *irâmâ I*: also known as *irâmâ ditugal*.
irâmâ mulur = *irâmâ wilet*.
irâmâ papat = *irâmâ rangkep*.
irâmâ rangkep **1** *irâmâ IV*: see *irâmâ* (3). **2** any *irâmâ* (3) where the density of decoration is doubled and the *balungan* speed is nearly halved. **3** (in *palaran*) = *ir I*. {*rangkep* = double}
irâmâ sabetan fast tempo; = *ir I*.
irâmâ sedheng a moderate tempo (cf. *irâmâ kenceng*, *irâmâ kendho*).
irâmâ seseg **1** = *irâmâ gropak*. **2** = *irâmâ lancar*. **3** = fast *irâmâ* (cf. *irâmâ tamban*).
irâmâ tamban slow *irâmâ*.
irâmâ tanggung *irâmâ I*; see *irâmâ* (3). {*tanggung* = intermediate, neither one thing nor the other}
irâmâ telu = *irâmâ wilet*.
irâmâ tikel = *irâmâ wilet*.
irâmâ wilet *irâmâ III*; see *irâmâ* (3).
irâmâ wilet rangkep = *irâmâ rangkep*.
ireng [*ng*] → *cemengan* [*kr*]
iringan accompaniment, e.g. *iringan tari* dance accompaniment.
irung-irungan **1** the top end of the *watangan* where it is attached to the *irah-irahan*, and containing the *bremårå*. **2** the edge against which the player's breath is directed in a *suling*.
isèn-isèn **1** = *abon-abon*. **2** parts played by elaborating instruments. **3** filling-in, referring to the functions of melodic instruments (cf. *baku*).
isèn-isèn balungan short phrase played by *balungan* instruments leading to an important note at the start of *palaran/rambangan*.
ISI (*Institut Seni Indonesia*) arts institutes at Yogyakarta, successor to ASTI, and at Denpasar, successor to STSI.
istana [*in*] palace.
istri = *lårånangis*.
iwak-iwakan the bend in a *kosok*, at the end away from the hand.

jågrå the frame on which a *bedhug* is hung.
jaipongan Sundanese popular song/dance style developed in late twentieth century, based on traditional *kethuk tilu* and other sources.
jaitan = *liyepan.*
jaler [*kr*] → *lanang* [*ng*]
jalumampang (section of *ayak-ayakan* in Yogya style) ?
jamang diadem; leather head ornament worn by dancer or *wayang kulit* puppet.
jamang(an) **1** the ring of rattan or bamboo that closes the top end of the hole where a *suling* is blown. **2** = *dodot* (1).
jamplakan = *ciblonan.*
janget **1** the cowhide straps, of round or square section, used to tension the heads of a drum. **2** = *pluntur.*
jånggå **1** [*ki*] → *gulu* [*ng*]. **2** see *kendhangan Jånggå.*
jangkep unabridged, complete.
janturan **1** narration by the *dhalang*, introducing a major scene in a *wayang kulit* performance, accompanied by a softly playing gamelan. **2** = *palaran, uran-uran.* **3** = *pinjalan* (1).
jaran [*ng*] → *kapal* [*kr*] horse.
jaranan [*ng*] → *kapalan* [*kr*] *wayang* scene representing departure of army.
jarik [*ng*] → *sinjang* [*kr*], *nyamping* [*ki*] *bathik* skirt.
jarik kawung a named *céngkok* on *gendèr*, etc,.
jarit = *jarik.*
jarwådhåså, jarwådhosok folk-etymology.
jas a short jacket worn by men as part of *pakaian jåwå.*
jathil(an) **1** a type of trance dance performed by male dancers on hobby horses. **2** hobby horse used in such dance.
jati [*ng*] → *jatos* [*kr*] teak.
jatos [*kr*] → *jati* [*ng*]
jédher, jédhor = *dhodhog.*
jegogan a Balinese gamelan instrument similar to a *slenthem.*
jejeging iråmå the keeper of the *iråmå*; refers to the function of some of the instruments in the gamelan.
jejer(an) a major scene in a *wayang kulit* performance, set (in most cases) in a royal court (cf. *adegan*).
jejer kedhatonan *wayang* scene set inside the royal palace.
jejer manyurå sepisan(an) opening scene in the third part of a *wayang.*
jejer pandhitå/pendhitå scene after the *gårå-gårå* in the second part of a *wayang*, in which the hero visits a holy man (*pandhitå*) at his hermitage.
jejer parwå the opening scene of a *wayang*, defining the story.
jejer paséban (n)jåbå [*ng*] → *jejer paséban (n)jawi* [*kr*]
jejer paséban (n)jawi [*kr*] *wayang* scene set outside the royal palace.
jejer sabrang(an) *wayang* scene set in a foreign (enemy) court.
jejer sepisan(an) first main scene in *wayang kulit.*
jejer srambahan miscellaneous scene in *wayang kulit.*
jejetan = *janget* (1), except made from rattan.
jembatan [*in*] = *srenten.*
jemblok = *kendhil grabah.*
jemblung imitation of the sound of a gamelan by about seven to ten voices: cf. *gamelan cangkem.*
jéndrå the lower-pitched string of the *rebab*, tuned to 2 or (for *pathet limå*) to 1.
jeneng = *watangan* (1).
jengkar kedhaton *wayang* scene representing the departure from the palace.
jengkar keputrèn *wayang* scene representing the departure from the residence of the royal ladies.
jengglèng sforzando playing (Yogya).
jengglong a Sundanese gamelan instrument, consisting of a set of horizontally suspended gongs in the shape of an L or U: can also be suspended vertically.
jidhor = *jédher.*
jindra = *lanang* (2).
jineman **1** a gamelan accompaniment for a song whose structure does not necessarily represent one of the regular formal structures of gamelan *gendhing.* **2** songs of a light character, which are accompanied by *gamelan gadhon*, without *rebab.* **3** a soft style of playing, without *rebab*, in which the *pesindhèn* has the prominent role: see *sekar lampah jineman.* **4** a song inserted into a *båwå*, with accompaniment on soft-style decorating instruments. **5** (?Yogya term) section towards the end of a *suluk* or a *båwå* in which the metre is regularised and all or some of the *kendhang, gong, kenong, kempul, kethuk* and soft instruments (except *rebab*) join the singer.
jinjingan handle of a *kendhang.*
jlèbèran description of metal at a stage intermediate between the *lakaran* and the final *pencon* form.
jogèd [*ng*] → *bekså* [*ki*] dance.
joglo **1** a traditional Javanese pitched roof form with two or more different slopes, the steepest part being in the middle. **2** the central part of such a roof.
jubah long robe worn, for example, by *wayang* puppets representing religious figures.
jublag a Balinese gamelan instrument similar to a *slenthem.*
jugag abbreviated (cf. *wantah*, *wetah*).
juluk to hammer from inside (for purposes of tuning).
jun = *kendhil grabah.*
juru bekså dancer.
juru demung a poetic verse-form of the category *sekar tengahan.*
kabupatèn 'regency'; local government division below province (*propinsi*), excluding cities, administered by a 'regent' (*bupati*).
kacang asin style of *celempung/siter* playing that fits the *pathet* but not the specific melodic line. {= salted peanuts}
kacu mas a ceremonial object in the royal palace, having the form of a handkerchief and symbolising the cleaning away of bodily or spiritual contamination.
kademung = *demung.*
kadhalan = *balungan ngadhal.*
kadipatèn residence of a crown prince (*adipati*).
kagok impur see *gagah impur.*
kagok kinantang see *alus kalang kinantang.*
kagok kinantang usap rawis a type of refined male dance (Yogya) for gods of a refined but dynamic character, such as Bathårå Indrå.
kagungan dalem royal possessions.
kain **1** cloth, fabric. **2** wrap-around skirt (cf. *sarung*).

kain bokongan skirt style worn by *wayang* puppets, with an exaggerated bulge at the rear.
kain panjang wrap-around skirt worn by men as part of *pakaian jåwå*.
kain polèng check-patterned *kain* (1) in black and white, e.g. as loincloth.
kajar a Balinese gamelan instrument similar to a *kethuk*.
KAKA (*Kawruh Karawitan*) educational institution at Surakarta.
kakawin sung poetry in Old Javanese (*kawi*), using metres based on Sanskrit prosody; = *sekar ageng kakawin*.
kålå **1** *kendhang*. **2** *kenong*.
kalajengaken **1** to change to a composition of a form differing from the preceding one. **2** to proceed from an *inggah* section of a *gendhing* (2) to a composition in a smaller formal structure. {*lajeng* = follow}
kalimat lagu **1** melodic sentence or phrase. **2** melodic line, contour.
kamanak = *kemanak*.
kambeng see *gagah kambeng*.
kambeng dhengklik a type of strong male dance (Yogya) for strong but calm monkey characters in the Ramayana story, such as Anoman.
kambeng usap rawis a type of strong male dance (Yogya) for strong gods of honest and tenacious character, e.g. Bathårå Bayu.
kampuh [*ki*] → *dodot* (1) [*kr*, *ng*]
kampung village, district, suburb, community.
kamus belt.
kamus bludiran embroidered belt worn by dancers.
kamus timang belt and buckle worn by male dancers in *wayang wong*.
kåncå gérong male singer.
kåndhå a narration by a *dhalang*, or a story-teller for a Yogyanese dance performance, giving the background to the events presented.
kåndhå sekar a sung *kåndhå*.
kangjeng title for nobles, equivalent to 'highness'; also for *pusåkå* gamelan.
kangsi **1** a single pot gong. **2** a pair of very small cymbals mounted on a frame.
kaniyagan a group of gamelan players.
kanjeng = *kangjeng*.
kanthil extreme top of *rebab*.
kapalan [*kr*] → *jaranan* [*ng*]
kapang-kapang majeng entrance of dancers in *bedhåyå* or *srimpi*.
kapang-kapang mundur exit of dancers in *bedhåyå* or *srimpi*.
kapungkas ending (with).
karawitan **1** gamelan music and associated singing, defined by the use of the *sléndro* and/or *pélog* scales. **2** group of performing musicians.
karah = *jamangan* (1).
kasambet [*kr*] → *kasambung* [*ng*] continuing (with).
kasambung [*ng*] → *kasambet* [*kr*]
kasar coarse, unrefined (opposite of *alus*).
kaseling = *selingan*.
Kasultanan (short name for) the court of the Sultan of Yogyakarta.
Kasunanan (short name for) the court of the Susuhunan of Surakarta.
kasuwuk ending (with).
katåmpå/katampan [*ng*] → *katampi* [*kr*]
katampi/katampèn [*kr*] → *katåmpå* [*ng*] using.
kåtå wilet the last word of the text of one phrase of the *sindhènan*; its pitch must correspond with the pitch of *dhong gedhé* of a given phrase.
kathok = *lancingan*.
katongan (*wayang kulit* puppets representing) royal personages.
kawåcå lagu the melodic structure for a dance.
kawat wire, string.
kawatan an ensemble consisting of two guitars, functioning as *gendèr* and *gambang*, a cello functioning as a *kendhang*, a *slenthem kawat*, a violin functioning as a *rebab*, and a *gong kemodhong*.
kawèng (cindhé) (silk) neckerchief with both ends crossing the chest, worn by male dancers representing *gagah* characters.
kawi the poetic vocabulary of Old Javanese.
kawin (Yogya) a type of *sulukan*, longer than *ådå-ådå* and invoking a calmer atmosphere.
kawiråjå **1** a court poet. **2** (competence in) delivery of the eulogy before a *wayang*; one of the skills of a *dhalang*.
kayon large 'puppet' in *wayang kulit*, representing trees, mountain, mouth of hell, etc., and used to mark beginning and end of 'acts'.
kayu wood, timber.
kébar **1** a lively style of *garap* used in *iråmå tanggung* (or in *iråmå dados* but with a double-density *balungan*), involving *ciblonan*, *imbal bonang*, extra *kempul strokes* and *keplok*. **2** = *gambyong* (1).
kebo giro the name for a *gendhing* played for special occasions such as weddings or to welcome an honoured guest.
kebudayaan [*in*] culture, civilisation.
kecapi a Sundanese plucked zither.
kecekan *siter* technique of damping a note while playing it; = *neceg* (2).
kecèr **1** a pair of small, round or eight-sided bronze plates hit with a mallet; = *rojèh* (1). **2** = *cèng-cèng*. **3** six tiny cymbals suspended from an iron bar and hit with a *saron* beater: also called *rojèh*.
kecèr bangkong a set of three *kecèr* shaped like large coconut shells on a frame, tuned to *limå*, *nem* and *barang*, or with seven notes, and played with a *saron* beater; found in *gamelan monggang* and *gamelan kodhok ngorek*.
kecèr bintang *kecèr* of eight-sided form. {*bintang* = star}
kecèr kambali *kecèr* of circular form, with a diameter of 10 to 12 cm, the lower set on a frame like a saron frame, and the other connected together by a cord; used in *wayang kulit* accompaniment.
kecèr rojèh *kecèr* shaped like large coconut shells of 40 cm diameter, in a set of six laid out in a line, and played with a *saron* beater; found in *gamelan monggang* and *gamelan kodhok ngorek*.
kecicèr = *kecèr*.
kecrèk **1** = *kecèr*. **2** = *kepyak*.
kecrek, kecrok a tambourine.
kedal enunciation, especially of vowels.
kedhaton = (inner part of) *kraton*.
kedhelèn description of an eye style, intermediate between *liyepan* and *thelengan*, for *wayang kulit* puppets. {*kedhelé* = soya bean}
kekayon = *kayon*.
kekecilan deliberate sharp playing on the *rebab*.
kekelèng a small bell used for signalling meditation.
kelat bahu ornament worn on upper arm by dancers and *wayang* puppets.
kelemahan the central part of a *wilah* (also *lemahan*).
kelinthing a small bell.

kelir the cloth screen used for a *wayang kulit* performance.

kemalo a form of *pendhok*, partially painted.

kemanak a small bronze instrument in the shape of a hollow banana, slit on one side, held in the left hand by a handle, and struck with a beater (similar to a *bonang* beater) held in the right hand; used in pairs tuned to adjacent notes, and played in alternation.

kembangan [*ng*] → *sekaran* [*kr*]

kembang sepasang a form of *pencon* instrument (*bonang*, *kenong*, *kempul*, *gong*, etc.) with only the *pencu* filed to a shiny surface.

kembang tibå a technique of *gendèr* playing, with reduced variation and liveliness, generally used in a *mérong* section.

kemben breast-cloth, part of costume of *bedhåyå* dancers.

kembul bojånå hold a celebratory feast, as in the final scene of *wayang*.

kemèng a high, thin, hoarse voice—a male voice of female character—that is not favoured for singing with the gamelan.

kemodhong one or two large bronze or iron knobbed keys suspended over a sounding box: see also *gong kemodhong*.

kemong a small gong: see *engkuk-kemong*.

kempalan [*kr*] → *kumpulan* [*ng*]

kempel concentrated, focused.

kempli a Balinese gamelan instrument similar to a small *kenong*.

kempling a small *rebånå*.

kempul a hanging gong, smaller than *gong ageng* and *gong suwukan*.

kempul adu manis = *kempul salah gumun*; also = *kempul kempyungan*.

kempulan four-note melodic unit ending with a *kempul* stroke, as in *ayak-ayakan* other than in *sléndro manyurå*.

kempul ancer = *kempul mbalung*.

kempul kempyungan a technique of playing the *kempul* in which the tones of the *kempul* are a *kempyung* distance above the tones of the *balungan*.

kempul mbalung a technique of playing the *kempul* in which the tones of the *kempul* coincide with the tones of the *balungan*.

kempul monggangan the technique of playing the *kempul* as heard in *gendhing monggang*, imitated as part of *ompak klénangan*.

kempul pinatut a technique of playing the *kempul* to anticipate a note in a vocal line.

kempul plèsèdan a technique of playing the *kempul* in which the tones of the *kempul* anticipate the succeeding tone of the *balungan*.

kempul salah gumun a technique of playing the *kempul* in which the pitch of the kempul is at the distance of one *salah gumun* (*gembyung*) above the pitch of the *balungan*.

kempul sungsun a technique of playing the *kempul* where each *kempul* note is repeated on the following *balungan* beat.

kempul susun = *kempul sungsun*.

kempul tunggal råså = *kempul mbalung*.

kempur a Balinese hanging gong, sometimes called *kempul*.

kempyang **1** the octave as conceived without intervening pitches: see *gembyang*. **2** an interval with four intervening keys as played on a *gendèr*. **3** an instrument of the gamelan, a rack with two, small, horizontally suspended gongs (Yogya) or one such gong (Solo). **4** two adjacent tones as played on the instrument *kempyang* (Yogya): also called *garo*. **5** the small head of a *kendhang*: see *tébokan kempyang*.

kempyung **1** an interval separated by two keys as played on a *gendèr*, e.g. 2–6. **2** the playing of 6̣ in addition to 2̣, or 1 in addition to 3̣, on the *bonang* (cf. *gembyung*).

kempyungan = *kempyung* (2).

kemudå one of the formal structures of gamelan *gendhing*, related to *srepegan*.

kencring = *genjring*.

kèndelan [*kr*] → *andhegan* [*ng*]

kendhang a generic term for drums.

kendhangan **1** drumming. **2** (Yogya) the term used to designate the type of pattern to be played for a given *gendhing*, such as *kendhangan Cåndrå*, the drum pattern *Cåndrå*; the *-an* suffix is sometimes attached to the generic term *kendhang*, and sometimes to the modifying term, e.g. *kendhang ladrangan/ kendhangan ladrang*, the *ladrang* drum pattern. **3** = *babad*.

kendhangan bandholan (Yogya) special *kendhangan* for certain *gendhing* in *sléndro* with three or five *kenongan* in the *gongan*, otherwise corresponding to *kt 2 kp mg 4* in Solonese terms.

kendhangan Barong (se)kepak a Yogya-style *kendhangan* for a few specific *gendhing* (2) in *sléndro*, corresponding to *kt 2 kp mg 4* in Solonese terms.

kendhangan bèbèr type of drumming used by itinerant players to attract attention.

kendhang bem = *kendhang gendhing*.

kendhangan Cåndrå a Yogya-style *kendhangan* for *gendhing* (2) in *sléndro*, corresponding to *kt 2 kp mg 4* in Solonese terms.

kendhangan Cåndrå tungkakan a Yogya-style *kendhangan*; = *kendhangan Barong (se)kepak*.

kendhangan Elå-Elå a Yogya-style *kendhangan* for *gendhing* (2) in *sléndro* or *pélog*, corresponding in Solonese terms to *gd ktw kt 2 kp* with *minggah ladrang* or *minggah ketawang*.

kendhangan Elå-Elå gandrung-gandrung a Yogya-style *kendhangan kalih* for *gendhing* (2) in *sléndro* or *pélog*, corresponding in Solonese terms to *gd ktw kt 2 kp mg ladrang*.

kendhangan Gandrung-Gandrung a Yogya-style *kendhangan kalih* for *gendhing* (2) in *sléndro* or *pélog*, corresponding to *kt 2 kp mg 4* in Solonese terms.

kendhangan gangsaran (Yogya) (variants of) drumming for certain *ladrang* performed with *gangsaran*.

kendhangan gembyakan (Yogya) a lively style of *kendhangan* using *kendhang batangan*.

kendhangan Jånggå a Yogya-style *kendhangan* for *gendhing* (2) in *sléndro*, corresponding to *kt 4 kp mg 8* in Solonese terms.

kendhangan Jånggå låråciblon a Yogya-style *kendhangan* for a few specific *gendhing* (2), corresponding to *kt 2 kp mg 4* in Solonese terms.

kendhangan kendhang ciblon = *kendhang ciblon*.

kendhangan kendhang kalih = *kendhang kalih*.

kendhangan kendhang satunggal = *kendhang satunggal*.

kendhangan Lålå = *kendhangan Elå-Elå*.

kendhangan Majemuk a Yogya-style *kendhangan* for *gendhing* (2) in *sléndro* or *pélog*, corresponding to *kt 2 kp mg 4* in Solonese terms, but with five *kenongan*.

kendhangan Mataram **1** any Yogya-style *kendhangan*. **2** (Solonese version of) Yogya-style *kendhangan* for loud-style *ladrang*, especially in *ir I*.

kendhangan Mawur a Yogya-style *kendhangan* for *gendhing* (2) in *sléndro* or *pélog*, corresponding in Solonese terms to *kt 4 ar mg 8*.

kendhangan Mawur tungkakan a Yogya-style *kendhangan* for certain *gendhing* (2) in *pélog*, corresponding in Solonese terms to *kt 4 ar mg 8*.

kendhangan pamijèn special *kendhangan* for a particular piece.

kendhangan Pangrawit a Yogya-style *kendhangan* for *gendhing* (2) in *pélog*, corresponding in Solonese terms to *kt 8 ar mg 16*.

kendhangan patut *kendhangan* selected from *ciblonan* elements to suit the piece.

kendhangan pematut = *kendhangan patut*.

kendhangan råjå (Yogya) drumming for certain *ladrang*, e.g. *Lunggadhung*.

kendhangan Råråciblon a Yogya-style *kendhangan* for a few specific *gendhing* (2), corresponding to *kt 2 kp mg 4* in Solonese terms.

kendhangan sabrangan (Yogya) drumming for *gati*.

kendhangan Såråyudå a Yogya-style *kendhangan* for *gendhing* (2) in *pélog*, corresponding to *kt 2 kp mg 4* in Solonese terms.

kendhangan Semang a Yogya-style *kendhangan* for *gendhing* (2) in *pélog*, corresponding in Solonese terms to *kt 4 kp mg 8* (= *Semang alit*) or *kt 8 kp mg 16* (= *Semang ageng*).

kendhang batangan **1** a term commonly used for the *kendhang ciblon* at Yogya, where this drum often has a relatively cylindrical form. **2** = *kendhang wayangan*. {*batangan* = cylindrical?}

kendhang ciblon (the usual term for) a medium-sized drum used for lively playing and for dance accompaniment: also = *kendhang batangan*.

kendhang cilik = *ketipung*.

kendhang gedhé (*gedhé* [*ng*] → *ageng* [*kr*]) the largest of the drums generally found in the gamelan.

kendhang gembyakan **1** a lively style of drumming (Yogya). **2** = *kendhang batangan*.

kendhang gembyangan = *kendhang batangan*.

kendhang gendhing = *kendhang gedhé*.

kendhang kalih **1** the drumming style played on *kendhang gendhing* and *ketipung*. **2** = *ketipung*. {= two drums}

kendhang ketipung = *ketipung*.

kendhang kosèkan = *kendhang wayangan*.

kendhang loro = *kendhang kalih*.

kendhang paneteg a drum of conical form, without a *rau* in the *klowongan*, used in *gamelan kodhok ngorèk* and *gamelan cårå balèn* (in two sizes; *kendhang paneteg ageng* and *kendhang paneteg alit*).

kendhang penunthung a drum similar in form to the *ketipung* but shorter.

kendhang sabet = *kendhang wayangan*.

kendhang salahan a *kendhangan* pattern for *lancaran*, used only once per cycle of *gongan*.

kendhang satunggal the drumming style played on the *kendhang gendhing* alone, or on the *kendhang gendhing* with *penunthung*. {= one drum}

kendhang teteg = *teteg*.

kendhang wayangan **1** the drum used to accompany *wayang kulit*, slightly larger than the *batangan*/*ciblon* drum. **2** the style of drumming used to accompany *wayang kulit*.

kendhil grabah an earthenware pot used as a resonator in certain instruments, e.g. *gong kemodhong*.

kendhili a ceremonial object in the royal palace, having the form of a rice cooker or lantern, and symbolising illumination in the hearts of the people.

kendho slow.

kengsèr a named *singgetan* for the *ciblon*.

kengsèr batangan a named *singgetan* for the *ciblon*.

kenong **1** a large, horizontally suspended gong. **2** = *kenongan*.

kenongan **1** a section of a *gongan* marked at the end by a stroke on the *kenong*. **2** the first word of a two-word, compound term designating style of playing the *kenong*. The suffix *an* is sometimes attached to the first word of the compound (*kenong*), sometimes to the second word, and sometimes is omitted altogether. **3** a *bonang*-type instrument (additional to *kenong*) in *gamelan monggang*, tuned to 5 and grouped with *penitir* and *banggèn*.

kenong(an) adu manis = *kenongan kempyungan*.

kenong(an) ancer = *kenongan mbalung*.

kenong(an) ater collective name for *kenong* notes that anticipate *gantungan* or vocal lines; = *kenongan plèsèdan*, *kenongan pinatut*.

kenong(an) banggèn = *kenongan sungsun*.

kenong(an) goyang = *kenongan sungsun*.

kenong(an) goyang sungsun = *kenongan sungsun*.

kenong(an) jumbuh = *kenong mbalung*.

kenong(an) kempyungan a style of playing the *kenong* in which the *kenong* tones are a *kempyung* above the tones of the *balungan*.

kenong(an) mbalung a style of playing the *kenong* in which the tones of the *kenong* are the same as the tones of the *balungan*.

kenong(an) nibani the style of playing the *kenong* as in the formal structures *ayak-ayakan*, *srepegan* and *kebo giro*; for example:

kenong(an) nitir a style of playing the *kenong* as in the formal structure *sampak*; for example:

kenong(an) nunggal råså = *kenong(an) mbalung*.

kenong(an) penuntun = *kenongan ater*.

kenong(an) pinatut a style of playing the *kenong* in which a *plèsèdan* note is played to harmonise with another melodic element, e.g. *sindhènan*.

kenong(an) plèsèdan a style of playing the *kenong* in which the *kenong* anticipates the succeeding *balungan* tone or the next *sèlèh* tone.

kenong(an) salah gumun a style of playing the *kenong* in which the *kenong* plays a pitch at the distance of one *salah gumun* (*gembyung*) interval above the pitch of the *balungan*.

kenong(an) sungsun a style of playing the *kenong* in which the *kenong* tone is reiterated after the first and second *kenong* stroke of a *ladrang* form, e.g.

kenong(an) susun = *kenongan sungsun*.

kenong(an) tunggal råså = *kenongan mbalung*.

kenong(an) tuturan a style of *kenong* (1) playing in which a *plèsèdan* note is used to indicate that the next *kenongan* differs from the previous three.

kenong jaler (*jaler* [*ng*] → *lanang* [*kr*]) = *kenong lanang.*

kenong japan(g) a large *kenong* (1) tuned usually to pitch *limå* (low register), found more commonly in ceremonial and Yogyanese gamelan, and played in loud-style pieces.

kenong jepang = *kenong japan.*

kenong lanang **1** any *kenong* (1) in the normal *kenong* range. **2** an archaic *kenong* (1) tuned to *nem* or *limå* an octave below *kenong japan.* {*lanang* = male}

kenong monggangan the style of playing the *kenong* (1) as heard in *gendhing monggang.*

kenong playon = *kenong wayangan.*

kenong plèsèdan = *kenongan plèsèdan.*

kenong rèntèng an instrument in the form of a *slenthem* (2), used as a substitute for a set of *kenong* (1) pots. {*rèntèng* = in a row}

kenong wadon = *kenong japan.*

kenong wayangan a single *kenong* (1) tuned to 6 and used in *gendhing lampah.*

kenthongan a slit gong made of either bamboo or wood and used as a signalling device.

kentrung frame drum.

kentrung jemblung performance by an itinerant singer of Islamic texts, accompanying himself with a *kentrung.*

kenut a single-row instrument of *bonang* type, providing notes 5 and 6, and used in conjunction with the *klénang*, which provides notes $\dot{1}$ and $\dot{2}$; found in the *gamelan cåråbalèn.*

kepandhitan = *jejer pandhitå.*

kepatihan see *titilaras kepatihan.*

keplok stylised, rhythmic, interlocking clapping employed to enliven a *gendhing.*

kepok description of a piece having similar melodic characteristics to another.

keprak **1** a small wooden slit drum, or box, struck with a wooden mallet, e.g. by dance master/mistress to keep time. **2** = *kepyak.*

kepyak a set of plates (e.g. Yogya, one wooden and one iron; Solo, four bronze) mounted on a box and struck by a *dhalang* with a metal beater held between the toes of the right foot; also a similar set of metal plates used by a dancer or another player.

kepyakan the sounds made by a *dhalang* while striking the *kepyak* during a *wayang kulit* performance, usually serving the same purpose as *dhodhogan.*

kepyak calapitå pieces of ivory that are held between the fingers.

kerajinan gamelan gamelan workshop.

kerep refers to one possible spacing of the *kethuk* strokes in the *mérong* of a *gendhing*, as marked by '*kethuk 2 (4, 8) kerep*': cf. *arang, awis.* {= frequent, at short intervals}

kerepan refers to the spacing of the strokes of the *kethuk* in a *gendhing* at even shorter intervals than *kerep*, e.g. in *minggah* sections and in *ketawang* and *ladrang.*

kerincing = *genjring.*

keris = *kris.*

keroncong = *kroncong.*

kesenian [*in*] the arts.

ketampèn = *katampèn.*

ketawang one of the formal structures of gamelan *gendhing* (1), with 16 *balungan* beats and two *kenongan* per *gongan.*

ketawang ageng = *ketawang gendhing.*

ketawang alit = *ketawang* (cf. *ketawang ageng*).

ketawang gendhing one of the formal structures of gamelan *gendhing* (1), belonging to the category of *gendhing* (2) with two *kenongan* per *gongan.*

ketawang rancagan *bentuk* used by some ceremonial gamelan, with two *gåtrå* per *kenongan* and two *kenongan* per *gongan.*

keteg(an) **1** heartbeat. **2** musical pulse. **3** one of the four beats of a *gåtrå* (1). **4** beats occurring at the rate of every second note of the *bonang barung* in *mipil.*

keter = *geter.*

kethoprak a semi-improvised theatrical genre invented in 1914, popular in central and East Java, accompanied by gamelan.

kethoprak humor version of *kethoprak* on television, with the emphasis on humour throughout.

kethu headgear worn by male *wayang* characters.

kethuk a small horizontally suspended gong.

kethukan stroke on an instrument.

kethuk banggèn a special style of playing the *kethuk* after the third *kenong* of the *inggah* section of *gendhing* (2) whose *inggah* are *kethuk 4*; for example:

```
+     +     +       +       +
. . . .  . . . .  . . . .  . . . (.)
```

kethuk kintel a *kethuk* tuned to 2.

kethuk kungkang a *kethuk* tuned to 1.

kethuk pothok describes a *gendhing* with the same structure in the *minggah* as in the *mérong.*

kethuk salahan a special style of playing the *kethuk* to signal approaching gong, for example (*ladrang* in *ir I* and *II*; also *ketawang* in *ir II*):

```
  +   +   +     +
.   .   .   .     .   .   .  (.)
```

kethuk susun a style of *kethuk* playing in *ladrang*, especially in ir II, where the normal stroke is followed by another on the next *balungan* beat.

kethuk tilu (Sunda) three *pencon* used in accompaniment for *tlèdhèk* dances. {= three *kethuk*}

kethu udheng headgear worn by *wayang* puppets representing court officials, and consisting of a cap (*kethu*) under an *udheng.*

ketipung a small drum used in conjunction with the *kendhang gedhé.*

ketrampilan [*in*] skill.

Ki abbreviation of *Kyai* (cf. *Ni*).

kidul south(ern).

kidung narratives usually sung in *sekar måcåpat* meters.

kidungan social gathering for the performance of *kidung.*

kidung sekar ageng *kidung* sung in *sekar ageng* metres.

kidung sekar kawi = *kidung sekar ageng.*

kijing(an) [*in*] style of frame with tall thin end-pieces, used for *gambang* and sometimes *saron* family. {*kijing* = tombstone}

kikir file.

kikir kesik fine file used to obtain the finish on the metal of gamelan instruments.

kikir patar coarse file.

kinantang alus see *kagok kinantang.*

kinantang dhengklik see *kalang kinantang dhengklik*.
kinanthi a *sekar mâcâpat* metre.
kinthilan **1** (Yogya) interlocking patterns played by a pair of *saron* (different from standard *saron imbal*): the second instrument repeats the note played by the first. **2** similar Solonese style with less close relationship between the parts played by the two players. {*kinthil* = follow}
kiprah *wayang wong* version of *gandrung* dance.
kiprahan style of *kendhangan* associated with *kiprah*.
kirap dress rehearsal.
KKI (*Konservatori Karawitan Indonesia*) = KOKAR, Solo.
klanthé **1** the cords that support the *kempul*, *gong suwukan* and *gong gedhé*. **2** the carrying handle of a *kendhang*.
klanthé cacing a *klanthé* made up of strands.
klanthé kålå a type of *klanthé* with a tassel on the end.
klanthé usus-usus a type of *klanthé* without a tassel on the end.
klénang **1** a Balinese instrument, a small, horizontally suspended gong. **2** a single-row instrument of *bonang* type, providing notes $\dot{1}$ and $\dot{2}$, and used in conjunction with the *kenut*, which provides notes 5 and 6; found in the *gamelan cårå balèn*. **3** instrument in the gamelan at Cirebon.
klénangan an old-fashioned style of *imbal bonang*, also known as *cårå balèn*.
klenèng(an) gamelan playing for pleasure, in contrast to playing for dance or theatrical accompaniment (Solo); also called *uyon-uyon* (Yogya).
klenèngan gobyog a *klenèngan* using pieces in a lively style.
klenèngan mådyå a *gamelan klenèngan* without *bonang barung*, *bonang panerus*, *demung* and *saron panerus*.
klenèngan tengahan = *gamelan wayangan* (1).
klening(an) = *klenèngan*.
klenong a small Balinese gong.
kliningan = *klenèngan*.
klithik see *wayang klithik*.
klowongan hole, opening.
kocapan = *caritå*.
kodhok ngorèk **1** a type of archaic gamelan. **2** the piece played on the gamelan of the same name, often used as a wedding piece and played on a modern gamelan. **3** a class of pieces performed in honour of special occasions at the palaces of Yogya and Solo, played on a *pélog* gamelan accompanied by *gendèr* or *gambang gångså* in *sléndro* (Solo), or a *saron barung* and *demung* in *sléndro* (Yogya).
KOKAR (*Konservatori Karawitan*) music high schools at Denpasar, Solo, etc.; now SMKI.
kombangan **1** refers to an extension of a melodic phrase: see *plèsèdan*. **2** the sustained syllables *'eeee'* or *'oooo'* of a *suluk* sung by a *dhalang*. **3** the humming of a *dhalang* on certain pitches, sometimes as a signal to the musicians to make a transition to a new section or piece. **4** see *senggakan kombangan*. **5** phrase played by *suling* to indicate a *gantungan*. {*kombang* = bumble-bee}
komplit complete, with all elements present, e.g. the full sequence of different treatments, *selingan*, etc.
komposisi [*in*] composition.
komposisi baru [*in*] new piece for gamelan using the conventional structures of *karawitan*: cf. *kreasi baru*; or these two terms may exchange definitions.
kondangan = *slametan*.

Konser = KOKAR, Solo.
ko(o)r chorus, *gérongan*.
kosèk alus **1** a Solonese style of drumming, slightly less lively and fast than *kosèk wayangan*, used in *ladrang* form and *inggah*, *irâmå III*. **2** a style of *kendhang satunggal* drumming used in the *inggah* section, *irâmå III*, of a *gendhing*.
kosèkan a fast, complex style of drumming played on the *kendhang wayangan* (Solo).
kosèk wayangan **1** the style of playing *kendhang wayangan* for *wayang* performance; = *kosèkan*. **2** *kosèkan*-style drumming for pieces in the formal structures *ladrang*, *kethuk kerep*, *mérong* and *inggah*.
kosok the bow of a *rebab*.
kosokan bowing of the *rebab*.
kosok(an) balèn = *kosok(an) wangsul*.
kosok(an) maju 'up-bow' on the *rebab*.
kosok(an) mbalung *rebab* bowing technique with one note per *balungan* note.
kosok(an) mbesut a *rebab* bowing technique.
kosok(an) milah *rebab* bowing technique with two notes per *balungan* note.
kosok(an) mlurut a *rebab* bowing technique.
kosokan mundur 'down-bow' on the *rebab*.
kosokan nduduk *rebab* playing technique with additional bow strokes inserted into a *céngkok* that otherwise has the rhythm of *kosokan milah*.
kosok(an) ngikik a *rebab* bowing technique.
kosok(an) ngrecek *rebab* playing technique where both open strings are played together for notes in the lowest register, i.e. $\underset{\cdot}{6}$ against $\underset{\cdot}{2}$, or $\underset{\cdot}{5}$ against $\underset{\cdot}{1}$.
kosok(an) ngungkak a *rebab* bowing technique.
kosok(an) nyelå a *rebab* bowing technique.
kosok(an) sendhul pancing a *rebab* bowing technique.
kosok(an) wangsul a *rebab* bowing technique.
kota [*in*] town, city.
kothak suårå sound box of an instrument such as *siter* or *celempung*.
kothak (wayang(an)) the box in which the *wayang* puppets and other equipment are kept, also used as a resonator for *dhodhogan*.
kothèkan **1** rhythmic interlocking patterns produced by several people striking a *lesung*. **2** interlocking rhythms played by two instruments.
kowi crucible used to melt bronze for instruments.
kraton royal palace; senior such palace at Yogya and Solo.
kreasi baru [*in*] new composition for gamelan ignoring the conventions of *karawitan*: cf. *komposisi baru*; or these two terms may exchange definitions.
Kridhå Beksa Wirâmå a dance teaching institute at Yogya.
Kridhå Mardåwå (in full, *Kawedanan Hageng Punakawan Kridhå Mardåwå*) arts office at the *kraton Yogya*.
kris [*ng*] → *dhuwung* [*kr*] wavy-bladed dagger, worn as part of *pakaian jawa* and dance costumes.
kris branggah a *kris* with a particularly wide hilt, worn by *alus* characters in Yogya-style dance.
kris gayaman a *kris* with a particular type of sheath, worn especially by *gagah* characters in *wayang wong*.
kromong = *bonang*.
krompyong = *byong*.
kroncong **1** a popular song style with strong Portuguese influence, usually

accompanied by a violin, ukulele, guitar, cello and flute. **2** ankle rings worn by *wayang* puppets. **3** = *byong*.

krucil see *wayang krucil*.

krumpyung see *gamelan krumpyung*.

kruwing(an) type of *wilah* with a *rai* and a concave *recep* separated by the *manis rai*.

kucu = *pencu*.

kudå képang (*kudå* [*kr*] → *jaran* [*ng*]) a hobby-horse made of plaited bamboo, used in dances including trance dances.

kudå lumping [*in*] a hobby-horse similar to *kudå képang*. {*lumping* = leather}

kudangan lullaby.

kuk mong = *engkuk-kemong*.

kulit leather. See *wayang kulit*.

kulit gudèl leather from water-buffalo calf, used for *wayang kulit*.

kulon west(ern).

kuluk [*ng*] → *kuthå* / *makuthå* / *panunggul* [*ki*] a type of headgear worn by men.

kumba pencu the rounded part of a *pencu* surrounding the *uceng*.

kumpulan [*ng*] → *kempalan* [*kr*] group; collection, e.g. of notation.

kumudå = *kemudå*.

kuncå tails of a *kampuh*.

kuncung a type of *blangkon* with a projecting fold of cloth at the front, known as *tumpangsari* or *adu mancung*.

kuningan brass.

kupingan a circular piece of wood of about 4 cm diameter that terminates the *mangol* on which a *rebab* string is wound. {= ear}

kusumå metrical phrase sung by *pesindhèn* at the end of an *andhegan*.

kuthå [*ki*] → *kuluk* [*ng*]

kuthuk a ceremonial object in the royal palace, shaped like a fish and symbolising the power of attraction.

kuthuk kuning (gembyang) a named *céngkok* (with octave ending).

Kya(h)i honorific title, usually translated as 'Venerable', given to men, also to gamelan and to *pusåkå* in general (cf. *Nyai*).

labuhan ceremony of offerings to Ratu Kidul by the Sultan of Yogya.

ladrang(an) **1** one of the formal structures of gamelan *gendhing* (1), with 32 *balungan* beats per *gongan*. **2** (according to some Yogya sources) one of the formal structures of gamelan *gendhing* (1), with 16 *balungan* beats per *gongan*: more commonly called *lancaran* or *bubaran*. **3** a type of sheath for a *kris*.

ladrang lancaran *lancaran* that includes a *ladrang* section played when the *irâmå* is slow.

lagon **1** a Yogyanese term for *pathetan* (1). **2** singing. **3** a *sasmitå* arranged as a melody.

lagon cekak = *lagon jugag*.

lagon jugag a shortened *lagon* (1).

lagon ngelik a *lagon* (1) set mainly in a high register, and usually used after a *lagon wetah*.

lagon tlutur a *lagon* (1) that evokes a sad atmosphere.

lagon pathet = *lagon* (1).

lagon wantah a long version of a *lagon* (1), the usual or normal form.

lagon wetah = *lagon wantah*.

lagu **1** melody, song. **2** an underlying or abstracted melody of a *gendhing* (= *lagu batin*). **3** a series of notes. **4** unstressed position in gamelan *gendhing*: alternates with *guru*, stressed position. **5** one *pupuh* or a set of *padeswårå* in *sekar* prosody. **6** the category *sekar ageng* or *kakawin*. **7** a particular *sekar ageng* or *kakawin*.

lagu baku = *lagu pokok*.

lagu batin inner melody.

lagu dolanan = *dolanan*.

lagu gecul a playful song.

lagu gedhé (*gedhé* [*ng*] → *ageng* [*kr*]) long melodies.

lagu gendhing melodies that originated in the instrumental, gamelan idiom.

lagu jonjang children's game songs.

lagu leutik (Sunda) short melodies.

lagu mati fixed melodies.

lagu pathet = *pathetan* (1).

lagu pokok = *balungan* (3).

lagu rerenggongan = *lagu leutik*.

lagu sedheng medium-sized melodies.

lagu sekar melodies that originated in the vocal idiom.

lagu seriosa solo songs in diatonic tuning, accompanied by Western instruments.

lagu tengah = *lagu sedheng*.

lajengan a continuation: see *kalajengaken*.

lakar(an) **1** metal blank for *wilah* or *pencon*, after casting and before forging. **2** blank *wayang kulit* puppet before carving and painting.

lakon a story delivered by a *dhalang* (in *wayang kulit* or *wayang wong*).

lakon carangan supplementary stories about traditional *wayang* characters.

lakon carang kadhapur supplementary *wayang* stories clearly related to *lakon pokok*.

lakon dhapur = *lakon pokok*.

lakon jejer = *lakon pokok*.

lakon lajer = *lakon pokok*.

lakon lugu = *lakon pokok*.

lakon pasemon *lakon* referring to real people.

lakon pokok core stories (cf. *lakon carangan*, *lakon sempalan*).

lakon sempalan apocryphal or inauthentic stories based on traditional *wayang* characters.

laku [*ng*] → *lampah* [*kr*]

laku bokong [*ng*] → *lampah pocong* [*kr*]

laku dodhok [*ng*] → *lampah pocong* [*kr*]

laku telu a *kendhangan* for *irâmå III*.

lalagon = *lagon*.

låmbå **1** a section of a *gendhing* with *balungan nibani*, usually just after the *bukå*, and preceding a *dados* section with *balungan mlaku* and a slower, stable tempo. **2** see *mipil låmbå*. **3** see *nacah låmbå*. **4** a style of *saron* playing. **5** see *gendèran låmbå*. {= single}

lamban relaxed tempo.

lambé **1** the free edge of a *pencon* instrument, surrounding the *lolohan*. **2** the long edges of a *wilah*.

lambé gajah the slit of the *kemanak*, where the thumb is applied to damp it. {= elephant's lips}

lambé tekèk the thin part of the slit of the *kemanak*. {= lizard's lips}

lambung [*in*] = *lemahan*.
lampah [*kr*] → *laku* [*ng*] **1** the ratio of instrumental strokes (e.g. *bonang, gendèr*) per *balungan* beat; e.g. *lampah* 4 = four strokes per *balungan* beat. **2** lines of poetry: see *pådå dirgå*. **3** the number of syllables per line in *slokå, kakawin*, or *sekar ageng* poetry. **4** stepwise: see *balungan lampah*. **5** (*lampah x*) in *x* style (e.g. *lampah soran*). **6** (*lampah x*) the number of *balungan* beats covered by a *céngkok* sung by a *pesindhèn*.
lampahan [*kr*] → *lakon* [*ng*]
lampah bedhayan (played in) *bedhåyå* style.
lampah pocong [*kr*] → *laku bokong, laku dhodhok* [*ng*] a squatting position, used in Yogya-style dance, with knees close together (female dance) or open (male dance).
lampah soran (played in) loud style; cf. *gendhing bonang*.
lamus **1** bellows used for the fire in a gamelan-maker's forge. **2** continuous (circular) breathing.
lanang(an) [*ng*] → *jaler* [*kr*] **1** a description applied to the normal range of the *kenong* (excluding the *kenong japan*) or the upper octave of the *bonang* (cf. *wèdokan*), also to certain instruments in ceremonial gamelan. **2** the higher-pitched (?) string of the *rebab*, tuned to *nem* (= 6), or to *limå* (= 5) in *pathet limå*. {= male}
lancaran one of the formal structures of gamelan *gendhing* (1).
lancingan (panji-panji) breeches worn by male dancer in *wayang wong*.
låndå Westerner. {from *Belåndå* = Holland}
langak with upturned gaze; description of *wayang kulit* characters of aggressive, impatient and irritable type.
langen driyå/driyan a dance-drama with dialogue in *sekar måcåpat* based upon the *Damar Wulan* story, performed exclusively by women, originally mainly in a squatting position.
langen måndrå wanårå a dance drama with dialogue in *sekar måcåpat* based upon the *Ramayana* story, originally performed mainly in a squatting position. {*wanårå* = monkeys}
langen sekar pieces in ¾ rhythm.
langgam **1** a kind of popular song, derived from *kroncong*, with the structure AABA and usually 4 *gåtrå* per *gongan*. **2** the central Javanese form of this, performed with gamelan accompaniment.
langgam jåwå **1** popular songs (*langgam*) accompanied by gamelan in the manner of *jineman*. **2** = *langgam* (2).
langkep = *jangkep*.
lapak ukel the form of *pangkon* used for the *saron* family, with scrolls at the ends.
laragan a gamelan player, usually a former *abdi dalem*, invited into the *kraton* to take part in performances.
lårånangis the string of the *rebab* tuned to *nem*, or to *limå* in *pathet limå*. {= weeping virgin}
laras **1** tuning system: see also *embat*. **2** scale: see also *pathet*. **3** note or degree of a scale. **4** pitch. **5** harmonious sound.
larasané numpang a slightly sharp tuning of the higher *rebab* string, relative to the rest of the gamelan.
larasané pleng = *laras mleng*.
laras bremårå = *laras mleng*.
laras cilik high-register tuning.
laras diatonis a *pélog* tuning found around Semarang, approximating to a diatonic scale where note 1 = Western E natural.
laras gedhé (*gedhé* [*ng*] → *ageng* [*kr*]) low-register tuning.
laras mådyå pieces with *sekar måcåpat* verse forms usually sung by men to the accompaniment of *terbang* and *kendhang* and sometimes *kemanak*: cf. *santiswara(n)*.
laras mleng perfectly tuned.
laras nyliring = *laras silir*.
laras pleng = *laras mleng*.
laras sedhengan medium-register tuning.
laras silir slightly out of tune but not necessarily undesirable.
laras umyung tuning appropriate for loud playing; see *umyung*.
larutan dragging of a thumbnail across the strings of the *siter* (etc.) to pluck a succession of notes instead of plucking them separately.
lat = *let*.
latihan [*in*] rehearsal.
lawak the crossed end-pieces of a drum stand (*placak* (4)).
lawé yarn, used to wrap beaters (*bindi*).
lawung ageng (*ageng* [*kr*] → *gedhé* [*ng*]) a dance in strong male style (Yogya), which depicts a group of men jousting with lances: also known as *beksan trunåjåyå*. {*lawung* = spear}
lawung alit a dance in refined male style (Yogya), which depicts a group of men jousting with lances.
låyå tempo: see also *iråmå* (1).
layang document.
lebdhå swårå = *wiråswårå*.
lèdhèk a female dancer of the *tayub* dance.
ledhung-ledhung lullaby.
lèhèr = *gulu* (2).
lekukan an indentation.
lelagon **1** = *lagon* (1). **2** = *lagu* (1).
lelangen = *langen*.
lemahan the centre portion of a *wilah*, between the two holes.
lengut Balinese melodic pattern, similar to *wilet*.
lénong type of folk theatre in the Jakarta area.
lentrèh slow.
lepet **1** the part of the *rebab* strings between the *srenten* and the bottom of the *rebab* (cf. *pengantèn anyar*). **2** = *seser*.
lèr [*kr*] → *lor* [*ng*]
lesung a rice mortar.
let interval of time or space.
lik = *ngelik*.
limå one of the tones of the gamelan scale, notated as 5. {= five}
lincip description of the long pointed nose of refined *wayang kulit* characters.
lirih(an) played in soft style: cf. *soran*.
liyepan description of the long narrow eyes of refined *wayang kulit* characters.
logondhang one of a number of melodies used in association with the *sinom sekar måcåpat* metre.
lolohan the opening in the underside of a *pencon* instrument.
lomba [*in*] contest, competition.

lombokan the point where the horsehair of a *kosok* is gathered together for attachment to the *béndhå*.

londo = *låndå*.

longok looking straight ahead, a description of *wayang* puppets representing characters intermediate between *tumungkul* and *langak* types.

lonthong (cindhé) (silk) sash worn around the waist by male dancers.

lor [*ng*] → *lèr* [*kr*] north(ern).

ludrug, ludruk a popular comic theatre style from East Java.

lugu plain, simple, ordinary.

luk = *eluk*.

lumpatan see *mipil lumpatan*.

lurah badhut leader of clowns in drama.

lurah gendhing the leader of an ensemble.

lurik a cotton homespun fabric with vertical stripes, used for jackets as part of *pakaian jawa*.

lurugan a scene showing the army preparing for battle; used in dance drama such as *wayang wong*.

luruh a description of a gamelan tuning with a relatively small interval between notes 1 and 2 (cf. *råtå, srigak*).

måcå kåndhå [*ng*] → *maos kåndhå* [*kr*] to read the *kåndhå* for a classical dance performance (Yogya).

måcåpat poetic metres and associated melodies: see *sekar måcåpat*.

måcåpatan social gathering for the performance of *måcåpat*.

madenda a Sundanese tuning.

mådyå låyå moderate tempo.

magak a named *singgetan* for the *ciblon*.

maguru gong.

maguru gångså one or two large bronze or iron knobbed keys suspended by cord; like *kemodhong* but without a sounding box.

mahasara = *gong*.

majeng gendhing [*kr*] → *maju gendhing* [*ng*]

maju either of the two weak beats of a *gåtrå*; = *dhing*.

maju gendhing [*ng*] → *majeng gendhing* [*kr*] the advance into battle; the first scene in a dance representing a battle (Yogya).

maketeg = *teteg*.

makuthå **1** crown. **2** headdress worn by demon kings in *wayang wong*. **2** [*ki*] → *kuluk* [*ng*]

malam midadarèni a ceremony in the evening before a wedding; also before some other commemorations.

malik a named *singgetan* for the *ciblon*.

mancer to play *pancer*.

mandheg = *andhegan*.

mandrakan an older style of *sindhènan*.

manggisan a decorative disc around the plaited hide strip where the handle (*cangkingan*) of a *kendhang* is inserted into the body. {*manggis* = mangosteen}

mangol a round wooden tuning peg on the *rebab*, the thickness of the little finger and about 25 cm long, with a hole at one end, through which the string is threaded.

manis **1** (Yogya) a term for the note $\dot{2}$. **2** arris, edge where two regions of a *wilah* or *pencon* instrument meet (see *manis dudu*, *manis rai*).

manis dudu the arris where the *dudu* meets the *recep* on a *pencon* instrument.

manis rai the arris where the *rai* meets the *recep* on a *wilah* or *pencon* instrument.

mantèn anyar the two grooves in the top of the bridge (*srenten*), where the strings are located.

mantu hold a wedding.

maos kåndhå [*kr*] → *måcå kåndhå* [*ng*]

mares = *gati*. {Dutch *mars* = march}

mas kumambang a *sekar måcåpat* metre.

mataram(an) in Yogya style. {from the name of the Muslim-Javanese kingdom founded in 1575 by Senopati, not to be confused with an earlier Hindu-Javanese kingdom of the same name}

mathet to damp the sound of a *wilah* when the next *wilah* is struck.

måtrå **1** metre. **2** pulse.

mawi with.

mayang to perform *wayang*.

mbalung to play the *balungan* as notated, subject to any necessary octave shifts. {= play the *balungan*}

mbalung nikeli a style of playing *bonang panerus*, *mbalung* style, twice as fast as the *bonang barung*.

mbandhul a Yogyanese *slenthem* playing style in which the instrument plays each note of *balungan nibani* on the preceding beat (cf. *gemakan* (1)).

mbanyu mili = *banyu mili*.

mbarang = *ngamèn* (1).

mbelèh a technique of playing the *rebab* (Yogya).

médoki the stroke that falls on the *dhong* beat in the playing of *imbal demung*: = *nglanangi*.

megar the sound of both open strings of the *rebab* being bowed.

mekak strapless bodice worn by female dancers in *wayang wong*.

mencug a dance rehearsal without gamelan accompaniment.

meneb ?move stealthily; settle down.

mengembat to *embat*.

menggembyang to *gembyang*.

méngkal to play *péngkalan*.

mentaraman = *mataram*.

menthak the resonator of the *rebab*, made of a piece of wood or coconut shell covered with a thin skin.

menur the highest part of the *rebab*, a round tapered piece of wood.

menur(an) the separate end-pieces on the ends of a *dudur*.

mérong a formal structure of gamelan *gendhing* (1), which cannot be played alone (it must be followed by an *inggah*), and is in one of the following formal structures: *kethuk 2 kerep*, *kethuk 2 awis*, *kethuk 4 kerep*, *kethuk 4 awis*, or *kethuk 8 kerep*: contrastive with *inggah*, *kethuk kerepan*.

mid = *blangkon*.

miji a player who specialises in one gamelan instrument, although capable of playing others; a rank among the *abdi dalem* at Solo.

miji punggåwå *wayang* scene where court officials are assigned their tasks.

milah **1** to play the keys (*wilahan*) of an instrument. **2** to play the *balungan*. **3** a *rebab* bowing-technique.

mineur = *minur*.

minggah = *inggah*.

minggah gendhing = *inggah gendhing*.

minggah kendhang = *inggah kendhang.*

minggah ladrang = *inggah ladrang.*

minir = *minur.*

minjal **1** a style of *balungan* decoration on the *saron.* **2** = *pinjalan.*

minur the sound of the *rebab* or voice using *barang miring* tuning. {Dutch *mineur* = minor}

mipil **1** a style of playing *bonang*, in which two notes taken from the first half or the second half of a *gåtrå* are repeated in various patterns according to *iråmå.* **2** = *pipilan* (1).

mipil baku (Yogya term) simple *mipil* playing on *bonang*, similar to Solonese *mipil* (cf. *mipil nglagu*).

mipil cegatan nggembyang = *gembyangan cegat.*

mipil cegatan tunggal single notes played on *bonang barung* in *gembyangan cegat* rhythm.

mipil låmbå a style of playing the *bonang*, as in the following example (*bonang barung, ir I*):

bonang	2 3 2 3 2 1 2 1
balungan	2 3 2 1

mipil låmbå mlampah = *mipil låmbå.*

mipil lumpatan = *mipil nibani.*

mipil ngedhongi *mipil* coinciding with the *sèlèh* note as in the following example:

balungan	. 1 . 6̣
mipil ngedhongi	. 1 . 5̣ 5̣ 1 . . 5̣ 1 5̣ . 6̣ 6̣ 1 6̣

mipil nglagu see *nglagu.*

mipil nibani Solonese style of *bonangan* used for *balungan nibani.*

mipil nikeli = *mipil rangkep.*

mipil rangkep a style of playing the *bonang*, as in the following example (*bonang barung, ir II*).

bonang	232..323212..121	(Solo)
	232.2323212.2121	(Yogya)
balungan	2 3 2 1	

mipil rangkep mlampah = *mipil rangkep.*

mipil rangkep nikeli a style of playing the *bonang*, as in the following example (*bonang barung, ir III*).

bonang	232.232.232.2323
balungan	2 3

miring **1** a notational device to indicate tones played on the *rebab* or sung, which are higher or lower than the indicated gamelan pitch. **2** the playing or singing of tones which are higher or lower than the indicated gamelan pitch. {= slanted}

mirong = *mérong.*

mitoni a celebration for the seventh month of a pregnancy, especially a first pregnancy. {*pitu* = seven}

mlaku [*ng*] → *mlampah* [*kr*] **1** see *balungan mlaku.* **2** = *mipil* (1). **3** a pattern played on the *ciblon.* **4** *balungan* embellished in the following style:

balungan	2 3 2 1	3 2 6 5
embellished	23532121	35321635

mlampah [*kr*] → *mlaku* [*ng*]: also = *mipil* (1).

mlathèn the ornamental tip of the *mangol*, outside the *kupingan.*

mlatuk a type of *åbå-åbå* from the *dhalang*, who also strikes the *kothak*, usually to request a piece or to signal the continuation of the scene. The sound of a *mlatuk* is: *dhog – dhog – dhog – dherodhog.*

mlåyå = *låyå.*

mlèsèd = *plèsèd.*

mligi ?= *kendhangan gandrung-gandrung.*

molak-malik to change between *sléndro* and *pélog* in mid-piece.

mondholan a hairpiece bound with cloth.

mondrèng a type of *slawatan.*

mondring texts used in *slawatan.*

monggang see *gamelan monggang.*

monggangan playing that imitates the melody of the *gamelan monggang*, e.g. a style of playing the *gendèr* in which notes are separated by a *pancer* tone.

mrabot a suite of pieces usually played together.

mradånggå = *kendhang.*

mrambat see *ngrambat.*

mrebot *bedhug* player.

mulai gérong entry of *gérongan.*

mulur see *balungan mulur.*

mulyåraras performance to honour a person.

mundå = *gong.*

mundur second beat of a *gåtrå.*

mundur gendhing the return from battle, the fourth stage of a Yogya-style dance suite representing a battle.

munggah = *inggah.*

munggah gendhing = *inggah gendhing.*

munggang(an) = *monggang(an).*

muraba = *kendhang.*

murada = *kendhang.*

murawa = *kendhang.*

nabuh hit with a *tabuh.*

nacah **1** a style of playing the *saron panerus* in pairs of strokes (see *nacah låmbå, nacah rangkep, nacah rangkep nikeli*). **2** = *kinthilan.* {= chopping}

nacah kembangan = *nyacah.*

nacah låmbå a style of playing the *saron panerus* with two strokes per *balungan* beat.

nacah rangkep a style of playing the *saron panerus* with four strokes per *balungan* beat.

nacah rangkep nikeli a style of playing the *saron panerus* with eight strokes per *balungan* beat.

nådå tone, note.

nådå dasar = *dhasar.*

nådå-nådå kelompok tone groupings.

nadantårå interval.

nådå sèlèh **1** the goal tone, or ending tone, of a melodic phrase. **2** the last pitch of any even-numbered *gatrå.*

någå snake with teeth, wearing a crown.

nångkå jackfruit, a timber used for drum bodies and the frames of instruments.

napas a style of *saron* playing, the same as *neceg* but with much-reduced volume.
nåwå small holes in the *penthat* of a *rebab*.
nawur to 'busk it'; to improvise a *garap*. {*tawur* = brawl}
nayågå = *niyågå*.
ndadi a state of trance used in some dances.
ndamel to play the *damel* part; = *gawé*.
ndhawah **1** to continue with. **2** = *dhawah*.
ndhawahi see *balungan ndhawahi*.
ndhedheg = *dhedheg*.
ndhodhog kothak to make *dhodhogan*.
nduduk **1** a type of *rebab* bowing in syncopated rhythm. **2** a *gendèr* melodic pattern. **3** a class of patterns on the *bonang*: see *nduduk gembyang* and *nduduk tunggal*. **4** = *gembyangan* (1).
nduduk gembyang **1** a *bonang* technique of playing octaves in rhythmic groupings of three. **2** collective term for *gembyangan låmbå*, *gembyangan dados*, *gembyangan rangkep* and *gembyangan rangkep nikeli*.
nduduk tunggal **1** a *bonang* technique of playing single tones in rhythmic groupings of three. **2** collective term for patterns corresponding to *nduduk gembyang* (2) but using single notes only.
neceg **1** a Yogyanese style of playing single notes or pairs of notes on *saron*, *demung* or *saron panerus* while damping (cf. *ngencot*). **2** to damp a note while playing it, e.g. on *bonang*, *celempung* or *siter*. {= to damp}
nèkeran a type of *sanggan*.
nem one of the tones of the gamelan scale, notated as 6. {= six}
nembang to perform *tembang*: also = *urå-urå*.
ngadhal see *balungan ngadhal*.
ngamèn **1** to perform in public from place to place, in a group of four or five players, e.g. on *siter*, *gendèr barut*, *kendhang* and *gong bumbung* or *gong kemodhong*; to busk. **2** see *suwuk ngamèn*. {= beggar, busker}
ngampat seseg gradual change of speed.
ngandhap [*kr*] → *ngisor* [*ng*]
ngantal to slow down.
ngaplak **1** a named *singgetan* for the *ciblon*. **2** a style of *kendhangan* for accompanying *trisig* movements in dance.
ngarep see *nyamleng*, *tabuhan ngarep*.
ngayati perform, prepare for.
ngecèk martelé, a bowing technique for the *rebab*.
ngecrèk = *ngecèk*.
ngedhasih a Yogyanese style of playing the *rebab*, relatively closer to the *balungan* (cf. *nyendari*).
ngédhé play left-handed.
ngedhongi **1** to play the on-beat part in *imbal demung* or *imbal saron* (cf. *nggawé*). **2** see *pinjalan ngedhongi*.
ngekik glissando up to the high register on the *rebab*.
ngelik **1** the section of a *gendhing* (1) that rises in pitch and is not optional. **2** an optional section of a *gendhing* (1), which is signalled by the rising pitch of the *rebab, gendèr, gambang, bonang* and *pesindhèn*. **3** a high-pitched voice. **4** (playing in) high register. **5** see *pathetan ngelik*. {= get smaller, go up in pitch}
ngempyung to play a *kempyung*.
ngencot to play (*saron, demung, saron panerus*) while simultaneously damping the note struck; the pattern played is usually anapaestic (cf. *neceg*). {= move feet up and down}
ngendhoni laras to lower a note on the gamelan, by filing the *kelemahan* part of a *wilah*, or the *rai*, *dudu* or *pok pencu* of a *pencon* instrument.
ngenyut = *gemakan* (1). {= laugh}
ngepok a variant of Yogya-style *demung imbal*.
nggandhul **1** a *rebab* bowing technique. **2** a delayed stroke of the *kenong*, *kempul* or *gong*. {= delay slightly}
ngganter-1 dividing *balungan* beats, as in *kethuk* strokes in *srepegan*.
nggantèr-2 dividing pairs of *balungan* beats, as in *kethuk* strokes for *lancaran*.
nggantung to play a special *bonang* treatment for a *balungan nggantung*.
nggantung låmbå a single *nggantung* pattern for the *bonang*.
nggantung rangkep a double *nggantung* pattern for the *bonang*.
nggawé to play the off-beat part in *imbal demung* or *imbal saron* (cf. *ngedhongi*, *nginthil*).
nggemak = *gemakan* (1).
nggembyang a style of octave playing by *gendèr, gambang* or *bonang*: see also *gembyang*.
nggembyang låmbå 'single' or fast *gembyang*.
nggembyang nyegat = *gembyang(an) cegat(an)*.
nggembyang rangkep 'double' or slow *gembyang*.
nggendhing to learn *gendhing*.
nggérong to sing *gérong*.
nggodhong see *bonang nggodhong*.
ngguguk continous playing of the *kempul*, as in *sampak*.
ngidung **1** sing. **2** compose poetry.
ngikik a *rebab* bowing-technique.
nginthil to play the on-beat part in *imbal demung* or *imbal saron* (cf. *nggawé*). {*kinthil* = follow}
ngisor [*ng*] → *ngandhap* [*kr*] **1** low register. **2** see *popor ngisor*.
ngiwå = *ngédhé*.
nglagu **1** a type of *mipil* for *bonang* in Yogya style, using three or more different notes for each pair of *balungan* notes. **2** patterns played on *bonang* for *balungan nibani*. **3** a Yogyanese style of *peking* playing. {= make a melody}
nglagu rangkep a style of *garap* for *peking* in Yogyanese style.
nglanangi the stroke that falls on the *dhing* beat in the playing of *imbal demung*; = *médoki*.
nglaras to tune an instrument.
ngracik **1** the style of playing the *bonang* in the opening section of a *gendhing* from the repertoire of *gamelan sekati*: see *racikan*. **2** a style of *saron* playing; see *balungan ngracik*. **3** a type of Yogya-style *bonang* playing, similar to doubling of density of *balungan* by *saron* in *kinthilan* (1). **4** a type of playing on *siter*, etc., similar to *mipil nglagu* on *bonang*; = *pipilan* (1). **5** a style of *ciblon* playing with doubled density.
ngrambat a type of Yogya-style *bonang* playing, realising a move to a higher register via a smooth contour instead of a *gembyang*. {= creep like a vine}
ngrangin a gamelan sound that is indistinct but also pleasant.
ngukel a technique of playing a *gendèr* or *gambang* line with a near-circular motion of the right hand, e.g. repeating the notes 6̣ 1 2 1.
ngungkung playing the *rebab* in the middle register.
ngunus keris to withdraw the *kris* from the sheath (*warångkå*).

nguthik a type of Yogya-style *bonang* playing, combining a change of register with *nglagu* patterns.

nguyu-uyu **1** a performance of *gendhing sabetan* on the day before a festival or celebration, or earlier in the same day (Solonese term). **2** (Yogyanese term) = *klenèngan*.

Ni abbreviation of *Nyai* (cf. *Ki*).

niågå = *niyågå*.

nibå = *dhawah*.

nibani **1** to play only on the strong beats (*dhong*). **2** see *balungan nibani*.

nikeli **1** a style of playing *bonang panerus*, playing the same tones as the *bonang barung* but twice as fast: see also *mbalung nikeli*. **2** a Yogyanese *peking* playing style. **3** see *gembyangan rangkep nikeli*, *mipil rangkep nikeli*, *nacah rangkep nikeli*. {= to increase, multiply}

nitir **1** a style of *kenong* playing in *sampak*, with two strokes on the *kenong* for every *balungan* note. **2** a 'rolled' style of *kethuk* playing, used in *irâmå II* or slower. **3** repetition of one note in the playing style of the *saron* or *peking*. **4** extended repetition of one note on *balungan* instruments in the *suwuk* of a *sampak*. {= sound repeatedly}

nitis a style of *saron* playing.

niyågå a gamelan musician.

njuluk = *juluk*.

noot/not/nut note, tone. {Dutch *noot*}

notasi [*in*] notation.

nunggal–misah to converge and separate, as of different parts in the texture of *karawitan*.

nungkak a *rebab* bowing technique.

nut = *noot*.

nut åndhå = *titilaras åndhå*.

nut ångkå **1** = *titilaras kepatihan*. **2** a notation system similar to *titilaras kepatihan*, used for notating Western music, especially for choral parts. {*ångkå* = number, cipher}

nut ranté = *titilaras ranté*.

nutur style of *kenong* playing that anticipates important notes within the lines of *palaran*.

nyacah patterns played by *saron* or *saron panerus* in certain forms such as *srepegan*, unrelated to *balungan* but coinciding with it at *sèlèh* points.

Nya(h)i honorific title, usually translated as 'Venerable', given to women and (rarely) to gamelan (cf. *Kyai*).

nyamat **1** gold knob at top of *tropong*. **2** see *pathet*, *pélog nyamat*.

nyamber a dance movement (Yogya).

nyamleng to present *uyon-uyon* especially with *tabuhan ngarep* instruments and vocalists.

nyampar a style of *balungan* decoration on the *saron*. {= poke with the foot}

nyamping [*ki*] → *jarik* [*ng*]

nyamping sérédan wide *bathik* cloth, reaching to ankles and to floor level at one edge, worn by female dancers in *wayang wong*.

nyarug/nyaruk **1** = *nyampar*. **2** in *bonangan*, a distortion of the expected rhythm, often found in *bukå*. **3** see *gembyangan sarug*. {*sarug* = drag the foot}

nyebrak to partially withdraw the *kris* from the *warångkå*.

nyeceg, nyecek = *neceg*.

nyekar verb form of *sekar*; = perform song.

nyelå a *rebab* bowing-technique.

nyendhal a style of playing the *rebab*.

nyendari a Solonese style of playing the *rebab*, relatively less close to the *balungan* (cf. *ngedhasih*).

nyengkléng a discordant combination.

nyenyepan a type of *sanggan*.

nyigar penjalin a form of *wilah* for *saron*, with a profile like split rattan; also used for *gendèr* in brass and iron. {*penjalin* [*ng*] = rattan}

nyodhèk = *sodhèkan*.

odangi(y)ah = *ådångiyah*.

ombak(an) **1** the beats of a sound vibration, especially those characteristic of a *gong ageng*. **2** the singing of the lengthened syllables *'aaaaaaa' or 'yaaaaaa'* by a *dhalang*, usually at the end of a *sulukan*, e.g. *ådå-ådå*: = *umpak* (4). {= wave (of the sea)}

ombak banyu vocal trill.

ompak = *umpak*.

ompak klénangan optional *garap* for the *ompak* section of certain *ketawang*, based on elements of *gamelan cåråbalèn*.

ompak-ompak = *embat*.

ompak-ompakan = *umpak-umpakan*.

ompak-ompak meråtå equidistant tuning.

oncèn string of flowers decorating the sheath of the *kris* in a dancer's costume.

orèn strand of hair as part of dancer's costume.

pådå **1** the end of a stanza. **2** a stanza. **3** a punctuation mark. **4** structural cell of a *palaran*. {= foot}

pådå dirgå two or more *pådå pålå*.

pådå lingså **1** the hook-shaped character of Javanese script commonly used as a comma. **2** a line of poetry.

pådå pålå a *gatrå*, or one line of poetry, consisting of two or more *wåndå* and two or more *pedhotan*.

pådåswårå the final vowel of one line of poetry.

padegongan ?

padeswårå a single verse consisting of two or more *pådå dirgå*.

padhang **1** an antecedent phrase that is followed by *ulihan*, a consequent phrase. **2** a question, an unresolved musical phrase. {*?(a)dhang* = wait}

padhang bulan = *padhang rembulan*. {= moonlight}

padhang rembulan a description of an instrument of *pencon* form with only the *pencu* and *rai* filed smooth.

padhat, padhet abbreviated; see *wayang padhat*.

padhoman guide, directive, standard.

padupan bowl containing incense.

paèsan a bevelled end on a *wilah* of *blimbingan* form.

pagan **1** a horizontal rail of a *rancakan*. **2** = *rancakan*.

pagelaran **1** presentation, event. **2** a north-facing open outer hall, part of the *kraton*.

pagongan two buildings on either side of the courtyard in front of the great mosque (*Mesjid Ageng*) on the northern *alun-alun* of the *kraton Yogya* and the *kraton Solo*, in which *gamelan sekati* are placed and played from 5 to 12 Maulud.

paguyuban association, club.

pahargyan celebration, festival.

pakaian jawa [*in*] 'court dress'; the most formal dress for men.

pakeliran presentation; the aspect of a *wayang* performance that deals with the action on the *kelir* rather than the literature.

pakeliran palat ?

pakem printed scenarios of some of the stories of the *wayang kulit* repertoire.

paku a post that stops the *wilah* of the *saron*, etc., from moving sideways; = *placak* (1). {= nail}

paku baut a threaded fastener, e.g. the eye bolt to which the *pluntur* are fastened in some *rancakan*.

pakurmatan ceremonial. {*kurmat* = honour}

palaran a style of singing *sekar måcåpat* in free rhythm accompanied by *gong, kenong, kempul, kethuk, gendèr, gambang, celempung* and *kendhang*, which may or may not be *rangkep* (Solo): the song is sung by a solo voice, or with a man and a woman alternating stanzas. Also called *uran-uran*, *janturan*.

palemahan = *pelemahan*.

palu a hammer used in gamelan-making.

pamangku = *pemangku*.

pamangku iråmå = *pemangku iråmå*.

pamangku lagu = *pemangku lagu*.

pamatut **1** = *kethuk*. **2** = *kendhang*.

Pamèran Kraton annual *kraton* festival.

pamijèn **1** special; unique to one piece. **2** see *gendhing pamijèn*. **3** see *kendhangan pamijèn*. {= singular, one of a kind; ?from *miji* = select, or *siji* = one}

Pamulangan Beksa Ngayogyakarta a private institute of Yogya-style dance education.

pamurbå leader, one who has authority.

pamurbå iråmå the instrument in charge of *iråmå*, i.e. *kendhang*.

pamurbå lagu the one who has authority over melody, the instruments that lead the melody (*lagu*), i.e. (a) *rebab*, *gendèr*, *bonang*, (b) *rebab*.

pamurbå yatmåkå the one who has authority in presenting the inner feeling of a *gendhing*.

pånå part of the *bau*, towards the *recep*, of a *pencon* instrument.

pånåkawan **1** the clown servants of a *wayang kulit* performance, usually Semar, Garéng, Pétruk and Bagong. **2** a term indicating the rank of a court musician (Solo).

pananggalan like the new moon: description of the eyes of certain *wayang kulit* characters.

panataan = *penataan*.

påncånåkå sharpened thumbnail of a *wayang kulit* puppet, especially Bimå, used as a weapon.

pancer a note, usually of constant pitch, played on the *pin* of *balungan nibani*; a similar pattern in *gendèran*. {?= marker post}

pandhé blacksmith, gamelan smith.

pandhé gångså gamelan smith.

pandhitå **1** priest. **2** holy hermit. **3** mystic teacher.

panembråmå a *gendhing* and a *gérongan* especially composed to welcome a distinguished guest.

panembung description applied to instruments pitched in low register within a family: see *bonang panembung*, *gendèr panembung*. {*tembung* = words}

panerus **1** description applied to instruments pitched in high register within a family: see *bonang panerus*, *gendèr panerus*, *saron panerus*, *siter panerus*. **2** = *bonang panerus*. **3** = *saron panerus*. {*terus* = continue}

panerusan instrumental parts that fill the gaps between the strokes of the slower instrumental parts; (soft-style) elaborating instruments.

panéwu gendhing a court official responsible for the care of the gamelan.

pangapit the individually mounted pots of the *bonang* in *gamelan sekatèn*. {*apit* = flank}

panggih temantèn the ritual meeting of the bride and groom at a wedding.

panggung stage.

pangkal [*in*] the end of a beater that is held.

pangkat dhawah = *angkat dhawah*.

pangkat inggah = *angkat dhawah*.

pangkat minggah = *angkat dhawah*.

pangkat munggah = *angkat dhawah*.

pangkat ndhawah = *angkat dhawah*.

pangkat unggah = *angkat dhawah*.

pangkon the wooden frame of the *saron demung*, *saron barung* and *saron penerus*.

pangkur **1** a *sekar måcåpat* metre. **2** the name of certain *gendhing* (1).

pangrakit arranger.

pangrawit = *niyågå*.

pangripta composer.

paningset [*ki*] → *sabuk* [*ng, kr*]

panjak a gamelan player, especially a player for *wayang kulit*.

panjanturan = *janturan* (1).

panji an expert in making metal gamelan instruments, the coordinator of the various workmen involved. {from Panji, a character in a cycle of traditional stories used in dance and *wayang*}

panjidhor = *jédher*.

pantun(an) poetic form of Malay origin, used especially in Sundanese music.

panunggul **1** one of the tones of the *pélog* scale: in *kepatihan* notation, *panunggul* = 1. **2** [*ki*] → *kuluk* [*ng*]. **3** middle finger. {= one}

påpå rårå a student of the gamelan who is starting from absolute basics.

papat four.

papathet = *pathetan*.

pårå = *pånå*.

paråmå kawi **1** literary scholar. **2** (competence in) the titles and names of the characters in *wayang*; one of the skills of a *dhalang*.

paråmå sastrå **1** grammar. **2** (competence in) the literature on which a *lakon* is based; one of the skills of a *dhalang*.

parang barong a diagonally striped *bathik* motif commonly used in costumes for kings in *wayang wong*, etc. {*parang* = machete, *barong* = giant}

parang rusak a *bathik* motif (cf. *parang barong*) for strong noble characters of royal descent, such as Gatutkåcå and Indrajid. {*rusak* = broken}

paré anom a coloured motif (yellow and green). {*paré* = bitter melon, *anom* = young, under-ripe}

parikan **1** a form of Javanese verse in rhyming couplets with 12 syllables per line, used by *pesindhèn* in some *céngkok*. **2** see *senggakan parikan*.

parikesit a *batik* motif (cf. *parang barong*) commonly used for a noble and refined character, e.g. Abimanyu

paringgitan an area of the *kraton* where *wayang kulit* performances take place.

påså = *recep.*

paséban (n)jåbå [*ng*] *wayang* scene outside the royal audience hall. {*jåbå* → *jawi* [*kr*]}

paséban (n)jawi [*kr*] → *paséban jåbå*

pasisir region stretching along much of the north coast of Java, characterised by greater influence from foreign cultures. {= coast}

pasu (rai) = *manis rai.*

patalon a sequence of pieces played before a *wayang* performance (cf. *talu*). {from *talu*}

patapukan = *wayang topèng.*

pathet **1** a modal classification system implying tonal range (tessitura), melodic patterns and principal notes: see table opposite. **2** = *pathetan.*

pathetan **1** one of the categories of songs (*suluk*), sung by a *dhalang* during a *wayang kulit* performance, accompanied by *rebab, gendèr, gambang* and *suling.* **2** similar passage played by the instruments alone as a prelude or postlude to *gendhing* outside the context of a *wayang* performance, and serving to establish or confirm the *pathet.*

pathetan jingking a *pathetan* starting and ending on 5.

pathetan jugag short *pathetan.*

pathetan ngelik *pathetan* in a high register.

pathetan wantah full-length *pathetan.*

pathet babon = *pathet induk.*

pathet barang highest of the *pathet* in *pélog*, with range from 3̣ to 3̇.

pathet bem collective description, applied mainly in Yogya, for *pathet* in *pélog* using the *bem* scale, otherwise categorised as *pélog pathet nem* or *pathet limå.*

pathet galong *pathet* higher than *manyurå*, used in final hour of *wayang* in Yogya style.

pathet induk 'native' pathet of a composition. {*induk* = mother}

pathet limå lowest *pathet* in *pélog*, with range from 1̣ to 2̇.

pathet manyurå **1** highest regular *pathet* in *sléndro*, with range extending from 3̣ up to 3̇ with occasional 5̇. **2** (in *pélog*) = *pathet nyamat.*

pathet manyuri ?= *pathet galong.*

pathet nem **1** lowest *pathet* in *sléndro*, with range from 2̣ to 3̇. **2** middle-pitched *pathet* in *pélog*, with range from 2̣ to 3̇.

pathet nyamat *pathet* in *pélog* with range from 3̣ up to 3̇, and other characteristics of *pathet manyurå* in *sléndro*: piece in this *pathet* are more commonly assigned to *pélog nem.*

pathet sångå **1** middle-pitched *pathet* in *sléndro*, with range from 5̣ to 2̇. **2** a *pathet* sometimes said to exist in *pélog*, with the characteristics of *sléndro sångå.*

pathet sendon = *sendon.*

pathokan = *padhoman.*

pati [*ng*] → *pejah* [*kr*]

patut [*ng*] → *pantes* [*kr*] suitable, fitting; implies a special pattern, *kendhangan*, etc., for one composition.

patut lima a type of *pélog* gamelan tuning, in Bali, in which there are five pitch-levels per octave.

Central Java [a]			
sléndro	*pathet nem*		lowest
	pathet sångå		↓
	pathet manyurå		
	pathet galong/manyuri		highest
pélog	*pathet limå/gangsal*	} *pathet bem* (Yogya)	lowest
	pathet nem		↓
	pathet barang		highest
	pathet manyurå/nyamat [b]		
	pathet sångå [c]		

a. The names used in Banyumas for the main *pathet* (the first three listed for each *laras*) are essentially the same. b. Equivalent of *pélog pathet nem* but with a range of 3̣ to 3̇: notation is the same as *sléndro manyurå.* c. Equivalent of *pélog pathet nem* but with a range of 5̣ to 2̇.

Madura		
sléndro	*pathet nem*	lowest
	pathet wolu	↓
	pathet sångå	highest
pélog	*pathet wolu*	lowest
	pathet nem	↓
	pathet sångå	highest

East Java		
sléndro	*pathet sepuluh*	lowest
	pathet wolu	↓
	pathet sångå	
	pathet serang	highest
pélog	*pathet pengasih/sorog/bem*	lowest
	pathet miring/sliring/barang	highest

pawang a dancer whose job is to lead and to 'bring round' trance-dancers.

pawon 'shoulder' of an instrument?

péci = *pici.*

pedhalangan the art of the *dhalang.*

pedhoman = *padhoman.*

pedhot = *pedhotan* (2).

pedhotan **1** the segments of a line of verse created by the caesura. **2** the caesura in the central section of a line of verse, used by the singer for taking a breath. **3** breath.

pejah [*kr*] → *mati, pati* [*ng*] description of a type of *imbal demung* with nothing played at the *sèlèh* point (cf. *gesang*). {= dead}

pekak(an) to grip a note to stop it sounding.
peking = *saron panerus.*
pekingan the part played by the *peking.*
pelandhan a water bath used for quenching the metal during manufacture of gamelan instruments.
pelatih [*in*] trainer; leader of a rehearsal.
pelemahan **1** the back of the central portion of a *wilah.* **2** the foot at the bottom of the *sikil* of a *rebab.* **3** the bottom of the *srenten* of a *rebab*, which rests on the *babad* (1).
pelengkap the upper neighbour of the most important pitch-level (*dhong*) of a given *pathet.*
pélog **1** tuning system in which the octave is divided into seven unequal intervals (cf. *sléndro*). **2** one of the tones of the *pélog* tuning system: in *kepatihan* notation, *pélog* = 4.
pélog barang **1** scale based on *pélog* notes 2 3 5 6 7. **2** = *pathet barang.*
pélog bem **1** scale based on *pélog* notes 1 2 3 5 6. **2** = *pathet bem.*
pemâcâ kândhâ the person who delivers the *kândhâ* in Yogya-style *wayang wong* (see *mâcâ kândhâ*).
pemain [*in*] player.
pemangku the one who holds something in his lap, i.e. the protector and upholder of a country or city, metaphorically extended to mean the upholder of *lagu* or *irâmâ* in gamelan music.
pemangku irâmâ (one of) the instruments that have the task of helping the *kendhang* present the form of the *gendhing* and of indicating the levels of *irâmâ*, i.e. *kethuk, kenong, kempul* and *gong.*
pemangku lagu (one of) the instruments that have the task of playing the basic melody (*lagu pokok, balungan*), sometimes designated as *saron demung, saron barung, saron peking* and *slenthem,* and at other times as *gendèr, bonang, gambang, celempung, gendèr penerus, bonang penerus, slenthem, saron demung* and *saron penerus.*
pembalung an instrument that plays the *balungan.*
pembonang *bonang* player.
pemurbâ irâmâ the instrument that controls *irâmâ*, i.e. the *kendhang.*
pemurbâ lagu an instrument that leads and determines the *lagu*, i.e. *rebab, gendèr* or *bonang.*
pén = *pin.*
penabuh player.
penacah **1** a small *saron.* **2** a type of *bonang.*
penangis a Sundanese tuning.
penari [*in*] dancer.
penata [*in*] arranger.
penataan [*in*] a suite of pieces, usually newly arranged rather than in a standard sequence such as a *talu.*
pencipta creator, composer.
pencon (instrument) with a *pencu.*
pencon gandhul a *pencon* instrument suspended from above, e.g. gong or *kempul.*
pencon pangkon a *pencon* instrument suspended by *pluntur* below, e.g. *kenong* or *kethuk.*
pencu the boss of a gong/pot such as *gong ageng, kempul, kenong, bonang, kethuk, kempyang*, etc.
pendhâpâ [*ng*], *pendhapi* [*kr*] pavilion with three or four open sides, and a *joglo* roof supported by pillars.
pend(h)awan interval between two adjacent notes.
pendhok a sheath for a *kris*, made of gold, silver or brass, and often decorated with a *bathik* motif.
pendhopo = *pendhâpâ.*
penerusan = *panerusan.*
peneteg small *kendhang* used in ceremonial gamelan.
pengantèn anyar **1** the two *rebab* strings together. **2** the *rebab* strings above the bridge (cf. *lepet*).
pengarah acara [*in*] master of ceremonies.
pengèjèr beats produced by Balinese instruments tuned as *pengisep* and *pengumbang.*
pengendhang drum-player.
pengeprak *keprak* player.
penggérong (male) singer of *gérong.*
penggesek [*in*] bow (of a rebab).
penghormatan [*in*] = *pakurmatan.*
pengirit the leader of a group of *kraton* gamelan players.
pengisep the tuning of the higher-pitched instrument of a pair of Balinese *gendèr*; when played with its mate (*pengumbang*) simultaneously on the same tone, acoustic beats will result.
péngkalan a Yogyanese style of playing *balungan* on the *saron*, with notes irregularly displaced to off-beats.
penglaras tuner.
pengumbang the tuning of the lower-pitched instrument of a pair of Balinese *gendèr*; when played simultaneously on the same pitch as its mate (*pengisep*), acoustic beats will result.
peniti gamelan = *anggong.*
penitil = *saron panerus.*
penitir a *bonang*-type instrument in *gamelan monggang*, tuned to 1 and grouped with *kenongan* and *banggèn*; the term may also be applied to the three instruments together.
penonthong a gong shaped like a *kenong* but suspended vertically by a cord; found in the *gamelan monggang* (two *penonthong*, tuned to 4 and 7), also in *gamelan kodhok ngorèk* (two *penonthong*) and *gamelan cârâ balèn* (one *penonthong*).
penthat the back of the *bathokan* of a *rebab.*
penunggul = *panunggul.*
penunthung **1** the smallest of the gamelan drums, essentially interchangeable with the *ketipung.* **2** the part played by such a drum in conjunction with *kendhang ageng* in *kendhangan* for *gendhing.*
penyacah **1** a Balinese gamelan instrument similar to a *gendèr.* **2** = *saron penacah.*
penyajian [*in*] performance, presentation (usually referring to the process: cf. *pertunjukan*).
penyusun composer, compiler, arranger.
peralihan [*in*] transition.
perampogan = *rampogan.*
perang ampyak scene representing the army in the forest, where the forest rather than the opposing army is the enemy, in the first part of a *wayang.*

perang amuk-amukan later, intense and conclusive stages of final battle in third part of a *wayang.*

perangan the third part, representing the battle itself, in a Yogya-style dance suite for a battle.

perang brubuh the final battle in a *wayang wong* story.

perang gagal indecisive battle that ends the first part of a *wayang.*

perangkat any gamelan ensemble.

perang kembang the main battle in the second part of a *wayang*, in which the hero defeats the ogre/monster of the forest.

perang lakon = *perang tanggung.*

perang pindho battle scene that ends the second part of a *wayang.*

perang sampak the later and conclusive stages of the final battle in a *wayang.*

perang simpangan ?= *perang gagal.*

perang tanggung earlier, inconclusive stages of the final battle in the third part of a *wayang.*

percobaan [*in*] session to try out a new gamelan before it is shipped.

pertunjukan [*in*] performance, show (usually referring to the event: cf. *penyajian*).

perunggu = *prunggu.*

pesindhèn **1** a solo female singer in the gamelan. **2** any singer, male or female, for example, the *pesindhèn bedhåyå.*

pesindhèn bedhåyå the group of male and female singers who perform the vocal parts in a *bedhåyå* suite.

petegakan = *klenèngan.*

pethetan rounded corner(s) of a *wilah.*

pethilan **1** an episode from a long drama, performed separately. **2** a duet dance for male and female dancers, usually representing a fight.

pewayangan [*ng*] = *pringgitan* [*kr*]

pici [*in*] rimless cap.

pidekså well-built, describing *wayang kulit* characters of medium size.

pilesan part of *ciblon* drumming for *iråmå III.*

pimpinan director, leader.

pin a dot in *kepatihan* notation: for most instruments, represents a continuation of the previous tone (i.e. the latter is not damped), but for some instruments means a rest. {from Dutch *punt*}

pindhah laras transpose.

pindhah pathet transpose.

pinggir edge, side.

pinjalan **1** a style of playing interlocking parts involving *slenthem*, *demung* and *saron.* **2** = *imbal* on *bonang* or *siter/celempung.* **3** a style of *gambang* playing in which the right hand plays twice as fast as the left hand.

pinjalan mbalung *pinjalan* (1) in which *saron* plays the *balungan* line.

pinjalan ngedhongi *pinjalan* (1) in which *saron* replaces the first note of the *gåtrå* with an anticipation of the second note, and the third note by an anticipation of the fourth note.

pin mundur *balungan* with *pin* occurring on the *dhong* rather than the *dhing.* {*mundur* = backwards, delayed}

pipi the curved side of the *kemanak* where it is struck by the beater.

pipilan **1** a technique on *gendèr* and *siter/celempung* in which the tones are not struck simultaneously by the two hands, but in succession, producing a single melodic line. **2** = *mipil* (1).

PKJT (*Pusat Kebudayaan Jawa Tengah*) cultural centre at Surakarta.

placak **1** a post holding the *pluntur* on the *grobogan* of *gendèr, slenthem, kenong rentèng*, etc. **2** posts fitted to the frames of the *saron* family and the *gambang* to hold the *wilah* in place. **3** tuning pegs to which the strings of *celempung*, etc., are attached. **4** a drum stand.

plajaran [*kr*] → *playon* [*ng*]

plancak = *tracak*; = *placak* (2).

plangkan **1** the generic term for the wooden frames of the instruments of the gamelan, i.e. *gayor, grobogan, pangkon, rancakan.* **2** the wooden frame for the *kendhang.* **3** the stand for the *kendhang.* **4** the stand for the *rebab.* **5** lid or entire box of *gong kemodhong.*

playon [*ng*] → *plajaran* [*kr*] a *bentuk* with a *kenong* stroke on every note, and a *kempul* stroke on the second note of every pair; the Yogya equivalent of a Solonese *srepegan.* {*layu* = run}

plencon = *pencon.*

pleng = *laras mleng, suårå pleng.*

plèsèd to slip off target; to hint or pun.

plèsèdan **1** the anticipation of a strong tone in the *gatrå* preceding the *gåtrå* that includes the strong tone. **2** the extension of a melodic phrase by the *pesindhèn* beyond the goal tone (*nådå sèlèh*) in which the final pitch of the *pesindhèn* is the same as the last pitch of the next *gatrå.* **3** notes on the *suling* that depart from the standard notes of the scale, achieved by partially closing a finger-hole. **4** anticipation of an important note by a special pattern.

plèsèdan céngkok *plèsèdan* (2) sung by the *pesindhèn* when there is a succession of repeated tones immediately after the *sèlèh* tone, but the repeated tones are not in stepwise relation to the *sèlèh* tone, for example, *balungan*:

2126̣̂ 33 . .

plèsèdan jujugan *plèsèdan* (2) sung by the *pesindhèn* when there is a succession of repeated tones immediately after the *sèlèh* tone, and in which the repeated tones are an octave or more distant from the *sèlèh* tone, for example, *balungan*:

. 16̣5̣̂ 66 . .

plèsèdan mbesut *plèsèdan* (2) sung by the *pesindhèn* when there is a succession of repeated tones immediately after the *sèlèh* tone, and the repeated tones are in stepwise relation to the *sèlèh* tone, for example, *balungan*:

2126̣̂ 11 . .

plèsèdan tungkakan *plèsèdan* (2) sung by the *pesindhèn* when there is a succession of repeated tones immediately after the *sèlèh* tone, and in which the tones leading to the *sèlèh* tone are too low for the *pesindhèn* to sing, for example, *balungan*:

. . 2̣3̣ 5̣6̣3̣5̣̂ 1̇1̇ . .

plèsèdan wilet *plèsèdan* (2) sung by the *pesindhèn* when the tones following the *sèlèh* tone are not repeated and the *pesindhèn* is guided by the *rebab*, for example, *balungan*:

. 1̇65̂ . 621

ploncon body of a *kendhang* before the drumhead is added.

pluntur the cords that support the *wilah* of the *gendèr* or *slenthem*, or the horizontal gongs of the *kenong, bonang*, etc.

pocapan **1** = *caritå.* **2** dialogue delivered by dancers in Yogya-style dance drama.

pokok 1 starting note of a scale? **2** see *lagu pokok*.
pok pencu the lowest part of the *pencu*, adjacent to the *widheng*.
polos see *wilah polos*.
ponthang see *rebab ponthang*.
popor ndhuwur the neck of the *rebab* below the *watangan* and connecting to the *menthak*, of tapering round shape, about 5 cm in diameter, and in several pieces.
popor ngisor a round stock similar to the *popor ndhuwur* but shorter, attached to the bottom of the *menthak*.
pråbå ornament worn on back by dancer or *wayang kulit* puppet, and symbolising holiness.
prådå gold plating or gilt used to decorate costumes.
pradånggå 1 = *niyågå*. **2** gamelan [in *båså kedhaton*].
prajuritan dance representing soldiers.
pranakan long-sleeved jacket in blue *lurik*, worn by *kraton* servants.
pranasmårå a sung theatrical genre invented in the twentieth century, based upon the stories of *wayang gedhog*, in which all parts are played by women.
prapèn the charcoal fire used in gamelan-making.
prenès with an intimate feeling; light-hearted (as description of mood of a piece).
pringgitan [*kr*] = *pewayangan* [*ng*] **1** description of reduced gamelan as used for *wayang* accompaniment. **2** area of *kraton* designated for performance of *wayang kulit*. {*ringgit* [*kr*] = *wayang* [*ng*]}
prunggu bronze: also called *gångså*.
pucuk pencu the boss of a *pencon* instrument, where the instrument is struck.
pujånggå court poet.
puksur frame drum played with a wooden mallet.
punakawan = *panakawan*.
pupuh 1 Balinese notation system using Balinese characters and the vocables *dhong*, *dhèng*, *dhung*, *dhang* and *dhing*: also called *pupuh dhong-dhing*. **2** a set of verses (*padeswårå*). **3** a group of lines (*pådå*) in *sekar ageng*.
purå palace (applied to the junior palaces at Solo and Yogya).
purwåkanthi text effects used for their sound quality alone.
purwåkanthi sastrå consonant alliteration in verse.
purwåkanthi swårå internal rhyme or assonance in verse.
purwåkanthi tembang repetition of syllables from the end of one line of verse at the start of the next.
pusåkå an object with magical power, considered an heirloom of the court, e.g. instruments, gamelan, dances, literary works, weapons.
puthut gelut/gelud a melodic pattern heard in *balungan* lines, realised with special patterns on decorating instruments. {= quarrelling disciples}
puthut semèdi a *céngkok* equivalent to the second half of *puthut gelut*.
putran *wayang kulit* puppets representing princes and nobles.
putrå-putri (of) mixed sexes. {*putrå* = male; *putri* = female}
putrèn *wayang kulit* puppets representing noblewomen.
putungan the ridges around the holes in a *wilah*.
rabånå = *terbang*.
racikan the opening section of a *gendhing* played by the *gamelan sekati*, consisting of several *gongan*, in which the *bonang* is the featured instrument and the *saron* play only on what would usually be the *kenong* tones.
racut see *suwuk racut*.
rai 1 the flat area surrounding a *pencu*. **2** the central strip of the top of a *wilah* of *blimbingan* form.
raket early form of dance drama, possibly without masks, distinct from *wayang wong*.
raksåså male ogre, e.g. as *wayang* character.
rambangan 1 = *uran-uran*, *palaran*. **2** = *palaran* using only one *iråmå*.
rambatan transition note.
rampak desirable balance between instruments in a gamelan; also see *tabuhan rampak*.
rampogan rectangular *wayang* puppet representing massed soldiers.
rancak 1 one set of gamelan instruments, either *sléndro* or *pélog*. **2** = *rancakan*.
rancak(an) the wooden frame of the *bonang barung*, *bonang penerus*, *kempyang*, *kethuk* and *kenong* (name also sometimes given to frames of *kenong rèntèng*, *saron*, etc.: cf. *pangkon*).
rångkå framework.
rangkaian [*in*] suite of pieces.
rangkep 1 see *iråmå rangkep*. **2** see *céngkok rangkep*. **3** see *thuthukan rangkep*. **4** see *balungan rangkep*. **5** see *gendèran rangkep*. {= double}
rangkung the wooden part of the bow of the *rebab*.
ranté see *titilaras ranté*.
raon = *rau*.
raos [*kr*] → *råså* [*ng*]
raras = *laras*.
råså [*ng*] → *raos* [*kr*] mood, feeling, taste, emotive quality.
rasukan short-sleeved jacket worn by female dancers in *wayang wong*.
råtå 1 a description of a gamelan tuning with an averagely sized interval between notes 1 and 2 (cf. *srigak*, *luruh*). **2** 'reciting note' in a *gåtrå* of *sekar*.
rau, raon a resonator cavity within the body of a drum.
rebab two-stringed fiddle: in a complete gamelan there are two *rebab*.
rebab blongsong = *rebab byur*.
rebab byur a *rebab* with an ivory or white wooden neck, which is played with a *pélog* gamelan.
rebab gadhing byur = *rebab byur*. {*gadhing* = ivory}
rebab ponthang a *rebab* with a black neck, or with ivory at the top and bottom and buffalo horn in the middle, played with a *sléndro* gamelan.
rebånå = *terbang*.
recep 1 the area of a *pencon* instrument between the *manis rai* and the *dudu*. **2** the area between the *manis rai* and the *lambé* of a *wilah* of *blimbingan* form.
recep nglengkèh a *recep* of concave form.
recep pajeg a *recep* of flat form.
refrein [*in*] chorus of a vocal piece.
reff = *refrein*.
regang = *kecèr*?
regu stately (as description of mood of a piece).
rejasa [*in*] tin.
rendah [*in*] low, low-pitched.
rengeng-rengeng 1 to sing *tembang* to oneself. **2** hum.
renggå = *rinenggå*.
renggep (competence in) handling puppets to keep the audience interested; one of the skills of a *dhalang*.

renyep = *recep.*
réog, réyog **1** performance in central Java using *kudå kepang.* **2** performance around Ponorogo in East Java using monster mask (*singåbarong*).
rerenggan refers to the function of certain instruments of the gamelan (see *instrumen rerenggå*). {= decoration}
rep = *sirep.*
repertoar, repertoir, repertorium [*in*] repertoire.
réyog = *réog.*
réyong **1** a Balinese gamelan instrument consisting of a single row of small horizontally suspended gongs. **2** a Balinese instrument consisting of two hanging gongs, found in *gamelan angklung.*
ricik see *saron ricik.*
ricikan **1** essential instrumental parts in gamelan playing. **2** instrument(s) of the gamelan. **3** *wayang kulit* puppets representing miscellaneous objects including armies and animals.
ricikan depan [*in*] = *instrumèn mukå.*
ricikan garap = *instrumèn mukå.*
rijal **1** small *saron.* **2** a single-row instrument of *bonang* type in *gamelan kodhok ngorèk* and *gamelan monggang.* **3** high pitch in the *Kodhok Ngorèk* melody.
rijalan a type of playing on *bonang panerus* during *gangsaran.*
rincik see *saron ri(n)cik.*
rinding an instrument made of bamboo with a hole as a resonator.
rinenggå decorated, especially of an elaborated version of an established composition.
ringgit **1** [*kr*] → *wayang* [*ng*]. **2** = *tlèdhèk.*
ringgit purwå = *wayang wong* or *wayang kulit.*
ringgit tiyang = *wayang wong.*
ringgit topèng = *wayang topèng.*
ringgit wacucal [*kr*] → *wayang kulit* [*ng*]
rodat regional folk dance form, involving dialogue between the solo dancer and a *dhalang*; see *ro'is.*
rog-rog asem a transition section, especially in *gangsaran.*
ro'is *dhalang* in *rodat.*
rojèh **1** an instrument found in certain *gamelan monggang* and *gamelan kodhok ngorèk* consisting of one or more round disks suspended from a centre hole and played with a hard mallet; = *kecèr* (1). **2** a pair of cymbals beaten with a hard mallet: same as *béri* (2). **3** = *kecèr* (3).
ronggèng a professional female dancer, accompanied by a small gamelan, who receives tips from the men with whom she dances: also known as *tlèdhèk.*
rong ulihan to perform a piece twice and then return to the start.
ros a node in a bamboo stem, e.g. at the top of a *suling.*
royal a technique of gamelan playing with switches between *sléndro* and *pélog*, e.g. in *gendhing Pangkur royal.*
RRI (*Radio Republik Indonesia*) state radio and TV stations.
rujak-rujakan a *sindhèn* and *gendèr* melodic pattern.
rumus a melodic formula more stereotyped than *wilet.*
ruwatan a ceremony or exorcism to protect a 'threatened' person, e.g. an only child.
sabetan **1** (competence in) physical manipulation of the puppets; one of the skills of a *dhalang.* **2** the four individual *balungan* beats of a *gatrå.* **3** the opening movements for various sections of a dance performance. **4** see *gendhing sabetan.* **5** *sesegan* section of a *gendhing bonang.*
sabetan balungan = *balungan.*
sabrangan see *kendhang(an) sabrangan.*
sabuk [*ng, kr*] → *paningset* [*ki*] a sash worn by men as part of *pakaian jåwå* and by some male dancers and *wayang* puppets.
sahuran **1** *kenong.* **2** *gong.*
saih pitu a type of Balinese *pélog* gamelan tuning in which there are seven pitches per octave.
sair = *syair.*
sajèn (bowls containing) offerings to the spirits, e.g. given before a *wayang* performance.
saji [*in*] present, perform.
sajian [*in*] performance.
sak ulihan to perform a piece and then return to the start.
salah **1** wrong, unexpected. **2** = *sèlèh.*
salahan an element of *garap* that breaks the usual pattern, e.g. *kethuk salahan*, typically signalling the end of the *gongan*; see also *gong salahan.*
salah gumun = *gembyung.*
salang gumun = *salah gumun.*
salendro = *sléndro.*
salisir **1** a poetic meter sometimes classified as one of the *sekar måcåpat* metres, sometimes classified as *sekar ageng.* **2** a *wangsalan* metre. **3** a five-toned mode of the Balinese *saih pitu* tuning system. **4** a category of *sekar ageng* metres.
salomprèt a wooden oboe, used in the *réyog* ensemble.
salop slippers, part of *pakaian jawa.*
salugi = *saron.*
salukat = *saron penerus.*
salundhing **1** a metallophone or xylophone with floating suspended keys, with or without resonating tubes: also called *salundhi.* **2** *kempul.* **3** *saron*: also see *gamelan salundhing.*
samopa = *gamelan.*
sampak one of the formal structures of gamelan *gendhing* (1), the densest of the 'editable' forms.
samparan a category of *sekar ageng* metres.
sampur a scarf worn by a female dancer; = *sondhèr.*
samswårå = *samyaswårå.*
samyåswårå **1** group singing. **2** chords.
sandiasmå name or message concealed in lines of *tembang*, as initial syllables (= acrostic), final syllables, syllables on either side of *pedhotan*, or combinations thereof.
sandiwara [*in*] drama, play, acting.
sånggåbuwånå = *pelemahan* (2).
sånggå wedhi (*sånggå* [*ng*] → *sanggi* [*kr*]) straps on a *plangkan*, supporting the *kendhang.*
sanggan a post made of metal, horn, etc., used to suspend the *wilah* of *gendèr* and *slenthem*, with or without a slit to allow the *pluntur* to be inserted; = *placak* (1).
sanggit *dhalang*'s creativity or ability to express the drama.
sanggul chignon worn by *pesindhèn.*

sångkå 1 gong. 2 *kethuk*. 3 conch-shell trumpet.
sangsangan ornament worn on upper chest by dancers and *wayang* puppets.
sangsangan sungsun chain of *sangsangan*, one above the other.
sangsangan tanggalan *sangsang* of half-moon form.
santen = *srenten*.
santi swårå, santiswaran pieces consisting of Islamic prayers, usually sung by men, to the accompaniment of drums including *terbang* or *kendhang* and sometimes *kemanak*.
sapangkon 1 a complete gamelan with both *sléndro* and *pélog* sections. 2 = *sarancak* (2).
saprangkat a complete gamelan with both *sléndro* and *pélog* sections.
saput a ceremonial object in the royal palace, symbolising alertness.
sarancak 1 a single gamelan instrument, e.g. a *saron* or a *bonang* (with its set of pots). 2 a set of gamelan instruments in one tuning, *sléndro* or *pélog*.
saraséhan discussion, seminar.
såråyudå the end of a *pathetan* accompanied by *kendhang* and *gong* or *kempul* and sometimes *kenong* and *kethuk*.
Såråyudå see *kendhangan Såråyudå*.
sari swårå see *titilaras sariswårå*.
Sarjana Karawitan first degree in *karawitan*, awarded by STSI, ISI, etc.
saron 1 any of a family of metallophones whose keys rest on low trough resonators. 2 = *saron barung*.
saron barung the middle-sized, medium-register *saron*.
saron demung the large-sized, low-register *saron*: also known as *demung*.
saron demung ageng (*ageng* [*kr*] → *gedhé* [*ng*]) a *saron* one octave lower than the *saron demung*, with a raised boss on each key.
saron demung lantakan a *saron demung* with five keys.
saron demung pencon a *saron demung* with a raised boss on each key.
saron panerus the small-sized, high-register *saron*.
saron peking = *saron panerus*.
saron penacah 1 = *saron wayangan* (2). 2 = *saron panerus*.
saron penerus = *saron panerus*.
saron ri(n)cik = *saron barung*.
saron sångå *saron wayangan* (2) with nine keys.
saron slenthem = *saron demung ageng*.
saron wayangan 1 a style of *imbal* played by two *saron barung* during the playing of *playon* or *srepegan*. 2 a *saron barung* with keys added in the upper register; = *saron sångå*.
sarug/saruk see *gembyangan sarug*.
sarugan see *nyarug*.
sarung a *bathik* piece with its two short sides sewn together, worn as a skirt, typically by men (cf. *kain*).
sasmitå 1 a partially disguised signal or hint, especially as used by a *dhalang* to indicate which *gendhing* is to be played next. 2 clue incorporated in a line of *tembang* to indicate which metre is being used, e.g. the words *brangti*, *dånå*, *kasmaran* or *kingkin* indicating *Asmarandånå*.
sastrå literature, writing.
satriyå nobleman; the nobility.
satriyå lumaksånå point in the second part of a *wayang* where the hero undertakes his task after consulting a holy man.
sawung a ceremonial object in the royal palace, having the form of a cockerel, and symbolising bravery.
sedheng 1 medium tempo. 2 medium register.
sègegan sforzando playing on the *rebab*.
sekar [*kr*] → *tembang* [*ng*] 1 classical verse. 2 song, generic term for vocal music.
sekar ageng [*kr*] → *tembang gedhé* [*ng*] a category of poetic forms based upon Sanskrit metres characterised by having two or four adjacent lines with the same number of syllables; the term *sekar ageng* was first used in the nineteenth century and may refer either to Old Javanese *kakawin* poetry or to nineteenth-century poetry based upon *kakawin* forms. {= large song}
sekar ageng kakawin = *sekar kawi*.
sekar ageng kawi miring nineteenth-century recreations of Old Javanese *kakawin*.
sekaran [*kr*] → *kembangan* [*ng*] 1 ornamenting patterns, either vocal or instrumental, at the end of a regular melodic pattern or at the end of an *imbal* sequence. 2 one of the numbered patterns used as components of *ciblonan*. 3 the usual type of pattern played on the *ciblon* drum (cf. *singgetan*). 4 melodies of instruments that elaborate the *balungan* melody. 5 see *gembyang(an) sekaran*. 6 patterns played on *bonang* for *balungan nibani*. 7 one style of Yogyanese *demung imbal*. {= flowering}
sekaran nyegat abridged *sekaran*, half-*sekaran*.
sekaran wetah complete *sekaran*.
sekar cilik = *sekar måcåpat*. {= small song}
sekar dhagelan = *sekar tengahan*.
sekard(e)limå an instrument consisting of small bells (*kelinthing*) arranged on a pole, and used in *gamelan kodhok ngorèk*.
sekar gedhé (*gedhé* [*ng*] → *ageng* [*kr*]) = *sekar ageng*.
sekar gendhing *gendhing* that are based upon melodies traditionally associated with the poetic forms *sekar tengahan* and *sekar måcåpat*, usually in the form of a *ladrang* or *ketawang*.
sekar kawi a subcategory of *sekar ageng* in the Kawi (Old Javanese) language, conforming precisely to the rules of Sanskrit prosody.
sekar lampah gendhing *sekar* that closely follow the *balungan* of the *gendhing*, usually in fast tempo, and in which the singing is somewhat intermittent.
sekar lampah jineman *sekar* that follow the melody of the *gendhing*, but in which the *saron* and *bonang* do not play, thus giving the impression that the gamelan is following the vocal melody.
sekar lampah lagon the style of singing *pathetan* (*lagon*) accompanied by *rebab*, *gendèr*, *gambang* and *suling*.
sekar lampah sekar the style of singing found in *gendhing kemanak* that accompanies *bedhåyå* and *srimpi* dances in which the *saron*, *slenthem* and *bonang* do not play.
sekar lampah sekar gendhing *sekar* that are sung continuously, usually in *iråmå rangkep*, and in which the gamelan follows the melody of the song.
sekar måcåpat a category of poetic forms, which, like *sekar tengahan*, is characterized by metres of varying numbers of syllables per line and different final vowels for each line.
sekar mådyå = *sekar tengahan*.
sekar palaran = *palaran*.
sekar pedhalangan the songs (*sulukan*) of the *dhalang*.

sekar tengahan a category of poetic forms, which, like *sekar måcåpat*, is characterised by metres of varying numbers of syllables per line and different final vowels for each line. {= medium-sized song}

Sekatèn festivities held on 6–12 *Mulud*, preceding commemoration (*Garebeg Mulud*) of birthday of the prophet Muhammad, and involving use of *gamelan sekati*.

Sekati see *gamelan sekati*.

sekawan four.

selah = *sèlèh*.

selang-seling a form of *garap* used by the *saron panerus*. {= alternating}

selatan [*in*] south(ern).

sèlèh see *nådå sèlèh*.

sèlèhan the cadence in a *gåtrå* of *sekar*.

sèlèh imbal = *sekaran* (1) used with *imbal bonang*.

seléndhang diagonal sash worn by dancers or *pesindhèn*.

selingan **1** (optional) insertion of a *gendhing* (1) with one formal structure into a *gendhing* (1) of another formal structure. **2** additional minor scenes inserted in a *wayang*. **3** = *selitan*. {*seling* = insert}

selisir = *salisir*.

selitan *céngkok* for *suling* used to indicate high register or a move to a high register.

selok a gong shape, used for *gong ageng*, where the *rai* is below the level of the *dudu*.

selukat = *saron panerus*.

semat = *mangol*.

sembådå description of the nose of *wayang kulit* characters of intermediate type.

sembah a gesture of greeting and respect, made by bringing the two hands together and touching the forehead or nose with the fingertips, while bowing.

sempalan = *lakon sempalan*.

senandhung måcåpat *sekar måcåpat* sung quietly or hummed.

senar wire, string.

sendarèn = *sundarèn*.

sendhal pancing a *rebab* bowing technique.

sendhon **1** one of the categories of *suluk*, sung by the *dhalang* to invoke a sad or moving atmosphere, accompanied by *gendèr*, *gambang* and *suling* (Solo) or *gendèr*, *gambang*, *suling* and *rebab* (Yogya). **2** like a *pathetan* but in the *pélog* tuning system, i.e. *sendhon limå*, *sendhon nem* and *sendhon barang*.

sendhon pathet *pathetan* specifically of vocal origin.

sendratari dramatic performance using dance accompanied by gamelan without narration, and based on *wayang wong*, e.g. the 'Ramayana ballet' presented at the Prambanan temples. {from *seni*, *drama*, *tari*}

seng zinc.

senggakan phrases or nonsense syllables inserted within the main vocal melody of a *gendhing* sung by members of the *gérong*; they may be one, two or four *gåtrå* in length.

senggakan colokan *senggakan* serving as continuation or appendix to a line of *sekar* or a *parikan* couplet.

senggakan kombangan *kombangan* used as *senggakan*, e.g. in *palaran*.

senggakan parikan *senggakan* consisting of a couplet of *parikan* form.

senggakan singgetan *senggakan* consisting of part of a couplet of *parikan* form.

sènggol **1** (Sundanese) melodic pattern, similar to *wilet*. **2** (Sundanese) vocal ornament, like a turn.

senggrèng = *rangkung*.

senggrèngan the last *rebab* phrase of a *pathetan*, often played as a brief prelude to the *bukå* of a *gendhing* or before the opening *pathetan* of a *gendhing*, cf. *grambyangan* on *bonang barung*.

seni [*in*] art, art form.

seniman male artiste.

seni rakyat folk art.

seni rupa [*in*] visual arts, fine arts.

seni tradisi traditional (court) arts.

seniwati female artiste.

senthing **1** = *bremårå* (1). **2** the lower point where the *rebab* strings are fixed.

serancak = *sarancak*.

serat kåndhå a book containing the texts of *lakon* for Yogya-style dances.

serimpi = *srimpi*.

sero/seru = *soran*.

seruling = *suling*.

sesaji dance performed in Buddhist celebrations for *Waiçak*.

seseg **1** fast: also see *iråmå seseg*. **2** = *sesegan*.

sesegan the fast section of a *gendhing*, often occurring at the end of the piece, especially the closing section (in *ir I*) of a *gendhing bonang*.

seser a string in the form of a ring joined to the two *rebab* strings to hold the *eneng* in place and to improve the sound.

setèm to tune. {Dutch *stemmen*}

setrèn = *wédokan*.

sewaragan (description of part of *mérong* of *gd Rondhon kt 4 ar sl 9*) ?

siaran broadcast.

siem = *siyem*.

sigar penjalin = *nyigar penjalin*.

sigrak a description of a gamelan tuning with a relatively large interval between notes 1 and 2 (cf. *råtå*, *luruh*); energetic.

sikil(an) **1** the support of a *rebab*. **2** the leg of a *rancakan*.

siliran interval between two adjacent notes (= *kempyang* (4)).

simpingan the arrangement of unused *wayang* puppets in the banana logs on either side of the screen.

sindhèn **1** = *sindhènan*. **2** = *pesindhèn*. **3** singing (of all types).

sindhènan **1** vocal parts sung by the *pesindhèn*. **2** vocal parts sung by the *pesindhèn* and/or *gérong*.

sindhènan baku 'basic' *sindhènan* (cf. *sindhènan isèn-isèn*).

sindhènan bedhåyå *sindhènan* as used for *gendhing* that accompany *bedhåyå* or *srimpi* dances, with *pesindhèn* singing in unison, and male singers singing in unison an octave below them.

sindhènan bedhayan = *sindhènan bedhåyå*.

sindhènan gawan *sindhènan* peculiar to one *gendhing*.

sindhènan isèn-isèn see *abon-abon*.

sindhènan limrah = *sindhènan srambahan*.

sindhènan patut *sindhènan* to fit, i.e. *sindhènan gawan*.

sindhènan sekar *sindhènan* texts that have their origin in *sekar* poetic forms sung with *gendhing*.

sindhènan srambahan *sindhènan* drawn from a repertoire of standard phrases, sung at accented points (cf. *sindhènan isèn-isèn*), and having the same importance as any other instrument of the gamelan (cf. *sindhènan gawan*). {*srambahan* = general-purpose, generic}

sindhur = *dodot*.

sindik peg that holds the *wilah* on the *pluntur* of instruments in the *gendèr* family (= *bremårå* (2), *cakilan* (1)).

sinenggakan = *senggakan*.

sinenggrèng = *senggrèngan*.

singgetan **1** sectioning. **2** section markers, referring to the function of some of the instruments of the gamelan. **3** patterns that mark boundaries, which are played on the *ciblon* drum. **4** transition. **5** see *senggakan singgetan*.

singir = *mondring*.

sinjang [*kr*] → *jarik* [*ng*]

sinom a *sekar mâcâpat* poetic form.

sirah **1** [*kr*] → *endhas* [*ng*]. **2** the upper part of the *watangan* of a *rebab*.

sirep **1** to play gamelan quietly (= *sirepan*). **2** a sudden drop in loudness of playing (cf. *udhar*).

sirepan quiet gamelan playing while the *dhalang* narrates in a *wayang kulit* or *wayang orang* performance.

siriran a category of *sekar ageng* metres.

siter a zither, a simpler version of the *celempung*.

siteran an ensemble consisting of *siter barung*, *siter peking*, *siter penembung*, a small *ciblon*, and *gong bumbung*. A *gong gendul* may replace the *gong bumbung*.

siter barung normal *siter*.

siter besar = *siter barung*.

siter dårå = *siter barung*?

siter panerus a small zither, tuned one octave above the regular *siter*.

siter peking = *siter panerus*?

siter penembung siter pitched an octave below *siter barung*?

siyak a signal from the *dhalang* or from the *kendhang* to switch a piece to a faster *irâmâ*, and then back to a slower one, in which only the *rebab*, *gendèr*, *kendhang*, *slenthem* and *gong* are played.

siyem see *gong siyem*.

skema [*in*] the sequence of elements, repetitions, transitions and *irâmâ* changes with which a particular piece or set of pieces is performed.

slah **1** = *selah*? **2** [*in*] trick.

slametan [*ng*] → *wilujengan* [*kr*] a ceremonial meal.

slawatan the singing, usually by men, of the *Qur'an* text concerning the birth of Muhammad, to the accompaniment of *terbang* or *kendhang*, and sometimes *kemanak*, while dancing in a sitting position (cf. *santiswaran*).

sléndro the tuning category in which the octave is divided into five intervals, which are more uniform than those of the *pélog* category.

sléndro miring = *barang miring*.

slenthem **1** a large-keyed, single-octave metallophone, tuned one octave below the *saron demung*, whose thin keys are suspended over bamboo or metal resonators (*gendèr* family), also (mainly in Yogya) called *gendèr panembung*. **2** a large-keyed, single-octave metallophone, of the *gendèr* family but with a raised boss (*pencon*) in the middle of each key; = *slenthem pencon*.

slenthem ageng (*ageng* [*kr*] → *gedhé* [*ng*]) **1** a *slenthem* that sounds an octave lower than the usual *slenthem*. **2** a knobbed, single-octave metallophone whose keys are suspended over a trough resonator (i.e. *saron* family), pitched an octave below *demung*: also called *saron demung ageng*.

slenthem gantung **1** a single-octave *slenthem* whose range is the same as the lowest octave of the *gendèr barung*. **2** same as (1) but with a raised boss in the middle of each key.

slenthem kawat instrument of *siter* family with low pitch and a function similar to *slenthem*.

slenthem pencon = *slenthem ageng* (2): see also *saron demung ageng*.

slenthem siter = *slenthem kawat*.

slentho = *slenthem ageng* (2): see also *saron demung ageng*.

slenthong = *slenthem ageng* (2): see also *saron demung ageng*.

slépé belt buckle worn by dancers.

slepeg(an) = *srepeg(an)*.

sliring deviating, out of tune.

slisir = *salisir* or *sekar mâcâpat*.

slokå = *kakawin*.

SMKI (*Sekolah Menengah Karawitan Indonesia*) high schools for the performing arts in various Indonesian cities (Banyumas, Solo, Yogya, Padang Panjang, Ujung Pandang, etc.).

sodhèkan a simple style of *gendèr* playing in which the movement of the hands 'is like a person pushing the ball in billiards'.

sondhèr (cindhé) (silk) dance scarf, stretching to the ankles.

songkok headdress worn by kings in *wayang wong*.

soran (played in) loud style, usually without *gendèr*, *rebab*, *gambang*, *suling* and *siter* (cf. *lirihan*).

sorog a Sundanese tuning category, with intervals similar to Sundanese *pélog* tuning but in a different sequence.

sorogan **1** interchangeable keys on the *gambang* (also sometimes on the *gendèr*) used in connection with the different *pathet* of the five-toned *pélog* scales. Pitch-1 keys for *pathet limå* and *pathet nem* must be exchanged (*disorog*) for pitch-7 keys when playing in *pathet barang*. **2** *pélog* tones that sometimes alternate with the usual tones of a given *pélog pathet*: these substitute, or *sorogan*, tones (accidentals in Western terminology) are as shown below.

pathet limå and *pathet nem*	7 is *sorogan* for 1
	4 is *sorogan* for 3
pathet barang	1 is *sorogan* for 7
	4 is *sorogan* for 5

srambahan **1** see *sindhènan srambahan*. **2** a *suluk* melody that can be used for several kinds of scenes or moods in a *wayang* performance. **3** *kendhangan* in which the pattern is played only once after the *bukå*, e.g. in *lancaran* and *ketawang*.

srawing = *eneng*.

srenten **1** the bridge of the *rebab*, of thin wood about 14 cm long, with two grooves on the central part to receive the strings; supports the two strings on the *tilam*. **2** the bridge of the *siter* or *celempung*.

srepeg(an) **1** one of the formal structures of gamelan *gendhing* (1), an 'editable' form with a density between *ayak-ayakan* and *sampak*. **2** in strictest Yogya style, a transition passage within *ayak-ayakan*.

srepegan rambangan = *rambangan*.

srigak = *sigrak*.

srimpi **1** a ceremonial dance from the central Javanese court tradition usually performed by four females, sometimes five. **2** dancers in such dances.

srisig = *trisig*.

srunten = *srenten*.

sruti **1** interval. **2** set of intervals.

sruwing = *eneng*.

stagèn wide sash or belt, e.g. as worn by men as part of *pakaian jawa*.

STKW (*Sekolah Tinggi Kesenian Wliwatikta*) arts institute at Surabaya.

STSI (*Sekolah Tinggi Seni Indonesia*) **1** arts institute at Solo, successor to ASKI. **2** arts institute at Denpasar, Bali, successor to ASTI, now ISI. **3** arts institute at Bandung.

suårå **1** sound, tone. **2** voice.

suårå berombak two pitches, sounding together, producing beats slightly out of tune but not necessarily undesirable.

suårå bléro two pitches, sounding together, very much out of tune.

suårå inggil high, thin vocal timbre.

suårå nyliring two pitches, sounding together, slightly out of tune but not necessarily undesirable.

suårå pleng two pitches, sounding together, perfectly in tune.

suh **1** rattan or rawhide plaited into a ring, used to tighten or loosen the head of a *kendhang*. **2** = *jamangan* (1).

suling an end-blown vertical bamboo flute.

sultan the ruler of the senior palace at Yogyakarta.

suluk (Yogya) a mood-song in the *sulukan* category, similar to *pathetan/lagon*.

suluk(an) a traditional song or songs sung by a *dhalang* during a *wayang kulit* or *wayang wong* performance, accompanied by *rebab*, *gendèr*, *gambang* and *suling*; may also be used in dance accompaniments.

sumber = *jamangan* (1).

sumpilan = *tawonan*.

sumping **1** = *eneng*. **2** ear ornament worn by dancers and *wayang kulit* characters.

sumpingan = *simpingan*.

sumping ron ear ornament of leaf form.

sunan = *susuhunan*.

sundaren self-sounding flute made of bamboo and attached to a kite.

sundari **1** a type of gamelan tuning: see *embat sundari*. **2** = *suling*.

sungu = *tanduk*.

supakan = *tumbengan*.

supitan part of the *bau*, towards the *lambé*, of a *pencon* instrument (where it is held by the tongs during forging?).

supit urang hairstyle of *wayang* puppets including a curl on the back of the head pointing forwards, and another on the front of the head pointing backwards. {= lobster claw}

surjan a long jacket, part of *pakaian jawa* (Yogya).

surupan Sundanese modal categories (cf. *pathet* in central Java).

susuhunan the ruler of the senior palace at Surakarta.

sutrå swårå finely woven sound.

suwekan the hole in the top (*tumbengan*) of a resonator tube under a *wilah*.

suwuk **1** the end of a piece. **2** the *gongan* on which a piece ends. **3** a special closing section added to the final *gongan* (*sampak*, *srepegan*, *ayak-ayakan*). **4** a substitute section at the end of the final *gongan*. {= end}

suwukan **1** a special section for ending a *gendhing*: see *suwuk* (2, 3). **2** *gong suwukan*. **3** a named *singgetan* for the *ciblon*.

suwuk gropak a *suwuk* that speeds up rather than slowing down.

suwuk ngamèn a widely applicable *suwuk*, signalled by the *kendhang*, to bring a piece to a quick end. {= beggars'/buskers' *suwuk*}

suwuk (ng)racut a *suwuk* that consists of a transition from *irâmå III* to a final *irâmå II*, and an associated signal on the *kendhang*.

swårå = *suårå*.

swarantårå intervals.

swårå nyorog note substituted by singer for a note that is too high to sing.

swåråwati the *pesindhèn* with a gamelan.

syair [*in*] poem; = *cakepan*.

tabang-tabang = *terbang*.

tabuh **1** a beater for striking instruments of the gamelan. **2** a Balinese classification system of the formal structures of gamelan pieces. Balinese terminology refers to the length of the unit marked off by a stroke on the largest gong, but is not used consistently between different genres of gamelan. For *gamelan gong* the *tabuh* classification is as given in the table below.

tabuh pisan (one)	8 strokes per *gongan*
tabuh dua (two)	32 strokes per *gongan*
tabuh telu (three)	48 strokes per *gongan*
tabuh pat (four)	64 strokes per *gongan*
tabuh kutus	twice the *gongan* length of *tabuh pat*

tabuhan, tetabuhan **1** an instrument or instruments of the gamelan struck with a beater. **2** process of striking a gamelan instrument; a stroke on an instrument.

tabuhan barangan instruments that play supporting parts.

tabuhan ngajeng [*kr*] → *tabuhan ngarep* [*ng*] an ensemble consisting of *rebab*, *gendèr barung*, *gendèr panerus*, *gambang*, *clempung* and *suling*.

tabuhan ngarep [*ng*] → *tabuhan ngajeng* [*kr*]

tabuhan penerusan = *tabuhan terusan*.

tabuhan rampak a style of gamelan playing where all the instruments are audible and in harmony with each other, no instrument being obtrusive. {*rampak* = uniform}

tabuhan reprepan = *gamelan tengahan*.

tabuhan ricikan instruments that play essential parts in the gamelan.

tabuhan tengah an ensemble consisting of *bonang barung*, *bonang panerus*, *bonang panembung* and *kendhang*.

tabuhan terusan instruments that fill in between the essential parts.

tabuhan wingking an ensemble consisting of *demung*, *saron penacah*, *peking*, *kethuk*, *kempyang*, *engkuk*, *kemong*, *kenong*, *kempul* and *gong*.

talèdhèk = *tlèdhèk*.

tali [*ng*] → *tangsul* [*kr*] string, cord.

talu a *gendhing* (1) or a series of *gendhing* played as an introduction to, or an opening of, a *wayang kulit* performance; the *gendhing* themselves are called *gendhing talu* or *gendhing patalon*.

tamban see *iråmå tamban*.

tampi = *niyågå*.

tampré = *genjring*.

tanceb kayon planting of the *kayon* in the banana log, as marker of divisions between acts of *wayang kulit*.

tandhak = *tlèdhèk*.

tandhes the anvil in a gamelan workshop.

tanduk animal (typically buffalo) horn, as used for head of *tabuh* for *peking*, for handle of *gambang* beater and for rods of *wayang kulit* puppets.

tanggel [*kr*] → *tanggung* [*ng*]

tanggung [*ng*] → *tanggel* [*kr*] see *iråmå tanggung*, *perang tanggung*.

tangsul [*kr*] → *tali* [*ng*]

tanjidhor = *tanjidhur*.

tanjidhur **1** musician. **2** type of European wind music.

tapak dårå two pieces of wood about 5 × 5 cm, one 60 cm long and the other shorter, joined together to provide support to the banana trunk in a *wayang kulit* performance.

tarawangsa Sundanese spiked fiddle.

tari [*in*] dance.

tari alus(an) refined male dance style, also (mainly?) danced by women.

tari gagah strong male dance style, rarely danced by women.

tari putri, tari putrèn female dance style.

tarupan setting-up for a ritual occasion.

tatabuhan = *tabuhan*.

tatajari [*in*] fingering (for *rebab*).

tawingan the side or end panel of a *rancakan*.

tawonan a cushion made of plaited rattan, about 5 × 5 cm and 1 to 3 cm thick, placed over the *placak* of a *saron*, etc., to isolate the *wilah* from the *pangkon*.

tayub(an) form of social dance involving men and professional female dancers, performed at ritual celebrations and somewhat deprecated for the associated drunkenness and immorality; also see *tlèdhèk*.

tayungan victory dance, typically by Bimå or Råmå, after the final battle in a *wayang*.

TBS Taman Budhaya Surakarta, a cultural centre in Solo.

TBY Taman Budhaya Yogyakarta, a cultural centre in Yogya.

tébokan drumhead.

tébokan bem the larger head of the *ciblon* drum.

tébokan kempyang the smaller head of the *ciblon* drum.

tèk = *pin*.

tekå njejak a *dhalang* who is called to perform by someone who already possesses all the other requirements for the performance—the puppets, the gamelan and the players.

tekes headdress of dancers in dance dramas.

tembågå [*ng*] → *tembagi* [*kr*] copper.

tembagi [*kr*] → *tembågå* [*ng*]

tembang [*ng*] → *sekar* [*kr*]

tembang dhagelan = *tembang tengahan*.

tembang gedhé (*gedhé* [*ng*] → *ageng* [*kr*]) = *sekar ageng*.

tembang måcåpat = *sekar måcåpat*.

tembang tengahan = *sekar tengahan*.

tembokan = *tébokan*?

tengah **1** the note numbered 3 in the *kepatihan* system; = *dhådhå*. **2** medium register. {= middle}

tengah pencu part of a *pencu*.

tepèn a type of *blangkon* with its *mondholan* covered with the same type of fabric.

terbang a frame drum; = *rebånå*.

terompong a Balinese gamelan instrument consisting of a row of small horizontally suspended gongs, similar to the Javanese *bonang*.

teropong = *tropong*.

terus continue, continuing with.

tetabuhan = *tabuhan*.

teteg, tètèg pivot between the parts of a *wayang kulit* puppet.

teteg, thetheg **1** a small *bedhug*. **2** *kendhang ageng* shaped like a *bedhug*.

tetegan soft *dodhogan*.

tetembangan singing.

tetesan female 'circumcision'.

thelengan description of the round wide-open eyes of coarse *wayang kulit* characters.

thetheg = *teteg*.

théthélilé = *centhé*.

thinthing to play notes to test them.

thinthingan **1** the playing of the four principal tones of the *pathet* in a descending order on the *gendèr*. **2** the style of accompanying *båwå* and *andhegan* on *gendèr*. **3** = *grimingan*.

thong-thong a bronze slit-gong struck with a wooden mallet.

thuthukan **1** instruments of the gamelan struck with mallets. **2** *balungan* beat.

thuthukan rangkep a style of playing *(saron, gendèr, gambang* and *bonang)* in which the patterns of one *iråmå* are doubled when played in the next highest *iråmå*.

thuthukan sabetan vigorous playing.

thuthukan sodhèkan see *sodhèkan*.

tik = *pin*.

tikel **1** the groove around a *pencu*: see also *widheng*. **2** the outer ridge of the *widheng* around a *pencu*. **3** see *iråmå tikel*.

tilam = *babad*.

timah putih tin.

timang a belt buckle worn by dancers with the *èpèk*.

timur [*in*] East(ern).

tindhih the leader of a gamelan for a performance in the *kraton*.

tingalan [*ki*] → *wetonan* [*ng*], *wiyosan* [*kr*] a celebration of a 35-day birthday.

tinggi [*in*] high, high-pitched.

tingkat iråmå levels of *iråmå*; i.e. *iråmå I, iråmå II, iråmå III* and so on.

tingkeb(an) = *mitoni*.

titik = *pin*.

titilaras notation.

titilaras åndhå step or ladder notation, invented at the Pakualaman palace, Yogyakarta.

titilaras daminå a variant of *sariswårå* notation compiled by Machjar Angga Kusumadinata.

titilaras kepatihan a system of cipher notation, devised by Radèn Mas Tumenggung Wreksadiningrat *c.* 1893 at the *Kepatihan* in Solo, based upon the Galin–Paris–Chevé system of 1844. {*Kepatihan* = residence of *patih* (prime minister)}

titilaras nutångkå = *titilaras kepatihan.*

titilaras ranté a system of notation using a staff of five or seven lines, invented during the time of Pakubawånå IX at Surakarta around 1870 or earlier.

titilaras sariswårå notation system based on a tonic, developed by Dr Ki Hadjar Dewantara, the founder of the Taman Siswa schools, in 1928.

titir a continuous sound.

titiraras = *titilaras.*

tlacapan the body of a *kendhang.*

tlapakan **1** = *pangkon.* **2** drumstand.

tledhak-tledhuk a technique of *gendèr* playing.

tlèdhèk **1** a female dancer/singer (or transvestite) who collects fees for street performances accompanied by a small gamelan: also called *ronggèng, tandhak.* **2** female dancer at *tayuban.* {= temptress}

tlèdhèkan social occasion including *tlèdhèk* dance.

tlèdhèk jaler young male professional dancer.

tlumpah the base of the *rancakan* of a *saron*, etc.

tlutur a form of melody, song or composition with a feeling of sadness: see *sendhon tlutur*, etc.

tonika tonic of a Western scale, sometimes used as equivalent of *dhasar.*

topèng a dance mask for a specific role, made of wood or paper and covering either the whole of the face or only the lower part (see *topèng congoran*).

topèng congoran a dance mask in Solonese or Yogyanese style covering the lower part of the face only.

topèng dhalang *topèng* dance with a narrator.

topong headdress worn by some types of male dance roles and *wayang kulit* puppets.

tosan [*kr*] → *wesi* [*ng*]

toyå mili ?(*toyå* [*kr*] → *banyu* [*ng*]) = *banyu mili.*

tracak **1** metal posts that hold in place the *wilah* of a *saron*, *gendèr*, etc. **2** = *placak* (2).

tratag performance area adjacent to a *pendhåpå.*

trenyuh moving.

trisig type of dance movement accompanied by characteristic *kendhangan* pattern.

triwikråmå transformation of a *wayang* character by magical powers.

trompong = *terompong.*

tropong = *topong.*

Trunåjåyå = *lawung ageng.*

tuding rods made of horn, attached to the arms of a *wayang kulit* puppet.

tudung = *suling.*

tukang nglaras gamelan tuner.

tumbengan **1** the closure (top) of a resonator (*bumbungan*) made from bamboo or sheet metal, or a similar structure in the mouth of the resonator of a *gong kemodhong.* **2** a partition introduced into a metal *bumbung*, dividing the tube in the same way as a node in a bamboo stem.

tumbuk (laras) the common tone or tones, with the same number, shared by a particular *sléndro* gamelan and a particular *pélog* gamelan.

tumbuk limå description of a gamelan with *tumbuk* note 5.

tumbuk nem description of a gamelan with *tumbuk* note 6.

tumungkul with bowed head, a description of *wayang kulit* characters of calm, patient and dedicated type.

tunggal **1** using a single note, in contrast to *gembyangan.* **2** see *nduduk tunggal.* {= single}

tunggal råså a style of *kenong* playing where the *kenong* note coincides in pitch with the *balungan* note.

tunjung a post that tapers from its central section towards the ends, serving as the foot of the *rebab.*

tuntunan instructions, manual, guide.

tutug, tutuk (competence in) delivery of dialogue and narration in *wayang*; one of the skills of a *dhalang.*

tutukan '*lik*', i.e. vocal, section of *langgam.*

tutupan rebab the stopping of the strings of the *rebab* by the fingers of the left hand.

tutupan suling the closing of the finger-holes of the *suling* to get the desired note.

tuturan see *kenong(an) tuturan.*

ubet-ubet long *bathik* breastcloth leaving shoulders bare, worn by female dancers.

uceng (pencu) the top of a *pencu.*

udhar return to normal loudness following a *sirep.*

udheng [*ki*] → *ikat* [*ng*]

ukel [*ki*] → *gelung(an)* [*ng,kr*] also see *ngukel.*

ukel pancaran a style of *gendèr* playing.

ukur sanak to tune a gamelan by relying solely on the ears of the gamelan tuner, without the use of measuring apparatus or a tuning fork; this is usually left to the gamelan maker.

ulem a soft, pleasant sound (whether of a voice or of a gamelan).

ulihan **1** a consequent phrase, preceded by *padhang*, an antecedent phrase. **2** the final part of a breath (*pedhotan*). {*ulih* [*ng*] = *antuk* [*kr*] = *kondur* [*ki*] = return home}

ulur-ulur **1** = *janget* (1). **2** long necklace worn by *wayang* puppets.

umbaran **1** bowing the open strings of the *rebab* for the purposes of tuning. **2** rapid left-hand playing in *gendèran rangkep.*

umbul a post used in gamelan-making.

umpak **1** an opening *gongan* of a composition (especially *ketawang* and *ladrang*), often played twice, followed by a *ngelik.* **2** a transition section of a *gendhing* (2); see *umpak inggah*, *umpak seseg.* **3** the metered *gendèr* part at the end of certain *sulukan.* **4** = *jineman* (4). **5** the first part of a transition section of a *gendhing* (2) in some *kt ar* forms, in which the *kethuk* structure is still the same as in the preceding part of the *mérong.*

umpak inggah **1** a transition section of a *gendhing* (2), which indicates the form of the following *inggah* (*dhawah*), consisting of one or two *kenongan* or a whole *gongan.* **2** the second part of such a transition in some *kt ar* forms, with an altered *kethuk* structure (cf. *umpak* (5)).

umpak ngandhap = *popor ngisor.*

umpak nginggil = *popor ndhuwur.*

umpak seseg the section of a *gendhing* at the end of the piece but preceding the *suwuk.*

umpak-umpak **1** = *embat*. **2** = *umpak*.

umpak-umpakan **1** a transition to an *inggah* in which the transition already has the structure and melody of the following *inggah*: = *umpak* (2). **2** a transition to a *sesegan*.

umpak-umpak merâtâ = *ompak-ompak merâtâ*.

umyung deliberately out of tune.

uncal kencânâ straps of *badhong*.

uncal wâstrâ tails of sash.

unggah [*ng*] → *inggah* [*kr*]

untu = *wilah*.

upacârâ **1** royal regalia (= *ampilan dalem*). **2** ceremony.

uran-uran the singing of *sekar mâcâpat* accompanied by *gendèr*, *gambang*, *kenong*, *kempul*, *gong* and *kendhang*: also called *rambangan* (Yogya) or *palaran* (Solo).

urâ-urâ **1** to sing for one's own pleasure in a quiet place such as the edge of a rice field or on a lonely road. **2** to sing non-classical songs. **3** = *uran-uran*.

urip [*ng*] → *gesang* [*kr*]

urung = *ploncon*.

usapan ornament on *suling*, made by removing fingers from holes.

utara [*in*] north(ern).

uyon-uyon **1** (Yogya) = *klenèngan*. **2** (Solo) loud-style gamelan playing as welcome at the start of a ceremony.

uyon-uyon gadhon playing gamelan *gadhon* for pleasure.

vokal vocal part(s) of a composition.

vokalis [*in*] vocalist.

waditrâ = *gamelan*.

wadon = *wédok(an)*.

wanârâ monkey.

wândâ **1** syllable. **2** one of the various moods exhibited by different *wayang kulit* characters. **3** different versions of the same *wayang* puppet character (representing different ages or different phases of the character's development), which may be changed between the acts of a performance.

wangkingan [*ki*] → *keris* [*ng*], *dhuwung* [*kr*]

wangsalan poetic riddle in pairs of lines, with twelve or sixteen syllables in each line, in which a word or group of words suggests through assonance or synonymity another word found later in the poem: often used as a *sindhèn* or *gérongan* text.

wangsul to return (to).

wantah ordinary, basic, unadorned, nothing added; applied to the full version of *pathetan*, *grambyangan*, etc. (cf. *jugag*).

waranggânâ female artiste, especially *pesindhèn*. {= fairy}

warângkâ a sheath for a *kris*: see also *branggah* and *gayaman*.

watak character, e.g. of a verse metre.

watangan **1** the tapering neck of the *rebab*, where it is held. **2** tournament held in front of *kraton*, involving dance.

wayang [*ng*] → *ringgit* [*kr*] **1** = *wayang kulit*. **2** a generic term referring to any traditional dramatic performance accompanied by gamelan. {= shadow}

wayang bèbèr a *wayang* performance where the scenes of the story are depicted upon painted cloth, which is unrolled during the performance.

wayang cinâ Chinese *wayang*.

wayang cokèk description of a street dance performance from the Jakarta area, similar to *tayuban*; see *gamelan cokèk*.

wayang dupara *wayang kulit* with stories about the kingdom of Surakarta.

wayang gedhog a shadow-puppet play accompanied by a *pélog* gamelan, depicting stories from the East Javanese *Panji* epic.

wayang golèk (a performance with) three-dimensional wooden puppets, representing stories from the Menak cycle.

wayang gremeng drama performances using voices but no instruments and no equipment.

wayang Jâwâ *wayang kulit* with stories about Prince Diponegoro.

wayang jengglong variant of *wayang kulit purwâ* found on the north coast, west of Semarang.

wayang kancil *wayang kulit* aimed especially at children, with stories about the mouse-deer Kancil.

wayang karetao New Zealand form of *wayang kulit* using Maori stories.

wayang klithik (a performance with) flat, wooden puppets depicting stories from the East Javanese *Damar Wulan* epic, traditionally accompanied by a *pélog* gamelan.

wayang krucil = *wayang klithik*.

wayang kulit [*ng*] → *ringgit wacucal* [*kr*] **1** (drama with) flat leather puppets that create shadows on a screen, traditionally accompanied by a *sléndro* gamelan, usually depicting stories from the *Mahabharata* and *Ramayana* epics. **2** any shadow-puppet drama, for example, *wayang gedhog* or *wayang mâdyâ*. **3** a puppet in such drama.

wayang (kulit) gedhog = *wayang gedhog*.

wayang (kulit) perjuangan *wayang kulit* using stories of the Indonesian independence struggle.

wayang (kulit) purwâ repertoire of shadow-puppet plays in which the stories are based upon (a) the Indian epics *Mahabharata*, *Ramayana* and *Bharata Yudâ*, (b) the *Arjuna Sâsrâ Bau* cycle, or (c) stories set in prehistoric Java, traditionally accompanied by a *sléndro* gamelan: often used interchangeably with *wayang kulit*.

wayang layar panjang *wayang kulit* with extra-long *kelir*.

wayang kuluk *wayang kulit* with stories about the Sultanate of Yogya.

wayang listrik *wayang kulit* using a large screen with multiple halogen lamps. {*listrik* = electricity}

wayang mâdyâ a *wayang kulit* tradition created in the nineteenth century, accompanied by a *pélog* gamelan playing pieces originally in *sléndro*; *wayang mâdyâ* stories begin at the point at which the *Mahabharata* stories end.

wayang menak *wayang kulit* with stories from the Menak cycle.

wayang orang = *wayang wong*. {*orang* [*in*] = *wong* [*ng*]}

wayang padhat/padhot a condensed form of *wayang kulit*.

wayang panca sila *wayang kulit* with stories illustrating the *Panca Sila* (political principles of Indonesian republic).

wayang planet novel form of *wayang kulit* using representations of real people and fictional characters from outside *wayang*, e.g. from TV programmes or strip-cartoons, in addition to traditional characters.

wayang potèhi = *wayang thithi*.

wayang purwâ = *wayang kulit purwâ*.

wayang ringkas [*in*] = *wayang padhat*.

wayang sandosa experimental form of *wayang kulit* with large screen and multiple *dhalang.*
wayang sasak *wayang kulit* performed in Lombok, using Islamic stories.
wayang suket performances using puppets made from grass.
wayang suluh modern-dress *wayang kulit* using stories overlapping and following on from *wayang perjuangan.*
wayang thithi *wayang* with stories of Chinese origin, delivered either in Chinese or in Indonesian.
wayang titi = *wayang thithi.*
wayang tiyang (*tiyang* [*kr*] = *wong* [*ng*]) = *wayang wong.*
wayang topèng old form of *wayang*, based on *wayang gedhog*, performed by dancers wearing masks.
wayang ukur *wayang kulit* with *dhalang* and puppets on either side of screen, and dancers. {*ukur* = measured}
wayang wahånå *wayang kulit* using stories focusing on contemporary social problems.
wayang wahyu Catholic religious *wayang* with gospel stories.
wayang wong dance-drama with spoken dialogue and stories based upon the *Mahabharata* and *Ramayana* epics, accompanied by both a *sléndro* and a *pélog* gamelan.
wayang wong golèk *wayang wong* in which dancers imitate movements of *wayang golèk* puppets.
wayang wong panggung *wayang wong* performed commercially on a proscenium stage (cf. *wayang wong pendhåpå*). {*panggung* = stage}
wayang wong pendhåpå *wayang wong* performed on the flat surface of a *pendhåpå* in a royal court.
wayang wong singkèk Chinese form of *wayang wong.*
wayang wwang early Hindu-Javanese form of dance drama with some characters in masks; presumed forerunner of *wayang topèng* and *wayang wong.*
wayuh = *tumbuk laras.*
wayuh jånggå = *tumbuk nem*; implies *tumbuk* on note 2 also.
wayuh nem = *tumbuk nem.*
wedalan [*kr*] → *tingalan* [*ki*], *wetonan* [*ng*]
wédokan female; a description applied to lower-pitched instruments in a family, e.g. the *kenong japan* or the lower octave of the *bonang* (cf. *lanangan*), also to certain instruments in ceremonial gamelan.
welå a gap in the colotomic structure.
wengkon the head of a *kendhang.*
wengku split bamboo made into a ring around the head of a drum.
wesi [*ng*] → *tosan* [*kr*] iron.
wetah complete, nothing left out (cf. *jugag*).
wétan east.
wetonan [*ng*] → *tingalan* [*ki*], *wiyosan* [*kr?*, *ki?*]
widådari angel.
widheng(an) **1** a groove around the base of a *pencu*, believed to improve the sound: see also *tikel.* **2** the flat outer part of a *kecèr.*
wilah the slab, bar or key of a gamelan instrument.
wilahan **1** = *wilah.* **2** the names of the tones in the *sléndro* and *pélog* tuning system, for example, *wilahan panunggul*, *wilahan gulu*, and so on. **3** the set of gamelan instruments.
wilah blimbingan **1** ribbed *wilah* as on the *slenthem* and *gendèr*, cf. *wilah polos.* **2** *wilah* of this type with flat *recep* (cf. *kruwingan*). {*blimbing* = starfruit}
wilah lugas = *wilah polos.*
wilah pencon *wilah* with a *pencu*, as found on *slentho*, *kenong rèntèng* and *gong kemodhong.*
wilah polos *wilah* with a curved upper profile, as on the *saron* and *demung* (cf. *wilah blimbingan*). {*polos* = plain, simple}
wilambitå låyå slow tempo.
wiled = *wilet.*
wiledan = *wiletan.*
wilet **1** = *céngkok* (1). **2** one specific realisation of a *céngkok* (1). **3** the two sections of a *céngkok*; the first *wilet* is called *padhang*, the second is called *ulihan.* **4** the melodic ornaments of a melody such as *luk* and *gregel.* **5** a category of vocal ornaments.
wilet ageng = *gongan.*
wiletan **1** the creation of melodic patterns (*wilet*) on a *gendèr*, *gambang* or *rebab.* **2** (Sundanese) *gåtrå.*
wilujengan [*kr*] → *slametan* [*ng*]
wiråmå **1** = *iråmå.* **2** (Balinese) Old Javanese or Sanskrit prosody observing long/short vowel qualities.
wiråswårå male singer.
wirèng(an) a combat dance performed by two dancers.
wiyågå = *niyågå.*
wiyosan [*kr?*, *ki?*] → *tingalan* [*ki*], *wetonan* [*ng*]
wolak-walik double-sided, as of a *siter peking* with *sléndro* strings on one side and *pélog* on the other.
wot = *supitan.*
wudhar = *udhar.*
wudelan the underside of a *wilah* on a *saron* with a burr from the creation of the holes that sit on the *placak*; usually found on old instruments where the holes were not drilled. {*wudel* = navel}
wwang (Old Javanese) = *wong*; see *wayang wwang.*
yågå = *niyågå.*
yogå the horse hair used in the bow of a *rebab.*

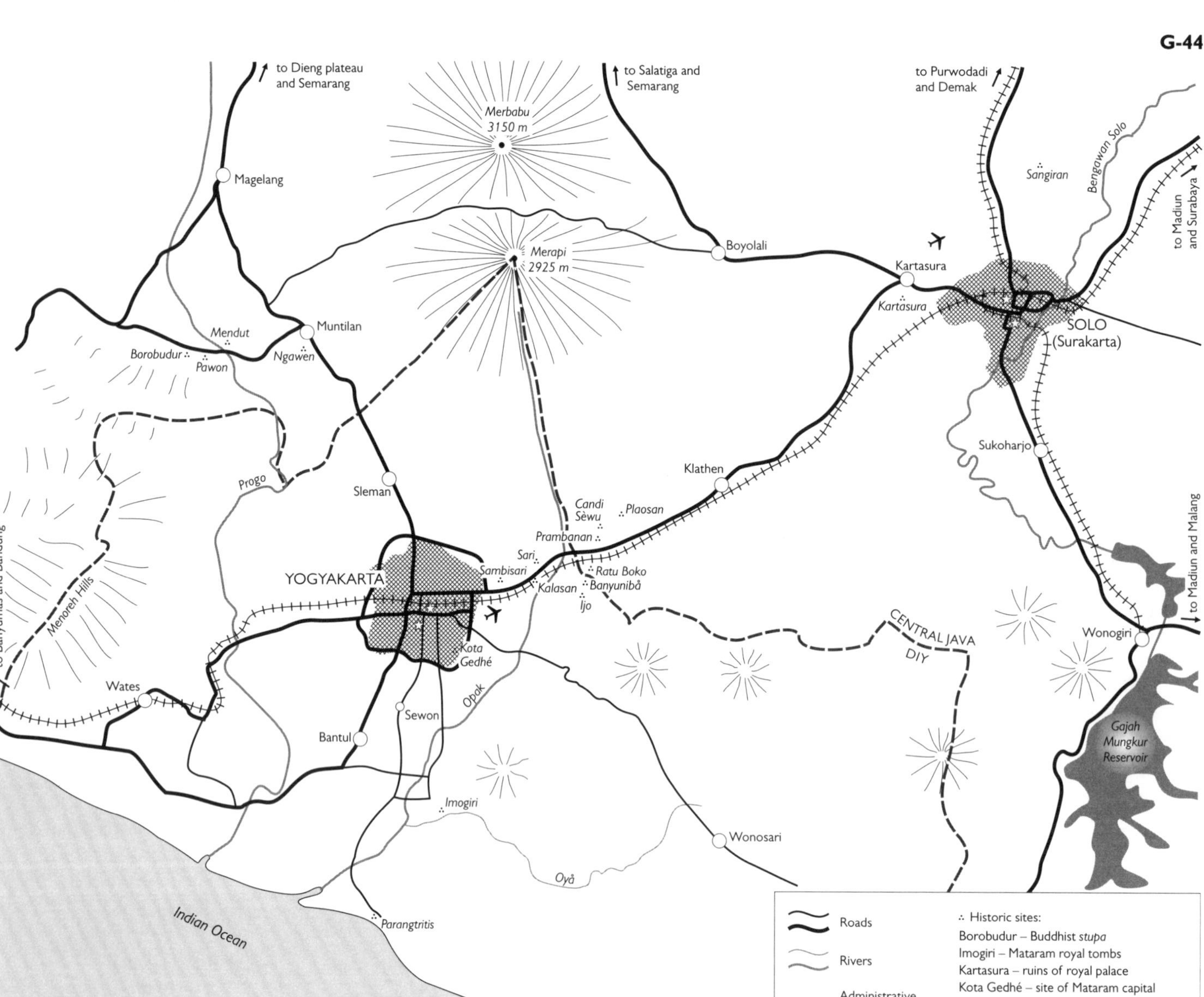
to Dieng plateau and Semarang
to Salatiga and Semarang
to Purwodadi and Demak
Merbabu 3150 m
Magelang
Sangiran
Bengawan Solo
to Madiun and Surabaya
Merapi 2925 m
Boyolali
Kartasura
Kartasura
SOLO (Surakarta)
Mendut
Muntilan
Borobudur
Pawon
Ngawen
Progo
Sleman
Klathen
Sukoharjo
Candi Sèwu
Plaosan
Prambanan
Sari
Sambisari
Ratu Boko
Banyunibå
Kalasan
Ijo
YOGYAKARTA
Menoreh Hills
to Banyumas and Bandung
Kota Gedhé
CENTRAL JAVA
DIY
Wonogiri
to Madiun and Malang
Wates
Sewon
Opak
Bantul
Gajah Mungkur Reservoir
Imogiri
Wonosari
Oyå
Indian Ocean
Parangtritis
Roads
Rivers
Administrative boundary
Railway
Mountain
∴ Historic sites:
Borobudur – Buddhist stupa
Imogiri – Mataram royal tombs
Kartasura – ruins of royal palace
Kota Gedhé – site of Mataram capital
Parangtritis – 'home' of Ratu Kidul
Ratu Boko – ruins of Buddhist monastery
Sangiran – 'Java Man' fossil discoveries
Others – Hindu and Buddhist temples
Palace
Airport
0 km 20
0 miles 10
©2003 Richard Pickvance

Map 3 The Principalities and their environs

Appendices

Not included in the printed book: see thumbnails on next page

A-2 Additional pages (A-3 to A-26) accessible via website

Appendix 1

Appendix 3

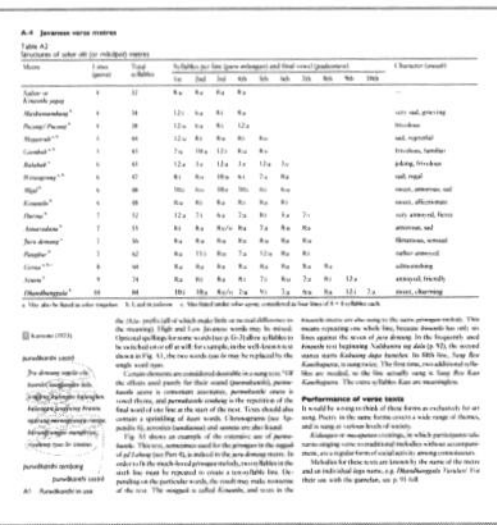

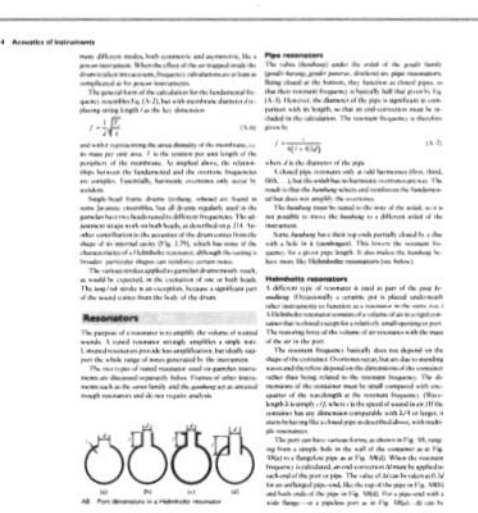

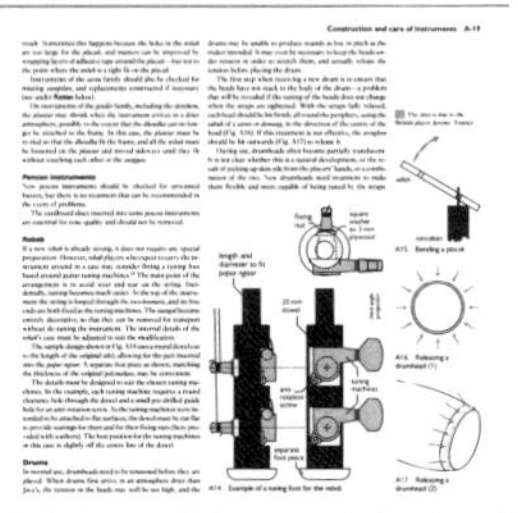

Appendix 6

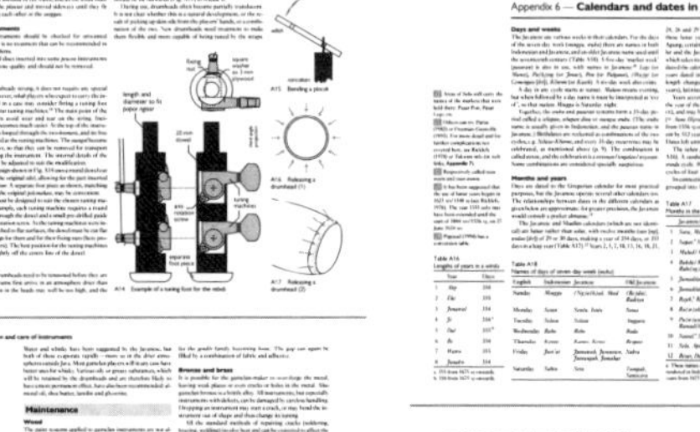

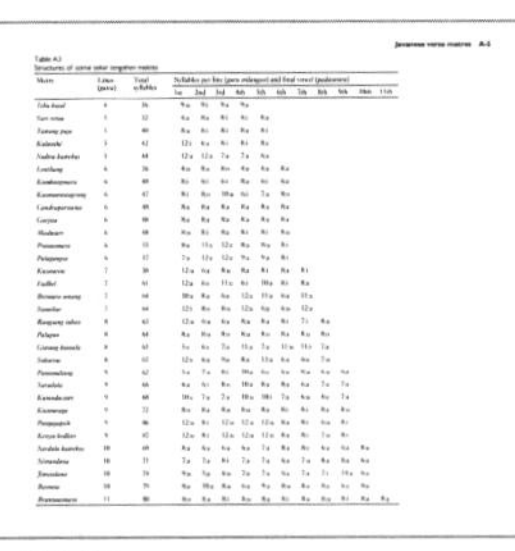

Appendix 4

Appendix 5

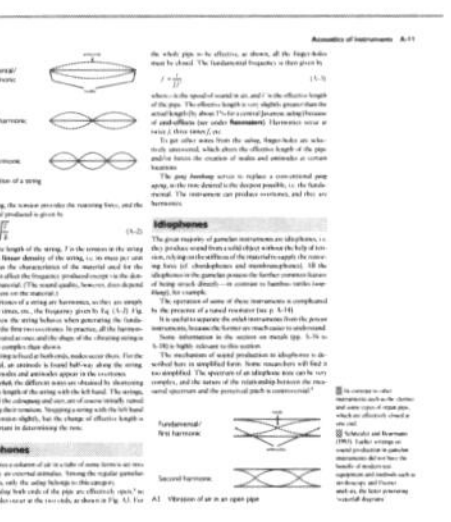

Appendix 2

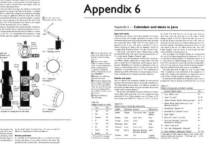

Appendix 7 — **Bibliography**

This bibliography is not comprehensive: it concentrates on material that follows up and/or complements the content of this book. Some dedicated bibliographies are listed below.

Dictionaries, grammars

Hans Herrfurth, *Djawanisch-Deutsches Wörterbuch*, VEB Verlag Enzyklopädie, Leipzig, 1972. Unfortunately for anglophones, still the best recent dictionary of Javanese into a Western language.

Elinor C. Horne, *Javanese-English Dictionary*, Yale University Press, New Haven, 1974.

Theodore Pigeaud, *Javaans-Nederlands Woordenboek*, KITLV, Leiden, 1938 (5th edn, 1994).

Stuart Robson, *Javanese Grammar for Students*, Monash University, Clayton, Australia, 1992.

Stuart Robson and Singgih Wibisono, *Javanese-English Dictionary*, Periplus, Hong Kong, 2002. An improvement on Horne (1974), but disappointing for gamelan students.

Sudarsono et al., *Kamus Istilah Tari dan Karawitan Jawa* [Dictionary of terms for Javanese dance and music], Jakarta, 1977/1978.

Other books, theses, dissertations, articles

Alit Djajasoebrata, *Shadow Theatre in Java: The Puppets, Performance and Repertoire*, Pepin Press, Amsterdam, 1999. A brief text, but with many fine colour illustrations.

Ben Arps, *Tembang in Two Traditions*, School of Oriental and African Studies, University of London, 1992.

Judith Becker, *Traditional Music in Modern Java*, University of Hawaii Press, Honolulu, 1980.

Judith Becker, *Gamelan Stories: Tantrism, Islam and Aesthetics in Central Java*, Arizona State University (*Monographs in Southeast Asian Studies*), 1993.

Judith Becker and Alan H. Feinstein (eds), *Karawitan: Source Readings in Javanese Gamelan and Vocal Music*, University of Michigan (*Michigan Papers on South and Southeast Asia*, nos. 23, 30 and 31), Ann Arbor: Vol. 1, 1984; Vol. 2, 1987; Vol. 3, 1988. Vols 1 and 2 contain translations from writings in Javanese and Indonesian; Vol. 3 contains a glossary, a collection of *balungan* notation, a large composite bibliography for Vols 1 and 2, and several indexes.

Art van Beek, *Life in the Javanese Kraton*, Oxford University Press (*Images of Asia* series), Singapore, 1990.

Marc Benamou, Rasa in Javanese musical aesthetics, PhD thesis, University of Michigan, 1998.

Clara Brakel, 'Court dances of Central Java: essential forms and concepts', *Archipel, 11* (1975) 155–67.

Clara Brakel-Papenhuyzen, *Classical Javanese Dance: the Surakarta tradition and its terminology*, KITLV, Leiden, 1995.

Benjamin Brinner, *Knowing Music, Making Music*, University of Chicago Press (*Chicago Studies in Ethnomusicology* series), Chicago, 1995.

Tim Byard-Jones, 'Developments in performance practice, the creation of new genres and social transformations in Yogyakarta *Wayang Kulit*', in *Indonesian Performing Arts: Tradition and Transition 1* (*Contemporary Theatre Review, 11.1* (2001)) 43–54.

Peggy Choy, 'Texts through time: the golèk dance of Java', in Stephanie Morgan and Laurie Jo Sears (eds), *Aesthetic Tradition and Cultural Transition in Java and Bali*, Center for Southeast Asian Studies, University of Wisconsin, Madison, 1984.

Jody Diamond, 'Out of Indonesia: global gamelan', *Ethnomusicology, 42.1* (1998) 174–83.

Neville Fletcher and Thomas Rossing, *The Physics of Musical Instruments*, Springer, New York, 2nd edn, 1998.

Malcolm Floyd (ed.), *World Musics in Education*, Scolar Press, Aldershot, 1996.

G. S. P. Freeman-Grenville, *The Islamic and Christian Calendars*, Garnet, Reading, 1995. Covers years 1–1650 AH.

[Garland] Terry E. Miller and Sean Williams (eds), *Garland Encyclopedia of World Music, Vol. 4, Southeast Asia*, Garland, New York, 1998. The Java section has a useful bibliography.

Clifford Geertz, 'Ethos, world view and the analysis of sacred symbols', *The Antioch Review, 17.4* (1957), reprinted in id., *The Interpretation of Cultures*, Basic Books, New York, 1973.

James Gleick, *Chaos*, Heinemann, London, 1988, and several other editions.

[Grove] Stanley Sadie (ed.), *New Grove Dictionary of Music and Musicians*, Macmillan, London, 20 vols, 1980. This was the first edition of Grove that covered ethnomusicology. Second edition with new articles, Macmillan, London, 29 vols, 2001: also available online (*www.macmillanonline.net/music*). Both editions contain substantial articles on several aspects of gamelan and *karawitan*, with bibliographies.

Sri Hastanto, The concept of pathet in Central Javanese music, PhD thesis, University of Durham, 1985.

Martin F. Hatch, Lagu, laras, layang: rethinking melody in Javanese music, PhD thesis, Cornell University, 1980.

Ron Hatley, 'Mapping cultural regions of Java', in *Other Javas away from the Kraton*, Monash University, Clayton, Australia, 1984.

Ernst Heins, *Music in Java: current bibliography 1973–1989*, University of Amsterdam, Ethnomusicologisch Centrum

'Jaap Kunst', 1989. Designed to continue the bibliography in Kunst (1973).

Ernst Heins, *Bibliography of Javanese Gamelan 1923–1990*, Amadeus Verlag, Basel, 1990.

Claire Holt, *Art in Indonesia: Continuities and Change*, Cornell University Press, Ithaca, NY, 1967. A broad survey with attention to links between art forms.

Mantle Hood, *The Evolution of Javanese Gamelan*, Noetzel, Wilhelmshaven, Germany: Vol. 1, *Music of the Roaring Sea*, 1980; Vol. 2, *The Legacy of the Roaring Sea*, 1984; Vol. 3, *Paragon of the Roaring Sea*, 1988.

Erich M. von Hornbostel and Curt Sachs, 'Systematik der Musikinstrumente: ein Versuch', *Zeitschrift für Ethnologie, 46.4-5* (1914) 553–90; trans. (rev.) A. Baines and K. P. Wachsmann as 'Classification of musical instruments', *Galpin Society Journal, 14* (1961) 3–29.

Jo Hoskin, 'Central Javanese court dance – a practical approach', in *Indonesian Performing Arts: Tradition and Transition 1* (*Contemporary Theatre Review, 11.1* (2001)) 55–66.

Georges Ifrah, *Histoire Universelle des Chiffres*, Editions Laffont, Paris, 1994; trans. as *The Universal History of Numbers*, Harvill Press, London, 1998.

E. Jacobson and J. H. van Hasselt, *De Gong-Fabricatie te Semarang*, Rijksmuseum voor Volkenkunde, Leiden, 1907; trans. A. Toth as 'The Manufacture of Gongs in Semarang', *Indonesia, 19* (1975) 127–172.

A. M. Jones, 'Towards an assessment of the Javanese pelog scale', *Ethnomusicology, 7.1* (1963) 22–5.

Margaret J. Kartomi, *Matjapat Songs in Central and West Java*, Australian National University Press, Canberra, 1973.

L. E. Kinsler and A. R. Frey, *Fundamentals of Acoustics*, Wiley, New York, 2nd edn, 1962.

Ward Keeler, *Javanese Shadow Plays, Javanese Selves*, Princeton University Press, Princeton, NJ, 1987. In-depth account of the cultural background to *wayang*, rather than *wayang* itself.

Ward Keeler, *Javanese Shadow Puppets*, Oxford University Press (*Images of Asia* series), Singapore, 1992. A brief introduction.

Jaap Kunst, *Hindu-Javanese Musical Instruments*, Martinus Nijhoff, The Hague, 2nd edn, 1968.

Jaap Kunst, *Music in Java*, Martinus Nijhoff, The Hague, trans. of 3rd edn of *De Toonkunst van Java*, 2 vols, 1973. The pioneering work; but based on fieldwork in the first third of the twentieth century, and Kunst did not play the gamelan.

Jennifer Lindsay, *Javanese Gamelan*, Oxford University Press (*Oxford in Asia* series), Kuala Lumpur, 1979; 2nd edn, Oxford University Press (*Images of Asia* series), Singapore, 1992. Another useful short introduction. The second edition is longer and has a completely new set of photographs.

Jennifer Lindsay, Klasik kitsch or contemporary: a study of the Javanese performing arts, PhD thesis, Sydney University, 1985.

William P. Malm, *Music Cultures of the Pacific, the Near East, and Asia*, Prentice-Hall, Englewood Cliffs, NJ, 2nd edn, 1977. Shows something of the relationships between Indonesian musical cultures and those of adjacent countries.

Frank Parise, *The Book of Calendars*, Facts on File, New York, 1982.

John Pemberton, 'Musical politics in central Java (or how not to listen to a Javanese gamelan)', *Indonesia, 44* (1987) 16–?30.

Marc Perlman, Unplayed melodies: music theory in postcolonial Java, PhD thesis, Wesleyan University, Middletown, CT, 1993; publ. as *Unplayed Melodies: Javanese Gamelan and the Genesis of Music Theory*, University of California Press, Berkeley and Los Angeles, 2004.

Stamford Raffles, *History of Java*, Black, Parbury, and Allen and John Murray, London, 1817 (2 vols); reprinted Oxford University Press, London, 1965; and other edns. Includes descriptions of music, illustrations of instruments and a few notations.

Merle C. Ricklefs, *Modern Javanese Historical Tradition: a study of an original Kartasura chronicle and related materials*, School of Oriental and African Studies, University of London, 1978.

Albrecht Schneider and Andreas Beurmann, 'Acoustics and tuning of gamelan instruments', in Ben Arps (ed.), *Performance in Java and Bali*, School of Oriental and African Studies, University of London, 1993.

Soekanto, *Bibliografi tentang Seni Karawitan* [Bibliography on the Art of *Karawitan*], Gadjah Mada University, Yogya, 1980 (in Indonesian).

Soesatyo Darnawi, *A Brief Survey of Javanese Poetics*, trans. from Indonesian, Balai Pustaka, Jakarta, 1982.

Ted Solís (ed.), *Performing Ethnomusicology: Teaching and Representation in World Music Ensembles*, University of California Press, Berkeley and Los Angeles, 2004.

Neil Sorrell, *A Guide to the Gamelan*, Faber and Faber, London, 1990; also published by Amadeus Press, Portland, OR, 1990; 2nd edn, Society for Asian Music, Ithaca, NY, 2000. A good short introduction, but new players will find that they soon progress beyond its technical coverage.

Henry Spiller, *Gamelan: The Traditional Sounds of Indonesia*, ABC-CLIO, Santa Barbara, CA, 2004. Focuses on Sunda and Cirebon, but the accompanying CD includes a performance of *ldr Pangkur* in central Javanese style, analysed in detail in the book.

Simon Steptoe, '*Gamelan* music in Britain', in *Indonesian Performing Arts: Tradition and Transition 2* (*Contemporary Theatre Review, 11.2* (2001)) 25–35.

Sumarsam, *Gamelan: Cultural Interaction and Musical*

Development in Central Java, University of Chicago Press (*Chicago Studies in Ethnomusicology* series), Chicago, 1995.

Sumarsam, 'Opportunity and interaction: the gamelan from Java to Wesleyan', in Solís (2004), pp. 69–92.

Rahayu Supanggah, Introduction aux styles d'interprétation dans la musique Javanaise [Introduction to performance styles in Javanese music], PhD thesis, Université de Paris VII, 1985. The most useful content is on musical education in Java and the role of music in weddings.

Rahayu Supanggah, *Bothèkan Karawitan I*, Masyarakat Seni Pertunjukan Indonesia, Jakarta, 2002 (in Indonesian). A series of essays on topics within *karawitan*. A volume II is promised.

Bernard Suryabrata [Bernard Ijzerdraat], *The Island of Music*, Balai Pustaka, Jakarta, 1987. This introductory work was published after the author's death, without any editing of the poor English and without proof correction. Captions for many music examples are included, but not the examples themselves, which would have been very valuable.

Hardja Susilo, '"A bridge to Java": four decades teaching gamelan in America', in Solís (2004), pp. 53–68.

R. Anderson Sutton, *Traditions of Gamelan Music in Java: Musical Pluralism and Regional Identity*, Cambridge University Press, Cambridge, 1991.

R. Anderson Sutton, Variation in Javanese gamelan: dynamics of a steady state, PhD thesis, University of Michigan, 1982; publ. as *Special report no. 28*, Centre for Southeast Asian Studies, N. Illinois University, DeKalb, 1993.

R. Anderson Sutton, 'Do Javanese gamelan musicians really improvise?', in Bruno Nettl and Melinda Russell (eds), *In the Course of Performance: studies in the world of musical improvisation*, University of Chicago Press (*Chicago Studies in Ethnomusicology* series), Chicago, 1998.

Joan Suyenaga, 'Patterns in process: Java through gamelan', in Stephanie Morgan and Laurie Jo Sears (eds), *Aesthetic Tradition and Cultural Transition in Java and Bali*, Center for Southeast Asian Studies, University of Wisconsin, Madison, 1984.

Eric Taylor, *Musical Instruments of South-East Asia*, Oxford University Press (*Images of Asia* series), Singapore, 1989.

Edward C. Van Ness and Shita Prawirohardjo, *Javanese Wayang Kulit: an Introduction*, Oxford University Press (*Oxford in Asia* series), Kuala Lumpur, 1980. Good on dramaturgy.

András Varsányi, Gong ageng. Herstellung, Klang und Gestalt eines königlichen Instruments des Ostens [Gong ageng. Manufacture, sound and design of a royal instrument of the East], PhD thesis, Tübingen University, 1999; publ. (*Tübinger Beiträge zur Musikwissenschaft*, 21) H. Schneider, Tutzing, 2000.

András Varsányi, 'Gong agung: gong making for Javanese and Balinese gamelan', *Sèlèh Notes, 11.2* (March 2004) 7–11.

Roger Vetter, Formal aspects of performance practice in central Javanese gamelan music, MA thesis, University of Hawaii, 1977.

Roger Vetter, Music for 'The Lap of the World': gamelan performance, performers and repertoire in the kraton Yogyakarta, PhD thesis, University of Wisconsin, Madison, 1986.

Roger Vetter, 'A retrospect on a century of gamelan tone measurements', *Ethnomusicology, 33.2* (1989) 217–27.

Graham Vulliamy and Ed Lee (eds), *Pop, Rock and Ethnic Music in School*, Cambridge University Press, Cambridge, 1982.

R. M. Wasisto Surjodiningrat et al., *Penjelidikan dalam pengukuran nada gamelan-gamelan djawa terkemuka di Jogjakarta dan Surakarta*, Gadjah Mada University Press, Yogyakarta, 1969; trans. as *Tone Measurements of Outstanding Javanese Gamelan in Jogyakarta and Surakarta*, Gadjah Mada University Press, Yogyakarta, 1972.

Ghulam-Sarwar Yousof, *Dictionary of Traditional South-East Asian Theatre*, Oxford University Press (*Oxford in Asia* series), Kuala Lumpur, 1994.

Journals

Journals giving most coverage of gamelan are marked with an asterisk. Gamelan material has occasionally appeared in the others. Journals increasingly provide online contents lists.

Archipel (Bandung, Indonesia) 1971– .

Asian Art and Culture (Arthur M. Sackler Gallery, Smithsonian Institution, Washington, DC, with Oxford University Press, New York) formerly *Asian Art*, 1987– .

**Asian Music* (Society for Asian Music, Cornell University, Ithaca, NY) 1968– .

Asia Pacific Journal of Anthropology, formerly *Canberra Anthropology* (Research School of Pacific and Asian Studies, Australian National University, Canberra) 1978– .

**Balungan* (American Gamelan Institute, Lebanon, NH) 1984– .

Bijdragen tot de Taal-, Land- en Volkenkunde (Nijhoff, 's-Gravenhage) 1852– .

Contemporary Theatre Review (Harwood Academic Publishers, Chur, Switzerland) 1992– .

Djawa (Weltevreden, Netherlands) 1921–41.

Drama Review (New York University, School of the Arts) 1957–?

East Asian Cultural Studies (Centre for East Asian Cultural Studies, Tokyo) 1962– .

**Ethnomusicology* (1957–1991 Society for Ethnomusicology; 1992– University of Illinois Press) 1957– .

Ethnomusicology Forum, formerly *British Journal of Ethnomusicology* (1992–2003 British Forum for Ethnomusicology; 2004– (with new title) Routledge) 1992– .

Ethnomusicology OnLine (University of Maryland) 1995– .

Galpin Society Journal (Galpin Society, Oxford) 1948– .

Hemisphere (Australian Government Publishing Service, Canberra) 1957–82?

**Indonesia* (Cornell University, Ithaca, NY) 1966– . N.B. several other journals share this title.

Indonesia Circle (School of Oriental and African Studies, London) 1973–1996; renamed *Indonesia and the Malay World* 1997– .

Journal of Musicological Research (Taylor & Francis, Philadelphia, PA), formerly *Music and Man*, 1973– .

Journal of Musicology (1982–7 Imperial Print. Co., St. Joseph, MI; 1987– University of California Press, Berkeley) 1982– .

Journal of Music Theory (Yale School of Music, New Haven, CT) 1957– .

Journal of Oriental Studies (University of Hong Kong) 1954– .

Journal of Royal Institute for the Indies (Koninklijke Vereeniging Indisch Instituut, Amsterdam).

Journal of Southeast Asian Studies (University of Singapore Press) 1970– .

Journal of the American Musicological Society (University of Chicago Press) 1948– .

Journal of the International Folk Music Council (Heffer, Cambridge) 1949–68.

Leonardo Music Journal (MIT Press, Cambridge, MA) 1991– .

Musica Asiatica (Oxford University Press, London; later Cambridge University Press, Cambridge) book series, 1977–91.

Music Perception (University of California, Berkeley) 1983– .

Musical Quarterly (various publishers; 1985– Macmillan) 1915– .

Oideion (Leiden, Netherlands), now an online multimedia journal (*http://www.iias.nl/oideion/journal/index-j.html*).

Orientatie (Bandung and 's-Gravenhage) 1947–49, 19??–1954.

Pacific Review of Ethnomusicology (University of California, Los Angeles) 1984– .

**Pélog*, see *Seleh Notes.*

Progress Reports in Ethnomusicology (University of Maryland, Baltimore) 1983– .

Review of Indonesian and Malayan Affairs (University of Sydney) 1967–82; renamed (... *Malaysian* ...) 1983– .

**Selected Reports in Ethnomusicology* (University of California, Los Angeles) 1966– .

**Seleh Notes* (UK Gamelan Network) 1993– ; successor to *Pélog*, 1984-1993.

Studies in Music (University of Western Australia, Nedlands) 1967– .

**Swara Bendhe* (Melbourne Community Gamelan Inc., Victoria, Australia) 2003– .

Viltis (??–1994 Lithuania; 1994– International Institute, Milwaukee) ?1950– .

World of Music (International Institute for Comparative Music Studies and Documentation, Berlin; publ. Mainz, Germany) 1959– .

Yearbook for Traditional Music, formerly *Yearbook of the International Folk Music Council* (International Council for Traditional Music, Urbana, IL) 1969– .

Web links

The initial *http://* before *www*... addresses has been omitted, as it is added automatically by the browser. Additional links are listed at *www.gamelan.org.uk*

American Gamelan Institute (*www.gamelan.org*): publishes the journal *Balungan*. The website lists gamelan groups and gamelan builders, offers *kepatihan* fonts, various writings, 'Gongcast' broadcast of music samples.

Asia/Pacific Cultural Centre for UNESCO (ACCU) (*www2.accu.or.jp/paap*): 'databank on traditional/folk performing arts in Asia and the Pacific'.

Ethnomusicology website list (*www.research.umbc.edu/eol/other/other.html*).

Gamelans of the Kraton Yogyakarta, by Roger Vetter (*http://web.grinnell.edu/courses/mus/gamelans/open.html*): photographs, information and sound samples.

Het Gamelanhuis [The Gamelan House] (*www.gamelanhuis.nl*): gamelan events in the Netherlands, also background information with sound clips and vintage photographs, mainly on central Javanese gamelan. In Dutch.

Gendhing Jawa (*www.calarts.edu/~drummond/gendhing.html*): notation for over 1000 pieces in downloadable .PDF files.

Indonesian Performing Arts (*www.indonesianperformingarts.org*): lists performances, performers and performing groups in the UK.

Joglosemar (*http://joglosemar.freeservers.com*, possibly *www.joglosemar.co.id*): a wide variety of information on central Java and its culture. The English is rough, and the event information is out of date. {Name derived from Jogyakarta, Solo and Semarang}

Marsudi Raras (*www.marsudiraras.org*): video and audio clips and notation for complete peformances of pieces, and descriptions of gamelan used (at Museum Nusantara, Delft, Netherlands); also an interactive virtual instrument.

Seleh Notes (*www.selehnotes.co.uk*): website of the journal for the UK gamelan community.

Takwim info (*http://eprints.anu.edu.au/archive/00002628/01/ahcen/proudfoot/Takwim.html*): information on calendars, including a conversion program.

UK Gamelan info (*www.gamelan.org.uk*): background information, UK gamelan locations and events, resources related to the gamelan, including this book; event information for gamelan-loving tourists in Java.

Wesleyan Virtual Instrument Museum, Wesleyan University

(*http://learningobjects.wesleyan.edu/vim*): video and audio clips, images and descriptions of gamelan instruments.

Directories of gamelan groups

List for most parts of the world are accessible via *www.gamelan.org*, but the following may be more up to date:

Australia and New Zealand: *http://danny.oz.au/gamelan*

Germany: *www.kulturkontakt-online.de/gamelan_e.htm*

Netherlands: *www.antenna.nl/indonet/bulletin.html*

Rest of Europe: *www.kulturkontakt-online.de/gamelan_e.htm*

UK: *www.selehnotes.co.uk* and *www.gamelan.org.uk*

Appendix 8 — **Discography**

The list below consists of commercially released recordings in LP, cassette or CD format. Some recordings have been issued in more than one format, and the latest is listed. The list is in order of date of recording (not release) if known. Recordings of gamelan began in the 78 rpm era, but few if any of the oldest recordings have been transferred to other formats. There is no implication that the recordings listed are available at the time of writing. With changes of company ownership, the numbers may change.

In all cases, the performers are wholly or largely Javanese and the recordings were made by Westerners. There are also recordings, not listed here, by ensembles based in the West:[29] these include

- groups playing Javanese gamelan and reproducing Javanese performance styles,
- groups playing their own music on Javanese instruments,
- groups who play various kinds of music on imitations of Javanese instruments,
- groups who play on Javanese gamelan instruments tuned to Western scales, with or without Western instruments too,
- groups using the name 'gamelan' but whose music has no other connection with Javanese gamelan.

Researchers have lodged their field recordings with various libraries, museums and educational institutions, some of which are open to the public. In London, for example, such collections exist in the National Sound Archive (part of the British Library), the Horniman Museum and the School of Oriental and African Studies (part of the University of London).

Recordings of gamelan can also be found in CD or DVD encyclopedias: these are likely to be extracts from commercial recordings listed below. Some gamelan websites (see **Appendix 7**) provide recorded excerpts for downloading.

In Indonesia there is a large recording industry, based mainly on cassettes although CDs are also now being issued. Supplies from the leading company, Lokananta, have been irregular since the late 1990s, but its recordings may reappear on other labels. (The numbers of some recordings have been changed.) No Indonesian recordings are listed here, partly because they are not regularly imported into Western countries, but mainly because they are balanced for local taste: the *pesindhèn* and the soft-style decorating instruments are prominent, but most of the other instruments can be difficult to hear, and the recordings are therefore not very helpful to the Western student of the gamelan. Technical quality is often poor. Both the balance and the recording quality are better on some of the CDs.

All recordings listed are in two-channel stereo unless otherwise indicated.

29 See, for example, the listing and review in Diamond (1998).

Java: Gamelans from the Sultan's Palace in Jogjakarta, Archiv 2723-017; 2 LPs, 1973?.

Java: Historic Gamelans, Philips 6586 004 (UNESCO series); LP.

Indonesia 1: Java Court Music (Musical Anthology of the Orient, 31), Bärenreiter-Musicaphon BM30 SL2031 (UNESCO collection); LP. *Gd bonang Wedhikèngser, gd Widåsari.*

Gamelan Music from Java, Philips 831-209-PY; LP.

Gamelan Garland, Fontana 858-614 FPY; LP.

Music of the Orient: Java, Parlophone MO 104; 78s.

Java: L'art du Gamelan, Playa Sound PS33507; LP.

Java: Palais Royal de Yogyakarta, Ocora/Radio France; CDs, 1970–1973. Jacques Brunet's recordings from the *kraton Yogya*: a valuable document, but sometimes affected by tentative performances, distortion and wandering volume levels, and the liner notes are unreliable. Compared with earlier formats, the CDs contain additional material. Main items:

Vol. 1, *Court dances*: *Gangsaran – ldr Roning tawang – ldr Bimå Kurdå* and *Srimpi Lobong*, C560067.

Vol. 2, *Instrumental music*: *Gd bonang Taliwångså pl 6* and *gd Lintang karahinan sl m* (*gd soran*), C560068.

Vol. 3, *Spiritual and sacred*: *Bedhåyå Gambirsawit sl 9*, etc., C560069.

Vol. 4, *Concert music*: *Gd Wasitah asih pl 6* and *gd Kabor manyarsih sl 9*, C560087.

Java: Music of Mystical Enchantment, Lyrichord LLCT7301; cassette. Mainly of interest for a choral performance of *gd Anglirmendhung* (cf. Dunya/Felmay 8041 below). Recording quality is poor.

Nonesuch (now Elektra Nonesuch) Explorer series; CD. The Court Gamelan series are classic recordings.

The Jasmine Isle, 79717-2; 1969?. Ten pieces, including six from central Java, some performed as solos. Some distortion. Total duration is short.

Javanese Court Gamelan Vol. I, *Pura Pakualaman, Jogjakarta*, 79719-2; 1971. Contains the *gd Téjånåtå – ldr Sembåwå – ldr Playon pl 5* sequence and *gd Mandulpati mg ldr Agun-agun sl 6*, plus shorter pieces.

Javanese Court Gamelan Vol. II, *Mangkunegaran, Solo*, 79721-2; 1976. Includes *gd bonang Babar layar pl 5*, *gd Elå-elå Kalibèbèr.*

Javanese Court Gamelan Vol. III, *Kraton Yogya*, 79722-2; 1976/1978. *Golèk Lambangsari* and shorter pieces.

Javanese Court Gamelan Vol. IV, *Kraton Solo*, recorded but not yet released.

Street Music of Central Java, Lyrichord LLCT7310; cassette,

1975. An excellent recording of a *siteran* ensemble, showing a different treatment of familiar classics such as *gd Gambirsawit*. Not to be confused with other recordings having similar titles.

Music of Indonesia 2: Kroncong, Dangdut and Langgam Jawa, Smithsonian/Folkways SF40056; CD, mid-1970s–1990. No gamelan, but examples of forms that have been adapted for the gamelan. One of an extensive series on regional music styles of Indonesia.

Java: Langen Måndrå Wanårå, Ocora C559014/5; 2 CDs, 1975.

Surinam: Javanese Music, Lyrichord LLST7317; LP, 1977.

Street Music of Java, Original Music OMCD 006; CD.

Music for Sale: Street Musicians of Yogyakarta. Kiwi Pacific TC HLS-91; cassette. From field recordings by Jack Body.

Suara: Environmental Music of Java, Kiwi Pacific/Hibiscus Records TC HLS-113; cassette, *c.*1978–1986. Compiled by New Zealand composer Jack Body from field recordings, with subsequent studio treatment. Very little actual gamelan, but several items of interest including folk elements that have influenced *karawitan*, and hocketing birds.

Java: Vocal Art, (reissue) Auvidis/UNESCO D8014, CD, 1979. *Mâcâpat* delivered in three styles from Yogyakarta: an unaccompanied version of the Dewaruci legend, and two *siteran* versions of *Gambirsawit* in *pélog* with male and female solo singers, the second being followed by *ldr Gonjang-ganjing* (?).

The Sultan's Pleasure, Music of the World, T-116; cassette, CD?, 1982/1983. An excellent recording of pieces in various styles from the *kraton Yogya*; major items are *gd Gålågothang sl m* (a *gendhing soran*) and *gd Genjung goling pl 6*.

Shadow Music of Java, Rounder CD5060; CD, 1991. Digital recording of a large selection of pieces that may be used in *wayang* accompaniment.

Gamelan of Surakarta, JVC VICG-5263; CD, 1992. Includes *Srimpi Jåyåningsih* and *Rånggålawé* suite.

The Music of K.R.T. Wasitodiningrat, CMP CMPCD 3007; CD, 1990.

World Music Library series, King Record Co., Japan. Mainly good digital recordings on CD. The English versions of the liner notes appear to be rather shorter than the Japanese.

The Javanese Gamelan, KICC 5129, 199?.

Court Music of Kraton Surakarta, KICC 5151, 1992. *Srimpi Sangapati*.

Chamber Music of Central Java (Gadhon), KICC 5152, 1992. *Gd Dånåråjå sl 9* and *gd Rimong pl 7* with a light *gadhon* ensemble from Surakarta (*gendèr barung* and *suling* but no *siter* or *gambang*); no singers.

Music of Mangkunegaran Solo I, KICC 5184. *Gd bonang* only: *gd Dhenggung Turularé, gd Sidåmukti, gd Parigentang*.

Klenèngan Session of Solonese Gamelan I, KICC 5185, 1992. *Gd Kembang mårå, gd Krawitan*.

Court Music of Kraton Surakarta II, KICC 5193, 1992?. *Bedhåyå Durådasih: gd kemanak Durådasih, ktw Kinanthi durådasih*.

Langendriyan, Music of Mangkunegaran Solo II, KICC 5194, 1992.

Gendhing Bonang, Court Music of Surakarta III, KICC 5238, 1992. *Gd Bremårå, gd Imåwinèndå*.

?*Rebab and female singing of Central Javanese Gamelan*.

Yogyakarta: Gamelan of the Kraton, Celestial Harmonies 13161-2; CD, before 1997. Excellent digital recording of *Srimpi Pandhelori* and pieces in *soran* style.

Gamelan of Central Java, Dunya/Felmay, CD. Digital recordings, mainly good.

I, Classical Gendings, FY8041, 2001. *Gd Dånåråjå sl 9, gd Tunggul Kawung pl 7* and an unusual version of *gd Anglirmendhung pl 7* with a solo *pesindhèn*. No *gérong*.

II, Ceremonial Music, FY8042, 1996 and 2001. Ceremonial gamelan at Surakarta—*gamelan sekatèn* from the *kraton*, and *gamelan munggang, kodhok ngorèk* and *cåråbalèn* at the Mangkunegaran. Some distortion.

III. Modes and Timbres, FY8043, 200?. Mostly *ladrang* and *ketawang*.

IV. Spiritual Music, FY8044, 200?. Mostly *sekatèn* pieces and *gendhing kemanak*.

Gamelan of Central Java, Arion ARN 64629; 3-CD boxed set, 1999–2002, with extensive and interesting notes:

Flowers: four complete pieces including all nine stanzas of *ktw Puspåwarnå*.

The Meditative Gendèr: short pieces featuring contributions by *gendèr*.

Colours: mostly short extracts illustrating the functions and timbres of individual instruments.

Gamelan from Central Java, Arc Music EUCD1902; CD, 1989–2004. Recordings of all types of ceremonial gamelan and various other compositions: mostly short tracks except for one recent piece. Some distortion, at least on earlier copies.

Index

Some subjects are so pervasive that it would be unhelpful to index every reference: gamelan, *garap*, *balungan*, *pathet*, *irâmâ*, etc. In these cases, the main theoretical coverage is indexed, plus selected key references elsewhere. As in the Glossary, entries are in letter-by-letter order, ignoring spaces.

- □ **Bold** entries: major coverage of a subject
- □ Underlined entries: in an illustration (figure, map, table)
- □ n after the page number indicates a note (marginal note or table footnote) on that page